Fodor's

GERMANY

FODOR'S
TRAVEL PUBLICATIONS

NEW YORK • TORONTO
LONDON • SYDNEY • AUCKLAND

WWW.FODORS.COM

136

CONTENTS

KEY TO SYMBOLS

- Map reference
- Address
- Telephone number
- Opening times
- Admission prices
- Underground station
- Bus number
- Train station
- Ferry/boat
- Driving directions
- Tourist office
- Tours
- Guidebook
- Restaurant
- Café
- Bar
- Shop
- Number of rooms
- Air conditioning
- Swimming pool
- Gym
- Other useful information
- ▷ Cross reference
- ★ Walk/drive start point

Understanding Germany **4**
Living Germany 13
The Story of Germany 27

On the Move **47**
Arriving 48
Getting Around 52
Visitors with a Disability 66

Regions **67**

Berlin **68**
Sights 74
Walks 102
What to Do 106
Eating 112
Staying 116

Northern Germany **120**
Sights 122
Walks and Drives 146
What to Do 152
Eating 156
Staying 160

Western Germany **162**
Sights 164
Walks 190
What to Do 194
Eating 200
Staying 206

Eastern Germany **208**
Sights 210
Walks and Drives 236
What to Do 246
Eating 250
Staying 254

Munich **258**
Sights 260
Walks 286
What to Do 290
Eating 294
Staying 298

Southern Germany **300**
Sights 302
Walks and Drives 330
What to Do 344
Eating 348
Staying 354

Practicalities **357**

Maps **398**

Index **417**

UNDERSTANDING GERMANY

Understanding Germany is an introduction to the country, its geography, economy, history and its people, giving a real insight into the nation. Living Germany gets under the skin of Germany today, while The Story of Germany takes you through the country's past.

Understanding Germany 6
The Best of Germany 10

Living Germany 13

The Story of Germany 27

Germany is not only blessed with varied and beautiful scenery, but also has a multifaceted past that has endowed it with a rich tapestry of historic buildings, art collections and fascinating towns and cities. Perhaps the most misrepresented country in western Europe, the new Germany has much to offer curious and open-minded visitors, from a bracing dip in the Baltic Sea off its northern shores to culture of every kind in Berlin, label-hunting in Munich's boutiques, and skiing and hiking in the Alps. Germany is divided into 16 administrative regions, known as *Länder*. Some of these *Länder*, like Berlin and Bremen, are city-states, while others, like Bavaria, cover hundreds of square kilometres. Some 130 years after Chancellor Otto von Bismarck brought the disparate German states together, regional identities remain strong, and visitors will still discover distinctive local traditions and accents today.

LANDSCAPE

With an area of 356,978sq km (137,829sq miles), Germany is one of western Europe's biggest nations. It is about 450km (280 miles) at its widest and some 853km (530 miles) long, and it has 907km (564 miles) of coastl along the North and Baltic seas. The old internal border separating the former German Democratic Republic (GDR) and Federal Republic of Germany (FDR) cut off 107,680sq km (41,575sq miles) to the east and ran for 1,393km (866 miles). Germany shares a border with nine other European countries: France, the Netherlands, Belgium, Luxembourg, Switzerland, Austria, the Czech Republic, Poland and Denmark.

North-flowing rivers delimit large stretches of both Germany's western and eastern borders, while the Bavarian Alps mark the country's southern edges and contain the Zugspitze, its highest peak at 2,962m (9,718ft). Along the western border is the Rhine valley, whose steep castle-topped banks are the quintessence of Romantic Germany. The Schwarzwald (Black Forest), and Swabian, Harz and Bohemian ranges are all lower than the Alps, but are still high enough for a variety of winter sports.

Elsewhere, the landscape is characterized by fertile valleys, hills cloaked in deciduous and spruce trees, and, to the north, low-lying plains.

POLITICS

Since reunification in 1989, political life has largely followed the relatively stable model established in post-war West Germany. The head of state is the president, elected for a five-year term by national and regional deputies. Day-to-day decision-making power, however, lies with the chancellor, who is elected by the Bundestag (lower house) on a proposal from the president. In the 2005 elections, the Christian Democrat Angela Merkel defeated the Socialist Party's Gerhard Schröder, to become the Federal Republic's first woman chancellor—indeed the first female German ruler of the modern era.

The Bundestag's 669 members are voted for in parliamentary elections, while the upper house, the Bundesrat, is made up of representatives from the 16 *Länder*. The two main post-war parties are the Christian Democrats (CDU) in alliance with the Bavarian Christian Social Union (CSU), and the Social Democrats (SPD). The Green Party, Free Democrats and The Left Party are strong minority parties. At regional level, each of the 16 *Länder* has its own state parliament, and these exert considerable influence through the Bundesrat. Built on consensus, the German federal system does not easily lend itself to swift or radical change, and has been criticized for holding back much-needed reform.

Clockwise from opposite *The façade of Köln cathedral; hikers' trail on Broken summit; a skiing trail in the mountains near Zugspitze*

ECONOMY

Germany's economy has stumbled as the 'miracle' of post-war reconstruction gives way to the harsh realities of globalization, an ageing workforce and increased labour unrest. Politicians have been unable or unwilling to administer a revamp of the generous state welfare system, while the banks and management press for urgent structural changes, lower taxation and greater flexibility in employment legislation. The CDU/CSU/SPD 'grand coalition' government formed in 2005 has been tackling some of these tough issues.

Growth has been slower than predicted in recent years, unemployment, though reducing, has stayed high, and the budget deficit exceeds 3 per cent. Despite this, the standard of living remains high, and Germany leads the motor vehicle, electronic goods, electrical machinery, metal chemical and pharmaceutical industries. Former industrial areas have suffered badly following the decline of heavy industry and mining, and regional authorities are making efforts to develop a strong tertiary sector—despite competition from eastern European countries with cheaper workforces

GERMANY'S REGIONS

NORTHERN GERMANY

Bremen is a city-state that was formerly a member of the Hanseatic League, an alliance of trade ports that stretched across northern Europe and the Baltics. The region consists of Bremen itself and the smaller town of Bremerhaven, a major port.

Hamburg, another city-state, is Germany's second-largest metropolitan area, with a long history that reflects its strategic maritime role. Shipping and trade continue to play dominant roles in the state's modern economy. Liberal, lively and full of parks, it's a cosmopolitan place with plenty of culture.

Mecklenburg-Vorpommern (Mecklenburg-Lower Pomerania) remains a largely agricultural state, with thousands of lakes and a diverse coastline edging the Baltic Sea. Visitors come to explore the white cliffs of Rügen, the Mecklenburg lakes and the state's superb architecture. Rapidly developing towns such as Rostock are helping to change the region's economic climate.

Niedersachsen (Lower Saxony) is second only to Bavaria in size, and stretches from the North Sea southeast to the Harz mountains. It is one of the least densely populated regions in Germany. Destinations such as the Harz Mountains, the Ostfriesische Inseln (East Frisian Islands) and the orchard-covered lowlands provide a varied natural setting, and make a pleasant contrast to Hannover, the state capital.

Below *Schloss Sanssouci at Potsdam, near Berlin was Frederick II's summer palace*

Schleswig-Holstein lies between the North and the Baltic seas, and as the most northerly of Germany's states, has complex linguistic and historical traditions. Lübeck's red-brick architecture is a major draw, as are the long beaches and opportunities for sailing.

WESTERN GERMANY

Hessen (Hesse) is a prosperous region that lies at the heart of modern German life: Frankfurt am Main is a major financial and commercial hub, while Kassel draws the international art world to its Documenta exhibitions. The wooded hills and waterways of Waldecker *Land*, meanwhile, provide a pleasant contrast to settlements such as Wiesbaden and Marburg. Vineyards play an important role in the state's economy.

Nordrhein-Westfalen (North Rhine-Westphalia) has the highest population of all of Germany's Länder. Although once dependent on heavy industry in the Ruhrgebiet (Ruhr District), service industries now employ more than 60 per cent of the workforce. Agricultural land covers more than half the territory, however, and there is a good balance of outdoor pursuits in areas such as the northern Eifel mountains and Teutoburger Wald (Teutoburg Forest), and fascinating cities such as Köln (Cologne) and Aachen.

Rheinland-Pfalz (Rhineland-Palatinate) is a wonderfully scenic region, where vine-covered slopes rise from the winding Rhine and tributaries such as the Mosel. Picturesque castles, wine routes and historic towns such as Trier are scattered around the state.

Saarland, the country's smallest region, nestles in the hilly triangle where Germany shares its borders with Luxembourg and France. It became part of the German Federal Republic in 1957. The state's industrial heritage is best seen at the Völklingen ironworks.

BERLIN

As the country's political hub, Berlin is at the heart of Germany's transformation. Wonderful museums, extensive parks and vibrant streets make it a fascinating place to visit.

EASTERN GERMANY

Brandenburg is a largely rural region, although its capital, Potsdam, contains some of Germany's most attractive palaces and formal gardens. The area's landscape is harmonious rather than dramatic, with lowland plains, the Spree and Havel rivers, and several nature reserves, including the Nationalpark Unteres Odertal (Lower Oder National Park).

Sachsen (Saxony) has the beautiful city of Dresden, while Leipzig is another city of historical and cultural interest. The population density is high here, and some places have been heavily industrialized. That said, the Erzgebirge Mountains lure visitors away from the urban areas.

Sachsen-Anhalt (Saxony-Anhalt) has a varied landscape, with the splendid Harz Mountains to the southwest, flat land to the north (the Altmark) and heavily industrialized areas to the east near Dessau and Halle. It is home to the historic town of Wittenberg and Magdeburg, the capital, which was rebuilt after wartime bombing.

Thüringen (Thuringia) is sometimes called the 'green heart' of Germany and preserves many aspects of its traditional lifestyles. It is largely rural, with the mountainous Thüringer Wald (Thuringian Forest) to the south, yet its medieval castles and abbeys speak of a rich history. Weimar, is one of the country's cultural treasures. Erfurt is the capital of this fairly compact state which also contains several winter sports resorts.

MUNICH

While not, strictly speaking, a separate region, München (Munich) has a vibrant urban atmosphere that distinguishes it from the rest of Bavaria. As an artistic and media hub, it contains superb galleries and museums, while its baroque and rococo churches attest to a long tradition of religious patronage.

SOUTHERN GERMANY

Baden-Württemberg is a prosperous and picturesque region of southern Germany. The Schwarzwald (Black Forest) and Bodensee (Lake Constance) are just two of its many attractive natural areas, while the towns of Stuttgart, Heidelberg and Freiburg also repay exploration.

Bayern (Bavaria) is Germany's largest state, and has some of the country's loveliest scenery. Once settled by Celts and Romans, the area was formerly divided into dozens of smaller territories. Modern Bavaria still retains a strong regional identity. The state's stunning Alpine scenery forms the backdrop for wonderful fairy-tale castles and some exceptionally rich ecclesiastical architecture.

BERLIN

Fernsehturm (▷ 76) Take in a 360-degree view of Berlin from the top of the television tower.

Brandenburger Tor (▷ 80) A symbol of historical and contemporary upheaval, the Brandenburg Gate is one of Berlin's most recognizable landmarks.

Gemäldegalerie (▷ 86–83) All the major European schools of painting are represented in this collection of masterpieces.

Jüdisches Museum (▷ 87) A museum with a disorientating and disturbing exterior, and an intelligently designed and thought-provoking interior.

Pergamonmuseum (▷ 90–95) The enormous Pergamon Altar and the stunning Ishtar Gate from Babylon are among this museum's highlights.

Reichstag (▷ 97) Weighted with historical significance and now topped with a symbol of transparent government, Germany's parliament building is a must-see.

Tiergarten (▷ 100–101) The green park in the heart of Berlin is the ideal spot for a relaxing stroll or a Sunday afternoon picnic.

NORTHERN GERMANY

Bremen (▷ 124–125) Wander around the Kunsthalle's impressive art collection, explore the quirky historic district of Schnoorviertel, or just count the ships at nearby Bremerhaven, one of Germany's busiest ports.

Hamburg (▷ 76–81) A bustling city with great architecture, a cosmopolitan feel and a strong maritime tradition.

Kiel (▷ 127) Try to visit during the Kieler Woche, the glamorous annual regatta held in June, when sailing ships compete with ferries for a place in the harbour.

Lübeck (▷ 136–137) This historically important town is famous for its wealth of brickwork architecture.

Nordfriesische Inseln and Ostfriesische Inseln (▷ 139 and 140) The low-lying North Frisian and East Frisian islands are two different archipelagos, but they share the same natural beauty and a reputation for summer fun.

WESTERN GERMANY

Aachen (▷ 164–165) Enjoy a Wednesday evening concert under the dome of Charlemagne's cathedral, or test your luck in the neoclassical casino.

Köln (▷ 172–175) Worth seeing just for its skyline, Cologne is best visited during the pre-Lenten Karneval; if the revellers get to be too much, explore the Dom, one of Europe's most splendid Gothic buildings.

Koblenz (▷ 176) The Mosel flows into the Rhine at Deutsches Eck, literally the 'German corner', and this attractive town has grown up at the confluence.

Saarland (▷ 181) This region's UNESCO-listed Völklinger Hütte steel mill commemorates a bygone industrial

heritage, while the interior of the Ludwigskirche in Saarbrücken is a white baroque dream.
Rheintal (▷ 182–183) The Rhine flows north along its valley past fortresses and steep vine-covered slopes. While the legendary singing siren may no longer be spotted near Lorelei rock, this remains an enticing and dramatic region.
Ruhrgebiet (▷ 184–185) The Ruhr has a fascinating industrial legacy, important design museums and art galleries, and, in the city of Dortmund, a long beer-making tradition.
Trier (▷ 186–188) Wonderful and extensive Roman ruins and the oldest cathedral in Germany are the main attractions of Trier, which was the birthplace of philposopher Karl Marx.

EASTERN GERMANY

Colditz (▷ 211) This grim prison fortress housed Allied prisoners during World War II, whose stories have provided inspiration for films and books ever since.
Dessau (▷ 218) This key location for Bauhaus architecture is surrounded by acres of landscaped park.
Dresden (▷ 212–217) Having overcome wartime bombing, flooding and neglect, Dresden is once again a visually stunning city with a renowned cultural heritage.
Potsdam (▷ 228–232) Brandenburg's capital is best known for its palaces and its magnificent Sanssouci park. It makes an excellent day trip from Berlin, although it is really best explored at greater leisure.
Sächsische Schweiz (▷ 233) Visit the untamed region of Saxon Switzerland to explore its bizarre rock formations, good hiking territory and attractive spa towns.
Spreewald (▷ 234) Take a trip around this UNESCO Biosphere Reserve and try some of the local pickled gherkins.
Weimar (▷ 235) This town is the historic heart of German literary and intellectual life.

MUNICH

Asamkirche (▷ 265) No other church in Germany can match this over-the-top feast of rococo architecture.
Hofbräuhaus (▷ 268) Come to this huge beer hall and shaded beer garden for the archetypal Bavarian experience.
Deutsches Museum (▷ 270–274) 'How does it work?' This vast and fascinating museum, full of interest for adults and children alike, provides the answers.
Englischer Garten (▷ 269) Surf, paddle, stroll or sunbathe in Munich's central park, a natural haven for busy city-dwellers.
Marienplatz (▷ 276–277) Sit over a beer or coffee in the summer, or hunt for presents in the Christmas market—this is the city's real heart.
Schloss Nymphenburg (▷ 284–285) Relax in the grounds of this vast baroque palace, or admire the models portrayed in the Schönheitsgalerie (Gallery of Beauties).

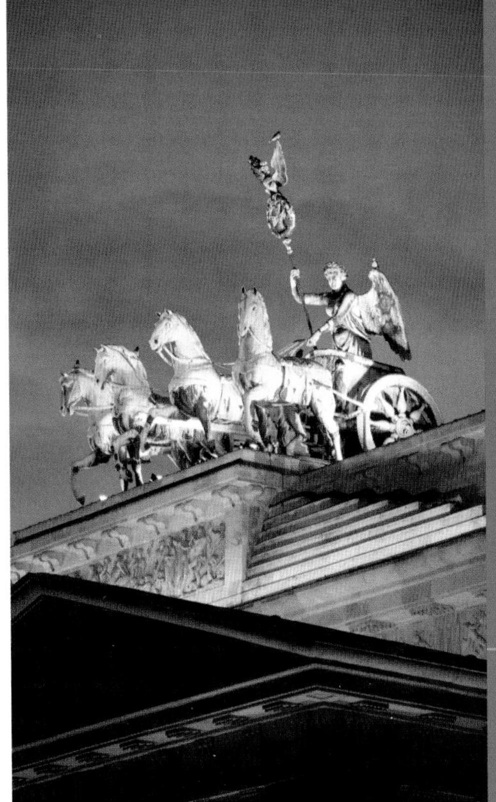

Clockwise from left to right *Ships gather in Kiel for the Full Ship Parade in 2008, a highlight of Kieler Woche; the copper Quadriga crowns Berlin's Brandendurger Tor*

SOUTHERN GERMANY

Baden-Baden (▷ 305) Take the waters in the outdoor pools used by Roman Emperor Caracalla, or try your luck in the classy casino.
Berchtesgadener Land (▷ 307) Alpine lakes, snow-covered peaks and scenic villages make this a spectacular place to explore.
Garmisch-Partenkirchen (▷ 314) Germany's winter sports capital has a well-deserved reputation: Come here for skiing, snowboarding or après-ski.
Heidelberg (▷ 312–313) Stroll along the Philosopher's Way, cross the Neckar on the old stone bridge or catch an open-air performance on the grounds of the imposing Schloss Heidelberg.
Nürnberg (▷ 316–317) Medieval and modern history combine in the busy town of Nuremberg. Its Christmas market is atmospheric and very popular.
Schloss Neuschwanstein (▷ 322–325) Ignore the crowds and soak up the atmosphere of the original fairy-tale castle and its beautiful setting.
Stuttgart (▷ 326–237) Pay homage to the German motor car industry at the Mercedes Benz or Porsche museums—even if you don't drive, you'll admire these beautiful cars.

TOP EXPERIENCES

Indulge in *Kaffee* und *Kuchen* (coffee and cakes) at a *Konditorei*, where you can choose from huge slices of mouthwatering cheesecake, rich Black Forest gateau or tangy fruit tart.

Hunt for presents at an atmospheric Christmas market, or simply chase away the end-of-year chill with a glass of warm *Glühwein* (mulled wine) and spicy *Lebkuchen* (gingerbread).

Relax in ornate 19th-century thermal baths, or splurge for a more modern spa experience; both are available at Baden-Baden (▷ 305) and other classic resorts.

Take a boat trip on one of Germany's many rivers and lakes. You can opt for anything from a one-hour round trip on Bodensee (Lake Constance; ▷ 308–309) to a week-long cruise down the Rhine or the Danube.

Examine artistic masterpieces from every era in Germany's excellent collections. Every region has at least one fine museum or art gallery, while art-lovers are spoiled for choice in the main cities.

Join in the pre-Lenten carnival atmosphere in towns and villages along the Rhine. Centuries-old traditions are revived each year as people dress up and entire communities look forward to the arrival of spring.

Wander around a castle or palace, choosing from among the dozens of historic monuments that are open to visitors—from stern fortresses and romantic ruins to the elegant homes of former rulers.

Hike or cross-country ski along mountain paths that have been marked out for sporting enthusiasts from the Schwarzwald (Black Forest) to the Harz Mountains.

Learn to distinguish between the hundreds of local beers, starting in Bamberg, with its dozens of breweries, and then joining thousands of drinking buddies at Munich's Oktoberfest (▷ 293).

Party all night to the latest techno rhythms in Berlin (its nightlife is one of the liveliest in Europe), or relax to the more traditional sounds of a world-class orchestra at one of the countless concert venues.

Escape to the mountains to climb a summit under your own steam, race downhill on a challenging ski run or simply enjoy the après-ski.

Take the easy way up on one of the funiculars (inclined railway) or cable cars that provide access to hilltop walks and stunning views. The narrow-gauge railway through the Harz Mountains adds another dimension to mountain climbing.

Island-hop in the North and Baltic seas. From car-less Helgoland to rugged Rügen, Germany's islands have a unique maritime history and a relaxing get-away-from-it-all atmosphere.

Window-shop for German fashion, as every city has a chic retail district as well as more affordable outlets. Düsseldorf is the fashion capital, while leading designers such as Jil Sander are based in Hamburg.

Partake in a wine-tasting at a local vineyard to see why Germany's wine-makers are winning a greater share of the international market.

Below *Sightseers on a tour boat travel along Berlin's Landwehrkanal*
Right *The bright lights and stalls of the Christmas market in Berlin*

LIVING GERMANY

Sports and Leisure 14
Fun and Festivals 16
German Culture 18
Traditional and Modern Architecture 20
Science and Technology 22
Economy, Politics and Europe 24
Green Germany 26

SPORTS AND LEISURE

Whether as enthusiastic spectators or hands-on participants, many Germans love sports. Good facilities exist for most activities, and organized sports clubs are very popular. The country's natural diversity allows for a full range of outdoor sporting activities, from bracing beach holidays by the North Sea to water sports in Alpine lakes and skiing and snowboarding in the mountain regions. The most keenly watched professional sport is soccer. Hopes of winning the UEFA European Football Championship for a fourth time were dashed in 2008, when the national squad were beaten by Spain in the final. Two years earlier, the team reached the semi-final of the World Cup, which Germany hosted. Tennis fans are hoping that a new generation of *Wunderkinder* such as Thomas Haas will replace Boris Becker and Steffi Graf. Motor-racing's Michael Schumacher became a sporting legend, but Formula 1 races in Hockenheim are watched as much for the cars as the drivers.

SUCCESSFUL STEERING

Behind every motor-racing champion is a team of technicians and design experts—not to mention a manager. Michael Schumacher, one of the world's highest-paid sportsmen, raced for the Italian firm Ferrari but was managed from 1983 by Bavarian Willi Weber. Weber recognized the young Schumacher's talent and took him into his Formula 3 WTS team in 1989, paying Schumacher's considerable costs for his first few seasons; in return, 'Schumi' agreed to hand over 20 per cent of his winnings. Schumacher moved to Formula 1 in 1991, and retired from the sport in 2006 as its most successful driver ever.

Clockwise from left to right *Snowboarding on the hills of Zugspitze; former Grand Prix motor-racing world champion Michael Schumacher; Berlin's Olympic Stadium*

GERMANS ON HOLIDAY

Post-war prosperity opened up leisure travel to West Germans, and the industry is now huge. Foreign travel declined after the terrorist attacks of September 2001, but Germans soon began returning to foreign destinations for their annual *Urlaub* (vacation). Spain, Italy, Austria and Greece are popular European destinations, but the number of Germans holidaying within their own country has risen in recent years. More than a third now take their main holiday in Germany (Mecklenburg-Vorpommern and Bavaria are top destinations). Reflecting ongoing economic differences, only half of East Germans go abroad, compared with two-thirds of West Germans. Habits are changing: People are taking shorter and less frequent breaks, and tend to organize their own trips with low-cost airlines, last-minute deals or discounted advance bookings.

HEALTH AND WEALTH

Baden-Baden (▷ 301) might be the country's best-known spa, but many other towns have built their economy around the 'wellness' industry, which now employs more than 600,000 people nationwide.

After World War II, a generous medical insurance system enabled some West Germans to take two- or three-week thermal 'cures' paid for by their health insurance company. The official Register of Health Spas identified those health resorts to which doctors could send patients to 'take the waters', and entitlement to visit a health spa was part of employment conditions.

Although the insurance companies have for the most part stopped paying for 'preventative' visits to health resorts, Germans are even entitled to go abroad if the specific treatment they need isn't available nationally—an option that has been confirmed by the European Court of Justice.

DAY OF REST

Germany's strict legislation on opening hours has long been a source of frustration. Until recently, most shops would close at lunchtime on Saturdays, and while a few stores were allowed to remain open until 4pm, further consumer spending had to wait until Monday. In 2003, the Bundestag (parliament) passed legislation enabling shops to remain open until 8pm on Saturdays, but Sunday trading is still only a rare exception. Trade unions have so far resisted calls for seven-day opening. Fuel stations are exempt, and make handsome profits from Sunday sales of bread, milk, beer and other products. In addition, retailers can now hold discount sales at any time, rather than during the traditionally designated end-of-season periods. As the country continues to experience recession, bargain-happy customers may be one way to keep the economy moving.

A PLACE TO DREAM

Munich's 1972 Olympic village was heralded as the most technologically and architecturally innovative design of its type: A high transparent roof swept over a 62,000-seat stadium, ice-rink, swimming complex and vast hall, and tall steel girders created a tent-like effect. After the ill-fated games (▷ 41), the city faced the challenge of ensuring that these purpose-built facilities benefited the Bavarian community and sporting enthusiasts. Two soccer teams came to the rescue: FC Bayern Munich, German and European cup winners; and TSV 1860 Munich, their lesser-known local rivals. For over two decades the teams shared the stadium, entertaining fans and attracting big-name visitors. The arrangement ended in 2004, when the city authorities decided that the entire Olympic complex needed a major facelift: The refurbished stadium is now used for other sports.

FUN AND FESTIVALS

Germans like to enjoy themselves. Of all the stereotypes about Germany, the image of a serious and angst-ridden nation is farthest from the mark. Although a deeply conventional streak runs through society, this is more than balanced by an equally strong interest in creativity, counter-culture and sheer fun. In Berlin, cabaret was developed into an art form, techno music first had its own city-wide parade and entire districts are known for their 'alternative' lifestyles. Throughout the country, the year is punctuated by great popular festivals that are as lively today as they ever were. These annual bouts of revelry and merry-making see thousands of ordinary people putting on fancy dress and letting their hair down in events that frequently tap into fairy-tales and pagan legends. Whether clubbing with Europe's trendiest DJs or waltzing to a small-town brass band, Germans believe in making the most of life. Reality shows, game shows and comedies fill the TV schedules, and the national sense of humour is alive and well (if sometimes impenetrable to non-German speakers).

Clockwise from left to right *A brass band in traditional Bavarian dress perform at a wedding; a traditionally dressed dray driver enjoys a stein of beer; crowds fill tables in a marquee at Munich's popular Oktoberfest*

ONE FOR ALL

In the ideological 1960s, anarchist and hippie communes were created in Berlin and Hamburg as a reaction against 'middle-class' values of individualism and consumerism.

Today, increasing numbers of young urban professionals are opting to join a housing-sharing community, but for different reasons. Berlin's 19th-century apartment blocks have numerous rooms; and renting one of these rooms, splitting bills and sharing a kitchen and bathroom facilities may be less expensive than finding a one-person flat (apartment).

Commitments of residents usually include a weekly meeting and may involve social activities, but the counter-culture has long disappeared.

WE'RE ONLY HERE FOR THE BEER

It's the Big Daddy of beer festivals: 16 days of frothing beer mugs, fairground rides and concerts. Munich's *Oktoberfest* began as a celebration of the future King Ludwig's wedding in 1810, and has grown into the world's largest annual party, with 6 million visitors descending on 14 beer tents in the Bavarian capital. The festivities open in mid-September with the arrival of horse-drawn brewery wagons, much pomp and the ceremonial tapping of a beer keg. Over the next two weeks, a folklore concert, a spectacular costume parade (with lots of *Lederhosen*) and brass-band concerts provide an ongoing excuse for downing even more beer—6 million litres (1.3 million gallons) are drunk by the first Sunday in October, when city life returns to normal and the six Munich breweries count their profits.

THE CAMERA NEVER SLEEPS

In recent years, 'reality' television shows have had as big an impact on Germany's screens as in other countries.

Big Brother, the series in which contestants live together and are gradually voted out by viewers, has been as controversial here as elsewhere—the leader of the Hesse region attempted to have it taken off the air in March 2000, arguing that it violated the constitutional provisions on human dignity. The series is filmed in a house outside Cologne, and has attracted celebrity visitors (such as Chancellor Schröder's half-brother) and fame-hungry competitors.

At least one marriage has taken place (after the second series), but producers must continually come up with new challenges, especially as each run now lasts a full 12 months.

WOMEN RULE THE RHINE

Cologne's pre-Lenten *Karneval* is one of the country's oldest and most boisterous festivals.

It begins on the Thursday before Ash Wednesday, and the first day's festivities are always the same: The day is called *Weiberfasnacht* and women are in charge of proceedings.

It's not clear when women began to enjoy this prerogative, but they have (almost) free rein to break everyday conventions. Men take precautions and don outlandish dress—anyone caught in business clothing is likely to have the end of his tie snipped off by trophy-collectors.

Along the Rhine valley, singing groups of women 'storm' their local government premises, where mayors symbolically hand over the keys to the city to them.

RAISING THE SPIRITS

In Germany, *Schnaps* (schnapps) is a general term for any kind of spirit that warms you up on the inside. A sixth of all Germany's schnapps distilleries are in the Freiburg region of Germany, most of them on Black Forest farms. An ancient church edict gave Black Forest farmers the right to produce their own schnapps, and the ruling still applies today. Farms with distillery rights are allowed to produce and sell locally 350 litres (77 gallons) a year. If a distillery falls into disuse, it cannot be revived and no further concessions are given. The best Black Forest schnapps is made from cherries (the famous Kirsch), but you can also find excellent varieties produced from damsons (Pfümli) and Williams pears (Williams).

Schnapps is served in small measures (2cl/ 0.7fl oz), but once a bottle has been opened, it gradually loses its taste, so it's best shared with friends.

GERMAN CULTURE

Contemporary German artists and musicians are following in the footsteps of a wealth of illustrious predecessors: In the fields of the visual arts, classical music and literature, Germany has been at the forefront of European artistic life for centuries. Ecclesiastical and aristocratic patronage enabled artists such as Albrecht Dürer (1471–1528) and Matthias Grünewald (*c*1470–1528) to flourish. Caspar David Friedrich (1774–1840) and Emil Nolde (1867–1956), to name but two, played important roles in the Romantic and Expressionist movements respectively. The country's role as a leader in the modern art world is confirmed by the Kassel Documenta, the Art Forum Berlin and the Kunstmesse Köln, which attract international artists. Composers such as Johann Sebastian Bach, Ludwig van Beethoven and Richard Wagner need no introduction, and the great orchestras of Berlin, Munich and Leipzig still generate controversy and enthusiasm. Music festivals, often concentrating on the work of a single composer, are held throughout the summer—the Wagner festival in Bayreuth is the best known.

Clockwise from left to right *A scene from* Die Meistersänger von Nürnberg (The Mastersingers of Nuremberg), performed at the Wagner festival in Bayreuth; *a poster for the Berlin Film Festival; the Documenta art exhibition is held in Kassel every four years (the next is in 2012)*

CANNES IN THE COLD

After Cannes and Venice, the Berlinale film festival is the third biggest in Europe. The location isn't as chic as the French Riviera (and in any case, the festival is held in February, so there's little chance of would-be starlets stripping down to their bikinis for the cameras), but according to the festival's organizers, 16,000 industry professionals from more than 100 countries come here to do serious business away from the awards ceremony. This makes sense, since Germany is Europe's largest market for films and is where big-money deals can be reached. On the artistic front, the Golden and Silver Bear awards are much prized, and recognition in Berlin often means further commercial and artistic success.

BRINGING ART TO THE MASSES?

In 2003, the Aldi discount supermarket chain commissioned seven contemporary artists to create 140,000 limited-edition etchings and graphic prints, each of which was to be signed and numbered by its creator. These original artworks and limited-edition prints went on sale for €10–€15 each in 1,500 of the chain's branches across southern Germany. Artists interested in this new 'retail outlet' included the controversial Felix Droese, who is particularly known for his 1981 installation *I Bumped Off Anne Frank*, which sparked strong criticism. Of the supermarket's idea, Droese told one journalist, 'I have the art and Aldi has the customers'. As a method of removing pictures from the sometimes élitist world of galleries and fairs, such 'off-the-shelf' originals typify the best of Germany's iconoclastic approach to affordable art.

TREES AS ART?

At first sight, the planting of *7000 Oaks* in and around Kassel in 1982 didn't have much to do with art. But when each tree was accompanied by a 1.2m (4ft) column of basalt stone, it became clear that this was no ordinary forestry scheme, but a sculpture project created to coincide with that year's Kassel Documenta. The man behind the idea was Joseph Beuys (1921–86), one of postwar Germany's best-known and most controversial artists, who represented his country at the Venice Biennale art exhibitions in 1976 and 1980. Intent on breaking down the barriers between ordinary life and the arts, Beuys argued that artists could help promote environmental change and urban renewal.

As his ideas on art's social role developed, he became involved in political activism and was closely connected with the founding of the German Green Party in 1979.

HOLLYWOOD ON THE ISER

Das Boot (*The Boat*), Wolfgang Petersen's claustrophobic submarine drama, has been one of German cinema's most successful exports since it first gripped movie-goers and television audiences in 1981. Based on an autobiographical bestseller by Lothar-Günther Buchheim (1918–2007), the six-hour production was the most expensive German film ever made at the time, at a cost of US$14 million. Shot at the Bavaria Filmstadt near Munich (▷ 278), home of German cinema since 1919, *Das Boot* rekindled discussion of U-boat crews' wartime role. Much of the set is still preserved at the studios, including the reconstructed submarine, which was composed of three separate sections to aid shooting. The submarine appeared at the end of Steven Spielberg's *Raiders of the Lost Ark* (1981).

SCHMALTZING ALONG

A source of amusement and irony inside Germany and abroad is *Schlager*, a form of popular music. Characterized by sentimental lyrics and uncomplicated, easily remembered tunes, the ballads are derived from 19th-century operetta, but are perhaps best described as a blend of pop and country-and-western music. The lyrics often incorporate a 'boy-meets-girl, girl-leaves-boy' scenario, and express feelings of loneliness, disillusionment or, conversely, hope.

Widely regarded as kitsch and musically unsophisticated, *Schlager's* catchy tunes nonetheless appeal to a sizeable audience (largely older people), and are a staple of German airwaves and restaurant sing-alongs. One of *Schlager's* most famous performers is Heino, best known for *'Schwarz-braun ist die Haselnuss'* ('Dark-brown is the Hazelnut').

TRADITIONAL AND MODERN ARCHITECTURE

Germany's regional diversity and plethora of independent states, all with leaders who wished to impress rivals or leave memorials to their piety, resulted in a multitude of wonderful buildings in a variety of styles. Even small towns find themselves with a Romanesque, Gothic or baroque place of worship, and the Renaissance and neoclassical styles are also well represented. In addition, German artists and architects played important roles in developing art nouveau (called *Jugendstil* here) and Modernism. Many fine churches, palaces and castles survived the 20th century's ravages, while others have been carefully reconstructed; one felicitous effect of this was a revival of interest in traditional building crafts. Modern German homes are generally built with great care, and environmentally friendly materials and designs are commonly used. On a grander scale, showcase buildings such as James Stirling's Staatsgalerie in Stuttgart demonstrate public investment in innovative design, and reunification provided a powerful impetus for rebuilding in Berlin, particularly Sir Norman Foster's glass dome on the Reichstag.

Clockwise from left to right *The Reichstag dome, designed by Sir Norman Foster; detail of the clock tower in Mainau; the west tower of Berlin's Kaiser-Whilelm-Gedächtniskirche*

INNER-CITY INDUSTRY

In December 2001, Volkswagen opened the Gläserne Manufaktur (literally 'glass factory') amid Dresden's baroque churches and palaces. Designed by the Munich architect Gunter Henn, the new assembly plant (for VW's luxury Phaeton model) is an ultramodern set of buildings, filled with light. A circular 40m (131ft) glass tower, in which completed cars are stored, rises from the main structure, while smaller pods emerge from the sides. The complex is in Strassburger Platz, and components are delivered on environmentally friendly freight trains. The futuristic VW factory marks a new departure in design. Here, industry is enhancing Dresden's heritage rather than detracting from the city's resurrected beauty.

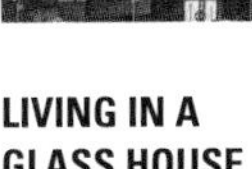

THE WASHING MACHINE

Post-reunification Berlin was both a giant construction site and an architect's dream—a space to be filled with state-of-the-art buildings. However, not all the new constructions have met with unanimous approval.

The contrete-and-glass Federal Chancellery, designed by Axel Schultes and Charlotte Frank and opened in May 2001 at a cost of €263 million, was described as 'too monumental' by the then Chancellor Schröder, who feared that the building's vast proportions would send out the wrong message about German ambitions. The newspaper *Die Welt* labelled it a 'concrete monster', and Berlin residents have given it their own name: the 'washing machine'. Yet the design is highly symbolic: A ribbon of government buildings brings together West and East, crossing the former line of division twice, and the spacious arches are intended to create an impression of governmental transparency.

PRESERVED HERITAGE

After World War II, East Germany's Communist rulers set to work redeveloping bombed cities such as their sector of Berlin and Leipzig, although frequently with unattractive results.

The former Hanseatic port of Wismar (▷ 145) was only slightly damaged by bombing and was therefore neglected by the authorities. This inadvertently preserved the town: Restoration work was left undone, but the buildings themselves remained.

Wismar's circular street layout has stayed unchanged for centuries, and about a quarter of the building façades in the middle of town are recognized for their historical importance.

Since reunification and an injection of European Union funds, Wismar and nearby Stralsund have been spruced up (without destruction) and designated UNESCO World Heritage Sites, bringing in cultural and historical visitors—and reassuring locals who felt that the money would have been better spent on direct job creation.

LIVING IN A GLASS HOUSE

One of the most innovative and radical buildings erected in Germany in recent years is a family home: House R 128 (alias Römerstrasse 128), on a hillside overlooking Stuttgart, was designed by the engineer Werner Sobek in 2000.

The minimalist four-floored house was intended to be recyclable, emission-free and self-sufficient in its use of energy. Built around a steel frame, it has no brick walls, merely glass panels. Except for the sanitary facilities, everything is open and visible. Triple glazing (rarely used in European housing) prevents overheating in the summer, and electricity is generated by 48 solar-power modules.

As a home, Römerstrasse 128 has little intimacy and even less furniture. As a contribution to environmentally sustainable futuristic lifestyles, however, it's a daring experiment—and, in its own way, a beautiful building.

BAUHAUS

Disillusioned with traditional 'academic' approaches to training, Walter Gropius (1883–1969) opened the Bauhaus school of architecture and applied arts in Weimar in 1919. With its emphasis on functionalism and the search for *Neue Sachlichkeit* (new objectivity), the Bauhaus's impact on modern architecture was immense, both inside and outside Germany. In 1927, some 16 architects—including Le Corbusier, Mies van der Rohe, Peter Behrens and Gropius himself—came together to design the Weissenhof Estate in Stuttgart. The 21-house project exemplified the movement's approach: clean lines, flat roofs, large windows and a daring use of new materials. The Nazis condemned the architects as 'decadent', and the school closed its doors in 1933. Wartime bombing destroyed several of the Weissenhof houses, but 11 can still be seen today.

Germany has been a leading industrial nation since the 19th century. However, it really came into its own as Europe's pre-eminent scientific and technological nation in the second half of the 20th century. While engineering and the chemical industry have formed the backbone of industrial progress, the IT industry and pharmaceutical and biomedical laboratories now attract international scientists, and the European Patent Office's location in Munich reflects Germany's standing as a heartland for innovative and applied research. Much of Germany's manufacturing output is destined for export, whether medical drugs and equipment, aircraft components or electronic goods. The port of Hamburg is the main hub of cargo transportation. Food processing, textiles and environmental technology are also important industries. But progress has brought moral dilemmas—pharmaceutical companies, for example, have been criticized for not sharing information about AIDS medication with poorer nations. Globalization is also raising challenges for both industrial giants and for the government, with jobs being outsourced to Eastern Europe and Asia.

BEETLING ALONG

The classic Beetle (*Käfer* in German) was the best-selling car of all time, and although the last model rolled off VW's Mexican production line in summer 2003, its status as a collector's item is assured. Vehicle design and technology, not to mention the automobile market, have moved on since Volkswagen sold the first *Käfer* in 1947 as a low-price model that would bring car ownership to the masses. In 1988, VW brought out the New Beetle (also known as the 'Newbie'). This model has retained elements of the original iconic design, but has been updated with a contemporary twist and more sophisticated features, such as airbags.

Top *The casing for an LNG compressor in the Siemens factory*

RUHR VALLEY FORTUNES

In its prime, the Ruhr was the most developed industrial region in the world.

While trade and service industries have partially replaced mines and furnaces, the human cost of deindustrialization has been high, and towns have been forced to find new uses for the steelworks and coal mines. Factories have been converted into nightclubs or housing, while other structures—including mines and model housing developments and pitheads—have been preserved as monuments to a proud industrial past.

Opened in 1932, the Zeche Zollverein colliery just outside Essen (▷ 185) has neo-Gothic façades and an art nouveau machine hall, showing the change from historicism to modernism. It is now a UNESCO World Heritage Site, preserving the past and providing a new kind of employment.

YOU ARE WHAT YOU DRIVE

The automobile industry may be built on engineering excellence, but it is driven by the Germans' love of cars and the pride and social prestige they associate with them. Germans bought 3.2 million cars in 2007, more than any other country in Europe—a figure that works out at 39.2 new cars for every 1,000 people. Most Germans in the former East have by now replaced their old Trabants with new Western cars. Where other countries have a class system, German professionals are judged by their cars. In this intensely competitive market, manufacturers such as Mercedes-Benz, BMW and VW are increasingly aware of the importance of image as well as technological superiority, and regularly issue next-generation models of their flagship vehicles in a bid to achieve and maintain brand loyalty.

NUCLEAR REACTION

Nuclear power has always divided Germany's citizens. The Green Party's emergence was closely linked to anti-nuclear protests, and the transportation of nuclear waste from France in 2001 mobilized hundreds of demonstrators. Yet Germany has 17 nuclear power stations of its own at 12 sites, accounting for about a quarter of the country's electricity production. Under the Green Party's influence, legislation was adopted in 2002 to phase out nuclear energy by 2021: No new nuclear plants are to be built, the operational life of existing plants has been restricted and there are caps on the amount of electricity each plant may produce. However, as alternative energy sources are not yet sufficiently developed to make up the shortfall, and as oil prices remain high, some politicians have called for a rethinking of the policy.

PUFFING AROUND THE MOUNTAIN

Saxony's Harz Mountains are home to the Harzer Schmalspurbahnen, a network of narrow-gauge railways that extends for more than 130km (80 miles). The railway connects the major settlements of Quedlinburg, Wernigerode and Nordhausen.

The most spectacular stretch is the Brockenbahn, which winds around northern Germany's highest mountain near the former East–West border. After decades of closure (the line had been deemed too close to a Soviet listening post), passenger services resumed in 1992. It is now very popular with visitors.

Most of the trains are pulled by steam locomotives introduced in the 1950s (when steam was already being phased out elsewhere). In a country that prides itself on high-speed inter-city links, they are a throwback to another era.

Below *A Mercedes-Benz CLK-Class cabriolet*
Right *Manufacturing wind-powered turbines*

For 45 years, West Germany experienced its *Wirtschaftswunder* (rapid economic growth), which made it the most prosperous and stable country in Europe. The post-World War II Marshall Plan injected 1.5 billion dollars into the economy, and bolstered by technological innovation and harmonious industrial relations, the country boomed. However, the cost of integrating 16 million people following reunification in 1990 has been high. Unemployment and taxes have both risen as billions of euros have been pumped into regenerating the eastern regions. A global economic slump and political unwillingness to tackle reform resulted in low economic growth, and Germany is slowly modernizing its labour regulations, immigration policy and welfare and taxation systems. The Communist legacy has gradually been overcome in much of the east, but more than 2 million first- and second-generation immigrants have still to be fully integrated into German society, where the issue of national identity remains fraught with tension. Meanwhile, the European Union has expanded eastward, opening up new markets and creating foreign policy challenges for Germany as it seeks to maintain its pivotal role in European development while renegotiating vital relationships with France and the United States.

Clockwise from left to right *East German cars at the former Berlin Wall; demonstrations against the government in Hamburg in 2002*

THE PENSION POT

Germany's pensioners are among the youngest and most prosperous in Europe, but a declining birth rate is raising the issue of who will pay for state pensions in the future.

Plans to raise the official retirement age from 65 to 67 have been announced beginning in 2012, and will be phased in between then and 2029. The average German retires just after 62, and pensions account for more than 10 per cent of GDP.

According to the Federal Statistics Office, there will soon be more Germans aged over 65 than under 15, so to maintain demographic stability and pension levels, Germany will have to accept large numbers of immigrants. Few young people want large families.

EAST BERLIN FROM THE INSIDE

In the years immediately after the 1990 *Wende* (change), Ossis (Easterners) had very mixed feelings about their past.

Some of this changed in 2003, when Wolfgang Becker's bitter-sweet comedy film *Good Bye Lenin!* was an unexpected critical and popular success throughout Germany. The story tells of Alex's staunchly Communist mother, who falls into a coma just before the collapse of the Berlin Wall, remaining unaware of reunification and the subsequent social transformations. When she comes round, Alex goes to extraordinary lengths to spare her any sudden shocks. *Good Bye Lenin!* swept the boards at the 2003 German film awards, and gave West Germans an insight into ordinary life in the former German Democratic Republic, helping to break down divisive stereotypes.

OUTSIDERS OR CITIZENS?

Germany's complex and ambiguous citizenship policies are seen most starkly in the situation of the Turkish *Gastarbeiter* (guest workers).

Following an agreement in the early 1960s between West Germany and Turkey, hundreds of thousands of Turks were invited to make up for Germany's manpower shortage and to rebuild the economy. Most intended to stay for only a few years, but ended up settling down, opening businesses and having children. Critics of Germany's *jus sanguinis* policy (by which nationality was conferred by blood rather than place of birth) point to the lower educational achievements and poor employment figures seen in this second-generation group.

A reformed nationality law passed in 2000 makes it easier for foreign nationals, especially those born in Germany, to be naturalized as citizens.

REBUILDING BRIDGES

When the Oder–Neisse line was chosen as the new Poland–German border in 1945, it drove a wedge between people who lived only a few hundred metres apart. At Germany's easternmost point, the Saxon town of Görlitz found itself divided: The historic heart lay on the west bank (and therefore in the GDR), while the residential districts on the opposite bank became the Polish town of Zgorzelec. The enlargement of the European Union has brought new challenges to the towns' mayors. The political culture and language may be different, but inter-municipal cooperation is both desirable and logical. Having seen a sharp rise in unemployment since 1990, many Germans are suspicious of a less expensive Polish workforce. Poles, on the other hand, tend to be more optimistic about the opportunities of an open market and visa-less travel.

WHO IS GERMAN?

For decades after World War II the small Black Forest town of Lahr was home to Canadian troops.

Since they withdrew in 1993, some 9,000 'Russian Germans' have moved into town, and now account for 22 per cent of the population. They are descended from German farmers who settled along the Volga in 1763, and were exiled to Siberia or Kazakhstan in 1941. Many gradually assimilated and married Russians, and the younger generations often hid their German origins.

Since the collapse of the Soviet Union, 2.4 million 'ethnic Germans' have taken advantage of an article in the German Constitution that enables them to claim citizenship, and they now constitute the country's biggest minority.

The German authorities introduced a language test in 1997 to control the influx, and a quota system is now also in place.

The majority of Germans share a genuine concern about the environment. Partly a legacy of the 19th-century Romantic movement, this consensus has found expression in the public's reaction to industrial pollution along the Rhine, tree disease in the 1970s and nuclear power. In 1994, a provision (Article 20a) was inserted into the constitution emphasizing the state's duty to preserve the country's natural resources, and Germans continue to be among Europe's most enthusiastic recyclers and exponents of alternative energy. Green Party leaders such as Petra Kelly (1947–92) and Joschka Fischer (1948–) have become household names, and no other Green Party in the world has had such a direct impact on national policy. Effort and expense have gone into landscaping rail lines, abandoned industrial sites have been turned into parks or leisure areas, and images of toxic waste from the eastern regions have prompted substantial clean-up efforts since reunification.

Above left to right *Recycling bins at a rail station in Berlin; wind turbines in the Saarland region*

HERE TO STAY

Many of Germany's native animal species, such as the beaver and wild cat, are threatened with extinction. Yet the numbers of one imported species, the raccoon, have increased so rapidly that it is now regarded as an urban menace.

A single pair of North American raccoons was released into the wild in 1934, and more escaped from a fur farm during a World War II bombing raid. With no natural predators, their numbers grew rapidly, and an estimated million of these scavengers are now at large, foraging through garbage and occasionally entering houses in search of food.

Kassel (▷ 176) is particularly badly affected, and has even appointed an official whose sole task is to deal with the pests.

DOING YOUR BIT

Environmental action in Germany goes much further than lip-service. German homes have a series of containers for household waste, which is separated into biodegradable or organic, plastics, glass, paper and other waste, and disposed of accordingly. Most people cooperate, and children are encouraged to conserve water and energy resources. Public waste bins also have separate sections, and plastic grocery bags are not generally available in supermarkets. Although transportation firms grumbled at the imposition of an 'ecology tax' on fossil fuels in 1999, individual drivers accepted the increase and the Constitutional Court backed the government, which claims that carbon dioxide emissions have fallen as a direct result.

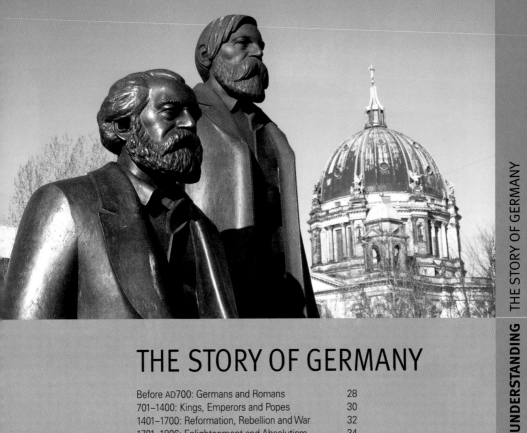

THE STORY OF GERMANY

Before AD700: Germans and Romans	28
701–1400: Kings, Emperors and Popes	30
1401–1700: Reformation, Rebellion and War	32
1701–1806: Enlightenment and Absolutism	34
1807–1870: Restoration, Revolution and Reaction	36
1871–1918: The German Empire	38
1919–1938: Between the Wars	40
1939–1948: Defeat and Division	42
1949–1989: Two Germanys	44
1989–Today: Germany Reunited	46

The remains of one of the very first inhabitants of the land now known as Germany were discovered at Neanderthal near Düsseldorf in 1856, and the place gave its name to an early species of man, *Homo Neanderthalensis*. From around the fifth century BC onwards, the Celts, widespread throughout western Europe, had to contend with Germanic tribespeople moving in from the north and east. By the first century BC nearby Celtic Gaul—today's France—had been incorporated into the Roman Empire. Seeking to extend their domain eastward, the Romans were soon in contact with the Germanic tribes. On more than one occasion, the legions marched east, but for the most part Roman civilization was confined to the lands west of the Rhine and south of the Danube. The end of the Roman Empire came in the fifth century AD, when, in the 'Migration of Peoples', the Roman troops were overwhelmed. But even today, traces of the long Roman presence can be discerned: In addition to relics like the Porta Nigra in Trier (▷ 187), some say there are subtle differences in culture and behaviour between the Romanized inhabitants of the Rhineland and their relatives to the east, where Rome's influence was never felt.

Top *The Roman Porta Nigra (Black Gate), built in the second century AD in Trier is one of several Roman ruins that make a visit to the city worthwhile*

THE ROMAN WALL

As they did at other extremities of their empire, the Romans attempted to hold their barbarian foes at bay by building formidable frontier barricades.

In Germany, the gap of several hundred kilometres between the natural boundaries of the Rhine and Danube was filled in the second century AD by an extraordinary wall called the Limes.

Reinforced by a palisade and a wide dry moat, the Limes was guarded by more than a thousand timber watchtowers and fortlets situated within hailing distance of one another. Some way to the rear of the frontier, around a hundred stone castles were built to house the troops of the border garrisons.

VINES ALONG THE RHINE

As the Romans transformed the area protected by the Limes (see The Roman Wall ▷ 28), they made sure their taste for wine was met, not just by importing it from Gaul and Italy, but by planting vines along the sunnier slopes of the Rhine and Mosel.

The fourth-century AD politician and poet Decimus Magnus Ausonius was so taken by the sight of the vineyards lining the Mosel that he composed the long poem *Mosella*, which compared this northern landscape to his native Bordeaux.

Archaeologists still continue to turn up objects associated with the wine trade of Roman times, although perhaps the most poignant are the inscriptions on tombstones that attribute a long and happy life to judicious consumption of the fruit of the vine.

FORMIDABLE FOES

The Romans were inclined to dismiss the Germans as idle, quarrelsome savages, at their happiest when eating and drinking to excess and fighting among themselves. Perhaps exposure to Roman ways might civilize them, they thought. Among selected German leaders invited to serve in the Roman army and even given citizenship was Arminius (*c*17BC–AD21; Hermann in German). But Arminius returned to his roots, raising the flag of revolt and defeating an army sent to teach the Germans a lesson. At the Battle of the Teutoburger Wald in AD9, a force of 20,000 was tricked into a swamp and cut to pieces by Arminius' men. In the 19th century, nationalists promoted Hermann as the first great German hero, and erected a huge monument to him on what was thought to be the site of his victory.

ATTILA THE HUN

The fiercest of the warrior folk who swarmed westwards across the Rhine as the Roman Empire crumbled were the nomadic Huns. Living, sleeping and fighting on horseback, they were led by the remorseless Attila (*c*AD406–453).

In AD451 he led his forces in a great rampage across northern France as far as the modern-day city of Orléans. Hearing that an army composed mostly of Germanic tribesmen was on his trail, Attila retraced his steps eastward.

The adversaries met on 20 September in one of the greatest massacres of ancient times, the Battle of the Catalaunian Fields.

Attila survived the slaughter of his army, but two years later he was dead, overcome in the arms of his bride by the effects of an over-sumptuous wedding banquet. A subsequent theory is that Attila was the victim of an assassination plot hatched to prevent him from attacking Constantinople.

FRANKS

The most powerful of the Germanic peoples inheriting the remains of the Roman Empire were the Franks. Originally just a group of tribes given to squabbling among themselves, they were eventually united under chieftain Clovis (*c*AD466–511), who slaughtered his rivals, routed the last Roman ruler of Gaul and was proclaimed king by being raised upon the shields of his warriors.

Clovis accepted Christianity, but many pagan beliefs persisted. He and his successors were thought to have magical powers, and could make crops flourish by walking over the fields.

From their power base in what is today's Belgium, the Franks extended their sway both east and west. They gave modern France its name (Frankreich in German) and settled in what is now Franken (Franconia). A fight with the heathen Saxons was settled when the Frankish army forded the River Main at what is now Frankfurt.

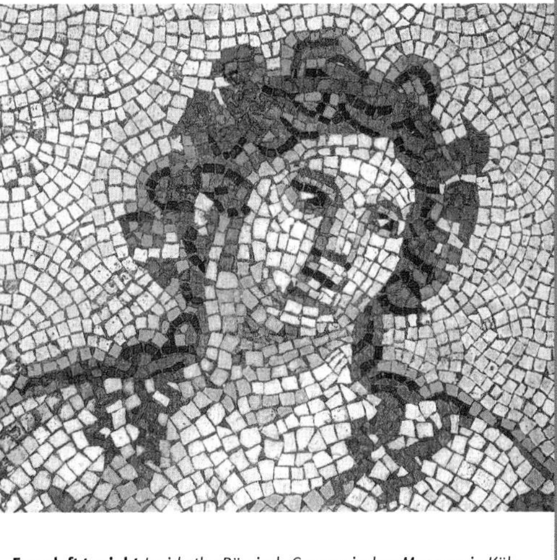

From left to right *Inside the Römisch-Germanisches Museum in Köln and a mosiac of Dionysus in the museum*

The memory of Rome's glory persisted long after its downfall, and in turbulent times the rulers of Germany were anxious to identify themselves with the empire's stability, culture and prosperity. The greatest of the Frankish kings was Charlemagne (AD747–814; Karl der Grosse in German), who united much of Europe, promoted learning and the arts and on Christmas Day AD800 was crowned Emperor of the West by the pope. But Germany was still too vast and diverse a land to be held together easily. After Charlemagne's death, the Frankish realm was split into three: an eastern part ruled by Louis the German; a western part—forerunner of modern France—in the hands of Charles the Bald; and a middle kingdom under Lothar (whose name survives in Lotharingen, the German name for the French province of Lorraine). Central power became ever weaker, and the responsibility for warding off attacks from Vikings and marauding Magyars (from modern-day Hungary) often fell to local leaders, whose domains eventually became powerful dukedoms such as Saxony, Franconia and Bavaria. These leaders were well able to resist the re-establishment of imperial power and prestige, not least because the Emperor's attention was often focused on his possessions outside Germany, notably in Italy.

Above *Charlemagne, the King of the Franks and Holy Roman Emperor who ruled much of Europe in the eighth century*

EVANGELIZING THE GERMANS

After the fall of Rome, Christianity continued to flourish on the edge of Europe, in Britain and Ireland, and it was from here that St. Boniface set out to convert the mostly heathen Germans. His first mission was to the Frisian coastlands of northern Germany, whose inhabitants were unreceptive to his teachings. Boniface had better luck in Hessen, where he demonstrated the impotence of the ancient gods by cutting down a sacred oak. When this awesome outrage was not avenged, the Hessians converted en masse. But Boniface's career came to an abrupt end. When he tried once more to exercise his persuasive powers on the Frisians in around AD754, they lost patience and put him to the sword.

CHARLEMAGNE

Charlemagne's rule as king of the Franks lasted from AD768 to 814. A great warrior-king, he fought dozens of battles, the bloodiest of which were against the Saxons, whose stubborn resistance was finally brought to an end in AD782 by the execution of more than 4,000 of their fighters.

Charlemagne exercised control over his vast territories by means of a mobile court, which settled periodically in one of his many estates. But his home base was the cathedral city of Aachen, to which he summoned wise men and scholars to create a great seat of learning, law-giving, art and architecture.

The glorious octagonal chapel he ordered to be built here has survived (▷ 164–165).

CANOSSA

Throughout the Middle Ages, popes, princes and emperors squabbled constantly about the extent of their respective powers. In the winter of 1077, faced with excommunication by Pope Gregory VII (*c*1020–85) and with rebellious dukes in Germany, King Heinrich IV (1050–1106) made his way to the castle at Canossa where Pope Gregory had sought refuge. In an astonishing ploy, Heinrich huddled in a hair shirt in the snow-packed courtyard for three days and nights until the puzzled pope ordered him to be let in. The monarch prostrated himself before the pope, begging for readmission to the Church. Moved, Pope Gregory granted the supplicant's wish. Ever since, *Canossa* has been a German byword for abject submission to a superior power (even though Heinrich subsequently succeeded in deposing Pope Gregory and replacing him with another pope).

THE HANSA

Germany prospered in the high Middle Ages, and German settlers and merchants moved throughout Europe, founding towns and trading hubs. Control of commerce around the Baltic was exercised by the Lübeck-based Hanseatic League, originally an association of harbour cities formed to secure the sea lanes and protect its shipping from pirates.

The most notorious of these buccaneers was Klaus Störtebeker, a kind of Robin Hood of the waves, who in the 15th century operated from his base on the Swedish island of Gotland. Störtebeker and his fellow freebooters were eventually overcome by a fleet sent by the Hanseatic League, and he was brought in triumph to Hamburg, where he was publicly put to death.

Hamburg is still proud of its Hanseatic traditions; cars licensed here carry plates labelled HH (Hansestadt Hamburg), and other old Hansa towns do likewise (HB is used in Bremen and HRO in Rostock).

BARBAROSSA

The most illustrious of medieval German rulers was the handsome and energetic Friedrich I (1122–90), known to his Italian subjects as 'Barbarossa' for his flowing red beard.

The splendour of Friedrich's court, his constant forays into Italy, his fearlessness in battle and his revival of the glories of Charlemagne's rule, together with his tragic death on his way to deliver Jerusalem from the Saracens, made him a legendary figure even in his own lifetime.

The legend was later added to, when the great emperor was thought not to be dead, but asleep, waiting for the moment when a German empire should rise once more.

Above left *Detail of Emperor's Otto's statue in Magdeburg*
Below *The exterior of the Romanesque Michaeliskirche in Hildesheim*

Before the devastation of the Thirty Years' War (1618–48), Germany was showing signs of national progress, with an increasingly vibrant cultural, intellectual and commercial life based around cities such as Nuremberg. The Habsburg Holy Roman Emperors still saw themselves as the successors to Charlemagne, but unlike him they had only limited power over the myriad states into which Germany was still divided. Nevertheless, the Holy Roman Empire remained an important player in the game of European power politics. As the Continent emerged from the Middle Ages, discontent with the Church grew and took a particularly radical form in Germany, the home of Martin Luther. The Reformation brought increasing political and religious tension, as many but by no means all territories converted to Protestantism, leaving Germany with a gaping confessional divide. The real catastrophe, however, was the Thirty Years' War, which devastated the country in a way not to be seen again until the 20th century, leaving cities in ruins and the population barely able to feed itself. In 1648, the Peace of Westphalia brought an end to this conflict, but this pattern of internal strife would be repeated.

Clockwise from left to right *A depiction of the death of Gustavus Adolphus, founder of the Swedish Empire and a Protestant leader, during the Battle of Lutzen in the Thirty Years' War; a desk and chair in Martin Luther's study in Fort Wartburg, Eisenach; a page from the Gutenberg Bible*

WALLENSTEIN

As the Thirty Years' War wore on, the religious passions that had inspired it were replaced by the lust for power and plunder. Many soldiers were brutal and unprincipled mercenaries—the notorious *Landsknechte*—drawn from the dregs of half of Europe.

Some of their commanders were little different, notably Albrecht von Wallenstein (1583–1634), the war's most successful general. Having wormed his way into the goodwill of Holy Roman Emperor Ferdinand II (1578–1637), this minor nobleman from Bohemia used every opportunity to enrich himself. When Wallenstein's troops showed more loyalty to their commander than to the emperor, Ferdinand ordered his elimination.

GUTENBERG

Originally endowed with the name of Gensfleisch (Gooseflesh), Johannes Gutenberg of Mainz (*c*1399–1468) was the man responsible for what has been called 'Germany's greatest single contribution to civilization'. His invention of modern printing and all the technology to go with it—presses, inks and, above all, moveable type cast in metal—revolutionized the production of books, which hitherto had been laboriously copied out by hand or printed from wooden blocks incapable of reuse. Basically unchanged until the 19th century, Gutenberg's technology made the rapid diffusion of the radical ideas possible, leading to the Reformation; his magnificent Bible dating from around 1455 is his greatest monument. But poor Gutenberg failed to profit from his genius. Greedy creditors reduced him to financial ruin, and he ended his days in the Mainz poorhouse.

THOMAS MÜNTZER

Originally a follower of Luther, the charismatic Thomas Müntzer (*c*1489–1525) later diverged from his master's teachings, propagating an apocalyptic version of Christianity and denouncing the worldly rule of princes and potentates. This made him a natural leader of the impoverished peasantry, many of whom had been reduced to the status of serfs. Under Müntzer they rose up against their lords in the Peasants' War of 1524–25, which, although vicious, was short. The peasant army was massacred at the Battle of Frankenhausen on 15 May 1525; Müntzer was taken to Mühlhausen, where, after expert torturers had persuaded him to recant, he was beheaded. Luther denounced him as a fanatic and tarnished his own reputation by condemnation of the peasants. Müntzer enjoyed a brief after-life of glory when he entered the GDR's pantheon of proto-Communist heroes.

MARTIN LUTHER

As a professor of theology at the University of Wittenberg, Martin Luther (1483–1546), like many other Germans, had become increasingly concerned with the serious failings and corrupt practices of the Catholic Church at that time.

The Reformation is said to have begun when he famously nailed his '95 Theses' to the door of the church in Wittenberg. Such an overt provocation soon saw him excommunicated and branded an outlaw, and his books were ordered to be burned.

He might easily have suffered the fate of so many other heretics had not Friedrich III, Elector of Saxony, given him a safe haven in the Wartburg (▷ 220).

Like other German princes, Friedrich had seen that a religious struggle could help him gain a greater degree of independence. Luther's pamphlets and his translation of the Bible into German were printed in large quantities by Gutenberg's press.

THE SACK OF MAGDEBURG

In April 1630, the prosperous Protestant city of Magdeburg was besieged by the Catholic Count of Tilly (1559–1632). General Tilly was a pious man of great personal rectitude, but his largely mercenary army was more interested in plunder than the rightness of their cause. When Tilly offered the Magdeburgers his personal protection if they opened their gates, they were inclined to submit, but they were overruled by the city's fanatical Protestant pastor, who preached resistance to the bitter end. Tilly reluctantly gave the order to attack, and the defences were duly stormed. But his men then ran amok, killing, raping, pillaging and destroying everything they could not steal. Carrying an infant that he had found in the arms of its murdered mother, the general rode through the burning city, powerless to halt the destruction. Magdeburg was reduced to ashes, and of its population of 30,000, only 5,000 survived.

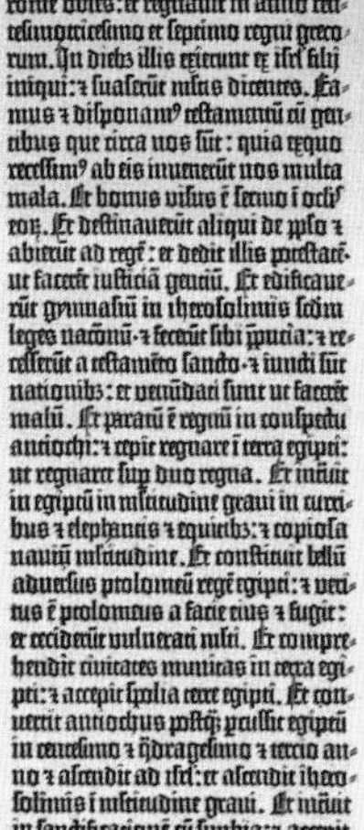

Under the absolute rule of King Louis XIV (1638–1715), France was Europe's undisputed super-power, and the style of his court at Versailles was imitated all over the Continent. However petty their realm, 18th-century German rulers also saw themselves as the heart of the state, answerable only to God. They competed with one another in the splendour of their palaces and formal gardens and in their promotion of the arts. Some became patrons of the Enlightenment, the philosophical movement based on reason rather than traditional belief, and surrounded themselves with the foremost thinkers and writers of the day, most notably at Friedrich II the Great's Potsdam and the Weimar of Goethe, Herder and Schiller. Music, too, owed much to princely patronage, though Bach's greatest days were spent in the service of the city of Leipzig rather than as a court musician. Throughout the century, Germany remained divided by political entities of every conceivable size and character. However, Prussia began a process that was to lead to its dominance over German affairs in the next century. In a series of internal reforms and successful wars, Prussia's Hohenzollern kings transformed their realm into a highly efficient, centralized state with a mighty army.

THE SERGEANT-KING

King Friedrich Wilhelm I of Prussia (1688–1740) was given the derisive name 'the Sergeant-King' by his fellow monarchs because of his obsession with all things military. A man of thuggish manners, Friedrich Wilhelm was at his happiest drilling his soldiers. His best-loved troopers were his *lange Kerle* (literally 'tall fellows'), recruited at great expense from all over Europe.

Despite the comic façade, the king built the hitherto insignificant Prussian army up into a formidable fighting force.

Above *Frederick II and Voltaire enjoyed discussions together; this painting is in the picture gallery at Sansoussi*

AUGUSTUS THE STRONG

Known as 'the Strong' not least for the hundreds of children he is said to have fathered with an array of mistresses, Friedrich August I of Saxony (1670–1733) was the most flamboyant of the absolute rulers in 18th-century Germany. Under his extravagant sway, his capital, Dresden, became one of the most beautiful cities of the baroque age—although his subjects groaned under the burden of taxation that funded the transformation. Augustus succeeded in his candidature for the throne of Poland by converting to Roman Catholicism, a step that caused offence in solidly Lutheran Saxony and proved the final straw for his pious wife Christiane, who left him. Augustus' body is buried in his Polish capital of Kraków, but his heart was brought to Dresden, where it is kept in the Court Church vaults.

BACH & CO.

The greatest musical genius of the German baroque period, Johann Sebastian Bach (1685–1750), was far from being the first musician in the family. Four generations of his forefathers had worked as organists, municipal bandsmen or court musicians, and one of his most influential teachers was his composer cousin Johann Christoph. The devout Bach not only mastered the craft of music but took it to increasingly sublime heights. He declared the purpose of music to be not only 'recreation of the spirit' but also 'praise of the Lord'. After his death, his music fell into neglect, and some of his numerous offspring were more highly regarded than their father. Revived in the mid-19th century by composer Felix Mendelssohn, Bach's music has reigned supreme ever since.

Above *The Bach House and garden in Eisenach*
Below left *Princess Luise von Mecklenburgh-Strelitz*

GOETHE IN WEIMAR

The giant of German literature, Johann Wolfgang von Goethe (1749–1832), was a master of poetry, the novel, drama, the essay and even autobiography. His questioning mind led him into every field of thought, and his scientific achievements included a famous treatise on colour, the elements of which were adopted by artists.

At the same time, Goethe's position as a high-ranking official in the ducal court at Weimar satisfied a parallel taste for practical action; he even managed to be present on the battlefield when a German army was defeated by the French at Valmy in 1792.

Still regarded as the greatest play in the German language, his *Faust* ends with the lines 'Whoever strives shall be redeemed'. Goethe saw his life as a work of art in which he strove to experience all the possibilities open to humankind.

A MUCH-LOVED QUEEN

Prussian monarchy generally presented a martial, ultra-masculine face to the world, but the pretty Princess Luise von Mecklenburg-Strelitz (1776–1810) made a pleasing exception. Married at the age of 16 to the future King Friedrich Wilhelm III in what was evidently a romantic love match, she soon won all hearts with her kindly nature and complete lack of pretension. Luise had brains as well as beauty. As queen while Prussia strove to modernize its creaking administration in the face of the Napoleonic onslaught, she stood firmly on the side of the reformers. Forced to flee from Potsdam by French invasion, in 1807 Luise bravely sought an audience with Napoleon and pleaded with him not to impose over-onerous terms on the defeated Prussia. The emperor responded to her charm but not to her plea; Prussia lost all its possessions west of the Elbe.

Napoleon's retreat from Moscow in 1812 was the signal for an outburst of patriotism among Germans. Anti-French riots broke out all over Germany, and volunteers flocked to join the army in what became a struggle for national liberation. Napoleon's fate was sealed at a series of battles, of which the greatest and deadliest on German soil was the so-called 'Battle of the Nations' at Leipzig in 1813. There were fervent hopes, particularly among patriotic students, that the post-Napoleonic order would not only mean an end to French domination but the establishment of a united and democratic Germany. But at the Congress of Vienna in 1815, representatives of the old regimes gathered with an agenda of restoration and reaction. Germany remained divided, though Prussia acquired territory that extended it westward as far as Aachen. The reinstalled regimes went to great lengths to stifle any opposition with strict censorship and control of education. Incongruously, these crypto-feudal regimes presided over a Germany that was entering the modern world. The reimposed old order was bound to be challenged sooner or later but a liberal revolution failed in 1848, and German unity was eventually imposed by Prussian military might, an ominous portent for the country's later development.

ROMANTIC GENIUS

Nowhere more so than in Germany did the Europe-wide Romantic movement find such intense expression and popular acclaim. Poets excelled in exploring the deeper recesses of the human soul, while among artists the reclusive painter Caspar David Friedrich (1774–1840) was perhaps most in tune with the spirit of the age. His canvases show humanity—frequently in the form of a single lonely figure—lost in contemplation of the vastness and mystery of nature. As the artist aged, his scenes became more melancholy, and Friedrich fell into a deep depression, eventually dying in a Dresden asylum.

Above *Detail of the Battle of Nations Memorial in Leipzig*

TOWARDS 1848

The outbreak of revolution in 1848 was heralded by large-scale unrest among working people, their poverty made all the more unbearable by the prosperity and complacency of the middle class.

In 1844, the decline of their industry in the face of British competition caused such desperation among the linen weavers of Silesia that they revolted, storming the factories. In the years following the revolt, a series of poor harvests meant near-starvation for tens of thousands.

There were food riots in a number of cities, including the Berlin 'Potato Revolution' of 1847. In that same year, the undernourished poor of Silesia were hit with a terrible typhus outbreak, which killed 16,000.

Above *A painting of the Battle of Koniggraz, 1866*
Right Wayfarer *by C. D. Friedrich painted c1818*

THE FRANKFURT TALKING SHOP

For a whole year, lasting from May 1848 to May 1849, some 600 delegates from all over Germany met in St. Paul's Church, Frankfurt, as members of the National Assembly, which everyone present hoped would result in the proclamation of a united Germany.

Although joined in their opposition to the reactionary regimes that had ruled since 1815, they soon fell out among themselves. Should the new Germany include Austria or just Prussia and the southern German states? Should it be a monarchy or a republic?

Most of the delegates were lawyers, professors and bureaucrats, and the discussions were interminable. By the time a constitution of sorts had been hammered out, conservative forces had regained their confidence. Those members of the National Assembly who had not had the good sense to return home were dispersed by Prussian troops.

AUF WIEDERSEHEN, DEUTSCHLAND!

Many of the leaders of the abortive 1848 revolution fled the country when the old regimes were re-established. In numerical terms, however, they made up only a tiny fraction of the total number of German emigrants who quit their homeland in their millions throughout the 19th century. Driven by rural overpopulation, poverty and unemployment, a total of 6 million Germans had left by 1913, most of them heading for the United States, though significant numbers went to Canada, South America, South Africa and Australia. Their departure was seen as a loss by patriotic fellow countrymen, who agitated for Germany to acquire colonies that could absorb surplus population. However, the rapid expansion of German industry in the latter part of the century provided employment at home, and by the 1880s the exodus had tapered off.

SEDAN

In the centuries-old struggle between France and Germany, the name of the settlement of Sedan became synonymous with French despair and German elation.

It was at this small town on the banks of the Meuse in September 1870 that the outcome of the Franco-Prussian War of 1870–71 was decided.

Surrounded by a superior Prussian force, their ranks raked by artillery firing, their commander wounded and Emperor Napoleon III in a state of utter exhaustion, the French fought desperately but without hope.

The defeat cost France 120,000 men and Napoleon III his throne.

Some 80 years later, in May 1940, fear struck the souls of Frenchmen once again, as German tanks swarmed across the Meuse at Sedan during the Battle of France.

Most Germans rejoiced when the Franco-Prussian War led to the unification of the country. Many saw the new Germany as the successor to the old Holy Roman Empire (the *Heiliges Römisches Reich*, or 'First Reich'), justifying its title of 'Second Reich'. But Austria was excluded, and not everyone was happy with the overwhelmingly Prussian character of the new empire. The united Germany was a federation of states, still ruled nominally by dukes, princes and kings (Ludwig of Bavaria only gave his assent to the arrangements on receipt of a bribe from Chancellor Bismarck). Holding the federation together was the Kaiser (emperor), who was also king of Prussia and head of the armed forces. The first Kaiser, Wilhelm I (ruled 1871–88), considered his new title a 'cheap decoration' and would have preferred to remain a king. But his grandson, Wilhelm II (ruled 1888–1918), relished the ostentation of his office; it was he who presided over an increasingly nationalistic and expansionist Germany, which flaunted its industrial and military muscle in the face of Britain and France. However, instead of achieving its 'Place in the Sun', with colonies to match, Germany's ambitions led to the Great War (1914–18), defeat and the replacement of the short-lived empire in 1918 by a democratic republic.

Above *A watercolour showing the sinking of the* Lusitania *off the coast of Ireland in 1915. Almost 1,200 civilians were killed and the event was a trigger for the United States to enter World War I*

GERMAN UNITY PROCLAIMED

The Palace of Versailles had long been the symbol of the French monarchy at the height of its powers—the glittering citadel from which Louis XIV had sent forth his armies to push France's frontier eastwards at Germany's expense. In 1871, to France's deep humiliation, it became the setting in which Germany's triumphant unification was proclaimed, even before the conclusion of the Franco-Prussian War. In the presence of Chancellor Bismarck, the man who had engineered this very moment, King Wilhelm I of Prussia was proclaimed Kaiser of the new Germany. An array of resplendently uniformed high-ranking officers raised their swords and cheered. The civilian presence was minimal, setting the militaristic tone of the German empire.

THE KAISER...

Emperor Wilhelm II embodied much of the flamboyant spirit of the German empire.

A grandson of Queen Victoria, he conducted a love-hate relationship with Britain, which he both admired (for its world-spanning empire and great navy) and detested (for the same reasons). The archaic ruler of a rapidly industrializing country, with a democratically elected parliament and active trade unions, he hankered for the power and glory of an absolute monarchy.

Going along with the game of great power brinkmanship in the years before 1914, he was nevertheless dismayed as war finally broke out: 'If grandma were alive, she would never have allowed it!' he cried.

...AND THE CAPTAIN

The German empire promoted discipline and obedience to orders. That this could have comic consequences was demonstrated in 1906 by the unemployed cobbler and former jailbird Wilhelm Voigt, who had acquired a discarded army captain's uniform. He donned it, and set off on an adventure that had all Germany laughing. Encountering some soldiers, Voigt ordered them to fall in and follow him. They instantly obeyed. Policemen were added to the troop, which he marched to the town hall at Köpenick just outside Berlin. Here, the 'captain' arrested the mayor and his staff, and confiscated Köpenick's Reichsmarks. Eventually arrested, Voigt was jailed, then lived off the proceeds of a successful autobiography.

THE *LUSITANIA*

Few passengers boarding the Cunard Line's mighty *Lusitania* in New York on 1 May 1915 had taken much notice of the ominous announcement by the 'Imperial German Embassy' that all vessels entering British waters were 'liable to destruction'. But as the *Lusitania* approached the Irish coast, she was struck by two torpedoes fired by a U-boat lurking beneath the surface. The great liner soon sank, taking almost 1,200 of the passengers with her. Of the dead, 129 were citizens of the still-neutral United States. Americans were outraged, and there were frenzied calls for war to be declared on Germany. For a while, U-boat skippers were instructed to choose their victims with greater care, but in spring 1917 Germany once more declared open season on all shipping approaching Britain. President Wilson called the German submarine campaign a 'war against all nations' and the United States entered World War I on the Allied side.

TYPES OF TRENCH

In spring 1918, after three-and-a-half years of stalemate on the Western Front in France, the German army embarked on its last attempt at victory.

The trenches from which the troops emerged to attack the British lines were testimony to Teutonic thoroughness. Penetrating far beneath the surface, they could even seem homey, with planked floors and panelled walls hung with pictures. But by 1918, Germany was running out of food and basic raw materials, and every soldier was aware of the sufferings and near-starvation of their families and other civilians back home.

As the soldiers overran the less solidly built British entrenchments, they found such evidence of plenty—coffee, whisky and tinned goods—that they soon grew demoralized.

The offensive eventually petered out in looting and drunkenness, and the remorseless Allied counterattack that was to end the war soon began.

Below left to right *German troops in a World War I trench in 1916; Wilhelm II was Kaiser during World War I*

The constitution of the post-war republic was drawn up in Weimar, to where the parliamentary delegates had fled from chaos in Berlin. Almost miraculously, the democratic Weimar Republic survived catastrophes such as the hyper-inflation of 1923 and attempted *coups d'état* from both left and right (including one in Munich, led by an obscure agitator named Adolf Hitler). In the second half of the 1920s, the country enjoyed a brief golden age of relative prosperity and outward social calm. But society remained deeply divided. After the Wall Street Crash in 1929, Germany was the country worst affected by the Great Depression. With industry crippled and 6 million unemployed on the streets, democracy was discredited. For many, Adolf Hitler (1889–1945) offered an alternative to renewed chaos and the prospect of Communist revolution. An alliance of conservatives and Nazis made him chancellor in January 1933. Within months, a totalitarian dictatorship—the 'third Reich'—was in place. The defeat of unemployment through rearmament and a massive schedule of public works, combined with a series of foreign policy triumphs, left most Germans in a state resembling euphoria, willing to follow the Führer wherever he went.

Above *Anti-religious protesters drive a vehicle painted with an abbreviated quotation from Karl Marx: 'Religion...is the opium of the people'*

PEACE FOR A TIME

The treaty ending World War I, signed in the Palace of Versailles in 1919, was a painful humiliation for a Germany whose unity had been proclaimed there half a century earlier. The terms of the treaty were humiliating, too. Germany lost about 20 per cent of its territory, including Alsace-Lorraine and industrial Upper Silesia. A wedge—the so-called 'Polish Corridor'—was driven between east Prussia and the rest of the country in order to provide Poland with access to the Baltic. Germany's pride, its great army, was reduced to a fraction of its former size and forbidden to patrol the Rhineland. Billions of dollars in reparations was to be paid to compensate the Allies for war damage. Here were the seeds of a future war.

TRILLION-MARK TRAGEDY

In early 1923, struggling to keep up reparations payments to the Allies and maintain public services, Germany resorted to printing money. Inflation, already rampant, now spiralled out of control. In January 1923, a loaf of bread cost RM250, compared with RM2 in 1920; by September 1923 its price had risen to RM1.5 million, and by December to nearly RM400 billion. People rushed from work to spend their wages before the passage of a few hours made them worthless. Barter became the norm, and middle-class folk were ruined when their investments evaporated. The disaster wrecked confidence in the new Weimar Republic and helped open the door to political extremism.

Above right *The 1936 Berlin Olympics were a triumph for Nazi propoganda*
Below *A bust of Ferdinand Graf von Zeppelin in the Zeppelin Museum*

GOODBYE TO WEIMAR

The most acute observer of the doomed world of Weimar society was the English-born writer Christopher Isherwood (1904–86), who lived in Berlin as Germany slid into the Great Depression and the embrace of the Nazis. His cast of barely fictionalized characters thronging the capital's seedy nightlife, in his collection of short stories *Goodbye to Berlin*, includes gigolos, rent boys, stage lesbians, Communist toughs in tight shorts, and Nazi thugs baying for blood. The most memorable creature among this nocturnal fauna is his friend Sally Bowles, throaty-voiced nightclub singer. With her green fingernails, champagne habit and utter unreliability, Sally was fated never to find the millionaire who would finance her breakthrough into cinematic stardom. However, she achieved immortality not only in the pages of Isherwood's book, but also in the play *I am a Camera* and the musical *Cabaret*.

BERICHT
in Wort und Bild
„Die 16 olympischen Tage"

EXTREMISM ON THE STREETS

The Nazis understood better than anyone the appeal—and effectiveness—of political violence. In addition to fighting for control of the streets against their rivals, their private militia, the Sturmabteilung (SA), impressed the German public with its smart uniforms, brass bands, catchy marching songs and apparent discipline. Some of its members were idealists, others came straight from the underworld, well versed in the use of the blackjack and knuckleduster. Many were drawn from the same social strata as their opponents in the equivalent Communist militia. The Red Front: 6 million unemployed proved willing recruits to movements offering comradeship and some real purpose in life. Such similarities failed to diminish the ferocity of the fighting on the streets, however, which the police seemed powerless to control.

OLYMPICS '36

But for the outbreak of World War I, Berlin would have hosted the Olympic games in 1916, although it's doubtful that the Kaiser's regime could have matched the Nazis' efforts when Germany's turn came around again in 1936. The Berlin games were a propaganda triumph, stage-managed with the consummate showmanship developed for the Nazi Party's Nuremberg rallies. As at Nuremberg, the spectacle was recorded in a documentary by the Führer's best-loved film-maker, Leni Riefenstahl (1902–2003). Careful concentration on key sports meant that Nazi Germany carried off the greatest number of medals, while its Axis allies Italy and Japan also excelled. However, to Hitler's intense annoyance, the real hero of the games was the black American athlete Jesse Owens (1913–80), who because of his race was considered in Nazi terms inferior; he won three gold medals.

In contrast to 1914, when crowds had cheered the troops on their way to the front, the mood on Berlin's streets in early September 1939 was sombre. Nearly all Germans had rejoiced at Hitler's achievements abroad and were glad that they had been accomplished without war. *Blitzkrieg* tactics led to easy victories over Poland, the Low Countries and France, and many assumed that Germany could now rest on its laurels. Hitler, however, had other plans: The subjugation of the East, the enslavement of Russia and the destruction of Europe's Jewish population remained his fundamental aims. For him, the Battle of Britain in 1940 was a sideshow; the real struggle began on 21 June 1941 when his armies marched into the Soviet Union. It was a fatal miscalculation. The Red Army proved more than a match for the *Wehrmacht* (armed forces), and with the Western Allies' invasion of Normandy in June 1944, the fate of Nazi Germany was sealed. After the war, fearful of a revival of German militarism, Germany's opponents considered dismantling the country's industry and returning it to what it had once been, a collection of largely agricultural, semi-independent states. In the end, Germany lost much of its eastern territory while the remainder of the country was divided into four occupation zones: Soviet, American, British and French. Living in the ruins of their towns and cities, a demoralized German population cared more about immediate survival than the political status of their country.

Clockwise from left to right *The Central Army Group of the German forces attack Moscow during the 1941–42 Russian campaign; people at the base of the Airlift Memorial commemorating Allied aid given during the Soviet blockade in 1948–49; an aerial view of central Dresden after bombing in May 1945*

HOW TO START A WAR

A grisly pretext for the attack on Poland that precipitated World War II was provided by SS chiefs Heinrich Himmler and Reinhard Heydrich, aided and abetted by secret police chief Heinrich Müller. Fitted out in Polish uniforms and sworn to secrecy, a squad of SS soldiers stormed a German radio station close to the border with Poland, at Gleiwitz (now the Polish town of Gliwice), locking the startled staff in the basement. A short broadcast was made in Polish, then the pseudo-Poles withdrew, leaving behind a German apparently killed while defending the transmitter. Nazi propaganda made the most of this outrage, putting the blame for the subsequent outbreak of hostilities squarely on Poland. In reality, the 'German' corpse was a concentration camp inmate, drugged and shot by Müller's minions before being dumped outside the radio station.

DECISION AT WANNSEE

A palatial lakeside residence in the exclusive Berlin suburb of Wannsee was the setting for the most monstrous single decision of the war.

America's entry into the conflict in December 1941 had confirmed Hitler's fantasy that an international Jewish conspiracy was bent on Germany's destruction.

On 20 January 1942, the SS convened a conference at Wannsee villa to make arrangements for the 'Final Solution' to the imagined 'Jewish Problem'.

With Adolf Eichmann taking heavily censored minutes that glossed over the real purpose of the meeting, Reinhard Heydrich outlined his frightful plans, expecting opposition from some delegates. But all concurred in setting up the administrative machinery for what was to be the murder of millions.

COUNT STAUFFENBERG

Behind its façade of unity, the Third Reich was opposed by individuals and groups, among them brave students and principled clergymen. But the only force capable of overturning the Nazi regime was the army, elements of which had plotted against Hitler since the 1930s.

After several abortive attempts to assassinate the dictator, on 20 July 1944 Colonel Count Claus von Stauffenberg seemed to have succeeded. The bomb he had placed beneath Hitler's conference table at the 'Wolf's Lair' in east Prussia exploded, apparently killing everyone around it.

Von Stauffenberg hastened to Berlin hoping to place the country under military control. But Hitler had survived. Inevitably, Stauffenberg was arrested and shot, his accomplices hunted down and all put to death.

HAMSTERS

'Enjoy the war, the peace is going to be terrible' was a common wisecrack as Germany's enemies closed in on her. And so it was. Cities and towns lay in ruins, released slave workers took their revenge on the population and there was no fuel for heating during the cold winters. Food was rationed, but supplies were erratic. City-dwellers swarmed into the countryside, on foot or clinging to the outside of infrequent and overcrowded trains. Dubbed 'hamsters', they carried rucksacks stuffed with precious possessions that they bartered for food from farmers ready to cut a deal. The lucky ones came back with butter, sides of ham or perhaps a sack of potatoes. Tales were told of cow byres carpeted with precious Persian rugs and of farmers' wives flouncing around the fields in furs.

THE BERLIN AIRLIFT

At the end of the war in May 1945, not only Germany but its erstwhile capital had been divided into four sectors: Soviet, American, British and French. As relations between Russia and the West deteriorated, the city became the principal theatre of the Cold War. In June 1948, in a test of the Western Allies' resolve, the Soviet authorities cut off power supplies and closed the land routes connecting the western sectors of Berlin with West Germany, knowing that only a few days' supply of essential provisions remained in the city. In a miracle of improvisation, the Americans and British organized hundreds of aircraft to fly in not only medicines and foodstuffs, but also heavy loads like coal; at one stage a plane was landing every 48 seconds. Berliners responded with enthusiasm to what they called *Die Luftbrücke* (the air bridge) and its *Rosinenbomber* (raisin bombers), and after a year the Russians lifted the blockade.

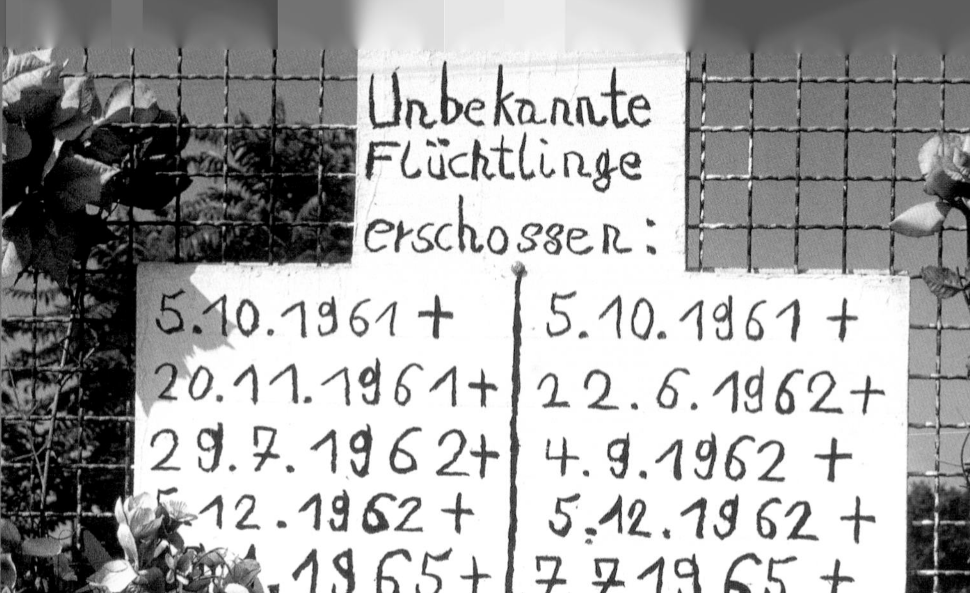

Unbekannte
Flüchtlinge
erschossen:
5.10.1961 +
20.11.1961+
29.7.1962+
5.10.1961 +
22.6.1962+
4.9.1962 +
5.12.1962 +
7.7.1965 +

The most important front line of the Cold War ran down the middle of Germany and through divided Berlin. As antagonism worsened between the Soviet Union and the West, each bloc sought to integrate 'its' Germany. West Germany rearmed and became a member of NATO, while East Germany, already highly militarized, became a formidable member of the Soviet-dominated Warsaw Pact. Ancient antagonism between France and Germany was replaced by genuine friendship and by cooperation as the leading partners in the Common Market, later the European Union. Professions of eternal friendship between the Soviet Union and the German Democratic Republic, the so-called 'First German Workers' and Peasants' State', were less convincing. Throughout the 1950s, East Germans voted against Communism with their feet, migrating across the still-open boundary between East and West Berlin. The building of the Berlin Wall in 1961 stopped the flow, and within a few years the GDR claimed to have created one of the world's strongest economies. Its population knew better, not least because they could watch Western television and see the realities of life in the West. When the USSR's President Mikhail Gorbachev loosened the reins of Soviet control in the late 1980s, pressure for change grew irresistible.

Clockwise from left to right *One of the white crosses erected adjacent to the Reichstag in memory of the people who died trying to cross the Berlin Wall; detail of a crest on the German unification flag; an anti-Olympic poster*

'TOO UGLY, TOO NOISY'

With these words, the British motor magnate William (later Lord) Rootes threw away Britain's chance of taking over production of what was to become the world's most successful automobile, the Volkswagen *Käfer*. The 'Beetle' had been conceived under the Nazi regime as the car to motorize the Master Race, but only a handful had been produced by the time war broke out.

In 1945, Rootes' reluctance was ignored by the British officer in charge of the run-down works in Wolfsburg. Scraping together a workforce and getting hold of materials, Major Ivan Hirst managed to restart production. By the 1950s, and with German management once more in charge, Volkswagen was selling hundreds of thousands of Beetles worldwide.

STRIKE ON THE STALINALLEE

While their Western counterparts were beginning to enjoy the fruits of prosperity, East German workers suffered shortages and were forced to work harder for less pay. Matters came to a head on 17 June 1953. Builders working on the Stalinallee, a prestigious Soviet-style boulevard in East Berlin, put down their tools and marched *en masse* through the streets. Their example was followed throughout East Germany, with strikes and demonstrations occurring in some 200 cities and towns. The Communist leadership panicked, and called for Russian help. Hurled cobblestones were no match for Soviet tanks, and the rebellion was soon crushed, though not before an unknown number of demonstrators had been killed. West German outrage was intense, and 17 June was declared a national day of commemoration, the 'Day of German Unity'.

THE WALL

In the early morning of 13 August 1961, not long after the East German leader Walter Ulbricht had proclaimed 'We have no intention of building a wall', workmen began constructing a barrier between East and West Berlin.

At first it consisted of crudely laid blockwork and barbed wire, and wasn't much of a deterrent to determined escapers. But later the barrier became a very formidable obstacle indeed.

Called the 'Anti-Fascist Defence Rampart' by its creators, it consisted of a virtually unclimbable smooth concrete wall 4m (13ft) high, backed by a 'death strip', tank and vehicle traps, tripwires and a second fence. Guards and their dogs patrolled constantly.

During its three decades of existence, the Wall claimed the lives of more than 200 would-be escapees to the West.

INTERRUPTED OLYMPICS

Germany's turn to host the Olympic games came around again in 1972. This time the venue was not Berlin, divided since 1961 by the Communists' Wall, but the southern city of Munich. All seemed set for what were to be the biggest games yet, with more than 7,000 athletes from 121 countries. Munich turned itself inside out in a frenzy of construction, building a glittering new U-Bahn to take visitors to the sensational stadium in the north part of the city, spectacularly set among swelling hills and lakes and overlooked by a tall tower that afforded an astonishing view of the distant Alps. But the exploits of the athletes were overshadowed by tragedy, when Palestinian gunmen stormed the Olympic village, killing 11 Israelis. This was an especially bitter blow to a Germany that had strived to build a positive relationship with the new state of Israel.

FROM STREET-FIGHTER TO FOREIGN MINISTER

Germany's 'Generation of 1968' was as radical as that of any other country and frequently more violent, with some of its members—including the Baader-Meinhof Gang—turning to terrorism. Others abandoned protest, preferring to work within the 'system', none more successfully than the charismatic, chameleon-like Joschka Fischer. He was in the front line of protest in the 1960s and 1970s, but later eschewed action on the street for politics. Fischer became a prominent member of Germany's influential Green Party, leading it into a government in 1998 in a coalition with the Social Democrats. As Foreign Minister (1998–2005), Fischer made a huge impact, encouraging reluctant fellow Greens into military action in Kosovo while publicly debating the Iraq war with pro-war US figures such as Donald Rumsfeld.

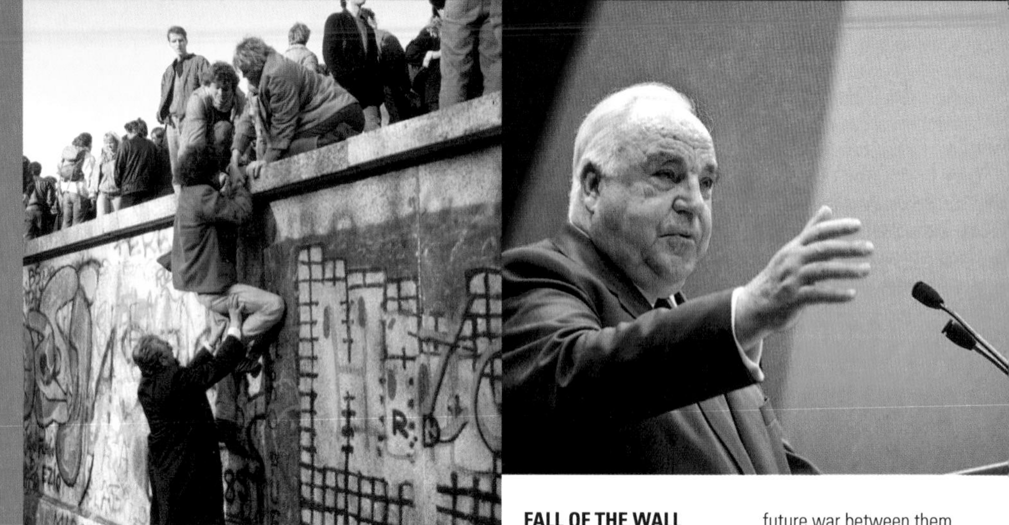

Euphoria at the fall of the Berlin Wall in 1989 and reunification in 1990 soon turned into disillusionment. On the one hand, West Germans resented paying extra taxes to support the shaky economy of the East; on the other, many East Germans were bitter about the loss of the comprehensive social security the Communist regime had provided, and some felt lost in the individualistic and competitive world of Western consumerism. The physical reality of the Wall might be gone, but a wall of sorts continues to exist in the minds of West Germans *(Wessis)* and Easterners *(Ossis)*. As Germany under Chancellor Angela Merkel, a native of 'East' Germany, faces up to the challenges of an ageing population and overdue economic reform, this impression of division is slowly taking on less importance.

Above left to right *The border in Berlin was opened and people smashed the Wall in 1989; Helmut Kohl, the former Chancellor of Germany, was determined to unify East and West Germany*

FALL OF THE WALL

As demands for total reform of the GDR intensified in the autumn of 1989, the Communist leadership twisted and turned in its attempts to remain in power. The long-serving leader, Erich Honecker, was forced to resign, but his successor, Egon Krenz, was equally out of touch. At a press conference on 9 November, a minister mumbled something about easing travel to the West. This was the signal for thousands of East Berliners to flock to the Wall, where confused guards had no option but to let them through. In the following days and weeks, a carnival atmosphere gripped Berlin as its long-separated populations mixed joyously.

CHANCELLOR KOHL

The towering figure of Chancellor Helmut Kohl dominated German politics for most of the 1980s and 1990s. He was determined to draw the nations of Europe together to make future war between them unthinkable. Kohl's greatest achievement was the unification of his country, which he steamrollered through when more cautious spirits advocated a long period of transition.

THE STASI

As the East German regime crumbled, its 'sword and shield'—the secret police known as the Stasi (short for STaatsSIcherheit, or State Security)—worked frantically to destroy evidence of its presence, shredding or burning files. Citizens' groups halted this activity, with records subsequently administered by commissions that have revealed the extent of Stasi surveillance and control. Some 100,000 uniformed and armed officials were backed by 500,000 'unofficial collaborators', members of the public who informed regularly on fellow workers, friends and even spouses. A further two million informers provided occasional information.

ON THE MOVE

On the Move gives you detailed advice and information about the various options for travelling to Germany before explaining the best ways to get around the country once you are there. Handy tips help you with everything from buying tickets to renting a car.

Arriving 48

Getting Around 52
- Getting Around in Berlin 52
- Getting Around in Munich, Hamburg and Frankfurt 54
- Driving 55
- Trains 58
- Long-Distance Buses, Taxis and Bicycles 61
- Regional Flights 62
- Domestic Ferries and Riverboats 64

Visitors with a Disability 66

ARRIVING BY AIR

Although Berlin has regained its status as Germany's capital city, the country's largest and most important airport is not here but in Frankfurt. As West Germany's financial hub, centrally located Frankfurt was the logical place to develop a major international airport, and its vast range of facilities and excellent accessibility have kept it ahead in the post-reunification period. It is here that the national airline, Lufthansa, has its base, and it is here that the majority of international flights arrive and depart, connecting with services to and from all major German cities.

Berlin is served not by a single airport, but by three, a reflection of the city's divided past. A pre-war, inner-city airport, Tempelhof, closed in 2008. Schönefeld was built by the Communist regime to serve East Berlin and much of the GDR, and is on the city's southeastern outskirts, some distance from central Berlin. It is used by a number of international carriers, including budget airlines and charter flights. Most international carriers land at Tegel, the modern airport built in the western suburbs to serve West Berlin.

Elsewhere in Germany, a number of regional capitals and other cities are served by international airlines, notably Munich and Düsseldorf, but also Cologne/Bonn, Hannover, Hamburg, Leipzig/Halle and Dresden. Budget airlines have exploited the low charges

GETTING INTO TOWN FROM THE AIRPORT

AIRPORT	FRANKFURT	BERLIN: TEGEL	BERLIN: SCHÖNEFELD
DISTANCE TO CITY	12km (7 miles)	8km (5 miles) to Zoologischer Garten	18km (11 miles) to Friedrichstrasse
TAXI	Price: €20–€25. Journey time: 20 min	Price: about €15 to Zoologischer Garten. Journey time: 20–30 min	Price: about €23 to Friedrichstrasse or Zoologischer Garten. Journey time: 30–40 min
TRAIN	From Regionalbahnhof: S-Bahn S8 or S9 to Hauptbahnhof (main train station), Offenbach or Hanau Frequency: 15 min. Price: €3.60. Journey time: 15 min From Fernbahnhof: frequent (two-hourly, hourly, half-hourly) intercity trains to major cities	n/a	Airport Express to Alexanderplatz, Friedrichstrasse, Zoologischer Garten. Journey time: about 35 min. S-Bahn line 9 to same destinations. Mainline rail connections
BUS	Services to towns in the region, e.g. Heidelberg, Mannheim	Express bus X9 (or local bus 109) to Zoologischer Garten or Jakob-Kaiser-Platz, with connections to U-Bahn, S-Bahn and DB (mainline railway). Express bus TXL to Unter den Linden and Alexanderplatz. Local bus 128 to Kurt-Schumacher-Platz U-Bahn station, then onward by U-Bahn to any city destination. Price €2.10 for a single ticket to anywhere in central Berlin	Local bus 171 to U-Bahn station Rudow, with onward connections to any city destination
CAR	Direct access to Autobahns A3 (Cologne–Munich) and A5 (Hannover–Basel), and to expressway B43	Direct access to A111 expressway, linking to national autobahn network and city streets	Direct access to Autobahn A113 (expressway towards middle of city is under construction)

of smaller airports such as Erfurt, Friedrichshafen (for Lake Constance), Hahn (for Frankfurt), Niederrhein and Lübeck (for Hamburg).

The major airports have generally good access and facilities for visitors with a disability. Let your travel agent or airline know your requirements before your trip and allow some extra time for check-in. (▷ 66 for more information).

Signs in airports are normally in English as well as German, although when arriving by car note that *Abflug* means 'departure', *Ankunft* means

Left *Ground crew prepare a Lufthansa aircraft for flight at Frankfurt airport*

MUNICH	**DÜSSELDORF-RHEIN-RUHR**	**HAMBURG**	**LEIPZIG-HALLE**
32km (20 miles)	10km (6 miles)	13km (8 miles)	15km (9 miles)
Price: €45–€50. Journey time: 45 min	Price: €16. Journey time: 20 min	Price: €17–€18. Journey time: 30 min	Price: €30. Journey time: 30 min
To city's Ostbahnhof (East Station): S-Bahn line 1 Frequency: 20 min. Price: €8.80. Journey time: 30 min To city's Ostbahnhof, Marienplatz and Hauptbahnhof: S-Bahn line 8 Frequency: 20 min. Journey time: 30–40 min. Price: €8.80	To Düsseldorf Hauptbahnhof (main train station): S-Bahn line 7 from S-Bahnhof Düsseldorf Flughafen Terminal Frequency: 20–30 min. Journey time: 13 min. Price: €2.20. To cities in region and beyond from Düsseldorf Flughafen mainline rail station: 350 local, regional and intercity trains daily	S-Bahn and U-Bahn links	Airport Express to Leipzig Hauptbahnhof (main train station) and Halle Hauptbahnhof (main train station) Frequency: 30 min (less at night). Journey time: 14 min (Leipzig), 16 min (Halle) Price: €3.60. Mainline train services from airport station to cities in region and beyond
Autobus Oberbayern to Schwabing and Hauptbahnhof Frequency: 20 min 6.20am–9.40pm. Journey time: 45 min. Price: €10.50. Buses to several cities in region and Austria	Local services. Express bus to Aachen	To Hauptbahnhof (main train station): Airport Express Frequency: 15–20 min daily 5am–9pm. Journey time: 30 min. Price: €5.50. To U-Bahn/S-Bahn station Ohlsdorf, with U-Bahn and S-Bahn connections with all destinations in Hamburg: City bus 110 Journey time: Airport to U-Bahn Ohlsdorf 11 min. Price: €2.60. Local bus services (e.g. 39 to Wandsbek Markt) and regional bus services to Kiel and Lübeck	Bus services to cities in region, including Havag Bus every hour into Halle
Direct access to Autobahn A92 (Deggendorf–Munich), leading south into city	Direct access to Autobahn A44, then expressway B8 into city	Expressway B433n south then B433 into city. Hannover–Kiel Autobahn A7 (interchange 23) 4km (2.5 miles) west	Autobahn A14 east, then south at interchange 17a on B2 to Leipzig. Autobahn A14 north-west, then west at interchange 11 on B100 to Halle

'arrival', and *Rückgabe Mietwagen* means 'rental vehicle return'.

Frankfurt (tel 01805 372 4636; www.airportcity-frankfurt.de) is 12km (7 miles) from downtown Frankfurt and officially known as Frankfurt-Rhein-Main. This gigantic international airport is not only the largest in Germany but also the busiest on mainland Europe, handling more than 50 million passengers annually. It has two terminals and a third will be complete in 2015. The sheer size of the airport means you should leave plenty of time to find your check-in desk and for connections. The terminals are linked by an overhead train called the Sky Line.

The range of facilities at the airport is impressive, and Frankfurt's public transportation connections are among the best in Europe. There are two train stations: beneath Terminal 1 is the Regionalbahnhof, which is served by local and regional trains, including the Frankfurt S-Bahn; some distance away, but accessible by covered pedestrian walkway, is the Fernbahnhof, used by intercity trains. From the Fernbahnhof you can travel swiftly to every major town in Germany (and to several in other countries), either directly or at most with just one change.

Below *Passengers with their luggage trolley (cart) at Munich airport*

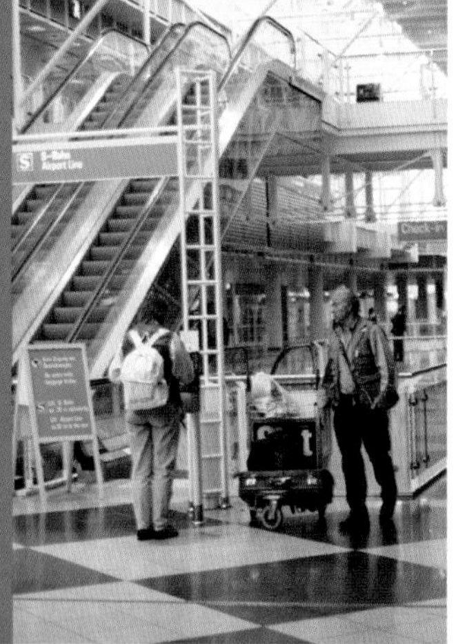

Berlin Tegel was built during the Berlin Airlift of 1948–49 (▷ 43). The airport is due to close in 2011. It's a modern complex in the northwestern suburbs, with easy access into the city, albeit without a direct rail link. It is promoted locally as Berlin's 'frequent flyer airport'. Tegel has a full range of services, including a tourist information desk (daily 5am–11pm), car rental desks, shops, banks and restaurants. This is the Berlin airport at which visitors from abroad are most likely to arrive, especially if they are coming on a scheduled flight by a national carrier.

Berlin Schönefeld is on the southeastern outskirts of the city and is sometimes referred to as 'Berlin's holiday airport'. It was built in GDR times as the international airport to serve East Berlin and much of East Germany. It now specializes in flights to and from holiday destinations in southern Europe and the Middle East, and is home to charter airlines and budget carriers. It has been brought up to date and now has most of the usual facilities. There are ambitious plans to redevelop it completely as Berlin's sole international airport—Berlin Brandenburg International—with facilities worthy of a capital city. A shuttle takes visitors to the train station (mainline and local services), which is also within walking distance. For more information on Berlin airports, either contact 01805 000186 or check online at www.berlin-airport.de.

Munich: Franz-Josef-Strauss-Flughafen (tel 01805 000186; www.munich-airport.de) was named after Bavaria's most famous post-war politician. This ultra-modern twin-terminal airport stands in open countryside well to the northeast of the city, to which it is linked by both S-Bahn and autobahn. Its lavish facilities and glittering architecture are in complete contrast to the old inner-city airport it has replaced, and it is now the country's second-busiest airport.

Düsseldorf Rhein-Ruhr (tel 0211 4210; www.duesseldorf-international.de) is a modern airport, just on the northern edge of Düsseldorf's built-up area, and well placed to serve the vast Ruhr conurbation and its 6 million inhabitants. The airport is linked by the fully automatic overhead Skytrain (ticket necessary) to its own mainline railway station, which is served by regional and intercity trains, making it easy to travel swiftly and conveniently to most towns in the region. Local trains depart from their own station right in the terminal. The airport has a range of facilities, including a stylish shopping arcade and a variety of places to eat and drink.

Hamburg-Fuhlsbüttel (tel 040 50750; www.ham.airport.de) is the fifth-busiest airport in the country and only 13km (8 miles) from the downtown area. There are flights to and from most large German cities and other mostly European destinations. There is also a good range of facilities. Planned extensions of the underground and S-Bahn networks will improve access into the city; in the meantime, a bus service runs frequently.

Leipzig-Halle (tel 0341 224 1155; www.leipzig-halle-airport.de), on the northern edge of the city, has been comprehensively modernized, and is still being extended to serve the cities of east-central Germany. It handles flights to and from major German cities and a number of European destinations. Facilities are excellent, and there are mainline train connections as well as a fast link into Leipzig and to the new trade fair grounds.

ARRIVING BY FERRY

There are currently no direct passenger ferry services from Britain to Germany. The nearest ferry ports, and the ferry lines that serve them, are: IJmuiden (DFDS Seaways, tel 0871 522 0955

MAJOR CAR RENTAL COMPANIES

COMPANY	TELEPHONE	WEBSITE
Avis	01805 217702	www.avis.com
Europcar	01805 80 0	www.europcar.de
Hertz	01805 333535	www.hertz.com
Sixt	01805 252525	www.e-sixt.de

Major international car rental companies have offices at all the main airports, in city downtown areas and at railway stations. Airport desks usually have extended opening hours and you can normally return a car at any time.

It may pay to reserve a rental car in advance, and you should certainly investigate any special deals that are being offered, perhaps through your airline. Otherwise, rates are somewhat higher than the European average. The German firm Sixt (linked to Budget) may offer slightly better rates. Check whether there is an additional fee for picking up a car at one point and returning it to another.

Insurance is compulsory, and drivers must have a current licence and be more than 21 (sometimes 25) years old. An international driver's licence is theoretically necessary, but it is unlikely you will be asked for one except possibly by a small rental firm. Additional drivers must be noted on any documentation.

Make sure you are certain about what fuel your car requires before you drive off, and familiarize yourself with the controls, particularly if you are used to a right-hand drive. The car should be equipped with a warning triangle and first-aid kit. Check also that there is no damage to the car's bodywork that has not already been noted in the contract. There are likely to be restrictions on which countries the car may be driven in; even countries in the European Union such as Poland may be excluded.

Rental cars are normally supplied with a tankful of fuel. You should fill up before returning the vehicle; if you leave this to the rental firm, they will charge you an additional amount, possibly double the cost of whatever topping-up is required.

in the UK; www.dfdsseaways.co.uk), Rotterdam Europoort (P&O Ferries, tel 0871 664 5645 in the UK; www.poferries.com), and Hoek van Holland (Stena Line, tel 08705 707070 in the UK; www.stenaline.com), in the Netherlands; and Zeebrugge (P&O Ferries, tel 0871 664 5645 in the UK; www.poferries.com; Superfast Ferries, tel 08702 340870 in the UK; www.superfast.com), and Ostend (Transeuropa Ferries, tel 01843 595522 in the UK; www. transeuropaferries.com; no foot passengers), in Belgium.

Scandlines (tel 01805 116688 in Germany; www.scandlines.de) run services linking the Baltic coast towns of Kiel with Klaipeda in Lithuania; Rostock with Gedser in Denmark, Liepaja in Latvia and Trelleborg in Sweden; Puttgarden with Rødby; and Sassnitz with Rønne, both in Denmark and Trelleborg in Sweden.

ARRIVING BY TRAIN

International trains connect most European countries to the German rail network. There is no direct link from Britain, but Eurostar services (tel 08705 186186 in the UK; www.eurostar.com) through the Channel Tunnel connect in Brussels with the high-speed Brussels–Aachen–Cologne line, making this route an attractive alternative to air travel. From Cologne there are good connections to all major German cities. An early evening train from London connects at Brussels with a DB Nachtzug sleeper train to a number of German cities, including Berlin and Hamburg. Eurostar trains currently depart from London St. Pancras. Check-in at St. Pancras is 30 minutes before departure, and you are allowed two suitcases and one item of hand luggage, all of which must be labelled with your name, address and seat number. You should not change your seat during the journey. Passports are required. Round-trip ticket prices London–Cologne are from around £100, and the journey time is around 6 hours.

ARRIVING BY CAR

To bring your own car to Germany you will need a valid driver's licence. Your home licence is normally sufficient if you are from other European countries or the US, but bring an international permit if you have one. Residents of other countries need an international permit and the vehicle registration document. Vehicles must be insured and display a nationality sticker.

Border patrols with EU countries have been progressively dismantled and controls relaxed, so border hold-ups are few. The most popular route for motorists driving from Britain begins with the Channel Tunnel or the short sea crossing from Dover to Calais. From Calais, the E40 leads through Belgium to Aachen, Cologne and beyond, while E42 and E25 lead through Belgium and Luxembourg to the central Rhineland and the southwest of the country.

Below *A rail line running parallel to a road in the Rhine area*

GETTING AROUND IN BERLIN

Berlin's fully integrated public transportation network makes it possible to explore the whole city without ever needing a car. The system is run by BVG (Berliner Verkehrs-Betriebe).

INFORMATION

There is a BVG information pavilion (tel 030 19449; www.bvg.de; daily 6am–10pm) at the entrance to the Hardenbergplatz bus station in front of Bahnhof Zoologischer Garten (Zoo Station) where the staff can provide you with tickets and travel information, including a basic public transportation map. There is also a public transportation information desk at Tegel airport (▷ 48).

Public transportation maps are also available at all stations, and tourist information offices dispense travel information.

THE NETWORK

Berlin's public transportation system is fully integrated, and many journeys will be made using a ticket or pass that allows you to change from one mode of travel to another.

» The S-Bahn (*Stadt-Bahn*, or City Rail), identified by a large letter 'S', runs through the middle of the city, linking it to the suburbs and beyond. It runs mostly on overground tracks. The elevated section from Savignyplatz and Zoologischer Garten in the west to Friedrichstrasse, Alexanderplatz and Ostbahnhof in the east is useful for visitors. Trains run at around 10-minute intervals between 4am and 1am. An hourly night service is provided on lines 3 to 10.

» The U-Bahn (*Untergrundbahn*, or Underground) comprises nine lines and 163 stations, the latter identified by a prominent letter 'U'. There is an elevated section between Nollendorfplatz and Warschauerplatz, which gives a view of the Landwehr canal and the attractions of Kreuzberg. Trains run at around 10-minute intervals between 4am and 1am. Lines 1, 9 and 15 provide an all-night service at 15-minute intervals.

» Berlin's yellow-painted double-decker buses run from 4.30am to 1am, as well as a number of night routes. Bus stops are identified by a green 'H' on a yellow background. Enter the bus by the front doors and leave by the middle or rear doors.

» There are 30 tram lines in eastern Berlin, some of which have been extended into western Berlin.

TICKETS

Tickets come in various forms, including short-distance, single-journey, day and week tickets, ranging from €1.30 to €32.30, and it is worth considering what trips you are likely to make during your stay before any purchase is made. All tickets except the short-distance ticket allow you to make as many transfers as you need between lines or from one mode of travel to another. Berlin is divided into three travel zones, A, B and C; most visitor trips will be within the two inner zones (A and B). The outer zone (C) includes Potsdam.

You can buy tickets that are valid for up to one day from the vending machines at station entrances. Instructions are in English as well as German. Coins and sometimes paper notes are accepted and change is given. Tickets must be validated before travel by being stamped in one of the red machines on the platform or aboard buses and trams. Single-journey and day tickets may also be purchased from bus drivers and on trams.

USEFUL TELEPHONE NUMBERS AND WEBSITES

Airports

» Madrid Barajas, tel 913 93 60 00
» Barcelona, tel 932 98 38 38
» Alicante, tel 966 91 90 00
» Málaga, tel 952 04 84 84
» Bilbao, tel 944 86 96 64

Airlines

» Iberia, tel 902 40 05 00, www.iberia.com
» British Airways, tel 902 11 13 33, www.britishairways.com
» American Airlines, tel 902 11 55 75, www.aa.com
» KLM, tel 902 22 27 47, www.klm.com
» Lufthansa, tel 902 22 01 01, www.lufthansa.com

Ferries

» Brittany Ferries (UK), tel +44 (0)8703 665 333, www.brittany-ferries.com
» P&O Ferries (UK), tel +44 (0)8705 202020, www.poferries.com
» Trasmediterránea, tel 902 45 46 45, www.trasmediterranea.es

Trains

» RENFE, tel 902 24 34 02 (international), tel 902 24 02 02 (national), www.renfe.es

Car rental offices

» Avis, www.avis.com
» Budget, www.budget.com
» EasyCar, www.easycar.com
» Europcar, www.europcar.com
» Hertz, www.hertz.com
» Málaga Car, www.malagacar.com
» Sur Rent, www.sur-rent.com

Taxis

» Madrid Barajas airport Officina Municipal del Taxis, tel 915 88 96 32
» Barcelona airport, tel 932 23 51 51
» Alicante airport, tel 965 25 25 11 or 965 91 01 23
» Málaga airport Radio Taxi, tel 952 04 08 04 Unitaxi, tel 952 33 33 33

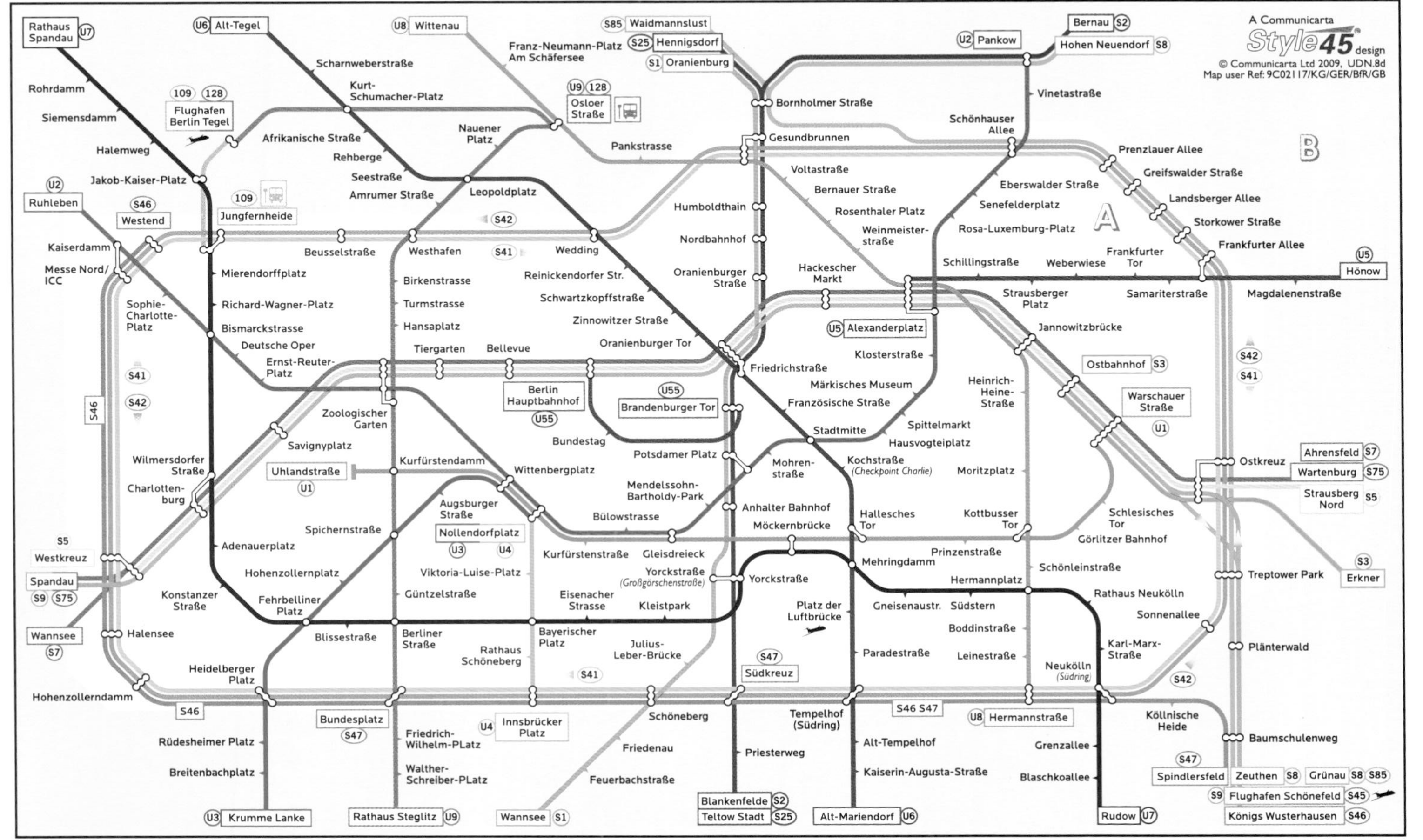
A Communicarta
Style45 design
© Communicarta Ltd 2009, UDN.8d
Map user Ref: 9C02117/KG/GER/BfR/GB
A
B
Rathaus Spandau U7
Rohrdamm
Siemensdamm
Halemweg
Jakob-Kaiser-Platz
U6 Alt-Tegel
Scharnweberstraße
Kurt-Schumacher-Platz
Afrikanische Straße
Rehberge
Seestraße
Amrumer Straße
Leopoldplatz
109 128
Flughafen Berlin Tegel
U8 Wittenau
Franz-Neumann-Platz Am Schäfersee
Nauener Platz
U9 128
Osloer Straße
Pankstrasse
S85 Waidmannslust
S25 Hennigsdorf
S1 Oranienburg
Bornholmer Straße
Gesundbrunnen
Voltastraße
Bernauer Straße
Rosenthaler Platz
Weinmeister-straße
Humboldthain
Nordbahnhof
Oranienburger Straße
U2 Pankow
Bernau S2
Hohen Neuendorf S8
Vinetastraße
Schönhauser Allee
Eberswalder Straße
Senefelderplatz
Rosa-Luxemburg-Platz
Prenzlauer Allee
Greifswalder Straße
Landsberger Allee
Storkower Straße
Frankfurter Allee
U5 Hönow
Magdalenenstraße
Samariterstraße
Frankfurter Tor
Weberwiese
Schillingstraße
Strausberger Platz
Jannowitzbrücke
U2 Ruhleben
S46 Westend
109 Jungfernheide
Kaiserdamm
Messe Nord/ICC
Sophie-Charlotte-Platz
Mierendorffplatz
Richard-Wagner-Platz
Bismarckstrasse
Deutsche Oper
Ernst-Reuter-Platz
Beusselstraße
Westhafen
Birkenstrasse
Turmstrasse
Hansaplatz
Tiergarten
Bellevue
S42
S41
Wedding
Reinickendorfer Str.
Schwartzkopffstraße
Zinnowitzer Straße
Oranienburger Tor
Friedrichstraße
Hackescher Markt
U5 Alexanderplatz
Klosterstraße
Märkisches Museum
Französische Straße
Stadtmitte
Spittelmarkt
Hausvogteiplatz
Berlin Hauptbahnhof U55
U55 Brandenburger Tor
Bundestag
Potsdamer Platz
Mohren-straße
Kochstraße (Checkpoint Charlie)
Heinrich-Heine-Straße
Moritzplatz
Ostbahnhof S3
Warschauer Straße U1
Ostkreuz
Ahrensfeld S7
Wartenburg S75
Strausberg Nord S5
Zoologischer Garten
Savignyplatz
Uhlandstraße U1
Kurfürstendamm
Wittenbergplatz
Augsburger Straße
Nollendorfplatz U3 U4
Mendelssohn-Bartholdy-Park
Bülowstrasse
Anhalter Bahnhof
Möckernbrücke
Hallesches Tor
Kottbusser Tor
Schlesisches Tor
Görlitzer Bahnhof
Prinzenstraße
Schönleinstraße
Treptower Park
S3 Erkner
S46
Wilmersdorfer Straße
Charlotten-burg
S5 Westkreuz
Spandau S9 S75
Adenauerplatz
Konstanzer Straße
Hohenzollernplatz
Fehrbelliner Platz
Spichernstraße
Viktoria-Luise-Platz
Güntzelstraße
Kurfürstenstraße
Gleisdreieck
Yorckstraße (Großgörschenstraße)
Yorckstraße
Eisenacher Strasse
Kleistpark
Mehringdamm
Hermannplatz
Rathaus Neukölln
Sonnenallee
Platz der Luftbrücke
Gneisenaustr.
Südstern
Boddinstraße
Leinestraße
Paradestraße
Karl-Marx-Straße
Neukölln (Südring)
Plänterwald
Wannsee S7
Halensee
Hohenzollerndamm
Heidelberger Platz
Blissestraße
Berliner Straße
Rathaus Schöneberg
Bayerischer Platz
Julius-Leber-Brücke
S47 Südkreuz
Tempelhof (Südring)
S46 S47
U8 Hermannstraße
Köllnische Heide
Baumschulenweg
Rüdesheimer Platz
Breitenbachplatz
Bundesplatz S47
Friedrich-Wilhelm-PLatz
Walther-Schreiber-PLatz
U4 Innsbrücker Platz
Schöneberg
Friedenau
Feuerbachstraße
Priesterweg
Alt-Tempelhof
Kaiserin-Augusta-Straße
Grenzallee
Blaschkoallee
S47 Spindlersfeld
Zeuthen S8
Grünau S8 S85
S9 Flughafen Schönefeld S45
Königs Wusterhausen S46
U3 Krumme Lanke
Rathaus Steglitz U9
Wannsee S1
Blankenfelde S2
Teltow Stadt S25
Alt-Mariendorf U6
Rudow U7

GETTING AROUND IN MUNICH, HAMBURG AND FRANKFURT

Most German cities have integrated public transportation systems based on buses and trams, while the larger cities and conurbations also have S-Bahn local trains and U-Bahn underground trains. Through-ticketing means that you can transfer between lines or change from one mode of travel to another on a single ticket.

Fare systems are usually based on zones, with tickets increasing in price the more zones are crossed. Ticket vending machines usually display a clear map of the network showing the different zones. The majority of visitor destinations in cities are likely to be within a single, central zone. Many vending machines have instructions in English, and they often accept paper notes as well as coins (and in some cases credit cards as well), and they give change. Before starting your journey, you must validate your ticket by inserting it into a stamping machine on the platform or on board the vehicle.

Single-journey tickets are available, but it will often be worth purchasing a *Tageskarte* (day ticket), *Familienkarte* (family ticket) or *Wochenkarte* (weekly ticket). A *Streifenkarte* (strip ticket) consists of a strip of usually 10 single-journey tickets at a reduced price. The real bargain in many cities is the Welcome Card, valid for between one and seven days, and giving concessions on entry to museums, galleries and other visitor attractions as well as unlimited use of public transportation. See individual entries for details.

Tickets are not checked before boarding, but non-uniformed inspectors are active, and on-the-spot fines are levied if you do not have a ticket or if the one you have is incorrect. Claiming that you are an ignorant tourist is unacceptable as an excuse.

MUNICH

www.mvv-muenchen.de

The MVV (Munich Transportation Authority) runs a comprehensive public transportation network comprising eight S-Bahn lines and six U-Bahn lines, plus trams and buses. Several S-Bahn lines run underground through the middle of the city, linking the Hauptbahnhof with Karlsplatz and the important hub of Marienplatz.

A single-journey ticket costs €2.30, a strip of 10 is €11, day tickets from €5 (depending on the number of zones) and a three-day ticket is €12.30.

✉ MVV (Münchener Verkehrs- und Tarifverbund), Hauptbahnhof (main train station) ☎ 089 4142 4344 🕒 Daily 7am–8pm

✉ Also at Marienplatz (below ground) 🕒 Mon–Fri 9–8, Sat 9–4

HAMBURG

www.hvv.de

The HVV (Hamburg Transport Authority) is responsible for a public transportation network comprising 15 S-Bahn and U-Bahn lines, more than 200 bus routes and several river and ferry services. Important hubs include the Hauptbahnhof (main train station), serving north and south sections, Jungfernstieg (S-Bahn station, close to Alster and Rathausplatz) and Landungsbrücken (for harbour trips and the promenade). A single-journey ticket for travel in the central zone costs €1.30.

✉ HVV (Hamburger Verkehrsverbund), Steinstrasse 7, 20095 Hamburg ☎ 040 194 49 🕒 Mon–Fri 8–6

✉ Also at the Hauptbahnhof (main train station) 🕒 Mon–Fri 6am–9pm, Sat, Sun 7am–9pm

FRANKFURT

www.rmv.de

The RMV (Rhine-Main Transportation Authority) administers public transportation in a vast area that is focused on Frankfurt and takes in the cities of the region around the Rhine and Main rivers, among them Wiesbaden, Bad Homburg and Darmstadt. In addition to trams and 100 bus routes, there are several S-Bahn and U-Bahn lines. Important interchange stations in central Frankfurt include the Hauptbahnhof, and there is also a direct S-Bahn link to the city's airport. A single-journey ticket for travel in the central zone costs €1.50.

✉ RMV (Rhein-Main Verkehrsverbund), An der Hauptwache, 60313 Frankfurt ☎ 01805 768 4636 (hotline) 🕒 Mon–Fri 9–8, Sat 9.30–6

Left *A tram on a narrow street in Munich*

DRIVING

The quality of the German road network makes driving an excellent way to explore the country. Although constant driving at high speed can be tiring, the autobahn makes it possible to cover long distances in a short time, enabling you to move easily from one area of interest to another. A car is the best way of getting around if you aim to explore smaller towns and villages and the countryside. If your interest is confined to a city or group of cities, public transportation will almost certainly be your better option.

The best-known feature of Germany's extensive and well-maintained road system is the autobahn, the network of toll-free motorways covering the whole country, but other roads like Bundesstrassen (national roads) and Landstrassen (main roads) are generally engineered to a high standard, with good surfaces and helpful signposting. Autobahns are identified by a white letter 'A' and a number on a blue background (e.g. A1, A2), and national roads by a black letter 'B' and a number (e.g. B1, B2) on a yellow background. The previously inadequate road network of eastern Germany has been transformed through the construction of motorways like the Ostseeautobahn, linking the Baltic coast to the rest of the country, and through the improvement of other roads. The downside to all this is the density of traffic; congestion can be acute in built-up areas like the Rhine–Ruhr and Rhine–Main conurbations, and anywhere at holiday times.

More than 100 named tourist routes crisscross the country. Some, such as stretches of the Deutsche Alpenstrasse (German Alpine Road), were intentionally built as scenic highways, although most are ordinary roads linking places of similar interest. The best known is probably the Romantische Strasse (Romantic Road), which runs from Würzburg in northern Bavaria to Füssen at the foot of the Alps, passing through picturesque, historic towns on the way. Even if they are not designated as such, many of the roads through the country's wooded uplands qualify as scenic routes, and extensive sections of the autobahn network (for example, Cologne–Limburg–Frankfurt, Munich–Salzburg and the Thuringian Forest autobahn) offer spectacular visual experiences.

Germans are fast drivers, and determined popular resistance among motorists has prevented the adoption of a speed limit on the autobahn. It can be unnerving when passing another vehicle at the suggested maximum speed of 130kph (80mph), only to glance in your mirror and spot a powerful vehicle coming up behind you at 200kph (125mph) or more. Most drivers are aware of what they are doing and respect the rules of the road, having passed the country's particularly rigorous driving test. Once you have become used to conditions, you will find the behaviour of fellow road-users fairly predictable.

BRINGING YOUR OWN CAR

Before You Leave

» If you have a right-hand drive car, adjust your headlights for driving on the right.
» Contact your car insurer or broker at least one month beforehand to make sure you will be covered to drive abroad.
» Have your car serviced.
» Fit a wing mirror on the left if you don't already have one.
» Ensure you have adequate breakdown assistance coverage, such as the Automobile Association's European Breakdown Cover (tel: 0800 085 2721; www.theaa.com).

You Will Need

» A valid national driver's licence (a translation may be required if you are from a non-EU country or from the US; check with your German National Tourist Office (▷ 370) before setting off) or international driver's licence.

SPEED LIMITS

AREA	BUILT-UP AREAS	OUTSIDE BUILT-UP AREAS	AUTOBAHNS
SPEED LIMIT	50kph (31mph) 30kph (18mph) in some residential and central areas	100kph (62mph)	Advisory limit is 130kph (80mph), otherwise there is no limit (though many heavily trafficked or curving stretches have speed limits of between 90kph (56mph) and 120kph (75mph))
SIGN	Indicated by the name of the town or village in black lettering on a yellow background (end of limit is shown by an identical sign with a diagonal red band through the place-name)		Minimum speed is indicated by a number on a blue circular sign

» The vehicle registration document if you are from a non-EU country.
» A vehicle insurance certificate; third-party coverage is the minimum required.
» A red breakdown triangle, spare headlight bulbs, reflective jacket and first-aid kit (including surgical gloves).
» A nationality sticker unless you have EU plates.
» Winter tyres (tires) for snow conditions (or potential snow conditions) and snow chains if you intend to drive in mountain areas during winter.

RULES OF THE ROAD

» Drive on the right.
» On roads without yellow diamond priority signs, give way to traffic from the right.
» Seat belts must be worn by all occupants of a vehicle.
» Children under 12 must use an appropriate safety seat.
» Halt at tram stops where there is no central (median) reservation and allow passengers to cross the road to board and disembark.
» Give way to trams and buses as they leave stops.
» Use dipped (low-intensity) headlights in poor visibility and in tunnels.
» Do not use side lights when driving.
» Give way to pedestrians when turning right or left at uncontrolled junctions (intersections).
» Do not drink and drive. The penalties are severe.
» Traffic lights are supplemented by priority signs, which must be obeyed when the lights are not functioning (e.g. at night or during weekends).
» A flashing light may indicate that a right turn is permitted when traffic lights are red, but you must give way to traffic coming from the other direction.
» Insulting behaviour to other drivers or police is an offence.
» Fines can be imposed on the spot by police and vehicles may be confiscated.

THE AUTOBAHN

With a total length of 12,500km (7,750 miles), the autobahn network connects all major cities and towns. Many places are linked to the system by more than one interchange (exit), and it is sensible to check the map to see which exit suits you best. Interchanges are numbered. Signs show the distance between service areas, which are generally closely spaced. In addition, there are rest areas with basic facilities, plus picnic areas, particularly on scenic stretches. Service areas vary in their facilities; some have hotels, and all have refreshments and well-maintained toilets. Vehicles joining the autobahn must give way to traffic already on it. Keep to the right-hand lane except when overtaking, and indicate your intention before you change lanes. Emergency telephones are placed at regular intervals, their location indicated by arrows.

PROBLEMS

If your car breaks down or you are involved in an accident, turn your hazard warning lights on and place your warning triangle at a safe distance behind the vehicle (200m/220 yards on the autobahn, less on other roads). You can obtain assistance by calling national German motoring organizations on one of the following numbers:
» ACE tel 01802 343536
» ADAC tel 01802 222222
» AvD tel 0800 990 9909
If an accident has occurred, exchange details with anyone involved (name, address, car details, as well as the name and address of both your insurance companies). If anyone is injured, the police must be called (tel 110). Call an ambulance (tel 110) or the fire brigade if required (tel 112). Do not admit liability even if you know you were in the wrong.

PARKING

There are strict rules for when and where you may not park. Parking is forbidden in many fairly obvious places, for example within 5m (5.5 yards) of a pedestrian crossing or road junction, or within 15m (16.5 yards) of a bus or tram stop. Less obviously, do not park on a main road in the countryside, or where parking restrictions may be indicated solely by the standard sign (which you may have to look for).

Competition for parking spaces can be harsh in densely built-up residential areas as well as in the middle of cities. In the former, many spaces will be reserved for residents, while in the latter you will usually have to pay a fee, and you may be limited to two hours or less. Payment for on-street parking is usually made by using a ticket machine (some accept credit cards), or less frequently by inserting coins in a parking meter. Where parking is free but limited in time, you may need to obtain a parking disc (from newspaper kiosks or filling stations) and set it to the correct time.

Rather than waste time driving around trying to find an on-street space, it may be better to park off the street. Specially built parking areas (*Parkhäuser*) are well marked, often with an indication of how

GLOSSARY OF ROAD SIGNS

GERMAN	ENGLISH
Abblenden	dip (lower) headlights
Alle Richtungen	all directions
Anfang	start
Anlieger frei	except residents
Ausfahrt	exit
Baustelle	works
Einbahnstrasse	one-way street
Einfahrt	entrance
Ende	end
Gefahr	danger
Links	left
Radweg	bicycle path
Raststätte	service area
Rechts	right
Rollsplitt	loose chippings (gravel)
Stau	hold-up, traffic jam
Steinschlag	falling rocks
Umleitung	diversion
Unfall	accident
Vorrang/Vorfahrt	priority
Vorsicht	careful
Zentrum	central city

many spaces are still available. The system usually involves taking a time-stamped ticket on arrival, then inserting it into the pay station just before departing, paying the sum indicated and retaining the ticket for use to raise the exit barrier. Parking areas may be closed at night.

Vehicles parked on the street must be clearly visible at night; leave side lights on in poorly lit areas.

FUEL

Germany pioneered the introduction of lead-free fuel, and leaded fuel is now unobtainable. On sale are *Normal* (91 octane)—not sold at all stations—and the same-priced *Super* (95 octane), *Super Plus* (98 octane), *Diesel* and—in 4,000 stations nationwide—*Autogas* (LPG). Most filling stations are self-service and often also function as mini-markets. Many are open 24 hours. When purchasing fuel, check the number of the pump and pay the cashier. Credit cards are normally accepted, but you need to check this before purchase, particularly in country areas. Prices vary slightly according to the degree of competition; the cheapest fuel comes from supermarket filling stations, the most expensive is on the autobahn or in remote areas. Avoid running out of fuel on the autobahn; you will incur a fine if you do. Fuel prices at the time of writing are volatile. Please check the prevailing rates before you travel.

MITFAHRERZENTRALE

This is the name given to offices in major cities that arrange car sharing for intercity trips. Drivers planning to undertake such a journey and who have a seat or seats to spare register with the office and are put in touch with others wishing to travel to the same destination. The fee is arranged between driver and passenger(s), and a fee is charged by the Mitfahrerzentrale, which also arranges insurance.

Below *Use the chart to work out the distance in kilometres (green) between major towns and estimated duration in hours and minutes (blue) of a car journey*

	Bonn	Bremen	Dresden	Düsseldorf	Erfurt	Frankfurt-am-Main	Freiburg	Hamburg	Hannover	Heidelberg	Köln	Leipzig	Mainz	München	Münster	Nürnberg	Regensburg	Rostock	Stuttgart	Würzburg
Berlin	552	400	216	530	310	535	741	254	306	615	543	211	545	552	441	426	453	219	617	453
Bonn		333	542	050	349	156	401	433	315	223	031	517	143	531	149	348	441	631	337	248
Bremen			432	309	441	441	658	128	134	521	323	344	451	725	153	549	626	326	629	453
Dresden				549	210	435	617	449	335	455	534	120	445	428	510	302	326	414	453	329
Düsseldorf					356	224	429	410	253	252	037	511	211	600	125	417	509	608	406	317
Erfurt						243	500	500	343	322	341	145	253	408	343	241	309	445	420	244
Frankfurt-am-Main							248	511	353	110	209	410	043	406	258	223	316	709	224	123
Freiburg								728	610	152	414	617	246	414	515	340	425	917	210	303
Hamburg									153	550	423	403	521	744	255	608	645	220	648	512
Hannover										433	306	247	403	628	204	450	529	351	531	354
Heidelberg											237	450	108	335	337	218	304	748	128	142
Köln												509	156	545	140	402	454	621	351	302
Leipzig													420	427	422	301	328	347	452	328
Mainz														419	308	236	328	719	222	136
München															634	155	128	729	241	256
Münster																451	543	453	451	355
Nürnberg																	111	602	216	113
Regensburg																		629	302	206
Rostock																			753	628
Stuttgart																				140

	Berlin	Bonn	Bremen	Dresden	Düsseldorf	Erfurt	Frankfurt-am-Main	Freiburg	Hamburg	Hannover	Heidelberg	Köln	Leipzig	Mainz	München	Münster	Nürnberg	Regensburg	Rostock	Stuttgart
Bonn	593																			
Bremen	391	342																		
Dresden	191	570	473																	
Düsseldorf	549	67	298	599																
Erfurt	299	366	469	215	395															
Frankfurt-am-Main	547	177	448	463	223	259														
Freiburg	805	426	715	677	472	526	276													
Hamburg	282	452	118	503	408	499	496	762												
Hannover	285	312	122	371	268	356	353	619	152											
Heidelberg	629	242	530	520	288	341	91	189	578	435										
Köln	566	26	316	568	35	364	191	441	425	286	256									
Leipzig	184	511	370	117	532	156	404	662	400	268	486	508								
Mainz	571	164	472	487	210	283	39	280	519	376	95	178	427							
München	588	572	775	460	618	419	410	416	805	673	336	586	445	434						
Münster	474	175	173	561	130	388	281	547	280	194	363	148	458	304	678					
Nürnberg	438	395	583	310	441	269	234	383	613	470	226	410	294	258	173	502				
Regensburg	481	501	667	345	547	312	339	474	697	565	317	515	337	363	132	607	112			
Rostock	226	640	306	447	596	500	684	1006	197	340	766	614	384	708	789	468	638	681		
Stuttgart	628	356	639	500	402	433	206	206	669	526	119	371	485	210	226	477	206	297	829	
Würzburg	497	288	485	369	334	279	127	321	515	372	164	303	353	151	285	404	109	214	697	144

TRAINS

Germany has a comprehensive rail network totalling some 42,000km (27,000 miles) of track linking all places of any size. Overall control is exercised by Deutsche Bahn (German Rail), which has several operating arms. There has been heavy public investment in the rail system over many years and services generally are of a very high standard. The efficiency and near-complete coverage of the system, combined with the availability of a range of special tickets, make travel by rail a very attractive option for a holiday in Germany. Nearly all trains have smoking coaches or compartments, and first- and second-class accommodation, and many also have toilets for people with a disability.

TYPES OF TRAIN

» InterCityExpress (ICE) are state-of-the-art trains that run at speeds up to 319kph (198mph). The latest has a first-class lounge giving passengers a spectacular driver's-eye view of the track.

» Metropolitan (MET) is a luxury train linking Hamburg with Essen, Düsseldorf and Cologne. There is a choice of three seating zones: 'Office', with fax, etc.; 'Silence', which is mobile- and computer-free; and 'Club', with DVD facilities, etc.

» InterCity (IC) trains are only marginally less luxurious and swift than ICE trains, and link major cities and towns across the country. They are air conditioned and have a restaurant or bistro.

» InterRegio (IR) fast trains connect regional hubs with the national network. They have buffet or bistro facilities or a refreshment trolley.

» RegionalExpress (RE) and StädteExpress (SE) are fast, limited-stop local trains, often with double-decker coaches.

» RegionalBahn (RB) local trains are usually diesel powered and stop at all stations.

» S-Bahn trains are the suburban trains in large cities and the Ruhr conurbation.

OVERNIGHT SERVICES

» DB Nachtzug (NZ) are domestic and international night trains with modern sleepers, couchettes or reclining seats.

» CityNightLine (CNL) has luxury cabin, standard and couchette accommodation on services between German cities and to Austria and Switzerland.

» DB AutoZug carries cars on double-decker wagons while passengers sit in coaches or stay overnight in sleeping accommodations. These trains link major German cities with popular summer and winter destinations in Germany and abroad.

TICKETS AND FARES

Travel by rail in Germany using standard tickets is not cheap, but you can significantly reduce the cost by choosing from the range of discount tickets. You can buy your tickets at train stations (from the booking office, travel office or a ticket machine), from some travel agents (who may charge a fee) or online (www.bahn.de). You can buy tickets on board some trains (but not on local services, where you will be fined if you are without a ticket), although only standard tickets are available and you will be charged a fee. Seats can be reserved on long-distance trains for a small fee—a good idea at peak times, such as weekends and national holidays.

» Standard tickets vary in cost depending on the length of journey—the longer the trip, the lower the price per kilometre. Fares on ICE trains are more expensive. Tickets are fully refundable. Accompanied children under 14 travel free. Groups of six or more people can save at least 50 per cent if they buy tickets seven days in advance and 70 per cent if they buy them 14 days in advance.

» Sparprice tickets allow you to make savings if you purchase your ticket in advance and limit yourself to a particular day and train—you can save 25 per cent (Sparprice 25) or 50 per cent (Sparprice 50) of the cost of a standard return ticket. There are weekend restrictions on the use of Sparprice 50. Up to two companions can travel with you at a 50 per cent discount. There are some restrictions on refunds.

» The €37 Schönes-Wochenende-Ticket ('Lovely Weekend' ticket) gives unlimited second-class travel on local trains for up to five people on Saturdays or Sundays. It is not valid on ICE and similar long-distance trains.

» The Länderticket costs €18–€23.50 for one person and €25–€33 for five people and gives unlimited second-class travel on local trains within a region for 24 hours between Monday and Friday.

RAIL PASSES

» The InterRail Germany is valid for travel on three, four, six and eight days in any one month on services within Germany (including ICE and IC). If purchased in the UK, the three-day pass costs £212 for first class and £157 for second class, while an eight-day pass costs £336 for first class and £249 for second class. This pass is worth buying if you intend to cover long distances during your stay.

» The Eurail Pass is intended only for visitors from outside mainland Europe and is available in multiple options, affording travel to Germany and from one to 19 additional countries, and from 5 to 10 days in a two-month period.

INFORMATION

There are several ways to obtain train information:

» Larger stations have a travel office (*Reisezentrum*) with English-speaking staff and a range of facilities.

» Timetables give information about departure times and platform numbers (yellow sheet) and arrivals (white).

» Train composition diagrams on the platform show the make-up of long-distance trains. Coaches (cars) are identified by a letter corresponding to a section of the platform, enabling you to position yourself at the exact spot where your coach will stop.

» Loudspeaker announcements in stations and on board trains give information in German and sometimes in English.

» The website www.bahn.de / international (in English) gives rail information and allows you to purchase tickets online.

OTHER POINTS

» In larger stations, the travel office (*Reisezentrum*) provides luggage storage (lockers as well as a manned office) and currency exchange.

» Up to 30kg (66lb) of personal luggage is carried free. The trolleys (carts) provided in larger stations take a coin (usually €1) deposit, which is returned when you replace the trolley (cart) at a collection point.

» Bicycles are carried on most but not all trains. Tickets for bicycles are inexpensive.

» Most long-distance trains run at regular intervals and the timetable is coordinated to make changing trains as straightforward as possible. Many changes can be made simply by crossing from one side of the platform to the other.

Clockwise from opposite *The high-speed train that runs between Köln and Hamburg; a heavily laden passenger at Köln station*

The chart below shows the duration in hours and minutes of a train journey between these destinations in Germany.

	Berlin	Bonn Hbf	Bremen Hbf	Dresden Hbf	Düsseldorf Hbf	Erfurt Hbf	Frankfurt (Main) Hbf	Freiburg (Breisgau) Hbf	Hamburg Hbf	Hannover Hbf	Heidelberg Hbf	Köln Hbf	Leipzig Hbf	Mainz Hbf	München Hbf	Münster (West) Hbf	Nürnberg Hbf	Regensburg Hbf	Rostock Hbf	Stuttgart Hbf	Würzburg Hbf
A437																					
A245		328																			
B158		613	534																		
A408		044	237	620																	
B253		356	405	214	404																
A329		137	321	426	137	210															
A549		328	553	651	336	435	203														
A210		359	054	441	305	415	319	600													
A131		304	058	412	235	244	207	429	110												
A431		210	423	537	218	321	052	134	421	308											
A417		019	259	555	021	339	110	310	326	243	148										
B132		500	414	107	508	102	313	538	400	252	424	440									
A405		125	411	504	149	248	029	216	409	256	050	117	353								
A618		450	546	649	458	430	323	418	558	434	304	431	458	338							
A325		207	117	606	117	348	300	458	216	144	336	143	454	311	619						
A439		348	413	505	358	246	205	421	413	254	301	328	314	239	139	443					
A543		450	517	618	458	401	305	528	517	358	409	431	414	344	126	547	057				
C243		709	331	508	615	610	550	901	213	340	707	636	443	642	901	458	716	821			
A455		234	459	557	242	341	118	153	459	346	039	214	446	122	212	404	211	320	747		
A345		251	315	418	259	202	108	329	319	200	215	231	307	142	228	345	050	153	622	212	

Bottom *An InterCityExpress train at Berlin's Hauptbahnhof*

Above *Bicycling is popular throughout Germany, with many bicycling paths*

LONG-DISTANCE BUSES, TAXIS AND BICYCLES

LONG-DISTANCE BUSES

The comprehensive extent of the German rail system means that the country has an under-developed long-distance bus network, certainly when compared with other countries. Local and regional bus services are operated by municipalities, an array of private companies and by Deutsche Bahn. Many bus routes make connections with rail services, and through (connecting) tickets may be available. Tickets can be obtained from bus offices and from the driver.

Berlin Linien Bus
www.berlinlinienbus.de
Buses run by Berlin Linien Bus connect the capital with 350 destinations in Germany, including major cities.
✉ Mannheimer Strasse 33–34, 10713 Berlin ☎ 030 861 9331

Zentraler Omnibusbahnhof Berlin (ZOB)
www.bvg.de
Berlin's central bus station.
✉ Masurenallee 4–6, 14057 Berlin (Charlottenburg) ☎ 030 302 5361

Deutsche Touring GmbH
www.deutsche-touring.de
As well as running guided tours of varying lengths, this company operates a limited number of long-distance luxury coach routes of interest to tourists (for example, along the Romantic Road from Frankfurt and from Würzburg to Füssen), with the possibility of unlimited stopovers.
✉ Am Römerhof 17, 60486 Frankfurt
☎ 069 790 3501

TAXIS

Universally identifiable by their cream paintwork, German taxis are available at stands in all towns and cities or can be ordered by phone. There are stands at rail stations, public transportation interchanges, airports and key downtown locations. It may not be easy to hail a taxi on the street. Licensing is carefully administered, and most vehicles are of a high standard (Mercedes or similar) and are well maintained.

Fares are shown on a meter and consist of a minimum fee of around €3 plus a charge per kilometre of around €1.60. Evening and weekend rates may be higher and there is a small extra charge for each item of luggage. It is customary to round up the fare as a tip. Public transportation operators in some larger cities can arrange for a taxi to meet passengers at a particular stop or station.

BICYCLES

Bicyclists are well provided for in Germany. The network of long-distance bicycling trails is well maintained and marked, and a bicycling holiday in Germany is an attractive proposition. Many Germans take their bicycles with them on vacation, particularly when camping, and use them for excursions. Bicyclists can be just as territorial as other vehicle users, and pedestrians are advised not to loiter on bicycleways!

Bicycles can be taken on most trains and on the Berlin U-Bahn, but you will usually need a special ticket. They can be rented in most places, and Deutsche Bahn operates a Call-A-Bike rental service in Berlin (▷ 108), Cologne, Frankfurt and Munich (tel 0700 0522 5522; www.callabike.de).

REGIONAL FLIGHTS

There are regular national flights between the major German cities. The majority of services are run by the national airline, Lufthansa, and many are designed to connect with its international hubs at Frankfurt and Munich. These flights are supplemented by services run by other airlines, which also serve a number of minor airports. Many flights are scheduled with business people in mind, and have early morning departures and late-afternoon/early evening return times. An impact on previously expensive fares has been made by the entry into the market of a number of budget operators, and some lower fares are available through advance and online booking; this makes a regional flight an alternative to the otherwise excellent rail services.

REGIONAL AIRLINES

AIRLINE	BASE	WEBSITE	TELEPHONE	AIRPORTS SERVED
Air Berlin	Berlin	www.airberlin.com	01805 737800	Berlin-Tegel, Bremen, Cologne, Dortmund, Dresden, Düsseldorf, Erfurt, Frankfurt, Hamburg, Hannover, Karlsruhe/Baden-Baden, Leipzig, Munich, Münster/Osnabrück, Nürnberg, Paderborn, Rostock-Laage, Saarbrücken, Stuttgart, Sylt
Cirrus (Lufthansa partner)	Saarbrücken	www.cirrus-airlines.de	06893 800440	Berlin-Tempelhof, Dresden, Erfurt, Frankfurt, Hamburg, Mannheim, Munich, Münster/ Osnabruck, Saarbrücken, Stuttgart
Germania Express	Hannover	www.gexx.de	01805 737100	Berlin-Tegel, Düsseldorf, Memmingen, Stuttgart
Germanwings	Cologne-Bonn	www.germanwings.com	0870 252 1250	Berlin-Schönefeld, Cologne-Bonn, Dortmund, Dresden, Hamburg, Leipzig, Munich, Rostock, Stuttgart
Lufthansa	Frankfurt	www.lufthansa.com	08105 838426	Augsburg, Berlin, Bremen, Dortmund, Düsseldorf, Dresden, Frankfurt, Friedrichshafen, Hamburg, Hannover, Hof-Plauen, Cologne-Bonn, Leipzig-Halle, Kiel, Munich, Nürnberg, Stuttgart
Luftverkehrsgesellschaft Walter	Dortmund	www.airberlin.com	01805 737800	Berlin-Tempelhof, Cologne-Bonn, Dortmund, Dresden, Düsseldorf, Erfurt, Hamburg, Nürnberg, Stuttgart, Westerland-Sylt
Ostfriesische Lufttransport	Bremen	www.olt.de	04921 89920	Bremen, Cologne, Dortmund, Frankfurt, Hamburg, Heringsdorf, Munich, Nürnberg, Seasonal services to the East and North Frisian Islands
Sylt Air	Westerland	www.syltair.de	01900 55677	Hamburg, Westerland (Sylt)

AIRPORTS

Major Airports

In addition to the international airports on pages 48–51, Germany has a number of well-located airports linked to other major cities, most with several daily national flights and some international services.

Bremen
Tel 0421 55950
www.airport-bremen.de

Dresden
Tel 0351 8810
www.dresden-airport.de

Hannover (Hanover)
Tel 0511 977 1899
www.hannover-airport.de

Köln-Bonn (Cologne-Bonn)
Tel 02203 404001
www.airport-cgn.de

Nürnberg (Nuremberg)
Tel 0911 93700
www.airport-nuernberg.de

Stuttgart
Tel 01805 948444
www.flughafen-stuttgart.de

Local Airports

With limited flights, these airports serve smaller cities and in some cases are located conveniently close to popular holiday areas.

Augsburg
www.augsburg-airport.de
Limited number of flights to Berlin and Düsseldorf.
☎ 0821 270 8111

Dortmund
www.dortmund-airport.de
Daily flights to Berlin, Dresden, Erfurt, Leipzig-Halle, Munich, Nuremberg and Stuttgart.
☎ 0231 921301

Erfurt
www.flughafen-erfurt.de
Limited number of flights to Berlin, Düsseldorf, Hamburg, Cologne and Munich.
☎ 0361 6560

Friedrichshafen
www.fly-away.de
Virtually in the lakeside town of Friedrichshafen, this airport serves the holiday towns and villages around the Bodensee (Lake Constance) and the western section of the German Alps. Daily flights to major cities.
☎ 07541 28401

Heringsdorf
www.flughafen-heringsdorf.de
This is the small airport for the Baltic holiday island of Usedom. It has infrequent flights to Berlin.
☎ 038376 2500

Hof-Plauen
www.airport-hof.de
On the outskirts of the northern Bavarian town of Hof. Limited number of daily flights to Frankfurt.
☎ 09292 95518

Kiel
www.airport-kiel.de
The airport of this city on the Baltic coast of Schleswig-Holstein has a limited number of flights to Frankfurt and Cologne.
☎ 0431 329190

Münster-Osnabrück
www.fmo.de
Just off the A1 Ruhr-Hamburg autobahn, midway between the cities of Münster and Osnabrück. Limited number of daily flights to Berlin, Frankfurt, Munich and Stuttgart.
☎ 02571 943360

Niederrhein
www.airportniederrhein.de
Just off the Düsseldorf–Netherlands autobahn, close to the old city of Kleve, the Lower Rhine airport is being developed for budget flights. Limited services to Berlin and Munich.
☎ 02837 666111

Saarbrücken
www.flughafen-saarbruecken.de
Limited number of flights to Berlin, Hamburg, Leipzig–Halle and Munich.
☎ 06893 83272

Above *Signs at airports are often in both German and English*
Opposite *A plane taking off at sunset*

Westerland-Sylt
www.flughafen-sylt.de
The airport serving the holiday island of Sylt offers mostly seasonal flights to major cities.
☎ 04651 920612

North Sea and Baltic Islands

A number of local companies operate small aircraft over short distances between the German mainland and holiday islands in the North Sea and Baltic.

LFH (Luftverkehr Friesland Harle)
www.inselflieger.de
Flights to Helgoland and to Wangerooge, Langeoog, Baltrum, Juist and Borkum in the Ostfriesische Inseln (East Frisian Islands) from Harlesiel.
☎ 04464 94810

FLN FRISIA-Luftverkehr
www.fln-norddeich.de
To Juist and Nordeney in the Ostfriesische Inseln (East Frisian Islands) from Norddeich.
☎ 04931 93320

DOMESTIC FERRIES AND RIVERBOATS

FERRIES

Ferries are the most popular and economical way of reaching Germany's holiday islands in the North Sea and Baltic. There are regular services all year round, though frequency decreases out of season. Timetables may be affected by tides and adverse weather.

Germany's great rivers are plied by a variety of craft, among them century-old paddle-steamers taking day visitors to nearby destinations and modern vessels providing luxurious accommodation for cruises of several days' duration. Most river trips are in the nature of excursions, with a return to the starting point, but steamers can be used as an alternative to rail in order to reach a particular destination, especially along the Rhine and Mosel.

Left to right *The tree-lined banks for Berlin's Landwehrkanal make an attractive sight for sightseers on a cruise boat; a vehicle and passenger ferry at dock in Travemunde*

ISLAND FERRY SERVICES

DESTINATION	FERRY COMPANY	MAINLAND PORT	DURATION	FARE
Ostfriesische Inseln (East Frisian Islands)				
Baltrum	Reederei Baltrum-Linie, Haus No. 278, 26579 Insel Baltrum (tel 04939 91300; www.baltrum-linie.de)	Nessmersiel	30 min	€16 round-trip
Borkum	AG Ems, Postfach 11 54, 26691 Emden-Aussenhafen (tel 01805 180182; www.ag-ems.de)	Emden	2.25 hr	€16.50 round-trip
Langeoog	Schiffahrt Langeoog, Kurverwaltung Langeoog, Hauptstrasse 28, 26465 Langeoog (tel 04972 6930; www.schiffahrt-langeoog.de)	Bensersiel	1 hr	€19.50 round-trip
Norderney	Reederei Frisia, Postfach 1262, 26534 Nordeney (tel 04931 9870; www.reederei-frisia.de)	Norddeich	55 min	€16
Spiekeroog	Spiekeroog Schiffahrt und Kurverwaltung, Noorderpad 25, 26474 Spiekeroog (tel 04976 919 3101; www.spiekeroog.de)	Neuharlingersiel	45 min	€19 round-trip
Wangerooge	Schiffahrt und Inselbahn Wangerooge, Kurverwaltung Wangerooge, Postfach 1620, 26480 Wangerooge (tel 04464 949411; www.wangerooge.de)	Harlesiel	1.25 hr	€18.20 round-trip
Nordfriesische Inseln (North Frisian Islands)				
Föhr and Amrum	Wyker Dampfschiffs-Reederei, Am fähranleger 1, 25938 Wyk auf Föhr (tel 04681 800; www.wdr-wyk.de)	Dagebüll	Wyk (Föhr) 1 hr, Wittdün (Amrum) 1.5–2 hr	Dagebüll–Wyk €12 round-trip, Dagebüll–Wittdün €17.50 round-trip
Pellworm	Fähre Pellworm, Postfach 69, 25849 Pellworm (tel 04844 753; www.faehre-pellworm.de)	Nordstrand	35 min	€10 round-trip
Hiddensee (Baltic coast)	Reederei Hiddensee, Fährstrasse 16, 18439 Stralsund (tel 0180 321 2150; www.reederei-hiddensee.de)	Stralsund, Schaprode (Rügen Island)	Stralsund 1 hr 30 min Schaprode 30 min	Stralsund €17.20 round-trip Schaprode €13.70 round-trip

RIVERBOAT SERVICES

RIVER	FERRY COMPANY	MAIN TOWN	ROUTES	DURATION	FARE
Danube	Donauschiffahrt Wurm & Köck, Höllgasse 26, 94032 Passau (tel 0851 929292; www.donauschiffahrt.de)	Passau (also Deggendorf)	Passau–Engelhartszell–Passau, Schlögen meanders, Passau–Linz –Vienna (Austria)	Passau–Linz: about 6 hr (return possible by train)	€22
Elbe	Sächsische Dampfschiffahrt GmbH, Hertha-Lindner-Strasse 10, 01067 Dresden (tel 0351 866090; www.saechsische-dampf schiffahrt.de)	Dresden	All towns between Seusslitz, Meissen, Dresden, Pirna, Bad Schandau and Decin (Czech Republic)	Dresden–Bad Schandau: 5.15 hr (single journey)	Dresden–Bad Schandau: €20.50 round-trip
Mosel	Personenschiffahrt Kolb, Georg-Schmitt-Platz 2, 54292 Trier (tel 0651 26666; www.kolb-mosel.com)	Trier	Local excursions on Mosel and Saar rivers	varies	round-trip from €8
Neckar	Rhein-Neckar-Fahrgast-gesellschaft, Untere Neckarstrasse 17, 69117 Heidelberg (tel 06221 20181; www.rnf-gmbh.de)	Heidelberg	Heidelberg–Neckarsteinach–Heidelberg	3-hr round-trip	€11.50 round-trip
Neckar	Berta Epple GmbH und Co. KG, Anlegestelle Wilhelma, 70376 Stuttgart (tel 0711 5499 7060; www.neckar-kaeptn.de)	Stuttgart	Local excursions on the Neckar from Bad Cannstatt near Stuttgart	daily from 10.30am 6-hr trip	from €14
Rhine, Main and Neckar	Frankfurter Personenschiffahrt primus Linie, Mainkai 36, 60311 Frankfurt (tel 069 133 8370; www.primus-linie.de)	Frankfurt	Frankfurt–Rhine Gorge, Frankfurt–Aschaffenburg, Frankfurt–Heidelberg	Frankfurt–Heidelberg–Frankfurt: 10.5 hr (9am–7.35pm)	Frankfurt–Heidelberg–Frankfurt: €29.50
Rhine and Mosel	Köln-Düsseldorfer Deutsche Rheinschiffahrt AG, Frankenwerft 35, 50667 Köln (tel 0221 208 8318; www.k-d.com)	Köln (Cologne)	All riverside towns between Cologne, Bonn, Koblenz and Mainz, and between Koblenz and Cochem on the Mosel	Cologne–Koblenz: 5 hr	Cologne–Koblenz: €37.40 (one way)
Weser	Flotte Weser GmbH und Co. KG, Deisterallee 1, 31785 Hameln (tel 05151 939 999; www.flotte-weser.de)	Hameln (Hamelin)	Most riverside towns between Bad Karlshafen, Hamelin, Minden and Bremen	Hamelin–Bodenwerder–Hamelin: day (10am –7pm), 4.5hr on board	Hamelin–Bodenwerder–Hamelin: excursion €31 round-trip

Compared with many other countries, Germany is well equipped to receive visitors with a disability, particularly in terms of public transportation and access to buildings. All modern facilities are designed to allow wheelchair access and many (but not all) older buildings have been suitably adapted. In addition, a wealth of information is available from a variety of sources to help visitors plan their trip and move easily around the country.

GENERAL ADVICE

» Think about where you are going to go and what you want to do well in advance, and make the necessary contacts. Specialist tour operators can help with this.

» If you are flying to Germany, let the airline know in good time about your requirements. They will inform the airport about what help and facilities you will need. Allow plenty of time to check in.

» Deutsche Bahn (German Railways) aims to make the use of its trains and stations as easy as possible for people with limited mobility. Most intercity trains have wheelchair access, and Nachtzug sleeping-car trains (▷ 58) have couchette compartments designed for wheelchair users. Help with boarding and luggage is available if requested in advance.

» In Berlin, S-Bahn and U-Bahn stations with good wheelchair access are indicated on the plan of the network, and some trams and buses have retractable ramps.

» Berlin's SonderFahrDienst services are available for people with limited mobility. Advance contact is necessary: SonderFahrDienst für Menschen mit Behinderung, SFD-Berlin, c/o WBT eG, Genthiner Strasse 36, 10785 Berlin (tel 030 2610 2300; www.sfd-berlin.de).

» Most other cities can provide comprehensive access information, including city plans showing wheelchair-accessible buildings and public toilets, and lists of wheelchair-accessible restaurants, hotels, museums and public buildings. Contact tourist information offices or use the relevant city website—see individual city entries for details. Most have information in English.

» Most of the German Länder (administrative regions) have travel information on their websites for visitors with a disability (sometimes only in German).

» The blue badge issued to drivers with a disability in Britain is valid throughout the EU. The leaflet accompanying the badge explains how to use it.

USEFUL ORGANIZATIONS

In Britain and the US

MOBILITY INTERNATIONAL USA
www.miusa.org
Information on travel and international exchange schemes for people with disabilities.
✉ 132 E. Broadway, Suite 343, Eugene, Oregon 97401, USA ☎ 541/343-1284

HOLIDAY CARE
www.holidaycare.org.uk
Information about the level of facilities and accessibility available at various destinations.
✉ Tourism for All, The Hawkins Suite, Enham Place, Enham Alamein, Andover SP11 6JS ☎ 0845 124 9971
Minicom 0845 124 9976

In Germany

BUNDESARBEITSGEMEINSCHAFT DER CLUBS BEHINDERTER UND IHRER FREUNDE E.V. (NATIONAL ASSOCIATION OF CLUBS FOR THE DISABLED AND THEIR FRIENDS)
www.bagcbf.de
Dispenses information about all aspects of travel for visitors with a disability. Offers lists of specialized travel operators and publications, including city access guides.
✉ Langenmarckweg 21, 51465 Bergisch Gladbach ☎ 02202 989 9811

BUNDESVERBAND SELBSTHILFE KÖRPERBEHINDERTER (NATIONAL ASSOCIATION DISABLED SELF-HELP)
www.bsk-ev.de
Provides advice and organizes travel for people with limited mobility, including provision of accompanying helpers.
✉ Altkrautheimer Strasse 20, 74238 Krautheim ☎ 06294 42810

TOURISTIK UNION INTERNATIONAL
www.tui.de
This large travel operator, with offices in many cities, has a comprehensive range of information about accessible travel and accommodation facilities, and can organize group and individual travel.
✉ Otto-Lilienthal-Strasse 17, 28199 Bremen ☎ 01805 884277

Below *Many U-Bahn stations have access for wheelchair users*

REGIONS

This chapter is divided into six regions of Germany (▷ 8–9). Places of interest are listed alphabetically in each region.

Germany's Regions	68–356
Berlin	68
Northern Germany	120
Western Germany	162
Eastern Germany	208
Munich	258
Southern Germany	300

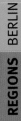

SIGHTS 74
WALKS 102
WHAT TO DO 106
EATING 112
STAYING 116

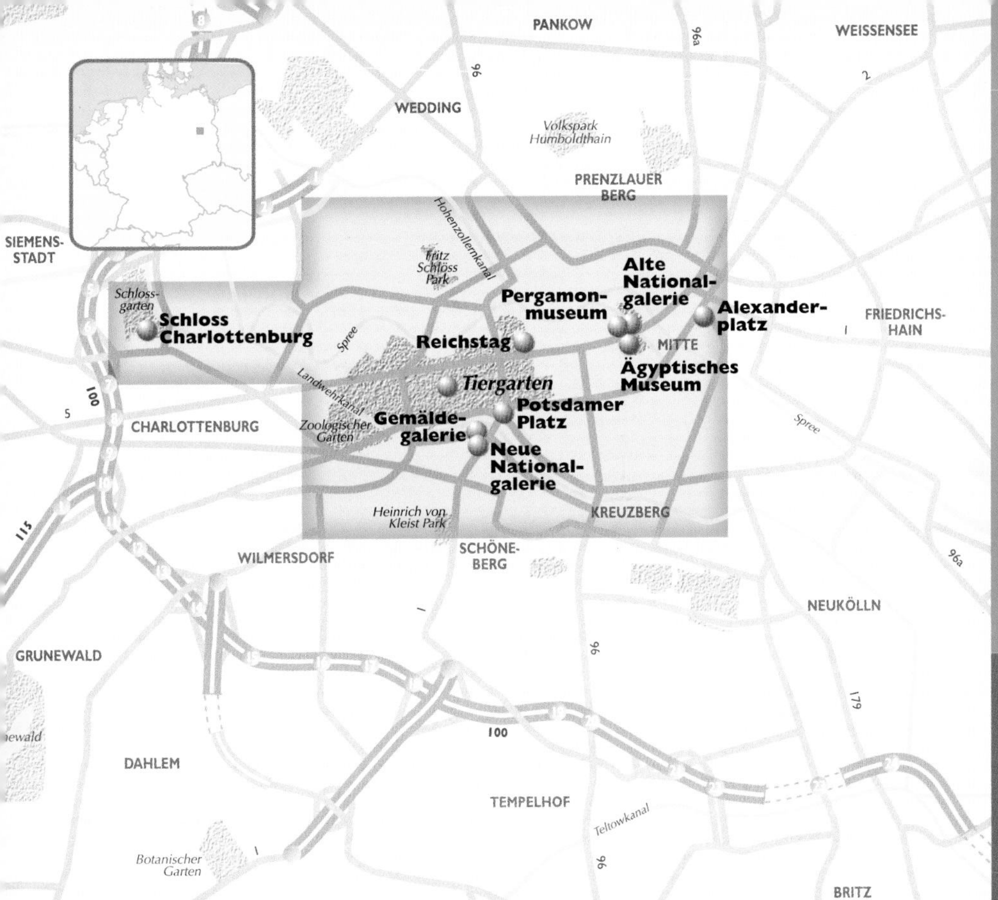

BERLIN

A great mix of old and new, Berlin is constantly redefining itself—and millions of visitors from around the world pour in every year to help. There's an unlimited energy on the loose here, a sense of the future being created this very minute. With the 20th century's many traumas now behind it, Berlin is able to look forward to the future. Important museums and vibrant cultural and nightlife scenes of every kind abound.

With a population of some 3.4 million, Greater Berlin covers an area of 890sq km (344sq miles), which makes it a relatively thinly populated city. This is most noticeable in the prevalence of large parks, like the Tiergarten and the Grunewald. Considering it suffered terribly from aerial bombardment and ground combat during World War II, the city retains, or has rebuilt, a surprising amount of its historical legacy. But much of Berlin is modern, and a significant part is built in cutting-edge architectural styles.

As befits its restored national capital status, this city-state is Germany's political hub. The service-orientated economy is increasingly dependent on a burgeoning tourist sector and on the federal government institutions—the two houses of parliament and important departments of state—which have set up shop here and brought in their wake well-heeled armies of lobbyists, consultants and journalists among others.

Berlin's 'Great Divide' is no longer easy to recognize on the ground, though a few short sections of the Berlin Wall do still exist. With the passage of years since the Wall was breached in 1989, the psychological divide between the two sides has slowly diminished, and for many Berliners life has moved on. The new challenges of living in a fast-changing, multicultural—or at least multi-ethnic—city at the crossroads of Europe, have taken over.

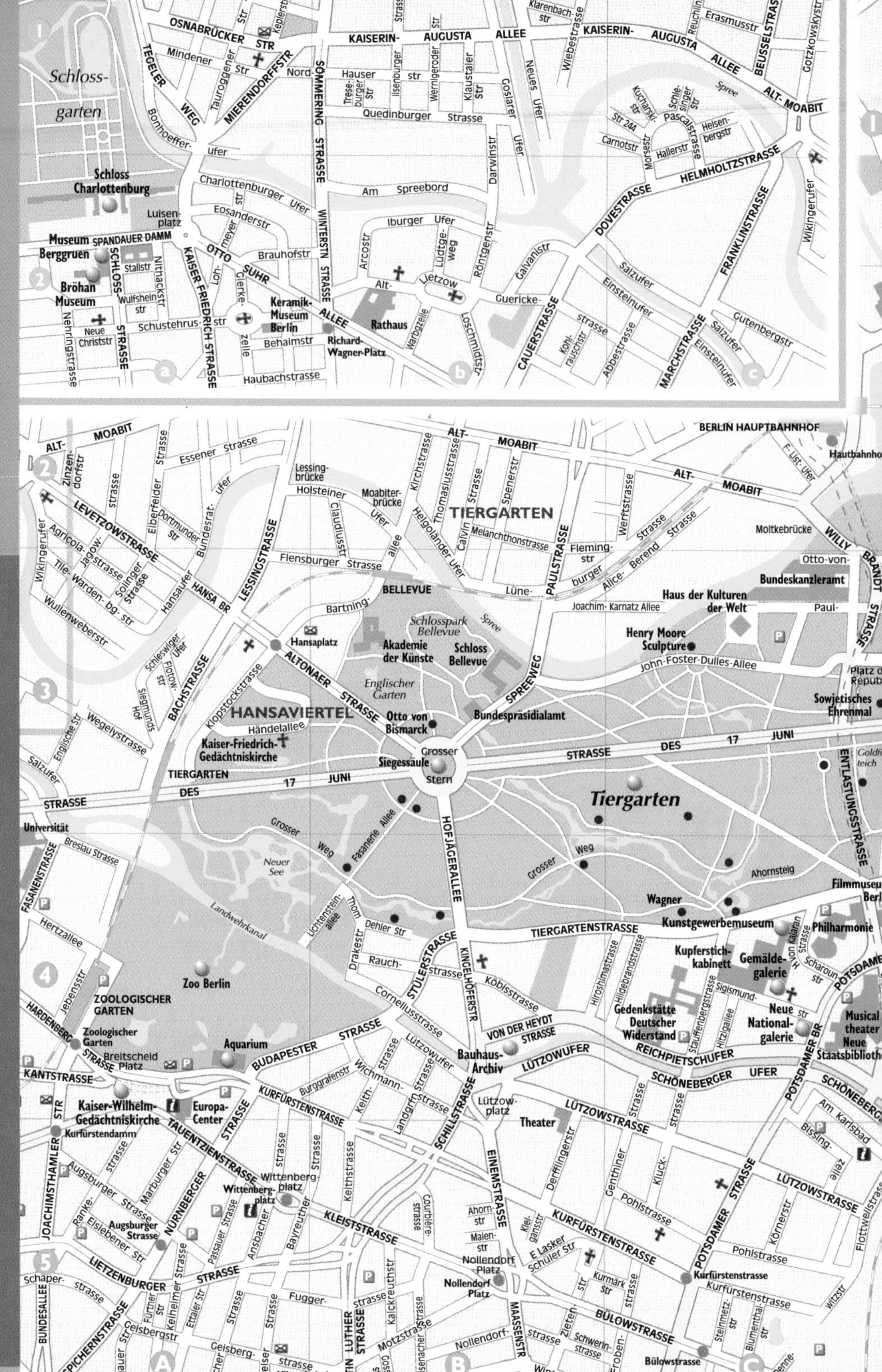
Mierendorffplatz
Keplerstrasse
OSNABRÜCKER STR
Mindener Str
TEGELER WEG
Tauroggener Str
MIERENDORFFSTR
Nord-
SÖMMERING STRASSE
KAISERIN- AUGUSTA ALLEE
Hauser str
Tresе-burger Str
Ilsenburger str
Wernigeroder Str
Klaustaler Str
Quedinburger Strasse
Goslarer Ufer
Neues Ufer
Wiebestrasse
Klarenbach-str
KAISERIN- AUGUSTA ALLEE
Reuchlinstr
Erasmusstr
BEUSSELSTRASSE
Gotzkowskystr
ALT- MOABIT
Spree
Kucharski-str
Schlesinger Str
Str 244
Pascalstrasse
Carnotstr
Morsestr
Hallerstr
Helsenbergstr
HELMHOLTZSTRASSE
Wikingerufer
Schloss-garten
Bonhoeffer-ufer
Schloss Charlottenburg
Charlottenburger Ufer
Am Spreebord
Darwinstr
Luisenplatz
Eosanderstr
Lohmeyer str
Iburger Ufer
Röntgenstr
DOVESTRASSE
FRANKLINSTRASSE
Museum Berggruen
SPANDAUER DAMM
Stallstr
Nithackstr
OTTO SUHR ALLEE
Brauhofstr
WINTERSTN STRASSE
Arcostr
Lüdtgeweg
Galvanistr
Salzufer
Bröhan Museum
SCHLOSS-STRASSE
KAISER FRIEDRICH STRASSE
Wulfsheinstr
Gierkezeile
Keramik-Museum Berlin
Alt-Lietzow
Guericke-strasse
Einsteinufer
Nehringstrasse
Neue Christstr
Schustehrusstr
Behaimstr
Richard-Wagner-Platz
Rathaus
Warbgzeile
Loschmidtstr
CAUERSTRASSE
Kohlrauschstr
Abbestrasse
MARCHSTRASSE
Gutenbergstr
Haubachstrasse
ALT-MOABIT
Zinzendorfstr
Essener Strasse
Lessingbrücke
Holsteiner Ufer
Moabiter-brücke
Kirchstrasse
Thomasiusstrasse
ALT-MOABIT
BERLIN HAUPTBAHNHOF
Hauptbahnhof
F.-List-Ufer
LEVETZOWSTRASSE
Elberfelder Strasse
Dortmunder Str
Bundesratufer
Claudiusstr
Helgoländer Ufer
Calvinstrasse
Spenerstr
TIERGARTEN
Melanchthonstrasse
PAULSTRASSE
Werftstrasse
Moltkebrücke
WILLY BRANDT STRASSE
Wikingerufer
Agricolastrasse
Jagowstrasse
Solinger Strasse
LESSINGSTRASSE
Flensburger Strasse
Flemingstr
Lüneburger Strasse
Alice-Berend-Strasse
Otto-von-Bismarck-Allee
Bundeskanzleramt
Tile-Wardenberg-str
Hansaufer
HANSA BR
Bartningallee
BELLEVUE
Joachim-Karnatz Allee
Haus der Kulturen der Welt
Paul-
Wullenweberstr
Schleswiger Ufer
Flotowstr
Hansaplatz
Akademie der Künste
Schlosspark Bellevue
Schloss Bellevue
Henry Moore Sculpture
John-Foster-Dulles-Allee
Platz der Republik
BACHSTRASSE
ALTONAER STRASSE
Englischer Garten
SPREEWEG
Sowjetisches Ehrenmal
Siegmunds Hof
Klopstockstrasse
HANSAVIERTEL
Händelallee
Otto von Bismarck
Bundespräsidialamt
Wegelystrasse
Kaiser-Friedrich-Gedächtniskirche
Grosser Stern
Siegessäule
STRASSE DES 17 JUNI
Goldfischteich
Englische Str
Salzufer
TIERGARTEN STRASSE DES 17 JUNI
Tiergarten
ENTLASTUNGSSTRASSE
Universität
Grosser Weg
Fasanerie Allee
HOFJÄGERALLEE
Neuer See
FASANENSTRASSE
Breslau Strasse
Ahornsteig
Filmmuseum Berlin
Wagner
Landwehrkanal
Thom
Lichtensteinallee
Dehler Str
Kunstgewerbemuseum
Philharmonie
Hertzallee
TIERGARTENSTRASSE
Drakestr
Rauchstrasse
STÜLERSTRASSE
KLINGELHÖFERSTR
Hiroshimastrasse
Hildebrandstrasse
Kupferstichkabinett
Gemäldegalerie
Von Karajan Strasse
Scharounstr
POTSDAMER
Jebensstr
Zoo Berlin
Köbisstrasse
Stauffenbergstrasse
Sigismundstr
ZOOLOGISCHER GARTEN
Corneliusstrasse
Gedenkstätte Deutscher Widerstand
Hitzigallee
Neue Nationalgalerie
Musical theater
Neue Staatsbibliothek
HARDENBERG STRASSE
Zoologischer Garten
VON DER HEYDT STRASSE
POTSDAMER BR
Breitscheid Platz
Aquarium
BUDAPESTER STRASSE
Bauhaus-Archiv
LÜTZOWUFER
REICHPIETSCHUFER
KANTSTRASSE
Burggrafenstr
Lützowstrasse
Wichmannstrasse
Lützowufer
SCHÖNEBERGER UFER
SCHÖNEBERGER
Kaiser-Wilhelm-Gedächtniskirche
Europa-Center
KURFÜRSTENSTRASSE
Keithstrasse
Landgrafenstrasse
SCHILLSTRASSE
Lützowplatz
Theater
LÜTZOWSTRASSE
Am Karlsbad
Bissingzeile
Kurfürstendamm
TAUENTZIENSTRASSE
Marburger Str
NÜRNBERGER STRASSE
Passauer Strasse
Keithstrasse
Courbierestrasse
EINEMSTRASSE
Derfflingerstr
Genthiner Strasse
Kluckstrasse
POTSDAMER STRASSE
LÜTZOWSTRASSE
Körnerstr
Flottwellstrasse
JOACHIMSTHALER STR
Augsburger Strasse
Rankestr
Eislebener Str
Augsburger Strasse
Wittenbergplatz
Ansbacher Strasse
Bayreuther Strasse
KLEISTSTRASSE
Ahornstr
Maienstr
Kleistgassestr
Pohlstrasse
KURFÜRSTENSTRASSE
Pohlstrasse
LIETZENBURGER STRASSE
Nollendorfplatz
E Lasker Schüler Str
Kurmärkische Str
Kurfürstenstrasse
Schaperstrasse
Fürther Str
Keilmeier Strasse
Ettaler Str
Fuggerstrasse
Kalckreuthstr
MARTIN LUTHER STRASSE
BÜLOWSTRASSE
Steinmetzstr
Blumenthalstr
Witzstr
BUNDESALLEE
SPICHERNSTRASSE
Geisbergstr
Geisbergstrasse
Welser Strasse
Motzstrasse
Eisenacher Strasse
Nollendorfstrasse
MASSENSTR
Zietenstrasse
Schwerinstrasse
Frobenstr
Bülowstrasse
Viktoria-Luise-Platz
Winterfeldtstr
Botanischer
Dennewitzstr

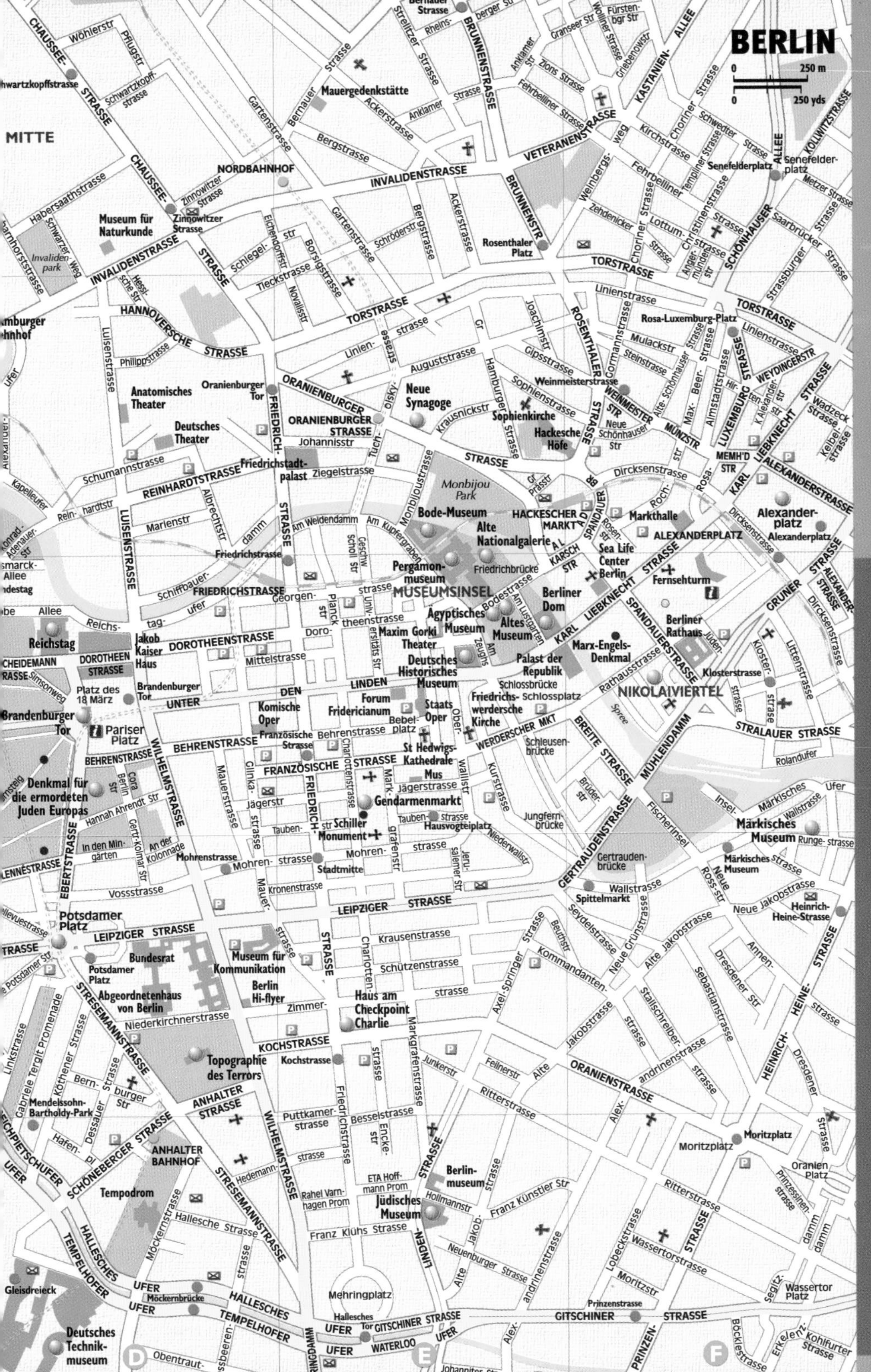
BERLIN
0 250 m
0 250 yds
MITTE
NORDBAHNHOF
Museum für Naturkunde
Invalidenpark
INVALIDENSTRASSE
CHAUSSEESTRASSE
Zinnowitzer Strasse
Mauergedenkstätte
Bernauer Strasse
Brunnenstrasse
Veteranenstrasse
Rosenthaler Platz
Senefelderplatz
Torstrasse
Hannoversche Strasse
Oranienburger Tor
Oranienburger Strasse
Anatomisches Theater
Deutsches Theater
Friedrichstadtpalast
Neue Synagoge
Sophienkirche
Hackesche Höfe
Weinmeisterstrasse
Rosa-Luxemburg-Platz
Monbijou Park
Bode-Museum
Alte Nationalgalerie
Pergamonmuseum
MUSEUMSINSEL
Hackescher Markt
Sea Life Center Berlin
Markthalle
Alexanderplatz
Fernsehturm
Berliner Dom
Altes Museum
Ägyptisches Museum
Maxim Gorki Theater
Deutsches Historisches Museum
Palast der Republik
Marx-Engels-Denkmal
Berliner Rathaus
NIKOLAIVIERTEL
Friedrichstrasse
Reichstag
Jakob Kaiser Haus
Unter den Linden
Brandenburger Tor
Pariser Platz
Platz des 18 März
Forum Fridericianum
Komische Oper
Staats Oper
St Hedwigs-Kathedrale
Friedrichswerdersche Kirche
Gendarmenmarkt
Schiller Monument
Hausvogteiplatz
Denkmal für die ermordeten Juden Europas
Märkisches Museum
Spittelmarkt
Stadtmitte
Potsdamer Platz
Leipziger Strasse
Bundesrat
Museum für Kommunikation
Berlin Hi-flyer
Abgeordnetenhaus von Berlin
Haus am Checkpoint Charlie
Topographie des Terrors
Kochstrasse
Mendelssohn-Bartholdy-Park
Anhalter Bahnhof
Tempodrom
Berlinmuseum
Jüdisches Museum
Moritzplatz
Oranienplatz
Mehringplatz
Hallesches Tor
Möckernbrücke
Gleisdreieck
Deutsches Technikmuseum
Prinzenstrasse
Wassertor Platz
Gitschiner Strasse
Oranienstrasse
Heinrich-Heine-Strasse
Stresemannstrasse
Wilhelmstrasse
D
E
F

BERLIN STREET INDEX

Street	Page	Grid
Abbestrasse	70	c2
Ackerstrasse	71	E1
A D Spandauer Br	71	F2
Agricolastrasse	70	A2
Aitlietzow	70	b2
Albrechtstrasse	71	D2
Alexanderplatz	71	F2
Alexanderstrasse	71	F3
Alexander-Ufer	71	D2
Alexandrinenstrasse	71	E5
Alice-Berend Strasse	70	C3
A L Karsch Strasse	71	E3
Almstadtstrasse	71	F2
Alte Jakobstrasse	71	E5
Alte Schönhauser Strasse	71	F2
Alt-Moabit	70	A2
Alt-Moabit	70	c1
Altonaer Strasse	70	A3
Am Karlsbad	70	C4
Am Lustgarten	71	E3
Am Spreebord	70	b2
Anhalter Strasse	71	D4
Annenstrasse	71	F4
Ansbacher Strasse	70	A5
Arcostrasse	70	b2
Augsburger Strasse	70	A5
Auguststrasse	71	E2
Axel-Springer Strasse	71	E4
Bachstrasse	70	A3
Bartningallee	70	B3
Bayreuther Strasse	70	A5
Bebelplatz	71	E3
Behaimstrasse	70	a2
Behrenstrasse	71	D3
Bergstrasse	71	E1
Bernauer Strasse	71	E1
Bernburgerstrasse	71	D4
Besselstrasse	71	E5
Beusselstrasse	70	c1
Bissingzeile	70	C5
Bodestrasse	71	E3
Bonhoefferufer	70	a1
Borsigstrasse	71	E1
Brahestrasse	70	a1
Brauhofstrasse	70	a2
Breite Strasse	71	F3
Breitscheid Platz	70	A4
Breslau Strasse	70	A4
Brunnenstrasse	71	E1
Budapester Strasse	70	A4
Bülowstrasse	70	B5
Bundesallee	70	A5
Calvin Strasse	70	B2
Carl Hertz Ufer	71	E5
Cauerstrasse	70	b2
Charlottenburger Ufer	70	a2
Charlottenstrasse	71	E3
Chausseestrasse	71	D1
Choriner Strasse	71	F1
Christinenstrasse	71	F1
Claudiusstrasse	70	B2
Corneliusstrasse	70	B4
Courbièrestrasse	70	B5
Darwinstrasse	70	b2
Dennewitzstrasse	70	C5
Derfflingerstrasse	70	B5
Dessauer Strasse	71	D5
Dircksenstrasse	71	F2
Dorotheenstrasse	71	E3
Dortmunder Strasse	70	A2
Dovestrasse	70	b2
Drakestrasse	70	B4
Dresdener Strasse	71	F4
Ebertstrasse	71	D4
Eichhornstrasse	70	C4
Einemstrasse	70	B5
Einsteinufer	70	c2
Eisenacher Strasse	70	B5
Elberfelder Strasse	70	A3
Englische Strasse	70	A3
Entlastungsstrasse	70	C3
Eosanderstrasse	70	a2
Erasmusstrasse	70	c1
Erkelenzdamm	71	F5
Essener Strasse	70	A2
Fasanenstrasse	70	A4
Fehrbelliner Strasse	71	F1
Fischerinsel	71	F3
Flemingstrasse	70	B2
Flensburger Strasse	70	A3
Flottwellstrasse	70	C5
Franklinstrasse	70	c2
Franz Klühs Strasse	71	E5
Franz Künstler Strasse	71	E5
Französische Strasse	71	D3
Friedrichbrücke	71	E3
Friedrich-List-Ufer	70	C2
Friedrichstrasse	71	D2
Frobenstrasse	70	C5
Fuggerstrasse	70	A5
Gabriele Tergit Promenade	71	D5
Galvanistrasse	70	b2
Gartenstrasse	71	D1
Geisbergstrasse	70	A5
Genthiner Strasse	70	C5
Georgenstrasse	71	E3
Gertraudenbrücke	71	F4
Gertraudenstrasse	71	E4
Gierkezeile	70	a2
Gipsstrasse	71	E2
Gitschiner Strasse	71	E5
Glinkastrasse	71	D3
Gormannstrasse	71	F2
Goslarer Ufer	70	b1
Gotzkowskystrasse	70	c1
Grainauer Strasse	70	A5
Gr Hamburger Strasse	71	E2
Grossbeerenstrasse	71	D5
Grosser Stern	70	B3
Gruner Strasse	71	F3
Guerickestrasse	70	b2
Gutenbergstrasse	70	c2
Habersaathstrasse	71	D1
Hallesche Strasse	71	D5
Hallesches Ufer	71	D5
Händelallee	70	A3
Hannah Ahrendt Strasse	71	D3
Hannoversche Strasse	71	D2
Hansa Brücke	70	A3
Hansaufer Bundesrat- Ufer	70	A3
Hardenberg Strasse	70	A4
Haubachstrasse	70	a2
Heinrichheinestrasse	71	F4
Helgoländer Ufer	70	B2
Helmholtzstrasse	70	c2
Hertzallee	70	A4
Hildebrandstrasse	70	C4
Hiroshimastrasse	70	B4
Hofjägerallee	70	B3
Holsteiner Ufer	70	A2
Iburger Ufer	70	b2
Ilsenburger Strasse	70	b1
Inselstrasse	71	F3
Invalidenstrasse	71	D2
Jägerstrasse	71	D3
Jägerstrasse	71	E3
Jagowstrasse	70	A3
Jebensstrasse	70	A4
Jerusalemer Strasse	71	E4
Joachimsthamler Strasse	70	A5
Joachimstrasse	71	E2
Johannisstrasse	71	E2
John-Foster-Dulles-Allee	70	C3
Jüdenstrasse	71	F3
Jungfernbrücke	71	E3
Junkerstrasse	71	E4
Kaiser Friedrich Strasse	70	a2
Kaiserinaugusta Allee	70	b1
Kalckreuthstrasse	70	B5
Kamminer Strasse	70	a1
Kantstrasse	70	A4
Kapelleufer	71	D2
Karl Liebknecht Strasse	71	E3
Kastanienallee	71	F1
Keithstrasse	70	B5
Kelheimer Strasse	70	A5
Keplerstrasse	70	a1
Kingelhöferstrasse	70	B4
Kirchstrasse	70	B2
Kirchstrasse	71	F1
Klaustaler Strasse	70	b1
Kleiststrasse	70	B5
Klopstockstrasse	70	A3
Klosterstrase	71	F3
Kluckstrasse	70	C5
Köbisstrasse	70	B4
Kochstrasse	71	E4
Kollwitzstrasse	71	F1
Kommandantenstrasse	71	E4
Körnerstrasse	70	C5
Köthener Strasse	71	D5
Krausenstrasse	71	E4
Krausnickstrasse	71	E2
Kurfürstenstrasse	70	A4
Kurstrasse	71	E3
Landgrafenstrasse	70	B5
Leipziger Strasse	71	D4
Lennéstrasse	70	D4
Lessingbrücke	70	A2
Lessingstrasse	70	A3
Levetzowstrasse	70	A2
Lietzenburger Strasse	70	A5
Lindenstrasse	71	E5
Linienstrasse	71	E2
Linkstrasse	71	D4
Littenstrasse	71	F3
Lobeckstrasse	71	F5
Lohmeyer Strasse	70	a2
Loschmidtstrasse	70	b2
Lottumstrasse	71	F1
Lüdtgeweg	70	b2
Luisenplatz	70	a2
Luisenstrasse	71	D2
Lüneburger Strasse	70	B3
Lützowplatz	70	B4
Lützowstrasse	70	B4
Lützowufer	70	B4
Maassenstrasse	70	B5
Marburger Strasse	70	A5
Marchstrasse	70	c2
Marienstrasse	71	D2
Markgrafenstrasse	71	E3
Märkisches Ufer	71	F3
Martin Luther Strasse	70	B5
Mauerstrasse	71	D3
Mauerstrasse	71	D4
Max-Beer-Strasse	71	F2
Mehringdamm	71	E5
Mehringplatz	71	E5
Memhardstrasse	71	F2
Mierendorffstrasse	70	a1
Mindener Strasse	70	a1
Mittelstrasse	71	D3
Moabiterbrücke	70	B2
Möckernstrasse	71	D5
Mohrenstrasse	71	D4
Moltkebrücke	70	C2
Monbijoustrasse	71	E2
Moritz Platz	71	F5
Moritzstrasse	71	F5
Morsestrasse	70	c2
Motzstrasse	70	B5
Mühlendamm	71	F3
Mulackstrasse	71	F2
Münzstrasse	71	F2
Nehringstrasse	70	a2
Neue Grünstrasse	71	F4
Neue Jakobstrasse	71	F4
Neuenburger Strasse	71	E5
Neue Rossstrasse	71	F4
Neue Schönhauser Strasse	71	F2
Neues Ufer	70	b1
Niederkirchnerstrasse	71	D4
Nithackstrasse	70	a2
Nollendorf Platz	70	B5
Nollendorfstrasse	70	B5
Nordhauser Strasse	70	a1
Nürnberger Strasse	70	A5
Obentrautstrasse	71	D5
Oberwalllstrasse	71	E3
Oranienburger	71	E2
Oranien Platz	71	F5
Oranienstrasse	71	F4
Osnabrücker Strasse	70	a1
Otto Suhr Allee	70	a2
Otto-Von-Bismarck-Allee	70	C3
Pariser Platz	71	D3
Pascalstrasse	70	c1
Passauer Strasse	70	A5
Paul-Löbe Allee	70	C3
Pflugstrasse	71	D1
Planck Strasse	71	E3
Platz der Republik	70	C3
Platz des 18 März	71	D3
Pohlstrasse	70	C5
Potsdamer Brücke	70	C4
Potsdamer Platz	71	D4
Potsdamer Strasse	70	C5
Prinzenstrasse	71	F5
Puttkamerstrasse	71	E4
Quedinburger Strasse	70	b1
Rankestrasse	70	A5
Rathausstrasse	71	F3
Rauchstrasse	70	B4
Reichpietschufer	70	C4
Reichstagufer	71	D3
Reinhardtstrasse	71	D2
Rheinsberger Strasse	71	E1
Ritterstrasse	71	E4
Rochstrasse	71	F2
Röntgenstrasse	70	b2
Rosa Luxemburg Strasse	71	F2
Rosenthaler Strasse	71	F2
Saarbrücker Strasse	71	F1
Salzufer	70	A3
Salzufer	70	c2
Schaperstrasse	70	A5
Scharnhorststrasse	71	D1
Scheidemann Strasse	71	D3
Schiffbauerdamm	71	D3
Schillstrasse	70	B5
Schlegelstrasse	71	D1
Schleusenbrücke	71	E3
Schlossbrücke	71	E3
Schlossplatz	71	E3
Schlossstrasse	70	a2
Schöneberger Strasse	71	D5
Schöneberger Ufer	70	C4
Schönhauser Allee	71	F2
Schumannstrasse	71	D2
Schustehrusstrasse	70	a2
Schützenstrasse	71	E4
Schwedter Strasse	71	F1
Sebastianstrasse	71	F4
Segitzdamm	71	F5
Senefelderplatz	71	F1
Seydelstrasse	71	F4
Sigismundstrasse	70	C4
Solinger Strasse	70	A3
Sömmering Strasse	70	b1
Sophienstrasse	71	E2
Spandauer Damm	70	a2
Spandauerstrasse	71	F3
Spenerstrasse	70	B2
Spichernstrasse	70	A5
Spreeweg Paulstrasse	70	B3
Stallschreiberstrasse	71	F4
Stauffenbergstrasse	70	C4
Steinstrasse	71	F2
Stralauer Strasse	71	F3
Strassburger Strasse	71	F2
Strasse des 17 Juni	70	A3
Strelitzer Strasse	71	E1
Stresemannstrasse	71	D4
Stülerstrasse	70	B4
Taubenstrasse	71	E3
Tauentzienstrasse	70	A5
Tauroggener Strasse	70	a1
Tegler Weg	70	a1
Tempelhofer Ufer	71	D5
Thomasiusstrasse	70	B2
Tieckstrasse	71	D2
Tiergartenstrasse	70	B4
Tilewarden-Berg-Strasse	70	A3
Torstrasse	71	E2
Tucholskystrasse	71	E2
Unter den Linden	71	D3
Veteranenstrasse	71	E1
Viktoria Luise-platz	70	A5
Von der Heydt Strasse	70	B4
Vossstrasse	71	D4
Wallstrasse	71	F4
Wassertor Platz	71	F5
Wassertorstrasse	71	F5
Waterloo Ufer	71	E5
Wegelystrasse	70	A3
Weinbergsweg	71	F1
Weinmeister Strasse	71	F2
Welser Strasse	70	A5
Werderscher Mkt	71	E3
Werftstrasse	70	C2
Weydingerstrasse	71	F2
Wichmannstrasse	70	B4
Wiebestrasse	70	b1
Wikingerufer	70	A3
Wikingerufer	70	c1
Wilhelmstrasse	71	D3
Willy Brandt Strasse	70	C2
Winterfeldstrasse	70	B5
Winterfeldtstrasse	70	B5
Winterstn Strasse	70	b2
Wittenbergplatz	70	A5
Wöhlerstrasse	71	D1
Wullenweberstrasse	70	A3
Ziegelstrasse	71	E2
Zietenstrasse	70	B5
Zimmerstrasse	71	E4
Zinnowitzer Strasse	71	D1

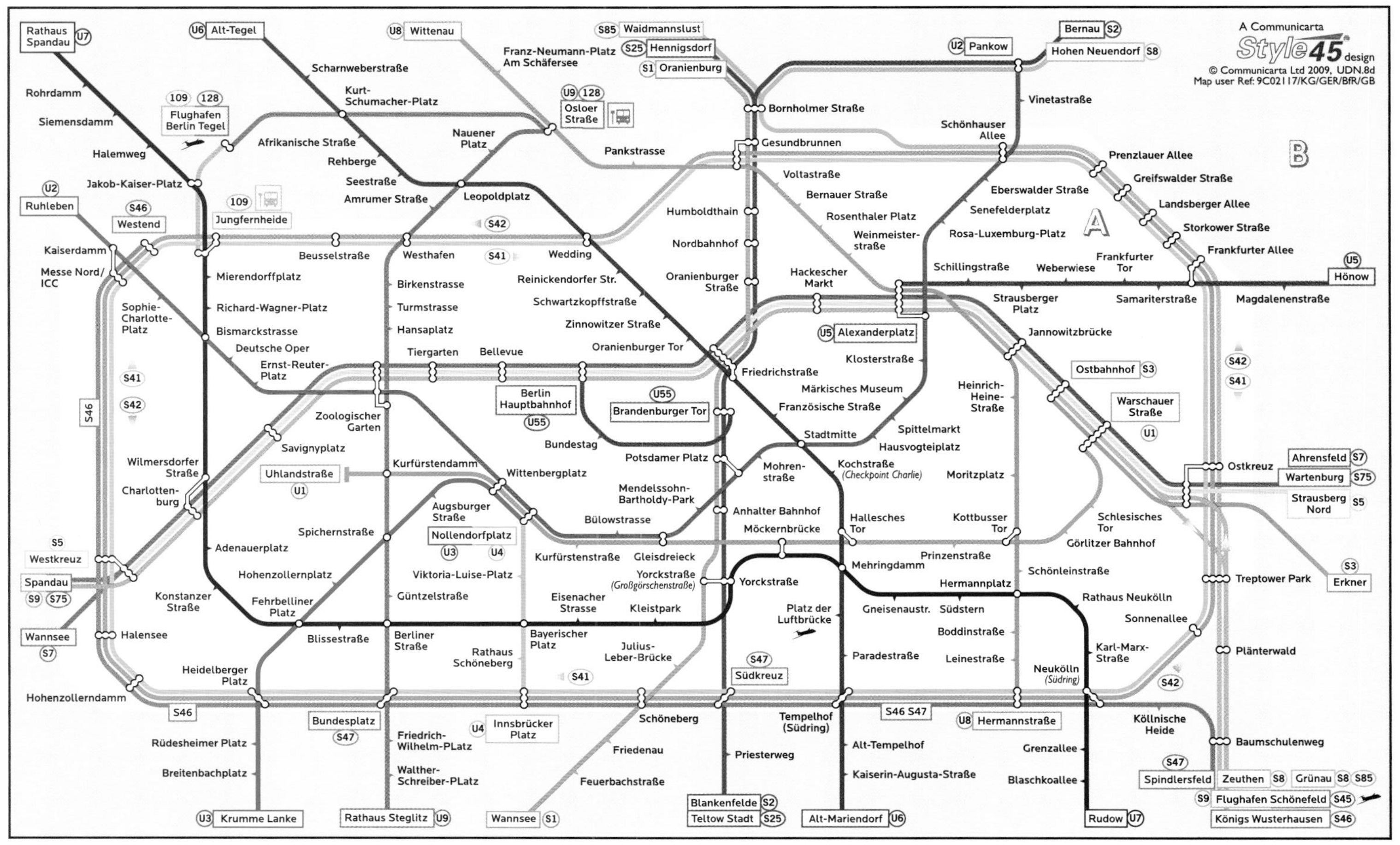

A Communicarta
Style45 design
© Communicarta Ltd 2009, UDN.8d
Map user Ref: 9C02117/KG/GER/BfR/GB
Rathaus Spandau U7
U6 Alt-Tegel
U8 Wittenau
S85 Waidmannslust
S25 Hennigsdorf
S1 Oranienburg
Bernau S2
Hohen Neuendorf S8
U2 Pankow
Rohrdamm
Siemensdamm
Halemweg
Jakob-Kaiser-Platz
109 128 Flughafen Berlin Tegel
Scharnweberstraße
Kurt-Schumacher-Platz
Afrikanische Straße
Rehberge
Seestraße
Amrumer Straße
Franz-Neumann-Platz Am Schäfersee
U9 128 Osloer Straße
Nauener Platz
Pankstrasse
Leopoldplatz
Bornholmer Straße
Gesundbrunnen
Vinetastraße
Schönhauser Allee
Prenzlauer Allee
Greifswalder Straße
Landsberger Allee
Storkower Straße
Frankfurter Allee
U2 Ruhleben
S46 Westend
109 Jungfernheide
Kaiserdamm
Messe Nord/ ICC
Sophie-Charlotte-Platz
Mierendorffplatz
Richard-Wagner-Platz
Bismarckstrasse
Deutsche Oper
Ernst-Reuter-Platz
Beusselstraße
Westhafen
Birkenstrasse
Turmstrasse
Hansaplatz
Tiergarten
Bellevue
S42
S41
Wedding
Reinickendorfer Str.
Schwartzkopffstraße
Zinnowitzer Straße
Oranienburger Tor
Voltastraße
Bernauer Straße
Rosenthaler Platz
Weinmeister-straße
Humboldthain
Nordbahnhof
Oranienburger Straße
Hackescher Markt
Eberswalder Straße
Senefelderplatz
Rosa-Luxemburg-Platz
Schillingstraße
Weberwiese
Frankfurter Tor
U5 Hönow
Strausberger Platz
Samariterstraße
Magdalenenstraße
U5 Alexanderplatz
Jannowitzbrücke
Klosterstraße
Friedrichstraße
Märkisches Museum
Französische Straße
Ostbahnhof S3
Heinrich-Heine-Straße
Warschauer Straße U1
S46
S41
S42
Zoologischer Garten
Savignyplatz
Berlin Hauptbahnhof U55
U55 Brandenburger Tor
Bundestag
Stadtmitte
Spittelmarkt
Hausvogteiplatz
Wilmersdorfer Straße
Charlottenburg
Uhlandstraße U1
Kurfürstendamm
Wittenbergplatz
Potsdamer Platz
Mohrenstraße
Kochstraße (Checkpoint Charlie)
Moritzplatz
Ostkreuz
Ahrensfeld S7
Wartenburg S75
Strausberg Nord S5
Augsburger Straße
Nollendorfplatz
U3 U4
Mendelssohn-Bartholdy-Park
Bülowstrasse
Anhalter Bahnhof
Möckernbrücke
Hallesches Tor
Kottbusser Tor
Schlesisches Tor
Görlitzer Bahnhof
S5 Westkreuz
Spandau S9 S75
Spichernstraße
Adenauerplatz
Hohenzollernplatz
Konstanzer Straße
Fehrbelliner Platz
Viktoria-Luise-Platz
Güntzelstraße
Kurfürstenstraße
Gleisdreieck
Yorckstraße (Großgörschenstraße)
Yorckstraße
Eisenacher Strasse
Kleistpark
Mehringdamm
Prinzenstraße
Hermannplatz
Schönleinstraße
Treptower Park
S3 Erkner
Gneisenaustr.
Südstern
Boddinstraße
Leinestraße
Rathaus Neukölln
Sonnenallee
Karl-Marx-Straße
Neukölln (Südring)
Plänterwald
Wannsee S7
Halensee
Heidelberger Platz
Blissestraße
Berliner Straße
Rathaus Schöneberg
Bayerischer Platz
Julius-Leber-Brücke
Platz der Luftbrücke
S47 Südkreuz
Paradestraße
Hohenzollerndamm
S46
Bundesplatz S47
U4 Innsbrücker Platz
Schöneberg
Tempelhof (Südring)
S46 S47
U8 Hermannstraße
Kölnische Heide
Baumschulenweg
Rüdesheimer Platz
Breitenbachplatz
Friedrich-Wilhelm-PLatz
Walther-Schreiber-PLatz
Friedenau
Feuerbachstraße
Priesterweg
Alt-Tempelhof
Kaiserin-Augusta-Straße
Grenzallee
Blaschkoallee
S47 Spindlersfeld
Zeuthen S8
Grünau S8 S85
S9 Flughafen Schönefeld S45
Königs Wusterhausen S46
U3 Krumme Lanke
Rathaus Steglitz U9
Wannsee S1
Blankenfelde S2
Teltow Stadt S25
Alt-Mariendorf U6
Rudow U7

ÄGYPTISCHES MUSEUM

This collection of 2,000 ancient masterpieces spans three millennia. Come here to admire the bust of Queen Nefertiti. In its refurbished premises in West Berlin, the Egyptian Museum presents one of Europe's finest collections of Egyptian antiquities.

Among the most memorable pieces are those recovered during excavations in Tell el-Amarna ranging from finds from Metjen's burial chamber, dating from around 2600BC, to Roman mummy masks from the first and second centuries AD. The undisputed highlight of the museum is the famous bust of Nefertiti.

NEFERTITI

The wife of Pharaoh Akhenaten, Queen Nefertiti was given more rights and responsibility than any other royal Egyptian consort before or after her. Her portrait bust was discovered in 1912, along with other royal portraits, in what had been the house of Thutmose, a sculptor. Made from limestone and plaster, the bust dates from around 1340BC and is almost perfectly preserved. The symmetrical model is thought to have functioned as a teaching tool for sculptors, hence the empty socket revealing the artist's techniques. Although precise, the bags under the eyes and the soft, warm skin lend vitality to the expression. The life-like portrayal appears to embody the contemporary western ideal of femininity and timeless beauty, and she has been a hit with visitors since the day she was first put on display in the 1920s.

QUEEN TIY

Composed of yew-wood, gold, silver, faience and horn, the portrait of Queen Tiy (New Kingdom, 18th Dynasty, *c*1355BC) may have less popular appeal than the portrait bust of Queen Nefertiti (▷ above), but is still fascinating. Tiy, the wife of Pharaoh Amenhotep III and mother of Pharaoh Akhenaten, is portrayed at an advanced age and wearing a crown in the shape of a solar disc, horns and two feathers, which take the sculpture's height to 22cm (8.5in). The superiority complex imparted by a lifetime of rule can be seen in her expression.

INFORMATION

www.egyptian-museum-berlin.com
71 E3 Neues Museum, 10178 Berlin (Mitte) 030 2090 5577
Daily 10–6 (Thu to 10) Adult €8, child (17–18) €4, under 17 free; combined admission to all Museumsinsel museums: Adult €12, child (17–18) €6, under 17 free; Thu from 6pm free to all S-Bahn Hackescher Markt 100, 200, TXL. Tram M1, M4, M5, M6, 12 Guided tours 030 2090 5566; free audioguide Gift shop selling souvenirs and books on Ancient Egyptian history and archaeology

TIP

» With so many museums clustered together on the Museumsinsel, there is a temptation to try to visit them all in one big, rushed tour. But the Egyptian Museum alone is worth at least a half day, and longer would be better.

Opposite *The famous bust of Nefertiti*
Above *The museum houses extraordinary antiquities*

INFORMATION

121 F3 10178 Berlin (Mitte) U- and S-Bahn Alexanderplatz M48, 100, 200, 248, TXL. Tram M2, M4, M5, M6 The rotating Telecafé in the Fernsehturm has spectacular views; there are many other restaurants, cafes and bars bordering the square

TIPS

» The entrance to the Fernsehturm is on the eastern side of the tower, opposite the station at Alexanderplatz.

» If you are going to the Telecafé you will need to check your coats and bags in at the cloakroom near the toilets in the viewing gallery. You may have to wait to be shown to a table during busy times.

» There are regular classical music recitals in the Marienkirche—pick up a leaflet, call 030 2345 7461 or check online (www.marienkirche-berlin.de) for the latest details.

ALEXANDERPLATZ

Modern architects have transformed this historic square into a bustling meeting place and transportation hub. Enjoy a panoramic view from the top of the Fernsehturm. Alexanderplatz was named after the Russian Tsar Alexander I in 1805. In the 1920s and 1930s it became a bustling crossroads for Berlin's traffic and a popular meeting place. Destroyed during World War II, it was transformed into a pedestrianized square during the 1960s, but today it is generally visited for the sights around it.

FERNSEHTURM

At 368m (1,207ft), the Fernsehturm (TV tower), affectionately known to locals as the Telespargel (Tele Asparagus), is the tallest building in Berlin (Mar–end Oct daily 9am–midnight; Nov–end Feb daily 10am–midnight; tel 030 242 3333). Inside, elevators whisk you to the viewing platform in the silver sphere, 203m (666ft) above the ground, at an ear-popping 5m per second (16.5ft per second) for a 360-degree view of the city. Above the viewing gallery is the Telecafé (daily 10am–midnight), where you can sit in the revolving restaurant and enjoy the panoramic view over *Kaffee und Kuchen* or a light meal.

MARIENKIRCHE

The Marienkirche (Apr–end Oct daily 10–9; Nov–end Mar daily 10–4; tel 030 242 4467) is the second-oldest parish church in Berlin, after the Nikolaikirche (▷ 88). It was first mentioned in records as early as 1294, but burned down in 1380 and was later rebuilt. Highlights include the alabaster baroque pulpit (1703) by Andreas Schlüter, decorated with reliefs of John the Baptist and personifications of the Virtues, and the *Dance of Death* (1485) fresco in the vestibule, which was rediscovered by August Stüler in 1860 behind the whitewashed walls.

ROTES RATHAUS

The Rotes Rathaus (Mon–Fri 9–6; closed during official events; tel 030 90260) is the official seat of the Mayor of Berlin and contains the magistrates' offices and state rooms. The frieze known as the 'stone chronicle' was added in 1879 and depicts historical figures and economic and scientific events that shaped the city. The building suffered extensive damage during World War II and was rebuilt in the 1950s, when it was the seat of the East Berlin authorities. After reunification the Rotes Rathaus became the base for the city's officials. Inside, climb the red-carpeted staircase to admire the modern stained-glass windows.

Below *A mural painted onto the house of a teacher in Alexanderplatz*

ALTE NATIONALGALERIE

The Alte Nationalgalerie holds a comprehensive collection of 19th-century German painting. There are French Impressionist works by Monet, Manet and Renoir. In 1861, the Berlin banker Joachim Heinrich Wilhelm Wagener left his collection of 262 paintings to Prince Wilhelm (later King and Emperor Wilhelm I). The gallery first opened its doors to the public on the king's birthday, 21 March 1876. From 2009, there is due to be an additional access to the gallery, via the reopened Neues Museum.

THIRD LEVEL

Begin at the top of the red-carpeted marble staircase on the third level. At the top of the stairs, lean on the balustrade and look across to Anselm Feverbach's huge painting *The Symposium* (1871–73). It illustrates an episode in Plato's *Symposium* when the poet Alcibiades makes a drunken entrance. The philosopher Socrates stands on the right, the poet is in the middle and the figure of Desire is depicted on the left. The elaborate frame is painted and incorporated into the picture, prompting the viewer to question the nature of reality and illusion. Room 3.06 is dedicated to the painter Caspar David Friedrich (▷ 36). The artist is famous for his night-time landscapes and depictions of moonlight reflected over water. *Moonrise over the Sea* (1822) shows two women and a man sitting on a rock, looking out to the sea and waiting for the returning ships. The group symbolizes companionship and safety, while the moonlight backdrop hints at the vast expanse of the universe. Return to room 3.04 and continue your tour clockwise around the third floor.

SECOND LEVEL

Room 2.03, the large room in the middle at the far end of the second level, is dedicated to the French Impressionists. Auguste Rodin's statue *The Thinker* (1881–83) is also in this room. A larger-than-life version stands on his grave, but this is the original. Look closely and you can detect Rodin's fingerprints and tool marks, left behind in the clay model before it was cast in bronze.

FIRST LEVEL

The first level focuses predominantly on realist painting, including works by John Constable, Gustave Courbet and Adolph Menzel. The main attraction is the neoclassical sculpture in the first long room you come to on the first floor, room 1.01. *Princess Luise and Princess Friederike of Prussia* (1797) by Johann Gottfried Schadow is the first life-size neoclassical double statue made.

INFORMATION

www.alte-nationalgalerie.de
www.smb.spk-berlin.de
71 E2–E3 Bodestrasse 1–3, 10178 Berlin (Mitte) 030 2090 5577
Tue–Sun 10–6, Thu 10–10 Adult €8, child (17–18) €4, under 17 free; combined admission to all Museumsinsel museums: Adult €12, child (17–18) €6, under 17 free; Thu from 6pm free to all
S-Bahn Hackescher Markt 100, 200, TXL. Tram M1, M4, M5, M6, 12
Guided tours 030 2266 3666
Small bookshop where they also serve coffee

Above *The Old National Gallery houses some of the best examples of modern painting and sculpture in Berlin*

ALTES MUSEUM

www.smb.spk-berlin.de

The Altes Museum is the oldest museum in Berlin. Completed in 1830, it was destroyed in World War II and rebuilt in the 1960s.

The focal point is the Rotunda, a perfect setting for the white marble statues of Roman gods.

The first compartment is dedicated to Greek prehistory, and contains sculpture and pottery from the Cycladic, Minoan and Mycenaean cultures (3000–2000BC). There is a large collection of Attic vases and ceramics dating from the early sixth and fifth centuries BC.

A perfectly preserved mosaic from the Villa Adriana in Tivoli, Italy (AD118–138), is in compartment 30, illustrating the ambush of a pair of centaurs by lions.

71 E3 Museumsinsel, Am Lustgarten, 10178 Berlin (Mitte) 030 2090 5277 Tue–Sun 10–6, Thu 10–10 Adult €8, child (17–18) €4, under 17 free; combined admission to all Museumsinsel museums: Adult €12, child (17–18) €6, under 17 free; Thu from 6pm free to all Friedrichstrasse TXL100, 147, 200; tram 1, 2, 3, 4, 5, 6, 7, 13, 52, 53 Free audioguide Small shop selling books and gift items

BAUHAUS-ARCHIV

www.bauhaus.de

The Bauhaus-Archiv celebrates the origins, techniques and work of the Bauhaus school of design, which ran from 1919 to 1933 (▷ 21). The school was open for only 14 years before the Nazi regime closed it down, but its founders and pupils were extremely influential.

This small museum is packed full of ground-breaking work by the masters and students of the Bauhaus, including Paul Klee (1879–1940), Vassily Kandinsky (1866–1944) and Oskar Schlemmer (1888–1943). The permanent exhibition traces the development of the Bauhaus style as expressed through design and art from architecture, household items and furniture to paintings, sculpture, graphic design and photography. The mysterious Light-Space modulator by László Moholy-Nagy has a prominent position at the heart of the collection. Moholy, who taught at the Bauhaus from 1923 to 1928, described this sculpture as 'an experimental apparatus for painting with light', which he captured in his film *Motion Picture Black-White-Grey*. The reconstructed kinetic sculpture is fully functional—press the red button to see it in action.

70 B4 Klingelhöferstrasse 14, 10785 Berlin (Tiergarten) 030 254 0020 Wed–Mon 10–5 Adult Sat–Mon €7/Wed–Fri €6, child (17–18) €4/2€, under 17 free U-Bahn Nollendorfplatz M29, 100, 106, 187 Café serving hot drinks, cakes, soups and sandwiches Bauhaus design books, gifts and household items

BERLINER DOM

www.berliner-dom.de

On the eastern edge of the Lustgarten (pleasure garden) is the Berliner Dom, the largest Protestant cathedral in Germany. Johann Bumann built the first cathedral on this site between 1747 and 1750.

The cross on top of its copper dome stands 114m (375ft) above the ground. Climb up the 270 steps to the outside viewing platform to enjoy the 360-degree view. The Sauer Organ, by Messrs Wilhelm Sauer, dominates the Sermon Church, the soaring congregational area. Its 113 registers and more than 7,200 pipes fill one of the huge Romanesque arches of the rotunda. The crypt was heavily damaged in 1945. After restoration it was reopened in 1999, and now contains around 100 sarcophagi and gravestones, including the tombs of the first king of Prussia, Friedrich Wilhelm I and Queen Sophie Charlotte

Look out for the dove in the stained-glass skylight of the Sermon Church.

71 E3 Am Lustgarten, 10178 Berlin (Mitte) 030 2026 9128 Mon–Sat 9–7 (until 8 in summer), Sun 12–7 (until 8 in summer) Adult €5, child (under 15) free S-Bahn Hackescher Markt 100, 200, 248, TXL. Tram M4, M5, M6 Concert tickets, books, guides, souvenirs

BODE-MUSEUM

The Bode-Museum, at the north end of Museum Island, was built by Ernst von Ihne between 1898 and 1904 and is named after its founder Wilhelm von Bode (1845–1929), art critic, writer and director of the royal Prussian museums. It contains the Museum für Byzantinische Kunst (Museum of Byzantine Art), the Münzkabinett (Coin Cabinet), the state sculpture collection, paintings from the early Middle Ages to the late 18th century and a children's gallery. In addition, there's the Skulpturensammlung's 1,700 separate pieces of European sculpture. Amid an array of German, Low Countries, French, Iberian and Italian works, the Florentine sculptor Donatello's marble *Madonna and Child* (*c*1418) stands out.

71 E3 Museumsinsel, Monbijoubrücke, Am Kupfergraben, 10178 Berlin (Mitte) 030 2090 5577 Daily 10–6 (Thu until 10) Adult €8, child (17–18) €4, under 17 free; combined admission to all Museumsinsel museums: Adult €12, child (17–18) €6, under 17 free; Thu from 6pm free to all S-Bahn Hackescher Markt; U-Bahn Friedrichstrasse 100, 200, TXL. Tram M1, 12

Left *A detail of the central dome of the neo-Gothic Berliner Dom*
Opposite *The Bauhaus-Archiv*

BOTANISCHER GARTEN

www.bgbm.org/bgbm
www.botanischer-garten-berlin.de

Berlin's Botanical Garden has more than 18,000 species of plants and 43.3ha (107 acres) of gardens.

It began as a 17th-century kitchen and herb garden of the former Berlin palace. The Kurfürst's garden, on your right as you pass through the south entrance, is a reconstruction of this original garden. Farther along, the art nouveau Dahlem Greenhouses were erected between 1900 and 1909. Look for the tropical waterfall in Greenhouse A, the huge spiky cacti in Greenhouses H and I, and the giant Amazonian water lilies in Greenhouse O. With a separate entrance at Königin-Luise-Platz 6–8, the Botanisches Museum (Botanical Museum; daily 10–6) takes a more focused scientific and educational approach to the work and collection of the garden. Models, dioramas and enlargements make it easier for non-specialists to understand what's being displayed.

Off 70 C5 Entrances on Königin-Luise-Platz and Unter den Eichen, 14191 Berlin (Dahlem) 030 8385 0100 May–end Jul daily 9–9; Apr, Aug daily 9–8; Sep daily 9–7; Mar, Oct daily 9–6; Feb daily 9–5; Nov–end Jan daily 9–4 Garden, museum: Adult €5, child (6–14) €2.50, under 6 free, family €10; museum only: Adult €2, child (6–14) €1, under 6 free, family €4 S-Bahn Botanischer Garten M48, X83, 101 Sun (free; in German only) Restaurant Landhaus (closed winter). The Bistro serves snacks and drinks Two shops; one selling books and gifts and the other plants and local produce

BRANDENBURGER TOR

Berlin's last remaining city gate is it's most symbolic and recognizable landmark. Carl Gotthard Langhans built the neoclassical arch for King Friedrich Wilhelm II between 1788 and 1791. In 1794, Johann Gottfried Schadow added the Quadriga, the statue of the four-horse chariot driven by Eirene, goddess of peace.

The gate's symbolic significance made it the backdrop for many victory parades, the scene of uprisings and a target during conflict. The gate barely survived World War II, and the Quadriga was destroyed except for one horse's head, which is now in the Märkisches Museum (▷ 87). After repairs in the early 1950s, a copy of the Quadriga was placed on top of the gate in 1958.

When the GDR closed the border to West Berlin in 1961, the Brandenburg Gate stood in no man's land just behind the Berlin Wall. When it was finally reopened on 22 December 1989, it became the venue for celebrations of freedom.

71 D3 Pariser Platz 1, 10117 Berlin (Mitte) Permanently Free U- and S-Bahn Brandenburger Tor M41, 100, 200, TXL

BRÖHAN-MUSEUM

www.broehan-museum.de

This intimate museum focuses on the art nouveau, art deco and Functionalism movements from 1889 to 1939, and has some of the finest examples of porcelain, sculpture and art from this time.

On the ground floor is an array of decorative arts. There are several pieces by the French designer and artist Jean Lambert-Rucki (1888–1967) who was strongly influenced by Cubism. The top floor is dedicated to art nouveau glass. The highlight is *Iris Vase* (1899), designed by Albert Klein. The large, green porcelain vase is inspired by the curling leaves and delicate flowers of an iris.

70 a2 Schlossstrasse 1a, 14059 Berlin (Charlottenburg) 030 3269 0600 Tue–Sun 10–6 (Thu until 8) Adult €5, child (13–18) €4, under 13 free; free on first Wed of month U-Bahn Sophie-Charlotte-Platz, Richard-Wagner-Platz; S-Bahn; Westend M45, 109, 309

DENKMAL FÜR DIE ERMORDETEN JUDEN EUROPAS

www.stiftung-denkmal.de

Better known as the Holocaust-Mahnmal (Holocaust Memorial), the Memorial for the Murdered Jews of Europe, just south of Pariser Platz and the Brandenburg Gate, is striking, thought-provoking and controversial. A 2sq km (0.7sq mile) field filled with 2,711 concrete stelae of varying heights recalls the Nazi slaughter of some 6 million European Jews.

Strolling through the constricted passageways of this maze is a sombre experience in which the visitor is seemingly hemmed in between massive gravestones or funerary monuments.

71 D3 Between Eberstrasse and Cora-Berliner-Strasse 030 2639 4336 Memorial permanently open. Information Centre April–end Sep Tue–Sun 10–8; Oct–end Mar Tue–Sun 10–7 Free Underground Information Centre U- and S-Bahn Brandenburger Tor M41, 100, 200, TXLL

DEUTSCHES HISTORISCHES MUSEUM

www.dhm.de

German history has been nothing if not eventful, but there is more to it than the wars and totalitarians that so shook the 20th-century. In its grand baroque home at the eastern end of Unter den Linden, the Zeughaus (Arsenal; 1706),

and an adjacent glass-walled cylindrical wing (2004) for temporary exhibitions (designed by I M Pei), the German Historical Museum takes a trip down Germany's memory lane. The exhibitions are organized into seven main historical periods. Three take the story from the Holy Roman Empire around 1200 to the Napoleonic era, and four cover the 19th century to the recent past. They are illustrated with excavated objects, antiques, models, maps, paintings, sculpture, clothing, weaponry, newsreels and photography. A Trabant car has a prominent place in the GDR section.
71 E3 Unter den Linden 2, 10117 Berlin (Mitte) 030 203040 Daily 10–6 Adult €5, child (under 18) free U- and S-Bahn Friedrichstrasse 100, 200, TXL; tram M1, 12

GEMÄLDEGALERIE

▷ 82–86.

GENDARMENMARKT

www.franzoesischer-dom-berlin.de
Friedrich Wilhelm's Gendarmenmarkt is a perfect piece of 18th-century town planning.

The Deutscher Dom (Tue 10–10, Wed–Sun 10–6, summer 10–7), to the south of the square, was built in 1708. The Französische Dom (Tue–Sat 12–5), in the north of the square, was erected around the same time and now also houses the Huguenot Museum (Tue–Sat 12–5, Sun 11–5; tel 030 22917). You can get a good overall view of the square from the Balustrade viewing platform (daily 9–7).

Built in 1774, the original Schauspielhaus (playhouse) and its replacement were destroyed by fire. The new theatre opened in 1821, and today is known as the Konzerthaus. It regularly plays host to the Berlin Symphony Orchestra.

In front of the Konzerthaus is the Schiller Monument (1869). Schiller is mounted on a pedestal, surrounded by allegorical figures of Poetry, Drama (with a dagger and cloak), Philosophy (with a covered head) and History (sitting on stone tablets).
71 E3 Gendarmenmarkt, 10117 Berlin (Mitte) U-Bahn Stadtmitte, Hausvogteiplatz, Französische Strasse M48, 100, 147, 200, 347, TXL

HAMBURGER BAHNHOF

www.hamburgerbahnhof.de
Completed in 1846, the Hamburger Bahnhof is the last remaining example of a railway station of this period in Berlin. After the war it became an art gallery, and in 1996 the Museum für Gegenwart Berlin (Museum of the Present) opened in the restored Hamburger Bahnhof.

The high-ceilinged rooms are filled with natural light, perfect for displaying large canvases and installations. The long gallery, with glass ceiling, leads along a tunnel of light to the wall dominated by Andy Warhol's screen print of *Mao* (1973).
70 C2 Invalidenstrasse 50–51, 10557 Berlin (Tiergarten) 030 3978 3411 Tue–Fri 10–6, Sat 11–8, Sun 11–6 Adult €8, child (17–18) €4, under 17 free; Thu 2–6 free U- and S-Bahn Hauptbahnhof 120, 147, 245

HAUS AM CHECKPOINT CHARLIE

www.mauermuseum.de
For more than 28 years, Checkpoint 'C', or 'Charlie' in the NATO phonetic alphabet, was a major crossing point through the Berlin Wall. It marked the main border between the Soviet sector in East Berlin and the American sector in the West.

Little is left today of the 155km (96 miles) of barricades that divided the city, and the Mauer Museum (Wall Museum) now occupies the creaky house that once sheltered the border guards. The rooms are small, but every inch of wall space is covered in newspaper articles, photographs and accounts of those affected by the Berlin wall (▷ 45).
71 E4 Friedrichstrasse 43–45, 10969 Berlin (Kreuzberg) 030 253 7250 Daily 9am–10pm Adult €12.50, child (6–18) €7.50, under 6 free U-Bahn Kochstrasse M29, M48, 347

Clockwise from left to right *The greenhouses of the Botanischer Garten; monumental buildings in Gendarmenmarkt*

INTRODUCTION

Containing some 2,700 European paintings, dating from the 13th to the 18th centuries, the Gemäldegalerie (Painting Gallery) can easily stand comparison with the world's greatest art museums. Stellar works by painters like Bruegel, Holbein, Rembrandt, Titian, Velázquez and Gainsborough grace its walls. The gallery is the centrepiece of the Museen der Europäischen Kunst (Museums of European Art), a key part of the Kulturforum cultural complex between the Tiergarten and Potsdamer Platz. You enter the maze-like, Modernist-style gallery from the Piazzetta, just off the square on which the 19th-century St. Matthäus-Kirche stands.

The collection began with various private bequests supplemented by those of the 17th-century Grosser Kurfürst (Great Elector) of Brandenburg Friedrich Wilhelm (1620–88), and the Prussian kings Friedrich der Grosse (1712–86) and Friedrich Wilhelm III (1770–1840). Following World War II, the paintings were divided between East and West Berlin, half in the Bode-Museum [▷ 78], and the other half in the former Asian Museum in Dahlem. In 1965, German architect Rolf Gutbrod (1910–99) won a competition to design the new Museums of European Art, to stand opposite the Philharmonie, but political and financial problems plagued the project and it wasn't until 1985 that construction began. Gutbrod's original drawings were reworked, and the museum finally opened to the public in 1998.

Allow at least a half-day for your visit, and preferably longer because you will need time to absorb all that is on display here. However, if time is short, visit the Digitalegalerie (Digital Gallery)—rooms 27, 33 and 42—to check out the exhibits onscreen before heading out to view the real thing. The room numbering system can be confusing: the larger inner rooms have Roman numerals and the outer, generally smaller rooms, called cabinets, have standard numbers. The 11 cabinets that make up the Studiengalerie (Study Gallery), where the displays change regularly, are in the basement in rooms 43–54.

WHAT TO SEE

THE FLEMISH PROVERBS BY PIETER BRUEGEL, IN ROOM 7

Bruegel brings together 100 proverbs in an absurd, slightly surreal village scene, reminiscent of the work of his predecessor Hieronymus Bosch. Look out for the egg with legs on the right-hand side of the painting, an image that often appears in Bosch's work. Painted in 1559, the painting was originally called *The Upside-Down World*, in reference to the inverted globe on the side of the house, reflecting the topsy-turvy scene. The devil occupies the chapel and takes confession, while Jesus sits outside on the right in front of a hut. A servant covers his face with a flax beard, the mask of a hypocrite. Chaos is the guiding principle, as money is thrown into the water and roses are cast before swine. Bruegel was constantly exploring the spiritual and moral questions of his time and this piece is no exception. The supposedly wise old sayings are used to illustrate man's foolishness and sinfulness in a world without the guidance of God.

CHILD WITH BIRD BY PETER PAUL RUBENS, IN ROOM 9

Rubens painted this portrait of his nephew Philip in 1624. Philip was born in 1611 and was the son of Rubens' brother, who died at a young age. Rubens captures the intuitive character of children through the boy's interaction with the bird and reflects his innocence with his white clothes, pale complexion and angelic features.

INFORMATION

www.smb.spk-berlin.de

70 C4 Kulturforum, Matthäikirchplatz, 10785 Berlin (Tiergarten) 030 266 2101 Tue–Sun 10–6, Thu 10–10 Adult €8, child (17–18) €4, under 17 free (price includes admission to all Kulturforum museums); Thu from 6pm free to all U- and S-Bahn Potsdamer Platz M48, 200, 347 Guided tours 030 266 3666; free audioguide Shop selling a wide range of art books, postcards and posters

TIP

» The air in the gallery is kept very dry to preserve the art, but you can take a break every so often by the water sculpture *5–7–9 Series* by Walter de Maria in the central hall.

Opposite *Portrait of* Der Kaufmann Georg Gisze (the Merchant George Gisze, *1532*) *by Hans Holbein the Younger*

GALLERY GUIDE

Rooms I–III and 1–4: German painting of the 13th to 16th centuries. *Die Madonna mit dem Zeisig* (*The Madonna and Child*) by Albrecht Dürer in room 2, *Die Geburt Christi* (*The Birth of Christ*) by Martin Schongauer in room 1, *Der Kaufmann Georg Gisze* (*The Merchant Georg Gisze*) by Hans Holbein the Younger in room 4, *Die Königin von Saba vor Salomon* (*The Queen of Sheba before Solomon*) by Konrad Witz in room I, *Der Jungbrunnen* (*The Fountain of Youth*) by Cranach the Elder in room III.

Rooms IV–VI and 5–7: Dutch, Flemish and French painting of the 14th to 16th centuries. *Die Madonna in der Kirche* (*The Madonna in the Church*) by Jan van Eyck in room 5, *Johannes auf Patmos* (*John on Patmos*) by Hieronymus Bosch in room 6, *Die Niederländischen Sprichwörter* (*The Dutch Proverbs*) in room 7.

Rooms VII–XI and 8–19: Flemish and Dutch painting of the 17th century. *Der Blumenstrauss* (*Bouquet of Flowers*) by Jan Bruegel the Elder in room 9, *Das Kind mit Vogel* (*Child with Bird*) by Peter Paul Rubens in room 9, *Der Mann mit dem Goldhelm* (*The Man with the Golden Helmet*) by Rembrandt in room 16,

Below *A portrait of Cornelius Anslo and his wife, painted in 1641 by Rembrandt*

LOVE VICTORIOUS BY CARAVAGGIO, IN ROOM XIV

Caravaggio's earthly figure of Love, painted between 1601 and 1602, shows him triumphing over the classical, intellectual love championed by the arts and sciences. Caravaggio's revolutionary portrayal was very controversial at the time: The down-to-earth, naked boy was kept behind a curtain and could only be viewed by men. A laurel wreath, the symbol of eternal fame and lyric poetry, is lying on the floor, while a sceptre and crown, emblems of worldly power, have been pushed to the right. The grubby, cheeky boy even has dirt under his toenails. The figure stands out bright against the dark background and appears to be illuminated by a spotlight, illustrating the chiaroscuro technique seen throughout Caravaggio's work. The painting offended his rival Giovanni Baglione, who was commissioned by a cardinal to communicate the established view. His critical response is on display in the same room, to the right of the door, while Caravaggio's interpretation is on the left. Baglione's painting, entitled *The Divine Eros* (1602–03), shows the angel-like eternal Eros dressed in armour, standing over Caravaggio's pale and beaten earthly love and preparing to finish him off with a bolt of lightning. The arrows belonging to earthly love lie broken on the floor and on the left in the background a demon, a symbol of base debauchery, is chained to the ground. Baglione's piece borrows some of Caravaggio's techniques, but remains faithful to the traditional over-stylized and formulaic portrayal of the ideal human form, which sets it apart from Caravaggio's emotional, natural interpretation.

LEDA AND THE SWAN BY ANTONIO CORREGGIO, IN ROOM XV

This piece was painted for the Duke of Mantua, Frederico Gonzaga II, in 1531. It is one of four classical amorous adventures painted by the artist. In this piece, Jupiter, in the form of a swan, is shown seducing Leda. Cupid is on the left holding a lyre. After Frederico's death, the painting made its way to Spain and was then passed around various European collections for the next 200 years. Philippe of Orléans, the Regent of France, acquired it in 1721. His son, Louis, found the portrait extremely distasteful. In a fit of religious rage he cut it up, completely destroying the head of Leda. The painter Coypel resurrected the painting by piecing it back together and filling in the missing sections, but

he left the head of Leda blank. Friedrich the Great purchased the traumatized painting for his gallery in Sanssouci (▷ 168–169) in 1755. Leda's head was finally repainted by the artist Jacob Sleschinger in 1830 before it was moved to the Museum am Lustgarten. Look very carefully and you will see some of the joins from where the painting was restored.

THE MAN WITH THE GOLDEN HELMET, IN ROOM 16

The Man With the Golden Helmet (1650–55) is one of the most popular paintings in the gallery, but there is now evidence to suggest that it was not actually the work of Rembrandt. During restoration in the 1980s, the painting was examined in detail and tests revealed that many of the brush strokes were inconsistent with the style of painting seen in Rembrandt's other works. The thickly applied paint on the helmet and the bright, reflected light demonstrate an exaggerated interpretation of Rembrandt's signature technique.

Down to Special Exhibitions

Digital Gallery

Down to Toilets

Lift

ENTRANCE

Minature Paintings

Junge Dame mit Perlenhalsband (*Young Woman with a Pearl Necklace*) by Jan Vermeer in room 18, *Moses mit den Gesetzestafeln* (*Moses with the Ten Commandments*) by Rembrandt in room X.

Rooms 20–22: French, English and German painting of the 18th century. *Der Tanz* (*The Dance*) by Jean Watteau in room 21, *Die Marsham-Kinder* (*The Marsham Children*) by Thomas Gainsborough in room 20, *Der Zeichner* (*The Draughtsman*) by Chardin in room 21.

Rooms XII–XIV and 23–27, 28: Italian, German, French and Spanish painting of the 17th and 18th centuries. *Der Campo di Rialto* (*Rialto Square*) by Canaletto in room XII, *Bildnis einer Dame* (*Portrait of a Lady*) by Velázquez in room XIII, *Amor als Sieger* (*Love Victorious*) by Caravaggio in room XIV, *Landschaft mit dem Evangelisten Matthäus* (*Landscape with Matthew the Evangelist*) in room 25.

Rooms XV–XVII and 29–32, 35–41: Italian painting of the 13th and 16th century. *Madonna Terranuova* by Raphael in room 29, *Vertumnus and Pomona* by Francesco Melzi and Der hl. *Sebastian* (*St. Sebastian*) by Sandro Botticelli in room XVIII, *Venus mit dem Orgelspieler* (*Venus with the Organ Player*) by Titian in room XVI.

Rooms 43–54: European painting of the 13th to 18th centuries. *Die Auffindung des hl. Sebastian* (*The Retrieval of St. Sebastian*) by De La Tour in room 43, *Venus* by Botticelli in room 50.

Room 34: *Miniaturmalerei* (Miniature Paintings)

Rooms 27, 33, 42: *Digitale Galerie* (Digital Gallery)

KEY

- Dutch and French artists
- European artists
- Flemish and Dutch artists
- French, English and German artists
- German artists
- Italian artists
- Italian, German, French and Spanish artists

VENUS WITH THE ORGAN PLAYER BY TITIAN, IN ROOM XVI

In this painting, Venus, accompanied by Cupid, is shown lying on a ceremonial couch against a red velvet curtain. A cavalier is sitting in front of the organ on the left-hand side with his hands on the keys and his eyes fixed on the goddess. Painted between 1550 and 1552, this is an extremely early example of Impressionism. Way ahead of its time, it has the artist's brush strokes visible in the painting. The piece moves away from the strict realistic or polished idealistic portrayal of the subject that was popular at the time. You will have to look carefully to detect Titian's experimental handiwork—he cleverly disguised it so as not to be shunned by the rest of the artistic community, who were staunchly committed to the style of realistic portrayal dominant at the time.

ARCHITECTURAL VIEW BY FRANCESCO DI GIORGIO MARTINI, IN ROOM XVIII

Set in a panel, this mysterious, idealized townscape appears to be inspired by the courts of Urbino in Italy. The painting has been attributed to Francesco di Giorgio Martini, who lived in Siena between 1439 and 1502, but critics are uncertain about the purpose of the painting and whether he is the artist. The theoretical piece plays with perspective and the three different viewpoints give the painting a sense of depth. Walk from the left to the right of the painting to fully appreciate the effect.

ST. SEBASTIAN BY SANDRO BOTTICELLI, IN ROOM XVIII

Botticelli painted his dedication to the martyr St. Sebastian in 1474 for the church of San Francesco Maggiore in Florence. The figure is shown in the *contrapposto* position, with his head and upper body twisted in the opposite direction to his hips and legs. Gazing into the middle distance with his head to one side and his eyebrows slightly raised, he appears to be calmly meditating his fate. His elongated legs and the low horizon bring him forward, making him look larger than life.

VERTUMNUS AND POMONA BY FRANCESCO MELZI, IN ROOM XVIII

Melzi painted this episode from Ovid's *Metamorphoses* between 1517 and 1520. Vertumnus, the god of vegetation, has changed his form to woo Pomona, the goddess of fruit and gardens. Pomona has retreated away from society and is living in an all-female community, so Vertumnus assumes the form of an old woman in order to get close to his love. In the middle is an elm tree with a vine wrapped around, a powerful symbol of union and co-existence at the heart of the painting. The artist, Melzi, was a student of Leonardo da Vinci, and you can clearly see the teacher's influence in Vertumnus' hands and Pomona's expression, reminiscent of Mona Lisa's famous smile. The manly neck and the young feet and hands of Vertumnus hint at his true identity.

Below Moses with the Ten Commandments *by Rembrandt*

THE PRELIMINARY WORKS, IN ROOMS 19 AND 10

The small circular rooms at the end of the hall contain preliminary works and drafts by famous artists. Many of the Italian masters, such as Michelangelo, made small preliminary works to show to their clients before embarking on the larger canvases, which were often completed by their students. These originals of the originals should not be overlooked.

THE VIRGIN AND CHILD WITH THE INFANT ST. JOHN THE BAPTIST AND A HOLY BOY BY RAPHAEL, IN ROOM 29

This circular painting was Raphael's first tondo, created in 1505 shortly after his arrival in Florence, where this style of composition was very popular. It is actually two paintings in one—Raphael completed the background scene first, then added the Madonna and Child and the Holy children on top afterwards.

JÜDISCHES MUSEUM

www.juedisches-museum-berlin.de

The Jewish Museum was designed by the Polish-born American architect Daniel Libeskind in 1989 for the exhibits on Jewish history from the Berlin Museum. Apart from being a museum space, the Postmodern structure stands as a monument to the plight of the Jews, with every space and aesthetic aspect designed with an emotional response in mind. From the outside, its zigzag shape resembles a bolt of lightning with windows cut through the shiny exterior-like cracks.

The Memory Void on the second level is the largest of the closed spaces that cut through the building. The narrowing empty space represents the expelled and murdered European Jews. The floor is covered with the installation *Shalechet* (*Fallen Leaves*, 1997–2001) by the artist Menashe Kadishman, made up of more than 10,000 faces cut out of sheet steel.

Although the subject matter is disturbing, the building and museum are intensely thought-provoking and designed with children in mind. The historical information is communicated interactively throughout, with photo light boxes, telephones that play historical recordings, and drawers and doors that beg to be opened and the contents explored. The traditional Jewish cuisine at the museum's excellent Restaurant and Café Liebermanns is worth experiencing.

71 E5 Lindenstrasse 9–14, 10969 Berlin (Kreuzberg) 030 2599 3300 Tue–Sun 10–8, Mon 10–10; closed on Jewish holidays and 24 Dec Adult €5, child (7–18) €2.50, under 7 free U-Bahn Hallesches Tor, Kochstrasse M29, M41, 248

KAISER-WILHELM-GEDÄCHTNISKIRCHE

The Kaiser Wilhelm Memorial Church is a mix of old and new architectural styles. Built at the end of the 19th century, the old church was destroyed by bombs in 1943. With insufficient funds to rebuild, the ruined tower became a war memorial. The new church was consecrated in 1961.

Unlike the old church the new buildings are dominated by straight lines and constructed from concrete and steel, covered with a honeycomb of deep blue stained glass. The walls of the hall of worship and the new tower are filled with 21,292 handmade panes of stained glass, and inside, the rich blue light envelops you. By contrast the entrance hall of the late 19th-century tower is covered in original mosaics. Most striking is the floor mosaic of the Archangel Michael slaying a dragon.

70 A4 Breitscheidplatz, 10789 Berlin (Charlottenburg) 030 218 5023 Church: daily 9–7; Gedenkhalle (Memorial Hall): Mon–Sat 10–4 Free U- and S-Bahn Zoologischer Garten; U-Bahn Kurfürstendamm M19, M29, M46, 100, 200

KUNSTGEWERBEMUSEUM

www.smb.spk-berlin.de

This museum displays European arts and crafts and interior design from the Middle Ages to the present day. The collection is spread over four floors in the Kulturforum museum complex. The star exhibit is the *Welfenschatz* (Guelph Treasure), a set of lavish gold and silver religious objects, some dating from the 11th century. This is closely followed by Lüneburg town council's 15th-century treasury of gold and silver reliquaries and other objects.

Delicate Renaissance and baroque pieces are in room IV, including a collection of intricate navigational instruments. On the ground floor, Postmodern retro furniture sits happily side-by-side with 1950s and 1960s style icons.

70 C4 Kulturforum am Potsdamer Platz, Matthäikirchplatz, (visitor entrance: Herbert-von-Karajan-Strasse 10), 10785 Berlin (Tiergarten) 030 266 2902 Tue–Fri 10–6, Sat, Sun 11–6 Adult €8, child (17–18) €4, under 17 free (includes admission to all Kulturforum museums) U- and S-Bahn Potsdamer Platz M48, 200, 347

MÄRKISCHES MUSEUM

www.stadtmuseum.de

The museum's permanent exhibition, Look at this city!, traces the history and cultural development of Berlin from the Middle Ages to the present day.

You are taken on a thematic journey through the city's history, exploring a variety of subjects including medieval sculpture, the development of the press, World War I, immigration, Berlin under the Swastika, the Cold War, and the destruction and reconstruction of Potsdamer Platz (▷ 96).

The one remaining original horse's head from the Brandenburger Tor is in the first room on the left at the top of the stairs (▷ 80). Another unusual piece is the Kaiserpanorama (*c*1900), a circular cabinet with 24 individual viewing stations used for watching stereoscopic images. You can sit and see them in operation.

Just south of the museum is the leafy compound where a pair of brown bears, Schnute and Maxi, are housed as symbols of the city.

71 F4 Am Köllnischen Park 5, 10179 Berlin (Mitte) 030 3086 6215 Tue–Sun 10–6 (Wed 12–8) Adult €4, child (6–15) €2, under 6 free, Wed free U-Bahn Märkisches Museum, Heinrich-Heine-Strasse; U- and S-Bahn Jannowitzbrücke 147

Below *The Postmodern Jewish Museum was designed by Polish-born US architect Daniel Libeskind*

MUSEUM BERGGRUEN

www.sammlung-berggruen.de

The Berggruen collection, also known as 'Picasso and his Time', is an intimate collection of early modern art by Pablo Picasso and his contemporaries. Heinz Berggruen was a close friend of Picasso and his collection was amassed over a period of 50 years.

The museum has rooms radiating out from the central spiral staircase. More than 100 works by Picasso, spanning 75 years of his career, form the basis of the collection. There is also a substantial number of works by Paul Klee and Henri Matisse, including several of Matisse's cutouts. Alberto Giacometti's *Femme Debout III* (1960), a tall, elongated bronze figure, dominates the rotunda on the ground floor, and is one of several pieces by him on display.

70 a2 Schlossstrasse 1, 14059 Berlin (Charlottenburg) 030 32 9580 Tue–Sun 10–6 Adult €6, child (under 17) free Richard-Wagner-Platz, Westend 109, M45, 309, X9 Free audioguide

NEUE SYNAGOGE

www.cjudaicum.de

The Neue Synagoge, opened in 1866, was once the place of worship for the largest Jewish community in Germany.

The National Socialists set fire to the building in 1938, although it was saved from total destruction. Services resumed until 1940, when the building was taken over and used as a Military Clothing Office. The rest of the building burned down after a bomb attack in 1943, and today the reconstructed front section of the building and dome stand as a memorial to Berlin's persecuted Jewish community.

The famous, glistening dome, a key landmark on Berlin's skyline, has been restored according to original plans, but the rest of the building has been only partially reconstructed and now contains the Centrum Judaicum. On the ground floor, the permanent exhibition, Open Ye the Gates, explores the history of the synagogue and Jewish life in Berlin. One of the most remarkable exhibits is the Ner Tamid, the eternal lamp, which was rediscovered in 1989 in the protective concrete ceiling when construction workers were removing rubble from the marriage chamber (men's vestibule).

71 E2 Oranienburger Strasse 28–30, 10117 Berlin (Mitte) 030 8802 8300 Apr–end Mar, Nov Sun–Fri 10–8; Sep–end Oct, Feb Sun–Fri 10–6; closed Sat and on Jewish holidays Adult €3, child €2 Hackescher Markt, Oranienburger Strasse, Oranienburger Tor Tram 1, 13 Guided tours in German Wed 4, Sun 2, 4 and on request 030 88 02 83 16; adult €1.50, child €1

NIKOLAIVIERTEL

On an island in Mitte, this faux old quarter of Berlin was rebuilt between 1981 and 1986 and is a mixture of refurbished old buildings, modern apartments, and arcades filled with craft and gift shops. The quarter's quiet streets and pristine buildings are a little too perfect for their reputed age, making the area feel a little like a film set.

At the heart of the quarter is the reconstructed Nikolaikirche (Mon–Thu 8–4, Sat, Sun 12–4; tel 030 2472 4529), the oldest parish church in Berlin. Inside, the Museum der Nikolaikirche (Tue–Sun 10–6; tel 030 2472 4529) explores the history of the church and its links to Berlin's famous personalities.

The Knoblauchhaus (Tue–Sun 10–6; tel 030 2757 6733), at Poststrasse 23, is the oldest surviving house in the Nikolaiviertel and the oldest building still standing in Berlin. Built between 1759 and 1761, it was reconstructed in the early 19th century and now displays a collection of household items and furniture owned by the aristocratic Knoblauch family, along with exhibits documenting the history of Berlin from the 18th to the 20th century.

71 F3 10178 Berlin (Mitte) Alexanderplatz, Klosterstrasse TXL, 100, 147, 148, 200

TOPOGRAPHIE DES TERRORS

www.topographie.de

The Topography of Terror is an open-air exhibition in the excavations of the former National Socialist government district and reveals the development and activities of the Nazi SS and police state.

Between 1933 and 1945, the genocide of the Jews and the persecution and murder of political opponents to Germany were planned here, and there was a Gestapo prison, used to detain and interrogate suspects. Towards the end of World War II, the buildings were damaged or completely destroyed. Following excavation of the site, the Topography of Terror exhibition was opened in 1987 in a pavilion. In 1995, the cornerstone was laid for a new building to house the Topography of Terror Foundation's International Documentation and Study Center. This project has been frozen for financial reasons, and a new architectural competition has been announced.

71 D4 Niederkirchnerstrasse 8, 10963 Berlin (Kreuzberg) 030 2548 6703 Oct–end Apr daily 10–6; May–end Sep daily 10–8 Free Potsdamer Platz, Kochstrasse 129, 248, 341 Audioguide in English

Below *The gilded dome of the Neue Synagoge was reconstructed along with other parts of the building after war damage*

NEUE NATIONALGALERIE

An outstanding collection of 20th-century painting and sculpture, with works by famous artists, such as Salvador Dalí, Paul Klee and Pablo Picasso. At the edge of the Tiergarten near the Kulturforum, the New National Gallery was designed by Bauhaus architect Ludwig Mies van der Rohe and built between 1965 and 1968. The square steel structure and glazed walls sit on a raised terrace, creating a spacious and versatile exhibition space for this collection, ranging from early Modernism to art of the 1960s and 1970s. Contemporary exhibitions are also held on the upper floor.

SCULPTURE

The Dancer (1911–12) made Georg Kolbe famous and established his reputation as a sensitive sculptor of the human form. It was first shown at the Berlin Secession in 1912 and was snapped up by the Nationalgalerie. Kolbe was inspired by the work of Rodin, particularly in the way in which he conveyed energy and the impression of fluid movement in his sculpture. You can also see one of Alexander Calder's mobiles, *Dancing Star* (1940), a carefully balanced and delicate sculpture made of thin wire and painted metal shapes that dance around with the slightest movement of air. Artist Käthe Kollwitz lost her son Peter, who was a soldier, in 1914. She confronts her loss in the sculpture *Pietà* (1937–38) by reworking the famous religious image into a universal expression of maternal grief. *Woman on a Bench* (1957) is one of Henry Moore's series of seated figures, which all refer to the struggle of life, and the pregnant woman is a comment on the natural process of birth, growth and decay.

PAINTING

Max Liebermann painted many self-portraits. *Self-Portrait* (1925) shows the 78-year-old artist, who was then president of the Prussian Academy of Arts, seated facing the viewer in his studio before a canvas with a brush and palette in his hand. There are two examples of Pablo Picasso's analytic Cubism on display, *Woman Seated in an Armchair* (1909) and *Woman Playing a Violin* (1911). *Potsdamer Platz* (1914), by Ernst Ludwig Kirchner, shows the famous square at night in autumn 1914. The building with the arcaded loggia in the middle is Potsdam Station. Two life-size female figures, intended to be prostitutes, stand on a traffic island in the foreground with the dark figures of potential clients in the background. These women contrast with the pink figures of the 'respectable' women in the distance.

INFORMATION

www.smb.spk-berlin.de
70 C4 Kulturforum am Potsdamer Platz, Potsdamer Strasse 50, 10785 Berlin (Tiergarten) 030 266 2651 Tue, Wed, Fri 10–6, Thu 10–10, Sat, Sun 11–6 Adult €8, child (17–18) €4, under 17 free (price includes admission to all Kulturforum museums); Thu from 6pm free to all U- and S-Bahn Potsdamer Platz; U-Bahn Mendelssohn-Bartholdy-Park M29, M480 Guided tours 030 266 3666 Small art bookshop

Above *A massive bronze,* Der Bogenschützze (The Archer, *1968) by Henry Moore is among major works in the sculpture garden at the Neue Nationalgalerie*

INFORMATION
www.smb.spk-berlin.de
71 E3 Museumsinsel, Am Kupfergraben, 10178 Berlin (Mitte)
030 2090 5577 Tue–Sun 10–6, Thu 10–10 Adult €8, child (17–18) €4, under 17 free; combined admission to all Museumsinsel museums: Adult €12, child (17–18) €6, under 17 free; Thu from 6pm free to all S-Bahn Hackescher Markt; U-Bahn Friedrichstrasse 100, 200, TXL. Tram M1, 12 Guided tours 030 2090 5566; free audioguide Two shops selling souvenirs and books

Above *The exterior of the museum*
Opposite *Glazed tiles depicting a lion from the Processional Way*

INTRODUCTION

One of the world's most impressive archaeological collections is assembled here on Museumsinsel. Visitors stroll through and around towering pieces of reconstructed monumental ancient architecture and interior design, among them the Pergamon Altar, Babylon's Ishtar Gate and Processional Way, Nebuchadnezzar's Throne Room, and the Market Gate of Miletus. In addition, there's Islamic art and architecture, from the early Caliphate to the Ottomans, and from Persia to Al-Andalus (Andalusia). The Pergamonmuseum actually consists of three museums—the Antikensammlung (Collection of Classical Antiquities), the Vorderasiatisches Museum (Museum of the Ancient Near East) and the Museum für Islamische Kunst (Museum of Islamic Art). Also, it fits in part of the Münzkabinett (Numismatic Collection) from the Bode-Museum (▷ 78). It would be hard to do justice to the famed collections in a visit of much less than a full day.

It wasn't until first phase of excavations at the Acropolis of Pergamon (Pergamum) were completed in 1886 that the question of where to keep these huge architectural discoveries was raised. At this time, Berlin's Collection of Greek and Roman Antiquities was on display in the Altes Museum and Neues Museum, but there was no way they could accommodate the Pergamon Altar. A provisional home for the collection was opened to the public in 1901 but was only just big enough for the reconstructed altar. Visitors could view it from just 8m (26ft) away, which meant it was difficult to get an overall impression. In 1908, the building had to be demolished when its foundations were found to be unstable, and it was another 22 years before the Pergamon Altar went on public view again.

Ludwig Hoffmann built the new and much bigger Pergamonmuseum between 1910 and 1930 based on designs by architect Alfred Messel (1853–1909). Between 1926 and 1930, the Market Gate of Miletus and the

GALLERY GUIDE
Upper Floor
Museum für Islamische Kunst
(Museum of Islamic Art)
Gallery 1: Lobby. Introduction
Gallery 2: Umayyad Art
Gallery 3: Abbasid and Fatimid Art
Gallery 4: Seljuk Art (Iran)
Gallery 5: Seljuk Art (Asia Minor), Ayyubid and Mamluk Art
Gallery 6: Alhambra Dome
Gallery 7: Il-Khanid and Timurid Art
Gallery 8: Spanish Carpets
Gallery 9: Mshatta Room and Sassanian Art. Mshatta façade
Gallery 10–11: Temporary exhibitions
Gallery 12: Early Ottoman Art
Gallery 13: Safavid and Mughal Art
Gallery 14: High Ottoman Art
Gallery 15–16: Aleppo Room

Main Floor (North Wing)
Antikensammlung
(Collection of Classical Antiquities)
Gallery 1 and 5: Lobby. History of Excavations
Gallery 2–4: Pergamon Room, Telephos Room and the Pergamon Altar
Gallery 6: Roman Architecture, Market Gate of Miletus
Gallery 7: Hall in the Trajaneum
Gallery 8: Hellenistic Architecture
Gallery 9–10: Archaic Sculpture
Gallery 11–12: Classical Greek Art
Gallery 13: Late Classical Sculpture
Gallery 14: Ancient Copies of Greek Masterpieces
Gallery 15: Ancient Copies, Portraits
Gallery 16: Hellenistic Sculpture
Gallery 17: Ancient Coins
Gallery 18: Roman Art

Ishtar Gate were pieced together and integrated into the museum's interior design. The museums were closed during World War II. Sandbags protected the altar, and many moveable valuables were put in storage in underground vaults. The Market Gate of Miletus could not be removed and was seriously damaged by the bombing. Also badly hit was the Pergamon room, and a bomb destroyed the altar's staircase. Luckily the protective walls sheltered the Ishtar Gate and the Processional Way, but large skylights in the roof were shattered throughout the museum and rain damaged many exhibits.

The Pergamonmuseum, along with the other museums on Museumsinsel, is a UNESCO World Heritage Site and, since the former West Berlin and East Berlin museums were reunited in 1990 both the exhibits and the museum itself have undergone extensive restoration. A rolling renovation project beginning in 2008 will cause parts of the museum to close, and the Market Gate of Miletus refurbishment is an ongoing project.

WHAT TO SEE

THE PERGAMON ALTAR

In 1876, Carl Humann began uncovering the remains of this ancient altar on the Acropolis of Pergamon in Turkey. The altar was built by King Eumenes II (197–158BC) and stood on the Acropolis in Pergamon. The altar was encircled by a relief frieze, over 2m (6.5ft) high and 120m (394ft) long, which illustrated the war between gods and giants that was finally settled by the heroic Hercules. Known as the Great Frieze, it captures the climax of the battle. Zeus' winged horses, driven by Hera, clear a path through the giants in the middle of the eastern frieze. From here the action moves to the central group, Zeus and his daughter Athena. To the left of Zeus you can just make out the huge figure of his son, Hercules, and to Athena's right is the war god Ares, preparing to charge into battle.

Another smaller frieze ran around the inner walls of the court of the Altar. In contrast to the Great Frieze, which captures the dramatic conclusion of a war,

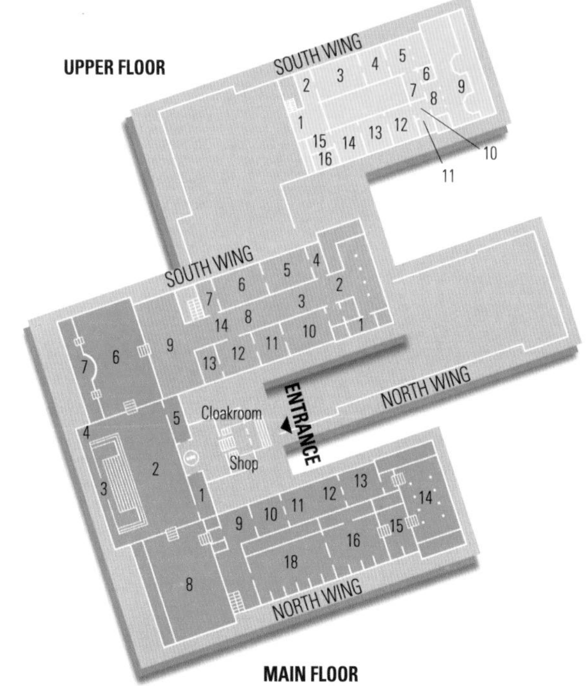

KEY

Collection of Classical Antiquities

Museum of Islamic Art

Museum of Ancient Near-Eastern Art

the Telephos Frieze tells the epic story of Telephos, Hercules' son, using trees or curtains to divide and separate each episode. Telephus was the product of a clandestine affair between Hercules and Auge, the daughter of King Aleos. King Aleos disowns his daughter and she is set adrift in the sea in a boat. The frieze begins with the building of Auge's boat and concludes with Telephos leading the Greeks into battle with Troy and returning victorious to found the city of Pergamon.

THE MARKET GATE OF MILETUS

The Market Gate of Miletus is currently being restored and is covered in scaffolding and netting. The ancient city of Miletus, whose ruins have been excavated, is 120km (75 miles) south of Izmir on the western coast of Turkey, at the mouth of the River Meander. Constructed around AD120, the gate provided access to the city's market, and when Emperor Justinian strengthened the fortifications of the city in AD538, he incorporated the gateway into the city walls. These walls, including the market gate, were destroyed during an earthquake in 1100. The buried fragments of the gate were uncovered between 1903 and 1905 by a team of archaeologists under the direction of Theodor Wiegand and Hubert Knackfuss. The main sections of the gate were brought back to Berlin and reconstructed in the Pergamonmusuem using much of the original material.

THE ISHTAR GATE

As early as 1851, French archaeologists working at Babylon found pieces of glazed bricks around the El-Kasr hill ruin that they believed formed part of a frieze. The Ishtar Gate is just one of at least eight double gates that led into the city of Babylon and formed the northern entrance into King Nebuchadnezzar II's capital. Because of its size, only the smaller outer gate could be reconstructed in the museum.

Ishtar was the Mesopotamian goddess of love and war and one of the protectors of Babylon, along with the city god Marduk and the weather god Adad. The fertile and passionate Adad is depicted on the gate in the form of a bull. The other god who appears on the gate, Marduk, was associated with the dragon Mushhushshu, who possessed the head of a viper, the paws of a lion, the claws of an eagle and the tail of a scorpion, signifying speed, strength, cunning and lethal danger.

THE FAÇADE OF THE THRONE ROOM

On the narrow walls on either side of the Ishtar gate are two sections of the reconstructed façade of the Throne Room from the southern palace of Nebuchadnezzar II. The Babylonian craftsmen who built the royal palace at Babylon in the sixth century BC coded each individual brick, which allowed Walter Andrae to reconstruct the façade of the throne room here between

Main Floor (South Wing)
Vorderasiatisches Museum
(Museum of the Ancient Near East)
Gallery 1: Rock Reliefs from Yazilikaya
Gallery 2: Finds from Syria, Asia Minor and Mesopotamia
Gallery 3: Esarhaddon-Stela from Sam'al
Gallery 4: Assyrian Royal Tombs
Gallery 5: Finds from Uruk and Habuba Kabira
Gallery 6: Babylonian Monuments
Gallery 7: Ancient Iranian Monuments
Gallery 8: Processional Way of Babylon
Gallery 9: Ishtar Gate of Babylon
Gallery 10: Finds from Assyria
Gallery 10a: Assyrian Tombs
Gallery 11: Assyrian Palace Room
Gallery 12: Finds from Assyria
Gallery 13: Urartian Monuments
Gallery 14: Stelae from Assur

Above *People viewing the relief frieze which encircled the Pergamon Altar*

Above *The carving on the cedar and poplar dome from the Alhambra is exquisite*

1899 and 1901. The palace façade was 56m (184ft) wide, but its true height remains uncertain—its present height is determined by the dimensions of the gallery space. Glazed tiles cover the wall, as they do on the Ishtar gate, and the lower section is decorated with a band of lions, reflecting the design of the Processional Way.

THE PROCESSIONAL WAY

The walled Processional Way ran north from the Ishtar Gate, and although only 8m (26ft) wide in the gallery, it was originally between 20m and 24m (65ft to 82ft) wide. The ceremonial road stretched for 250m (820ft) from the Ishtar Gate to a temple on the northern outskirts of the city. In Babylon, the New Year began in early spring and was welcomed with a huge festival, during which the king would be re-enthroned. The festival revolved around the worship of the statues of the city gods, who enjoyed a rapturous reception, as it was believed that the fortunes of the king and the people depended on their welfare. The statues were given pride of place during the festivities and then carefully carried back to the temple on highly decorative thrones, along the Processional Way and through the Ishtar gate, accompanied by musicians and crowds.

THE MSHATTA FAÇADE

The Mshatta façade first came to the world's attention in 1873. The ruin was threatened by the construction of a railway that was planned to pass right through the site, linking Damascus with the holy cities of the Arabian Peninsula. German archaeologists appealed to Wilhelm II and the Berlin museums to finance a rescue mission for most of the façade. The rest of the palace remains in its original location. Mshatta Palace was built for the Caliph al-Walid II (AD743–744) 25km (15 miles) from Amman in what is now the Jordanian desert. It was never finished as the Caliph died unexpectedly. The outer wall and some of the interior structures were incomplete, and an earthquake in AD746 reduced most of the building to rubble.

The elaborate decoration on the façade was designed to demonstrate the wealth of the Caliph, and the zigzag band, with rosettes in each triangle, is typical of the decoration seen on early Islamic palaces. Various animals drink out of the basins in the middle of the rosettes, from cattle and lions to mythical beasts such as centaurs, griffins and peacock dragons, creatures seen in pre-Islamic Iranian art. The section of the façade that was closest to the palace prayer niche is more restrained, as it was forbidden to show depictions of animals or people on sacred monuments or religious buildings.

THE ALEPPO ROOM

The wall panelling, 35m (115ft) in length, once covered the lower part of a function room in a house of a Christian broker working for merchants in Aleppo, in northwest Syria, at the beginning of the 17th century. The inscription to the left of the entrance in the right wing reveals his name, 'Isa ibn Butrus', Jesus Son of Peter. Sections are dated as being painted in 1600, 1601 and 1603, making it the oldest and best-preserved painted wall panelling from a Syrian house.

The right-hand section of the panelling is decorated with scenes from the Old and New Testaments. They are very similar to illustrations found in Islamic books at the time and, although the style of painting is Ottoman, the figures depicted resemble those seen in Persian art. The left-hand panels focus on aristocratic life and are decorated with depictions of rulers and hunting scenes. There are various inscriptions on the panels, including Psalms 1, 2 and 117 and proverbs. In the anteroom there is a video installation showing a reconstruction of the entire house, so you can get a sense of what the room was like in its original context.

MORE TO SEE

THE HEPHAISTION MOSAIC

This second century BC mosaic in the Museum of Classical Antiquities is a rare example of a signed work—look for the inscription on what appears to be a peeling label, which reads 'Hephaistion Eppoie', meaning 'Hephaistion made this'. Unfortunately, the central area of the mosaic has not survived, but the ornamental bands that frame it are in excellent condition. Wave patterns border a black saw-tooth design, followed by a three-dimensional meander band and creepers filled with butterflies and winged cupids.

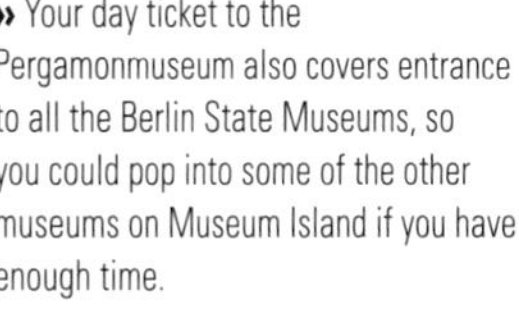

TIP

» Your day ticket to the Pergamonmuseum also covers entrance to all the Berlin State Museums, so you could pop into some of the other museums on Museum Island if you have enough time.

THE XANTEN BOY

Named after the German town of Xanten in Westphalia where it was found, this is an extremely rare example of a bronze statue from the first century AD. Many other bronze pieces made around this time were melted down during preparations for war when metal was in short supply. The Hellenistic tradition of child portrayal was popular with the Romans and it is likely that this statue stood in a Roman villa and performed the service of a dumb waiter, where he would hold a tray during banquets.

THE MEDEA SARCOPHAGUS

Made in Rome between AD140 and 150, the carving on the surface of the sarcophagus tells the grisly story of the princess and sorceress Medea. Medea fell in love with Jason (of Argonauts fame), but he left her to marry Creusa. Spurned, Medea sought revenge by lacing Creusa's dress with poison. The carving shows Creusa with her hair in flames, burning alive from the effects of the poison. Medea, meanwhile, is leaving the scene in a winged chariot, taking the bodies of her and Jason's two dead children with her. Look closely and you can see their tiny limbs sticking out of the side of the carriage.

THE DOMED ROOF FROM THE ALHAMBRA

This intricately carved cedar and poplar dome, dating from the early 14th century, covered one of the towers in the Alhambra, the Moorish palace that overlooks Granada in Spain. The dome has a repeated inscription, which reads 'There is no victor but God'. Sixteen panels radiate from a star set in a polygon at the top of the dome.

THE QIBLA

This turquoise blue Qibla (prayer niche) comes from the Beyhekim mosque in Konya, built in the mid- to late 13th century, and is covered in geometric motifs and the words of the Prophet Mohammed. The technique, known as faience mosaic, is the combined work of calligraphers and expert tile cutters.

Below *Decorated panelling in the Aleppo Room*

INFORMATION

www.potsdamerplatz.de
www.sonycenter.de
www.potsdamer-platz-arkaden.de
71 D4 10785 Berlin (Tiergarten)
U- and S-Bahn Potsdamer Platz
M41, M48, 200, 347

TIPS

» The cafés and restaurants on Potsdamer Platz are a short walk from the Kulturforum, making it the ideal place to wind down after time spent in the museums.

» If you want to change from the U-Bahn to the S-Bahn or vice versa you will need to come up to street level and walk between stations.

» Throughout December there is a Christmas market here, with an outdoor ice-skating rink and stalls selling decorations, gifts, *Glühwein* and *Wurst*.

Above *The stunning steel-and-glass dome of the Sony Center*

POTSDAMER PLATZ

This redeveloped area is constantly expanding, and is rapidly growing into a cultural hotspot and sleek business district. Potsdamer Platz was once the heart of the city, a major crossroads for the traffic of Berlin. The 'Stammbahn' rail route, which passed through the newly built Potsdamer Station towards Potsdam (▷ 228–232), was opened in 1838, and brought the first signs of hustle and bustle to the square. Potsdamer Platz marked the point where five major roads intersected and provided a link between the middle of the city and the developing West. Famous hotels, department stores and restaurants lined the streets, and the area became popular with artists and the politicians and diplomats who were based nearby. A line of metal plaques imbedded in the street paving marks where the Berlin Wall once stood.

REBUILDING

Most of the buildings in Potsdamer Platz were destroyed by bombing raids during World War II and the wall between East and West Berlin ran right through the middle of the square, so that the few buildings that remained standing fell into disrepair. Shiny skyscrapers of big corporations such as Daimler Benz now dominate the skyline, and the square has become a key financial and business district.

THE SONY CENTER

Designed by Helmut Jahn and built between 1996 and 2000, the Sony Center is one of Berlin's greatest architectural attractions. The steel and glass dome measures 4,013sq m (43,195sq ft) and shelters the light, spacious piazza beneath. The fountains and trees at its heart are surrounded by gleaming office buildings, alfresco dining establishments and the glass-fronted Sony Style Store, packed with the latest home entertainment gadgets.

FILM

Movie buffs will find plenty here to keep them occupied. There is a plethora of cinemas to choose from, including two 3D Imax theatres in the Sony Center and an art-house cinema on the ground floor of the Filmhaus, underneath the Berlin Film Museum (Fri–Wed 10–6, Thu 10–8; tel 030 300 9030). The museum, too, is an audiovisual feast; catch the film *Asphalt* by Joe May (1929) in room 4, which re-creates Potsdamer Platz at its prime in the late 1920s. At the heart of the museum is a shrine to the German film star Marlene Dietrich.

REICHSTAG

Walk up Sir Norman Foster's dome, an impressive architectural statement, to get an inside look at the seat of the German Parliament. The original Reichstag was built in 1894 by Paul Wallot as the seat of the German Parliament. An inscription above the wide staircase, cast in bronze in 1916, reads '*Dem Deutschen Volke*', meaning 'To the German People'. The building was damaged by fire on 27 February 1933 and was completely devastated as a result of heavy fighting around the building during World War II. After extensive restoration, the building was handed over to the Federal Administration in 1973, and the first session of the reunified German Parliament was held here on 4 October 1990.

SIR NORMAN FOSTER

In June 1993, the British architect Sir Norman Foster was awarded the commission to restore the Reichstag. Foster preserved the original features and functions of the building, while adding glass walls, a symbol of the transparency of democracy, and a glass roof and chamber that bring light to the heart of the structure. Sections marked by bullet holes and Red Army graffiti have been left exposed in the lobbies and corridors as a reminder of the building's turbulent history.

The new building is self-sustaining and nothing is wasted. The water supply, heating and electricity for the parliament complex is powered by two engines fired by rapeseed oil, a clean and renewable energy source. Any excess heat generated in the summer is stored for the winter in a brine lake 300m (985ft) below ground.

THE DOME

Foster's dome is visible for miles around and has a powerful presence on Berlin's skyline. It has also become a symbol of popular rule, and every day thousands of people climb to the top. Visitors are reflected in the central mirrored funnel as they walk up the gently sloping spiral walkway. From the top you can look down into the chamber, representing open democratic rule. There are information panels around the base of the funnel documenting the history of the Reichstag, and you can walk out of the dome onto the roof terrace to appreciate the view over the city.

The 21m (69ft) flag-like panel in the western hall, called *Black, Red and Gold* (1999), by German artist Gerhard Richter is made from recycled glass.

INFORMATION

www.reichstag.de

71 D3 Platz der Republik, 11011 Berlin (Tiergarten) 030 2273 2152 Daily 8am–midnight, last admission 10pm Free U- and S-Bahn Brandenburger Tor; U-Bahn Bundestag M41, 100, TXL Lectures by prior arrangement

TIPS

» All visitors have to pass through security checks before entering the building, so be prepared to wait.

» An elevator takes you up to the public roof terrace and the base of the dome, but you have to walk up the sloping spiral path to reach the top.

» The Reichstag is open until midnight (last entry at 10), and there are some great night-time views of the city from the viewing gallery.

Below *The glass dome of the Reichstag is a popular sight for visitors*

Clockwise from left to right *Gates and statues herald the main façade of Schloss Charlottenburg; the formal gardens and lawns in the grounds of the palace*

INTRODUCTION

The focus of Berlin's leafy Charlottenburg district, graceful Schloss Charlottenburg is where Prussia's kings and queens had their restful country villa on what was then the city's edge. Its diverse elements combine to create one of Berlin's most memorable sights. Fine furniture and art from the 17th to the 20th centuries fill every room of this extensive palace complex's ornate private apartments of kings and queens, princes and princesses.

The largest palace of Prussia's and later Germany's ruling Hohenzollern royal dynasty started out in 1699 as Lützenburg, a modest summer country retreat for the intellectually inclined Sophie Charlotte of Hannover (1668–1705), the wife of Kurfürst Friedrich III (1657–1713), who in 1701 was crowned as the first 'King in Prussia', Friedrich I. He gave the palace the name Charlottenburg after his wife's death, and he and future Prussian kings, among them Friedrich II the Great (1712–86), and later the German emperors, extended and beautified it. Schloss Charlottenburg was badly damaged in World War II and restored in a long-running post-war saga.

It takes at least a day to see everything in the palace and its extensive garden, the Schlossgarten, behind the palace, and you will still need to be selective if you have a limited amount of time. You can only visit the royal apartments with a guide, but it is worth paying extra to see the lavish private rooms of King Friedrich I and Queen Sophie Charlotte. Round off your visit with a relaxing stroll around the gardens.

The currently homeless Hohenzollernmuseum, the historical collections of the Hohenzollern dynasty, will be established permanently in Schloss Charlottenburg at an as yet undetermined date in the future.

WHAT TO SEE

THE STATE ROOMS AND APARTMENTS

After passing through the guest suite, you come to the Glass Bedchamber of Queen Sophie Charlotte, decorated with alternating strips of mirrored glass and green damask. From the intimate surroundings of the Queen's Apartments you pass into the more formal chambers of King Friedrich I. The tour of the intersecting rooms on the ground floor, from east to west, ends with the Porcelain Cabinet. It once contained 3,000 examples of Chinese and Japanese porcelain dating from the second half of the 17th century, but the room was badly damaged in 1943, and the collection is now made up of pieces acquired after the war, a project that was finally completed in 1993. Thankfully, the lavishness of this room has been preserved.

THE WHITE HALL

The White Hall on the top floor of the Neuer Flügel (New Wing) was Friedrich II the Great's banqueting hall and throne room. The room suffered extensive damage during World War II and was reconstructed using the paintings of Friedrich Wilhelm Höder as a guide. The light-filled hall is lined with arched windows and Corinthian pilasters topped with gold stucco capitals. Originally bright pink, the room has faded to white, and the austere Classicism contrasts with the elaborate flourishes of the Golden Gallery next door.

THE GOLDEN GALLERY

Next to the White Hall is the Golden Gallery, the venue for dancing and musical recitals during Friedrich II the Great's banquets and parties. The gallery is one of the best examples of a rococo banqueting hall in Germany, its long, bright hall lined with floor-to-ceiling windows and console mirrors increasing the sense of space and reflecting the baroque gardens outside. Look for Flora and her entourage above the entablature over the chimney on the west wall and the cheeky cherubs climbing trees along the cornice.

THE WINTER ROOMS

In 1796, King Friedrich William II converted the former First Apartments of Friedrich II the Great into his winter quarters: They all face south, so benefit from sunshine in the winter months, and are one of the few examples of early Prussian Classicism in existence. The rooms were damaged during World War II but the furnishings survived, and in 1983 the interior was re-created from archived documents. The small rooms all have marble heating stoves and patterned inlaid parquet floors made from maple, elm and mahogany. Every room is filled with paintings, furniture, fabrics and tapestries, and all still have their original crystal chandeliers.

The Haute-Lisse rooms, to the right of the staircase, are hung with four tapestries illustrating the life of Don Quixote. Made in Paris, they were presented to Prince Henry, the brother of Friedrich the Great, as a gift from Louis XVI of France.

THE GARDENS

The palace grounds were originally laid out in 1697 in the French baroque formal style, with swirling paths and neatly trimmed hedges. In 1819, Friedrich Wilhelm III employed the landscape architect Peter Joseph Lenné, who had previously designed the gardens of Sanssouci (▷ 229–230) and Potsdam (▷ 228–232). The parallel avenues and large pool flanked with baroque statues near the Altes Schloss have been preserved, but a network of geometric paths beyond the palace was replaced with wider curving footpaths running around the parks edge. Broad lawns and forest areas, akin to those seen in English romantic gardens, replaced the topiary and circular flowerbeds. Today, the palace garden is a peaceful public park, popular with joggers and dog-walkers.

INFORMATION

www.spsg.de
70 a2 ✉ Spandauer Damm 10–22, 14059 Berlin (Charlottenburg)
☎ 030 320910 Altes Schloss Tue–Sun 9–5 (royal apartments on ground floor can be visited only by guided tour, see below); Neuer Flügel Apr–end Oct Tue–Sun 10–5; Nov–end Mar Tue–Sun 11–5; Neuer Pavillon Tue–Sun 10–5; Mausoleum Apr–end Oct Tue–Sun 10–5; Belvedere Apr–end Oct Tue–Fri 12–5, Sat, Sun 10–5, Nov–end Mar Tue–Sun 12–4; Museum für Vor- und Fruhgeschichte Tue–Fri 9–5, Sat, Sun 10–5 Altes Schloss: Adult €10, child (7–14) €7, under 7 free; Neuer Flügel: Adult €6, child €5; Neuer Pavillon: Adult €2, child €1.50; Mausoleum: €1; Belvedere: Adult €2, child €1.50; Schlossgarten: free at the time of writing, but plans for an admission fee have been proposed and widely opposed; Museum für Vor- und Fruhgeschichte: Adult €3, child (16–18) €1.50, under 16 free; combined admission to all State Museums of Berlin museums in Charlottenburg (this does not include Schloss Charlottenburg): Adult €6, child (16–18) €3, under 16 free U-Bahn Sophie-Charlotte-Platz, Richard-Wagner-Platz; S-Bahn Westend M45, 109, 309 Guided tours of the royal apartments in German (information sheets available in other languages, including English), see 'Prices' above; Neuer Flügel admission includes free audioguide
Restaurant in the Kleine Orangerie
Porcelain, posters, postcards, souvenirs, books on Prussian history and the Hohenzollerns

INFORMATION

www.zoo-berlin.de

70 C3 10785 Berlin (Tiergarten) S-Bahn Tiergarten, Bellevue, U- and S-Bahn Brandenburger Tor; U-Bahn Hansaplatz; U- and S-Bahn Potsdamer Platz M41, 100, 106, 187, 200, 347

INTRODUCTION

Berlin's green haven, the city's oldest and largest urban park, has gardens, wooded areas and lakes, and is speckled with sculptures and monuments placed here over the centuries. Established as a royal hunting reserve in 1527 by Kurprinz Joachim der Jüngere, the 'Animal Garden' became a public park in the 18th century. In 1818, landscape architect Peter Joseph Lenné redesigned it in the naturalistic English landscape style. During World War II, the park was chewed up by bombing and ground combat and the post-war years of shortage saw its trees chopped down for firewood.

The Tiergarten's rebirth began in 1949 with new trees being planted. Since then, its monuments have been restored and new ones built, and today the park is a popular refuge for people who want to relax, exercise or picnic. Its 200ha (500 acres) of prime Berlin real estate is divided laterally by the Strasse des 17 Juni. This boulevard intersects other roads at central Grosser Stern, with its towering Siegessäule (Victory Column). A network of footpaths and bicycle routes criss-crosses the park.

WHAT TO SEE

SIEGESSÄULE

www.monument-tales.de

This column, in the middle of the Tiergarten, is at the heart of Berlin. King Wilhelm I ordered the construction of the monument, which originally stood in Platz der Republik, in 1864, following the victory of Prussia and Austria over Denmark. In 1938, it was moved to the Grosser Stern in the Tiergarten to make room for the rebuilding of the city under the Third Reich. The monument survived World War II, and, more recently, has become a popular meeting place during the Berlin Love Parade. The Siegessäule, designed to convey German strength and dominance, is now a symbol of peace and acceptance.

The four sides of the base of the column are decorated with bas-reliefs cast from captured bronze cannons, and illustrate scenes from the Danish–German

War (1864), the Austro-Prussian conflict (1866) and the Franco-Prussian War (1870–1871). The interior walls of the spiralling staircase are covered in graffiti left behind by summer revellers, which will keep you entertained during the strenuous climb to the top. The walls of the column on the first viewing platform are covered in a detailed mosaic showing key events in the creation of the German Empire.

Continue climbing to the top and you will reach the final viewing platform, beneath the gilded angel of Victory, designed by Friedrich Drake in 1870. The main attraction is the 360-degree view. If you look down Strasse des 17 Juni towards Brandenburger Tor (▷ 80), you can see all the way down Unter den Linden, with the Reichstag (▷ 97) on the left and the Fernsehturm (▷ 76) in the distance.

To the north, in a wooded area, is the Schloss Bellevue (not open to the public). Built for Prince Ferdinand of Prussia in 1786, it is now the official residence of the President of the Federal Republic of Germany.

70 B3 Grosser Stern, 10785 Berlin (Tiergarten) 030 391 2961 Apr–end Oct Mon–Fri 9.30–6.30, Sat, Sun 9.30–7; Nov–end Mar Mon–Fri 10–5, Sat, Sun 10–5.30 Adult €2.20, child (12–18) €1.50, under 12 free

ZOO BERLIN

www.zoo-berlin.de

The zoo dates back to 1841, when Friedrich Wilhelm IV, the King of Prussia, donated his pheasant gardens and exotic animal collection to the citizens of Berlin. It suffered serious damage during World War II: After rebuilding, it has developed into one of the most important zoos in the world, with over 14,000 animals and 1,500 species represented.

Moats and trenches rather than bars and cages define the outdoor enclosures, creating a sense of openness and giving visitors a good view of the animals. The hippopotamus house is the most modern in Europe. Completed in 1997, the two glass domes cover the steamy, climate-controlled home of the common and pygmy hippopotamuses. A glass wall in the viewing gallery allows you to watch them swimming under water. The polar bears and seals are also free to swim around in their homes, and the seals even have their own wave machine.

The stars of the zoo are the two giant pandas, Bao Bao the male and Yan Yan the female.

70 A4 Hardenbergplatz 8 and Budapester Strasse 34, 10787 Berlin (Tiergarten) 030 254010 Mid-Mar to mid-Oct daily 9–6.30; mid-Oct to mid-Mar daily 9–5 Adult €12, child (16–18) €9, child (5–15) €6, under 5 free; small family €20, large family €32; combination ticket with Aquarium: Adult €18, child (16–18) €14, child (5–15) €9, under 5 free, small family €30, large family €45; reduced admission after 5.30 Jul to mid-Sep Guide book and plan Restaurant, cafeteria, snack bars Souvenir shop selling posters, postcards and educational toys Pets not allowed

AQUARIUM

www.aquarium-berlin.de

A huge statue of an iguanodon, which became extinct 90 million years ago, guards the entrance here. The aquarium is occupied by a huge variety of fish, frogs, lizards, snakes, crocodiles and turtles from all over the world. The Komodo dragons dominate the reptile area on the second floor. Measuring 3m (10ft) in length, they are the largest lizards in the world and capable of eating prey as large as deer.

70 A4 Budapester Strasse 32, 10787 Berlin (Tiergarten) 030 254010 Daily 9–6 Adult €12, child (16–18) €9, child (5–15) €6, under 5 free; small family €20, large family €32; combination ticket with Zoo: Adult €18, child (16–18) €14, child (5–15) €9, under 5 free, small family €30, large family €45; reduced admission after 5.30 Jul to mid-Sep Cafeteria Souvenir shop

TIPS

» The climb up to the top of the Siegessäule is quite challenging, but there are seats to rest on at regular intervals and it is worth it for the panoramic view of the park at the top.

» The zoo covers a large area, so if you want to see the animals being fed, plan your visit around those times. From April to end September the feeding times are: seals 11, 1.30, 3.15; penguins 1.30; polar bears 10.30; apes 3.30; monkey house 11, 2, 3.30; carnivore house 2.30; pandas 11.30, 3; hippos 2; pelicans 3.30; cormorants 2; crocodiles 3.30 every Mon. Alterations and winter feeding times are posted on notice boards just inside the gates.

» Smoking is forbidden in the animal houses in the zoo.

Clockwise from left to right *Relaxing in the Tiergarten; the gilded bronze statue of* Winged Victory *on the Siegessäule; a mosaic on the first viewing platform of the tower*

BERLIN MITTE

This route takes in all the major sights in Berlin Mitte, from the Brandenburg Gate and the historic Unter den Linden avenue in the west to Alexanderplatz and the towering Fernsehturm around the former heart of the city in the east.

THE WALK
Distance: 5.5km (3.5 miles)
Allow: 1 hour 30 min (not including stops)
Start at/end at: Brandenburger Tor

HOW TO GET THERE
Brandenburger Tor U and S-Bahn stations; buses M85 or 100.

★ With your back to Pariser Platz and the Brandenburg Gate (▷ 80) walk down the left side of Unter den Linden. After 150m (165 yards), pass Hotel Adlon and the Russian embassy on the right. Cross Neustädtische Kirchstrasse. A little farther on, you'll see, on the left, the courtyard of the Staatsbibliothek zu Berlin (Berlin State Library). Just ahead on the left is Humboldt University, and in the middle of the street is the equestrian statue of Frederick the Great (1851). On the opposite side is Bebelplatz.

❶ Bebelplatz was where, on 10 May 1933, the group 'Action Against the Non-German Spirit' burned piles of books and journals by authors on Hitler's 'black list'.

Another 50m (55 yards) down Unter den Linden is the Neue Wache (New Guardhouse).

❷ The Neue Wache was built between 1816 and 1818. A large sculpture by Käthe Kollwitz (1867–1945) in the middle is a memorial to the victims of war and tyranny.

Cross Hinter dem Giesshaus, passing the Zeughaus (Arsenal) on the left, now the Deutsches Historisches Museum.

❸ The Arsenal was designed in 1706 by Johann Arnold Nering. The exhibits in the square, baroque-style building provide insights into the country's turbulent past.

Unter den Linden now becomes Schinkelallee, which takes you over the River Spree. Continue ahead, keeping Museum Island and the Berliner Dom (▷ 78) on the left. Pass over the Liebknecht bridge and cross to the right-hand side of the road to the Marx-Engels-Forum.

❹ The sculpture group by Ludwig Engelhart of Karl Marx and Friedrich Engels, was placed in the square in 1986.

Face the Fernsehturm (TV Tower, ▷ 76). Cross Spandauer Strasse, walk past the Neptunbrunnen (Neptune Fountain) and around to the main entrance of the Fernsehturm. This is a good place to stop for a break. Go back south, re-crossing Spandauer Strasse at the crossing nearest the Rotes Rathaus. Turn left, with the arcades on the right. At Am Nussbaum turn right into the pedestrian-only Nikolaiviertel (▷ 88). Walk towards Nikolaikirche.

❺ From the Nikolaikirche, turn right

onto Propstrasse and walk west. Continue towards the River Spree until you reach the equestrian statue of St. George slaying the dragon. At the river turn right and walk down Spree Ufer towards the Berliner Dom. Head northwest along the river, turn left onto Rathausstrasse and cross the bridge.

6 The Palast der Republik, seat of the GDR's parliament, once stood here. The site will remain empty, pending the reconstruction of the Berliner Stadtschloss, the old imperial palace, which was damaged in World War II and knocked down by the Communist authorities.

Walk west towards the red-brick twin towers of the Friedrichswerdersche Kirche, crossing Breite Strasse. On the right is the Bauakademie monument. Next to this is the Friedrichswerdersche Kirche.

7 The Friedrichswerdersche Kirche, designed by Friedrich Schinkel and built between 1824 and 1830, was the first neo-Gothic church in Berlin.

Proceed along Werderscher Markt. The Hedwigskirche is on the right.

8 Berlin's Catholic cathedral, St. Hedwigs-Kathedrale, was consecrated in 1773. It was rebuilt after damage during World War II.

Head back onto Werderstrasse on the right; this becomes Französische Strasse. Continue along here for a little more than 150m (165 yards) and then turn left into Markgrafenstrasse and cross over into the square known as Gendarmenmarkt (▷ 81). From the Schinkel monument in the middle, walk northwest, leaving the square between the Konzerthaus (Concert Hall) and the Französische Dom. Turn right on to Charlottenstrasse. Cross over to the other side of the road and walk until the road rejoins Französische Strasse. Turn left and keep going as far as the traffic lights. You can end the walk here, at the Französische Strasse U-Bahn station. Alternatively, turn right into Friedrichstrasse, which leads back to Unter den Linden and the Brandenburg Gate.

WHEN TO GO

This walk can be done any time of day, all year round.

PLACES TO VISIT

DEUTSCHES HISTORISCHES MUSEUM

www.dhm.de
✉ Unter den Linden 2, 10117 Berlin (Mitte) ☎ 030 203040 ⌚ Daily 10–6 Adult €5, child (under 18) free U- and S-Bahn Friedrichstrasse 🚌 100, 200, TXL. Tram M1, 12

FRIEDRICHSWERDERSCHE KIRCHE-SCHINKELMUSEUM

✉ Werderscher Markt, 10117 Berlin (Mitte) ☎ 030 208 1323 ⌚ Daily 10–6 Free Hausvogteiplatz 🚌 100, 147, 200, TXL

ST. HEDWIGS-KATHEDRALE

www.hedwigs-kathedrale.de
✉ Bebelplatz, 10117 Berlin (Mitte) ☎ 030 203 4810 ⌚ Mon–Sat 10–5, Sun 1–5 Free U-Bahn Hausvogteiplatz, Französische Strasse; U- and S-Bahn Brandenburger Tor 🚌 100, 147, 200, TXL

WHERE TO EAT

At the top of the Fernsehturm is the Telecafé, where you can enjoy a snack or a light meal and take in the view in the revolving restaurant (Fernsehturm Alexanderplatz, Panoramastrasse 1A, 10178 Berlin (Mitte) tel 030 242 3333). The ice-cream sundaes, and coffee and cake selections are particularly good. Café Einstein (▷ 113) on Unter den Linden is something of a German institution and a great place for a snack. Sit back and enjoy a coffee or tea and—to revitalize yourself on a cold, wet day—warm apple strudel with vanilla sauce.

Opposite *The Fernsehturm dominates the skyline*

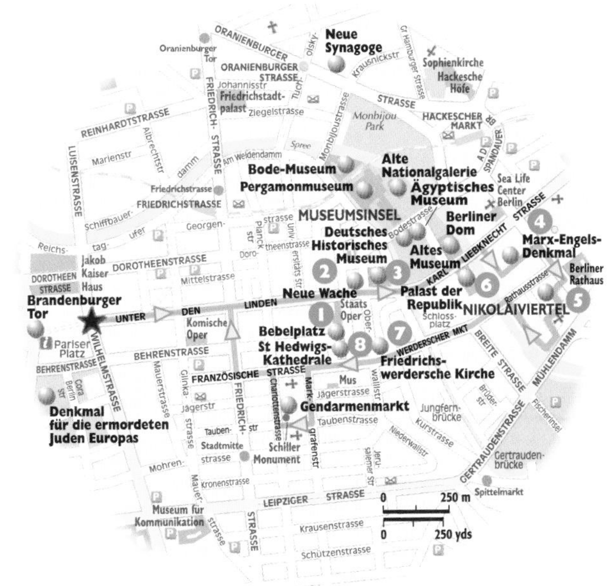

THROUGH THE TIERGARTEN

Heading west along the north side of Berlin's large central park (▷ 100–101), then back east along the south side, this largely traffic-free walk allows you to enjoy the Tiergarten purely as a park while taking in its highlights along the way.

THE WALK
Distance: 7km (4.5 miles)
Allow: 2 hours (not including stops)
Start/end: Brandenburger Tor

HOW TO GET THERE
Brandenburger Tor U- and S-Bahn stations; buses M85 or 100.

★ Standing in Platz des 18 März and facing west from the Brandenburger Tor (▷ 80), you are looking down a long boulevard, Strasse des 17 Juni, that bisects the Tiergarten from east to west. Go north on Ebertstrasse and left on Scheidemannstrasse.

❶ The Reichstag (▷ 97), Germany's historic parliament building, has a modern glass dome designed by British architect Sir Norman Foster.

Go left into the Tiergarten, towards the point where Strasse des 17 Juni joins Yitzhak-Rabin-Strasse.

❷ The Sowjetisches Ehrenmal (Soviet Memorial), surmounted by a colossal bronze statue of a Red Army infantryman, and 'guarded' by a pair each of artillery pieces and T-34 tanks, is a tribute to the Russian soldiers who died in the Battle of Berlin in April and May 1945.

Cross Yitzhak-Rabin-Strasse and go northwest through the trees back to Scheidemannstrasse and its continuation which turns into John-Foster-Dulles-Allee.

❸ The Haus der Kulturen der Welt (House of World Cultures) is a multi-purpose cultural space. Note the Henry Moore sculpture *Large Divided Oval: Butterfly* (1986) in the pond at the front.

John-Foster-Dulles-Allee now skirts the south bank of the Spree, passing a playground on Grossfürstenplatz. Continue west to Spreeweg.

❹ Schloss Bellevue (▷ 101), a neoclassical palace that's the official residence of Germany's federal president, occupies a handsome location along the Spree. Behind the palace are the green spaces of Schlosspark Bellevue and the Englischer Garten (English Garden).

You pass the presidency's administrative building, the Bundespräsidialamt, on the way to Grosser Stern.

❺ The Siegessäule (Victory Column) occupies the middle of this large

Above *People enjoying the sunshine and shade in the Tiergarten*

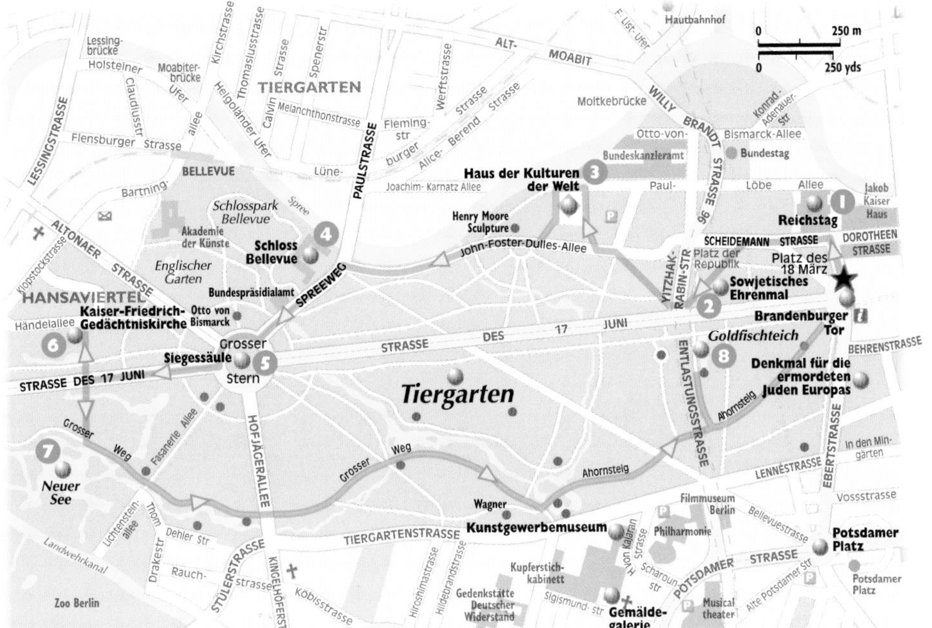

roundabout (traffic circle), which is the Tiergarten's focal point. You can climb the column's interior steps for a fine outlook on the Tiergarten from the viewing platform. Across on the north side of Grosser Stern (Large Star) is an austere sculpture (1901) of Otto von Bismarck (1815–98), the 'Iron Chancellor', who orchestrated the unification of Germany under Prussian leadership.

Go west on Strasse des 17 Juni to the Fauler See, a small lake, and then follow the path north through the trees.

❻ The neo-Gothic Kaiser-Friedrich-Gedächtniskirche (1895), with its entrance on Handelsallee, is dedicated to the memory of Kaiser Friedrich III (1831–88).

Return to Strasse des 17 Juni and the cross to the south side of the street.

❼ The Neuer See is the park's largest lake. Between the lake and Grosser Stern is a series of sculptures on hunting themes.

Go east on Grosser Weg, a pathway that skirts the park's southern edge and passes a sculpture (1903) of composer Richard Wagner (1813–83). The pathway becomes Ahornsteig and crosses a small island, Luiseninsel, on which stand monuments to the much-loved Queen Luise of Prussia (1776–1810) and to Crown Prince Wilhelm (1882–1951).

Cross Yitzhak-Rabin-Strasse.

❽ The tree-shaded Goldfischteich (Goldfish Pond) is the final body of water in this stretch of the park.

A continuation of Ahornsteig leads back to the Brandenburger Tor, passing a sculpture (1870) of Johann Wolfgang von Goethe (1749–1832).

WHEN TO GO

You can do this walk at any time during daylight hours.

PLACES TO VISIT

BRANDENBURGER TOR

Pariser Platz 1, 10117 Berlin (Mitte) 030 2026 9128 Permanently Free U- and S-Bahn Brandenburger Tor M85, 100

REICHSTAG

www.reichstag.de
Platz der Republik 1, 11011 Berlin (Tiergarten) 030 2273 2152 Daily 8am–midnight (last admission 10pm) Free U- and S-Bahn Brandenburger Tor M85, 100

SIEGESSÄULE

www.monument-tales.de
Grosser Stern, 10785 Berlin (Tiergarten) 030 391 2961 Apr–end Oct Mon–Fri 9.30–6.30, Sat, Sun 9.30–7; Nov–end Mar Mon–Fri 10–5, Sat, Sun 10–5.30 Adult €2.20, child (12–18) €1.50, under 12 free U-Bahn Hansaplatz 100, 106, 187

WHERE TO EAT

A Bavarian-style Biergarten, the lakeside Café am Neuen See is a people-magnet in good weather (Liechtenstein Allee 2, 10787 Berlin (Tiergarten, tel 030 254 4930). The rooftop Käfer Dachgarten is a chic restaurant inside the Reichstag where the politicos hang out (Platz der Republik 1, 11011 Berlin (Tiergarten), tel 030 2262 9935).

Above *The book department in the Kaufhaus des Westens*

SHOPPING

ERZGEBIRGISCHER FACHHANDELS RASCHKE

www.erzgebirge-berlin.de

If you miss out on Berlin's Christmas markets (▷ 111), you can still find traditional wooden, handmade Christmas decorations in this magical shop, which is stuffed from floor to ceiling with painted wooden toys, figurines, advent carousels and armies of wooden soldiers. Children will love coming here.

✉ Neuer Hackescher Markt, Dircksenstrasse 50, 10178 Berlin (Mitte) ☎ 030 2838 8010 🕒 Mon–Fri 11–7, Sat 11–4 Ⓢ S-Bahn Hackescher Markt 🚌 Tram M1, M4, M5

FASSBENDER & RAUSCH

www.fassbender-rausch.de

Founded in the 19th century, this luxury chocolate shop and confectioners near the Gendarmenmarkt (▷ 81) is always busy. If you can't decide what to buy, treat yourself to their delicate truffles and chocolate cake.

✉ Charlottenstrasse 60, (corner of Mohrenstrasse), 10117 Berlin (Mitte) ☎ 030 2045 8443 🕒 Mon–Sat 10–8, Sun 11–8 Ⓤ U-Bahn Stadtmitte 🚌 M48, 147, 347 ☕

GALERIES LAFAYETTE

www.lafayette-berlin.de
www.galerieslafayette.de

This glass-roofed shopping arcade dominates the stylish shopping district of Friedrichstrasse. Every exclusive item you desire is here, from designer shoes to fine porcelain. In the delicatessen you can sip champagne, sample exquisite pastries and track down some of the smelliest French cheese in the city.

✉ Friedrichstrasse 76–78, 10117 Berlin (Mitte) ☎ 030 209480 🕒 Mon–Sat 10–8 Ⓤ U-Bahn Französische Strasse 🚌 147

KADEWE—KAUFHAUS DES WESTENS

www.kadewe.de

KaDeWe is the largest department store in mainland Europe. This consumer paradise is spread over eight floors. Its legendary delicatessen is popular with visitors and locals alike, who are attracted by the feast of luxury chocolates, vintage wines and spirits and the variety of the gourmet ingredients. Exhibitions, fashion shows and book signings are regular occurrences. There is a great view across the rooftops of the Kurfürstendamm from the top-floor café when you are all shopped-out.

✉ Tauenzienstrasse 21–24, 10789 Berlin (Schöneberg) ☎ 030 21210 🕒 Mon–Fri 10–8, Sat 9.30–8 Ⓤ U-Bahn Wittenbergplatz 🚌 M19, M29, M46 ☕

MARKT AM WINTERFELDPLATZ

www.winterfeldt-platz.de

This bustling market attracts a diverse crowd in search of organic fruit and vegetables, freshly baked wholemeal bread and freshly squeezed juices. There are clothes and craft stands, but the highlights are the delicatessen stands.

✉ Winterfeldtplatz, 10781 Berlin (Schöneberg) 🕒 Wed 8–1 or 2, Sat 8–4 Ⓤ U-Bahn Nollendorfplatz 🚌 M29, 171, 194

SCHÖNUNDGUT

www.post-art.de

This shop has a huge range of unusual postcards and cards. There is also an entertaining and kitsch collection of gifts, trinkets and accessories, such as souvenirs bearing the green and red 'Ampelmann' logo, the cult

hat-wearing celebrity from Berlin's pedestrian crossings.
✉ Prenzlauer Allee 225, 10405 Berlin (Prenzlauer Berg) ☎ 030 4171 4684 ⊙ Mon–Fri 12–8, Sat 12–10, Sun 2–7 Ⓤ U-Bahn Senefelderplatz 🚌 Tram M2

SERGEANT PEPPERS
www.sgt-peppers-berlin.de
Sergeant Peppers, in the funky Kastanienallee shopping street, is the place to shop for authentic 1960s clothing. It has an excellent selection of original antique clothing for men and women.
✉ Kastanienallee 91–92, 10435 Berlin (Prenzlauer Berg) ☎ 030 448 1121 ⊙ Mon–Fri 11–8, Sat 11–6 Ⓤ U-Bahn Eberswalder Strasse 🚌 Tram M1, M10, 12

TÜRKISCHER BASAR
The Turkish Bazaar, popular since the 1970s, is the liveliest and cheapest market in Berlin. It is a great place to sample Turkish cuisine, soak up exotic sights and smells, and get a genuine feel for Berlin's multicultural way of life.
✉ Maybachufer, 12047 Berlin (Neukölln) ⊙ Tue, Fri 12–6.30 Ⓤ U-Bahn Schönleinstrasse 🚌 140

ENTERTAINMENT AND NIGHTLIFE

ARSENAL
www.fdk-berlin.de
This art-house cinema screens films by up-and-coming German directors during the Berlin International Film Festival (▷ 111). For the rest of the year, its shows classic films, historical documentaries and cinematic lectures.
✉ Potsdamer Strasse 2, 10785 Berlin (Tiergarten) ☎ 030 2695 5100 ⊙ Performance times vary: Mon–Fri from 7pm, Sat, Sun from 4pm ✋ Adult €8, child (under 12) €4 Ⓤ U- and S-Bahn Potsdamer Platz 🚌 M41, M48, 200, 347

BAR AM LÜTZOWPLATZ
www.baramluetzowplatz.com
Designed by architect Jürgen Sawade, this sophisticated cocktail bar is one of the largest in Berlin and boasts 126 different varieties of champagne. Happy hour attracts many of Berlin's business types seeking a tipple in stylish surroundings after work. The bartenders have made serving drinks an art form.
✉ Lützowplatz 7, 10785 Berlin (Tiergarten) ☎ 030 262 6807 ⊙ Daily 2pm–4am. Happy hour: 2pm–9pm Ⓤ U-Bahn Nollendorfplatz 🚌 M29, 100, 106, 187

BERLINER ENSEMBLE
www.berliner-ensemble.de
In 1952, this theatre became the home of the Berliner Ensemble, founded by Bertolt Brecht and Helene Weigel in the late 1940s. It focuses on the works of Brecht, William Shakespeare and Austrian playwrights. There are also film screenings and exhibitions.
✉ Theater am Schiffbauerdamm, Bertolt-Brecht-Platz 1, 10117 Berlin (Mitte) ☎ 030 2480 8155 ⊙ Mon–Fri 8–6, Sat, Sun and holidays 11–6 ✋ €6–€30 Ⓤ U- and S-Bahn Friedrichstrasse 🚌 147. Tram M1, 12

B-FLAT
www.b-flat-berlin.de
This club was founded in 1995 by two musicians, Jannis and Thannasis Zotos, and by the actor Andre Hennicke. It is in the heart of the city and has acoustic music and jazz. Drinks are cheaper before 10pm, and happy hour is between 1am and 2am. There are open-mike sessions on Wednesday nights; the club screens art-house films and shorts on Thursday; and Sunday night from 10pm is 'Tango Time'. The live music schedules change weekly.
✉ Rosenthaler Strasse 13, 10119 Berlin (Mitte) ☎ 030 283 3123 ⊙ Sun–Thu from 8pm, Fri, Sat from 9pm ✋ €4–€5; free Wed–Thu Ⓤ U-Bahn Weinmeisterstrasse, Rosenthaler Platz 🚌 240. Tram M1

CINEMAXX
www.cinemaxx.de
A modern mutiplex showing a selection of the latest film releases in their original version. As it is easy to end up in the wrong screening, make sure you get the 'OV—Originalversion' (original version) ticket for your film, and check it and the screen number carefully. There is a café and a bar.
✉ Potsdamer Strasse 5, 10785 Berlin (Tiergarten) ☎ 01805 2463 6299 ⊙ Daily; performance times vary ✋ Varies depending on the day: Adult €5–€7.50, child (under 12) €4.50, student and school student €5–€6, family (Sun only) €4.50 per person; supple supplement for special seats Ⓤ U- and S-Bahn Potsdamer Platz 🚌 M41, M48, 200, 347

DEUTSCHE OPER BERLIN
www.deutscheoperberlin.de
www.staatsballett-berlin.de
The Deutsche Oper company has been staging classical and modern opera and ballet, plus symphony and chamber concerts, since 1912. Performances since World War II have been held in Fritz Bornemann's contemporary glass-fronted building. Even in the cheap seats you get a great view of the stage and can appreciate the fantastic acoustics.
✉ Bismarckstrasse 35, 10627 Berlin (Charlottenburg) ☎ 030 3438 4343 (Deutsche Oper); 030 2035 4555 (Staatsballett Berlin) ⊙ Mon–Sat 11–1 hour before performance, Sun 10–2 and 1 hour before performance ✋ €10–€115 Ⓤ U-Bahn Deutsche Oper, Bismarckstrasse 🚌 101, 109

FRIEDRICHSTADTPALAST
www.friedrichstadtpalast.de
This is Berlin's largest cabaret theatre and the largest costume revue venue in Europe. The show is a fantastic glitzy spectacle of dance, circus, music and chorus. The theatre has its own troupe of 66 dancers, plus an orchestra.
✉ Friedrichstrasse 107, 10117 Berlin (Mitte) ☎ 030 2326 2326 ⊙ Ticket hotline: Mon 10–6, Tue–Sat 10–7, Sun 10–6, and 1 hour before evening performances; main revue: Tue–Fri 8, Sat 4, 8, Sun 4 ✋ €17–€70 Ⓤ U-Bahn Oranienburger Tor; U- and S-Bahn Friedrichstrasse 🚌 147. Tram M1, 12

HAVANNA
www.havanna-berlin.de
This welcoming Latin club in Schöneberg has three floors, and

you can dance the night away to salsa, merengue, bachata, funk and soul. They also hold dance classes.
✉ Hauptstrasse 30, 10827 Berlin (Schöneberg) ☎ 030 784 8565 ⏲ Fri, Sat from 10pm, Wed from 9pm ✋ €3–€7.50 🚇 U-Bahn Kleistpark; S-Bahn Schöneberg 🚌 M48, M85, 104, 106, 187

MAXIM GORKI THEATER

www.gorki.de

Completed in 1827, this former singing academy, with its beautiful classical façade, has been a theatre since 1952. The main theatre stages plays by contemporary dramatists and classical German playwrights, while experimental theatre and performance art is held at the Gorki Studio.
✉ Am Festungsgraben 2, 10117 Berlin (Mitte) ☎ 030 2022 1115 (box office) ⏲ Mon–Sat 12–6.30 and 1 hour before performance, Sun and holidays 4–6.30 ✋ €10–€30 🚇 U- and S-Bahn Friedrichstrasse 🚌 147. Tram M1, 12

PHILHARMONIE

www.berliner-philharmoniker.de

Hans Scharoun's eye-catching yellow building was built between 1960 and 1963. The Philharmonie is now home to the Berlin Philharmonic Orchestra, and plays host to classical and modern orchestral concerts, chamber music and solo performances.
✉ Herbert-von-Karajan-Strasse 1, 10785 Berlin (Tiergarten) ☎ 030 2548 8999 ⏲ Mon–Fri 3–6, Sat, Sun and holidays 11–2 ✋ €8–€138 🚇 U- and S-Bahn Potsdamer Platz 🚌 200, 347

PONY BAR

www.pony-bar.de

Pony Bar is the brainchild of a couple of once unemployed architecture students. They have completely transformed this bar in Mitte, creating a postmodern 1970s-to-1980s-inspired interior with floral tablecloths and funky lamps.
✉ Alte Schönhauser Strasse 44, 10119 Berlin (Mitte) ☎ 0163 775 6603 ⏲ Mon–Sat from noon, Sun from 6pm 🚇 U-Bahn Rosa-Luxemburg-Platz, Weinmeisterstrasse 🚌 M1

SO 36

www.so36.de

Besides the regular weekly line-up of club nights—techno, Asian vibes, 1980s revival, hip-hop and house—this club also plays host to ska, rock, new metal and punk bands. Up-and-coming German bands make their mark here, as well as a few headline acts.
✉ Oranienstrasse 190, 10999 Berlin (Kreuzberg) ☎ 030 6140 1306 ⏲ Concerts from 8pm; party nights from 11pm; special events from 5pm (7pm in summer) ✋ Concerts: €10–€25; other events €3–€8 🚇 U-Bahn Kottbusser Tor, Görlitzer Bahnhof 🚌 M29, 140

ZAPATA

www.cafe-zapata.de

This chilled-out café by day and offbeat bar and music venue by night attracts hundreds of people to listen to experimental DJs or up-and-coming live music acts. It is decorated with barbed wire, tins and artworks made from recycled materials. They serve a wide selection of beers, and a beer garden open in the summer.
✉ Oranienburger Strasse 54 (in Tacheles art gallery), 10117 Berlin (Mitte) ☎ 030 281 6109 ⏲ Daily noon–late 🚇 U-Bahn Oranienburger Tor; S-Bahn Oranienburger Strasse 🚌 147, N6. Tram M1, M6

SPORTS AND ACTIVITIES

ALBA BERLIN

www.albaberlin.de

The Albatrosses won the German basketball championships seven times running up to 2003. If you fancy checking out their skills, head for O2 World, one of the best sports venues in the city.
✉ Stadium: O2 World, Helene-Ernst-Strasse, 10243 Berlin (Friedrichshain). ☎ 030 300 9050 (club); 030 971 8400 (stadium) ⏲ One mid-week and one weekend match per week year round ✋ €7.50–€32 🚇 U- and S-Bahn Warschauer Strasse; S-Bahn Ostbahnhof 🚌 240, 347. Tram M10, M13

CALL-A-BIKE

www.callabike.de

If you have a mobile phone and fancy renting a bicycle to explore the city, you can hop on one of the red-and-white high-tech bicycles distributed around the city. Deutsche Bahn's fleet of 2,000 bicycles are found near S-Bahn and long-distance train stations, and at major crossroads. You need to register by ringing Call-a-Bike's hotline, giving them your credit card details or bank account number. Then call the number in the red circle on the cover of the lock of the bicycle you want to rent, and you will be given a code to unlock it. Once you have finished pedalling, return the bicycle to any major crossing and lock it to a fixed object such as a traffic sign or one of the stands provided. Open the protective cover of the lock and a message will appear in the electronic display reading 'Rückgabe Ja/Nein' ('Return Yes/No'). Press 'Ja' to return the bike and you will be given a receipt code. Dial the number circled in red on the cover of the lock again, and give Call-a-Bike the receipt code and the location of the bicycle (the names of both roads at the crossing). Your credit card or bank account will then be charged for the amount of time you used the bicycle.
☎ 0700 0522 5522 ✋ 8¢ a minute, €15 per day

EISBÄREN BERLIN

www.eisbaeren.de

Ice hockey is very popular in Germany and is a big-money sport. Berlin 'Polar Bears', one of 15 Deutsche Eishockey-Liga clubs, won the league for the second time in a row in 2006. They play their home games through the winter at the new O2 World stadium
✉ Stadium: O2 World, Helene-Ernst-Strasse, 10243 Berlin (Friedrichshain) Club: Friedrichstrasse 76, 10117 Berlin (Mitte) ☎ 030 971 8400 ⏲ Jan–end Mar, Fri, Sat or Sun evenings ✋ Adult €15–€30, senior and other concessions €8–€30, child (6–12) €5–€30, under 6 free–€30 🚇 U- and S-Bahn Warschauer Strasse; S-Bahn Ostbahnhof 🚌 240, 347. Tram M10, M13

HERTHA BSC

www.herthabsc.de

Berlin's largest soccer club has moved away from its past, which was dogged by allegations of bribery and match fixing. The club battled back from bankruptcy in 1994 with the aid of media giant UFA, and the team are now fighting to stay at the top end of the Bundesliga table. Hertha has had a good run in the European Champions League and has moved to the renovated stadium of the Olympiastadion complex, which was completed in time for the 2006 soccer World Cup.

Olympiastadion, Olympischer Platz 3, 14053 Berlin (Charlottenburg) Ticket hotline 01805 189200 Alternate Sats during the season (Aug to mid-May) €7.50–€60 U-Bahn Olympia-Stadion; S-Bahn Olympiastadion (two separate stations) M49, X34, X49, 218

RBB LAUFBEWEGUNG

www.rbb-laufbewegung.de

Run with the crowd and participate in this weekly communal event. This is the largest running and walking club in Berlin, and meets every Saturday at 2pm at the Siegessäule. Yellow-clad crew members are on hand to guide runners on a circuit of the Tiergarten. Whether you are old or young, training for a marathon or a complete beginner, there is a time and pace to suit you.

RBB-Laufbewegung, 14046 Berlin Every Sat at 2 Free U-Bahn Hansaplatz; S-Bahn Bellevue, Tiergarten 100, 106, 187, 343

STERN- UND KREISSCHIFFAHRT

www.sternundkreis.de

Berlin is intersected by the River Spree and crisscrossed with a network of canals, so there are plenty of opportunities to view the city from the water. Take in the contrasting historic and modern sights on a boat trip from Treptow to Charlottenburg, or explore the heart of Berlin on a one-hour boat tour with commentaries in German and English departing from/to Nikolaiviertel. Alternatively, join one of the short tours of the River Spree and Landwehr canal that leave every half hour from Jannowitzbrücke.

Puschkinallee 15, 12435 Berlin (Treptow) 030 536 3600 Historical City Tour: mid-Mar to end Oct, departures range from 5 daily in low season to 14 daily in high season Adult €9.50, child (6–14) €4.75, under 6 free S-Bahn Treptower Park 104, 147, 166, 167, 194, 265

STRANDBAD MÜGGELSEE

You can wallow and splash to your heart's content in this open-air bathing area on the Müggelsee, Berlin's largest natural lake (20ha/50 acres). There are sandy beaches to lie on, footpaths to explore and sports facilities to make use of, and you can have a sauna.

Fürstenwalder Damm 838, 12589 Berlin (Köpenick) 030 648 7777 Mid-May to mid-Sep daily 9–6 Free S-Bahn Rahnsdorf Tram 61

TRABRENNBAHN MARIENDORF

www.berlintrab.de

The betting is fast-paced and the tension high during trotting meetings at the Mariendorf Derby Course. Ladies and gents come out in their hats on summer weekends, while on Fridays entry is free and things are more relaxed.

Mariendorfer Damm 222–298, 12107 Berlin (Mariendorf) 030 740 1212 Competition days vary from week to week: Mon 6pm, Fri 1pm, Sat 1pm, 8pm, Sun 1pm Adult €2.50, child (under 14) free S-Bahn Marienfelde M76, X76, 179

HEALTH AND BEAUTY

THERMEN AM EUROPA-CENTER

www.thermen-berlin.de

Indulge in cosmetic treatments or a massage, and enjoy the warm salt springs and chlorine-free rooftop pool of the Europa Center in the west of town. With aqua aerobics, Jacuzzis, saunas, steam rooms, solariums and mud baths, there is all you need here to help you relax.

Nürnberger Strasse 7, 10787 Berlin (Charlottenburg) 030 257 5760 Mon–Sat 10am–midnight, Sun 10–9 Multi-hour and day ticket €14–€29.80, family €15–€50, massage €21–€109 U-Bahn Wittenbergplatz, Kurfürstendamm M19, M29, M46, 100, 200

FOR CHILDREN

KINDERTHEATER CHARLOTTCHEN

www.charlottchen-berlin.de

While parents sip coffee or enjoy lunch in blessed tranquillity at the restaurant attached to this theatre, their children can be culturally improved in an adjacent room at performances of theatre and puppet theatre, and by clowns, magicians, and more. In addition, children

Left *Shelves of neatly stored ties for sale in a store on Kurfürstendamm*

can celebrate their birthday in the restaurant, let off steam in the play room, and take in a kid's film at the children's cinema.
✉ Droysenstrasse 1, 60129 Berlin (Charlottenburg) ☎ 030 324 4717
🕘 Restaurant: daily from 10am; children's theatre: Mon–Fri from 3pm, Sat, Sun from 10am 🎫 Adult €5, child (4–15) €4 🚇 S-Bahn Charlottenburg; U-Bahn Adenauer Platz, Wilmersdorfer Strasse 🚌 109, 309

MUSEUM FÜR NATURKUNDE

www.museum.hu-berlin.de

Pick up a free audioguide and explore the 6,000sq m (64,500sq ft) of this natural history museum, filled with geology, palaeontology and zoology exhibits. Get close to the largest assembled skeleton of a brachiosaurus in the world and Germany's biggest collection of meteorites.
✉ Invalidenstrasse 43, 10115 Berlin (Mitte) ☎ 030 2093 8591 🕘 Tue–Fri 9.30–5, Sat, Sun and holidays 10–6 🎫 Adult €5, child (6–18) €3, under 6 free, family €10
🚇 U-Bahn Zinnowitzer Strasse 🚌 120, 123, 240, 245. Tram M6, M8, 12 🍴

SEA LIFE BERLIN AND AQUADOM

www.sealifeeurope.com

Berlin's Sea Life Center has an extra fascination to go along with its 4,000 sharks, rays, sea horses and other denizens of the deep. It shares the DomAquarée complex with the Radisson SAS Berlin and the hotel's fabulous lobby AquaDom. This cylindrical acrylic glass tank is 14m (45ft) tall and holds 2,600 tropical fish representing 56 species. An elevator goes up and down through the middle of the tank.
✉ Spandauer Strasse 3, 10178 Berlin (Mitte) ☎ 030 992800 🕘 Apr–end Jul daily 9–7; Aug–end Mar daily 9–6 🎫 Adult €15.95, senior €14.95, child (3–14) €11.50, under 3 free 🚇 S-Bahn Hackescher Markt 🚌 M48, 100, 200, 248, TXL. Tram M4, M5, M6

ZEISS GROSSPLANETARIUM

www.astw.de

The shows in the auditorium transport you into space. Learn more about astronomy, from ancient interpretations of the heavens to modern theories of the origins of the earth.
✉ Prenzlauer Allee 80, 10405 Berlin (Prenzlauer Berg) ☎ 030 4218 4512
🕘 Shows: Mon–Fri 9.30am, 11am (also afternoon shows Wed, Sat, Sun) 🎫 Adult €5, child (6–16) €4, family €15 🚇 S-Bahn Prenzlauer Allee 🚌 156. Tram M2

ZOO BERLIN AND AQUARIUM

▷ 101.

Above *The neon lights of the Sony Center, on Potsdamer Platz, inviting visitors inside*

FESTIVALS AND EVENTS

JANUARY/AUGUST

LANGE NACHT DER MUSEEN

www.lange-nacht-der-museen.de

More than 100 museums stay open until midnight. Accompanying events include concerts, readings, lectures, theatre and parties.

☎ 030 2474 9888 ⊙ Late January and late August

FEBRUARY

INTERNATIONALE FILMFESTSPIELE BERLIN

www.berlinale.de

Two weeks of classic films, lectures, previews and directorial debuts are held around the Filmhaus (▷ 96) in Potsdamer Platz and in various other city cinemas.

☎ 030 259200 ⊙ Early to mid-February

MAY

KARNEVAL DER KULTUREN

www.karneval-berlin.de

This three-day festival in Kreuzberg celebrates the city's multicultural character. Enjoy the parades, singing and dancing.

☎ 030 6097 7022 ⊙ Late May (Whitsun)

JUNE

LESBIAN & GAY CITY-FESTIVAL

www.csd-berlin.de

The lesbian & gay pride week takes place every year at the end of June around Nollendorfplatz. The carnival spreads down Motzstrasse, Fuggerstrasse, Kalkreutstrasse and Eisenacher Strasse, and the party culminates with the CSD: Christopher Street Day gay and lesbian parade.

☎ 030 2362 8632 ⊙ One week in late June

AUGUST

LANGE NACHT DER MUSEEN

www.lange-nacht-der-museen.de

See January, above. The same events take place.

⊙ Late August

SEPTEMBER

BERLIN MARATHON

www.berlin-marathon.com

More than 40,000 runners, wheelchair competitors and power walkers from 100 countries take part in the Berlin Marathon which starts and finishes near the Brandenburg Gate, the Federal Chancellery and the Reichstag, and passes many of Berlin's major sights. An in-line skating marathon is held around the course on the Saturday before the main Sunday marathon.

☎ 030 3012 8810 ⊙ Late September

U-and S-Bahn randenburger Tor

MUSIKFEST BERLIN

www.berlinerfestspiele.de

Part of the Berliner Festspiele series of events, the Musikfest brings multiple top orchestras and soloists from around Germany and the world to Berlin's concert halls, for a veritable feast of classical music.

☎ 030 254890 ⊙ From early to late September

OCTOBER

ART FORUM BERLIN

www.art-forum-berlin.de

This contemporary art fair at the Berlin Exhibition Grounds showcases the work of young and experimental artists from around the world.

☎ 030 3038 2066 ⊙ First week of October S-Bahn Messe Nord/ICC, Messe-Süd; U-Bahn Theodor-Heuss-Platz

X34, X49, M49, 104, 139, 218, 349

NOVEMBER

JAZZFEST BERLIN

www.berlinerfestspiele.de

This annual three-day jazz festival attracts artists from all over the world and takes place at various venues across the city.

☎ 030 254890 ⊙ Early November

NOVEMBER/DECEMBER

CHRISTMAS MARKETS

www.weihnachtsmarkt-deutschland.de/berlin.html

During the month before Christmas, Berlin's squares are filled with fairground rides and market stands selling traditional Christmas decorations and Glühwein (warm spiced wine). The largest Christmas market in Europe is in Altstadt Spandau, while the market around the Gedächtniskirche is great for an evening stroll. Alexanderplatz has a fairy-tale market selling sweets, warm punch and Brockwurst, and there is an outdoor skating rink to get you in the mood. For more nostalgia, head for the market at the Opernpalais on Unter den Linden.

✉ Weihnachtsmärkte (Christmas Markets)

⊙ 24 November–28 December

WINTERWELT (WINTER WORLD)

www.winterwelt-berlin.de

In addition to a Christmas market and animation, Potsdamer Platz gets a downhill ski and toboggan run and an ice-skating rink.

☎ 030 2554 2342 (co-ordinator at Daimler Potsdamer Platz) ⊙ First week November to first week of January

DECEMBER

NEW YEAR'S EVE

www.weihnachtsmarkt-deutschland.de/silvester-berlin.html

Every year on the evening of 31 December there is a huge party around the Brandenburg Gate to welcome in the New Year. Expect huge crowds and plenty of fireworks, light shows and live music.

✉ Silvesterparty am Brandenburger Tor

⊙ 31 December

EATING

Above *Alfresco dining at café terraces near the Hackescher Markt*

PRICES AND SYMBOLS

The restaurants are listed alphabetically (excluding Le, La and Les). The prices given are the average for a two-course lunch (L) and a three-course dinner (D) for one person, without drinks. The wine price is for the least expensive bottle. All the restaurants listed accept credit cards unless otherwise stated.

For a key to the symbols, ▷ 2.

AMRIT

www.amrit.de

Warm surroundings, friendly and attentive staff, excellent food and fruity cocktails make this Indian restaurant a popular choice with both locals and visitors. The spicy dishes, whisked to your table on sizzling hot plates, are sure to awaken the senses. If you prefer something milder, they also prepare some creamy coconut curries. There is another branch in Mitte at Oranienburger Strasse 45.

✉ Oranienstrasse 202–203, 10999 Berlin (Kreuzberg) ☎ 030 612 5550 🕐 Daily noon–1am L €15, D €35, Wine €18 U-Bahn Görlitzer Bahnhof 🚌 M29, 140

AROMA

This large Chinese restaurant on the corner of Kantstrasse is the place to go for dim sum and the Cantonese dishes are first class. The sweet-and-sour soup and the chicken soup with fine glass noodles are great lunchtime fillers.

✉ Kantstrasse 35, 10625 Berlin (Charlottenburg) ☎ 030 3759 1628 🕐 Daily noon–3am L €12, D €27, Wine €18 S-Bahn Savignyplatz 🚌 M49, X34

BOCCA DI BACCO

www.boccadibacco.de

This is the most exclusive restaurant in the city for Italian food. The food and the surroundings are stylish, the staff are friendly and welcoming, and the clientele are relaxed. Black chairs, gleaming white tablecloths and fruit-inspired art add to the clean, modern feel. The finest Italian ingredients are lovingly prepared and beautifully presented. Reservations are essential for dinner.

✉ Friedrichstrasse 167–168, 10117 Berlin (Mitte) ☎ 030 2067 2828 🕐 Mon–Sat 12–12, Sun 6–midnight L €35, D €65, Wine €25 U-Bahn Französische Strasse 🚌 147

BORCHARDT

A. F. W. Borchardt founded this top-quality French restaurant on the eastern side of Mitte in 1853. High ceilings, plush maroon benches, art nouveau mosaics and marble columns re-create the 1920s café culture. Reservations are essential.

✉ Französische Strasse 47, 10117 Berlin (Mitte) ☎ 030 8188 6262 🕐 Daily 12–12 L €20, D €50, Wine €20 U-Bahn Französische Strasse 🚌 147

CAFÉ BRAVO

American artist Dan Graham created this sculpture garden-cum-café in the courtyard of the Kunst-Werke Institute of Contemporary Art between 1995 and 1998. The two cube-shaped areas form a contemporary meeting- and eating-space at the heart of the institute. Enjoy coffee, cake or a light meal in the bright, calm surroundings

of this unique gallery café.
✉ Auguststrasse 69, im Kunst-Werke Berlin, 10117 Berlin (Mitte) ☎ 030 2345 7777 ⏰ Daily 11am–midnight 🖐 L €12, D €26, Wine €12 🚇 U-Bahn Französische Strasse 🚌 147

CAFÉ EINSTEIN

www.einsteinudl.com

This café is an institution, popular with business lunchers during the week and with brunchers on Sunday. It has a touch of art nouveau elegance with a modern twist. Snuggle into one of the booths, or get a table by the window. They have a great selection of exotic teas and coffees, and their home-made apple strudel is a great comfort on a cold days.
✉ Unter den Linden 42, 10117 Berlin (Mitte) ☎ 030 204 3632 ⏰ Daily 9am–1am 🖐 L €18, D €30, Wine €20 🚇 U-Bahn Nollendorfplatz 🚌 M19, 106 187

CAFÉ DE FRANCE

www.peugeot-avenue.de

A meal here is an affordable, stylish and romantic treat. The dishes are traditional French but the surroundings are totally modern. Red chairs, walls and ceilings contrast with the white tablecloths and sparkling glasses. You can enjoy a pre-dinner drink in their sleek bar area.
✉ Unter den Linden 62–68, 10117 Berlin (Mitte) ☎ 030 2064 1391 ⏰ Mon–Sat 10–10, Sun 10–6 🖐 L €16, D €30, Wine €17 🚇 U- and S-Bahn Brandenburger Tor 🚌 M41, 100, 200, TXL

CAFFÈ E GELATO

www.caffe-e-gelato.de

Eat in or take away at this café and ice-cream parlour on the top floor of the Potsdamer Platz Arkaden. Alternatively, share a towering sundae or sample their cakes and generous Italian coffees.
✉ Potsdamer Platz Arkaden, Alte Potsdamer Strasse 7, 10785 Berlin (Tiergarten) ☎ 030 2529 7832 ⏰ Sun–Thu 10am–11pm, Fri, Sat 10am–midnight 🖐 €1 per scoop 🚇 U- and S-Bahn Potsdamer Platz 🚌 M48, M85, 200, 347

CAFÉ-RESTAURANT WINTERGARTEN IM LITERATURHAUS

www.literaturhaus-berlin.de

On the ground floor of a beautiful 19th-century villa, this traditional coffee house is one of Berlin's most popular Sunday brunch hotspots. Try the extensive cake buffet. The ceilings are lined with gilt stucco and there is a wonderful early 20th-century conservatory, so you can enjoy the view out to the garden.
✉ Fasanenstrasse 23, 10719 Berlin (Charlottenburg) ☎ 030 882 5414 ⏰ Daily 9.30am–1am 🖐 L €25, D €30, Wine €16 🚇 U-Bahn Uhlandstrasse 🚌 M19, M29, X10, 109, 110, 249

CAFÉ AM UFER

www.cafe-am-ufer.de

This garden café on the Paul-Lincke-Ufer (*Ufer* means 'riverbank') is a great place to be if the weather is warm, when you can bask in the sunshine over a coffee or iced tea. In spring and summer, the café's terraces are packed, but it is worth waiting for a place so you can enjoy the breakfast, light lunch or an evening meal outside.
✉ Paul-Lincke-Ufer 42, 10999 Berlin (Kreuzberg) ☎ 030 6162 9200 ⏰ Summer 9am–after midnight; winter 10am–midnight 🖐 L €12, D €20, Wine by the glass 🚇 U-Bahn Kottbusser Tor, Schönleinstrasse 🚌 140

IL CASOLARE

The service here is excellent and everything comes with a smile. The house wine is very good, and the pizzas are the best you will find in Berlin at the most reasonable prices. If you don't fancy pizza, try the venison ragout with mushrooms. Reserve a table in the evenings to avoid disappointment.
✉ Grimmstrasse 30, 10967 Berlin (Kreuzberg) ☎ 030 6950 6610 ⏰ Daily 12–12 🖐 L €15, D €25, Wine €11 🚇 U-Bahn Schönleinstrasse 🚌 M41

FACIL

www.themandala.de

Mediterranean cuisine with a French twist is served at the Hotel Mandala's superb restaurant. You'll be treated to first-class service in this tranquil glasshouse in a bamboo-filled quadrangle at the heart of the hotel. Reserve ahead for this Zen oasis.
✉ Hotel Mandala, Potsdamer Strasse 3, 51234 Berlin (Tiergarten) ☎ 030 5900 50000 ⏰ Mon–Fri 12–3, 7–11 🖐 L €50, D €70, Wine €22 🚇 U- and S-Bahn Potsdamer Platz 🚌 M48, M85, 200, 347

GOURMET RESTAURANT LORENZ ADLON

www.hotel-adlon.de

Sample some of the best gourmet fusion food at this exclusive experimental restaurant (pictured left) in the surroundings of the Adlon Kempinski (▷ 116). Seafood from Brittany, Bresse poultry, fine wines, lobster, caviar and regional dishes are all on the menu.
✉ Hotel Adlon Kempinski, Unter den Linden 77, 10117 Berlin (Mitte) ☎ 030 2261 1960 ⏰ Tue–Sat 7pm–10.30pm 🖐 D €85–€150, Wine €45 🚇 U- and S-Bahn Brandenburger Tor 🚌 M41, 100, 200, TXL

HACKESCHER HOF

www.hackescher-hof.de

This wine bar and café has been tastefully modernized, yet still preserves reminders of the 1930s boomtime of Berlin's coffee houses and music halls. There is an excellent selection of wines and the late opening hours are attractive to those seeking a meal when everything else is shut.
✉ Rosenthaler Strasse 40–41, 10117 Berlin (Mitte) ☎ 030 283 5293 ⏰ Mon–Fri 7am–3am, Sat, Sun 9am–3am 🖐 L €20, D €30, Wine €18 🚇 S-Bahn Hackescher Markt; U-Bahn Weinmeisterstrasse 🚌 Tram M1, M6

HENNE

www.henne-berlin.de

A rollicking old pub this Kreuzberg institution, with its wood décor and cozy nooks, specializes in tender organic chicken, roasted and deep-fried, and accompanied by a local beer and a schnapps from the Fassobstler barrels. It witnessed

the rise and fall of the Berlin Wall right outside its front door on grassy Leuschnerdamm. Sit outside in a tree-shaded beer garden in summer.
✉ Leuschnerdamm 25, 10999 Berlin (Kreuzberg) ☎ 030 614 7730 ⏲ Tue–Sat 7pm–1am, Sun 5pm–1am ✋ D €20 Ⓤ U-Bahn Moritzplatz, Kottbusser Tor 🚌 M29, 347

HUGOS

www.hugos-restaurant.de
Hugos is a gourmet restaurant at the top of the Hotel Inter-Continental and is considered one of Berlin's best. Enjoy a cocktail or a glass of champagne in the sophisticated low-lit bar before you are shown to your table in the restaurant, which has a 360-degree view. Head chef Thomas Kammeier has created a diverse and enticing menu with an emphasis on light Mediterranean food. You can start with cold-smoked salmon with leeks and Périgord truffles, and then move on to fillet of sole with salsify and truffle fondue, or saddle of suckling pig on saffron-fennel vegetables and olive gnocchi. For dessert, try the blood-orange terrine with marinaded orange fillets and Grand Marnier ice cream.
✉ Hotel InterContinental, Budapester Strasse 2, 10787 Berlin (Tiergarten) ☎ 030 2602 1263 ⏲ Mon–Sat 6–10.30 ✋ D €150 (4 courses), Wine€28 Ⓤ U- and S-Bahn Zoologischer Garten 🚌 200

KAISERSAAL

www.kaisersaal-berlin.de
Kaisersaal is housed in one of few structures in Potsdamer Platz to survive World War II bombing. With its new glass exterior, it has become one of the top places to eat in Berlin. There are only 40 seats, so reservations are essential. The superior cuisine is based on the classical German-French style. Begin with tomato cappuccino with king prawns or fried scallop with kohlrabi, then try the red snapper with bean cassoulet or the poached turbot on fennel with crayfish ravioli. There is a huge variety of delicate desserts.
✉ Sony Center, Bellevue Strasse 1, Potsdamer Platz, 10785 Berlin (Tiergarten) ☎ 030 2575 1454 ⏲ Daily 7pm–midnight ✋ D €139, Wine €26 Ⓤ U- and S-Bahn Potsdamer Platz 🚌 M48, M85, 200, 347

KARTOFFEL KISTE

www.katoffelkiste-berlin.de
Hearty and wholesome German cooking is served in traditional surroundings. Every dish contains potato in some shape or form, but vegetarians will struggle to find a dish without meat too.
✉ Europa Center, 1 Étage, 10789 Berlin (Mitte) ☎ 030 261 4254 ⏲ Daily 11.30am–midnight ✋ L €15, D €25, Wine €19 Ⓤ U-Bahn Wittenbergplatz, Kurfürstendamm 🚌 M19, M29, M46, 100, 200

LAFIL

www.lafil.de
This Spanish restaurant is great value for money. Its extensive cocktail and wine menu rivals any found in a gourmet restaurant, and the fish and lobster dishes are fantastic. The finest fresh Mediterranean ingredients are used, and the relaxed and friendly staff and clientele make this a great place to start your evening.
✉ Wörther Strasse 33, 10405 Berlin (Prenzlauer Berg) ☎ 030 2859 9026 ⏲ Mon–Fri 1pm–2am, Sat, Sun 6pm–2am ✋ L €14, D €36, Wine €18 Ⓤ U-Bahn Senefelderplatz 🚌 Tram M2

MAO THAI STAMMHAUS

www.maothai.de
This is universally regarded as the finest Thai restaurant in Berlin, with top-class service and elegant surroundings. It is a bit pricey, but the food is delicious and deserves its excellent reputation.
✉ Wörther Strasse 30, 10405 Berlin (Prenzlauer Berg) ☎ 030 441 9261 ⏲ Daily 12–12 ✋ L €20, D €30, Wine €18 Ⓤ U-Bahn Senefelderplatz 🚌 Tram M2

MARY SOL

www.marysol-berlin.de
Come here for Spanish cooking and the tastiest and fastest tapas in the city. The food is authentic and the crowd is loud. There is an extensive list of Andalucian delicacies to choose from. It is always busy, so reservations are essential, particularly on the weekend.
✉ Savignyplatz 5, 10623 Berlin (Charlottenburg) ☎ 030 313 2593 ⏲ Daily 11am–1am ✋ Tapas €2–€10, L €15, D €25, Wine €16 Ⓤ S-Bahn Savignyplatz 🚌 M49, X34

MARGAUX

www.margaux-berlin.de
Head chef Michael Hoffman and his expert team create fabulous avant-garde and classic French dishes at this excellent restaurant. The service is quick, discreet and professional, and the contemporary furnishings add to the sophistication. Choose from four to eight courses, and the sommelier is happy to help you select from the 750 vintage wines. You will need to reserve a table in advance.
✉ Unter den Linden 78, 10117 Berlin (Mitte) ☎ 030 2265 2611 ⏲ Mon–Sat 7–10.30 ✋ D €100, Wine €25 Ⓤ U- and S-Bahn Brandenburger Tor 🚌 100, TXL

MARJELLCHEN

www.marjellchen-berlin.de
It would be hard to partake in more traditional German dining than at this much-admired eatery a few blocks southwest of Savignyplatz, which specializes in the regional cuisines of Germany's forfeited eastern lands in Eastern Prussia, Pomerania and Silesia. Soups, hearty meat-and-potato dishes, fried lake and Baltic fish, and weighty desserts are served in a relatively formal if slightly frayed Prussian setting.
✉ Mommsenstrasse 9, 10629 Berlin (Charlottenburg) ☎ 030 883 2676 ⏲ Mon–Sat 5–11.30pm ✋ D €32, Wine €21 Ⓤ S-Bahn Savignyplatz 🚌 M19, M29, M49, X10, X34, 109, 110

MERHABA

www.merhaba-restaurant.de
One of Berlin's finest Turkish restaurants offers Anatolian cuisine—goat's cheese, grilled lamb, yoghurt, and more—and enough

genuine ambience that members of the local Turkish community are among its regular patrons. Less authentic, though nonetheless welcome on a hot and sunny day, is the Turkish beer garden.
✉ Wissmannstrasse 32, 12049 Berlin (Kreuzberg/Neukölln) ☎ 030 692 1713 ⊕ Daily 12–12 L €26, D €36, Wine €12 U-Bahn Hermannplatz, Boddinstrasse M29, 104, 171, 194, 344

MIRCHI

www.mirchi.de

At this Indian and Singaporean fusion restaurant and cocktail bar in Mitte, the dishes have been toned down to suit the Western palate, so it isn't exactly authentic, but the food is still very good. .
✉ Oranienburgerstrasse 50, 10117 Berlin (Mitte) ☎ 030 2844 4482 ⊕ Daily noon–1am L €15, D €40, Wine €18 U-Bahn Oranienburger Tor; S-Bahn Oranienburger Strasse 147, 240. Tram M1, M6, 12

OSSENA

www.ossena.de

Bustling at any time of day, Ossena is filled with people who return again and again for the warm welcome and surroundings, prompt service and excellent Italian food at affordable prices. If yo have space for dessert, try the deliciously light tiramisù.
✉ Oranienstrasse 39, 10999 Berlin (Kreuzberg) ☎ 030 615 2622 ⊕ Sun–Thu 12–12, Fri, Sat noon–1am L €15, D €30, Wine €2.80 per glass U-Bahn Moritzplatz, Kottbusser Tor M29, 140

OSTWIND

The menu at this relaxed restaurant with a subdued Asian décor just off Kollwitz Platz covers Chinese, Thai and Vietnamese cuisine and adds elements from neighbouring countries, yet comes over as authentic in each.
✉ Husemannstrasse 13, 10435 Berlin (Prenzlauer Berg) ☎ 030 441 5951 ⊕ Mon–Sat 6pm–1am, Sun 10am–1am L €15, D €23, Wine €14 U-Bahn Eberswalder Strasse, Senefelderplatz Tram M1, M2, M10, 12

OXYMORON

www.oxymoron-berlin.de

Classic Italian food is on the menu at this 1920s-style restaurant-bar. The buffalo mozzarella on a bed of salad leaves with chilli and leek cream is delicious, and the rosemary and honey parfait with marinaded figs is divine. For a long night out, enjoy a wonderful meal, relax in the sophisticated lounge and then party into the night on the dance floor of the stylish bar.
✉ Hackesche Höfe, Rosenthaler Strasse 40–41, Hof 1, 10178 Berlin (Mitte) ☎ 030 2839 1886 ⊕ Daily 11am–midnight L €27, D €34, Wine €22 S-Bahn Hackescher Markt; U-Bahn Weinmeisterstrasse Tram M1, M6

SARAH WIENER

www.sarahwieners.de

Sarah Wiener is in a wing of the Hamburger Bahnhof, and is a great place for a meal after a morning's modern art appreciation. Enjoy some classic Austrian cuisine in stylish contemporary surroundings. There are plenty of newspapers, magazines and art books to browse while you dine.
✉ Hamburger Bahnhof, Invalidenstrasse 50–51, 10557 Berlin (Tiergarten) ☎ 030 7071 3650 ⊕ Tue–Fri 10–6, Sat 11–8, Sun 11–6 L €26, D €32, Wine €12 U- and S-Bahn Hauptbahnhof 120, 147, 245

SODA

www.soda-berlin.de

Part of the KulturBrauerei's Soda nightclub, the lobby restaurant and cocktail bar offers its hip young clientele fusiony continental dishes—such as burgers made with Kobe beef—and cocktails, in a large, sparely lit space fitted out in a cool modern style, or in summer on an outside terrace. There is also a club, which is accessed via a glass elevator, where you can dance until the early hours.
✉ KulturBrauerei, Schönhauser Allee 36, 10435 Berlin (Prenzlauer Berg) ☎ 030 4431 5100 ⊕ Thu, Sun 7pm–late, Fri, Sat 7pm–11pm D €25, Wine €15 U-Bahn Eberswalder Strasse Tram M1, M10, 12

SUFISSIMO

www.sufissimo.de

There is a wealth of Middle eastern and North African eateries in Kreuzberg, but this café and Persian restaurant is one of the best. Spicy couscous, traditional lamb dishes and freshly prepared, healthy options are on the menu, and vegetarians will also find plenty of interesting choices. Round off your meal with an aromatic and energizing herbal tea.
✉ Fichstrasse 1, 10967 Berlin (Kreuzberg) ☎ 030 6162 0833 ⊕ Daily 4pm–late D €20, Wine €14 U-Bahn Südstern M41

SUMO

www.s-u-m-o.com

This modern, stylish sushi bar has an excellent choice of expertly prepared raw fish, along with a great selection of Japanese beers and green teas. All sushi is charged by the plate. There are also soups and salads—try the Eiersuppe, with glass noodles, tofu, seaweed and shrimps.
✉ Bergmannstrasse 89, 10961 Berlin (Kreuzberg) ☎ 030 6900 4963 ⊕ Daily 12–12 L €and D €12, Wine by the glass U-Bahn Gneisenaustrasse 140, 248

WEINSTEIN

www.weinstein.eu

One of the best wine bars in the city is also a bistro and restaurant. The classic German and French food is very good, but customers are happy to come here simply for the quality wine list and the atmosphere. The elegance and service, reminiscent of the restaurants and brasseries of Paris in the late 19th and early 20th centuries, will make this a meal to remember.
✉ Lychener Strasse 33, 10437 Berlin (Prenzlauer Berg) ☎ 030 441 1842 ⊕ Mon–Sat 5pm–2am, Sun 6pm–2am D €25, Wine €14 U-Bahn Eberswalder Strasse Tram M10, 12

PRICES AND SYMBOLS
The prices are the lowest and highest for a double room for one night including breakfast, unless otherwise stated. All the hotels listed accept credit cards unless otherwise stated. Note that rates can vary widely throughout the year.

For a key to the symbols, ▷ 2.

AGON AM ALEXANDERPLATZ
www.agon-alexanderplatz.de
This monolithic 1960s-style building is a few blocks north of the Fernsehturm. The guest rooms are functional and have everything you need for a comfortable stay. The suites have a small kitchenette.
Mollstrasse 4, 10178 Berlin (Mitte) 030 275 7270 €73–€179 150 U- and S-Bahn Alexanderplatz 200, 240, TXL; tram M4, M5, M6, M8

ADLON KEMPINSKI
www.hotel-adlon.de
The original Hotel Adlon was opened in 1907 at a ceremony attended by Kaiser Wilhelm II. It was one of the most luxurious hotels in the world. In May 1945 a fire demolished part of the hotel and in 1984 it was torn down. The current building (pictured above), equally luxurious, opened in 1997. Its Gourmet Restaurant Lorenz Adlon (▷ 113) is one of the best in the city.
Unter den Linden 77, 10117 Berlin (Mitte) 030 2261 1111 €380–€500, excluding breakfast 382 Indoor U- and S-Bahn Brandenburger Tor 100, 200, TXL

ALAMEDA-BERLIN
www.alameda.de
Relax after sightseeing in this rooftop haven in the heart of the city. The light, spacious rooms, which take up a top-floor conversion, have sloping ceilings, arched windows, balconies and great views. The hotel is within walking distance of all the major sights around Mitte.
Michaelkirchstrasse 15, 10179 Berlin (Mitte) 030 3086 8330 €80–€128 17 U- and S-Bahn Jannowitzbrücke; U-Bahn Heinrich-Heine-Strasse 147

ALEXANDER PLAZA
www.alexander-plaza.com
This is one of the few good mid-range hotels in the area of Hackescher Markt, so reserve in advance. You'll get an excellent standard of service and an impressive range of facilities, including a guest room that is modern and functional, with a stylish bathroom suite. The hotel has two restaurants: the à la carte Wintergarten Restaurant and the Bistro, which serves lighter meals and snacks. Bicycles can be rented.
Rosentrasse 1, 10178 Berlin (Mitte) 030 240010 €160–€190 92 (16 non-smoking) Indoor €15 per day S-Bahn Hackescher Markt 100, 148, 200, TXL; tram M2, M4, M5

Above *The public areas of the Adlon Kempinski are airy and elegant*

ANDECHSER HOF
www.andechserhof.de
The rooms at this hotel near Alexanderplatz and Hakescker Markt have been modernized and are clean and spacious. The breakfast buffet includes Bavarian treats and organic and healthy options.
Ackerstrasse 155, 10115 Berlin (Mitte) 030 2809 7844 €89–€134 22 U-Bahn Rosenthaler Platz 240; tram M8, 12

ART'OTEL BERLIN MITTE
www.artotel.de
Primary shades and contemporary design leave a lasting impression at

at this ultramodern art hotel in Mitte, which attracts both business guests and independent visitors. The modern art on display throughout the hotel is by the German artist Georg Baselitz (born 1938), who also has works in the Deutsche Guggenheim in Berlin and the Museum of Modern Art in New York. The Factory Restaurant, in the covered courtyard and decorated with pop art, serves international cuisine; its grand breakfast buffet is open throughout the morning.
Wallstrasse 70–73, 10179 Berlin (Mitte) 030 240620 €130–€260, excluding breakfast 109 U-Bahn Märkisches Museum 147, 248, 347

ARTE LUISE KUNSTHOTEL

www.luise-berlin.com
Different well-known artists have designed each room in this hotel for art buffs. The hotel was built in 1825 as a city palace, and is only a few minutes' walk from Friedrichstrasse, Unter den Linden and Brandenburger Tor. The lobby is filled with sculptures, the large hall is often used for exhibitions and events, and philosophical maxims decorate the main stairwell. The restaurant, Habel Weinkultur, serves ambitious and creative German cuisine and has an excellent selection of fine wines.
Luisenstrasse 19, 10117 Berlin (Mitte) 030 284480 €79–€150, excluding breakfast 32 Some rooms U- and S-Bahn Friedrichstrasse 147, TXL

ARTIST RIVERSIDE HOTEL AND SPA

www.tolles-hotel.de
All the rooms in this small, romantic artists' hotel on the bank of the River Spree have been individually designed and decorated with antique furnishings. The hotel gives discount rates to creative guests such as artists, film production companies and designers.
Friedrichstrasse 106, 10117 Berlin (Mitte) 030 284900 €99–€249, excluding breakfast 32 Spa Some rooms U- and S-Bahn Friedrichstrasse 147, TXL

BERLINER CITY-PENSION

www.berliner-city-pension.de
The rooms in this renovated budget hotel, close to Mitte and Alexanderplatz, are very clean, airy and light, and have high ceilings and large windows. The furnishings are practical. Some rooms have a shower and toilet; cheaper ones have shared facilities.
Proskauer Strasse 13, 10247 Berlin (Friedrichshain) 030 4208 1615 €40–€55, excluding breakfast 24 U-Bahn Samariterstrasse, Frankfurter Tor Tram 21

BOULEVARD

www.ahc-hotels.com
This Austrian-owned hotel offers excellent service, clean and spacious rooms and a convenient location—just off Kurfürstendamm and close to the action, making it great value for money. The hotel's main selling point is its rooftop café terrace, a great spot for relaxing and admiring the view on a summer's evening.
Kurfürstendamm 12, 10719 Berlin (Charlottenburg) 030 884250 From €99, excluding breakfast 57 U-Bahn Kurfürstendamm M19, M29, M46, X10, 109, 110, 204, 249

CIRCUS HOSTEL

www.circus-berlin.de
Choose from a dormitory bed or a two- or four-bedroom apartment with private bathroom at this popular, well-maintained hostel close to the sights, restaurants and nightlife of Mitte. Some rooms even have a rooftop terrace and their own kitchen. The rooms are clean, functional and bright.
Weinbergsweg 1a, 10119 Berlin (Mitte) 030 2839 1433 €19–€23 per dormitory bed, €56–€66 doubles, excluding breakfast 180 beds U-Bahn Rosenthaler Platz 240; tram M1, M8

CITY HOSTEL BERLIN

www.meininger-hostels.de
City Hostels are the best-value modern and stylish hostels in the city. The one-, two-, three-, four- and five-bed rooms or dormitories have bright, coordinated furnishings and are very clean. All rooms have their own shower and toilet. An all-you-can-eat breakfast is included in the price; there is a bar, internet access and table football.
Meininger Strasse 10, 10823 Berlin (Schöneberg) 030 6663 6100 €12–€17 per dormitory bed, doubles €41 51 Beer garden in summer U-Bahn Rathaus Schöneberg, Bayerischer Platz M46, 104

FLOWERS BOARDINGHOUSE MITTE

www.flowersberlin.de
These modern apartments are ideal for a longer stay in the capital. They are within easy reach of all the major attractions, and there are plenty of restaurants, cafés and bars nearby. Choose from studios, apartments or maisonettes spread over two floors.
Mulackstrasse 1, 10119 Berlin (Mitte) 030 2804 5306 €89–€129 apartment, plus 20 per cent during high season and important conventions 20 apartments U-Bahn Rosa-Luxemburg-Platz, Weinmeisterstrasse 240; tram M8

FRAUENHOTEL ARTEMISIA

www.frauenhotel-berlin.de
This was the first hotel in Germany to cater exclusively for women and it still accepts only female guests. It lies within easy reach of the Kurfürstendamm. It is on the third, fourth and fifth floors of a renovated building accessed by an elevator. Changing exhibitions of paintings by female artists decorate the rooms and halls. Two of the modern, light and bright rooms have shared bathroom facilities, but the rest have their own shower and toilet. During the summer you can have breakfast outside on the sundeck.
Brandenburgische Strasse 18, 10707 Berlin (Wilmersdorf) 030 873 8905 €78–€108, excluding breakfast 12 U-Bahn Konstanzer Strasse 101, 104

GENDARM

www.hotel-gendarm-berlin.de
If you want to be close to

Gendarmenmarkt, this four-star hotel is a good-value option. It may be a little chintzy, but co-ordinating blue-, white- and yellow-striped classic fabrics give the rooms a regal edge, and the white bathrooms are clean and functional. You can rent bicycles here.
Charlottenstrasse 61, 10117 Berlin (Mitte) 030 206 0660 €160, excluding breakfast 27 Sauna and solarium U-Bahn Stadtmitte M48, 147, 347

GRAND HOTEL ESPLANADE

www.esplanade.de

This is an exclusive choice for those who want the comforts and services of a luxury hotel. Rooms are stylishly decorated with contemporary furnishings. The hotel has a huge reception area with a water wall. There are two bars: Harry's New York Bar, one of the best in Berlin, attracts a chic crowd; and the Eck-Kneipe, a traditional Berlin pub, has a great selection of German beers.
Lützowufer 15, 10785 Berlin (Tiergarten) 030 254780 €195–€305, excluding breakfast 385 Indoor U-Bahn Nollendorfplatz M29, 100, 106, 187

GRAND HYATT

www.hyatt.com

José Raphael Moneo, the Pritzker Prize-winning Spanish architect, designed this luxury hotel, which was built in the late 1990s. It is opposite the casino, musical theatre and Imax cinema. There are two restaurants—the intimate Tizian Italian Restaurant and Lounge and the Vox Restaurant.
Marlene-Dietrich-Platz 2, 10785 Berlin (Tiergarten) 030 2553 1234 €230–€350 342 With spa Indoor U- and S-Bahn Potsdamer Platz M48, M85, 200, 347

HILTON BERLIN

www.hilton.de

Next to Stadtmitte U-Bahn station and overlooking the historic Gendarmenmarkt square, this popular hotel oozes stylish elegance. Art nouveau touches, dark wood, stained glass, classic lighting and a waterfall surrounded by tropical palms create a lasting impression in the marble atrium. The waterfall is flanked by two wide staircases, leading up to the dining areas and guest rooms.
Mohrenstrasse 30, 10117 Berlin (Mitte) 030 20230 €129–€325, excluding breakfast 589 Indoor Spa 20 U-Bahn Stadtmitte M48, 147, 347

HONIGMOND GARDEN HOTEL

www.honigmond-berlin.de

The main attraction of this small family hotel in the heart of the Scheunenviertel is its beautiful garden and intimate surroundings. The owners provide excellent service, and also run a smaller, less expensive hotel above their restaurant and café on Tieckstrasse.
Invalidenstrasse 122, 10115 Berlin (Mitte) 030 281 0077 €89–€199 9 (all non-smoking) S-Bahn Nordbahnhof; U-Bahn Zinnowitzer Strasse 245, 247; tram M6, M8, 12

HOTEL-PENSION SAVOY

www.hotel-pension-savoy.de

The Savoy is in the west of the city off Kurfürstendamm, and is within walking distance of the Kaiser Wilhelm Gedächtniskirche and the city's zoo and aquarium. An impressive entrance hall greets you as you enter this friendly guest house. The furnishings have a predominantly floral theme and the rooms are clean and comfortable.
Meinekestrasse 4, 10719 Berlin (Charlottenburg) 030 8847 1610 €109, €129, €149: starting rate for various double room types 21 U-Bahn Uhlandstrasse, Kurfürstendamm M19, M29, X10, 109, 110, 204, 249

INTERMEZZO—HOTEL FÜR FRAUEN

www.hotelintermezzo.de

This small, down-to-earth bed-and-breakfast is for women only, and is a short walk from Friedrichstrasse and Unter den Linden. The rooms are simply furnished and each has a shower room.
Gertrud-Kolmar-Strasse 5, 10117 Berlin (Mitte) 030 2248 9096 €75–€90, excluding breakfast 17 U- and S-Bahn Potsdamer Platz; U-Bahn Mohrenstrasse M48, M85, 200, 347

LETTE'M SLEEP HOSTEL

www.backpackers.de

This relaxed backpacker hostel in Prenzlauer Berg attracts a friendly crowd of guests. In addition, there is a beer garden in the summer, a basketball court and table tennis. All rooms have hand basins, and you are guaranteed a hot shower at any time of the day. There is no curfew, and the multilingual staff (on hand 24 hours) are helpful.
Lettestrasse 7, 10437 Berlin (Prenzlauer Berg) 030 4473 3623 €11–€20 per dormitory bed, doubles €40–€69, excluding breakfast 46 beds, 10 rooms U-Bahn Eberswalder Strasse; S-Bahn Prenzlauer Allee Tram M2, M10, 12

THE MANDALA HOTEL

www.themandala.de

A waterfall cascading behind frosted glass greets you as you walk into this contemporary hotel. The grey, brown and black minimalist furnishings and marble-topped tables in the bar are lifted by slowly changing red, blue, yellow and green lighting. The rooms sit around a quadrangle, with balconies overlooking the bamboo garden and the conservatory that houses the renowned restaurant Facil (▷ 113). The hotel prides itself on its discreet, quality service.
Potsdamer Strasse 3, 10785 Berlin (Tiergarten) 030 5900 50000 €195–€455 165 Spa U-and S-Bahn Potsdamer Platz M48, M85, 200, 347

MIT-MENSCH

www.mit-mensch.com

This hotel has been designed to accommodate people with disabilities. Information is provided in Braille, seven of the 15 modern and functionally furnished rooms are wheelchair-accessible and all have a television and telephone. The bathrooms are also fully adapted for

wheelchair users. A shuttle service operates to and from the airport or train station and sightseeing tours are in buses adapted for wheelchairs.
Ehrlichstrasse 48, 10318 Berlin (Karlshorst) 030 509 6930 €72–€93 15 Free (priority for wheelchair users) S-Bahn Karlshorst 396; tram 21

MONDIAL
www.hotel-mondial.com
Mirrors, plush red leather chairs, chandeliers and glass coffee tables give an air of sophistication to the lobby of this four-star hotel. The large, elegant guest rooms have a contemporary feel, while the restaurant is reasonably priced and serves traditional German cuisine, international dishes and bistro fare. This hotel caters to wheelchair users: All public areas are accessible, and some bedrooms are designed to assist visitors who have a disability.
Kurfürstendamm 47, 10707 Berlin (Charlottenburg) 030 884110 €140–€245 75 Indoor Sauna, solarium U-Bahn Adenauerplatz, Uhlandstrasse; S-Bahn Savignyplatz M19, M29, X10, 109, 110

NH BERLIN-MITTE
www.nh-hotels.com
The four-star NH Berlin-Mitte is close to all the major sights of Mitte. The rooms in this business hotel are tastefully decorated, and have large bathrooms. You can admire the view of the city from the roof terrace. The restaurant serves international, local and seasonal dishes and has a well-stocked wine cellar.
Leipziger Strasse 106–111, 10117 Berlin (Mitte) 030 203760 €119–€259 392 Sauna, solarium U-Bahn Stadtmitte

PALACE BERLIN
www.palace.de
Built in the late 1960s, the Palace Berlin is close to amenities and public transportation.
Budapester Strasse 45, 10787 Berlin (Charlottenburg) 030 25020 €200–€335 282 Indoor Spa U- and S-Bahn Zoologischer Garten; U-Bahn Kurfürstendamm 100, 200

PEGASUS HOSTEL
www.pegasushostel.de
This hostel has a lot on offer: a garden, excellent cooking facilities, apartments and the choice of private or shared showers. Formerly a school founded in 1903, it has a beautiful courtyard. Rooms are bright, comfortable and quiet.
Strasse der Pariser Kommune 35, 10243 Berlin (Friedrichshain) 030 297 7360 From €10 per dormitory bed, €58–€70 double, excluding breakfast 25 U-Bahn Weberwiese 240, 347

PROPELLER ISLAND CITY LODGE
www.propeller-island.de
The owner of this fantastic hotel, artist Lars Stroschen, has designed every room to a different theme. All the furnishings are handmade and some rooms also contain sound sculptures. Staying here is an experience you are unlikely to forget.
Albrecht-Achilles-Strasse 58, 10709 Berlin (Wilmersdorf) 030 891 9016 €74–€205, excluding breakfast 45 Art and design gallery U-Bahn Adenauerplatz, Konstanzer Strasse M19, M29, X10, 104, 110

SAVOY
www.hotel-savoy.com
An elegant establishment that opened in 1929 just off the Kurfürstendamm shopping street, the Savoy offers an updated version of 1930s plush, and has many of the amenities of the city's top hotels. The Times Bar is a comfy setting in which to peruse *The Times* of London and other newspapers. A roof terrace affords a fine view.
Fasanenstrasse 9–10, 10623 Berlin (Charlottenburg) 030 311030 €130–€250, excluding breakfast 125 Some rooms U- and S-Bahn Zoologischer Garten M49, X34

SOFITEL AM GENDARMENMARKT
www.accorhotels.com
The rooms in this hotel are contemporary, with an emphasis on dark marble and frosted glass. Don't miss the views of the Gendarmenmarkt from the fifth floor. The glitzy Delphinium function room is often used for film award ceremonies. The 1920s Aigner café-restaurant was transported from Vienna piece by piece; its traditional Austrian and international menu attracts politicians and diplomats from the nearby government district.
Charlottenstrasse 50–52, 10117 Berlin (Mitte) 030 203750 €245–€300 92 (44 non-smoking) U-Bahn Französische Strasse 100, 148, 157

SWISSÔTEL BERLIN
www.swissotel-berlin.de
The minimalist, Oriental-style wood-and-glass interior is clean and contemporary, while sculptures and paintings by the Austrian artist Luepertz (1941–) decorate corridors and foyers. Upper rooms have good views. Restaurant 44 serves a mixture of classic European and Asian cuisine, as well as a few experimental combinations.
Augsburger Strasse 44, 10789 Berlin (Charlottenburg) 030 220100 €180–€290, excluding breakfast 316 Spa U-Bahn Kurfürstendamm M19, M29, X10, 109, 110, 204, 249

TRANSIT LOFT
www.transit-loft.de
This modern yellow-brick building with a glass tower has been converted into a budget hotel. It is close to the restaurants, cafés, pubs, bars, cinema and cabaret venues of Prenzlauer Berg. Five floors are filled with bright, clean and functional furnishings. There are spacious, single-bedded dormitory rooms for price-conscious guests. The rate includes a buffet breakfast.
Immanuelkirchstrasse 14, 10405 Berlin (Prenzlauer Berg) 030 4849 3773 €21 per dormitory bed, doubles €72 50 U-Bahn Senefelderplatz 200, TXL. Tram M4

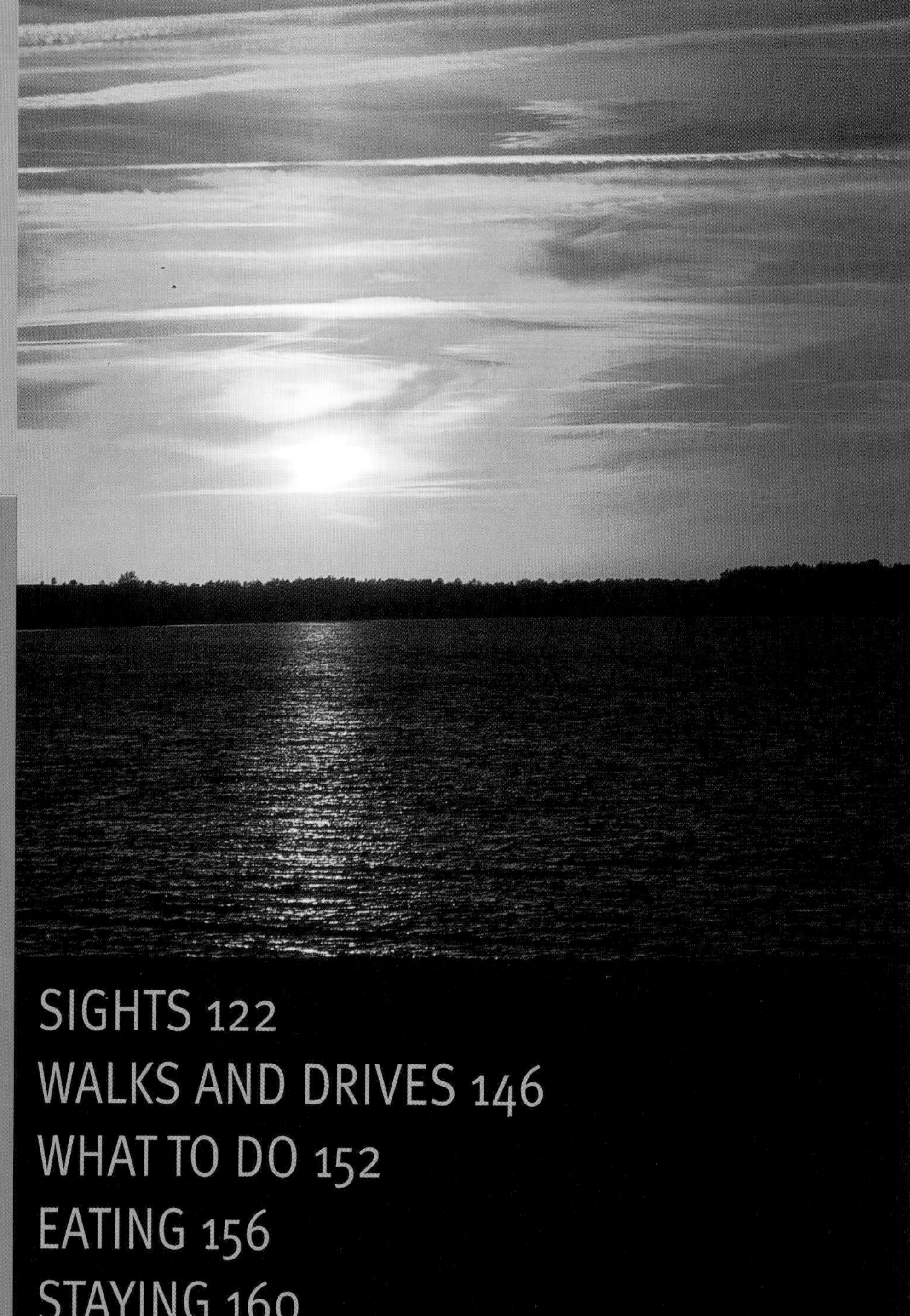

SIGHTS 122
WALKS AND DRIVES 146
WHAT TO DO 152
EATING 156
STAYING 160

NORTHERN GERMANY

Comprising the states of Niedersachsen, Schleswig-Holstein and Mecklenburg-Vorpommern, and the city-states of Hamburg and Bremen, northern Germany is mainly flat, or at best rolling, and takes in the country's entire maritime coastline. Its bustling port towns, once members of the powerful Hanseatic League, are complemented by an agricultural hinterland and market towns. Sailing, windsurfing and other water sports are a big attraction. Bicycling and hiking are popular, too, and the generally unchallenging terrain makes them feasible for most age groups. But as there are no mountains, and not even many high hills, open-air winter sports are limited to ice-skating when waterways and lakes freeze, and some Langlauf (cross-country) skiing.

Hamburg is one of Germany's style capitals, and the city's opera and concert hall are stars among the nation's cultural icons. Undoubtedly the most notorious nightlife area in the country is Hamburg's red-light district, focused on the Reeperbahn, but this by no means represents all the city has to offer. Its clubs have a reputation for cutting-edge music that dates back to the time when the Beatles were learning their trade here. Nowhere else in the North can match the range and vigour of this port city's nightlife, though the other big cities have good scenes as well. Lübeck adds a superb tradition of church and choral music. Both Rostock and Schwerin were culturally important in the former East Germany and retain that character today.

When it comes to dining, the north has a 'home-ground' advantage for fresh seafood, accompanied by the salty tang of sea air, at its many fishing ports. Large, multiethnic cities like Hamburg, Bremen and Hannover have plenty of ethnic dishes to browse. The range of local beers is huge, and towns like Jever and Einbeck are famed for their brews. Rostock produces excellent *schnapps*.

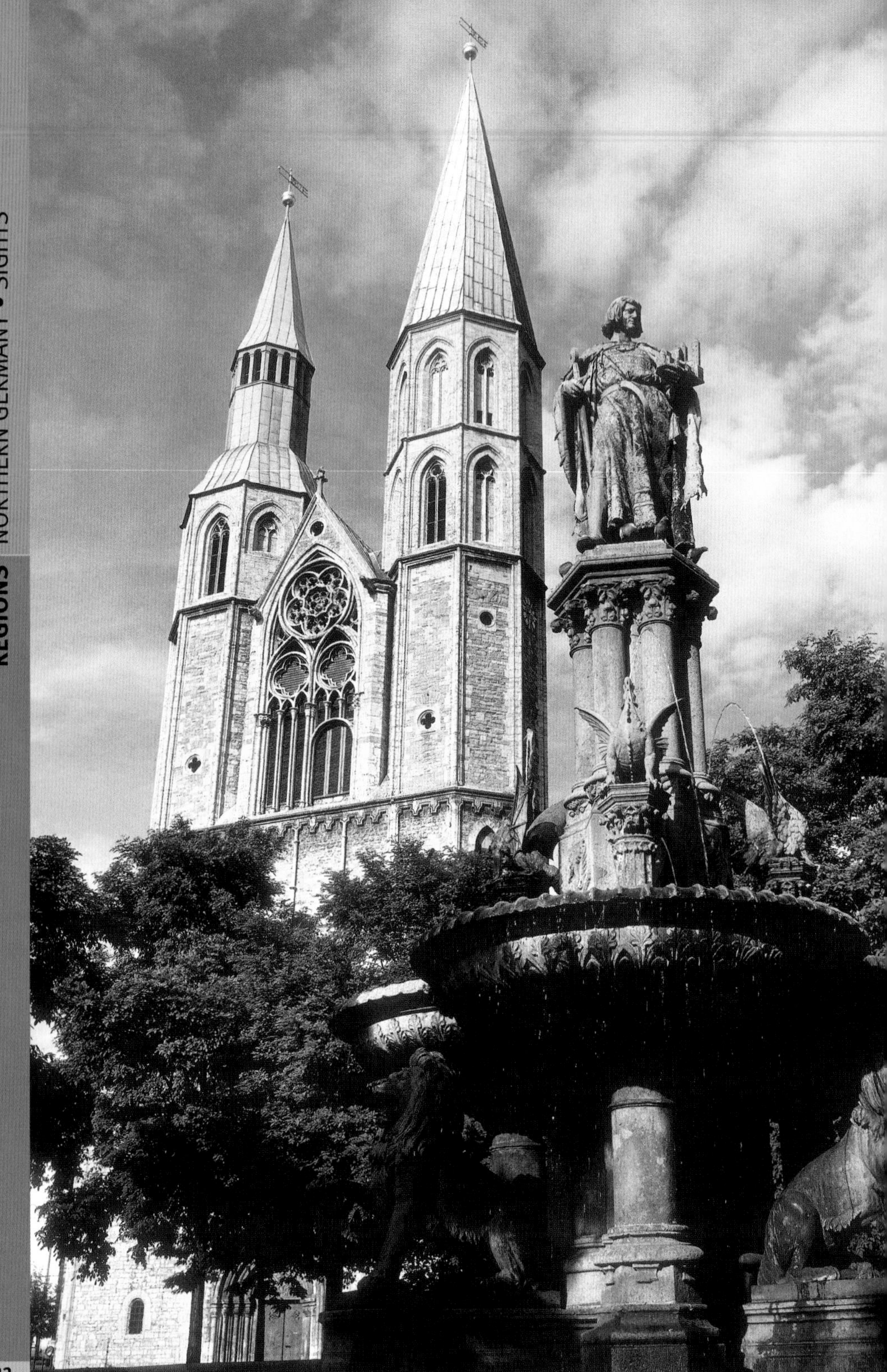

BRAUNSCHWEIG

www.braunschweig.de

Heinrich der Löwe, ruler of the short-lived Duchy of Saxony and Bavaria, gave Braunschweig (or Brunswick in English) an early political boost by making it his residence in 1166. It was 1753 before this town on the River Oker again experienced political power, when the Duchy of Brunswick was established here.

Braunschweig's response to the destruction of its Altstadt (old town) in World War II was to rebuild in modern style, interspersed with Traditionsinseln—islands of traditional architecture—a combination that gives the town a patchwork feel while maintaining some of its former character. The Gewandhaus (Cloth Hall) on Altstadtmarkt, originally built in 1303, was redesigned and decorated in an intricate Renaissance style in 1591. It faces two fine Gothic monuments across Altstadtmarkt: the 14th-century, two-floor Altes Rathaus and the 12th- to 14th-century Martinikirche. To the east, on Burgplatz, stands the Gothic and Romanesque Dom, begun in 1173, containing the side-by-side tombs of Heinrich der Löwe (died 1195) and his English wife Mathilde (died 1189).

406 F6 Vor der Burg 1, 38100 Braunschweig 0531 470 2040 Braunschweig

BREMEN

▷ 124–125.

CELLE

www.touristsinfo-celle.de

This town, 45km (28 miles) northeast of Hannover, at the southern extremity of the Lüneburger Heide (▷ 138), has a well-preserved roster of 16th- to 18th-century *Fachwerkhäuser* (half-timbered houses). The Altstadt is a virtual open-air museum of 480 such houses, many ornately decorated and inscribed. Those on Zöllnerstrasse are among Germany's finest; Hoppenerhaus (1532) at Poststrasse 8 is a superb example.

For more than three centuries to 1705, Celle was a residence of the dukes of Braunschweig and Lüneburg, and their graceful, many-gabled Schloss (guided tours hourly Apr–end Oct Tue–Sun 11–3; Nov–end Mar Tue–Fri 11 and 3; Sat, Sun 11, 1 and 3; tel 05141 550714), west of the Altstadt, survives. Dating from the late 14th century, it was rebuilt in Renaissance style and contains a beautiful baroque theatre.

405 F6 Markt 14–16, 29221 Celle 05141 1212 Celle

FLENSBURG

www.flensburg-tourismus.de

Germany's northernmost town has belonged off and on to Denmark, and Danish character still shines through. Always an important harbour town, Flensburg is still orientated towards the sea, though now mostly as a base for pleasure craft. Past maritime trading glories are recalled in the Museumwerft, a wharf lined with old ships, and in the neatly restored 17th- to 19th-century merchants' courtyards and warehouses, many of them converted to apartments, offices and artists' studios. In one such warehouse at Schiffbrücke 39, the Schiffahrtsmuseum (Apr–end Oct Tue–Sun 10–5; Nov–end Mar 10–4; tel 0461 852970) celebrates the town's nautical traditions, while the Rum-Museum in its cellar does the same for rum-making.

Try to leave time to visit 16th-century Schloss Glücksburg (May–end Sep daily 10–6; Oct Tue–Sun 10–6; Nov–end Apr Sat–Sun 10–5; tel 04631 442330), 9km (6 miles) northeast of Flensburg. Inside the brilliantly white, moated castle, are 18th-century Flemish tapestries.

401 E2 Rathausstrasse 1, 24937 Flensburg 0461 909 0920 Flensburg

GOSLAR

www.goslar.de

On the northwestern foothills of the Harz Mountains (▷ 236–237), Goslar, a former residence of Germany's Holy Roman Emperors, has both fresh air and historic

significance in abundance. Begin your stroll through the handsome Altstadt (old town), a UNESCO World Heritage Site, at the Marktplatz. In the gable of the Kämmereigebäude (treasury) across the square, a glockenspiel is accompanied by a parade of mechanical figures representing an emperor, knights and miners. The streets leading from here are full of *Fachwerkhäuser*, 16th-century half-timbered houses with ornate carvings.

On the southern edge of the old town, on a broad stretch of grass, the stone-built Kaiserpfalz (Apr–end Oct daily 10–5; Nov–end Mar 10–4; tel 05321 311 9693) is an imposing but overly pristine 19th-century reconstruction of the 11th-century Romanesque imperial palace. Its 12th-century chapel is more authentic-looking and contains the heart of Kaiser Heinrich III (1017–56). Just out of town, the Bergbaumuseum Rammelsberg (guided tours daily 9– 6, last tour begins at 4.30; tel 05321 7500), also a UNESCO Site, recalls the mines here that were worked for a thousand years for silver, tin, zinc, copper, lead and even gold.

405 F7 Markt 7, 38640 Goslar 05321 78060 Goslar

Opposite *A statue in front of the Katherinenkirche in Braunschweig*
Above *Half-timbered houses in Celle*

INFORMATION

www.bremen-tourism.de

405 D5 Bremen Touristik-Zentrale (BTZ), Findorffstrasse 105, 28215 Bremen 01805 101030; Mon–Fri 8.30–6, Sat 9.30–1 Hauptbahnhof; Mon–Fri 9–7; Sat, Sun 9.30–6 Obernstrasse/ Liebfrauenkirchhof; Mon–Fri 10–6.30, Sat, Sun 10–4 Bremen

Above *The 17th-century Rathaus stands on one side of the paved Marktplatz*

INTRODUCTION

Bremen stands on the River Weser, 94km (58 miles) southwest of Hamburg. Founded near the end of the eighth century during Charlemagne's campaigns to subdue the Saxons, it soon became an important port and trading town, and later was an important member of the Hanseatic League—it is still known as the Freie Hansestadt Bremen (Free Hanseatic City of Bremen). Nowadays, most port activities take place downstream in Bremerhaven, at the mouth of the Weser, which is joined with Bremen as a federal state.

The city was hard-hit by Allied bombs during World War II and most monumental buildings had to be rebuilt. Many venerable buildings in the handsome pre-war Altstadt (old town) vanished for good, but Bremen has a character that combines old and new in ways attractive to the eye. Most sights are in the Altstadt, on the Weser's north bank, between the waterfront and a line of angular ponds that once formed a moat, and particularly around the central Marktplatz, where you find the Rathaus, the Dom and other monumental buildings. Just east of this core, is the Schnoorviertel, a district of 15th- to 18th-century higgledy-piggledy houses once inhabited by the town's fisherfolk, now gentrified and partly given over to trendy shops, cafés and restaurants.

WHAT TO SEE

FOCKE-MUSEUM

www.focke-museum.de

This museum—also known as the Bremer Landesmuseum für Kunst und Kulturgeschichte—is on the eastern edge of the city, but the trip out there is well worth it. The museum holds a varied and fascinating collection of regional

art, history, archaeology, decorative art and more. The diverse collection covers more than a thousand years of Bremen history. Maritime history, from the city's rich Hanseatic period up to the days of the great ocean liners taking German emigrants to the US, is given plenty of space.
Schwachhauser Heerstrasse 240, 28213 Bremen 0421 699 6000 Tue 10–9, Wed–Sun 10–5 Adult €4, child (6–18) €2, under 6 free, family €7 Tram 4, 5

KUNSTHALLE BREMEN

www.kunsthalle-bremen.de
One of Germany's most important art collections is housed in this museum in the eastern reaches of a park area known as the Wallanlagen, just outside what used to be the city walls. There's a fine collection of 19th- and 20th-century paintings, including Camille Pissarro's *Girl Lying on a Grassy Slope* (1882), Eugène Delacroix's *King Rodrigo* (1833), and Claude Monet's *Camille* (1866). There are also works by artists of the local 19th-century Worpswede School.

In 2001, artworks belonging to the museum, which had been looted by Russian troops from a storage depot during World War II, were returned after turning up on the black market in New York. They include etchings by Rembrandt and watercolours by Albrecht Dürer, and are now on display again.
Am Wall 207, 28195 Bremen 0421 329080 Tue 10–9, Wed–Sun 10–5 Adult €5, child (14–18) €2.50, (6–14) €2, under 6 free, family €8 24, 25. Tram 2, 3, 4, 6, 8

MARKTPLATZ

Photographers trying to capture the essence of this beautiful old square do their best to exclude the architecturally challenged 1966 state parliament building, the Haus der Bürgerschaft. That proviso noted, the rest of the square, which is dominated by the Rathaus and the St. Petri Dom (see below), rewards closer study. Out on the cobblestones is a monumental sculpture (1404) of Roland, a nephew of Charlemagne, who is seen as the protector of the city. A sculpture (1953) in bronze of four animals—a donkey, a dog, a cat and a cockerel—standing one atop the other, is that of the Bremer Stadtmusikanten, characters in a Brothers Grimm fairy-tale who set out to be town musicians.

RATHAUS

www.rathaus-bremen.de
Behind the Town Hall's Weser Renaissance façade from 1612 lurks an original Gothic building from 1410, but it's no surprise that the magnificent façade is what people notice, along with the great bronze roof and the decorative gables. The sculptures of Charlemagne and seven Electors of the Holy Roman Empire are, however, copies (the originals are in the Focke-Museum; see left).
Am Markt 21, 28195 Bremen 01805 101030 Tours generally Mon–Sat 11, 12, 3, 4, Sun 11, 12; times may vary—check in advance Adult €5, child (under 13) free 24, 25. Tram 2, 3, 4, 5, 6, 8

ST. PETRI DOM

On the eastern edge of Marktplatz rise the twin towers (98m/321ft) of the imposing Dom, dedicated to St. Peter. It was begun in 1219, but has been altered and added to over the centuries so that today it presents a mix of styles. Once frequented by the emperor and the archbishop, the cathedral acquired decorative elements appropriate to its status, including a fine pulpit and organ. In the *Bleikeller*, a lead-lined cellar, are the mummified bodies of workers said to have been killed in accidents during the building's construction.
Sandstrasse 10–12, 28195 Bremen 0421 365040 Apr to mid-May, mid-Oct to mid-Nov Tue–Sat 10–12, 2–4, Sun 11–12, 2–4; mid-May to mid-Oct Mon–Sat 10–5, Sun 11–12, 2–4; mid-Nov to end Mar daily 11–12 and 2–3 Cathedral: free; Tower: adult €1, child (6–18) €0.75, under 6 free; Bleikeller: adult €1.40, child (6–18) €1, under 6 free 24, 25. Tram 2, 3, 4, 5, 6, 8

HELGOLAND

The red sandstone cliffs of Helgoland (Heligoland), a tiny island out in the Deutsche Bucht (German Bight), are a distinctive sight. A fishing port and holiday resort, Helgoland can be reached by tour boat, ferry or fast catamaran from Bremerhaven and numerous other ports on Germany's North Sea coast. You can stroll easily around the island and its two small villages, breathing in the sea air, and visit an aquarium and Lange Anna, a tall sandstone rock on the north coast. Düne, a neighbouring even smaller islet, consists mainly of sand dunes.

Below *Outdoor exhibits at the Schiffahrtsmuseum (Ship Museum)*

GÖTTINGEN

www.goettingen-tourismus.de

A prominent university town, Göttingen is notable for the all-hours activity a big student population creates. On the River Leine, the town has a handsome setting, fine medieval and neoclassical architecture and traditional *Fachwerkhäuser* (half-timbered houses). The Georg-August-Universität was founded in 1734 by the Hanoverian King of Britain (and Elector of Hannover) George II, but the town was founded in 953 as the Saxon village of Gutingi.

In the trim Markt, in front of the arcaded Altes Rathaus, begun around 1270 as a trading hall and completed as the town hall in 1443, stands the famous *Gänseliesel-Brunnen*. This bronze fountain (1901) is in the shape of a girl carrying geese and a basket—male students traditionally kiss the girl when they receive their doctorates.

405 E8 Altes Rathaus, Markt 9, 37073 Göttingen 0551 499800 Göttingen

GREIFSWALD

www.greifswald.de

Close to the Baltic, on the banks of the River Ryck, this old Hanseatic League town has a neatly restored Altstadt. In the central zone around the Markt, the towers of a cathedral and two churches—the 15th-century *Backsteingotik* (brick-built Gothic) Dom Sankt-Nikolai, 14th-century Marienkirche and 13th-century Jacobikirche—form a distinctive triptych. The Romantic landscape painter Caspar David Friedrich (1774–1840) was born in Greifswald, and you can see a few of his works, including *The Ruins of Eldena Abbey in the Riesengebirge* (1815), in the Gemäldegalerie of the Pommersches Landesmuseum (May–end Oct Tue–Sun 10–6; Nov–end Apr Tue–Sun 10–5; tel 03834 83120), in Rakower Strasse, just east of the Markt.

403 J4 Rathaus, Am Markt, 17461 Greifswald 03834 521380 Greifswald

Above *The Pied Piper on a sign outside the Rattenfängerhaus restaurant in Hameln*

GÜSTROW

www.guestrow-tourismus.de

Memories of Güstrow's former wealth and status as the seat of the Duchy of Mecklenburg-Güstrow abound in the Altstadt's elegant patrician houses. The town, 60km (37 miles) northeast of Schwerin, avoided damage from World War II bombs and East Germany's Communist planners alike, and its buildings have been spruced up to something like their former distinction. Their highlight is the fine Schloss Güstrow (mid-Apr to mid-Oct daily 10–6; mid-Oct to mid-Apr Tue–Sun 10–5; tel 03843 7520), built in a variety of styles by Italian and Dutch architects between 1558 and 1588, and set in ornamental French gardens. A tour of the graceful interior reveals many pieces of furniture that have always been in the castle, along with decorative art elements from the collection of Schwerin's State Museum.

Nearby, the 13th- to 14th- century *Backsteingotik* (brick-built Gothic) Dom (Apr to mid-May and mid-Oct to mid-Nov Tue–Sun 10–12, 2–6; mid-May to mid-Oct daily 10–12, 2–4; mid-Nov to end Mar daily 11–12, 2–3; tel 03843 682433) towers over the town. Inside, look for the oak figures of the Apostles from around 1530 and a replica (the original was destroyed) of Ernst Barlach's striking bronze *Hovering Angel* (1927).

403 H4 Domstrasse 9, 18273 Güstrow 01805 681068 Güstrow

HAMBURG

▷ 128–133.

HAMELN

www.hameln.de

Although attractive enough, and dotted with buildings in the flamboyant 16th- to 17th-century *Weser Renaissance* style, Hameln doesn't have many superlatives —apart from the fairy-tale of its *Rattenfänger*, the infamous Pied Piper of Hamelin. For many children, this will be ample. The story goes that in 1284 Hameln was infested with rats, which the Pied Piper agreed to get rid of in return for a generous payment. Playing his magic pipe, he drew the rats after him to the River Weser, where they drowned. When the townsfolk went back on their financial agreement, he played his pipe once more, this time luring 130 of the town's children into a cave, never to be seen again.

Every Sunday at noon (May to mid-Sep), you can watch a free costumed Pied Piper play performed on the terrace of the Hochzeitshaus on Osterstrasse (mid-May to mid-Sep), and at 4.30pm on Wednesdays, there's a short musical entitled *Rats*. Three times every afternoon, the Hochzeitshaus's glockenspiel plays and mechanical figures emerge from the upper façade to re-enact the tale.

403 E7 Deisterallee 1 (Bürgergarten), 31785 Hameln 05151 957823 Hameln

HANNOVER

▷ 134–135.

HILDESHEIM

www.hildesheim.de

Until 22 March 1945, Hildesheim, 30km (19 miles) southeast of Hannover, was the pride of North German Renaissance architecture, with thousands of beautiful ornamented *Fachwerkhäuser* (half-timbered houses). On that day, near the end of World War II, Allied aircraft dropped bombs on the town, igniting a firestorm that reduced 95 per cent of the Altstadt to rubble. A few post-war reconstructions give an idea of what was lost. On the central Marktplatz, the famed Knochenhaueramtshaus, the Butchers' Guildhouse, was rebuilt in the 1980s along the lines of the 1529 original, all of wood. It looks a little too pristine, but is an impressive reconstruction. Next door is the Bäckeramtshaus, the Bakers' Guildhouse, from 1451, but restored to its 1800 form.

Hildesheim's role as a key ecclesiastical town, which began in AD815 when Emperor of the Franks, Louis the Pious, founded the bishopric, is recalled in a quartet of imposing churches in the Altstadt. These are the Romanesque Michaeliskirche, a UNESCO World Heritage Site, founded by St. Bernward in the 11th century and containing the tomb of the saint and a mostly original painted ceiling; the Romanesque Dom, begun in the 11th century, also a UNESCO site, with sculpted bronze doors and an illustrated bronze column; the 14th- to 16th-century Gothic Andreaskirche; and the 12th-century Godehardikirche.

The town has one of Germany's most notable museums, the Roemer und Pelizaeus-Museum (daily 10–6; tel 05121 93690), at Am Steine 1, in a modern building on the edge of the Altstadt. It contains a fine collection of ancient Egyptian relics, including several mummies, Inca finds and Chinese porcelain. The museum is best known, though, for its temporary exhibitions.

403 E7 Rathausstrasse 18–20, 31134 Hildesheim 05121 17980 Hildesheim

HUSUM

www.husum-tourismus.de

A busy fishing port at the point where the River Mühlenau flows into the Heverstrom fjord, Husum is a sailing and holiday destination on the Schleswig-Holstein coast. Watching boats in the harbour is a popular pastime, but a stroll through town reveals other charms. Around the central Markt and nearby streets, elegant 16th- to 17th-century patrician houses testify to the wealth seafaring brought to the town. Ferries depart from Husum for the Nordfriesische Inseln (▷ 139) and Helgoland (▷ 125).

An interesting excursion is to Friedrichstadt, 12km (7 miles) south on the River Eider. It was founded in 1621 by Dutch religious refugees, at the invitation of Duke Friedrich III, who had visions of creating a trading powerhouse like Amsterdam. That didn't work out, but with its canals and gabled houses, the town remains a transplanted piece of Golden Age Holland.

401 E3 Historisches Rathaus, Grossstrasse 27, 25813 Husum 04841 89870 Husum

RÜGEN

▷ 142–143.

JEVER

www.stadt-jever.de

This pretty Frisian town—best known in Germany for its Jever pilsener beer—makes a good, if brief, stopping point on the road from Oldenburg or Bremen to the Ostfriesische Inseln (▷ 140). Along with taking a stroll through the central area around the Neuer Markt, you should visit Schloss Jever (Tue–Sun 10–6, plus Mon in Jul, Aug; tel 04461 969350). This magnificent rose-and-white palace was begun as part of a 14th-century fortification (since demolished). In the 16th century, local ruler Maria von Jever transformed it into a Renaissance-style palace. It has an imposing tower with an onion-shaped dome and is set in fine gardens. A tour of the rooms gives a good idea of aristocratic lifestyles from the 16th to the 19th centuries.

400 D4 Alter Markt 18, 26441 Jever 04461 71010 Jever

KIEL

www.kiel-tourist.de

Founded in 1233, Kiel received its town charter in 1242 and later became a member of the Hanseatic League (▷ 31). It might have remained a minor port town, but in 1865 it became the main Baltic base of Germany's fast-expanding navy.

The Nord-Ostsee-Kanal (Kiel Canal) opened in 1895, affording both the fleet and commercial shipping a secure passage between the North Sea and the Baltic, and it is still a busy trading artery today. Kiel's naval installations brought about its destruction by Allied air raids in World War II, and today, it has little of historical interest, though the art nouveau Rathaus and Gothic Nikolaikirche are worth exploring. Kiel is Germany's busiest ferry port, and popular with sailboats, particularly during the annual June *Kieler Woche*, the world's largest regatta.

402 F3 Andreas-Gayk-Strasse 31, Neues Rathaus, 24103 Kiel 01805 656700 Kiel

Below *A small sail viewed across yachts tied up in the shelter of the harbour (Olympiahafen) at Kiel*

INTRODUCTION

Germany's second most populous city after Berlin, Hamburg covers a spread-out expanse on the north bank of the River Elbe, straddling its confluence with the River Alster. Although it stands 120km (74 miles) from the North Sea, it is Germany's busiest port. A great part of its waterfront is occupied by docks, port installations and warehouses. Vessels ranging in size from ocean-going cargo ships to barges that ply the inland waterways come and go constantly. This maritime tradition gives Hamburg a rakish air that extends from the old salts who sing the praises of harbour tours at the Elbe Landungsbrücken to the Reeperbahn's notorious red-light haunts. But behind this rough and ready façade, the city is wealthy, sophisticated and cosmopolitan, adding a dynamic creative sector to its trade and distribution portfolios.

Hamburg traces its origins to the fortress of Hammaburg, an outpost established at this strategic point early in the ninth century by Charlemagne during his military campaigns against the Saxons. A settlement grew up around the fort, and its history as a port began in 1189 when Holy Roman Emperor Friedrich I Barbarossa granted it trading privileges and fishing rights on the Elbe. This role received a major boost in the 14th century, when Hamburg joined the Hanseatic League, eventually growing to rival and surpass that medieval trade federation's leader, Lübeck. Proclaimed a free imperial city in 1618, Hamburg continued to grow in importance, aided by a shift in trade patterns towards the west and across the Atlantic. In 1842, the city was devastated by fire, a destruction that was repeated 101 years later during World War II, when Allied aircraft dropped thousands of bombs that created a horrific firestorm.

Still one of the world's major ports today, and a German federal state in its own right, it recalls its proud history by calling itself the Freie und Hansestadt Hamburg (Free and Hanseatic City of Hamburg).

Most places of interest lie within, or just outside, a semicircle of boulevards that traces the curve of the demolished city walls. This oldest part of town is divided into the Altstadt (old town), a tiny kernel whose origins date from Hamburg's earliest days, and the outer Neustadt (new town), settled a mere 300 years later.

INFORMATION

www.hamburg-tourismus.de

402 F4 · Hamburg Tourismus, Hauptbahnhof (Kirchenallee) · 040 3005 1300 · Mon–Sat 8am–9pm, Sun 10–6 · St.-Pauli Landungsbrücken (Harbour) Apr–end Oct daily 8–6 · Hamburg-Fuhlsbüttel Airport, Terminal 1 and 2 (Arrivals area); daily 6am–11pm · Hamburg

Opposite *Hamburg's cityscape*
Above *Old houses overlooking the Nikolaifleet channel*

Above *The modern Chilehaus office building blends well with Hamburg's historic architecture*

WHAT TO SEE

BINNENALSTER AND AUSSENALSTER

The Binnenalster is the smallest of these two connected lakes, which stretch from the middle of the city out to the northeast. Its shores are lined by elaborate houses, hotels (including the famed Vier Jahreszeiten) and offices, and its surface peppered by tour boats and small pleasure craft (and in winter by ice skaters if the water freezes). Next to the bustling street called the Jungfernstieg on the south shore is a pier from which tour boats leave on cruises through the two lakes and along the River Alster. The lakeside Alex im Alsterpavillon café-restaurant here is invariably crowded with people enjoying both the good things on offer inside and the view over the water. A stroll around the lake is a popular pastime.

Larger than the Binnenalster, the outer lake, the Aussenalster, has a number of jetties dotted around its shores, where the tour boats from the Jungfernstieg stop to take on and disembark passengers. A particularly good place to stop for a while in good weather is the Alstervorland, a large park on the northwest shore, close to a district of fine 19th-century villas.

✚ 131 C1 and 131 D1

KUNSTHALLE

www.hamburger-kunsthalle.de

Between the Hauptbahnhof and the northeastern corner of the Binnenalster, this vast art gallery, which opened in 1869, is the most important in North Germany. There are 144 exhibition rooms, so even if you spend no more than a minute in each one, allowing for walking between them, you're looking at a minimum visit of 3 hours. Be selective and use the museum's floor plan to identify the areas you want to concentrate on. The museum's elegant Café Liebermann is worth visiting, either for a light meal or just coffee and cake.

While there are masterpieces by many international artists—such as Anthony van Dyck's *The Adoration of the Shepherds* (*c*1632), Rembrandt's *Simeon and Hanna in the Temple* (*c*1627), one of Edvard Munch's 20th-century series, *Girls on a Bridge*, and Edouard Manet's *Nana* (1877)—there are many stellar paintings by German artists. Look for the superb Grabow altarpiece (1383) from Hamburg's Petrikirche, by Master Bertram of Minden, its multiple panels depicting scenes from the Creation and early Jewish history. A strong collection of work by Caspar David Friedrich includes his striking *Polar Sea* (1824), showing the flotsam of a wooden ship's collision with an iceberg, and the foreboding *Winter* (1834), a fine example of his North German landscapes. Among a few works by the short-lived Hamburg painter Phillip Otto Runge (1777–1810) is *Morning* (1809), the only completed piece of a planned series, the *Phases of the Day*.

Connected to the older gallery by an underground passage, the Galerie der Gegenwart, opened in 1997, focuses on modern art from 1960s pop art onwards.

✚ 131 D1 ✉ Glockengiesserwall, 20095 Hamburg ☎ 040 4281 31200 ◷ Tue–Wed and Fri–Sun 10–6, Thu 10–9 ✋ Adult €6, child (under 18) free, family €9 Ⓠ U-and S-Bahn Hauptbahnhof

LANDUNGSBRÜCKEN

On the Elbe waterfront of the St.-Pauli district, west of the Neustadt, this long pier connected to the shore by a series of bridges affords a marvellous view of the busy river and is the home base of fleets of boats that offer *Hafenrundfahrten* (harbour tours). There are plenty of variations in these tours, but the primary division is established by the kind of boat you take. The small, old-fashioned and grubby boats moored on the landward side of the pier, and generally piloted by an idiosyncratic Hamburg riverman with sardonic wit to match, putter their way into the nooks and crannies of the harbour on a typically one-hour jaunt. These tours have more character than those operated by the sleek, powerful cruisers moored on the river side of the pier, some of which have fancy restaurants and bars on board, and power their way up and down on the often choppy waters of the Elbe.

On the shore, close to the western end of the Landungsbrücken, is a handsome bronze-domed building that is the north-bank entrance to the Alter Elbtunnel. From here, people and cars descend on elevators before taking the tunnel under the river.

131 A3 U-and S-Bahn Landungsbrücken

MICHAELISKIRCHE

www.st-michaelis.de

The copper-sheathed spire of the originally 17th-century baroque St. Michael's Church, dubbed the 'Michel', in the southwestern reaches of the Neustadt soars 132m (433ft) and is a distinctive symbol of Hamburg. From an observation platform two-thirds of the way up there are great views across the city and along the Elbe. The church was destroyed in World War II, but has been beautifully rebuilt. you can descend into the vaults for a sound-and-slide show on Hamburg history, and to see where the composer Carl Philipp Emanuel Bach (1714–88) is buried.

Across the street from the church, in Krayenkamp, you will find the Krameramtswohnungen, a closed alley of half-timbered cottages that together once formed an almshouse. They are now occupied by boutiques, galleries and cafés.

131 A3 Englische Planke 1a, 20459 Hamburg 040 376780 Church and tower: May–end Oct Mon–Sat 9–8, Sun 12.30–8; Nov–end Apr Mon–Sat 10–6, Sun 12.30–6; Vaults: May–end Oct Mon–Sat 11–5, Sun 12.30–5; Nov–end Apr Sat 11–5, Sun 12.30–5; Hamburg History sound-and-slide show: daily 12.30–3.30 Church: free; tower: Adult €3, child (6–16) €1.50, under 6 free; tower and Hamburg History: Adult €4.25, child (6–16) €34, under 6 free; tower, vault and Hamburg History: Adult €5, child (6–16) €3.50, under 6 free

TIP

» One way to trim expenses is to buy the Hamburg Card, which offers free use of public transportation, reductions on city and harbour tours and reduced admission to several museums and attractions. The card, which is valid for one adult and up to three children under 15, costs €8 for one day, €18 for three days and €33 for five days, and is available at tourist offices, offices of the HVV public transportation company and many hotels.

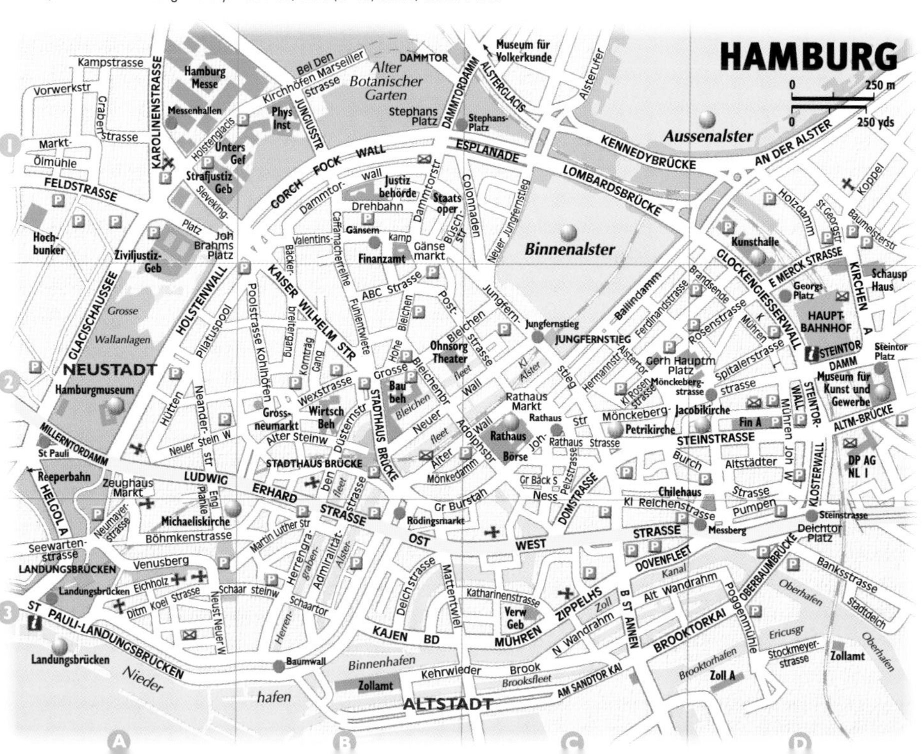

REEPERBAHN

This central axis of the St.-Pauli red-light district and the streets leading off it, where the sex industry is exposed in all its garishness, might not appeal to everyone. Hamburg is a port city and such places have traditionally had their district of low-life haunts for sailors on shore leave. So the Reeperbahn and the streets diverging off it, with their bordellos, strip clubs, sex shows and video parlours, are merely following in a long if not exactly noble local tradition. Some of the sex clubs are quite tame, while others are pornographic in the extreme, but you don't need to partake of the sexual services for sale to get something out of a visit here: It's become the latest meeting place for young Hamburgers and tourist crowds, and there's plenty of nightlife in the bars, dance clubs, theatres and restaurants that intersect with the flesh trade only by way of their proximity.

Below *The Swedish Church and landmark copper spire of Michaeliskirche*

HAMBURGMUSEUM

www.hamburgmuseum.de

A clear focus on Hamburg's history gives this museum, in the Grosse Wallanlagen park between the Michaeliskirche and the St.-Pauli district, its special character. A visit here lends context to what can be a bewilderingly large and complex city. The most instructive displays are the models of Hamburg at various periods of time, and particularly those that show the changing face of the port, which has always driven the city's development. It's interesting to compare the model waterfront scene from 1497, for instance, with its gabled houses and warehouses, small wooden ships, cranes and horse-drawn carts, with the full-scale industrial reality of today. And you can enter the lifestyles of the past, by visiting living quarters that range from an elegant 17th-century merchant's home to a World War II air-raid shelter. The model railway display should have special appeal for children.

131 A2 Holstenwall 24, 20355 Hamburg 040 4281 3223-80 Tue–Sat 10–5, Sun 10–6 Adult €7.50 (Fri €4), child (under 18) free, family €12 (Fri €6) U-Bahn St.Pauli

MUSEUM FÜR KUNST UND GEWERBE

www.mkg-hamburg.de

Just south of the Hauptbahnhof, this large museum houses a wide range of art and applied art from a variety of periods and cultures, beginning with ancient Greece and Rome and including the Orient, though there's an inevitable focus on Germany. The medieval section has superb religious reliquaries in bronze and silver, along with sculptures and embroideries. Gold objects and jewellery, textiles, furnishings and some of the finest works of German porcelain grace the collections that cover the Renaissance and baroque periods, and extend into the 19th century. A memorable highlight is the separate exhibit on antique keyboard instruments. Art nouveau (or *Jugendstil*, as the genre was known in Germany) objects and design, and an extensive section on photography, bring this eclectic experience up to the present time.

131 D2 Steintorplatz 1, 20099 Hamburg 040 4281 3427 32 Tue, Wed, Fri–Sun 10–6, Thu 10–9 Adult €8 (Tue from 4pm, Thu from 5pm €5), child (under 18) free, family €13 U- and S-Bahn Hauptbahnhof

MUSEUM FÜR VÖLKERKUNDE

www.voelkerkundemuseum-hamburg.de

The ethnography collections at this museum are wide-ranging, stretching as far as the South Pacific, where Germany once had colonies. Their traditional exhibits, such as those of ceremonial masks from the South Sea islands, are complemented by others that treat the communities in a modern context and examine some of the problems they face. The museum's guiding principle is 'a roof for all cultures', and there are sections on Europe, Africa, the Arab world, Asia, and North and South America.

Off 131 C1 Rothenbaumchaussee 64, 20148 Hamburg 01805 308888 Tue–Wed, Fri–Sun 10–6, Thu 10–9 Adult €5 (Fri from 4pm free), child (under 18) free

RATHAUS

Standing on an inverted forest of 3,780 pinewood piles sunk into the marshy soil, the imposing but somewhat overdone neo-Renaissance structure dates from 1897 and stands in a large square at the heart of the Altstadt. This is the fifth in a succession of Hamburg town halls, its predecessors over the centuries having been destroyed by war, fire or both, as indeed this one's predecessor was in World War II. On guided tours (when parliament is not in session) you can visit some of its 600 rooms, including the council chamber. On the north side is the Alsterfleet canal, and adjoining the southwest face is Hamburg's stock exchange, the Börse.

131 C2 Rathausmarkt 1, 20095 Hamburg 040 4283 12064 Guided tours hourly

in English Mon–Thu 10.15–3.15, Fri 10.15–1.15, Sat 10.15–5.15, Sun 10.15–4.15 Adult €3, child (under 14) 50¢, family €6 U-Bahn Rathaus

MORE TO SEE

JACOBIKIRCHE

www.jacobus.de

Built in the 14th to 15th centuries and all but destroyed during World War II, St. James's Church, in the east of the Altstadt, has a re-created exterior and a plain, mostly modern, interior. However, some medieval altars and decorative elements remain.

131 D2 Jacobikirchhof 22, 20095 Hamburg 040 303 7370 Mon–Sat 10–5 Free U-Bahn Steinstrasse

PETRIKIRCHE

www.sankt-petri.de

Although missing its superb medieval altarpiece (now in the Kunsthalle ▷ 130), the central St. Peter's Church—originally Gothic on a Romanesque foundation but rebuilt after World War II—is still worth visiting. Artworks in the church include a 14th-century bronze doorknocker and a 15th-century Madonna.

131 C2 Mönckebergstrasse, 20095 Hamburg 040 325 7400 Mon, Tue, Thu, Fri 10–6.30, Wed 10–7, Sat 10–5, Sun 9–9 Free U-Bahn Mönckebergstrasse

THE FAB FOUR

Hamburg revels in its association with the Beatles' early days. It was in the clubs of St.-Pauli between 1960 and 1962 that the group began to make a musical impact. At that time there were five members: John Lennon, Paul McCartney, George Harrison, Stuart Sutcliffe and Pete Best. Sutcliffe and Best later left. Ringo Starr, who joined at the end of the Hamburg period, completed the 'Fab Four' line-up. A monument named Beatles-Platz opened in 2008 at the junction of Reeperbahn and Grosse-Freiheit.

Below *A ferry comes in to dock alongside other vessels at the St.-Pauli ferry terminal*

INFORMATION

www.hannover.de
405 E6 Ernst-August-Platz 8, 30159 Hannover 0511 1234 5111; Mon–Fri 9–6, Sat 9–2, Sun (Apr–end Sep) 9–2 Hannover

Above *The Neues Rathaus (new town hall) has a lakeside view*

INTRODUCTION

Close to the middle of Niedersachsen, Hannover is one of northern Germany's principal cities. Trade fairs at the congress and exhibitions complex on the city's southern edge have long brought foreign visitors to town, a modern tradition that was given a huge boost by the successful Expo 2000. It's a spread-out city, with relatively few stellar sights for the large area it covers. Two places that are well worth a visit are the superb Herrenhäuser Gärten (Herrenhaus Gardens) to the northwest, and the Maschsee, a large lake in the south.

Although it gained its town charter in 1241, Hannover was for a long time a minor market town on the trade route from the Netherlands through Braunschweig and Magdeburg to Berlin. That changed in 1636, when members of the ambitious Calenberg family, who were dukes of Braunschweig and Lüneburg, made it their seat. The Calenberg ruler Ernst Augustus was made an imperial elector in 1692, and in 1714 his son and successor Georg Ludwig ascended the British throne as King George I. In the 19th and early 20th centuries, Hannover grew to be an important industrial city. Heavily damaged by World War II bombing, it was rebuilt along mostly modern lines.

WHAT TO SEE

HERRENHÄUSER GÄRTEN

Hannover's reputation as a green city owes much to the gardens and parkland of the Herrenhausen district in the northwest. These cover 135ha (334 acres) and are connected by Herrenhäuser Allee, an avenue lined with lime trees. The baroque French-style Grosser Garten, begun in 1666, was extended and embellished during the next 50 years. Its harmonious array of flower beds, lawns, paths, statuary and hedges is enlivened by fountains—one of which, the Grosse Fontäne, spurts 80m (260ft) high. In a neighbouring opulent mansion from 1721, the Fürstenhaus Herrenhausen-Museum (pre-arranged group tours only; tel 0511 1684 7743) retains surviving elements of the gardens' Hanoverian palace destroyed during World War II. The adjacent, English-style Georgengarten was laid out in the mid-19th century as a 'natural' landscaped park.

✉ Herrenhäuser Strasse 4, 30419 Hannover ☎ 0511 1684 7743 🕐 Grosser Garten and Berggarten: daily Nov–end Jan 9–4.30; Feb 9–5.30; Mar, Oct 9–6; Apr, Sep 9–7, May–end Aug 9–8 (Grotto in Grosser Garten closes 30 min earlier Sep–end Apr; one hour earlier May–end Aug) 🎫 Apr–end Sep Adult €4, child (under 15) free; Oct–end Mar Grosser Garten free, Berggarten and Grotto Adult €2, child (under 15) free 🚌 Tram 4, 5

LEINESCHLOSS

The seat of Lower Saxony's state parliament, the Leineschloss dates from the 17th century, but was largely remodelled in neoclassical style in the mid-19th century. It is not open to the public.

✉ Hinrich-Wilhelm-Kopf-Platz 1, 30159 Hannover 🚌 Tram 3, 7, 9

MASCHSEE

Created between 1934 and 1936 by diverting the waters of the River Leine, this artificial lake, 2.4km (1.5 miles) long and about 500m (1,620ft) wide, begins just south of the Neues Rathaus.

Appropriately, it's a great place of diversion for the people of Hannover. In summer, the banks are invariably humming with activity, and they're popular for weekend and evening strolls at any time of the year. Restaurants and cafés line the shores and there's a casino on the north bank. All kinds of small pleasure craft use the waters, and tour boats sail between several landing stages around the shore.

🚌 100, 200

NEUES RATHAUS

The 'New' Town Hall is an extravagantly ornate neo-baroque structure begun in 1901 and completed in 1913. The original was an expressive representation of the high point of Germany's wealth and self-confidence in the period just before World War I, but this is a reconstruction following the original's destruction in World War II.

You can tour the elegant interior to admire its rich decorative detail, and ride to the top of the bronze-domed cupola on a curving elevator. In the domed entrance hall are four large and fascinating models of Hannover at different periods in its history: the walled town in 1689; the pleasant regional capital in 1939; the war-devastated city in 1945; and the modern commercial city today.

✉ Trammplatz 2, 30159 Hannover ☎ 0511 1684 5333 🕐 Mar–end Oct Mon–Fri 9.30–6, Sat, Sun 10–6.30; Nov–end Feb daily 11–4.30 🎫 Town Hall: free; Dome elevator: Adult €2.50, child (6–18) €2, under 6 free 🚌 100, 200

NIEDERSÄCHSISCHES LANDESMUSEUM

www.landesmuseum-hannover.niedersachsen.de

The Lower Saxony State Museum's multifaceted collection—which covers geology, natural history, marine biology, art and more—gives you a broad insight into a considerable swathe of north Germany.

A fine aquarium is a reminder that the land has an extensive North Sea coastline, though it covers the world's oceans more generally. Among some fascinating prehistoric exhibits are several preserved corpses recovered from the region's peat bogs.

The museum's art gallery has paintings by Low Countries masters like Rembrandt, Rubens, Ruysdael and Van Dyck, and Italian painters Botticelli and Tiepolo.

✉ Willy-Brandt-Allee 5, 30169 Hannover ☎ 0511 980 7686 🕐 Tue, Wed, Fri–Sun 10–5, Thu 10–7 🎫 Adult €4, child (5–18) €3, under 5 free, family €9, Fri 2–5 free 🚌 100, 200

TIP

» A great excursion from Hannover is to the Steinhuder Meer, a scenic lake 30km (19 miles) northwest of the city. The waters of this large lake are good for swimming and sailing, and the lakeside villages have plenty of restaurants and cafés with outdoor terraces. A local delicacy is smoked Steinhuder eel.

Below *Water, water everywhere at the Herrenhäuser Gärten*

INFORMATION

www.luebeck-tourismus.de
402 F4 Lübeck und Travemünde Marketing, Welcome Center (Touristbüro), Holstentorplatz 1, 23552 Lübeck
01805 889 9700; Jan–end May and Oct–end Dec Mon–Fri 9.30–6, Sat 10–3; Jun–end Sep Mon–Fri 9.30–7, Sat 10–3, Sun 10–2 Lübeck

Above *Life in Lübeck still revolves around the water*

INTRODUCTION

Situated south of the Baltic, 66km (41 miles) east of Hamburg, and with good road and rail connections from around northern Germany, Lübeck is easy to get to and is a gateway to the nearby Baltic coast resorts. Thanks to its compact Altstadt (old town) and a relaxed urban pace, it's also easy to explore. Radiating from the central Marktplatz, a network of main streets reaches out to a moat formed by the River Trave and its connecting canals. The city's main attractions lie within or just beyond the island created by this moat.

Lübeck was founded in 1143 by Graf Adolf von Schauenburg und Holstein near the site of an earlier Slavic settlement, Liubice, which had been destroyed in 1138. Almost immediately, the new town near the mouth of the Trave began to develop as a trading hub, attracting merchants from as far away as Westphalia, the Rhineland and Holland, but its growth was cut short for a time by a disastrous fire in 1157. By 1226, Lübeck had been made a free imperial city. In the same century it rose to leadership of the Hanseatic League [▷ 31]. Vast wealth flowed into Lübeck and its civic pride was expressed in great red-brick Gothic churches filled with art and topped with mighty gilded spires, and in elaborate civic and mercantile buildings. A significant part of the Altstadt was destroyed by Allied air raids in 1942 but it was rebuilt and restored and is now a UNESCO World Heritage Site.

WHAT TO SEE

BUDDENBROOKHAUS

www.buddenbrookhaus.de

This is a place of pilgrimage for lovers of *Buddenbrooks*, the 1901 novel by Lübeck native Thomas Mann (1875–1955), which tells the story of the rise and fall of a Lübeck merchant family. The 16th century townhouse, rebuilt in gabled baroque style in 1758, was owned by Thomas Mann's grandparents.

Mengstrasse 4, 23552 Lübeck 0451 922 4100 Jan–end Mar daily 11–5; Apr–end Dec daily 10–6 Adult €5, child (6–18) €2, under 6 free, family €6–€9 1, 4, 11, 21, 31, 32, 34

HAUS DER SCHIFFERGESELLSCHAFT

www.schiffergesellschaft.de

You might easily think you've strayed back in time to Hanseatic Lübeck when you enter the late-Gothic Sea Captains' Guild House from 1535, now an excellent, if touristy, restaurant (▷ 159). Behind the red-brick façade, model sailing ships hang from the beamed ceiling, and medieval furnishings complete the picture.

✉ Breite Strasse 2, 23552 Lübeck ☎ 0451 76776 🕒 Daily 10am–1am 🚌 1, 3, 4, 11, 12, 21, 30, 31, 32, 34, 40

HOLSTENTOR

Guarding the western entrance to the Altstadt, the twin-towered city gate, built between 1464 and 1478, was influenced by Flemish models like those of Bruges, fostered by Hanseatic trade connections. It seems to have been as much a monumental statement of civic wealth and pride as a practical means of controlling entry to the city. Traffic now passes around instead of through it, but the gate retains its symbolic function. Its twin towers and central step gable form an enduring image of Lübeck, and it stands in a green space that sets it off nicely for photographers. Inside the squat brick walls, which on the city side are elaborately decorated with terracotta friezes, is the Museum Holstentor. This skips through a thousand years of municipal history, focusing strongly on the Hanseatic period, and displays a superb model of 17th-century Lübeck.

✉ Holstentorplatz 23552 Lübeck ☎ 01805 929200 🕒 Jan–end Mar Tue–Sun 11–5; Apr–end Dec daily 10–6 ✋ Adult €5, child (6–18) €2, under 6 free, family €6–€9 🚌 1, 2, 4, 5, 6, 7, 9, 10, 11, 16, 17, 19, 21, 30, 31, 34, 40

MARIENKIRCHE

A masterpiece—perhaps *the* masterpiece—of the *Backsteingotik* (brick-built Gothic) style, the Lutheran St.-Marien zu Lübeck (St. Mary's) church was built between 1200 and 1350 on the town's highest point, just north of the Rathaus. Very nearly brought to the ground by World War II bombing, the vast church was largely restored after the war. Its twin towers, each 125m (410ft) high, are Lübeck's loftiest. In the south tower, two giant bells that came crashing down during the war have been left where they fell, in what is now a memorial chapel. The central nave is a vast space, supported on great columns and suffused with light during the day. Danish-born composer Dietrich (born Diderik) Buxtehude (1637–1707), who lived for a considerable part of his life in Lübeck, and influenced both Bach and Händel, was appointed church organist in 1668. His tradition of Advent organ recitals is continued to this day.

✉ Marienkirchhof (Schüsselbuden 13), 23552 Lübeck ☎ 0451 77391 🕒 Apr–end Sep daily 10–6; Oct daily 10–5; Nov–end Mar daily 10–4 ✋ Free 🚌 1, 4, 11, 21, 31, 32, 34

RATHAUS

Dating from 1230, but extended and rebuilt several times over the centuries, the multi-turreted, red-and-black-brick Town Hall is mostly Gothic, but has earlier Romanesque elements and a later Renaissance sandstone loggia. It's a fantastical, rambling building that was not completed until 1571. From the Marktplatz you can take in the L-shaped ensemble as a whole, before moving in for a close-up look at some of its ornamental details: graceful pillars and arcades, intricate carved decorations, sculptures and coats-of-arms, medallions on the façade, and an external stone staircase in Breite Strasse. Inside there's rococo decoration from 1756 to 1760, including graceful chandeliers, in the Audienzsaal. A superbly atmospheric, traditional German restaurant occupies the cellar (▷ 159).

✉ Rathausplatz (Breite Strasse 64), 23552 Lübeck ☎ 0451 122 1005 ☛ Tours: Mon–Fri 11, 12, 3, Sat, Sun 1.30 ✋ Adult €1.50 🚌 1, 3, 4, 11, 12, 21, 30, 31, 32, 34, 40

TIPS

» Take advantage of Lübeck's proximity to the Baltic coast by visiting the beaches and seafood restaurants at nearby Travemünde, and the sea cliffs of the Brodtener Steilufer (▷ 146).

» Lübeck has been famous for its marzipan since the 16th century. The Niederegger Marzipan Salon has a fantastic selection and has been at Breite Strasse 98, across from the Rathaus, since 1806.

Below *The Holstenstor still guards the Alstadt*

LUDWIGSLUST

www.stadtludwigslust.de

Duke Friedrich von Mecklenburg-Schwerin moved in 1764 from his ancestral palace in Schwerin (▷ 140) to this purpose-built town 34km (21 miles) to the south. He later set up house at Schloss Ludwigslust (daily 10–6; tel 03874 57190), built between 1772 and 1776. The castle's stately late-baroque sandstone exterior is complemented by its setting in a 19th-century English-style landscaped garden, where water in fountains, ponds and canals is the main focus.

Money got tight before Duke Friedrich's dream castle was finished. In a brilliant solution, much of the castle's interior ornamentation was produced from a specially formulated papier mâché. You might think the results would be shoddy, but the hard-wearing substance is indistinguishable from marble, filigreed carved wood and other noble materials, and is in near perfect condition.

402 G5 Schlossstrasse 36, 19288 Ludwigslust 03874 526252 Ludwigslust

LÜNEBURG

www.lueneburg.de

Just east of the Lüneburger Heide (see below), Lüneburg received its town charter in 1247 and was a member of the Hanseatic League (▷ 31). Untouched by World War II, and isolated from the main currents of the post-war economic miracle, Lüneburg has kept many of its past graces. Construction of the Rathaus on the Markt, in the north of the town, was begun in the 13th century, and work continued until the 18th century.

A tour of the surrounding district, with its traditional brick houses, can be complemented by a stroll among the warehouses and mills of the atmospheric Wasserviertel, the old harbour along the River Ilmenau. Look for the Abtswasserturm from 1531, which employed a water wheel to collect river water for Lüneburg's breweries. Salt has been mined in the Lüneburger Heide since the 10th century and this 'white gold' was the principal source of the town's prosperity during the Hanseatic period. The Deutsches Salzmuseum (May–end Sep Mon–Fri 9–5, Sat, Sun 10–5; Oct–end Apr daily 10–5; tel 04131 45065), in the southwest of the town, takes you through the local history and economic importance of salt extraction.

402 F5 Rathaus, Am Markt 7, 21335 Lüneburg 04131 207 6620 Lüneburg

Above *The Lüneburger Heide's natural-looking heathland is manmade*

LÜNEBURGER HEIDE

www.lueneburger-heide.de

The Lüneburger Heide's heaths, glades and forests cover 775sq km (299sq miles) west and southwest of Lüneburg.

What seems the epitome of a natural north German landscape was, in fact, manmade. Before the Middle Ages, the entire area was covered by forest, but the trees were cut down, creating grazing land for sheep and cattle. A local strain of moorland sheep, known as *Heidschnucken*, still keep the heather down and the forests away. The best way to experience the heathland is to load up a backpack with a picnic and water, and hike its many signposted trails; you can also get around on a more limited trail network by bicycle.

The Bergen-Belsen Konzentrationslager (Concentration Camp) stood on the southern reaches of the Heide, and is recalled in the Gedenkstätte (Apr–end Sep daily 10–6; Oct–end Mar daily 10–5; tel 05051 47590), where documentation illustrates the history of the camp and its prisoners. Among the many thousands of victims of this Nazi death camp was a young Jewish diarist: Anne Frank.

401 F5 Wallstrasse 4, 21355 Lüneburg 04131 309960

MÜRITZ-NATIONALPARK

www.nationalpark-mueritz.de

The central part of Mecklenburg-Vorpommern, midway between Berlin and the Baltic coast, known as the Mecklenburgische Seenplatte, is thickly speckled with lakes—around 1,000 of them—created by glaciation during the last Ice Age. They range in size from little more than ponds to the 117sq km (45sq miles) of the Müritzsee, southeast of Güstrow (▷ 126). Ironically, this lake, the largest fully inside Germany's borders, takes its name from the Slav for 'small lake'.

East of the lake and focused around Neustrelitz, a baroque gem of a town, the national park's 322sq km (124sq miles) encompass a still largely undeveloped landscape of lakes, forests, heathland, marshes and traditional villages. This is a paradise for birdwatchers, particularly during the migration and breeding seasons for waterbirds. Guided nature tours leave from the park's visitor centres.

403 J5 Schlossplatz 3, 17237 Hohenzieritz 039824 2520

NEUBRANDENBURG

www.neubrandenburg-touristinfo.de

Founded in 1248, the town presents a stark contrast between the old and the new. The Stadtbefestigung, a circuit of medieval town walls, 2.3km (1.4 miles) long, is one of the finest in Germany. Sadly, little of the once character-rich Altstadt survived World War II, and the East German authorities replaced it with character-free buildings. But the walls themselves are worth seeing.

You can stroll around the circuit on Ringstrasse, just inside the walls, and in a park on the outside. The four original 14th- to 15th-century gates—the Friedländer Tor, Neues Tor, Stargarder Tor and Treptower Tor—are its most impressive features. Both the Friedländer Tor and the Neues Tor are decorated on their interior faces with terracotta sculptures. Built into the walls were 57 Wiekhäuser (defensive strongpoints). Most of these were later rebuilt as half-timbered houses, and 26 have been restored. Inside the walls, the 13th-century Gothic Marienkirche, near the middle of the city, and the 14th-century Johanniskirche, beside the walls to the north, have been restored. At the southwestern edge of town is the Tollensesee, a lake that stretches for 10km (6 miles).

403 J4 Stargarder Strasse 17, 17033 Neubrandenburg 01805 170330 Neubrandenburg

Below *Neubrandenburg's Treptower Tor, at the western end of the Altstadt, is one of four city gates*

NORDFRIESISCHE INSELN

www.wattenmeer-nationalpark.de

A group of barrier islands, each with a different character, the North Frisian islands form the above-water segment of the Nationalpark Schleswig-Holsteinisches Wattenmeer. The remainder is a zone of inter-tidal mudflats bathed by a shallow sea, a haven for seabirds and wading birds stretching the length of Schleswig-Holstein's west coast. The islands are, from south to north, Nordstrand, Pellworm, Hooge, Langeness, Amrum, Föhr and Sylt.

Sylt, the largest and most northerly island, has long had the reputation of being a party island, an anything-goes kind of place, a paradise for gay people, naturists and fashionistas. It is also a place of great natural beauty, with long white-sand beaches, dune landscapes and red cliffs and a sandy moorland interior. One reason for the frenetic summer partying in the main resort of Westerland and the chic village of Kampen might be the fear that Sylt won't always be around. The wiry salt grasses that defend it from wind and tidal erosion are slowly losing their battle. Sylt is connected to the mainland by the Hindenburgdamm railway causeway.

401 D2 Landesamt für den Nationalpark Schleswig-Holsteinisches Wattenmeer, Schlossgarten 1, 25832 Tönning 04861 61670 Westerland (Sylt)

OLDENBURG

www.oldenburg-tourist.de

At the southeastern gateway to the East Frisian peninsula, this former capital of the Grand Duchy of Oldenburg-Holstein-Gottorp belonged to Denmark for a period until 1773. Today it's a pleasant-looking and lively university town with several interesting museums. South of the central Markt, over which towers the late-Gothic Lambertikirche, the old grand-ducal Schloss is an attractive but sober mix of Renaissance, baroque and neoclassical styles. It houses the Landesmuseum für Kunst und Kulturgeschichte (Tue, Wed, Fri 9–5, Thu 9–8, Sat, Sun 10–5; tel 0441 220 7300), which contains classical-revival paintings by the local artist Johann Heinrich Wilhelm Tischbein (1751–1829), along with works by Dutch and Italian Old Masters. Across from the castle is the Schlossgarten, an English-style landscaped garden.

401 D5 Markt 22, 26122 Oldenburg, 0441 3616 1340 Oldenburg

OSNABRÜCK

www.osnabrueck.de

Osnabrück hosted part of the negotiations that led to the 1648 Peace of Westphalia and brought the Thirty Years' War to an end. Later, it was the home town of author Erich Maria Remarque (1898–1970), whose novel *All Quiet on the Western Front* (1929) is an anti-war classic. This tale of war and peace continued in World War II, when the town was heavily bombed.

In the Markt, a triangular 'square' in the middle of town, are rebuilt gabled mansions and guildhouses, the 16th-century Rathaus (where the Peace of Westphalia was announced) and the Gothic Marienkirche. Nearby streets host most of the surviving half-timbered houses, and the 12th- to 16th-century Dom St. Petrus, with one Romanesque and one Gothic tower.

At Kalkriese, 10km (6 miles) north of Osnabrück, the Varusschlacht Museum und Park (daily 10–6; tel 05468 92040) is located on what archaeologists believe to be the site of the Battle of the Teutoburgerwald (AD9), in which German tribes led by a turncoat Roman ally, Arminius (or Hermann), ambushed and wiped out three Roman legions commanded by Publius Quinctilius Varus (▷ 29).

404 C6 Bierstrasse 22–23, 4907 Osnabrück 0541 323 2202 Osnabrück

OSTFRIESISCHE INSELN

www.die-nordsee.de

Seven low-lying islands, havens of natural beauty, are connected by ferry across the shallow Wattenmeer from harbours on the Ostfriesland peninsula. In a line from west to east, they are: Borkum, Juist, Norderney, Baltrum, Langeoog, Spiekeroog and Wangerooge, plus a few uninhabited sand banks.

The archipelago, the Wattenmeer and the adjacent coastline belong to the Nationalpark Niedersächsisches Wattenmeer. Large areas are protected zones for wildlife and plants. Enough remains outside these domains to ensure that the islands are a holiday zone *par excellence*, as are the mainland fishing ports and ferry harbours. Their long sandy beaches are the islands' most popular assets, but hiking on the dunes, birdwatching, seal-watching and sailing have plenty of devotees.

Borkum is the busiest and most developed of the islands, with casinos, a marina and hotels ranging from 19th century to the most modern. Second in size is Norderney, where handsome villas, grand hotels and a casino recall the island's 19th-century heyday as a resort for the rich and powerful. All the other islands are car-free; you get about on foot or by horse-drawn cart. Borkum, Langeoog and Wangerooge have little railways.

400 C4 | Postfach 2106, 26414 Schortenss | 01805 202096

SCHLESWIG

www.ostseefjordschlei.de

Schleswig, 40km (25 miles) northwest of Kiel, was founded by the Vikings in the ninth century on the Schlei, a long Baltic fjord. The Dom (May–end Sep Mon–Sat 9–5, Sun 1.30–5; Oct–end Apr Mon–Sat 10–4, Sun 1.30–4; tel 04621 599030), begun in the 12th century and completed in the 15th, contains the oak triptych Bordesholm altarpiece by Hans Brüggemann from 1521, a masterpiece of Gothic sculpture, and has a spire 112m (367ft) high.

Schloss Gottorf, the rambling 16th- to 18th-century seat of the dukes of Schleswig-Holstein-Gottorf (Apr–end Oct daily 10–6; Nov–end Mar Tue–Fri 10–4, Sat, Sun 10–5; tel 04621 8130), on a tiny islet in the Bergsee on the western edge of town, houses two fine museums: the Landesmuseum für Kunst und Kulturgeschichte, with a collection of local art and applied art, and the Archäologisches Landesmuseum, which has a small boat from around AD350 and a gruesome collection of preserved corpses recovered from peat bogs.

401 E2 | Plessenstrasse 7, 24837 Schleswig | 04621 850056 | Schleswig

SCHWERIN

www.schwerin-tourist.de

The capital of Mecklenburg-Vorpommern is 54km (33 miles) southeast of Lübeck, on the shore of the Schweriner See. Its undoubted highlight is the Schweriner Schloss (Tue–Sun 10–5; tel 0385 525 2920), on an island in the Burgsee, an inner arm of the lake. Built in 1843, this former seat of the grand dukes of Mecklenburg-Schwerin, who ruled from Schwerin for most of the period 1318–1918, is a vast and fantastical conglomeration of revival styles—primarily neo-Renaissance but with a dab of neo-Gothic and a touch of neo-baroque—enlivened by spires, gables and domes. The island has its own garden, but an even finer one, the Schlossgarten, lies across the south bridge.

Strolling through the heart of town, look out for the 19th-century mock-Tudor Rathaus and the 13th- to 15th-century Gothic Dom. The Galeriegebäude (Tue–Sun 10–6; tel 0385 59580), at Alter Garten 3 just across the north bridge from the Schloss, has a notable collection of paintings, including *The Sentinel*, 1654 by Rembrandt's pupil Carel Fabritius, and Lucas Cranach the Elder's *Venus and Cupid with a Honeycomb* (1527).

402 G4 | Am Markt 14, 19055 Schwerin | 0385 592 5212 | Schwerin

STADE

www.stade-tourismus.de

On the banks of the River Schwinge close to where it flows into the Elbe, Stade, 36km (22 miles) northwest of Hamburg, is an old Hanseatic town (▷ 31) that has retained much of its historic character. It has few outstanding sights, but shines rather as an ensemble and an almost perfect example of a traditional north German town—even if it has been a bit too pristinely renovated. Half-timbered houses line the streets of the Altstadt, particularly along riverside Alter Hafen, the old harbour, many of them converted into restaurants and trendy shops and galleries.

The Schwedenspeicher-Museum (Tue–Fri 10–5, Sat, Sun 10–6; tel 04141 3222), at Wasser West 39, in a warehouse from 1705 whose name recalls Stade's period of Swedish occupation during the Thirty Years' War, has displays on local history.

401 E4 | Hansestrasse 16, 21682 Stade | 04141 409170 | Stade

Left *Schweriner Schloss, the former home of the dukes of Mecklenburg-Schwerin, is set on an island on an arm of the Schweriner See*

ROSTOCK

Rostock's bustling waterfront along the River Warnow is a reminder of its past maritime trading glories. Rostock, 90km (56 miles) northeast of Lübeck, stands on the south bank of the River Warnow at the point where it opens into a broad estuary. It has been a maritime city since the 13th century when it joined the Hanseatic League (▷ 31) and has retained that distinction to the present day. That the town has an attractive character at all today owes much to the extensive rebuilding undertaken by the former East German government to repair heavy damage inflicted by Allied air raids during World War II.

THROUGH THE ALTSTADT

The primary places of interest are in the Altstadt, within the city walls, a section of which survives in the southwest of the old town. The Rathaus, a rambling affair consisting of three 13th- to 14th-century gabled houses and seven towers, behind an 18th-century baroque façade, is in the central Neuer Markt. Across the way, the St.-Marien-Kirche (Mon–Sat 10–12.30, 2–4, Sun 11.15–12; tel 0381 492 3396), built between 1300 and 1550 is mostly original, having escaped serious damage in the war—though it was damaged badly enough during construction when the nave collapsed.

Pedestrianized Kröpeliner Strasse, leading west from Neuer Markt, is the town's main street, and its parade of gabled 16th- to 19th-century houses has been beautifully restored. It passes by a fountain in Universitätsplatz that is a popular meeting point for the town's students (the university dates from 1419). Note also on the triangular 'square' a sculpture of local hero Marshal Blücher, who commanded the Prussian army at Waterloo.

MAKING HISTORY

The Schiffbau- und Schiffahrtsmuseum (Tue–Sun 9–6; tel 0381 1283 1364), at Schmarl-Dorf 40, celebrates Rostock's maritime traditions from its earliest days but focuses on the 19th and 20th centuries. Among many model ships on display are *Hansekoggen* sailing ships and battleships from World War I's High Seas Fleet. The Kulturhistorisches Museum (Tue–Sun 10–6; tel 0381 203590), off Universitätsplatz, is housed in the Gothic Kloster zum Heiligen Kreuz, a former Cistercian convent and church founded in 1270. Its collection covers religious art, folk art and works by local artists. Among its finest pieces is the 15th-century Three Kings altarpiece.

INFORMATION

www.rostock.de

403 H3 Tourismuszentrale Rostock and Warnemünde, Neuer Markt 3, 18055 Rostock 0381 381 2222 May, Sep Mon–Fri 10–6, Sat, Sun 10–4; Jun–end Aug Mon–Fri 10–7, Sat, Sun 10–4; Oct–end Apr Mon–Fri 10–6, Sat 10–3 Rostock

TIP

» Boat tours of Rostock harbour and as far north as the port, fishing harbour and busy seaside resort of Warnemünde, 10km (6 miles) to the north on the Baltic Sea, leave from jetties at Stadthaven on the River Warnow (known as the Unterwarnow at this point).

Above *The modern fountain in the middle of Universitätsplatz*

INFORMATION

www.ruegen.de
www.nationalpark-jasmund.de
403 J3 Tourismuszentrale Rügen (TZR), Bahnhofstrasse 15, 18528 Bergen auf Rügen 03838 80770 Mon–Fri 10–6 Bergen

INTRODUCTION

Germany's largest island, Rügen lies in the Baltic Sea, close enough to the Mecklenburg-Vorpommern mainland to be connected by road and rail via a chain of islets, a causeway and bridges from Stralsund. The varied scenery includes sea cliffs, coastal plains, forested and agricultural land, low hills, moors and beaches. National parks and nature reserves protect several sites of scenic and wildlife importance. Rügen is very nearly cut in two by a long jagged inlet, the Grosser Jasmunder Bodden, and by the smaller nearby Kleiner Jasmunder Bodden on the other side of a land bridge—both stretches of water are good places for birding. All these attributes, and more, have inevitably given Rügen the status of a popular and busy vacation island.

Shaped by the advance and retreat of Ice Age glaciers, Rügen was occupied by the Huns as they pressed west during the early fifth century AD. It was in Slavic hands until the 12th century, and later shuttled back and forth between Danish and Swedish rule before falling to Prussia at the end of the Napoleonic Wars. Members of German society liked to be seen at its bathing resorts right up to the start of World War II, but in 1936, Rügen's truly insular status was lost when the causeway across the straits from Stralsund was completed.

On such a large island, getting around by car affords the most flexibility, but you can also go by bus, train (including narrow-gauge railway), taxi and, if you are up to the long distances, by bicycle.

WHAT TO SEE

KAP ARKONA

www.kap-arkona.de

Beyond Putgarten, the scenic, cliff-fringed northern tip of the island sports a brick lighthouse from 1829, and a more functional-looking, striped model from the turn of the 20th century. About 1km (0.6 miles) southeast of Putgarten, and accessible on foot or by horse and carriage, is the handsome little fishing village of Vitt, its thatched cottages seemingly suspended in time.

Am Parkplatz 1, 18556 Putgarten (Rügen) 038391 4190

Above *A memorial stands at the heart of the village green at Putbus, an example of 19th-century town planning*

NATIONALPARK JASMUND

www.nationalpark-jasmund.de

Dense forests of beech and oak cover the Jasmund peninsula north of Sassnitz and reach right to the edge of the sea. They end at a line of white chalk sea cliffs called the Stubbenkammer, which is marked by a series of lofty viewpoints connected by a clifftop path. The finest of these is the Königsstuhl, a cliff at the midpoint, 119m (390ft) above the sea. As the peninsula curves away to the west, the cliffs give way to sands around the resort of Glowe. From the port at Sassnitz, ferries sail to various points around the Baltic.

Nationalpark-Zentrum Königsstuhl, Stubbenkammer 2, 18546 Sassnitz 038392 661766 Easter–end Oct daily 7–7; Nov–Easter daily 10–5

TIP

» Take a trip on the steam train of the narrow-gauge railway that runs from Putbus in the southeast to the nearby Ostseebäder resorts of Binz, Sellin, Baabe and Göhren.

OSTSEEBÄDER

From the early 19th century until well into the 20th, a cluster of four bathing resorts in the southeast of the island were popular watering holes among well-to-do Germans, primarily because of their excellent sand beaches. The resorts are Binz, Sellin, Baabe and Göhren, and although their popularity declined after World War II period, they have been making a comeback. The restored fin-de-siècle mansions are now more likely to hold hotels, apartments or restaurants than to be privately owned. In keeping with the island's modern tradition of caring for its natural treasures, the resorts lie within the Biosphärenreservat Südost Rügen, a reserve that protects the forests and wildlife of the area.

Binz is the most popular resort town and has the longest beaches. On the southern edge of the town you'll find the Jagdschloss Granitz (May–end Sep daily 9–6; Oct daily 9–4; Nov–end Apr Tue–Sun 10–4; tel 038 3932263), a hunting lodge from 1836 in the shape of a neo-Gothic Tudor fantasy castle. You get a fine vista from the high viewing platform in the courtyard.

PUTBUS

www.putbus.de

On the way to the Ostseebäder (▷ above), you may pass through this town, which was built in the early 19th century by Prince Wilhelm Malte. The prince's castle is no more, but the planned neoclassical town that was created around it survives, though many of its flamboyant villas have been turned into hotels and apartments. On the coast 3km (2 miles) to the southeast, the village of Lauterbach retains traces of the grandeur Malte gave it as a bathing resort.

Orangerie, Alleestrasse 35. 18581 Putbus 038301 431

HIDDENSEE

www.insel-hiddensee.de

By German standards, this island just off Rügen's west coast is big at 17km (11 miles) long by a maximum of 2km (1.25 miles) wide, but by comparison with nearby Rügen it seems like no more than an islet. However, on the ground, you have to get around on foot, by bicycle or by horse and cart (the island is car-free). Dubbed the 'pearl of the Baltic' for its isolation, tranquillity and variety of landscapes, Hiddensee can be reached by boat from Stralsund and Zingst on the mainland and from Schaprode and Wiek on Rügen. Boats sail between one and three times per day. The island is an outpost of the Nationalpark Vorpommersche Boddenlandschaft, which extends across to the ancient forests of the Zingst peninsula on the mainland, and is a prime zone for observing migrating birds. A lighthouse from 1888 stands on the Dornbusch hill, 72m (236ft) high, on the north coast, and a number of resorts that get busy in summer and are built around fishing and farming villages—Grieben, Kloster, Vitte and Neuendorf—are strung along the island's spine.

Norderende 162, 18565 Vitte 038300 64226 Jan–end Mar and Nov–end Dec Mon–Fri 9–3; Apr, Oct Mon–Fri 9–4; Apr–end Sep Mon–Fri 8.30–5, Sat 10–noon Kloster, Neuendorf, Vitte

Below *The coastline of the Jasmund National Park, Rügen Island*

STRALSUND

www.stralsundtourismus.de

Gateway to the Baltic holiday island of Rügen (▷ 142–143), Hanseatic Stralsund maintains the maritime bustle resulting from its fantastic natural harbour, though these days it is filled primarily with fishing boats and pleasure craft. In the Altstadt, ringed by lakes and the sea, are many Gothic buildings that are fully the equal of those in Lübeck (▷ 136–137) and Rostock (▷ 141), the Katharinenkloster, a former abbey at Katharinenberg, hosts the Deutsches Meeresmuseum (Jun–end Sep daily 10–6; Oct–end May daily10–5; tel 03831 265 0210). This fine oceanographic museum has sections on the fish and plant life of the Baltic, but also covers the other oceans. The large tropical aquarium and the turtle pool are particular highlights.

West of here, and stretching north, are the finest surviving sections of Stralsund's medieval walls. These protected, among other things, two superb Gothic buildings: the 13th- to 14th-century Rathaus in Alter Markt and the 13th-century Nikolaikirche.

404 J3 · Alter Markt 9, 18439 Stralsund · 03831 24690 · Stralsund

USEDOM

www.usedom.de

This developing Baltic holiday island, 60km (37 miles) east of Greifswald, has two distinguishing characteristics: a strip of land in the east belongs to Poland, and it was one of the birthplaces of rocketry. At the Peenemünde research base on the island's west coast, Wernher von Braun, the engineer whose expertise would later help to put Americans on the moon, developed the World War II V2 rocket that bombarded London. A Historisch-Technisches Informationszentrum (Apr–end Sep daily 10–6; Oct–end Mar daily 10–4; tel 038371 5050) details the history of Peenemünde's rocket projects and their role in the history of space exploration.

Elsewhere, the island has a variety of landscapes: moors, dunes, forests and extensive beaches along the Baltic shore. The sands are edged by a string of resorts with elegant architecture. Its popularity, which extended from the 19th century to just before World War II, is being revived in particular at the Kaiserbäder (Imperial Resorts) of Bansin, Heringsdorf and Ahlbeck.

403 K4 · Waldstrasse 1, 17429 Seebad Bansin · 038378 47710

WISMAR

www.wismar.de

Founded in 1229 and later a wealthy member of the Hanseatic League (▷ 31), this Baltic harbour town went into decline and became little more than a fortified Swedish outpost from 1648 until 1803. A new period of decline set in under the neglectful rule of the East German government, but since 1989 the Altstadt has undergone a revival, with renovation and restoration giving it back its historic shine.

The wide open space of the large, central Markt is surrounded by an array of gabled guildhouses and mansions in a variety of styles that span the centuries. But your attention is likely to be drawn first to the domed, Dutch Renaissance Wasserkunst pavilion from 1602 that contains a spring outlet. From there, explore the white stone of the neoclassical Rathaus from 1819, and the red-brick Gothic Alter Schwede mansion (now a traditional restaurant) from around 1380.

Restoration of the war-damaged Gothic Georgenkirche, dating from 1295, west of the Markt is still in progress. But the vast 14th- to 15th-century Nikolaikirche at Hinter dem Chor, just north of a watercourse called the Grube, is complete. It contains the fine Krämergilde altarpiece from 1430. A stroll around the old town and its harbour will complete the picture of Wismar.

402 G4 · Am Markt 11, 23966 Wismar · 03841 19433 · Wismar

WOLFENBÜTTEL

www.wolfenbuettel-tourismus.de

Wolfenbüttel is notable for its Weser Renaissance *Fachwerkhäuser*. More than 500 examples of these decorated half-timbered houses survive, many of them from the 16th century. Between 1432 and1753 the town was the seat of the Duchy of Brunswick and Lüneburg. This period saw the construction of some fine monumental buildings. First among them is the Renaissance and baroque ducal Schloss Wolfenbüttel (Tue–Sun 10–5; tel 05331 92460), which stands on extensive grounds at the western edge of the Altstadt, and is now a museum retaining the 18th-century appearance of the state apartments.

Just north of the Schloss stands the Herzog-August Bibliothek (Tue–Sun 10–5; tel 05331 8080), founded in 1644 by Duke Augustus and added to over the centuries. The library holds 860,000 volumes, many of them rare and valuable, including the 12th-century illuminated Evangelistary (Gospel) that belonged to Heinrich der Löwe (▷ 123).

406 F7 · Stadtmarkt 7, 38300 Wolfenbüttel · 05331 86280 · Wolfenbüttel

Clockwise from left to right *The baroque Schloss Wolfenbüttel; Stralsund was once an important member of the Hanseatic League*

BRODTENER STEILUFER

The curving Brodtener promontory jutting into the Lübecker Bucht between Travemünde and Niendorf is rimmed with low sea cliffs. The easily managed walk along here gives you superb views of the Baltic coast.

THE WALK

Distance: 4km (2.5 miles)
Allow: 1–2 hours
Start at: Travemünde
End at: Niendorf

Note: You can follow the clifftop path or walk on the beach, directly alongside the sea. Both routes end at the same place. However, the beach route is rocky and the going is hard in places, while the views are less spectacular. The descriptive detail that follows is based on a walk along the clifftop path. In either case, as long as you keep the sea to your right, it's hard to get lost.

★ Start at the Mövenstein parking area alongside the sailing school at the north end of Travemünde beach (there is a public toilet here). Go up on Helldahl, a path that ascends easily into the trees. You're soon on the clifftop path, the start of which is marked near a sign that says *Landschaftsschutzgebiet*, indicating that this is a protected landscape. The cliffs and the sea are just off to your right.

❶ On the clifftop, try to resist the temptation to peer over the cliff edge. Signposts warn of an *abbrechendes Steilufer*—meaning that the edge is subject to collapse and that you approach it at your own peril. The cliffs are no more than 20m (66ft) high, but a fall from that height could easily prove fatal. As you come level with the practice range of a golf course off to your left, an information board (in German) provides background about the geography and wildlife of the Brodtener coastline.

About 100m (110 yards) beyond the intersection of the cliffside path with a path that goes off to the left through a forested area—the Heidenhof—you'll see a stone inscribed with the text of Psalm 93, verse 4, which extols the greater power of the Lord in comparison even with that of the sea. Some 50m (55 yards) beyond here is a section of the cliff that is lower and less steep, where it's possible to scramble down to the beach and back up again—as long as you go carefully. Back on top, little side paths branch off from the main path through the trees to the cliff edge.

❷ Hermannshöhe, a café-restaurant that sits on a wide lawn overlooking the sea, is at about the midpoint and is a good spot for a break.

Continuing, the path curves away from the sea a little and you pass what looks like a broken-down vacation home on your right, before regaining the shore.

❸ Large broken concrete blocks down on the beach, and others a little way inland, are the remnants of an old coastal defence system, the Buschkoppel. In this more open country, you'll see a pond in a field off to your left, and beyond that the village of Brodten. As the promontory curves westward, a view over another arm of the Lübecker Bucht opens up, across to Timmendorfer Strand and beyond.

Some 50m (55 yards) after passing, on your left, a holiday home for young people, the red-brick Jugendheim 'Seeblick', a flight of wooden steps leads down to the beach. Staying on the path, you emerge from a cluster of bushes, with Niendorf just ahead. The path becomes enclosed and seaside homes appear on the left as you enter the resort.

WHEN TO GO

The best season for this walk is undoubtedly summer, but you could also tackle it on a fine spring or autumn day. In winter, be prepared for wind and cold temperatures; in bad weather, conditions could be very unpleasant.

WHERE TO EAT

Café-Restaurant Hermannshöhe (tel 04502 73021) is the ideal point for a mid-walk break, either inside or on the outside terrace.

Below *The setting sun reflects on the Baltic Sea*

HAMELN

Associations with the Pied Piper, the legendary medieval ratcatcher immortalized in English in Robert Browning's much-loved poem, are a big part of Hameln's attractions. But they are not the whole story, as this tour goes to show.

THE WALK
Distance: 3km (2 miles)
Allow: 1 hour
Start/end at: Tourist Information Hameln, Deisterallee, at the eastern end of the Altstadt (old town)

★ From outside the tourist office, cross busy Kastanienwall via the pedestrian tunnel at the top end of Deisterallee. This brings you onto Osterstrasse, the Altstadt's main thoroughfare. Walk to the corner with Bungelosenstrasse.

❶ The Rattenfängerhaus, on the corner, was built between 1602 and 1603 in Weser Renaissance style. The Pied Piper's House, which takes its name from an inscription recounting the legend, is now a restaurant. On the other side of Osterstrasse is the Garrisonkirche (1713), the baroque former garrison church, now a bank. A few doors along, at Osterstrasse 18, is a building from 1577 (now a health-food store) with a bas-relief carving of a dragon and a lion on the façade.

Continuing along Osterstrasse, pass the post office and a bronze sculpture of the Pied Piper.

❷ The richly ornamented Weser Renaissance Leisthaus, at Osterstrasse 9, was built between 1585 and 1589. It houses the Museum Hameln, which has a collection of items from the town's history, including exhibits relating to the Pied Piper. The museum continues in the next house, known as the Stiftsherrenhaus (Canon's House, 1556–58), which has a café on the ground floor.

At Osterstrasse's western end, on the other side of the street, is the massive bulk of the Hochzeitshaus.

The 'Wedding House', built in Weser Renaissance style from 1610 to 1617 as a ceremonial hall, now fulfils a rather dull purpose as civic offices. But crowds gather outside every day at 1.05, 3.35 and 5.35 to hear its carillon play and to watch mechanical figures re-enact the legend of the Pied Piper. Facing this building across Osterstrasse, in Pferdemarkt, is the Gothic Marktkirche St-Nicolai. Originally dating from 1200, the church was rebuilt in the 1950s. It's well worth a visit, as is Pferdemarkt itself, especially on a Saturday, when there is a lively market.

❸ Adjoining Pferdemarkt is Am Markt. The Dempterhaus on the corner of Am Markt is a graceful sandstone and half-timbered house built in Weser Renaissance style in 1607 to 1608 for Tobias van Dempter, who in 1629 was mayor of Hameln.

Take Zehntopfstrasse at the side of the Dempterhaus and at its end cross over to the Weserpromenade, where there's an uninspiring view of the river from the bridge. Go south along the riverfront for 100m (110 yards) or so, past the Pfortmühle, a 19th-century mill that houses the library, and cross over Sudetenstrasse to Kupferschmiedestrasse.

❹ The Weser Renaissance Bürgerhaus at Kupferschmiedestrasse 13 dates back to 1560. Once a brewery, this rambling building now houses a restaurant, the Kartoffelhaus. Around the corner at Wendenstrasse 8 is the half-timbered Lückingsches Haus (1638–39), with painted motifs and an inscription from Psalm 127 on its façade.

Turn right into Bäckerstrasse for a look at the Löwenapotheke, dating from 1300, directly ahead, and at the Rattenkrug (1250, rebuilt 1568–69), Hameln's oldest café-restaurant. A few steps on, go left on Alte Marktstrasse, a street of half-timbered residential houses. This leads back by way of Bungelosenstrasse to the Rattenfängerhaus and Osterstrasse, from where you retrace your steps to return to the tourist office.

WHEN TO GO
You can do this walk at any time of the year. The streets are quieter in winter but you miss out on the outdoor café terraces and other street animation.

PLACES TO VISIT
Museum Hameln (▷ 126).

WHERE TO EAT
The Rattenfängerhaus (▷ 158) and the Kartoffelhaus (▷ 158) are both excellent choices.

THE BALTIC COAST

Beginning near Lübeck and ending near Rostock, this tour covers a scenic section of eastern Germany's quickly developing Baltic coast and its agricultural hinterland. At about the midpoint, it passes through the particularly attractive small town of Wismar.

THE DRIVE
Distance: 160km (100 miles)
Allow: 6–8 hours
Start at: Travemünde
End at: Heiligendamm

★ In Travemünde, you cross from the west to the east bank of the River Trave on a vehicle ferry, the *Priwallfähre*. On the east bank, go straight ahead; after about 2km (1.2 miles), you cross the old border with East Germany, which is marked by a memorial stone with the inscription *Nie Wieder Geteilt* (Never Again Divided).

Go right, following the signs for Pötenitz and Dassow, with intermittent views of the waters of the Dassower See off to your right, into Dassow. At the first major intersection, go left onto the B105 in the direction of Wismar, but only for 200m (220 yards) or so before going left again, following signs for Neuenhagen and Kalkhorst. Pass through Neuenhagen and continue to Kalkhorst.

❶ The handsome village of Kalkhorst is worth stopping at to look at its impressive red-brick Gothic Sankt-Laurentius church.

Just beyond the church turn left, then quickly right again, onto the road to Brook. This brings you to the coastal forest of Naturschutzgebiet Brooker Wald (Brook Forest Nature Reserve). The minor road continues through Warnkenhagen and Elmenhorst before regaining the coast road to Wismar just short of Klütz (watch for the Dutch-style windmill on your left just before you enter the village).

❷ In Klütz, the 13th-century Sankt-Marienkirche is of interest, as is Schloss Bothmer, and, for railway enthusiasts, there are the steam trains of the Klützer–Ostsee–Eisenbahn. A pleasant side-trip from the village is north to the Baltic resort of Boltenhagen.

From Klütz the coastal road runs southeast towards Wismar, making a gentle curve around the coast of the Wohlenberger Wiek. Part of this section of the drive is on scenic roads lined by avenues of trees—*Alleenstrassen*. Just beyond the village of Proseken, turn left onto the E22/B105 for the run into Wismar.

❸ The old heart of Wismar (▷ 145), a former Hanseatic town, is one of the most handsome on this coast.

Take the coastal road north out of town, following the signs for Insel Poel. Some 10km (6 miles) farther, the road splits at Gross Strömkendorf and you follow the signs left for Poel, across a causeway to the island.

❹ Once on Poel, follow the signs for Wangern and Timmendorf along a road between wide, flat fields dotted with large farmhouses. At Kirchdorf, park next to the fishing harbour, where you may find fishermen selling freshly caught fish. Stroll around the harbour and into the remnants of a star-shaped fortification next to it, which dates from 1620. Driving on, you eventually come to the end of the road at Timmendorfer-Strand, a small resort with a fine, sandy beach.

Retrace your route back over the causeway to Gross Strömkendorf, where you head north once more along the coast road, following the signs for Neubukow. At Wodorf, you pass several fine *Heidekaten*—traditional thatched farmhouses—and at Stove there is a Dutch-style windmill from 1889. At Boiensdorf, take the road to your left for short trip of 2km (1.2 miles) to the Boiensdorfer Werder peninsula, where there's parking right beside the beach. Back on the coastal road, the stretch to Neubukow is on a scenic *Alleenstrasse*.

❺ Neubukow, where there is another old windmill, was the birthplace of Heinrich Schliemann (1822–90), the archaeologist who discovered and excavated the ancient Greek sites of Troy and Mycenae.

Take the road north to Kühlungsborn, passing the lighthouse at Bastorf.

❻ The coastal resort of Kühlungsborn is a curious mix of decrepit old buildings,and well-restored art nouveau and belle époque villas.

Drive 9km (5.5 miles) east to Heiligendamm.

❼ Heiligendamm was founded in 1793 as a bathing resort, and is even more exclusive than nearby Kühlungsborn.

From here it's just 6km (3.5 miles) to Bad Doberan along the E22/B105, for a fast return via Wismar, or on to the autobahn interchanges (exits) around Rostock.

PLACES TO VISIT

KLÜTZER–OSTSEE–EISENBAHN

✉ Bahnhofstrasse 4, 23948 Klütz
☎ 038825 3201

POEL ISLAND

www.insel-poel.de
ℹ Wismarsche Strasse 2, 23999 Kirchdorf/Poel ☎ 038425 20347

KÜHLUNGSBORN

www.kuehlungsborn.de
ℹ Ostseeallee 19, 18225 Ostseebad Kühlungsborn ☎ 038293 8490

BAD DOBERAN (FOR HEILIGENDAMM)

www.bad-doberan.de
ℹ Severinstrasse 6, 18209 Bad Doberan
☎ 038203 62154

WHEN TO GO

Any time between spring and late autumn is ideal, but note that the roads and resorts are at their busiest in summer. In winter, many attractions in the coastal regions are closed, but if weather conditions are good, the coast does have more of an untamed beauty then.

WHERE TO EAT

Lübeck and Rostock, respectively close to the start and the end of the drive, and Wismar in the middle all have good eating possibilities (▷ 159). There are places to eat in the resorts of Travemünde, Kühlungsborn and Heiligendamm too, though they tend to be more tourist-oriented. A great choice is the Alter Schwede (▷ 159) in Wismar.

Opposite *Gabled houses on Wismar's main square*

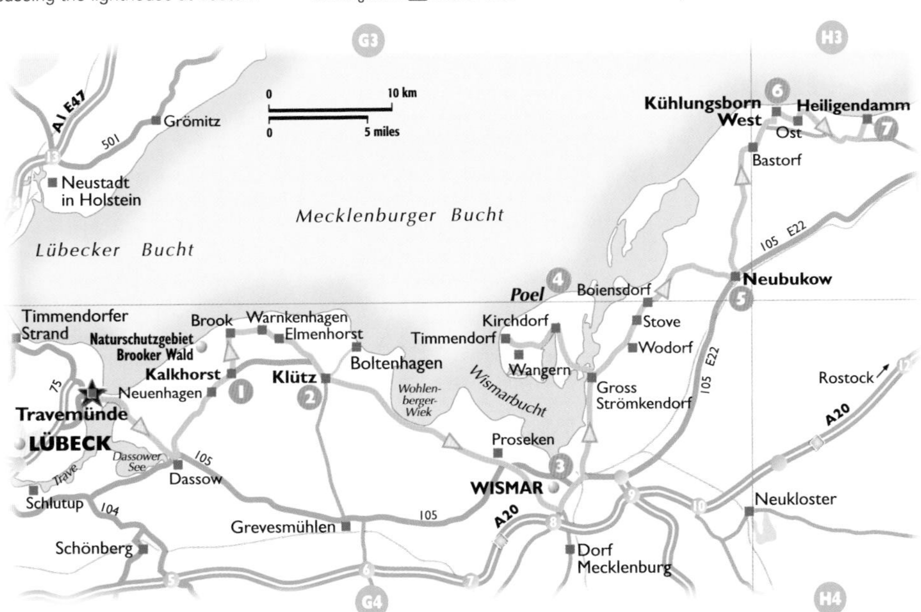

Above *The Weser river valley is a fertile and attractive area, well suited to a car tour*

THE WESERBERGLAND

Beginning and ending close to the E45/A7 north–south autobahn, this route winds through the gentle hill country of the Weser river valley. This is an inland holiday area, rich in nature parks and other protected landscapes, and dotted with towns full of interest for their literary associations, romantic half-timbered buildings and architectural treasures in the style known as Weser Renaissance.

THE DRIVE
Distance: 166km (103 miles)
Allow: 5–8 hours
Start at: Hildesheim
End at: Hannoversch Münden—the distance from here to Hildesheim along the E45/A7 is 110km (68 miles)

★ Hildesheim (▷ 127), an important ecclesiastical town during the Middle Ages, retains a quartet of fine churches from that period, two of which are UNESCO World Heritage Sites. The partially reconstructed central Marktplatz is a reminder of what was one of Germany's largest and finest collections of centuries-old half-timbered houses before it was destroyed in World War II.

From central Hildesheim, follow the signs west for Hameln, leaving town along the B1. About 6 m (3.5 miles) along the road, as you pass the twin villages of Gross Escherde and Klein Escherde, you can see off to your left the low forested hills of the Hildesheimer Wald. After a further 6km (3.5 miles), you cross over the River Leine at Burgstemmen, before pressing on through the village towards Elze and the southern edge of the Osterwald. From here the B1 curves northwest through Coppenbrügge in the valley between the Osterwald and the Oberberg (494m/1,620ft). It then angles westward for the final 14km (8.5 miles) into Hameln. Find the old heart of the town by following signs to *Historische Altstadt* and *Zentrum*.

❶ Hameln (▷ 126), on the banks of the River Weser at the southern edge of the Naturpark Weserbergland-Schaumburg-Hameln, is famous for its legend of the Pied Piper (*Rattenfänger*). The attractive, bustling heart of town is invariably filled with visitors. There are sites associated with the tale of the ratcatcher, and enough places of interest to justify an hour or two strolling around.

You leave Hameln to the south, along the B83, following the signs for Höxter. This road hugs the west (left) bank of the Weser all the way to Höxter, so it's hard to go wrong. The road twists through the alternately flat and hilly country of the Weserbergland (pictured above). Sometimes you are looking down on the river, while at other times it is hard to see. Small ferries take cars and passengers across the stream at several points, and tour boats take off at riverside towns and villages. At the hamlet of Risch, 8km (5 miles) south of Hameln, signs point off to the right for the village of Hämelschenburg, with its fine Weser Renaissance Schloss

(May–end Sep Tue–Sun 10–5; Apr, Oct Tue–Sun 11–4; tel 05155 951690) dating from 1613. A visit here makes a worthwhile diversion of just 4km (2.5 miles) in total. Some 19km (11.5 miles) southeast of Hameln, you arrive at Bodenwerder.

❷ Bodenwerder is noteworthy because of its connection with Baron Münchhausen (1720–97), after whom the disorder Münchhausen's syndrome is named. This spinner of tall tales has been immortalized in literature and film, and his family seat, now the Rathaus, has a museum devoted to him.

After the village of Stahle, 29km (18 miles) south, either go left into Holzminden for a look at its half-timbered houses or keep to the right on the B83 and continue for 8km (5 miles) into Höxter to do the same, passing Kloster Corvey, an abbey founded in 820, on the way. At Godelheim, 5km (3 miles) south of Höxter, watch for a left turn near the end of the village, with signs for Hann. Münden. Take this to remain on the B83 riverside road. Continue through Beverungen and Herstelle. At Bad Karlshafen, go left across a bridge over the Diemel, a tributary of the Weser, and on into the town. At this point you leave the B83 for the B80 (marked for Hann. Münden).

❸ Elegant Bad Karlshafen is a spa town that was founded in 1699 as a community for French Protestant Huguenot refugees, and many of its baroque buildings survive. Among these is the Rathaus, which was formerly the hunting lodge of Landgrave Karl von Hessen. Close to here, in a former cigar factory, is the Deutsches Hugenottenmuseum, which records the town's history and the role of the Huguenots here.

The B80 continues through Bad Karlshafen and emerges once more alongside the Weser. The road curves east and south, between the river and the Reinhardswald,

sometimes passing over hills and sometimes through flat country. After a drive of about 40km (25 miles), you approach Hannoversch Münden, which you enter by staying on the B80 when it turns sharp left, crossing the Weser. Follow signs to *Innenstadt* and *Zentrum*.

❹ Hannoversch Münden (or Hann. Münden) lies at the foot of wooded hills in the gorge where the Fulda and Werra rivers merge to form the Weser. The Reinhardswald is to the northwest, the Bramwald to the northeast and the Naturpark Münden to the east and south. The town's centuries-old half-timbered houses give it character, though there are few remaining examples.

From Hannoversch Münden, it is 10km (6 miles) along the B496 to intersection 76 on the E45/A7 *autobahn* if you are heading south, and 20km (12 miles) to intersection 75, for those going north.

WHEN TO GO

Spring and autumn are good times to go, as the roads are quieter than in summer. The advantages of a summer trip are that more places to visit are open.

PLACES TO VISIT

MUSEUM HAMELN

✉ Osterstrasse 8–9, 31785 Hameln ☎ 05151 202 1215 🕐 Tue–Sun 10–4.30 🎟 Adult €3, child (6–12) €1.50, under 6 free

MÜNCHHAUSEN MUSEUM

✉ Münchhausenplatz 1, 37619 Bodenwerder ☎ 05533 40541 🕐 Apr–end Oct daily 10–1, 2–5 🎟 Adult €2, child (6–14) €1.50, under 6 free

WHERE TO EAT

The towns and villages of the Weserbergland have many hotels, restaurants and cafés. Good choices are the Knochenhaueramtshaus in Hildesheim (▷ 158), the Rattenfängerhaus in Hameln (▷ 158) and the restaurant of Hotel Schlosschänke (Vor der Burg 3–5, 34346 Hann. Münden; tel 05541 70940), across from the River Werra and the Welfenschloss on the north edge of the Altstadt. It serves traditional German cuisine.

AMRUM

WINDSURFING

www.amrum.de

One of the outer islands of the Nordfriesische Inseln chain (▷ 139), Amrum is amply exposed to bracing North Sea winds, and windsurfers pile in by ferry in summer to extract the maximum advantage from its position. Both of the laid-back windsurfing locations have a small windsurfing school attached, but the beach is better at Nebler Strand.

✉ Nebler Strand and Norddorf, on the island's west coast 🕑 May–end Oct 🖐 Free ⛴ Wyker Dampfschiffs-Reederei car ferry from Dagebüll to Wittdün

BREMEN

CASINO BREMEN

www.casino-bremen.de

Try your luck here at French and American roulette and blackjack. The casino is housed in a fine building dating from 1927, just off Martinistrasse in the Altstadt's pedestrian zone. You'll need to take your passport, and men are required to wear a jacket and tie.

✉ Böttcherstrasse 3–5, 28195 Bremen ☎ 0421 329000 🕑 Daily 3pm–3am 🖐 Admission €2.50 🚋 Tram 2, 3, 4, 6, 8

DIE GLOCKE

www.glocke.de

This old concert hall just south of the Dom is the home of two fine orchestras—the Deutsche Kammer-philharmonie Bremen, which performs chamber music, and the Bremer Philharmoniker symphony orchestra. The venue has been described as one of the three finest in Europe, with a fine chandelier-hung entrance hall.

✉ Domsheide 4–5, 28195 Bremen ☎ 0421 33699 🕑 Box office: open 1 hour before performances 🖐 €15–€110 🚋 Tram 2, 3, 4, 5, 6, 8

Above *The Universum Science Center Bremen is a popular attraction for children and adults alike*

SCHÜTTINGER

www.schuettinger.de

Although it has only been in existence since 1990, the Erste Bremer Gasthausbrauerei home brewery, in the Altstadt, has a reputation for its fine Schüttinger pilsener and a range of special beers. The bar has a rustic atmosphere and you sit at long wooden tables. There's simple pub food, and the kitchen can rustle up something for groups of six or more.

✉ Hinter dem Schütting 12–13, 28195 Bremen ☎ 0421 337 6633 🕑 Mon–Fri 12–12, Sat, Sun 11am–2am 🚋 Tram 2, 3, 4, 5, 6

SV WERDER BREMEN

www.werder-online.de
www.weserstadion.de

The home ground of the 2004 Bundesliga soccer champions and winners of the German Cup is the fine Weserstadion, just north of the River Weser.

Am Weserstadion 7, 28205 Bremen 01805 937337 Information: Mon–Fri 9–6. Tickets: Mon–Fri 10–6, Sat 11am–30 minutes before the game, Sun 3pm–30 minutes before the game €11–€55 2, 3, 10

THEATER AM LEIBNIZPLATZ

www.shakespeare-company.com

The Bremer Shakespeare Company is unique in Germany. Its productions of Shakespeare plays attract visitors from all over the country. All performances are in German.

Leibnizplatz 28, 28066 Bremen 0421 500333 Tue–Sat 3–6 €8–€30 Tram 4, 5, 6

THEATER BREMER

www.theaterbremen.de

This large venue, just outside and to the southeast of the Altstadt, is actually a multi-theatre complex, the different elements of which stage opera, dance, musicals and theatre (occasionally in English) among other events.

Am Goetheplatz 1–3, 28203 Bremen 0421 365 3333 Mon–Fri 11–5, Sat 11–2 €10–€90 Tram 2, 3

UNIVERSUM SCIENCE CENTER BREMEN

www.universum-bremen.de

Visit this high-tech, interactive facility for an introduction to the mysteries of the universe and the way humans act to uncover the truth. Some 250 different hands-on exhibits explore problems and solutions in three main scientific areas: planet Earth, the human race and the cosmos.

Wiener Strasse 2, 28359 Bremen 0421 33460 Mon–Fri 9–6, Sat, Sun 10–7 Adult €15.50, child (6–18) €10.50, under 6 free, family €39.50 Tram 6

BREMERHAVEN

ZOO AM MEER BREMERHAVEN

www.zoo-am-meer-bremerhaven.de

The primary focus of this marine-oriented zoo beside the Weser is its aquarium, home to seals and sea lions, but there are also animals from the Arctic and the northern seas, such as polar bears, Arctic foxes and Arctic hares.

H.-H.-Meier-Strasse 5, 27568 Bremerhaven 0471 308 410 Apr–end Sep daily 9–7; Mar, Oct daily 9–6; Nov–end Feb daily 9–4.30 Adult €6.50, child (4–14) €3.50, under 6 free; Mon (except holidays) €5, €2.50

HAMBURG

ALSTERHAUS

www.alsterhaus.de

Under the ownership of the Karstadt chain, Hamburg's long-established flagship department store took a leap into the future and a further step towards chicdom during 2004. Rebuilding gave it a more modern look, and the product range was refined to focus on quality fashion and accessories, perfumes, lifestyle items and gastronomy.

Jungfernstieg 16–20, 20354 Hamburg 040 35901 Mon–Sat 10–8 Jungfernstieg

AM ROTHENBAUM

www.dtb-tennis.de

The Masters Series Hamburg tournament, one of the key competitions on the international men's professional tennis circuit, takes place here every May. The venue is in the north of the city, off Rothenbaumchaussee and close to the Aussenalster, and can seat 13,000 spectators.

Hallerstrasse 89, 20148 Hamburg 040 411780 Tickets: Mon–Fri (also some Sat and Sun) 10–6 From €40 Hallerstrasse

COTTON CLUB

www.cotton-club-hamburg.de

Hamburg's oldest jazz club was founded in 1959 and has been called the Cotton Club since 1963. It has changed venue several times, before ending up at its present location across the Herrengraben canal from the middle of town. Live jazz is performed by highly regarded local combos and international names.

Alter Steinweg 10, 20459 Hamburg 040 343878 Daily from 8.30pm (music from 9pm) €6–€15 Stadthausbrücke

ENGLISH THEATRE OF HAMBURG

www.englishtheatre.de

Founded by two Americans in 1976, this is the only dedicated English-language theatre company in northern Germany. It puts on both modern and classic works. The theatre building, in the Uhlenhorst district east of the Aussenalster, has just 160 seats. Most performances are in the evening, but there are matinees on Tuesdays and Fridays.

Lerchenfeld 14, 22081 Hamburg 040 227 7089 Box office: Mon–Fri 10–2, 3.30–7.30, Sat 3.30–7.30 €7 (previews)–€28.50 Mundsburg

FISCHMARKT

www.hamburger-fischmarkt.de

The venerable St.-Pauli fish market is renowned throughout Germany, so much so that it has gone on the road, taking its inimitable brand of street-trader charm (and cheek) to other cities. But back home on the Elbe waterfront is where it makes its principal mark, selling not only fish but also many other different kinds of food products and flea-market goods.

Fischmarkt (and nearby streets), 22767 Hamburg May–end Oct Sun 5am–9.30am; Nov–end Apr Sun 7am–9.30am Landungsbrücken

GROSSE FREIHEIT 36

www.grossefreiheit36.de

Big, brash and beautiful, this club just off the Reeperbahn in the city's red-light district is world famous, not least for its connection with the early days of the Beatles. It is a top venue for visiting performers of international renown. There is live music by less well-known performers in the downstairs Kaiserkeller, and a dance club.

✉ Grosse Feiheit 36, 22767 Hamburg ☎ 040 3177 7811 🕐 Concerts: from 7 or 8pm (in the Kaiserkeller, from 10pm) 🖐 €15–€30 🚇 Reeperbahn

HAMBURG DUNGEON

www.hamburgdungeon.com

An underground boat trip at this attraction in the Speicherstadt takes you on a tour through some of the grislier aspects of Hamburg's 1,200 years of history. Ghosts, torture, death, the Black Death, the Inquisition, fire and flood are depicted by actors and through displays, making for a pretty scary show. Not recommended for children under 10 or those of a squeamish disposition.

✉ Kehrwieder 2, 20457 Hamburg ☎ 040 3600 5520 🕐 Daily 11–6 (from 10 Jul–end Aug) 🖐 Adult €18.95, child under 14 (must be accompanied by an adult) €14.45 🚇 Baumwall

HAMBURGER GOLF-CLUB

www.hamburgergolf-club.de

This is a top-notch, 18-hole course, in the suburb of Blankenese west of the city.

✉ In de Bargen 59, 22587 Hamburg ☎ 040 812177 🕐 Daily 9–5 🖐 Green fees: €45–€55 🚇 Sülldorf ☕

HAMBURGISCHE STAATSOPER

www.hamburgische-staatsoper.de

The home of the Hamburgische Staatsoper and Ballettcompagnie John Neumeier (Hamburg's ballet company) was built in the 1950s and is in the northern part of the Neustadt. The opera company itself was founded in 1678 and stages everything from classics to contemporary works while the ballet company specializes in modern dance.

✉ Grosse Theaterstrasse 25, 20354 Hamburg ☎ 040 356868 🕐 Box office: Mon–Sat 10–6.30 and 1 hour before performances 🖐 €7–€146 🚇 Gänsemarkt ☕

LAEISZHALLE-MUSIKHALLE HAMBURG

www.musikhalle-hamburg.de

On the northwest edge of the Neustadt, beside the Wallanlagen gardens, is this ornate concert hall dating from 1908. It is the home of the Hamburger Symphoniker, the Philharmonisches Staatsorchester Hamburg and the NDR Sinfonieorchester, and attracts some of the world's great ensembles.

✉ Johannes-Brahms-Platz, 20355 Hamburg ☎ 040 346920 🕐 Box office: Mon–Fri 10–6 and 1 hour before performances 🖐 €12–€80 🚇 Stefansplatz, Gänsemarkt ☕

TIERPARK HAGENBECK

www.hagenbeck-tierpark.de

Dating back to 1907, this large and impressive zoo in northwest Hamburg was a pioneer in the more modern presentation of exotic animals in habitats modelled on those in the wild. On its 27ha (67-acre) site, it continues to develop novel approaches to keeping animals, and there are numerous activities for children.

✉ Lokstedter Grenzstrasse, 22527 Hamburg ☎ 040 530 0330 🕐 Mar–end Oct daily 9–5 (as late as 7 when the weather is fine); Nov–end Feb daily 9–4.30 🖐 Adult €15, child (4–16) €10, under 6 free, family €45–€51 🚇 Hagenbecks Tierpark

HANNOVER

AALRÄUCHEREI HODANN

www.hodann.de

Smoked eel from the Steinhuder Meer is a byword for taste throughout Germany, and no one does it better than this traditional smoke-house. Find it in the fishing village and resort of Steinhude, some 30km (18 miles) west of Hannover (▷ 134–135). You can visit the smoking facility and buy some of the goods at the on-site shop.

✉ Alter Winkel 1, 31515 Steinhude ☎ 05033 8246 🕐 Mon–Fri 8–6, Sat, Sun 9–6

LEIBNIZUFER FLOHMARKT

A long stretch along the west bank of the Leine, just outside Hannover's Altstadt (old town), is taken up every Saturday with the stands of this popular general market and flea market.

✉ Leibnizufer, 30169 Hannover 🕐 Sat 7–2 🚌 Markthalle

NIEDERSÄCHSISCHES STAATSTHEATER

www.staatstheater-hannover.de

This palatial theatre is Hannover's premier venue for opera, classical music, ballet and theatre. The Niedersächsisches Staatsorchester often performs here.

✉ Opernplatz 1, 30159 Hannover ☎ 0511 9999 1111 🕐 Mon–Fri 10–7.30, Sat 10–4 🖐 €13–€105 🚌 Kröpcke ☕

LÜBECK

FIGURENTHEATER LÜBECK

www.figurentheater-luebeck.de

Just off Holstenstrasse, and a few doors along from the Theaterfiguren Museum (▷ opposite), is this superb puppet theatre, which is aimed as much at adults as it is at children. The magical performances of pieces like *The Little Prince* and *The Barber of Seville* should appeal to all ages, although they are spoken and sung in German.

✉ Kolk 20–22, 23552 Lübeck ☎ 0451 70060 🕐 Tue 9–noon, Wed–Fri 9–12, 1.30–3, Sat, Sun 1.30–3 (except 1st Sun of month 🖐 €5–€7 🚌 1, 3, 11

NIEDEREGGER

www.niederegger.de

Lübeck has been famed for its marzipan since Hanseatic times, and nowhere is it better made than in this jewel of a place across from the Rathaus, in business since 1806.

Downstairs, marzipan is available in an astonishing range of pastries and confections; upstairs, you can eat it in an elegant café; and in the top-floor museum you can chew over its provenance.

Breite Strasse 89, 23552 Lübeck 0451 530 1126 Mon–Fri 9–7, Sat 9–6, Sun 10–6 5, 7, 11, 14, 16

SEA LIFE TIMMENDORFER STRAND

www.sealife-timmendorf.de

This, one of five Sea Life centres in Germany, is at a Baltic coast resort just north of Lübeck. Rays, small sharks and sea horses are among the denizens of the deep in the various display tanks. A unique element of the exhibition is a section on the endangered sea that was organized in cooperation with Greenpeace.

Kurpromenade 5, 23669 Timmendorfer Strand 01805 6669 0101 Jul, Aug daily 10–7; Apr–end Jun, Sep, Oct daily 10–6; Nov–end Mar daily 10–5 Adult €12.95, senior €11.95, child (3–14) €9.50, under 3 free

THEATERFIGUREN MUSEUM

www.tfm.luebeck.com

This appears to be associated with the nearby Figurentheater Lübeck, but in fact it is a fascinating collection of more than 2,000 puppets from around the world, both antique and modern. The proprietors are accomplished puppet-masters and their love for their subject shows in the range and quality of the exhibits.

Kolk 14–16, 23552 Lübeck 0451 78626 Fri–Wed 11–8 Adult €4, child (4–12) €2, under 4 free 1, 3, 11

ROSTOCK

ZOO ROSTOCK

www.zoo-rostock.de

This zoo is the largest in northern Germany, with some 1,500 animals in woodland and gardens. Every year a different theme from the natural world is explored through exhibitions and educational activities.

Rennbahnallee 21, 18059 Rostock 0381 20820 Apr–end Oct daily 9–7; Nov–end Mar daily 9–5 Adult €11, child (3–16) €6, under 3 free, family €21–€31 Tram 3, 6

VERDEN

RENNBAHN VERDEN

www.rennverein-verden.de

The town of Verden, southeast of Bremen, is so closely connected with horses that it is known as Reiterstadt (Horse-Riders' Town) Verden. The connection, with the German army's cavalry, with stud farms and with horse racing, goes back centuries. Race meetings are held at the racetrack here.

Lüneburger Weg, 27266 Verden 04231 63195 On race days 1–6 From €5

WALSRODE

VOGELPARK WALSRODE

www.vogelpark-walsrode.de

Located just outside the small town of Walsrode, between Hamburg, Bremen and Hannover, this theme park sets its main attractions—birds—amid multihued gardens and fountains. Some 5,000 birds from 750 species are the star performers, literally in the case of performances with hawks and other raptors. A petting zoo and adventure playground complete the picture.

North of Walsrode (Autobahn A27/E234 exits Walsrode West and Bad Fallingbostel), 29655 Walsrode 05161 60440 May–end Sep daily 9–7; Apr, Oct daily 9–6; Nov–end Mar daily 10–4 Adult €14, child (4–17) €9, family €28–€42

WILHELMSHAVEN

OCEANIS

www.oceanis.de

The port town that was Germany's most important naval base through two world wars is an appropriate place to host an introduction to the sea. Here, you enter a virtual underwater research station—it's actually onshore, in a purpose-built harbour facility. Innovative technology and a hands-on approach help illuminate the wonders of the sea and its creatures.

Bontekai 63, 26382 Wilhelmshaven 04421 755055 Mid-Mar to mid-Nov, Christmas, New Year and holidays, daily 10–6 Adult €8.90, child (6–14) €5.90, family €21.90

FESTIVALS AND EVENTS

JULY

TRAVEMÜNDER-WOCHE

www.luebeck-tourism.de

Lübeck's Sailing Week has been attracting sailors to this maritime town for over 100 years. More than 800 boats from 16 countries attend this annual sailing regatta and yachting event.

01805 889 9700 Late July

JULY/AUGUST

SCHLESWIG-HOLSTEIN MUSIC FESTIVAL

www.shmf.de

Germany's northernmost Land celebrates classical music with 100 concerts held in a variety of locations, from barns and stables to churches and country estates.

Lübeck 0451 389570 July and August Varies

OCTOBER

BREMEN FREIMARKT

www.bremen-tourism.de

Although primarily based around the Bürgerweide and Marktplatz, the oldest folk festival in Germany takes over the whole city, with music, dancing and general gaiety. The highlight of the festival is the parade on the second Saturday.

Bürgerweide and Marktplatz 01805 101030 Two weeks from mid-October

Opposite *A wrought-iron folly offers shade in the rose garden at the Herrenhausen Gardens in Hannover*

Above *In good weather, cafés and restaurants set out tables and chairs on Hildesheim's square*

PRICES AND SYMBOLS

The restaurants are listed alphabetically (excluding Le, La and Les) within each town. The prices given are the average for a two-course lunch (L) and a three-course dinner (D) for one person, without drinks. The wine price is for the least expensive bottle. All the restaurants listed accept credit cards unless otherwise stated.

For a key to the symbols, ▷ 2.

BAD KARLSHAFEN

HESSISCHER HOF

www.hess-hof.de

Dine in the white-themed restaurant, the light-suffused Wintergarten or on the outside terrace of this hotel restaurant. The menu majors on regional cuisine, such as game in season, along with a sprinkling of international choices that run as far as Bombay rice.

Hessischer Hof Hotel, Carlstrasse 13–15, 34385 Bad Karlshafen 05672 1059 Daily 11–2, 5.30–10 L €18, D €27, Wine €16

BRAUNSCHWEIG

BRODOCZ

www.restaurant-brodocz.de

If you relish vegetarian and vegan food, you'll enjoy this small restaurant a few blocks west of the Rathaus. The atmosphere inside its stone walls and half-timbered frame is informal. There is a play table for children. Some of the interior seating is fixed, and the swivel chairs could be a little more comfortable, but in fine weather, you can sit out on the tree-shaded terrace. The menu is Mediterranean with some Asian flourishes.

Stephanstrasse 1, 38100 Braunschweig 0531 42236 Mon–Sat 11.30–10 L €15, D €25, Wine €11

BREMEN

MEIEREI IM BÜRGERPARK

www.meierei-bremen.de

In an area northeast of the Hauptbahnhof, where 19th-century villas abound, you can combine a stroll in the English-style Bürgerpark (1866) with lunch or dinner at this smart but casual restaurant. The gabled Swiss-style wood-built villa dates from 1881 and was once an aristocrat's summer hideaway. Tranquillity and relaxation are guaranteed while you choose from the fine seafood, meat (the sautéed squab is particularly good) and vegetarian dishes on the varied Continental menu. Eat in one of the four traditional interior rooms, or on the verandah with a garnish of fresh air and a view of the park. Coffee and cake are served between mealtimes. Visa is the only card accepted.

Bürgerpark, 28209 Bremen 0421 340 8619 Tue–Sun 12–12 L €25, D €35, Wine €23

RATSKELLER

www.ratskeller-bremen.de

Often considered the best of Germany's many traditional Ratskeller (town-hall cellar) restaurants, Bremen's vaulted establishment, with secluded niches, has been in business since 1408. Seafood—including smoked fish—has a prominent place on the menu, but so, too, does that Hamburg favourite, *Labskaus* (▷ 389). More than 600 different German wines are served, some from barrels.

Rathaus, Am Markt, 28195 Bremen 0421 321676 Daily 11am–midnight L €15, D €25, Wine €20

CELLE

HISTORISCHER RATSKELLER

www.ratskeller-celle.de

Rustic, wood-hewn, and decorated with old paintings and antiques, the atmospheric restaurant in this vaulted cellar of the stone-built town hall is plush in a faded kind of way. It serves German cuisine such as local roast game and *Heidschnucken* lamb, but also includes some international dishes—if items such as steak with various sauces and scallops au gratin can be so described—and a mixed seafood platter that's a bit of both. Dustin Hoffman passed this way once and apparently departed satisfied, and there's every reason to suppose you will too. It's also popular with locals. Be sure to sample one of the fine German wines.

Markt 14, 29221 Celle 05141 29099 Mon–Sat 10am–midnight, Sun 10–3 L €12, D €20, Wine €17

EINBECK

BRODHAUS

One way to celebrate the local brewing tradition in this small walled town filled with 16th-century half-timbered houses, is to dine on plain but hearty German fare in one of the beer-barrel booths in this rustic pub, inside one of the most beautiful buildings in the heart of town—it was originally the Bakers Guildhouse. The natural choice for an accompanying drink is one of Einbeck's own Einbecker beers.

Marktplatz 13, 37574 Einbeck 05561 924169 Daily 11am–midnight L€14, D €19, Wine €14

GOSLAR

DIE WORTH

www.kaiserworth.de

The in-house restaurant of this 500-year-old lodging is a touch of class on the venerable market square. Gothic arches define the interior, but far from being gloomy it is bright and elegant, with fine table settings and attentive service. Given the proximity of the Harz Mountains, with their forests, rivers and lakes, it is no surprise that roast venison and other game is on the menu in season, and grilled trout year round. If the weather is fine try for a seat on the outside terrace, under the building's arches on the square.

Kaiserworth Hotel, Markt 3, 38640 Goslar 05321 7090 Daily 11.30–11 L €15, D €25, Wine €16

HAMBURG

CASA MADEIRA

Amid an enclave of ethnic restaurants on a bustling street just inland from the Landungsbrücken, this small but personable place stands out for its authentic Portuguese cuisine. The interior recalls many such plain but satisfying eateries in Portugal. The atmosphere achieved by having a television set tuned to a Portuguese satellite station won't appeal to every diner, but menu items such as garlic scampi certainly should.

Ditmar-Koel-Strasse 14, 20459 Hamburg 040 7404 1880 Mon–Fri 9.30am–2am, Sat, Sun 8am–2am L €12, D €20, Wine €9 Landungsbrücken

FISCHEREIHAFEN

www.fischereihafenrestaurant.de

Just off the England-Kai in Altona, this modern, family-owned seafood restaurant has been a fixture in Hamburg since 1981. The extensive menu covers traditional and some international dishes, including the popular grilled fillet of *Zander* (pike-perch) on spinach with a caper and tuna sauce and potatoes. The mixed seafood platter (for two) is a good way to sample different items from the menu. You can have a pre-meal drink in the *gemütlich* (friendly) Oysterbar, and dine indoors or (from May to late September) on the balcony, which has fine views.

Grosse Elbstrasse 143, 22767 Hamburg 040 381816 Sun–Thu 11.30–10, Fri, Sat 11.30–10.30 L €20, D €45, Wine €25 112 to Elbberg

LANDHAUS DILL

www.landhausdill.com

A country-style villa across a wide street from the Elbe is the setting for this elegant restaurant, focusing mainly on German and Austrian cuisine. Despite the proximity to the river, there's no real view of the water. The garden terrace separated from the traffic by a hedgerow is a fine place to dine on a warm summer's day, while at other times, the flower-bedecked interior is better. Seafood dishes, including sushi, complement standards such as roast lamb with herbs. The wine list has 250 choices.

Elbchaussee 94, 22763 Hamburg 040 390 5077 Tue–Sun 12–3, 5.30–10.30 L €30, D €45, Wine €23 Altona Bus 36 Susettestrasse

OLD COMMERCIAL ROOM

www.oldcommercialroom.de

It would be difficult to find a place that's more replete with traditional Hamburg atmosphere than this venerable seamen's tavern not far from the port, facing the landmark Michaeliskirche. With its intimate wood-panelled interior, tables in convivial proximity to one another and old photographs adorning the walls, this is the place to sample that traditional Hamburg dish of *Labskaus*. Seafood dishes, including fine sole and wild salmon, are on the menu, and meat-eaters won't go wrong by choosing a simple steak with all the trimmings.

Englische Planke 10, 20459 Hamburg 040 366319 Daily 12–12 L €20, D €40, Wine €25 St. Pauli

VAPIANO

www.vapiano.de

Ideal for a break while shopping, or for a quick but far from bland dinner, this breezy self-service Italian restaurant, one of a fast-growing chain, is a cut above a mere fast-food joint and has a trendy cachet all its own. Freshly made pasta and pizza, and some interesting wines, make Vapiano stand out from the crowd. You don't pay directly but put your purchases on a house card, and settle up before leaving.

Hohe Bleichen 10, 20345 Hamburg 040 3501 9975 Mon–Sat 11.30am–midnight, Sun 11.30–10 L €8, D €12, Wine €12.50 Gänsemarkt

HAMELN

KARTOFFELHAUS IM BÜRGERHAUS

www.kartoffelhaus-hameln.de

You might find it difficult to persuade yourself to enter this restaurant, so handsome is the outside of the old half-timbered townhouse on the west side of the Altstadt. The scene is equally good beneath the wooden beams on the two floors inside, where you dine on unambitious but tasty traditional fare such as the *Kartoffelhaus pfanne*, which is based around tender grilled pork fillet and the restaurant's signature potatoes. There's a good view of the nearby *Fachwerkhäuser* (half-timbered houses) from the window tables upstairs, but the downstairs nooks are perhaps cosier.

Kupferschmiedestrasse 13, 31785 Hameln 05151 22383 Tue–Sat 11.30–2.30, 6–10.30, Sun 11.30–2.30, 6–9 L €10, D €20, Wine €15

RATTENFÄNGERHAUS

www.rattenfaengerhaus.de

Indelibly associated with the Pied Piper, if for no other reason than the inscription on its 1603 façade, this bustling, touristy but memorable restaurant on the main street takes full advantage of Hameln's legend. Things are perhaps taken too far, as some dishes and set-price menus contain the rather unappetizing word 'rat' in their names. Traditional German dishes such as schnitzel and roast game (in season) abound on the menu, but you can also choose light snacks.

Osterstrasse 28, 31785 Hameln 05151 3888 Mon–Wed 10–3, 6–11, Thu–Sun 10am–midnight L €10, D €22, Wine €14

HANNOVER

BASIL

www.basil.de

This chic restaurant is in the unlikely but graceful setting of a former Prussian army riding establishment in the northeast of Hannover. Up to 100 diners can be seated here among iron pillars, under a vaulted brick ceiling in a room suffused with natural light. The menu is hard to define—'international fusion' would be one way—since it changes every few weeks and the chef roams Europe and Asia in spirit for inspiration. Cuisines, styles and ingredients are mixed and matched to intriguing effect, complemented by wines from around the world. In good weather, there's a fine outdoor terrace.

Dragonerstrasse 30a, 30163 Hannover 0511 622636 Mon–Sat 6.30pm–2am, Sun during important trade fairs only L€20, D €40, Wine €18 Tram 8

CLICHY

www.clichy.de

This downtown restaurant is one of the most admired and consistent in Hannover, pulling in local foodies, business people and visitors alike for a dining experience that's memorable without being overly formal. The owner-chef speaks of trying to create an elegant bistro ambience, and there seems little doubt that he succeeds, aided by waiters who are attentive, but not to a fault. Goose livers, truffle sauces and similar gourmet fare have their place on the menu, but so too does pan-fried chicken in a curry sauce with vegetables. American Express and Visa are accepted.

Weissekreuzstrasse 31, 30161 Hannover 0511 312447 Mon–Fri 12–2.30, 6–11, Sat 6–11 L €30, D €45, Wine €22 Tram 3, 7

HILDESHEIM

KNOCHENHAUERAMTSHAUS

www.knochenhauer-amtshaus.de

Dining at this café-restaurant in the central square is something of an event thanks to the building it is in. The medieval masterpiece *Fachwerkhaus* (half-timbered house), the old Butchers' Guildhouse, was one of the loveliest buildings in Germany. Destroyed during World War II, it was rebuilt in the 1980s, and has plenty of nooks and crannies where you can keep apart from fellow diners, and open spaces where you can join them. You can settle for just a beer and a snack inside or, in good weather, outside on the cobbled square. Alternatively, you can also have a meal from the limited menu. Visa is the only card accepted here.

Markt 7, 31134 Hildesheim 05121 288 9909 Daily 9am–10pm L €10, D €15, Wine €10

KIEL

FISCHERS FRITZ

www.hotel-birke.de

Although the name is based on a German tongue-twister—*Fischers Fritz isst frische fische* (Fischer's Fritz eats fresh fish)—the seafood here is easier on the tongue, melt-in-the-mouth even. Sadly, the restaurant hasn't got a waterfront setting but is landlocked in Kiel's Hasseldieksdamm district. It's as bright and airy as a sea breeze, though, and further compensates with sophisticated dining, employing a variety of fish from the nearby Baltic and from Schleswig-Holstein's rivers and lakes.

Hotel Birke, Martenshofweg 8d, 24109 Kiel 0431 533 1435 Daily 11.30–2, 6–10pm L €28, D €38, Wine €18

Below *You can't miss the Basil restaurant in Hannover*

LÜBECK

MIERA

www.gulara.com/miera

Hidden away up a flight of stairs in an old merchant's townhouse just east of the Markt, Miera shines both as a setting and for its food. Graceful dining rooms edged with stucco display touches of artful shabbiness and are adorned with modern art that veers towards the risqué. The menu changes every few days, drawing on a mix of Continental influences and paying significant homage to Mediterranean cuisine and wines, although it deliberately eludes easy categorization—venison might share the day's list with bouillabaisse and rocket (arugula) salad. The restaurant is only open for lunch and dinner, but there is also a bistro, which is open all day (Mon–Sat 9.30am–midnight).

✉ Hüxstrasse 57, 23552 Lübeck ☎ 0451 77212 ⌚ Mon–Sat 9.30am–midnight 🖐 L €20, D €35, Wine €16 🚌 1, 4, 11, 21, 24, 31, 32, 34, 39

SCHIFFERGESELLSCHAFT

www.schiffergesellschaft.de

An armada of models of old sailing ships is suspended from the ceiling and other antique maritime memorabilia grace the wood-panelled walls in this restaurant of the step-gabled Hanseatic League-era Haus der Schiffergesellschaft (Sea Captains' Guild House; ▷ 137), dating from 1535. Dine convivially at long oak tables, or at your own four-person table. Expect hearty servings of heavy but tasty traditional fare, such as grilled pork fillets and roasted lamb with thick sauces and all the trimmings, alongside lighter fish dishes and salads.

✉ Breite Strasse 2, 23552 Lübeck ☎ 0451 76776 ⌚ 10am–1am 🖐 L €20, D €35, Wine €21 🚌 1, 2

RATSKELLER ZU LÜBECK

www.ratskeller-zu-luebeck.de

This cellar restaurant, with an entrance at the side of the medieval Rathaus (▷ 137), has a choice of dining spaces: in an open room, in a more discreet space close to the kitchen, and in total privacy in a series of booths whose doors are marked with the insignia of once-prominent local families. Whichever you choose, you'll be basking in traditional style and dining on old-fashioned northern German cuisine. Meat dishes predominate, but there are a few vegetarian choices; among the fish options, the grilled *Zander* (pike-perch) is a special house dish, and the smoked-fish soup is also well worth trying. The restaurant accepts Visa and MasterCard.

✉ Markt 15, 23552 Lübeck ☎ 0451 72044 ⌚ Daily 11am–midnight 🖐 L €20, D €30, Wine €14 🚌 1, 2

LÜNEBURG

NEPTUNS FISCHHAUS/ MARISQUEIRA

That 'Marisqueira' tag reveals the Portuguese roots of this fine little seafood restaurant, close to the old Wasserviertel river port, though much of the fish comes from the North Sea and the Baltic. Choose your fish from a glass-fronted cabinet in which the day's offerings are displayed on ice, and you can watch the lady of the house as she cooks your selection. The interior is plain, but the plants on the tables are real. In fine weather, you can dine outside. Fish soup, grilled scampi, *Matjes* (fresh raw herring) and grilled tuna are just a few of the dishes on offer. The restaurant doesn't accept credit cards.

✉ Bei der Abtspferdetränke 1, 21335 Lüneburg ☎ 04131 408528 ⌚ Mon–Thu 10–9, Fri, Sat 10–10, Sun noon–9am 🖐 L €20, D €30, Wine €10

ROSTOCK

ZUR KOGGE

www.zur-kogge.de

If a location at the harbour and a name that recalls the *Hansekoggen* (Hanseatic League cog ships) of yore isn't enough of a give-away, you'll be convinced that you've entered a maritime world the moment you step through the door. This 150-year-old sailors' bar-turned-restaurant is Rostock's oldest such establishment. Model sailing ships hang from the ceiling, and all kinds of seagoing mementoes lie among the polished wood and burnished brass. The menu includes pan-fried Baltic herring and the *Labskaus*, and many different pork dishes, but it manages to fit in some vegetarian choices too. American Express is not accepted here.

✉ Wokrenterstrasse 27, 18055 Rostock ☎ 0381 493 4493 ⌚ Mon–Sat (also Sun Apr–end Dec) 11.30am–11pm 🖐 L €15, D €25, Wine €12 🚌 Tram 11, 12

SCHWERIN

UHLE 1751 WEINHAUS

www.uhle1751.de

This restaurant in the old town, close to the cathedral, is in an elegant rococo building dating from 1740 that later became a wine shop and tasting house. The renovated main dining room is decorated in a bright, *Jugendstil* (art nouveau) style. Upstairs is the medieval-style Rittersaal (Knights' Hall), used on special occasions and for groups. Regional dishes include pan-fried Schweriner eel and *Zander* (pike-perch), as well as roast Mecklenburg duck. The couple who run the restaurant are notable for their German *Gastfreundschaft* (hospitality).

✉ Schusterstrasse 13–15, 19055 Schwerin ☎ 0385 477 3030 ⌚ Daily 12–3, 6–12 🖐 L €20, D €35, Wine €18

WISMAR

ALTER SCHWEDE

www.alter-schwede-wismar.de

The oldest building in town (1380) and a visitor attraction in its own right contains one of the most characterful restaurants on the Baltic coast. The 'Old Swede' has a traditional, wood-panelled interior and a warm and sophisticated atmosphere. The portions of Baltic seafood, marinaded roast pork and other traditional dishes are hearty. In warm weather, you can dine outdoors on the square, with a view of the Wasserkunst pavilion.

✉ Am Markt 19–20, 23966 Wismar ☎ 03841 283552 ⌚ Daily 11.30am–late 🖐 L €15, D €25, Wine €17

Above *The café terrace of the Kaiserworth hotel in Goslar*

PRICES AND SYMBOLS

The prices are the lowest and highest for a double room for one night including breakfast, unless otherwise stated. All the hotels listed accept credit cards unless otherwise stated. Note that rates can vary widely throughout the year.

For a key to the symbols, ▷ 2.

BREMEN

BUTHMANN IM ZENTRUM

www.hotel-buthmann.de

Although it is short on amenities, this small hotel in a renovated townhouse compensates with a friendly welcome and the personal touch from its long-time family owners. It's on a quiet side street on the edge of the Altstadt. The guest rooms are clean and comfortable. It's best to reserve in advance.

Löningstrasse 29, 28195 Bremen
0421 326397 €75–€85 9
1, 4, 5, 10

PARK HOTEL BREMEN

www.park-hotel-bremen.de

This hotel has a grandiose 19th-century style, but it actually dates from the 1950s. There's a small lake, the Hollersee, and the 19th-century park makes a quiet retreat. The public spaces are graceful, and the large, elegant rooms are fully equipped. Restaurants include the Meierei im Bürgerpark (▷ 156).

Im Bürgerpark, 28209 Bremen
0421 34080 €230–€350 177
Spa; limousine
5, 6

CELLE

FÜRSTENHOF CELLE

www.fuerstenhof.de

Since you're visiting a town where the main attraction is the fantastical ducal seat of the house of Brunswick and Lüneburg (▷ 138), you may as well pamper yourself by staying at this high-end establishment. The guest rooms of the 17th-century salmon-hued mansion, south of the castle, are a shade less distinguished than the public spaces, but they have garden views. The French restaurant, Endtenfang, is excellent.

Hannoversche Strasse 55–56, 29221 Celle 05141 2010 €185–€265
73  Indoor Spa

GOSLAR

KAISERWORTH

www.kaiserworth.de

This hotel stands out on the main square, where it occupies the Gothic Tailors' and Weavers' Guild Hall (1494). It easily combines traditional looks and service in its public spaces with modern facilities in the guest rooms. Front rooms look onto the Markt. Additional assets include the fine Die Worth restaurant (▷ 157), a bar, wine bar and a café terrace.

Markt 3, 38640 Goslar 05321 7090
€105–€175 66

HAMBURG

AUSSEN ALSTER

www.aussenalster.de

In the St.-Georg district on the southeastern shore of the Aussen Alster, this boutique hotel in a dazzlingly white, renovated 19th-century mansion has earned plaudits for care and attention to detail. The ambience is that of a sophisticated country villa, a feeling enhanced by the courtyard garden. Hidden in the cellar is the exquisite Schimilinsky Mediterranean and Italian restaurant.

Schmilinskystrasse 11, 20099 Hamburg
040 241557 €130–€165 27
Sauna, solarium; bicycle, boat rental Lohmühlenstrasse

FAIRMONT HOTEL VIER JAHRESZEITEN
www.hvj.de
The superb Four Seasons is renowned in Germany. Public spaces are all but dripping in antiques, and guest rooms are individually styled. Alongside fine restaurants and tradition since 1897, there are views of the Binnenalster from many of the rooms.
Neuer Jungfernstieg 9–14, 20354 Hamburg 040 34940 €300–€385, excluding breakfast 157 Spa Gänsemarkt

HAMELN

HOTEL ZUR KRONE
www.hotelzurkrone.de
This hotel, behind a half-timbered façade is ideal for exploring. Most rooms have a comfortable, modern style but some have exposed wooden beams and more stylish fittings. The restaurant serves continental and German dishes.
Osterstrasse 30, 31785 Hameln 05151 9070 €95–€99 32

HANNOVER

MARITIM GRAND HOTEL HANNOVER
www.maritim.de
This lies just a block from the heart of the old town, amid shops, restaurants, theatres and museums, and close to the Maschsee lake. All this and a personable staff help compensate for a 1960s exterior, and a business-hotel ambience.
Friedrichswall 11, 30159 Hannover 0511 36770 €115–€275 285 €13.60 per day Markthalle/Landtag

LÜBECK

KAISERHOF
www.kaiserhof-luebeck.de
On a busy street just outside the ring canal, two graceful mansions house a fine hotel. Rooms are individual and pleasant in a pastel, chintzy way. There's a lounge, bar, attractive terrace overlooking the garden and a heated pool. Try to get a room in the main hotel.
Kronsforder Allee 11–13, 23560 Lübeck 0451 703301 €100–€135 60 Indoor 2, 7, 16

RINGHOTEL JENSEN
www.ringhotel-jensen.de
In a gabled townhouse across the canal from the Holstentor, the Jensen is well placed for exploring. The large, comfortable rooms overlook either the canal or gardens. The restaurant serves seafood.
An der Obertrave 4–5, 23552 Lübeck 0451 702490 €85–€117 42 1, 3, 11

ROSTOCK

HOTEL VERDI
www.hotel-verdi.de
This hotel, in a baroque house, is close to the Petrikirche. The family owners offer a friendly welcome and a commitment to comfort and value. The low-on-frills modern rooms are comfortable and clean. Some are small apartments with a kitchen.
Wollenweberstrasse 28, 18055 Rostock 0381 252240 €74–€98 10 Bicycle rental

RÜGEN

STEIGENBERGER RESORT HOTEL RÜGEN
www.steigenberger.com
An all-inclusive resort in the Nationalpark Jasmund, which forms its own self-contained world. The focal point is a restored villa, with rooms and apartments around it.
Neddesitz 4, 18551 Sagard-Rügen 038302 95 €105–€160 145 rooms, 155 holiday apartments Indoor and outdoor

SCHLESWIG

STRANDHALLE
www.hotel-strandhalle.de
A small hotel, ideally placed for a visit to the Schlei inlet on the Baltic. The neat little rooms are furnished in a modest modern style, and front rooms look over the waterfront. The restaurant specializes in seafood.
Strandweg 2, 24847 Schleswig 04621 9090 €103–€127 25 Indoor Bicycle, boat rental

SCHWERIN

HOTEL ARTE SCHWERIN
www.hotel-arte.de
A 19th-century country inn that has been modernized but hasn't lost all its traditional character. The hotel is close to the Ostorfer See and is handy for the outer ring road. Guest rooms are comfortable. The Fontane restaurant serves seasonal and regional cuisine.
Dorfstrasse 6, 19061 Schwerin-Krebsförden 0385 63450 €82–€119 40

NIEDERLÄNDISCHER HOF
www.niederlaendischer-hof.de
The hotel, dating back to 1901, is on the west bank of the Pfaffenteich, a small inland lake between the Old Town and Hauptbahnhof. Oceans of marble define the bathrooms in the luxurious rooms. Relax in front of the fireplace in the stately library-lounge. The restaurant has a reputation for its cuisine.
Alexandrinenstrasse 12–13, 19055 Schwerin 0385 591100 €106–€147 32

SYLT

MIRAMAR
www.hotel-miramar.de
This island of calm is on the western edge of Westerland. The hotel has been owned by one family since 1903 and tradition and family pride are much in evidence. The large guest rooms are modern.
Friedrichstrasse 43, 25890 Westerland-Sylt 04651 8550 €184–€388 93 Indoor Wellness

WISMAR

STEIGENBERGER HOTEL STADT HAMBURG
www.steigenberger.com
In an unbeatable position on Wismar's central square, the Stadt Hamburg has become ever more exclusive. Rooms have every modern comfort and there's a restaurant that serves everything from superior snacks to haute cuisine.
Am Markt 24, 23966 Wismar 03841 2390 €105–€165 104

SIGHTS 164
WALKS AND DRIVES 190
WHAT TO DO 194
EATING 200
STAYING 206

WESTERN GERMANY

In the states of Hessen, Nordrhein-Westfalen, Rheinland-Pfalz and Saarland, western Germany can lay claim to much more than the economic powerhouses of Düsseldorf, Frankfurt (Germany's financial capital) and Köln (Cologne). Bonn was the capital of the former West Germany. It has competition in the former-capital stakes, though—from Trier, Constantine the Great's seat when he ruled half of the West Roman Empire, and Aachen, capital of Charlemagne's Empire of the Franks. Both cities are speckled with ruins and monuments from those distant times.

This is frontier territory, sharing borders with France, Luxembourg, Belgium and Holland, producing a different, more open kind of German experience at the interface. The Rhine and Mosel rivers course through the west, their wine-producing valleys and castles an invitation to imbibe and explore. In the interior are the natural treasures of the Sauerland, the Eifel and the Taunus Mountains, complementing Cologne's cathedral, Düsseldorf's K20 museum and Beethoven's birthplace in Bonn.

The region abounds in things to see and do beyond its best-known buildings, monuments and museums. Both Düsseldorf and Frankfurt have exclusive designer districts, while Essen and Cologne offer a choice of mainstream stores and small, independent boutiques. And Cologne is the place to sample eau de Cologne, the world's most famous perfume. If all this sounds a little tame, there's the legendary Nürburgring, where members of the public can drive their own car around a Formula One racing circuit.

Nordrhein-Westfalen is proud of its culinary trademark, *Eisbein* (knuckle of pork), served with mashed potato and *Sauerkraut* (pickled white cabbage), which seems to be on the menu of every tavern. Wash this and other dishes down with a glass of Frankfurt's heady *Apfelwein* (cider), or Cologne's dark Alt or light frothy Kölsch beers. In the Rhine and Mosel valleys, welcoming *Weinstuben* (wine bars) have tastings of local wines, such as the Ahr valley's Spätburgunder and the Rhine's fresh and fruity Riesling.

AACHEN

One of the oldest-established spa towns in western Germany, dating back to AD60, with a superb domed cathedral that was the country's first ever UNESCO World Heritage Site.

HISTORY

It was the Romans who first realized the therapeutic potential of Aachen's foul-smelling springs (local tribes thought that the water came directly from hell), founding the spa town of Aquis Granum here in the middle of the first century AD (Grannus was the Celtic god of healing and water). After the fall of the Roman Empire, Aachen gradually fell into ruin, until Charlemagne revived the city's fortunes by establishing his capital here in AD794; 11 years later, he consecrated the city's cathedral, which became an important pilgrimage site following his death in AD814. In 1165, Aachen was granted market rights and became an important city for copper production. In the 19th century, Princess Elisabeth, wife of Wilhelm IV, made bathing in Aachen fashionable again, and it has been a thriving resort town ever since. Aachen was all but destroyed during World War II. However, much of the Altstadt has since been restored, and these days it is a thriving commercial town.

AACHENER DOM

At the heart of Aachen Cathedral (Mon–Sat 11–7, Sun 1–7; tel 0241 4770 9127) is Charlemagne's magnificent octagonal chapel, which at the time of its consecration in AD805 was the largest domed structure north of the Alps. It consists of a two-level arcaded gallery, embellished throughout with Italian marble and gilt trim. Almost as important as the building itself, however, are its relics: Mary's robe, Christ's swaddling clothes and the decapitation cloth of John the Baptist are all said to have been brought here by Charlemagne (▷ 31). In the 13th century, his remains were interred in the elaborately gilded Karlschrein, commissioned by Friedrich I. Charlemagne's white marble throne, which between 936 and 1531 was ascended by 30 German kings, also survives, but can only be seen on a guided tour.

Further highlights include the huge 12th-century chandelier (also commissioned by Friedrich I) and the intricately decorated choir, which was added in the 15th century to commemorate the anniversary of Charlemagne's death (and to accommodate the sheer numbers of pilgrims flocking through the church). With its striking tracery windows (at 27m/89ft high, they were then the tallest north of the Alps), it became known as 'The Glass House of Aachen.' The Dom was granted World Heritage status in 1978.

INFORMATION

www.aachen.de

✚ 404 A8 ℹ Information Office Elisenbrunnen, Friedrich-Wilhelm-Platz, 52062 Aachen ☎ 0241 180 2960 🕑 Oct–end Mar Mon–Fri 9–6, Sat 9–2; Apr–end Sep Mon–Fri 9–6, Sat 9–2, Sun and public holidays 10–2 🚉 Aachen

TIP

» To fully appreciate the cathedral's serenity, time your visit to coincide with one of its Wednesday evening concerts (details from the tourist information office, or from the notice board in the cathedral's main entrance hallway).

Opposite *The magnificent Aachener Dom*
Above *The interior of the cathedral, famous for its association with Charlemagne*

INFORMATION

www.bonn.de

436 B9 Bonn Information, Windeckstrasse 1, Wolfenbüttel, 53111 Bonn 0228 775000 Mon–Fri 9–6.30, Sat 9–4, Sun, public holidays 10–2 Bonn region Welcome Card: one day: €12.30 individual, €16.40 family; three days: €23.50 individual and family Bonn

TIP

» Bonn's Haus der Geschichte der Bundesrepublik Deutschland (Tue–Sun 9–7; tel 0228 91650) brings the last 50 years of Germany's history to life with interactive exhibits. Particularly memorable is a film about the fall of the Berlin Wall—you won't have to speak German to appreciate the emotions involved.

BONN

Bonn was the capital of the former West Germany, and the birthplace of composer Ludwig van Beethoven. It's thought that Bonn was first settled more than 6,000 years ago, but it wasn't until the Romans tramped into town in the first century BC that it became a major player in the region's history. The town's patron saints, Cassius and Florentius, were both Roman soldiers executed in Bonn for refusing to participate in the persecution of Christians. The 11th-century cathedral is built on the site where they are said to have been buried.

Bonn is also famous for being made the capital of the newly formed West German state in 1949, a distinction it retained until East and West Germany were reunified in 1990 (▷ 46). Following reunification, six of the government's 15 ministries remained in Bonn, and as a result the city still plays an important part in German political life.

BONNER MÜNSTER

Bonn's Altstadt is dominated by the five spires of its lofty basilica, begun in the 11th century and not completed until two centuries later (Mon–Wed, Fri 9–noon, Thu 9–noon, 4–7; tel 0228 985880). It has a Romanesque (round-arched) nave, three tiers of arches, and aisles with a single tier. Many of the more flamboyant decorative elements, such as the high altar and the splendid apse mosaic, were added in the 19th century. The highlight, though, is the crypt, which is said to house the remains of Cassius and Florentius, contained in a wooden shrine encased in decorative lead plating (if the latter looks a little modern to be found in a Romanesque cathedral, that's because it is: It was designed in 1971).

BEETHOVEN-HAUS

Ludwig van Beethoven was born in Bonn on 17 December 1770, and today it's hard to escape the great man's influence, what with the imposing Beethovendenkmal (memorial) in the middle of Münsterplatz, the ultra-modern Beethovenhalle concert hall just to the north of the city, and the annual Beethovenfest (founded by fellow composer Franz Liszt in 1845). But the first port of call for any music-lover has to be the Beethoven House (Apr–end Oct Mon–Sat 10–6, Sun, public holidays 11–6; Nov–end Mar Mon–Sat 10–5, Sun, public holidays 11–5; tel 0228 971750), where the composer was born and spent the first few years of his life. Part museum, part restored family home, it chronicles Beethoven's life in a series of numbered rooms, complete with portraits, instruments and original scores.

Below *Inside the Beethoven-Haus, the partly restored birthplace of the great composer*

Above *The fortified Burg Eltz was attacked only once, in the 14th century*

BURG ELTZ

www.burgeltz.de

Perched high in a forested valley overlooking the River Mosel, Burg Eltz is one of Germany's most romantic-looking castles, its sheer walls supporting a series of slate-roofed towers grouped around a diminutive courtyard. Tours take you through wonderfully preserved halls and rooms. Highlights include the Rübenach Lower Hall, with an impressive 15th-century wooden ceiling; the Rübenach Bedroom with filigreed frescoes; the Knights' Hall, with weapons and armour; and the 15th-century vaulted ceiling of the Banner Hall.

404 B10 Gräflich Eltz'sche Kastellanei, Burg Eltz, 56294 Münstermaifeld 02672 950500 Easter–end Oct daily 9.30–5.30 Tours: Adult €8, child (6–18) €5.50, under 6 free, family €24; Moselkem; from here, it's a one-hour walk to the castle (signed)

COLOGNE

Köln, ▷ 172–175.

DARMSTADT

www.darmstadt.de

Darmstadt's bustling pedestrian precinct is focused around the vast, cobbled Luisenplatz and the 39m (128ft) Ludwigsmonument, built in 1844 to commemorate local duke Ludwig I, who was responsible for the baroque façade of the palace that still dominates the 14th-century Marktplatz.

But the city's highlight, and the reason for its continued renown, lies 1km (0.6 miles) to the east, at Mathildenhöhe. Here, in 1899, Grand Duke Ernst Ludwig founded an artists' colony, which went on to become the heart of the *Jugendstil* (art nouveau) movement. Today, it is home to a superb Museum Künstlerkolonie (Artists' Colony museum, open Tue–Sun 10–5; tel 06151 133385), in the Ernst-Ludwig-Haus (1901), with posters, paintings and designs by the likes of Joseph Olbrich, Peter Behrens and Hans Christiansen. Also worth exploring are the grounds and nearby streets, to see sculptures and buildings designed by the artists-in-residence.

408 D10 Info Darmstadt, Im Carrée, 64283 Darmstadt 06151 134513 Darmstadt

EIFEL

www.eifel.info

Hemmed in by the Mosel, the Rhine and the Belgian border, the Eifel is the westernmost of Germany's upland massifs. Its forests and deep valleys provide opportunities for escaping the crowds and offer excellent hiking, particularly around Hohe Acht, the region's highest point at 747m (2,450ft).

Many visitors make Monschau their first stop. The village straddles the River Rur at the foot of a steep valley 27km (17 miles) south of Aachen. Monschau's old, half-timbered, slate-roofed houses and cobbled streets are fairy-tale scenic.

The Eifel is known for its Spätburgunder wine, the finest of Germany's otherwise undistinguished reds. An ideal place to sample some is Altenahr on the banks of the River Ahr. Altenahr is the start of the Rotweinwanderweg, or Red Wine Hiking Trail, which follows the Ahr tos Bad Bodendorf—35km (22 miles). You can get maps from local tourist information offices.

The southern Eifel, around Gerolstein and Daun, is known as the Vulkaneifel for its many volcanoes—some extinct, some dormant. Smoke from the last of 270 eruptions stained the sky 10,000 years ago. Solidified lava flows and *maaren* (volcanic lakes) abound. Gerolstein's volcanic springs are the source of a popular bottled mineral water. The Eifel-Vulkanmuseum (Mar to mid-Nov Tue–Fri 1–4.30, Sat, Sun 11–4.30; 26 Dec–6 Jan Tue–Fri 1–4.30; tel 06592 985353) in Daun has the story.

404 A10–B9 Eifel Tourismus, Kalvarienbergstrasse 1d, 54595 Prüm 06551 96560

FRANKFURT AM MAIN

▷ 170–171.

FULDA

www.tourismus-fulda.de

A small city with a fascinating history, Fulda is within an hour's drive of Frankfurt. It was founded as a Benedictine monastery in AD744 by St. Boniface, an English missionary who was later martyred in Friesland, northern Netherlands. His remains were returned to Fulda, which became an important pilgrimage site.

A rather gruesome object purported to be his skull can be seen in the Dom Schatzkammer (Treasury, open Apr–end Oct Tue–Sat 10–5.30, Sun 12.30–5.30; Nov–end Mar Tue–Sat 10–12.30, 1.30–4, Sun 12.30–4; tel 0661 87207); you can also catch a glimpse of the foundations of the original basilica, built at the end of the eighth century to house the saint's remains. The basilica was torn down in 1704 and rebuilt in the baroque style by Johann Dientzenhofer, who is said to have worked from a model of St. Peter's in Rome (Apr–end Oct Mon–Fri 10–6, Sat 10–3, Sun 1–6; Nov–end Mar Mon–Fri 10–5, Sat 10–3, Sun 1–6).

405 E9 Tourism Fulda, Bonifatiusplatz 1, 36037 Fulda 0661 102 1813 Mon–Fri 8.30–6, Sat 9.30–4, Sun 10–2 Fulda

INFORMATION

www.duesseldorf-tourismus.de
404 B8 Tourist Information Hauptbahnhof, Immermannstrasse 65b, 40210 Düsseldorf 0211 172020 Mon–Fri 9.30–6.30, Sat 9–3
Tourist Information Altstadt, Marktstrasse (at Rheinstrasse), 40213 Düsseldorf 0211 172020 Daily 11–6 Düsseldorf

TIPS

» Get a great view of the city from the viewing gallery at the top of the Rheinturm. A café serves snacks and hot drinks, and there's a restaurant on the top floor, 180m (590ft) above the Rhine.

» The Düsseldorf WelcomeCard affords free use of public transportation in the city and admission to many museums, plus other reductions. Available from tourist offices, the card costs €9 for 24 hours, €14 for 48 hours and €19 for 72 hours; the respective rates for families are €18, €28 and €38.

Above *The K20 art museum*

INTRODUCTION

Affluent Düsseldorf rivals Cologne as an artistic and cultural hub. First mentioned in archives in 1135, Düsseldorf has long been the capital of the northern Rhine region, but it was Elector Palatine Johann Wilhelm II (1679–1716), known as Jan Wellem, who put the city on the map with his building schemes and his enthusiastic patronage of the arts. A statue outside the Rathaus commemorates him. Much of Wellem's town planning was laid waste during Allied bombing raids in 1944, but Düsseldorf has risen from the ashes. Today, its wealth is reflected in the über-trendy boutiques and malls on Königsallee. The restored Altstadt (Old Town), the heart of the cultural and culinary scenes, is compact and largely traffic-free, making it easy to explore.

WHAT TO SEE

K20

www.kunstsammlung.de

The K20 building (1986), close to the Hofgarten in the northern part of the Altstadt, is a distinctive sight, and home to one of Germany's most important collections of 20th-century art, the Kunstsammlung Nordrhein-Westfalen (North Rhine-Westphalia Art Collection). Particularly well represented are pop protagonist Andy Warhol, abstract expressionist Jackson Pollock, expressionist Ernst Kirchner, Max Beckmann of the new objectivity movement, and abstract artist Paul Klee, along with works by Henri Matisse, Piet Mondrian, Pablo Picasso and others. Top billing, though, goes to Düsseldorf native Joseph Beuys (1921–86), whose works include the intriguing *End of the 20th Century* (1983): natural basalt columns with small, cone-shaped holes drilled into their sides, which have been roughly repaired by wrapping the removed cones in cloth and replacing them. If abstract ideas start to hurt your head, seek out the dreamy works of Pierre Bonnard and André Derain on the top floor.

Grabbeplatz 5, 40213 Düsseldorf 0211 838 1130 Tue–Fri 10–6 (1st Wed in month 10–10), Sat, Sun 11–6 Adult €6.50, child (6–18) €4.50, under 6 free, family €15 U-Bahn Heinrich-Heine-Allee Tram 703, 706, 712, 713, 715

K21

www.kunstsammlung.de

If you like your art even more cutting-edge, take a second bite at the Kunstsammlung Nordrhein-Westfalen farther south in the Altstadt. K21, housed in the former Rheinland parliament building (1880), focuses on international contemporary art from about 1970 onwards and presents a growing permanent collection—with works by Marcel Broodthaers and Nam June Paik, among others—alongside temporary exhibitions.

Ständehausstrasse 1, 40217 Düsseldorf 0211 838 1600 Tue–Fri 10–6 (1st Wed in month 10–10), Sat, Sun 11–6 Adult €6.50, child (6–18) €4.50, under 6 free, family €15 SB85. Tram 703, 704, 706, 709, 712, 713, 715, 719

MEDIANHAFEN (MEDIA HARBOUR)

If you stroll along the east bank of the Rhine, through Düsseldorf's redeveloped inland port south of the Rheinkniebrücke road bridge,you will see the three asymmetrical buildings of the Neuer Zollhof (New Toll House; 1999), which appear to be in danger of keeling over into the water. This is merely the design signature of architect Frank O. Gehry (1929–), whose postmodern office complex mainly houses media, design and legal firms. The former Zollhafen (Customs Harbour), once the busiest part of the port, has been transformed into a yacht harbour. At its eastern end, the Rheinturm (Rhine Tower; 1982) television tower (daily 10am–11.30pm; tel 0211 84858), 240m (790ft) above the river, contains an enclosed viewing platform and a rotating restaurant.

Stromstrasse 26, 40221 Düsseldorf Tram 704, 709

HOFGARTEN (COURT GARDEN)

Curling around the north end of the Altstadt (enter from the north end of Königsallee), this large park is bordered by museums and other cultural establishments. It began as a French-style baroque garden in 1769 and has been extended several times and laid out anew in the English garden style. The Hofgarten is speckled with fountains, ponds and monuments to artists, thinkers and other prominent persons. Among these is the bronze statue *Harmonie* (1944) by Aristide Maillol, in the park's northern reaches, dedicated in 1956 as a memorial to Düsseldorf-born poet Heinrich Heine (1797–1856).

Hofgartenstrasse (and nearby streets), 40479 Düsseldorf Permanently Free Tram 701, 703, 706, 711, 712, 713, 715

Below left *An exhibition in the K20 museum*

Below *A portrait of Johann Wilhelm, Elector of the Palatinate, painted in 1700 by Adriaen van der Werff*

INFORMATION

www.frankfurt-tourismus.de

409 D10 Tourist Information Hauptbahnhof, 60329 Frankfurt am Main 069 2123 8800 Mon–Fri 8am–9pm, Sat, Sun, public holidays 9–6 Tourist Information Römer, Römerberg 27, 60311 Frankfurt am Main 069 2123 8800; Mon–Fri 9.30–5.30, Sat, Sun, public holidays 10–4 Frankfurt Card (free public transportation, 50 per cent discount at 21 museums, plus other discounts): €8.70 for one day or €12.50 for two days Frankfurt

Above *Modern Frankfurt's skyline at night*

INTRODUCTION

Frankfurt am Main (pronounced 'Mine'), the economic heart of Germany, is among the country's most cosmopolitan cities. Known locally as Mainhattan, it is the closest thing western Germany has to a high-rise metropolis. A striking skyline takes in the Commerzbank and the Main Tower, headquarters of the European Central Bank. The city is home to the Bundesbank (Germany's central bank) and the stock exchange, and is renowned for its trade fairs. Not surprisingly, this world of commerce is reflected in the designer stores. But beyond the Wolkenkratzer (literally 'cloud-scrapers') and bright lights of the financial district lies a city with a medieval core, and plenty to interest visitors.

The first official mention of Frankfurt was made in AD794, but it wasn't until 1240 that Emperor Friedrich II declared it a market city and granted it other privileges. In a charter dated 1356, Frankfurt was named as the electoral site of all German kings, a privilege it retained until the dissolution of the German Holy Roman Empire in 1806. In 1848, Germany's first democratically elected parliament convened at the Paulskirche (St. Paul's Church), which is now considered to be the birthplace of democracy in Germany. More than three-quarters of the city was destroyed in World War II bombing raids, and despite the rapid reconstruction of commercial institutions, the meticulous restoration of the Römerberg wasn't completed until 1983.

WHAT TO SEE

RÖMERBERG

The focus of Frankfurt's compact Altstadt is the beautifully restored Römerberg, a cobbled, octagonal square that's known locally as the Gut Stubb, or Great Parlour. Market fairs were held here as early as the ninth century, and the striking Town Hall (daily 10–12, 2–5), made up of three buildings united

by a Gothic gable, was originally built in the 15th century. It was here that coronations were celebrated in the days of the Holy Roman Empire. This is a perfect starting point for exploring the rest of the city.
U-Bahn Dom/Römer Tram 11, 12

STÄDEL-MUSEUM

www.staedelmuseum.de

At the heart of Frankfurt's Museum Embankment, this is one of Germany's leading fine-art museums. The collection contains more than 600 masterpieces of European art from the 14th to the 20th centuries, including works by Albrecht Dürer, Lucas Cranach, Jan van Eyck, Sandro Botticelli, Andrea Mantegna and Canaletto. Don't miss Hans Holbein's *Meyer Madonna* (*c*1526).
Schaumainkai 63, 60596 Frankfurt am Main 069 605 0980 Tue, Fri–Sun 10–6, Wed, Thu 10–9 Adult €10, child (12–18) €8, under 12 free, family €18 U-Bahn Schweizer Platz Tram 15, 16, 19

MUSEUM FÜR MODERNE KUNST

www.mmk-frankfurt.de

The Museum of Modern Art is in a striking triangular building, designed by Viennese architect Hans Hollein. The core of the collection is American and European art from the 1960s and 1970s, with works by Andy Warhol, Roy Lichtenstein and Joseph Beuys among the highlights. Alongside these well-known names are works by contemporary artists.
Domstrasse 10, 60311 Frankfurt am Main 069 2123 0447 Tue, Thu–Sun 10–5, Wed 10–8 Adult €7, child (6–18) €3.50, under 6 free U-Bahn Dom/Römer Tram 11, 12

DEUTSCHES ARCHITEKTURMUSEUM

www.dam-online.de

Most of the gallery space in this splendid museum is used for temporary shows, but the permanent exhibition is excellent. Twenty-five brilliant models of some of the world's famous buildings offer you a tour of architectural history, from mud huts to skyscrapers. Highlights include Speyer Cathedral (▷ 189), the Royal Cresent in Bath, England, and New York's Chrysler building.
Schaumainkai 43, 60596 Frankfurt am Main 069 2123 8844 Tue, Thu–Sun 11–6, Wed 11–8 Adult €6, child (6–18) €3, under 6 free U-Bahn Schweizer Platz Tram 15, 16, 19

MORE TO SEE

KAISERDOM

www.dom-frankfurt.de

Frankfurt's 13th-century cathedral served as the electoral site for German kings from 1356, and as the coronation site of emperors from 1562 to 1792 (hence the name). The striking late Gothic tower (currently closed for restoration) was added following a fire in 1867; it is 95m (312ft) tall, a climb of 324 steps.
Domplatz 14, 1 60311 Frankfurt 069 297 0320 Tue–Fri 10–5, Sat, Sun 11–5 Free U-Bahn Dom/Römer Tram 11, 12

HISTORISCHES MUSEUM

www.historisches-museum.frankfurt.de

This museum is worth visiting in its own right, but you can pay just €1 to see the splendid model of Frankfurt in the 1930s, and a second model of the city as it looked at the end of the war, when 80 per cent of it had been destroyed. Off to one side is the tiny 12th-century Saalhof Chapel, Frankfurt's oldest building, and in a separate room there is a stunning collection of silverware.
Saalgasse 19 (Römerberg), 60311 Frankfurt am Main 069 2123 5599 Tue, Thu–Sun 10–6, Wed 10–8 Adult €4, child (6–18) €2, under 6 free U-Bahn Dom/Römer Tram 11, 12

TIPS

» For a great view of the city, head up to the observation platform at the top of Main Tower (Apr–end Sep Sun–Thu 10–9, Fri, Sat 10–11; Oct–end Mar daily 10–7; tel 069 3650 4771), or have dinner or drinks at the ever-so-elegant Main Tower Restaurant and Bar (▷ 202).

» Many of the city's museums are free one day each month. Check with the tourist office for details.

Below *A brightly painted tram travels past the Messe tower*

INFORMATION

www.koeln.de

404 B8 Kardinal-Höffner-Platz 1, 50667 Köln (Dom) 0221 2213 0400 Mon–Sat 9–8, Sun 10–5 WelcomeCard (free public transportation and cut-price tours, plus reductions in many museums, concert venues and churches): €9 for 24 hrs (family €18), €14 for 48 hrs (family €28) Köln

Above *Looking from the east bank of the Rhine towards the spires and towers of the cathedral quarter of Köln*

INTRODUCTION

Cologne's skyline is dominated by the delicately filigreed twin spires, 157m (515ft) tall, of its mighty cathedral, the Dom, which is without doubt one of Germany's greatest architectural treasures. To this, the city can add stylish shops, fabulous restaurants, a thriving cultural scene, and a handsome and historic location along the River Rhine. Strung out along the riverfront and surrounding the medieval Altermarkt, the immaculately restored Altstadt (old town) is crammed with intimate cafés, welcoming bars and superb traditional restaurants. Across the river are the wide open spaces of the Rheinpark, and the warm, soporific waters of the Claudius Thermal Baths.

Founded by the Romans in 38BC, Cologne was granted city status less than a hundred years later by Julia Agrippina, the wife of Emperor Claudius, who was born and raised here. Its importance as a Roman outpost is reflected in the exquisite workmanship of the vast Dionysus Mosaic, which today forms the focus of the Römisch-Germanisches (Roman-Germanic) Museum, home to one of the most important Roman collections in Europe. By the Middle Ages, Cologne had become the largest city in Germany, an accolade it held well into the 19th century. In 1942, the city was the target of the first Allied 1000-bomber raid, and over the next three years 90 per cent of the buildings in the Altstadt were destroyed; remarkably, the 700-year-old cathedral seemed to withstand the worst of the blasts, but it suffered structural damage that continues to plague it to this day.

After the war, the Altstadt was sympathetically restored, although the rest of Cologne seems to have been rebuilt with varying degrees of sensitivity (and success). However, its former street pattern has been preserved, a measure which has helped it to retain some of its historic feel.

WHAT TO SEE

KÖLNER DOM

www.domforum.de

Cologne Cathedral was begun in the 13th century, but because of funding problems it wasn't actually completed until the end of the 19th century. Throughout this time, however, far-sighted architects remained faithful to the original drawings, which miraculously survived. (The original drawing of the west front still hangs in the ambulatory, but is kept behind a curtain to protect it from the light.) The resulting harmony of structure and decoration, achieved on such a massive scale, made it one of the most awe-inspiring and audacious Gothic monuments ever built, and at the time of its completion in 1880, it was the tallest structure in the world (although it was superseded just 10 years later by the Eiffel Tower).

Externally, its sheer mass is relieved by the miraculous delicacy of its flying buttresses and its lace-like masonry, while internally it seems hard to believe that the towering nave is barely a quarter of the height of the soaring spires. Indeed, the best way to appreciate just how tall these spires are is to climb the 519 steps to the platform at the base of the southern steeple. On the way, you'll pass St. Peter, the largest working bell in the world. Sadly, the platform itself is badly graffitied, but this doesn't detract from the magnificent views that it commands.

The cathedral's other highlights include its vast expanses of priceless stained glass, which if laid flat would cover the floor of the cathedral twice over; the Gerokreuz (Gero Cross), a wooden crucifix dating from AD970, which is unusual for showing Christ with his eyes closed, not as a resplendent Messiah but as a dying man; the Shrine of the Three Magi, an unimaginably ornate, jewel-encrusted sarcophagus built between 1180 and 1225 and said to contain the bones of the Three Kings; and the largest choir stalls in Germany, carved from oak at the beginning of the 14th century. More modern, but no less striking, is the vast floor mosaic in the choir and ambulatory. Made by Villeroy & Boch at the end of the 19th century, its allegorical scenes depict important events from throughout the cathedral's history.

Look for the workshop, at the southeast corner of the cathedral. Only by seeing the individual blocks of masonry on the workshop floor can you fully appreciate the scale of the walls and buttresses above. Something you can't fail to miss, however, is the scaffolding that clings precariously to various parts of the building. For first-time visitors this can be something of a disappointment, but the locals are used to the constant repair work and have a saying: 'The day the cathedral is finished will be the day of Judgement.'

175 B1 Domforum, Domkloster 3, 50667 Köln 0221 9258 4720 Mon–Fri 10–6.30, Sat 10–5, Sun 1–5 Cathedral: free; Tower: Adult €2, child (6–18) €1, under 6 free Guided tours (Mon–Sat 10.30, 2.30, Sun 2.30): Adult €6, child (6–18) €4, under 6 free (in English); Multivision multi-media show, in English (Mon–Sat 11.30, 3.30, Sun 3.30): Adult €2, child (6–18) €1, under 6 free U- and S-Bahn Dom/Hauptbahnhof

RÖMISCH-GERMANISCHES MUSEUM

www.museenkoeln.de

If you are interested in ancient history, or indeed Roman art and architecture, a visit to the Roman-Germanic Museum is a must. Built in 1974 on the south side of the Dom, over the exquisite Dionysus Mosaic, it is home to the best collection of Roman ruins and everyday items on the Rhine. The mosaic itself was discovered in 1941 during the building of an air-raid shelter; it measures a remarkable 10m (33ft) by 7.5m (25ft), and is one of the best-preserved examples of its kind. It takes its name from the images of Dionysus, the Greek god of wine. It is thought to have been the dining-room floor of a merchant's villa in AD220–230.

Under the Romans, Cologne was an important area of glass production,

TIPS

» It's a good idea to take a quick guided tour of Cologne. The city is so full of history, and so rich in significant sites, that only a local expert can really do it justice. The same goes for the cathedral, which is crammed from top to bottom with fascinating little details.

» The best time to see the outside of the cathedral is at night, when the whole place gives off a green, ethereal glow. It looks most striking from the footpath that crosses the railway bridge (or Hohenzollernbrücke) at the east end of the cathedral, or from the far side of the Rhine, from where you can really appreciate the intricacies of the flying buttresses that surround the ambulatory.

Below *A street artist puts the finishing touches to his portrait of Beethoven outside the cathedral*

KÖLSCH

As well as being the name of the intractable dialect spoken by natives of Cologne, Kölsch is also the name of the city's traditional beer, which is served in every single bar, bistro and restaurant in town. A light, refreshing brew, it is invariably served in small, narrow glasses. Since 1986, the name Kölsch has been protected by law, and can only be given to beer brewed in or near Cologne.

so the museum also has a collection of glassware. The most famous items on display are the Serpentine Thread Glasses dating from the second century AD, and the fourth-century Cage Cup, with its astonishingly intricate surface decoration. Equally beguiling are everyday items like jewellery and toys, which help to give everything a more human context. Exhibit labels are in English as well as German.

Nearby are the ruins of the Roman gateway at Domplatz, and the foundations of the old city walls that have been preserved in a parking area beneath the main square.

175 B1 Roncalliplatz 4, 50667 Köln 0221 2212 4438 Tue–Sun 10–5 Adult €6, child (6–18) €3.50, under 6 free

WALLRAF-RICHARTZ-MUSEUM AND FONDATION CORBOUD

www.museenkoeln.de/wallraf-richartz-museum

Founded in 1861, the museum is the oldest in Cologne, but its original home was destroyed in World War II. It wasn't until 2001 that it finally found a permanent home, in a purpose-built, post-modern building designed by Cologne's architect of the moment, Oswald Mathias Ungers. His simple design, with its clean lines and wide, open spaces, has been a hit with architects and gallery-goers alike. The building was deliberately positioned at the heart of the Altstadt, which during the Middle Ages would have housed the workshops of the Cologne Masters, whose works form an important part of the museum's collection. Peter Paul Rubens and Rembrandt are also well represented, as are early 19th-century romantic painters like Caspar David Friedrich.

175 B2 Obenmarspforten (at Kölner Rathaus) 1a, 50667 Köln 0221 2212 1119 Tue, Wed, Fri 10–6, Thu 10–10, Sat, Sun 11–6 Adult €7.50, child (6–18) €5, under 6 free U-Bahn Heumarkt

MUSEUM LUDWIG

www.museenkoeln.de.museum-ludwig

The museum, with its vast underground concert hall and industrial-looking roofline, houses one of the best collections of 20th-century art in Germany. Andy Warhol is much in evidence, as are German postmoderns Georg Baselitz and Max Beckmann. There's also plenty on offer for those who prefer the early years of modern art, with the likes of Marc Chagall, Pablo Picasso and Paul Klee all getting a look in. There's little information provided about the paintings or artists, so unless you're an expert, you'd be well advised to get an audioguide. Its intimate café is popular (▷ 202).

174 B1 Heinrich-Böll-Platz, 50667 Köln 0221 2212 6165 Tue–Sun 10–6 (first Fri of each month 10–10) Adult €9, child (6–18) €6, under 6 free, family €18 U- and S-Bahn Dom/Hauptbahnhof

SCHOKOLADENMUSEUM

www.schokoladenmuseum.de

Officially known as the Imhoff-Stollwerck-Museum, Cologne's fabulous Chocolate Museum, on the banks of the Rhine just south of the Altstadt, is a must for children of all ages. In a well-ordered sequence of exhibits, it tells the fascinating story of chocolate production, from the harvesting of cocoa beans to the making of Easter eggs, and all the information is presented in English as well as German. To start with there's just too much information to take in, but once you get to the working production line, all you have to do is look on in wonder as ingredients are mixed, heated, rolled and churned, before being moulded, cooled, wrapped and bagged. Many of the machines have perspex-protected cutaways so you can see what's going on inside them, and it's also possible to sample rationed amounts of liquid chocolate from a chocolate fountain.

175 C3 Am Schokoladenmuseum 1a, 50678 Köln 0221 931 8880 Tue–Fri 10–6, Sat, Sun, public holidays 11–7 Adult €6.50, child (6–18) €4, under 6 free U-Bahn Severinsbrücke

DEUTSCHES SPORT UND OLYMPIA MUSEUM

www.sportmuseum.info

Right next door to the Chocolate Museum, this enthralling sports museum is the perfect opportunity to work off any calories—both real and imagined—that might have been gained gazing at tumbling truffles. You are guided through a series of exhibition areas that follows a time-line from ancient Greece to the present day. Many of the labels are in English as well as German, and there's not so much information that you feel overwhelmed.

Obviously, the focus is on German sport, but this only serves to make it all the more interesting, particularly when it comes to the role sport played in the rise of the Third Reich (▷ 41). The Berlin Olympics of 1936 are well covered, and there is a section on Jesse Owens (▷ 41). But the highlights are the interactive exhibits: the triple-jump runway showing how far Britain's Jonathan Edwards jumped when he set a world record of 18.29m (60ft) at the 1995 Gothenburg World Championships; the wind tunnel, where you can cycle until your legs scream; and the multi-media screen, where you can watch a selection of the best goals ever scored by German soccer players. Just don't try the standing jump too many times, or you might not be able to walk properly the next day.

175 C3 Im Zollhafen 1, 50678 Köln 0221 336090 Tue–Fri 10–6, Sat, Sun and public holidays 11–7 Adult €5, child (6–18) €2.50, under 6 free, family €12.50 U-Bahn Chlodwigplatz

EAU DE COLOGNE

The world's most famous fragrance was first manufactured by an Italian immigrant early in the 18th century and was originally sold for medicinal purposes, to treat everything from gout to gangrene. In 1810 Napoleon decreed that the formula of all medicines must be revealed for the good of the people, something which the manufacturers of the Eau Admirable were understandably keen to avoid. Their simple but ingenious solution was to re-classify it as a product 'for the care of the body.' Overnight, miracle water became toilet water, and eau de Cologne was born.

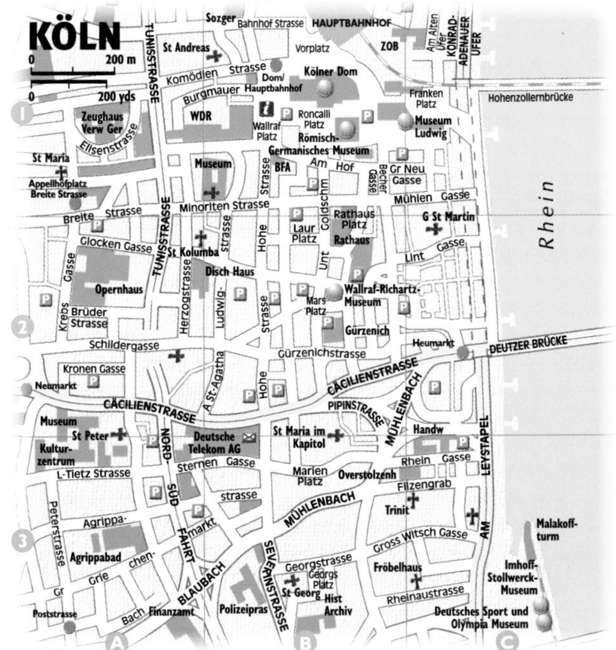

Below *People at café tables in the square in front of brightly painted houses and the circular tower of Gross St. Martin*

Above *Looking across the river to Limburg's cathedral*

KASSEL

www.kassel.de

Just 130km (80 miles) north of Frankfurt, workaday Kassel was badly damaged during World War II and has since been subjected to some pretty unflattering reconstruction. Its saving grace is its stunning setting, best appreciated at Park Wilhemshöhe, 6km (4 miles) west of the city. A sweeping, romantic landscape created for Willhelmshöhe Palace in the 18th century, it has a statue of Hercules on top of an enormous octagonal amphitheatre (mid-Mar to mid-Nov Tue–Sun 10–5; tel 0561 312456), which can be reached by climbing a seemingly endless series of steps (or by road if you prefer). The views are spectacular. The palace (Tue–Sun 10–5; tel 0561 316800) was once the home of Wilhelm II (▷ 39), and now houses an impressive exhibition of paintings by Renaissance masters such as Albrecht Dürer, Titian, Anthony van Dyck and Peter Paul Rubens, not to mention the largest Rembrandt collection in Germany.

Kassel hosts the highly regarded three-month-long Documenta modern art exhibition, which takes place every 10 years; the next will be in 2017.

✚ 405 E8 ℹ Kassel Tourist, Obere Königsstrasse 8, 34117 Kassel ☎ 0561 707707 🚉 Kassel

KOBLENZ

www.koblenz-touristik.de

Historic Koblenz, at the confluence of the Rhine and the Mosel, can trace its origins back to 9BC, when the Romans first built a fortress here. In subsequent years, it was captured by the Franks, became an important commercial district under Germany's prince electors, and was overrun by the French, a history that reflects the changing fortunes of much of the region.

It's perhaps fitting, then, that Koblenz is home to the Mittelrhein-Museum (Tue–Sat 10.30–5, Sun, public holidays 11–6; tel 0261 129 2520), which houses a superb art collection relating to the river, including works by English artists such as George Clarkson Stanfield, whose much-vaunted *View of the Balduin Bridge in Koblenz* (1858) epitomizes the 19th-century notion of the Romantic Rhine.

From here, a short walk along the Mosel leads you to its confluence with the Rhine at Deutsches Eck, or German Corner, dominated by an equestrian statue of Emperor Wilhelm I (*c*1897). The statue itself was destroyed in 1945, and a replica was erected in 1993.

✚ 404 C9 ℹ Koblenz Tourist Information, Bahnhofplatz 7, 56068 Koblenz ☎ 0261 31304 ℹ Tourist Information Rathaus, Jesuitenplatz 2, 56068 Koblenz ☎ 0261 130920 🚉 Koblenz

KÖLN

▷ 172–175.

LEMGO

www.lemgo.net

One of the best-preserved medieval towns in northern Germany, lively Lemgo was once a member of the Hanseatic League (▷ 31). This brought considerable wealth to Lemgo throughout the Middle Ages, and because the town escaped damage during World War II, many of its medieval merchants' houses and administrative buildings can still be seen. The most famous of these is the Hexenbürgermeisterhaus, or House of the Witches' Mayor (Tue–Sun 10–5; tel 05261 213276).

The house takes its name from one Hermann Cothmann who, during his stint as Mayor of Lemgo (from 1667 to 1683), sentenced no fewer than 90 women to death for alleged witchcraft.

✚ 405 D7 ℹ Lemgo Tourism, Kramerstrasse 1, 32657 Lemgo ☎ 05261 98870 🚉 Lemgo

LIMBURG

www.limburg.de

Standing on the south bank of the River Lahn, in an open section of the otherwise rugged Lahn Valley, Limburg is a handsome small town, rich in traditional Fachwerkhaüser (half-timbered houses) dating from the 13th to the 18th centuries. It is best known for its striking orange and white Dom St. Georg (Apr–end Sep daily 8–7; Oct–end Mar daily 9–5; guided tours Tue–Fri 11, 3, Sat 11, Sun 11.45; tel 06431 929983), which is perched on a rocky spur overlooking the river. Built during the transition from Romanesque round arches to Gothic pointed ones, it is a fine example of its type and has 12th-century paintings.

Rising in the Sauerland (▷ 181), the River Lahn flows for much of its length through a pretty wooded gorge, and is much less commercialized than the Rhine or the Mosel. Upstream, between Limburg and Marburg (▷ 181), is Weilburg, which is dominated by a 16th-century, early Renaissance Schloss. Although the palace's interior is impressive, the real draw here is its gardens, which march down to the river in a series of sweeping terraces. Boat traffic can bypass the promontory on which the palace is built by taking a shortcut through a 235m (771ft) tunnel.

✚ 404 C9 ℹ Limburg Tourism, Hospitalstrasse 2, 65549 Limburg an der Lahn ☎ 06431 6166 🚉 Limburg

MAINZ

The stunning stained-glass windows by Marc Chagall, in one of the city's churches, are an unexpected highlight. Mainz has long been a city of economic importance, thanks in part to its strategic position at the confluence of the Rhine and Main rivers. The Romans founded a military garrison here in the first century BC, and since the Middle Ages it has been the seat of a succession of archbishops, many of whom are entombed in the city's vast cathedral. Much of the city was destroyed during World War II, but has since been meticulously rebuilt. Today, Mainz is a thriving university town with pleasant, pedestrianized areas and an exceptionally mild climate.

GUTENBERG-MUSEUM

The city's most famous son is undoubtedly Johannes Gutenberg (1397–1468), who in around 1438 became the first European to print books using moveable type (▷ 33). The Gutenberg-Museum (Tue–Sat 9–5, Sun 11–3; tel 06131 122640) in Liebfrauenplatz has a series of exhibits outlining his work and the evolution of modern printing. Labels are in German only, but in some sections there are explanations in English.

DOM MAINZ

Dominating the city's Altstadt is its Dom St. Martin (Mar–end Sep Mon–Fri 9–6.30, Sat 9–4, Sun 12.45–3, 4–6.30; Oct–end Feb Mon–Fri 9–5, Sat 9–4, Sun 12.45–3, 4–5; tel 06131 253412), a mountain of red sandstone that was begun in AD975, though most of what survives was built in the 12th and 13th centuries. Apart from its sheer size, the most impressive thing about the cathedral is its collection of archbishops' tombs, which document the gradually evolving styles of memorial design between the 13th and 19th centuries, from Gothic to baroque and rococo.

CHAGALL'S STAINED GLASS

If it's serenity you're after, head for the St. Stephan Church (Mar–end Oct Mon–Sat 10–5, Sun 12–5; Nov–end Feb Mon–Thu 10–12, 2–4.30, Fri, Sat 10–4.30, Sun 12–4.30; tel 06131 231640), about 10 minutes' walk to the southwest of the Dom. The church itself is pleasant enough, but the sublime blues of Chagall's stained glass), made between 1978 and 1984, when the artist was in his 90s, are simply breathtaking.

INFORMATION

www.mainz.de

408 C10 Touristik Centrale Mainz, Brückenturm am Rathaus, 55116 Mainz
06131 286210 Mon–Fri 9–6, Sat 10–4, Sun 11–3 Mainz Card (free entry to many museums, free public transportation, free guided city tour, plus a free hotel drink): €9.95 for 48 hours, family €25 Mainz

Below *The Gutenburg-Museum has displays of equipment and describes early printing*

Clockwise from left to right *The meandering Mosel passes the village of Krov; grapes ripening in one of the vineyards in the valley; a Mosel River boat tour*

INTRODUCTION

Rising high in the Vosges Mountains of eastern France (where it is called the Moselle), the River Mosel follows the border between Luxembourg and Germany before flowing through the ancient city of Trier. From here, it cuts through the low Hunsrück and Eifel mountains in a series of dramatic loops until it merges with the Rhine at Koblenz. The whole stretch of 200km (125 miles) is lined with vineyards, which cling to the steep south-facing slopes of the valley, and these vineyards produce the region's famous Mosel wines.

The Mosel is a romantic river, and one of the best ways to reach the towns and villages along its banks is by boat. The two main departure points are Koblenz (▷ 176) and Trier (▷ 186–188): From either city it's possible to take a cruise either up- or downstream before returning by boat or train to where you started. To avoid the worst of the summer crowds but still make the most of the sunny weather, plan your trip for late May to early June or late September to early October.

WHAT TO SEE

BOAT TRIP TO COCHEM

Unless you want to spend only 40 minutes in Cochem (the time available if you're going back to Koblenz by boat the same day), you have three options: stay overnight and take the boat back to Koblenz the following afternoon; catch a train back to Koblenz later that day or the next morning; or catch an early train from Koblenz to Cochem and then return by river that afternoon. If you've only got a day to spare, the last is arguably the best option, as it allows time to explore the town and have lunch at one of Cochem's riverside restaurants, before putting your feet up on the boat as it bears you gently back to Koblenz. Trains between Cochem and Koblenz (and vice-versa) run at least once an hour between 7am and 10pm, with the journey taking a little less than an hour. If you are staying in Cochem, the friendly, family-run Hotel Am Hafen (www.hotel-am-hafen.de) has rooms with balconies overlooking the river and the castle. More modern, but without the views, is the Hotel Café Germania (www.mosel-hotel-germania.de) on Moselpromenade.

COCHEM'S SIGHTS

Approaching Cochem downstream of the town, it's impossible to miss its magnificent castle, Reichsburg Cochem, perched on a steep-sided, vine-clad hill high above the right bank. Originally built in around 1000, it became an imperial castle in 1151 under the Hohenstaufen dynasty. It was later destroyed by marauding French forces in 1689, and wasn't rebuilt until 1868. Today it houses a fine museum (daily 9–5; tel 02671 255; guided tours). The walk up from the river takes about 15 minutes, and although it's quite steep, the views from the hilltop are worth the effort, even when the castle is closed.

Another, less strenuous, way to get great views of the town and valley is to take the chairlift (mid-Mar to end Nov daily, varies from between 9.30 and 11 to between 4 and 7; adult €4.30 one way, €5.80 round trip, child (4–14) €1.90 one way, €2.70 round trip, under 4 free, family €16 round trip; tel 02671 989065 up to the Pinnerkreuz, a memorial cross on a high knoll just downstream of the castle. The bottom of the chairlift is on Endertstrasse (which eventually becomes Moselbrücke, the town bridge).

THE WINE TRAIL

It's possible to walk back down to Cochem through the vineyards—detailed maps can be obtained from the local tourist information office. A wine-tasting is an essential part of any visit to the Mosel and there are half a dozen cellars to choose from. One of the most inviting is Beim Weinbauer (daily 10–late; tel 02671 7448), a *Weinstube* (wine bar) and restaurant on the Moselpromenade, between the bridge and the castle. If you have any time to spare, you could also visit the 19th-century Historisches Senfmühle (mustard mill: daily 10–6; tel 02671 607665) on the east bank of the river.

INFORMATION

www.cochem.de

404B10 Tourist Information Ferienland Cochem, Endertplatz 1, 56812 Cochem 02671 60040 Apr Mon–Fri 9–5; May–end Jul Mon–Fri 9–5, Sat (May to mid-Jul) 9–3, Sun 10–12; Aug–end Oct Mon–Thu 9–5, Fri 9–6, Sat (mid-Jul to end Oct) 9–5, Sun 10–12; Nov–end Mar Mon–Fri 9–1, 2–5 Cochem Boat trip between Koblenz and Cochem: Adult €23.90 one way, €28.20 round-trip, child (4–13) €4.30, under 4 free. Boats depart Koblenz 9.45, arrive Cochem 3, depart Cochem 3.40, arrive Koblenz 8

MÜNSTER

This attractive, beautifully restored university town is home to Dom St. Paul, which has a working astronomical clock that's almost 500 years old. Founded as a monastery in AD793 by one of Charlemagne's cohorts (the name comes from the Latin word *monasterium*), Münster became a bishopric just 12 years later. Today, Münster is a lively and attractive university town, where immaculately renovated baroque buildings jostle for attention on spacious, cobbled streets, while high overhead false gables hide steeply pitched slate rooftops. Don't miss the impressively gabled Rathaus (Tue–Fri 10–5, Sat, Sun and holidays 10–4; tel 0251 492 2724) which in 1648 bore witness to the signing of the Peace of Westphalia bringing the Thirty Years' War to an end (▷ 32). Damaged during Allied air raids, it was restored in the 1950s. Today, it's one of the finest examples of secular Gothic architecture in Germany. The Hall of Peace, where the treaty was signed, contains the original carved panels.

INFORMATION

www.marketing.muenster.de
432 C7 Münster Information, Heinrich-Brüning-Strasse 9, 48143 Münster 0251 492 2710 Mon–Fri 9.30–6, Sat 9.30–1 Münster

DOM ST. PAUL

Münster's massive cathedral (Mon–Fri 6.30–6, Sun 6.30am–7.30pm; tel 0251 495322) was built mostly in the 13th century, and is a mixture of Romanesque round arches and blind arcading and Gothic pointed arches and windows. Inside, visitors are greeted by a huge (5m/16ft) baroque statue of St. Christopher (*c*1627) by Johann von Bocholt. Even more impressive is the vast and intricate astronomical clock (*c*1542) on the south side of the ambulatory. The inscription in its gable explains that the clock shows the time, the position of the sun and the planets and the phases of the moon, and has a calendar calibrated until the year 2071. Remarkably, it's still clunking away and chimes every 15 minutes.

GRAPHIKMUSEUM PABLO PICASSO

The only museum in the world dedicated solely to Picasso's graphic works, the Pablo Picasso Graphics Museum (Tue–Fri 11–6, Sat, Sun, and holidays 10–6; tel 0251 414 4710) was established in 2000 to exhibit a permanent collection of some 780 lithographs bequeathed by Westphalian native and graphic artist Gert Huizinga. This is an absolute must for those who can't get to grips with modern art: Picasso's famous series sketches lead you on a journey through the stages of pictorial representation, from a detailed drawing of a realistic-looking bull (for example) to the four or five lines that are needed to depict the bull's essence. In addition to its light and airy gallery spaces, the museum has a small bookshop dedicated to the father of Modernism, and a designer café.

Below *Burg Vischering is one of many moated castles in the Münster region* **Opposite** *A fountain in the forecourt of the Schlossplatz in Saarbrücken, capital of Saarland*

MARBURG

www.marburg.de

Medieval Marburg, an hour's drive north of Frankfurt, has more than its share of historic highlights, including Germany's earliest Gothic church and Europe's first Protestant university. The latter was founded in 1527 and is now in buildings scattered throughout the town.

The Elisabethkirche (Church of St. Elisabeth, open Apr–end Sep daily 9–6; Oct daily 10–5; Nov–end Mar daily 10–4; tel 06421 65573) was built between 1235 and 1283 on the tomb of St. Elisabeth (1207–31), who founded a hospice in Marburg. Such was the impact of her short life that she was canonized just four years after her death. Its exterior is dominated by lofty twin towers, bolstered by massive buttresses.

Much of the town, including the beautifully preserved, half-timbered Altstadt, is built on a hillside, with steep steps leading to the 13th-century castle (now a local history museum), with fantastic views.

✚ 405 D9 ℹ Tourism Marburg, Pilgrimstein 26, 35037 Marburg ☎ 06421 99120 🚉 Marburg

RHEINTAL

▷ 182–183.

RUHRGEBIET

▷ 184–185.

SAARLAND

www.tourismus.saarland.de
www.die-region-saarbruecken.de

While the Rhine and Mosel regions are more popular, Saarland isn't without its charms, and in the high season it offers a nice change of pace from the tourist stampede of the nearby towns. The region's capital is Saarbrücken, an unprepossessing, industrialized city that offers little in the way of cultural highlights. If you're passing through, however, it's worth stopping at the Schloss to visit the city's excellent Historisches Museum Saar (Tue, Wed, Fri, Sun 10–6, Thu 10–8, Sat 12–6; tel 0681 506 4501), which charts the changing fortunes of the region from 1914 to 1959.

Beyond Saarbrücken, other attractions worth seeking out include the superb museum of industrial heritage at the former Völklinger ironworks (daily 10–7; tel 06898 910 0111), which is a UNESCO World Heritage Site. The Keramikmuseum at Mettlach (Mon–Fri 9–6, Sat, Sun 9.30–6; tel 06864 811294), is a stone's throw from the headquarters of Germany's leading ceramics manufacturer, Villeroy & Boch (there are four factory outlets in Mettlach). The panorama at nearby Cloef, overlooks a spectacular bend in the River Saar.

✚ 408 B11 ℹ Tourism Saarland, Franz-Josef-Röder-Strasse 17, 66119 Saarbrücken ☎ 0681 927200 ℹ Tourism Saarbrücken, Rathaus St. Johann, Rathausplatz 1, 66111 Saarbrücken ☎ 01805 722727 🚉 Saarbrücken

SAUERLAND

www.sauerland.com

A gently rolling range of forested hills to the southeast of the Ruhrgebiet, the Sauerland is made up of five nature parks, the most scenic of which is the Naturpark Rothaargebirge. At the heart of this region is Winterberg, which has the best winter sports facilities north of the Alps, including a 1,600m (5,248ft) bobsleigh run (▷ 198). In the winter, the whole place has a lively, après-ski feel, while in the summer it makes a great base for trekking and mountain biking.

One of the most accessible (but also one of the busiest) trails leads to the top of Kahler Asten, the second-highest point in Sauerland at 841m (2,762ft). The plateau summit, which takes about an hour to reach on foot, is swathed in trees, which restrict your view, but for €1.80 you can climb to the top of the weather station for a more expansive vista. The weather station has a couple of cafés and a small regional museum (information in German only), and there's parking for those who'd prefer to drive up.

✚ 405 C8–D8 ℹ Sauerland Tourism, Johannes-Hummel-Weg 1, 57392 Schmallenberg ☎ 02974 96980 🚉 Schmallenberg, Bad Fredeburg

SOEST

www.soest.de

Historic Soest, with its half-timbered Altstadt and its narrow, cobbled lanes, was once the most important market town in northern Westphalia, and today it is home to architectural and cultural treasures.

Chief among these are its churches, which dominate the skyline for miles around. The twin Romanesque cathedrals of St. Petri and St. Patrokli face each other across Rathausstrasse, but neither is as interesting as the 14th-century Church of St. Maria zur Wiese, known locally as the Wiesenkirche (daily 11–4). As well as being one of the most exquisitely decorated Gothic churches in Germany, it's also home to the *Westphalian Last Supper*, a 14th-century stained-glass window that shows Jesus and his disciples tucking into a meal of beer, ham and pumpernickel.

✚ 407 C7 ℹ Tourist Information Soest, Teichsmühlengasse 3, 59494 Soest ☎ 02921 6635 0050 🚉 Soest

SPEYER

▷ 189.

INFORMATION

www.romantischer-rhein.de

404 B9–C10 Romantischer Rhein Tourismus, Loreley Besucherzentrum, 56346 St. Goarshausen 06771 959 9111

INTRODUCTION

In addition to being one of the biggest wine-producing regions in the country, the Rhine Valley is packed with half-timbered houses and romantic castles. The mighty River Rhine originates high in the Swiss Alps, following first the Swiss-German border and then the French-German border before delving into Germany proper near Karlsruhe. Between Bingen and Bonn the river is at its most scenic, and it is here that the notion of the 'Romantic Rhine', with its dramatic, castle-clad crags and its impossibly steep vineyards, first flourished. These days, it's busy with visitors in the summer, but if you travel out of season, or head even a little way off the beaten track, you'll find a region that's every bit as picturesque as it was when British and French artists first started visiting in the 18th and 19th centuries.

The Rhine has long provided an important trade route between the Alps and the North Sea, and most of the towns and castles along its banks owe their existence to commerce. Throughout the Middle Ages, wealthy barons added to their coffers by extorting taxes from those transporting goods along the river; at one time there were as many as 15 stations between Koblenz and Bingen alone.

It was the Romans who first brought wine to the region, although it wasn't until the sixth century that people began to cultivate vines here. The steep, manmade terraces that are so typical of the Rhine Valley have dominated the landscape since the 12th century. The most famous grape grown in the region is Riesling, which typically produces white wine with a lively, fruity bouquet, and can range in taste from very dry to very sweet.

WHAT TO SEE

LORELEY BESUCHERZENTRUM

www.loreley-touristik.de

The first major landmark along the Rhine gorge as you travel north from Bingen is the famous Lorelei Rock, an unremarkable slab of granite presiding over a

Above *Burg Rheinfels affords superb views of the river*

particularly tight bend in the river. According to legend, a flaxen-haired siren once lured sailors to their deaths here with her seductive singing. The best views of it are from the west bank, but even from there it's nothing to write home about. More impressive is the state-of-the-art visitor centre on the east bank, which has a multi-media myth room, plus other displays on navigation, wine, and flora and fauna in the region. (There are regular ferries across the river at St. Goar if you find yourself on the opposite bank.)

✉ Auf der Loreley, 56346 St. Goarshausen ☎ 06771 599093 🕐 Mar–end Oct daily 10–6; Nov–end Feb Sat, Sun 11–4 ✋ Adult €2.50, child (6–18) €1.50, under 6 free

BURG RHEINFELS

www.burg-rheinfels.com

Perched high above the village of St. Goar are the ruins of spectacular Burg Rheinfels, once the biggest and most impressive castle on the Rhine. Begun in 1245 as a customs house, it went on to be an important administrative town throughout the Middle Ages. In 1692, it was the only fortress on the west bank not to fall to Louis XIV's troops, but less than a hundred years later it was handed over to Napoleon's forces without a struggle, and much of it was blown up. Apart from its sheer size, its most impressive feature is its labyrinth of tunnels and trenches, which you can still visit.

✉ Schlossberg, 56329 St. Goar ☎ 06741 7753 🕐 Mid-Mar to mid-Oct daily 9–6; mid-Oct to end Oct daily 9–5; Nov to mid-Mar Sat, Sun 11–5 ✋ Adult €4, child (6–14) €2, under 6 free, family €10

BOPPARD

www.boppard.de

Boppard is an attractive medieval town, complete with half-timbered houses and a lovingly preserved late-Romanesque church—don't miss the 13th-century Triumphal Crucifix hanging above the altar, which is unusual for showing Christ as a suffering man rather than a resilient king. But the highlights of Boppard lie beyond the town. For great views of the Rhine, take the chairlift at the west end of town to the top of the Vierseenblick (Apr–end Oct daily 9.30 or 10 until between 5 and 6.30; tel 06742 2510).

Another worthwhile excursion is by train to Buchholz. The scenic, 10-minute journey takes you across two viaducts and through no fewer than five tunnels during its 330m (1,083ft) ascent. The walk back through woodland is all downhill, and brings you out at a great viewpoint overlooking the town (it's well signed, but good maps can be obtained from the tourist information office). After this, the path narrows, and traverses some steep slopes, so be sure to wear shoes with good grip if it's wet.

✚ 404 C10 ℹ Boppard Tourismus, Marktplatz (Altes Rathaus), 56154 Boppard ☎ 06742 3888 🕐 May–end Sep Mon–Fri 8–6, Sat 9–1; Oct–end Apr Mon–Fri 8–4

FRIEDENSMUSEUM BRÜCKE VON REMAGEN

www.bruecke-remagen.de

Remagen is a must for history buffs. In 1945, retreating German troops tried desperately to blow up every bridge across the Rhine, but the bridge at Remagen was secured by American troops and survived shelling, bombing and frogmen for 10 days before finally falling into the river. By this time Allied forces had managed to establish a bridgehead on the west bank. Hitler suspected sabotage, and had five of his officers court-martialled and shot. The bridge was never rebuilt, but one of its towers now houses a Peace Museum, with displays on the bridge's dramatic final days (labels are in English and German, and a leaflet in English is available free of charge).

✉ Brücke von Remagen, 53424 Remagen am Main ☎ 02642 20159 🕐 May–end Oct daily 10–6; Mar, Apr, Nov daily 10–5 ✋ Adult €3.50, child (6–18) €1, under 6 free, family €7

TIP

» Reserve a place on a night-time tour of Rheinfels castle (Apr–end Oct Fri). Tours can be arranged in English for groups of 10 or more.

Below *The two towers of St. Kastor Church in Koblenz*

INFORMATION

Essen

www.essen.de

404 B7 Touristikzentrale Essen, Hauptbahnhof 2, 45127 Essen 0201 19433 Mon–Fri 9–5.30, Sat 10–1 RuhrTOPCard (free public transportation and free or reduced price entry to 120 attractions throughout the Ruhr): Adult €34, child (6–14) €29, under 6 free for three days, plus other offers and reductions for a year Essen

Dortmund

www.dortmund-tourismus.de

404 C7 Dortmund Tourismus, Königswall 18a, 44137 Dortmund 0231 1899 9111 Mon–Fri 9–6, Sat 9–1 TouristCard (free transportation and free or reduced-price entry to numerous attractions): €8 for 1 day, €14 for 3 days Dortmund

Above *The exterior of Villa Hugel at Essen, home to Alfred Krupp, a 19th-century arms manufacturer*

INTRODUCTION

Densely populated, modern and commercial, the Ruhr has a rich industrial heritage. Named after the river running along its southern boundary, the Ruhr comprises a narrow corridor of industrialized cities between Dortmund in the east and Duisburg in the west.

Though coal and steel are no longer as important as they once were, this corridor is still referred to as Germany's Kohlenpott, or Black Country, and industry still characterizes much of the landscape. Having said that, the region is making a real effort to overcome its reputation as a cultural wasteland, not by denying or destroying its industrial heritage, but by embracing and celebrating it.

The Industrial Heritage Trail, linking a series of manufacturing museums, preserved pitheads and technological curiosities, is just one way to explore the area's legacy. Attempts have also been made to consolidate the area's green spaces and to make them more accessible, with footpaths and bicycleways linking them to cities throughout the region.

Many of the Ruhr towns and cities stood on an important medieval trade route, but it wasn't until the 19th century that the region's rich deposits of coal propelled it to the forefront of the nation's economy. With the extraction of coal came the production of steel, and it wasn't long before the Ruhr's mines and factories became the most productive in the world. This made them a prime target for Allied bombing raids, and most of the region's cities were all but obliterated during World War II.

The rapid rebuilding that followed left little room for architectural sensitivity, and for decades the Ruhrgebiet was seen as a wasteland of mills and belching smoke stacks. Today, technology and banking have all but replaced coal and steel as the mainstays of the region's economy, and cities like Dortmund and Essen are enjoying an economic and cultural revival that's well worth experiencing.

WHAT TO SEE

ESSEN

Essen is a heaving, industrial city in the heart of the Ruhr, 20km (12 miles) northeast of Düsseldorf. Essen enjoys a lively cultural scene, thanks to its plethora of superb venues, and is a great shopping district. But the best way to appreciate the city's—and the region's—heritage is to pay a visit to Zeche Zollverein. When Shaft XII opened in 1932 it became the largest coal-mining operation in the world. The mine workings and its buildings are designed in the Bauhaus style (▷ 21), and are considered to be a landmark of industrial architecture. The mine remained open until 1986, and, 15 years later, it was designated a UNESCO World Heritage Site. Today it's home to the fantastic Red Dot Design Museum at the Design Centre Nordrhein-Westfalen (Tue–Thu 11–6, Fri–Sun and holidays 11–8; tel 0201 301 0425).

In the Design Centre, conceived by British architect Sir Norman Foster, are masterpieces of modern design, from bicycle frames to bath-tubs, exhibited alongside rusting girders, red-brick walls and massive industrial piping. It's not obvious which route you're supposed to take, but it's still impressive, and is a must for anyone interested in design.

Zollverein's Shaft XII has its own visitor centre (Apr–end Oct daily 10–7; Nov–end Mar Sat–Thu 10–5, Fri 10–7; tel 0201 830360), which leads guided tours of the colliery itself (Apr–end Oct Mon–Fri 2, 4, Sat, Sun 11, 1, 2, 3, 4; Nov–end Mar Mon–Fri 2, Sat, Sun and holidays 11, 1, 2, 3, 4; tel 020 1830 3636). If you miss a tour, or if you can't get enough people together to arrange one in English, it's still worth exploring the site on your own, along designated footpaths, to marvel at the scale of the complex.

Essen's excellent Museum Folkwang (Goethestrasse 41; Tue–Sun 10–6; tel 0201 884 5301) has a collection of paintings, prints and sculptures from the 19th and 20th centuries. The museum also has a rare collection of early photographic prints.

✚ 404 B7

DORTMUND

Dortmund is one of Germany's biggest beer-producers, with six breweries producing well over 500 million litres (132 million gallons) of beer a year. The brewers of Dortmund and their predecessors have quenched the thirst of generations of miners as can be gleaned from a visit to the city's Brauerei-Museum (Brewery Museum: Tue, Wed, Fri, Sun, holidays 10–5, Thu 10–8, Sat 12–5; tel 0231 840 0200), housed in the old Hansa-Brauerei in the north of the town.

No less fascinating, though harrowing, is the Steinwache (Tue–Sun 10–5; tel 0231 502 2159), a former Gestapo prison where some 30,000 people were tortured and executed during World War II; the cell blocks survived Allied air raids and can still be seen (an information leaflet is available in English).

Other historic highlights of Dortmund include a trio of medieval churches: near the station is the 14th-century Petrikirche (Tue–Fri 12–5, Sat 11–4; tel 0231 721 4173), whose magnificent 16th-century altar is adorned with more than 500 gilded figures and 50 relief images carved into the wood. Nearby is the Romanesque Reinoldikirche (daily 10–7; tel 0231 523733), dominated by its steeple (100m/328ft); it's named after the city's patron saint, who is depicted in a life-size statue inside the church, opposite a statue of Charlemagne.

Finally, the 12th-century Marienkirche (Tue–Fri 10–12, 2–4, Sat 10–1; tel 0231 526548) is thought to be the oldest vaulted church in Westphalia, and has an altarpiece triptych (*c*1420) by local artist Conrad von Soest. Although the original was cropped in 1720 to fit its existing baroque frame, it remains one of the finest altarpiece paintings in western Germany, thanks to its unusual composition and its rich blue and gold hues.

✚ 404 C7

Below *Essen's Zeche Zollverein*

INTRODUCTION

Straddling the River Mosel, Trier is the birthplace of Karl Marx and is reputed to be Germany's oldest town. It is for certain one of the finest medieval cities in the country. At the heart of the beautifully restored Altstadt (old town) is the Markt, hemmed in by Renaissance and baroque buildings. But Trier's highlight is undoubtedly its collection of Roman ruins—prime among them the Porta Nigra (Black Gate)—which are worth at least a day's exploration on their own.

Founded as Augusta Treverorum under Emperor Augustus in 16BC (Treveri was the name of the local tribe), it later became the capital of half of the West Roman Empire. In the fourth century AD, Constantine the Great, Rome's first Christian emperor, made it Germany's first bishopric and indeed, after centuries of stagnation following the fall of the Roman Empire, it was the bishops of Trier who re-established the city's power in the 13th century.

WHAT TO SEE

PORTA NIGRA

Built at the end of the second century AD, the monumental Porta Nigra, or Black Gate, is one of four gates that once defined the axes of ancient Augusta Treverorum (see Background). Remarkably, no mortar was used, the massive sandstone blocks instead being held together by small iron clamps. Many of the city's Roman monuments were plundered for building materials in the Middle Ages, but the Porta Nigra survived thanks to St. Simeon, who in 1028 incarcerated himself inside the gate for seven years as an act of penance. After his death, it was transformed into a church in his memory (only its Romanesque apse now remains), and as such it was saved from looting by

INFORMATION

www.trier.de

408 A10 Tourist-Information Trier, An der Porta Nigra, 54290 Trier 0651 978080 Jan–end Feb Mon–Sat 10–5, Sun 10–1; Mar–end Apr and Nov–end Dec Mon–Sat 10–6, Sun 10–3; May–end Oct Mon–Thu 9–6, Fri, Sat 9–7, Sun 10–5 Trier Card (free public transportation, 50 per cent reduction on Roman monuments, 25 per cent reduction on museums, plus other discounts): €9 per person, €15 per family, valid for 3 days Trier

Opposite *One of the mismatched towers of the Dom*

Above *The Roman ruins of Kaiserthermen*

TIPS

» If you've got time, take a guided tour—the city is so rich in history, and so packed full of fascinating buildings and details, that it's simply impossible to do it justice here. Ask the tourist office for details.

» If you're in Trier on a Friday, Saturday or Sunday in summer (Apr–end Oct), head to the Roman amphitheatre (a short walk to the east of the Kaiserthermen) at 6pm (4.30 in Oct) to see a re-enactment of a gladiatorial contest. Full details from the tourist office.

» A nice spot for a picnic is the Schlosspark Quint, which are presided over by the striking, pink and cream façade of the magnificently kitsch Schloss Quint (*c*1768).

local builders. It even survived the heavy hand of Napoleon, who was told it was a building of Gallic origin and therefore worthy of preservation. The black staining, caused by a combination of weather and pollution, is at its worst at the southwest corner, the direction of the prevailing wind.

✉ Porta Nigra Platz, 54290 Trier ☎ 0651 75424 🕐 Apr–end Sep daily 9–6; Mar, Oct daily 9–5; Nov–end Feb daily 9–4 ✋ Adult €2.10, child (6–18) €1, under 6 free, family €5; combination ticket to all the Roman monuments (valid indefinitely): Adult €6, child (6–18) €2.50, under 6 free, family €14.80 🚌 1, 2, 3, 5, 6, 7, 8, 12, 13, 14, 16, 40, 82, 83, 85, 87

BASILIKA

Trier's remarkable Roman basilica was probably built at the end of the third century AD as Constantine's throne room, and was once part of a larger complex. It is the second-largest enclosed Roman building in existence, after the Pantheon in Rome. Unusually, it was made entirely of brick. The arched sections at ground level are remnants of an under-floor heating system. Inside, it looks even bigger than it does from the outside, thanks largely to the fact that there are no aisles or other obstructions to limit the sense of space. The windows at the east end are also slightly smaller than those at the sides, to make it look even longer than its 72m (236ft). Today it is a Protestant church, a function that is very much in keeping with its spare, spartan feel.

✉ Konstantinplatz, 54290 Trier ☎ 0651 72468 🕐 Apr–end Oct Mon–Sat 10–6, Sun and holidays 12–6; Nov–end Mar Tue–Sat 11–12, 3–4, Sun 12–1 ✋ Free 🚌 2, 10, 30, 33, 84, 87

KAISERTHERMEN

The Imperial Baths are impressive not for what remains above ground, but for what lies below. Originally intended as a massive spa complex and later relegated to serve as a military garrison, the vast courtyard area is crisscrossed with a maze of catacombs. Many of these labyrinthine corridors are almost perfectly preserved, and some sections are over 100m (328ft) long.

✉ Im Palastgarten, 54290 Trier ☎ 0651 44262 🕐 Apr–end Sep daily 9–6; Oct, Mar daily 9–5; Nov–end Feb daily 9–4 ✋ Adult €2, child (6–18) €1, under 6 free, family €5 🚌 2, 6, 7, 8, 10, 16, 30, 33, 82, 84, 87

KARL MARX HAUS

The Karl Marx House is a must for anyone interested in social history. A numbered sequence of rooms guides you through the life and times of both Marx (1818–83) and Engels (1820–95), and a leaflet is available in English. You can also see a 20-minute documentary on Marx's work. Highlights include a collection of the *Communist Manifesto* in various languages, a first edition of his *Das Kapital*, which was to prove so influential, and letters and articles.

✉ Brückenstrasse 10, 54290 Trier ☎ 0651 970680 🕐 Mid-Mar to end Oct daily 10–6; Nov to mid-Mar Tue–Sun 10–1, 2–5, Mon 2–5 ✋ Adult €3, child (6–18) €2, under 6 free 🚌 1, 3, 5, 6, 7, 8, 13, 15, 16, 40, 82, 83, 87

DOM

www.dominformation.de

Trier's Romanesque cathedral, with its curiously mismatched towers (a result of 15th-century one-upmanship directed at nearby St. Gangolf Church), contains a curious mix of architectural styles, from its fabulous Romanesque tympanum in the south aisle to its gigantic art deco organ (1974) hanging from the ceiling. But once again the highlight is Roman: The foundations of a third-century church, beneath the visitor centre, make this the oldest cathedral site north of the Alps.

ℹ Dom Information Trier, Liebfrauenstrasse 12, 54290 Trier ☎ 0651 979 0790 🕐 Apr–end Oct daily 6.30–6; Nov–end Mar daily 6.30–5.30 ✋ Free admission; hour-long tours (German only) daily in summer at 2pm: adult €3, child (4–16) €1, under 4 free, family €7. Tours in other languages can be booked through Dom Information 🚌 2, 5, 10, 30, 33, 84, 86, 87

Below *The Dom has Roman remains of an earlier church beneath its visitor centre*

SPEYER

www.speyer.de

Ancient Speyer, founded around 2,000 years ago, is renowned for its magnificent Kaiserdom, the largest surviving Romanesque cathedral in Europe (Apr–end Oct Mon–Sat 9–7, Sun 1.30–7; Nov–end Mar Mon–Sat 9–5, Sun 1.30–5; tel 06232 102397).

Founded in 1030, it was redesigned at the end of the 11th century to include four towers and two domes, and later became one of Germany's three imperial cathedrals (the other two being at Worms and Mainz). It is an astonishing 134m (440ft) long (best appreciated from the top of the steps leading up to the transept), with a nave height of 33m (108ft), but its deceptively plain design makes it look more massive still. Even the crypt, with its simple walls, banded arches and solid cylindrical columns, is bigger than many parish churches. The ante-crypt, accessed via a gloomy set of steps from the main crypt, houses the modest tombs of eight Salian dynasty emperors.

Beyond the cathedral's west front stretches Maximilianstrasse, a wide, cobbled avenue, lined with shops and cafés, that terminates at the 13th-century Altpörtel, Speyer's only remaining medieval gateway. Just to the south of the cathedral is the town's Historisches Museum der Pfalz, which charts the history of Speyer from Roman times to the present day (Tue–Sun 10–6; tel 06232 13250). Highlights include the remarkably ornate Golden Hat of Schifferstadt, which dates from the 14th century BC, and a third-century intact bottle of wine.

408 C11 Tourism Speyer, Maximilianstrasse 13, 67346 Speyer 06232 142392 Speyer

WIESBADEN

www.wiesbaden.de

The ancient spa town of Wiesbaden was founded by the Romans in AD40 and it has provided a welcome retreat for the old and infirm ever since. These days, most of the city's thermal baths are housed in hotels, but two can be visited by the public: the restored traditional Kaiser Friedrich Therme in the city (Sat–Thu 10–10, Fri 10–midnight; tel 0611 172 9660), and the renovated Thermalbad Aukammtal, about 1km (0.6 mile) to the northeast (Fri, Sat 8am–midnight, Mon, Wed, Thu, Sun 8am–10pm, Tue 6am–10pm; tel 0611 172 9880). Decked out like a Roman bathhouse the former encourages 'textile-free bathing.' The latter has a more modern feel and welcomes those who prefer to keep their textiles on!

The town is dominated by the lofty Marktkirche, a Gothic-revival monstrosity built by Karl Boos in the mid-19th century (Tue, Thu, Fri 2–6, Wed 10.30–12, 2–6, Sat 10–2, Sun 2–5; tel 0611 900 1611); it is built entirely in brick, which makes it look even higher than its 92m (300ft).

Of far greater artistic integrity is the splendid Kurhaus, an early 20th-century neoclassical masterpiece that now houses a convention venue and casino. The Museum Wiesbaden (Tue 10–8, Wed–Sun 10–5; tel 0611 335 2250) is home to a collection of vibrant paintings by Russian expressionist Alexej von Jawlensky (1864–1941), who lived in Wiesbaden for the last 20 years of his life.

408 C10 Tourist Information Wiesbaden, Marktstrasse 6, 65183 Wiesbaden 0611 172 9780 Wiesbaden

WORMS

www.worms.de

Over the centuries, the unassuming city of Worms has probably borne witness to more history than any other town in western Germany. Originally settled by the Celts and then the Romans, in the fifth century AD it became the home of the Nibelungen, a tribe whose demise was immortalized in the epic poem *Nibelungenlied* (c1200), which in turn inspired Wagner's equally epic opera cycle *Der Ring des Nibelungen* (1854–76).

As one of three imperial cities on the Rhine (along with Mainz and Speyer), Worms hosted over a hundred imperial *Diets*, or assemblies, the most famous of which took place in 1521, when Martin Luther was banned from the Empire for refusing to renounce his beliefs (▷ 33). Worms is also the home of Liebfraumilch (literally 'milk of our lady'), the white wine that takes its name from the 14th-century Liebfrauenkirche.

Highlights include the city's magnificent 12th-century cathedral (Apr–end Oct daily 9–6; Nov–end Mar daily 10–5; tel 06241 6115), and in particular the imposing Romanesque Kaiserportal on the north side; the Gothic frieze of the south porch, with detailed biblical scenes; and, inside, the extravagant altarpiece, designed and built by baroque master Johann Balthasar Neumann in 1742.

The Lutherdenkmal (Luther Memorial) in Lutherplatz (*c*1868) shows the great reformer addressing his detractors. The pedestal is inscribed with what are thought to be his closing words: 'Here I stand. Can do no other. May God help me. Amen.'

408 C11 Tourist Information Worms, Marktplatz 2, 67547 Worms 06241 25045 Worms

Below *One of the square towers that are surviving remnants of the city walls that surrounded Worms*

SAUERLAND AND WINTERBERG

This drive takes you across the gently rolling hills of the Naturpark Arnsberger Wald to the lively ski resort of Winterberg and to Kahler Asten, the highest peak in western Germany. From here, the drive crosses back over the Arnsberger Wald to reach Möhnesee-Damm, which holds back the waters of a manmade lake that's a popular vacation spot.

THE DRIVE
Distance: 180km (112 miles)
Allow: 8 hours
Start/end at: Soest

★ To find your way out of the labyrinth that is central Soest, follow signs for the B1 towards Bad Sassendorf and then the B475 towards the A44. Continue straight under the A44, following signs to Meschede, passing wind turbines.

❶ The wind turbines you see are evidence of the German government's ongoing commitment to green energy. Germany leads the world in wind-power production, generating six per cent of the nation's electricity this way.

Some 10km (6 miles) beyond the A44, you come to a crossroads; turn left here, following the B7 towards Brilon. After 20km (12 miles) the route starts to wind up into the Arnsberger hills. At the traffic lights just before Brilon, turn right towards Winterberg, along the B480. In Altenbüren, turn left at the lights. A steep climb brings you to the brow of a hill with views over Olsberg.

Continue through Olsberg as far as the traffic lights, then turn left along the B480. The next stretch follows the bottom of a pretty wooded valley, and is lined with car parking areas and footpath signs. At Winterberg, follow signs for *Zentrum* and park where you can find a spot.

❷ Winterberg is a friendly resort town with some of the best winter sports facilities north of the Alps. There's also great hiking and bicycling in the summer months. From Winterberg, take the B236 towards Kahler Asten. To reach the top of Kahler Asten (841m/2,758ft), take the first right after the Bob-Bahn and then first left up a steep hairpin road.

To continue the drive, return to the B236 and turn right towards Olpe. Stay on the B236 for the next 20km (12 miles). After about 10km (6 miles), some exciting hairpin driving provides fine views. Drive through the tiny, half-timbered villages of Oberkirchen and Winkhausen and continue as far as the traffic lights in Gleidorf. Turn right here, towards Bad Fredeburg, on the B511. After 3km (2 miles), take the first right to get to the heart of Bad Fredeburg.

❸ Bad Fredeburg's spa is Sauerland-Bad, which you reach by continuing along the B511 until you see it marked to the right. Spas are still very much part of the health and leisure scene in Germany.

Beyond Bad Fredeburg, a fast, sweeping road winds along the Wenne valley as far as Bremke. At Bremke, turn left on the B55 and, after 2km (1.2 miles), take the left turn that doubles back under the B55 towards Freienohl. Just after you cross the Ruhr into Freienohl, turn left at the traffic lights and continue to Arnsberg.

If you want to visit the town, continue as far as the traffic lights at the end of the road and head right, following signs for *Zentrum*. At the end of a tunnel turn left up a gentle hill, and park as close to the top as you can. The town square is at the end of this road.

❹ Arnsberg is a pleasant place to stop for a stroll. History enthusiasts might like to visit the Sauerland-Museum in a whitewashed neoclassical building just off Altermarkt. The poorly marked tourist office (which publishes some leaflets in English) is on the north side of the town square.

To continue to Soest along the B229 without stopping in Arnsberg, turn hard right up a hill at the first traffic lights as you come into the town. This is a steep, winding road, taking you over a pass and into the heart of the Naturpark Arnsberger. Just beyond the first Möhnesee bridge, at the top of a hill, is an information board with a map of the reservoir. At the end of the second bridge, turn left at the roundabout to reach the Möhne Dam.

❺ The Möhnesee-Damm was one of a number of dams in the region targeted by the RAF's 617 Squadron during World War II. They used bouncing bombs to destroy it, a feat later dramatized in the 1954 film *The Dambusters*. There's ample parking, and an information board at one end explains (in English and German) exactly what happened to the dam—and to the villages below it—on the morning of 17 May 1943.

To return to Soest, retrace your route from the dam, and go left along the B229 for 10km (6 miles).

WHEN TO GO

Although January and February are probably the best months for skiing, driving in the hills can be hazardous after particularly heavy snow. The summer is the best time for driving, bicycling, walking and water sports. If you want to avoid the crowds, May is recommended (also for trekking before the weather gets too warm) along with September, which is good for sailing and windsurfing too (when the water has had the whole summer to warm up).

PLACES TO VISIT

SAUERLAND-BAD

www.sauerland-bad.de
Sportzentrum 1, 57392 Bad Fredeburg
02974 96800 Mon–Fri 10–10 (Wed from 7am), Sat, Sun and holidays 9am–10pm
Adult €7.50, child 4–14 €4.50, under 4 free, family €13.50, €18.50; lower adult and child prices available for 1.5, 2 and 4 hours

SAUERLAND-MUSEUM

www.sauerland-museum.de
Alter Markt 24–26, 59821 Arnsberg
02931 4098 Tue–Fri 9–5, Sat 2–5, Sun 10–6 Adult €2, child (6–18) €1, under 6 free

MÖHNESEE

www.moehnesee.de
Küerbiker Strasse 1, 59519 Möhnesee
02924 497

WHERE TO EAT

In Winterberg, the bistro Täglich Café (Hellenstrasse 2, tel 02981 820990) is a welcoming eatery, serving anything from snacks and coffees to cocktails.

The Goldener Stern in Arnsberg (Alter Markt 6, tel 02931 530020), a luxurious café/restaurant, has an impressive range of starters and main courses, plus cakes and waffles.

Opposite *The flower-filled fields of Sauerland*

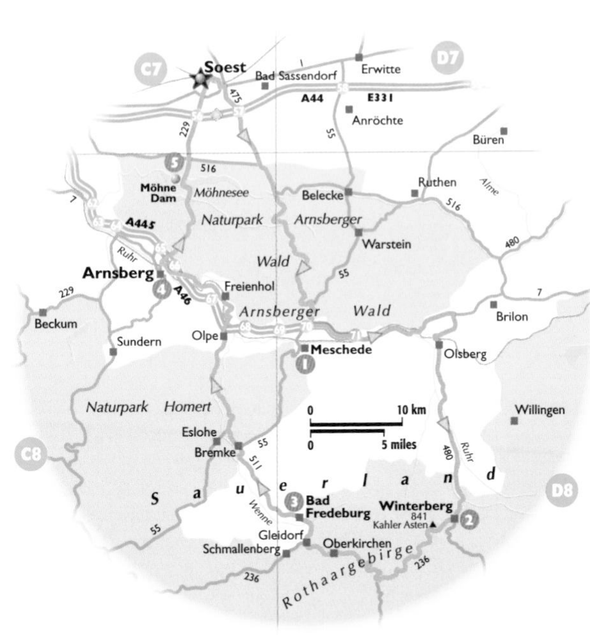

THE EIFEL

The high hills and low mountains of the Eifel, a sparsely populated region that lives off agriculture, forestry and tourism, make for great driving country. This tour begins amid World War II battlefields and courses through a volcanic terrain before arriving at a scenic lake district.

THE DRIVE
Distance: 262km (162 miles)
Allow: 8 hours, including stops
Start/end at: Aachen

★ Head south from Aachen towards Roetgen on L233, before joining B258 southbound beyond Schmithof.

❶ Roetgen is a sprawling village on the Belgian border. The dense Hürtgenwald (Huertgen Forest) east of here was the setting for a ferocious World War II battle, as the US army infantry struggled through strong German positions in the autumn and winter of 1944–45.

Stay on B258—which briefly passes through a piece of Belgium—heading south and out of the forest to Konzen and Imgenbroich, before descending on the steeply curving road into Monschau.

❷ Monschau's quaintly timbered, slate-roofed houses are traditional, and its setting in the River Rur valley picture-postcard perfect.

Leave Monschau on B258 southbound through Höfen. You now enter the landscape of the World War II German Ardennes Offensive, better known as the Battle of the Bulge, in the winter of 1944–45. The road takes a long eastward loop, becoming L159 before entering Hellenthal.

❸ Hellenthal stands at the eastern end of the Oleftalsperre, an artificial lake in a scenic part of the Deutsch-Belgischer Naturpark (German-Belgian Nature Park).

Take B265, heading south through Hollerath, and then drive along the German-Belgian border, beyond the forest-fringed crossroads at Losheimergraben, and down to Losheim.

❹ Now a paragon of peace and quiet, tiny Losheim was a strategic point in December 1944. The elite German 1st SS Panzer Division jumped off from the village at the start of the Battle of the Bulge, before blasting through thin American forces posted just across the border in Belgium.

Opposite *Timbered houses line the River Rur in Monschau*

Stay on B265 south to its intersection with L20. Go right on this forest-fringed road, which runs atop a ridge called the Schneifel, or Schnee Eifel (Snow Eifel).

❺ The Schneifel culminates in the Schwarzer Mann,which at 697m (2,286 feet) is the third-highest mountain in the Eifel. Abundant snow here most winters creates a sports zone centered on downhill and *langlauf* (cross-country) skiing.

Follow L20 south. Just before the hamlet of Schneifel, go left on L17, through Sellerich, then right on B265 south into Prüm. This road leads into an area where explosions of a far different kind once impacted the landscape—the Vulkaneifel, a dormant volcanic hotspot.

❻ Prüm, a focus for tourism, is known for its Benedictine Fürstabtei (Princely Abbey), founded in 721 by Bertrada, a great grandmother of Charlemagne (Karl der Grosse).

Leave Prüm to the east on B410, driving amid rolling farming country, through Büdesheim, to Gerlostein.

❼ Following the Sarresdorfer eruption 60,000 years ago, lava flowed to the edge of present-day Gerolstein, which is noted for its volcanic springs and as the source of Gerolsteiner mineral water.

Go east and north on B410 to Pelm, then right on L27. On the way to Daun, you curve around the Eifel's second-highest mountain, the Erresberg, 699m (2,292 feet) high.

❽ Daun's Eifel-Vulkanmuseum (⊳ 167) is worth a visit. If you have time, you might also wish to see one of the three Maaren—low-lying volcanic craters filled with shallow lakes—just south of the town.

Go north on B421 through Hillesheim to Stadkyll; switch to B51/E29 northeast to Blankenheimerdorf; then B258 northwest to Schleiden; then L207 and B266 to Einruhr. This drive of 80km (50 miles) brings you back to the hilly, forested northern Eifel.

❾ From Einruhr, a village on the Obersee lake on the edge of the Nationalpark Eifel, you can take a boat cruise on the lake, relax on a lakeside café terrace, or press north to Rurberg to explore more of the Rursee lake district.

Return to Aachen on B266 to Lammersdorf, then L12 to Kornelimünster, and the B258, which becomes Trierer Strasse in the heart of Aachen.

WHEN TO GO

Spring, summer and autumn all have a different charm in this hilly, forested landscape. Winter can be problematic for such a long drive, especially around the Schneifel.

PLACE TO VISIT

EIFEL-VULKANMUSEUM

⊳ 167.

WHERE TO EAT

In Gerlostein, at about the midpoint of the tour, try the family-run Brunnenstübchen (Am Brunnenplatz, Raderstrasse 7, 54568 Gerolstein, tel 06591 5319) for decent German food from an extensive menu.

The Imbiss am Damm (Am Damm, 52152 Simmerath (Rurberg), tel 02473 2476), won't win many culinary awards, but the café-snack bar's dramatic position overlooking the Rursee dam compensates for the menu.

Above *Rhine Meadows in Bonn is a perfect place to relax, and it also hosts several festivals throughout the year*

AACHEN

CAROLUS THERMEN

www.carolus-thermen.de

Built in 2001 to look like an original Roman bath, Carolus Thermen is the perfect place to pamper aching limbs and tired muscles. This cutting-edge spa complex features 10 outdoor and indoor pools (all filled with thermal mineral water at a balmy 38°C/100°F), outdoor sun terraces, a Baltic sauna landscape, an Oriental bathing world, a solarium and an inviting café. There's also a Mediterranean restaurant and beer garden.

Passstrasse 79, 52070 Aachen 0241 182740 Daily 9am–11pm (last entry 9.30pm) €10–€29 Bus to Carolus Thermen

FORUM M

www.mayersche.de

This great bookshop is just north of the tourist information office. It has a newspaper and magazine section with foreign editions. Many of its books on art, photography and travel are in English. It also sells gifts, postcards, and there is a café.

Buchkremerstrasse 1–7, 52062 Aachen 0241 4777 7145 Mon–Sat 9.30–8

LEONIDAS PRALINEN

www.leonidas.com

Belgian Leonidas pralines are among the most delicious—and calorific—chocolates in the world. They taste smooth and creamy because they're made with cream instead of milk, which also means that they have to be kept refrigerated. They're available in dozens of different sizes and guises.

Markt 45, 52062 Aachen 0241 72032 Mon–Fri 9.30–6.30, Sat 9.30–4

BONN

BEETHOVENHALLE

www.beethovenhalle.de

This domed building on the banks of the Rhine has been Bonn's main concert arena and congress hall since it opened in 1959, and today is home to the world-renowned Beethoven Orchestra. The biggest of the four halls can seat 2,000.

Wachsbleiche 16, 53111 Bonn 0228 72220 Performances most days €15–€55 Tram to Wilhelmsplatz

EN'TE BAR

www.ente-bonn.de

The En'te Bar is tucked away in Kaiserpassage, a mall adjacent to Bonn's university. It's more of a bistro than a bar, with its menu of snacks and main meals, but it also serves a comprehensive range of cocktails, shots and beers. The intimate candlelit atmosphere makes it ideal for a romantic drink. There is live jazz every Wednesday night from 9pm to 1am.

Kaiserpassage, Kaiserplatz, 53113 Bonn 0228 639322 Mon–Sat 10am–1am, Sun and holidays 10am–8pm Tram to Hauptbahnhof

KAMMERMUSIKSAAL

www.beethoven-haus-bonn.de

Two doors down from the Beethoven House (▷ 166) is the Beethoven Chamber Music Hall. The focal point of the building is the Hermann J. Abs Music Hall. An unusual agenda includes special performances for children. It's also home to the Beethoven Archive, the Beethoven House collection and the Beethoven Library.

Bonngasse 18–26, 53111 Bonn 0228 981750 Performances every 7–14 days €5–€20 Tram to Bertha von Suttner Platz

RHEINAUE FREIZEITPARK

This lovingly landscaped park on the banks of the Rhine boasts 45km (28 miles) of footpaths (the riverside promenade alone is over 5km/3 miles long), a boating lake (ideal for rowing in the summer), a Japanese garden and a garden for the blind. For kids there's a crazy golf course and a playground. The park is open 24 hours year round.

✉ Herbert-Wehner-Platz (at Ludwig-Erhard-Allee), 53175 ☎ 0228 374030 🕑 Daily 24 hrs 🚋 Tram to Rheinaue 🍴

DÜSSELDORF

AQUAZOO

www.duesseldorf.de/aquazoo

This superb sea life attraction combines the presentation techniques of a zoo with the sort of information you'd usually expect to find at a natural history museum. Exhibition rooms from A to Z are alphabetically ordered and themed according to region or species, making them easy to explore.

✉ Kaiserswerther Strasse 380, 40200 Düsseldorf ☎ 0211 899 6150 🕑 Daily 10–6 ✋ Adult €6, child (6–18) €4, family €12 Ⓢ Aquazoo

GOLFPLATZ LAUSWARD

www.gsvgolf.de

Within sight of downtown Düsseldorf and the Rheinturm (▷ 168) is Lausward Golf Course, established in 1978 as the first public golf course in Germany. It has a nine-hole, par-35 course and a 250m (275-yard) driving range. Clubs and hand carts can be rented.

✉ Auf der Lausward 51, 40221 Düsseldorf ☎ 0211 410529 🕑 Mar–end Nov daily ✋ 18 holes: Mon–Fri €24, Sat, Sun €30 🚋 Tram 708 to D-Hamm, then bus 725 to Auf der Lausward

KÖNIGSALLEE

Düsseldorf's tree-lined Königsallee, known locally as the Kö, prides itself on being a shoppers' paradise. The street itself is lined with achingly fashionable boutiques, while nearby malls take shopping to a whole new level. Almost every designer label you can think of is represented here, and the Kö's cafés and restaurants are every bit as chic as its shops.

Ⓢ Königsallee 🍴 ☕

RENNBAHN GRAFENBERG

www.duesseldorf-galopp.de

This is one of the loveliest and most important racecourses in Germany. Race meetings are held from March to late October, but check the website before you go. The track is on the B7, about 6km (4 miles) to the west of the A3 autobahn.

✉ Rennbahnstrasse 20, 40629 Düsseldorf ☎ 0211 622885 or 177260 🕑 Race meetings: Mar–end Oct Sat, Sun ✋ Adult €5, under-16 free, family €7.50 🚋 Tram to Staufenplatz, then shuttle bus 894 to the Rennbahn (racecourse)

EIFEL

NÜRBURGRING

www.nuerburgring.de

The world-famous Nürburgring is in the heart of Germany's Eifel region. Built between 1925 and 1927 it is 21km (13 miles) long and contains no fewer than 73 bends. It was the venue for the German Grand Prix from 1950 to 1976, when it was finally deemed too dangerous following Niki Lauda's spectacular crash. Today, Nürburgring is still used for the European (or Luxembourg) Grand Prix, and as a test track and occasional racetrack, and at certain times it can be driven by the public. For those who'd prefer not to be in the driving seat, it is possible to be chauffeured around the circuit in a Ringtaxi (tel 02691 932020), at speeds of up to 330kph (205mph). There's also a motoring museum here, plus a 450m (1,475ft) indoor go-cart track.

✉ Nürburgring GmbH, 53520 Nürburg ☎ 02691 3020; Ticket Hotline 01805 770750 🕑 Track: most weekends year round, plus some additional days ✋ Self-drive: €22 (reduction for more circuits). Ringtaxi: €200 for up to three people. Formula One tickets €77–€277

ESSEN

CITY CENTER ESSEN

www.citycenter-essen.de

With its vast downtown shopping precinct, Essen is rightly regarded as a magnet for shopaholics. In the heart of it all is City Center Essen, a state-of-the-art mall with a multiplex cinema, fast-food outlets and more than 80 shops, selling everything from sports equipment to lingerie. There's little in the way of designer gear on offer, however.

✉ Porscheplatz 67, 45127 Essen ☎ 0201 747670 🕑 Mon–Sat 10–8 Ⓢ Porscheplatz

FRANKFURT AM MAIN

MARKETS

Frankfurt's popular Saturday flea market has kitsch art and assorted knick-knacks. Those who like their food fresh will relish a tour of Kleinmarkthalle, a vast, indoor grocery market selling meat, fish, vegetables, fruit and exotic herbs and spices.

SHOPPING DISTRICTS

Frankfurt is home to some of Germany's most profitable shopping districts. Chief among these is the famous Zeil Promenade, lined with department stores, retail outlets and specialist shops. Nearby is Goethestrasse, which has exclusive designer boutiques and expensive jewellery stores. Also worth exploring is Schweizer Strasse, in the Sachsenhausen district. And for those who prefer to do all their shopping under one roof, the gleaming Zeilgalerie, at the west end of the Zeil, has over 50 shops on eight levels.

EINTRACHT FRANKFURT

www.eintracht-frankfurt.de

Although the Eintracht Frankfurt soccer team has had a yo-yo career in recent years, its die-hard fans continue to turn out in droves to show their support. In 2006, Eintracht moved to its new home at the impressive Commerzbank Arena stadium just to the south of the city off Junction 51 of the A3 autobahn.

✉ Commerzbank Arena, Moorfelder Landstrasse 362, 60528 Frankfurt am Main ☎ 069 955030 🕑 Home games: Aug–late May Sat or Sun every few weeks ✋ €16–€56 🚋 Bus to Arena

ENGLISH THEATRE

www.english-theatre.org

Billed as the largest English-language theatre in mainland Europe, Frankfurt's English Theatre presents a varied schedule of plays and musicals throughout the year. Many of the shows performed here have come from Broadway or London's West End, and they regularly feature famous faces from television and film.

✉ Gallusanlage 7, 60329 Frankfurt am Main ☎ 069 2423 1620 ⏲ Shows Tue–Sat 7pm, Sun 6pm 💶 €21–€44 🚇 Willy Brandt Platz

EXPLORA MUSEUM

www.exploramuseum.de

Hidden in a former air-raid bunker is the brilliant Explora Museum, with an outstanding collection of interactive exhibits, including optical illusions, puzzle pictures and holograms, 3D photography, 3D stereo art and 3D magic-eye dots (you'll have to go to find out what these are), and even a famous Ames room, where things are never quite what they appear. The museum is about 1km (0.6 mile) to the north of the Römerberg, and is a must for both curious kids and adults.

✉ Glauburgplatz 1, 60318 Frankfurt am Main ☎ 069 788888 ⏲ Tue–Sun 11–6 💶 Adult €12, child (6–12) €6, family €33 🚇 Glauburgstrasse

FRANKFURTER GOLF CLUB

www.fgc.de

There are more than half a dozen golf courses in and around Frankfurt that welcome non-members, but the one closest to the downtown area is the Frankfurt Golf Club. It's also one of the oldest, since it was established in 1913. During the 1970s and 1980s, the German Open tournament was held here on a number of occasions. Guests must have a handicap of 32 or better. Carts and caddies are available to rent.

✉ Golfstrasse 41, 60528 Frankfurt am Main ☎ 069 666 2318 ⏲ Daily 💶 €80 Mon–Fri, €100 Sat, Sun 🚋 Tram to Niederrad

JAZZKELLER

www.jazzkeller.com

Established in 1952, this jazz club, in the heart of the city's shopping district, is the oldest in Germany. Over the years it has played host to such luminaries as Louis Armstrong, Dizzy Gillespie and Frank Sinatra. A small, intimate venue with a relaxed, earthy feel, it continues to present the very best in local and world jazz on an almost nightly basis.

✉ Kleine Bockenheimer Strasse 18a, 60318 Frankfurt am Main ☎ 069 288537 ⏲ Wed–Sun from 9pm 💶 €5–€15 🚇 Opernplatz

KING KAMEHAMEHA

www.king-kamehameha.de

Specializing in Latin jazz and house music, the King Kamehameha is one of the most popular clubs in Frankfurt. This vast contemporary venue attracts a trendy crowd and some of the country's best bands and DJs. There's a restaurant (food until 11pm) and cocktail bar (drinks until 4am). King Kamehameha is to the east of Ostbahnhof.

✉ Hanauer Landstrasse 192, 60314 Frankfurt am Main ☎ 069 480 0370 ⏲ Mon–Fri 3.15–midnight, Sat, Sun 10–midnight 💶 Around €10, depending on show 🚇 Ostbahnhof

NATURMUSEUM SENCKENBERG

www.senckenberg.de

The Senckenberg Natural History Musuem, about 1km (0.6 mile) west of the city, is one of the largest museums of its kind in Europe. As well as an impressive display of freestanding dinosaur skeletons, it has exhibitions on animals, vegetables and minerals, on specific mammal species and on the origins of the Earth and the evolution of humans.

✉ Senckenberganlage 25, 60325 Frankfurt am Main ☎ 069 75420 ⏲ Mon–Wed 9–8, Thu, Fri 9–5, Sat, Sun and holidays 9–6 💶 Adult €6, child (6–16) €3, under 6 free 🚇 Bockenheimer Warte

TIGERPALAST

www.tigerpalast.com

Frankfurt's famous Tigerpalast is a variety theatre. Accompanied by a resident orchestra, five to seven different artists from all over the world feature in a performance that lasts around two hours. It's great fun if you're in the mood for something a bit different. Tigerpalast is also home to an excellent late-night restaurant (Tue–Sat 6pm–1am), an American cellar bar (Tue–Sun 5pm–3am) and an underground bistro (Tue–Sun 5pm–2am), both of which are grat in the early hours.

✉ Heiligkreuzgasse 16–20, 60313 Frankfurt am Main ☎ 069 920 0220 ⏲ Two performances per night Tue–Sun, plus midnight reviews Mon–Fri 💶 Adult €51–€55, under 12 half-price, student 25 per cent discount (subject to availability) 🚇 Konstablerwache

ZOO FRANKFURT

www.zoo-frankfurt.de

Frankfurt Zoo is in a spacious park just beyond the east end of the Zeil Promenade. It has a big cat jungle, elephant and hippo enclosures, and an impressive free-flying aviary, plus a sea-cliff environment (visible from both above and below water) and a specially designed house for nocturnal animals.

Water-filled ditches or panes of glass are used around the zoo, so visitors don't feel cut off from the animals.

✉ Alfred-Brehm-Platz 16, 60316 Frankfurt am Main ☎ 069 2123 3735 ⏲ Apr–end Oct daily 9–7; Nov–end Mar daily 9–5 💶 Adult €8, child (6–18) €4, under 6 free family €20 🚇 Alfred-Brehm Platz 🍴

KÖLN (COLOGNE)

SHOPPING DISTRICTS

Bearing in mind Cologne's size (it's the fourth-largest city in Germany), it has a reassuringly compact downtown area.

Its three main shopping precincts are the area around Domplatz, at the northern end of the Altstadt; Hohe Strasse and its offshoots, stretching to the south of Domplatz for almost 1km (0.6 mile); and the area around Neumarkt, about 1km (0.6 mile) to the west of Hohe Strasse.

Domplatz itself is dominated by

glitzy designer shops, but as you head south, you'll see the more mainstream stores of Hohe Strasse, including Benetton, Gap and Zara. Neumarkt is home to the Neumarkt Passage, a small, street-like mall specializing in gifts, clothes and shoes. Beyond Neumarkt, dozens of little side-street shops sell everything from fine art to furniture.

4711

www.4711.com

Eau de Cologne was first manufactured in the city at the start of the 18th century by Italian immigrant Paolo Feminis. Soon dozens of other companies began distilling the so-called *eau admirable* using similar methods.

One of the biggest of these companies was run by the Mülhens family, whose laboratory on Glockengasse was given the number 4711 by Napoleon's troops during the French occupation of Cologne in 1794. This number went on to become a world-famous trademark, although the building itself was destroyed during World War II. It was rebuilt in 1964 in neo-Gothic style and is now the flagship store for 4711.

✉ Glockengasse 4711, 50667 Köln ☎ 0221 925 0450 🕐 Mon–Fri 9–7, Sat 9–6 🚋 Tram to Appellhofplatz

Below *A colourful crane, one of many birds that can be seen in Zoo Frankfurt, which is set in a park*

BRASSERIE BRUEGEL

www.bruegel.de

The effortlessly cool Brasserie Bruegel, just to the north of Rudolfplatz, doubles as a jazz bar from 11pm until late every night. One end of its elegantly furnished main dining area is overlooked by a lofty gallery lined with candlelit tables for two. The seasonal menu focuses on fish dishes, and theme nights help to spice things up a little. Aside from the food, of course, Breugel also serves up some of the country's biggest names in jazz and soul. For the best seats, reserve in advance and ask for a gallery table.

✉ Hohenzollernring 17, 50672 Köln ☎ 0221 252579 🕐 Mon–Fri noon–3am, Sat, Sun 6pm– 3am 🖐 €15–€25 🚋 Tram to Rudolfplatz

BIRKENSTOCK & BERKEMANN

www.birkenstock.de

As anyone who's ever owned a pair of these well-designed and enduringly popular shoes knows, the numerous felt and leather layers used to make up the soles soon mould themselves to your feet, resulting in a perfect fit. There are dozens of different designs.

✉ Breite Strasse 80, 50667 Köln ☎ 0221 252529 🕐 Mon–Fri 10–8, Sat 10–4 🚋 Tram to Domplatz

CLAUDIUS THERME

www.claudius-therme.de

Tucked away in a corner of Cologne's restful Rheinpark, these thermal baths are an oasis of calm. Characterized by bright tiles, marble paving and stone columns, the facilities here include a spa area with massage jets, neck showers and a whirlpool, plus a sauna area offering all kinds of steam rooms. The thermal water is state-accredited, and comes from two springs 364m (1,194ft) and 1,027m (3,370ft) underground. There's a café overlooking the main pool.

✉ Sachsenbergstrasse 1, 50679 Köln ☎ 0221 981440 🕐 Daily 9am–midnight 🖐 €14–€16 for 2 hours, €19.50–€21.50 for 4 hours, €25.50–€27.50 for day pass 🚌 Bus to Claudius Therme ☕

DEUTSCHES SPORT UND OLYMPIA MUSEUM

www.sportmuseum-koeln.de

This cleverly conceived museum is on the banks of the Rhine just a short walk south of Cologne's Altstadt (▷ 172–175). Sports-mad kids can enjoy the interactive exhibits, from the bicycling wind tunnel and the triple-jump runway to the boxing ring and soccer cinema.

✉ Im Zollhaven 1, 50678 Köln ☎ 0221 336090 🕐 Tue–Fri 10–6, Sat, Sun 11–7 🖐 Adult €5, child (6–16) €2.50, family €12.50 🚋 Tram to Heumarkt ☕

FC KÖLN

www.fc-koeln.de

The RheinEnergieStadion, situated in Müngersdorf to the west of the city, is home to Cologne's professional soccer team, Cologne FC. For tickets and additional information, log onto the website.

✉ RheinEnergieStadion, Aachener Strasse 999, 50933 Köln ☎ 01805 325656 (club/tickets); 0221 7161 6300 (stadium) 🕐 Cologne FC games: Aug–late May generally Sat or Sun every few weeks 🖐 Soccer tickets: €8–€51 🚋 Tram to Stadion

HOTELUX SOVIETBAR

www.hotelux.de

This plush, bright red bar, steeped in Soviet nostalgia, serves 28 different sorts of vodka and over 40 different cocktails. A host dressed as a seaman from the Soviet battleship *Potemkin* greets guests, and the bar area is clad in military memorabilia. At Von-Sandt-Platz, on the other side of town, the Hotelux Soviet Restaurant (Mon–Thu 6pm–1am, Sat, Sun 6pm–3am) serves Russian staples such as *pelmeni* (a kind of stuffed pancake) and borscht.

✉ Rathenauplatz 22, 50674 Köln ☎ 0221 241136 🕐 Daily 8pm–5am 🚋 Tram to Zülpicher Platz

PHILHARMONIE

www.koelner-philharmonie.de

This vast, cavernous concert hall, next door to the cathedral beneath Heinrich-Böll-Platz Promenade, is home to two world-renowned

orchestras: the Gürzenich Orchestra Cologne and the WDR Symphony Orchestra Cologne. The hall puts on more than 350 concerts a year.
✉ Bischofsgartenstrasse 1, Köln 50667 ☎ 0221 204080 ⌚ Performances almost daily year round ✋ €9–€47 depending on concert/seat 🚋 Tram to Domplatz or Hauptbahnhof

PUPPENSPIELE

www.haenneschen.de

This historic puppet theatre dates from 1802 and is a Cologne institution. Tickets for the annual *Puppensitzung*, or puppet festival, at the beginning of February go on sale at the end of September. The event is so popular that people camp outside the theatre for days to ensure they don't miss out. Tickets for other shows are easier to get, but it's still worth reserving well in advance. There are two matinees a day for kids and an evening show for adults. The shows aren't in English, but you can follow what's going on.
✉ Hänneschen-Theater, Eisenmarkt 2–4, 50667 Köln ☎ 0221 258 1201 ⌚ Children's performances: twice daily Wed–Sun. Adult shows: once daily Wed–Sun ✋ €7.50–€22.50 🚋 Tram to Heumarkt

SCHOKOLADENMUSEUM

www.schokoladenmuseum.de

Cologne's chocolate museum (▷ 197) is right next door to the sports museum (above). The beauty of this museum lies in watching the inner workings of a fully functioning, miniature chocolate factory, which takes visitors through the various stages of chocolate production, from mixing the raw ingredients to wrapping the final truffle.
✉ Rheinauhafen, 50678 Köln ☎ 0221 931 8880 ⌚ Tue–Fri 10–6, Sat, Sun 11–7 ✋ Adult €6.50, child (6–16) €4, under 6 free 🚋 Tram to Heumarkt ☕

WOLTERS SCHOKO EXPRESS

www.bimmelbahnen.de

Kids young enough to appreciate the finer things in life should try the Bimmelbahn, or 'small train', which winds its way through Cologne's Altstadt to either the chocolate museum or zoo. The round-trip takes around two hours and departs from Roncalli Platz, just to the south of the cathedral. Expert commentary is in both English and German.
✉ Malteserstrasse 28, 50859 Köln ☎ 02234 77226 ⌚ Mar–end Nov daily 10–6; Dec–end Feb Sat, Sun 10–6 ✋ Round-trip: adult €5, schoolchild €3 🚋 Tram to Domplatz or Hauptbahnhof

ZOOLOGISCHER GARTEN KÖLN

www.zoo-koeln.de

Set in magnificent parkland to the north of the cathedral, the zoo houses a huge variety of animals. It is best known for its primate collection, aquarium and big-cat enclosure. Next door is the botanical garden, which contains around 12,000 different plant species.
✉ Riehler Strasse 173, 50735 Köln ☎ 01805 280101 ⌚ Apr–end Oct daily 9–6; Nov–end Mar daily 9–5. Aquarium: daily 9–6. Botanical Gardens: daily 8–dusk ✋ Adult €13, child (4–14) €6 🚋 Tram to Zoo or Flora 🍴 ☕

MÜNSTER

ALLWETTERZOO, DELPHINARIUM UND PFERDEMUSEUM HIPPOMAXX

www.allwetterzoo.de

A few kilometres southwest of the city is Münster's All-Weather Zoo, also home to the Dolphinarium and Horse Museum. Zoo highlights include the orang-utan enclosure, with its unique tropical forest and 6m-high (19ft) viewing platform, and two walk-through enclosures housing smaller primates. There is also a roofed, all-weather route that goes past all the main enclosures.
✉ Sentruper Strasse 315, 48161 Münster ☎ 0251 89040 ⌚ Apr–end Sep daily 9–6; Mar, Oct daily 9–5; Nov–end Feb daily 9–4 ✋ Adult €12.50, child (3–17) €6.30, under 3 free 🚋 To Allwetterzoo 🍴

HOT JAZZ CLUB

www.hotjazzclub.de

In a basement next door to Grosse Freiheit 26, the Hot Jazz Club, one of Münster's premier music venues, has international jazz and blues on an almost nightly basis. Staff members are friendly and knowledgeable, and resident DJs keep things moving.
✉ Hafenweg 26b, 48155 Münster ☎ 0251 6866 7909 ⌚ Tue–Sat 7pm–late, Sun 3pm–late ✋ Around €9–€30

LWL LANDESMUSUEM UND PLANETARIUM

www.naturkundemuseum-muenster.de

Right next door to the zoo (above) is the State Museum and Planetarium. Inside, the natural history of the Rhine is brought to life by a well-presented display on dinosaurs and other prehistoric animals. There's also an ongoing schedule of temporary exhibitions. The planetarium features a varied selection of shows for both kids and adults in German.
✉ Sentruperstrasse 285, 48161 Münster ☎ 0251 59105 ⌚ Tue–Sun 9–6 ✋ Landesmuseum: adult €4, child (6–18) €2, family €9; Planetarium: adult €4, child (6–18) €2, family €9 🚋 To Allwetterzoo ☕

RADSTATION MÜNSTER

You can rent bicycles at a number of places in Münster, but the outlet with the biggest stock is the Radstation, a vast, underground bicycle park enclosed by a striking glass triangle opposite the city's main train station. Numbered routes crisscross the city and the surrounding area—maps are available at the Radstation and the tourist information office (▷ 180).
✉ Berliner Platz 27a, 48153 Münster ☎ 0251 484 0170 ⌚ Mon–Fri 5.30am–11pm, Sat, Sun and holidays 7am–11pm ✋ Bicycles: €8 per person per day. Tandems: €16 per day

SAUERLAND

BOBBAHN WINTERBERG HOCHSAUERLAND

www.bobbahn.de

The Olympic bobsleigh run at Winterberg is 1,600m (1,750 yards) long and has an average gradient of 10 per cent. It has been the venue for a number of German and European championships,

and you too can discover exactly what it feels like to be fired down a narrow barrel of rock-hard ice at speeds of up to 130kph (81mph). All participants are accompanied by an experienced driver. You must be at least 16 years old and 1.5m (5ft) tall, and have no heart or spinal problems.
Kapperundweg, 59955 Winterberg
0291 941559 Nov–end Feb daily
€78 per person Winterberg

SPEYER

SEA LIFE SPEYER

www.sealife.de
This facility on the banks of the Rhine embraces the 'learning can be fun' philosophy. Imaginative displays take visitors on an underwater journey from the upper reaches of the Rhine to the deep Atlantic. Among Sea Life Speyer's highlights are its shark population, and a hands-on tank for curious children.
Im Hafenbecken 5, 67346 Speyer
01805 6669 0101 Mon–Fri 10–5, Sat, Sun 10–6 Adult €12.95, senior €11.95, child (3–14) 9.50, under 3 free

TECHNIK MUSEUM SPEYER

www.technik-museum.de
Visitors to Speyer can't miss the sprawling Technology Museum, just to the south of the town, with its enormous collection of trains, planes and automobiles. Among the displays that kids can explore are a full-size, walk-in jumbo jet, a U-boat and a gigantic Antonov 22 transporter. Additional attractions include 70 more aircraft and helicopters, vintage cars, fire engines and trains. A café serves snacks and hot meals, and there are IMAX cinemas (films are in German).
Am Technik Museum 1, 67346 Speyer
06232 67080 Mon–Fri 9–6, Sat, Sun, holidays 9–7 Museum only: Adult €12.50, child (6–14) €10.50, under 5 free; Museum and IMAX Dome: Adult €17, child (under 15) €13

TRIER

COYOTE CAFE

www.coyote.de
This centrally located bar, on a quiet street near Marktplatz, is popular with well-heeled students and young professionals. It serves a Tex-Mex menu of burgers, burritos and steaks, plus an all-day breakfast menu and a changing lunch menu. The theme is continued in the terra-cotta-toned vents that snake around the ceiling and in the large mural of Arizona's Monument Valley opposite the entrance. But the focal point for late-night visitors is the long and well-stocked bar, which serves dozens of different cocktails, spirits and beers.
Nikolaus Koch Platz, 54290 Trier
0651 994 7606 Sun–Thu 10am–1am, Fri, Sat 10am–3am

SPIELZEUGMUSEUM

www.spielzeug-museum-trier.de
Do you remember Meccano? And the USS *Enterprise*? And the scale model of the space shuttle with the working bay doors? All these toys and thousands more like them at this splendid toy museum take curious kids and nostalgic adults on a journey back in time. Other highlights include an astonishingly detailed model railway, a clockwork animal kingdom and some 19th-century life-size dolls. Note that the museum is above the Café Restaurant Zur Steipe (▷ 205).
Dietrichstrasse 51, 54290 Trier 0651 75850 Apr–end Dec daily 11–6; Jan–end Mar Tue–Sun 11–5 Adult €4, child (11–18) €2, (4–11) €1.50, family €10

WIESBADEN

SPIELBANK WIESBADEN

www.spielbank-wiesbaden.de
With its opulent red carpet, enormous crystal chandeliers and lofty coffered ceiling, the Spielbank Wiesbaden is the oldest casino in Germany, not to mention one of the most lavish. It's housed in the magnificent, neoclassical Kurhaus, which was built in 1907 and restored in 1987 in accordance with the plans of original architect Friedrich von Thiersch. Men are required to wear a jacket and tie, and guests must be at least 21. Free taster sessions take place on Friday and Saturday night.
Kurhausplatz 1, 65189 Wiesbaden
0611 536 100 Gaming tables: Daily 2.45pm–3 to 4pm; slot machines: Daily noon–4am Gaming tables €2.50; slot machines €1 Bus to Kurhaus

FESTIVALS AND EVENTS

APRIL/MAY

MUSIKTRIENNALE

www.musiktriennalekoeln.de
This musical extravaganza is held every three years: the next event is in 2010. Orchestras from all over the world come here to take part in some of the 130 concerts at 14 venues around the city.
Bischofsgartenstrasse 1, 50667 Köln
0221 925 7160 Late April to late May

AUGUST

CHIO INTERNATIONAL EQUESTRIAN CHAMPIONSHIPS

www.chioaachen.de
Held over five days in August, Aachen's premier equestrian event covers both show jumping and dressage. Each year, the show is themed around a foreign country.
Aachen-Laurensberger Rennverein, Albert-Servais-Allee 50, 52070 Aachen
0241 91710 Late August
€10–€40

SEPTEMBER/OCTOBER

BEETHOVEN FESTIVAL

www.beethovenfest.de
Inaugurated in Bonn by composer Franz Liszt in 1845, the festival features some 50 concerts performed in a variety of venues all over the city and the surrounding region.
Three to four weeks, September/October €11–€125

Above *A table laid and waiting for diners*

PRICES AND SYMBOLS

The restaurants are listed alphabetically (excluding Le, La and Les) within each town. The prices given are the average for a two-course lunch (L) and a three-course dinner (D) for one person, without drinks. The wine price is for the least expensive bottle. All the restaurants listed accept credit cards unless otherwise stated.

For a key to the symbols, ⊳ 2.

AACHEN

BESITOS

www.besitos.de

Although it is part of a chain, this bustling bistro feels like a family-run restaurant, with its warm lighting, Spanish music and imaginatively decorated interior. It is on the broad sweep of the Kapuzinergraben, near the imposing neoclassical theatre. Diners can choose to sit either at tall wooden tables with stools (ideal for a quick snack) or at more formal tables with cushioned chairs. The menu includes tapas and main courses, from succulent Iberian ham to mouthwatering paella.

✉ Kapuzinergraben 19, 52062 Aachen ☎ 0241 445 3682 🕑 Daily 10am–1am 🖐 L €12, D €24, Wine €10

NOBIS PRINTEN

www.nobis-printen.de

Nobis Printen takes its name from a local culinary delicacy—a soft and spicy gingerbread. As well as baking the gingerbread, this popular bakery also serves a huge range of sandwiches and baguettes, plus traditional *Kaffee und Kuchen* (coffee and cakes).

Sample them upstairs in the snug café with its bouncy leather seats and great views of the cathedral square.

✉ Münsterplatz 3, 52062 Aachen ☎ 0241 968000 🕑 Mon–Fri 7–7, Sat 7.30–6, Sun 9–6 🖐 Cakes, rolls €2–€4

POSTWAGEN

www.postwagen-aachen.de

This sweet little restaurant, upstairs in the city's sole surviving half-timbered building (dating from 1657), with its spiral wood columns and wavy, leaded-glass windows, seems more suited to hobbits than humans. The 'Stage Coach' occupies a corner extension, something like an enclosed loggia, attached to the corner of the Rathaus (Town Hall) and overlooking the Markt.

Wiener Schnitzel is a typically popular dish here, though there's fish too, such as grilled Zander (pike-perch), on the menu.

✉ Krämerstrasse 2, 52062 Aachen ☎ 0241 35001 🕑 Daily 9.30am–1am 🖐 L €27, D €36, Wine €18

BONN

CAFÉ BISTRO PENDEL

www.cafe-bistro-pendel.de

This intimate little café in the heart of Bonn's Altstadt is just around the corner from the tourist information office.

It attracts a young crowd, and has a great range of dishes, from fresh snacks, salads and baguettes to steaming bowls of chilli, gnocchi and pasta. The low lighting and dark wooden interior, complemented by an impressive collection of antique clocks, give the place a snug, old-fashioned feel in winter, while in summer visitors can sit outside and watch the world go by, or plan their next excursion.

✉ Vivatsgasse 2a, 53111 Bonn ☎ 0228 976 6064 🕑 Mon–Thu 9am–1am, Fri, Sat 9am–2am, Sun and holidays 10am–1am 🖐 L €10, D €18, Wine €8

ROSES RESTAURANT

www.roses-bonn.de

More classy than Café Pendel is this restaurant, which serves reasonably priced food in elegant surroundings. Soft lighting and clean lines characterize the interior, while the menu includes a tantalizing array of pasta, fish and meat dishes, ranging from dark tagliatelle with shrimp in a mascarpone sauce to pork medallions draped in orange slices. An extensive breakfast menu is served daily until 3pm. A mezzanine looks out over Martinsplatz and the basilica, as does a cobbled patio.

✉ Martinsplatz 2a, 53113 Bonn ☎ 0228 433 0653 ⏲ Sun–Thu 9am–1am, Fri, Sat 9am–2am 💶 L €13, D €22, Wine €14

DARMSTADT

BORMUTH CAFÉHAUS

www.bormuth.de

This ultra-elegant bakery has a bustling *Stehcafe* (stand-up café) downstairs for quick bites and coffee. There is a seating area upstairs for those who prefer to take their time. The interior is simple yet sumptuous, with dark leather booths, marble-topped tables and subtle yellow lighting. The extensive menu includes breakfasts, cakes, baguettes and hot specials, plus more than a dozen sorts of tea, each with a name like 'Sport Cup' (which apparently contains 10 different vitamins).

✉ Marktplatz 5, 64283 Darmstadt ☎ 06151 17090 ⏲ Mon–Fri 7.30–7, Sat 7–6, Sun 10.30–6 💶 Snacks €3–€5, breakfasts and main courses €5–€8

DARMSTÄDTER RATSKELLER

www.darmstaedter-ratskeller.de

Although established only in 1989, this centrally located pub overlooking Darmstadt's spacious Marktplatz has an old-fashioned feel, with solid wooden tables and walls, apron-wearing waiters and, of course, home-brewed beer. Ratsbräu Spezial Dunkel is a sweet, slightly malty brew that is wonderful in cold weather, while Ratsbräu Premium Hell has a more refreshing aftertaste, and is a great warm-weather thirst-quencher. Simple but tasty German food is served all day, every day, and in the summer the pub spills out onto the bustling square.

✉ Marktplatz 8, 64283 Darmstadt ☎ 06151 26444 ⏲ Daily 10am–midnight 💶 L €10, D €18, Wine €12

DÜSSELDORF

RESTAURANT BRAUEREI ZUM SCHIFFCHEN

www.stockheim.de

Founded in 1628, Zum Schiffchen is the oldest restaurant in Düsseldorf, and it's also one of the best. Traditional *Alt* beer is brewed on the premises and served direct to your table until you say you've had enough; even then, the waiter will probably ask again, just to make sure. Special local dishes include pork leg with mashed potato and sauerkraut: Portions are on the generous side, so make sure you come with a really hearty appetite. The restaurant is just off Bergerstrasse, one block to the south of Uerige.

✉ Hafenstrasse 5, 40213 Düsseldorf ☎ 0211 132421 ⏲ Mon–Sat 11.30am–midnight 💶 L €15, D €25, Wine €21 🚇 Heinrich-Heine-Allee

UERIGE OBERGÄRIGE HAUSBRAUEREI

www.uerige.de

Extremely popular with locals in both summer and winter, the Uerige oozes Rhenish charm, from the intricately carved wooden wall panels to the copper detailing that is used almost everywhere else. Deliciously dark beer is brewed on the premises and is poured from wooden barrels on top of the bar. A wide range of snacks is also available, including platters of *Liverwurst* and gouda sandwiches for larger groups. Reserve in advance for *Schweinshaxe* (knuckle of pork). Uerige can be found one block to the south of Markplatz.

✉ Bergerstrasse 1, 40213 Düsseldorf ☎ 0211 866990 ⏲ Daily 10am–midnight 💶 Snacks: €3–€6 🚇 Heinrich-Heine-Allee

EIFEL

WINZERGENOSSENSCHAFT MAYSCHOSS-ALTENAHR

www.winzergenossenschaft-mayschoss.de

Established in 1868, the wine cooperative in Altenahr is a great place to sample the region's renowned Spätburgunder wine, a velvety-smooth red that is considered to be among Germany's best. The region's white wine, meanwhile, typically comes from Riesling, Müller-Thurgau and Silvaner grapes, while *Eiswein* (ice wine) is made from specially selected grapes that have been allowed to freeze on the vine. The latter is considered an aromatic delicacy, and a half-bottle will set you back at least €30, but is a wonderful accompaniment to desserts. The cooperative itself is housed in a fine brick building overlooking the Ahr.

✉ Ahrrotweinstrasse 42, 54508 Mayschoss ☎ 02643 93600 ⏲ May–end Oct daily 9–6; Nov–end Apr Mon–Fri 8–6, Sat, Sun 10–6 💶 Cellar tour and tasting costs €2.50–€16 per person, depending on size of group and number of wines tasted 🚆 Altenahr

ESSEN

CAFÉ SOLO

www.cafe-solo-essen.de

Despite its young, vibrant feel, Café Solo is popular with people of all ages, thanks to its relaxed atmosphere, wholesome food and friendly service. It's always busy but never overwhelmingly so, and the whole place is bathed in a warm, welcoming glow. Snacks such as bagels, panini and salads are the mainstay of the menu, but burgers and pasta dishes are also available, and the delicious spicy Chinese specials are superb value. Solo's location, at the heart of Essen's main shopping precinct, makes it a great place for alfresco dining in the summer, while in the winter outdoor heaters keep the cold at bay.

✉ Kettwiger Strasse 36, 45127 Essen ☎ 0201 747 6666 ⏲ Mon–Fri 8am–1am, Sat 9am–3am, Sun 10am–1am 💶 L €8, D €8, Wine €13 🚇 Hauptbahnhof

CASINO ZOLLVEREIN

www.casino-zollverein.de

This *über*-chic restaurant and café has an effortlessly elegant dining area and bar among the pipes and pillars of a former industrial boiler room. *Kaffee und Kuchen* (coffee and cakes) are available during the day, but to appreciate the atmosphere here fully it's best to come at night, when crisp white tablecloths and flickering candles provide inviting islands of light in an otherwise dark and cavernous space. The imaginative menu has a mixture of international and German cuisine, which is exquisitely prepared and presented. Zollverein itself is a few kilometres to the northeast of Essen, and can be reached via tram from anywhere in the downtown area.

✉ Gelsenkirchener Strasse 181, 45309 Essen ☎ 0201 830240 🕐 Tue–Sun 11.30am–midnight 🖐 L €30, D €38, Wine €19 🚌 Bus or tram 7 to Zollverein

FRANKFURT AM MAIN

HAUS WERTHEIM

This intimate little pub just to the south of the Römerberg is the oldest inn in the city, and was one of the few buildings to survive the Allied bombing raids of World War II. Inside, it looks as if it hasn't changed in centuries: Beer jugs and brass fittings dangle from every available beam, while kitsch, back-lit paintings made of stained glass bathe everything in a warm, ethereal light. The house dish is *Wiener schnitzel* in green sauce, which comes with boiled potatoes and eggs, and is indescribably delicious, not to mention generous to a fault. Because there are only half a dozen tables, it's often a good idea to reserve in advance.

✉ Fahrtor 1, 60311 Frankfurt am Main ☎ 069 281432 🕐 Daily 11–11 🖐 L €18, D €25, Wine €21 🚇 Römerberg

MAIN TOWER RESTAURANT AND BAR

www.maintower-restaurant.de

Perched 200m (650ft) above Frankfurt's teeming streets, the Main Tower Restaurant offers a breathtaking dining experience. Tables for two are arranged near floor-to-ceiling windows on the 53rd floor, with superb views of the city and its surroundings. The modern, imaginative menu isn't cheap, but for a treat it's hard to beat. Main courses might include scallops and caviar with beetroot ravioli and horseradish sauce, or breast of duck with creamed potatoes and wild garlic in a honey mushroom sauce. For dessert, choose from the likes of chocolate and rhubarb risotto, or coconut, banana and lime compote. After, you can take a stroll on the open observation deck. Main Tower is a short walk south of Opernplatz.

✉ 53rd floor, Helaba Building, Neue Mainzer Strasse 52–58, 60311 Frankfurt am Main ☎ 069 3650 4777 🕐 Tue–Thu 5.30pm–1am, Fri, Sat 5.30pm–2am 🖐 D menus €48–€98, Wine €27 🚇 Willy-Brandt-Platz

RAMA V

International restaurants abound near the train station and around Fressgasse, the pedestrianized precinct between Opernplatz and An der Hauptwache, but for a real treat make your way farther east to Rama V. This popular Thai restaurant is characterized by candlelit tables, dark, wood-panelled walls and cool white tablecloths, although its relaxed atmosphere ensures it never feels too formal. The menu is available in English and German, and lists an overwhelming variety of dishes at very reasonable prices. The service is impeccable, and the portions are more than generous. For a taste sensation, try the deep-fried banana with coconut ice-cream.

✉ Vilbeler Strasse 32, 60313 Frankfurt am Main ☎ 069 2199 6488 🕐 Mon–Sat 12–3, 6–11.30, Sun 6–11.30 🖐 L €21, D €28, Wine €16 🚇 Konstablerwache

ZUM GEMALTEN HAUS

www.zumgemaltenhaus.de

There are literally dozens of pubs, restaurants and bars in Frankfurt's Sachsenhausen district, to the south of the river, but the best place to sample *Apfelwein and Handkäse mit Musik* (▷ 346) is arguably Zum Gemalten Haus. Set back a little from the street, it has wall-to-wall wood-panelled paintings with a distinctly Dutch feel. The cider is served in large, tilting jars that are left on your table.

✉ Schweizer Strasse 67, 60594 Frankfurt am Main ☎ 069 614559 🕐 Tue–Sun 10am–midnight 🖐 Snacks €2–€5, main courses €8–€12, cider €1.60 for 300ml (12fl oz) 🚇 Schweizer Platz

KOBLENZ

KAFFEEWIRTSCHAFT

www.kaffeewirtschaft.de

The friendly Kaffeewirtschaft is in a prominent position overlooking Münzplatz, in the heart of the old town. The café is fronted by a stunning colonnade and has a striking candlelit interior with dark wooden chairs, marble table tops and blood-red walls. It serves everything from breakfasts and baguettes to pasta dishes and steak specials, so it provides the perfect place to rest at any hour of the day or night. In the summer, drinks here on the square are a must.

✉ Münzplatz 14, 56068 Koblenz ☎ 0261 914 4702 🕐 Mon–Thu 9am–midnight, Fri, Sat 9am–2am, Sun and holidays 10am–midnight 🖐 L €8, D €14, Wine €12

KÖLN

CAFÉ HOLTMANN'S

www.holtmanns.com

Housed in Cologne's famous Museum Ludwig, Café Holtmann's is one of the most popular and relaxing eateries in the middle of the city, and as such is worth a visit in its own right. It serves a wide range of cakes, baguettes, quiches and salads, all at surprisingly reasonable prices considering its location. The sofas lining one of the walls provide the perfect place for burying your head in a book or newspaper, and live jazz is played every Friday, Saturday and Sunday afternoon.

✉ Museum Ludwig, Bischofsgartenstrasse 1, 50667 Köln ☎ 0221 2509 9977 🕐 Tue–Sun 10–6 🖐 Snacks/lunches €3–€7 🚌 Bus/tram to Domplatz

GRANDE MILANO

www.ristorante-grande-milano.de

For a culinary treat, head to this chic Italian restaurant on the Hohenstaufenring, a few blocks to the south of Rudolfplatz. The interior is elegant yet understated, characterized by soft spot lighting, crisp white tablecloths and immaculately framed black-and-white prints, giving the whole place a relaxed, informal feel. The restaurant's chef, Dottore Minotti, specializes in truffles. Reservations are recommended. If the main restaurant seems a bit pricey, there's also a bistro right next door.

✉ Hohenstaufenring 29–37, 50674 Köln ☎ 0221 242121 🕐 Mon–Fri 12–3, 6.30–midnight, Sat 6.30–midnight 🖐 L €25, D €40, Wine €17 🚍 Bus/tram to Zülpicher Platz

PETERS BRAUHAUS

www.peters-brauhaus.de

Just to the northeast of the Altermarkt, Peters Brauhaus is one of the traditional taverns in Cologne's Altstadt, and it's also one of the best, thanks to its friendly service, welcoming atmosphere and excellent food. Not surprisingly, traditional staples such as *bratwurst* with *sauerkraut* and *Wiener schnitzel* with potatoes are the mainstay of the menu here, and everything is invariably washed down with a few glasses of *Kölsch*, the city's local brew—the number of beers you drink is marked on your beer mat with a pencil and added up at the end of the meal.

✉ Mühlengasse 1, 50667 Köln ☎ 0221 257 3950 🕐 Daily 11am–12.30am (food served 11.30am–midnight) 🖐 L €12, D €15, Wine by the glass 🚍 Hauptbahnhof

MAINZ

PIZZA PEPE

www.pizzapepe.de

This tiny pizza place just a short walk to the east of the cathedral may not look like much from the outside, but it's actually one of the most popular places in town. This is largely because of its great-tasting pizzas, which are made to order from fresh ingredients, although the booming voice of the proprietor also helps to keep the atmosphere fun and frantic. There's a vast array of toppings to choose from, and the mini pizzas (18cm/7in) are ideal for those with smaller appetites. All the staff wear white uniforms and tall paper hats, and can usually be seen flinging dough around the kitchen as though their lives depended on it. Pasta dishes are also available, and food can be ordered until midnight.

✉ Augustinerstrasse 21, 55116 Mainz ☎ 06131 229986 🕐 Sun–Thu 11am–1am, Fri, Sat 11am–2am 🖐 Small pizzas from €3, large pizzas from €5

MÜNSTER

FREIHEIT 26

Münster's once-derelict docklands have been transformed into a trendy but understated meeting place for students, jazz-lovers and other assorted night owls. At the heart of Hafenweg, the area's main drag, is Grosse Freiheit 26, a romantic, candlelit eatery that rubs shoulders with the Hot Jazz Club, the city's best basement jazz venue, on one side (▷ 198) and a Harley Davidson shop on the other. Overlooking the canal, this vibrant, popular restaurant has intimate but informal seating in a converted industrial space, complete with brick walls and internal piping. The young staff are friendly and attentive, the food is excellent, and the atmosphere is relaxing.

✉ Hafenweg 26, 48143 Münster ☎ 0251 747 4919 🕐 Daily 6pm–1am 🖐 D €25, Wine €19

Below *Kaffeewirtschaft in Koblenz is open for breakfast and into the evening*

IPANEMA

www.ipanema-muenster.de

Specializing in Latin American food, this lively restaurant just a short walk to the north of the train station is very popular. Wicker chairs, an artificial waterfall and beach-hut bamboo give a relaxed, informal feel, and the extensive menu—with everything from generously stuffed tortillas to mouthwatering steaks—is unbelievably good value for money. Fast and friendly service and lively Latino music complete the scene in this inexpensive gem.

✉ Mauritzstrasse 24, 48143 Münster ☎ 0251 40409 ⌚ Daily 12–12 ✋ L €15, D €20, Wine €11

MARKT CAFÉ

The café is opposite the cathedral in the heart of Münster's pedestrian precinct, and is far more inviting than its uninspired façade suggests. Frequented by students, work colleagues and families in equal measure, it serves everything from cake and hot drinks to baguettes and pizzas, not to mention all manner of beers, cocktails and spirits. In summer, the whole café spills out onto the square, making it a great place to quaff a quick beer or soft drink just a stone's throw from the cathedral.

✉ Domplatz 6–7, 48143 Münster ☎ 0251 57585 ⌚ Mon–Fri 9am–1am, Sat 8am–1am, Sun and holidays 10am–1am ✋ L €18, D €12, Wine €17

RHEINTAL

RESTAURANT ZUM GOLDENEN LÖWEN

www.goldener-loewe-stgoar.de

With its pink candles and curtains, and its old-fashioned furnishings, this friendly establishment on the banks of the Rhine is like a flashback to the 1950s, although it's no less charming for all that. The menu is a little on the pricey side, but the Goldenen Löwen is one of the few places near Lorelei rock and has a terrace overlooking the river. It is also a hotel dating from 1728, with 12 immaculate double rooms.

✉ Heerstrasse 82, 56329 St. Goar ☎ 06741 1674 ⌚ Apr–end Nov daily 8am–10pm; Dec–end Mar Fri–Wed 8am–10pm ✋ L €15, D €22, Wine €13 🚉 St. Goar

RISTORANTE DA FRANCO

www.ristorante-dafranco.de

If you find yourself feeling a little peckish in Remagen, look no further than Ristorante da Franco, one of a handful of eateries with a view of the Rhine. It's housed in a fine baroque building painted an eye-catching (if rather incongruous) yellow, while the interior is littered with little knick-knacks, from oversize bottles of wine to giant jars of pasta. Home-made pizza is the order of the day here, but if you just want a snack, the soup—accompanied by freshly baked dough balls—is also excellent.

✉ Rheinpromenade 43, 53424 Remagen ☎ 02642 22422 ⌚ Daily 10.30am–midnight ✋ L €21, D €26, Wine €17 🚉 Remagen

SCHWARZWALD (BLACK FOREST)

WANDERHÜTTE SATTELEI

www.bareiss.com

Finding this luxurious-rustic, wood-built hiker's restaurant deep in the Black Forest would be an unlikely stroke of luck—except that it's a dependency of the tony Hotel Bareiss, whose staff can provide foolproof guidance for the uphill trail-trek of about three-quarters of an hour. Once arrived at an altitude of 706m (2,316ft), your 'reward' is a plate of homemade Schwarzwald sausage, cheese and other snacks, or a slice of their *Schwarzwälder Kirschtorte* (Black Forest Gateau).

✉ Hotel Bareiss, Gärtenbühlweg 14, 72200 Baiersbronn-Mitteltal ☎ 07442 470 ⌚ Daily 11–5 ✋ Snacks €4.50–€7.50

SPEYER

DOMHOF HAUSBRAUEREI

www.domhof.de

With its tendril-clad façade, flower-draped ceilings and solid wooden beams, this historic establishment opposite Speyer's magnificent cathedral is popular with locals and visitors. The Domhof is staffed by friendly female waitresses who are young (or young at heart). A wide range of traditional German food is available, with sausages and *Sauerkraut* much in evidence, along with delicious home-brewed beer by the barrelful.

✉ Grosse Himmelsgasse 6, 67346 Speyer ☎ 06232 67440 ⌚ Mon–Thu 11am–midnight, Fri 11am–1am, Sat 10am–1am, Sun 10am–midnight ✋ L €23, D €28, Wine by the glass

MAXIMILIAN CAFÉBAR UND RESTAURANT

www.cafe-maximilian.de

With its dark wooden tables, shallow-domed ceilings and art nouveau theme, this intimate bar has all the charm of a busy Parisian café. In addition to snacks and main courses, from buffalo wings to burritos, it also does a fine line in doughnuts and cakes. Its hot drinks include a whole range of teas, plus flavoured hot chocolates with apt names like 'One Night in Heaven' (laced with caramel and toffee).

✉ Korngasse 15, 67346 Speyer ☎ 06232 100 2500 ⌚ Mon–Fri 8am–1am, Sat, Sun 9am–1am ✋ L €10, D €17, Wine €17

SOEST

LAMÄNG BRASSERIE

www.lamaeng-brasserie.de

This intimate, welcoming café is decorated in art nouveau style, with deep, comfortable sofas, stained glass and assorted Gustav Klimt prints hung tastefully on the walls. It does a nice menu of hot baguettes, as well as breakfasts, waffles and *Apfelstrudel*. In terms of drinks, it seems your imagination really is the limit here: Beers, wine and cocktails are served alongside coffees, milkshakes and there are no fewer than 17 different types of tea. Candlelight in the evening adds to the relaxed atmosphere.

✉ Kungelmarkt 6, 59494 Soest ☎ 02921 767283 ⌚ Sun, Mon 9am–1am, Fri, Sat 9am–3am ✋ L €8, D €12, Wine €14

Opposite *Enjoying the sun outside Café Restaurant Zur Steipe in Trier*

TRIER

CAFÉ RESTAURANT ZUR STEIPE

www.zur-steipe.de

Zur Steipe is a relaxed restaurant that also has a café and cake shop. It is housed in one of the most historic buildings in Trier: The Steipe itself was built in the 15th century, and has an imposing crenellated façade with a striking colonnade of arches on the ground floor. Between these arches are statues of the city's patron saints, and above them, at the corners of the building, are two knights, one of whom faces the cathedral with his visor down, an act of defiance that symbolized the animosity between Church and State during the Middle Ages. The restaurant is arranged around a stunning courtyard. Cakes and sandwiches are served in the café, with more substantial fare offered in the main restaurant.

✉ Hauptmarkt 14, 54290 Trier ☎ 0651 145 5456 🕑 Daily 8am–10pm 🖐 L €11, D €18, Wine €14

ZUM DOMSTEIN

www.domstein.de

As well as serving traditional German fare and offering wine-tasting by the glass, Zum Domstein, overlooking Trier's historic Market Place, also has a separate dining area devoted entirely to Roman cuisine. Menus are printed in Latin, English and German, all the dishes are taken from an original Roman recipe book, and the intimate cellar where the food is served is decked out with replicas of Roman objects that were unearthed in the cellar when it was excavated just a few years ago. A typical set-price menu might include pine-kernel sausages with artichoke hearts, green beans in a fish sauce, lamb cutlets in a wine and date marinade, and soufflé of pears topped with crème caramel and pepper (which, believe it or not, tastes rather good). Meals are accompanied by wine and a Roman 'aperitif', a sweet liqueur with a faintly aniseed taste.

✉ Hauptmarkt 5, 54290 Trier ☎ 0651 74490 🕑 Daily 8.30am–midnight 🖐 L €15, D €25, Wine €9

WIESBADEN

LUMEN RESTAURANT

www.lumen-gastronomie.de

In the middle of Marktplatz at the base of the imposing Marktkirche is Lumen, a glass and chrome haven in the heart of Wiesbaden. It's popular with smartly dressed business people and ladies who lunch, but it retains a relaxed atmosphere thanks to its light and spacious feel. It's not particularly cheap, but the constantly changing menu is imaginative, and the food delicious. If you just fancy a snack, the soup, served with warm bread, is highly recommended.

✉ Marktplatz, 65183 Wiesbaden ☎ 0611 300200 🕑 Mon–Thu 9am–1am, Fri, Sat 9am–2am, Sun 10am–1am 🖐 L €22, D €32, Wine €14

Above *The entrance to the delightful Mozart hotel in Bonn*

PRICES AND SYMBOLS

The prices are the lowest and highest for a double room for one night including breakfast, unless otherwise stated. All the hotels listed accept credit cards unless otherwise stated. Note that rates can vary widely throughout the year.

For a key to the symbols, ▷ 2.

AACHEN

BENELUX

www.hotel-benelux.de

This immaculate designer hotel is just a few minutes' walk south of the cathedral. As well as an elegant restaurant and bar, it has a fitness room and roof garden. The rooms have contemporary furniture and original art. Packages that include a visit to Carolus Thermen (▷ 194) are available.

✉ Franzstrasse 21–23, 52064 Aachen ☎ 0241 400030 €103–€148 33 Chinese and Mongolian

DÜSSELDORF

BEST WESTERN HOTEL SAVOY

www.savoy.bestwestern.de

The renovated Savoy has a striking neoclassical façade and is between Düsseldorf's main train station and the Königsallee shopping precinct (▷ 195). Its young staff are friendly and helpful, and its immaculate rooms have dark wooden furniture, pale yellow walls and crisp white linen. There is a small health suite.

✉ Oststrasse 128, 40210 Düsseldorf ☎ 0211 388380 €95–€165 114 Daily 5pm–midnight Indoor pool, sauna, solarium Oststrasse

BONN

MOZART

www.hotel-mozart-bonn.de

In a stunning townhouse a short walk west of the main train station, this hotel has bags of charm, thanks to its antique furniture and sumptuous wallpaper and carpets. The bright, lofty rooms have sparkling renovated bathrooms.

✉ Mozartstrasse 1, 53115 Bonn ☎ 0228 659071 €65–€95 39 (16 non-smoking) Small private garage beneath hotel, €6 per night Hauptbahnhof

ESSEN

ESSENER HOF

www.essener-hof.com

A palatial hotel, opposite the main train station, that has been in the Bosse family since its foundation in 1883. It's arranged around a quiet courtyard, and all the rooms have muted tones with tasteful, contemporary furniture. The snug restaurant serves a wide choice of beers and freshly cooked meals. The Moonlight Express Bar is laid out like an art deco railway carriage.

✉ Am Handelshof 5, 45127 Essen ☎ 0201 24250 €135–€185 130 rooms, 3 apartments Hauptbahnhof

FRANKFURT AM MAIN

MIRAMAR GOLDEN MILE

www.miramar-frankfurt.de

The Miramar is near the 'museum embankment', the central shops and the famous Sachsenhausen district. This four-star hotel is small but its rooms are comfortable.

✉ Berliner Strasse 31, 60311 Frankfurt am Main ☎ 069 920 3970 €110–€140 (prices double during trade fairs) 39 Nearby underground parking area, €18 per 24 hours Römerberg

KOBLENZ

BRENNER

www.hotel-brenner.de

The unprepossessing façade of this hotel belies its beautifully restored rococo interior, characterized

by elaborately gilded furniture, delicately painted floral wall panels and crisp white linen. Most rooms are light, airy and spacious and are excellent value. It's just south of the Friedrich-Ebert-Ring, 10 minutes' walk from downtown Koblenz.
✉ Rizzastrasse 20–22, 56068 Koblenz ☎ 0261 915780 €68–€78 24

MERCURE KOBLENZ

www.mercure.de

The imposing, ultramodern Mercure is set on the banks of the Rhine and is a few minutes' walk from the middle of Koblenz and Deutsches Eck (▷ 176). Cheerful rooms with all modern conveniences are complemented by a lobby bar, a public area with free internet access, and a small fitness room. The riverside location makes up for what the hotel lacks in charm.
✉ Julius-Weleger-Strasse 6, 56068 Koblenz ☎ 0261 1360 €72–€149 168 Sauna and gym

KÖLN

CITYCLASS HOTEL CAPRICE

www.cityclass.de

The Caprice offers understated luxury in the heart of Cologne's Altstadt. All rooms are simply but stylishly furnished, and have gleaming bathrooms. Try for a room overlooking Eisenmarkt.
✉ Auf dem Rothenberg 7–9, 50667 Köln ☎ 0221 920540 €60–€110 53 Sauna, whirlpool and Jacuzzi Bus/tram to Heumarkt

DAS KLEINE STAPELHÄUSCHEN

www.koeln-altstadt.de/stapelhaeuschen

One of Cologne's oldest and most romantic hotels is in the heart of the old town, it's full of wood-panelled walls, antique furniture and creaking floorboards. Many of the rooms have beamed ceilings and some come with enormous old baths. The friendly owners run an intimate restaurant on the first floor, serving traditional dishes, such as pork knuckle with sauerkraut and potato.
✉ Fischmarkt 1–3, 50667 Köln ☎ 0221 272 7777 €64–€108 30 Bus/tram to Heumarkt

RHEINTAL

BELLEVUE RHEINHOTEL

www.bellevue-boppard.de

The whitewashed Bellevue, with its steeply pitched gabled roof and first-floor balconies, has been looking after guests since 1887. One of the most elegant and inviting hotels on the Rhine, it has rooms that range from old-fashioned opulence to modern simplicity, as do its two restaurants (one with live piano music) and its wood-panelled bar. There's also a wine cellar for tastings and a health spa with sauna, steam room and swimming pool.
✉ Rheinallee 41, 56154 Boppard ☎ 06742 1020 €86–€160 92 Indoor Sauna, steam bath and fitness room Two restaurants Boppard

MÜNSTER

KAISERHOF

www.kaiserhof-muenster.de

Opposite the city's main train station, the Hotel Kaiserhof makes for a memorable stay. Owners Peter and Anne Cremer have combined their unerring eye for design with meticulous attention to detail. The result is calming tones, clean lines and contemporary design features.
✉ Bahnhofstrasse 14, 48143 Münster ☎ 0251 41780 €102–€153, excluding breakfast 100 Sauna

SAARBRÜCKEN

HOTEL AM TRILLER

www.hotel-am-triller.de

This hotel is unique in Germany. The reception area isn't remarkable, but the rooms are: Many of them are themed according to seasons and to artists.
✉ Trillerweg 57, 66117 Saarbrücken ☎ 0681 580000 €115–€294 110 (60 non-smoking) Sauna, solarium and gym €8.50 per day

SOEST

HOTEL RESTAURANT 'IM WILDEN MANN'

www.im-wilden-mann.com

If it's tradition you're after, you can't go wrong with this half-timbered hotel in the heart of Soest. Some rooms are beamed, and they all have a rustic, romantic feel. The restaurant is equally atmospheric and serves traditional Westphalian dishes (such as bratwurst with savoy cabbage and fried potatoes).
✉ Am Markt 11, 59494 Soest ☎ 02921 15071 €74–€90 12 €5 per day

SPEYER

DOMHOF

www.domhof.de

Almost next door to the beer hall of the same name (▷ 204), this is the most attractive hotel in Speyer thanks to its cobbled courtyard, terrace and medieval details. All the rooms are individual, and many have antique furniture and window shutters. The combination of a room here with a meal at the Domhof Hausbrauerei is hard to beat.
✉ Bauhof 3, 67346 Speyer ☎ 06232 13290 €115–€125 49

HOTEL AM TECHNIK MUSEUM

www.hotel-am-technik-museum.de

Although it doesn't look much more than a whitewashed concrete building from the outside, this hotel is surprisingly well appointed. The refurbished rooms are clean and comfortable, the young, helpful members of staff all speak excellent English, and the hotel is just a short walk from the middle of town. It is ideal for families, or for those on a budget.
✉ Am Technik Museum 1, 67346 Speyer ☎ 06232 67100 €85 105 Free

TRIER

PARK PLAZA TRIER

www.parkplaza-trier.de

In the heart of Trier, this is a contemporary, stylish hotel. Clean lines and warm tones characterize the beautifully designed rooms, each of which has a replica of a Roman object unearthed in the city. The fourth floor has a sauna and steam room.
✉ Nikolaus-Koch-Platz 1, 54290 Trier ☎ 0651 99930 €114–€124, excluding breakfast 150 Sauna and steam room

SIGHTS 210
WALKS AND DRIVES 236
WHAT TO DO 246
EATING 250
STAYING 254

EASTERN GERMANY

The states of Brandenburg, Sachsen, Sachsen-Anhalt and Thüringen now positively welcome visitors—a sharp contrast to the decades of Communist control when this territory belonged to the former East Germany. Much of the region has caught up, and its most famous destinations—Dresden and Potsdam—have recovered much of their charm. Other key attractions include Leipzig, popular with lovers of classical music, and Weimar, a name that became synonymous with a weak and doomed democracy, and which was once the hub of Germany's artistic Golden Age.

The region has wonderfully varied countryside, and tempting recreational opportunities abound: rock-climbing in Saxon Switzerland; hiking in the Harz Mountains or the Thuringian Forest; or floating around in boats more or less everywhere, but particularly in watery Brandenburg, with its many lakes and slow-flowing rivers. Rail buffs are well catered to, with several lines still served by steam engines

Eastern Germany's theatres, opera houses and concert halls are some of the best in the country, and an evening spent at the Semperoper in Dresden or the Gewandhaus in Leipzig is sure to be memorable. Culture of another kind is available in the student clubs of the region's university cities—lively complexes like the Moritzbastei in Leipzig, the Rosenkeller in Jena and the Kasseturm in Weimar. An evening stroll along Dresden's Münzgasse or Leipzig's 'Drallewatsch' affords convincing proof that these cities are every bit as lively as those in the rest of Germany.

Strong local musical traditions mean that there are several first-rate classical music festivals, and Dresden's annual Dixieland jamboree is one of the biggest of its kind in the world. Folk traditions survived and often flourished under Communism. Miners still parade through the streets of Freiberg arrayed in their traditional finery, while old customs and costumes survive among the Sorbs, the Slav population of the Spreewald and Lusatia.

BAUTZEN

www.bautzen.de

High above a bend in the River Spree, this picturesque thousand-year-old town has substantial remains of the medieval fortifications once necessary in this much-contested border region. Within the many-towered walls are romantic streets and cobbled alleyways lined with baroque mansions and red-roofed houses, as well as a late-Gothic cathedral, shared, unusually, between Catholics and Protestants.

The castle is home to the Sorbski Musej, a museum of the local Slav minority, the Sorbs; a look at its attractive displays will give you a good idea of the culture of this ethnic group. Bautzen has its very own leaning tower, the tall Reichenturm (Apr–end Oct daily 10–5; tel 03591 460431); the reward for climbing its 135 steps is a fine view of the city.

Grim aspects of the more recent past are revealed at the Gedenkstätte Bautzen, the prison where, successively, opponents of Nazis, Soviets and the Stasi were held, often in horrible conditions (Tue–Thu 10–4, Fri 10–8, Sat, Sun, holidays 10–6; tel 03591 40474).

407 K9 Tourist-Information, Hauptmarkt 1, 02625 Bautzen ☎ 03591 42016 Mar–end Oct Mon–Fri 9–6, Sat, Sun 9–3; Nov–end Feb Mon–Fri 9–5, Sat, Sun 9–2 Bautzen

BRANDENBURG

www.stadt-brandenburg.de

Lakes, rivers and woodlands combine to give this millennium-old city one of the most inviting settings in Germany. Brandenburg was built on a series of islands, first by Slavs, then by Germanic rulers such as 12th-century Albert the Bear, who made it the base for farther eastward colonization and conversion to Christianity.

Despite intense industrialization, severe pollution and neglect during GDR times, Brandenburg's medieval street pattern remains intact. Its islands are linked by bridges over the channels of the River Havel and graced by splendid brick-built Gothic churches and other historic buildings. Restoration has proceeded apace, and more and more visitors make the trip here. It's an easy day excursion from Berlin, around half an hour by express train, but more fun, if longer, by boat.

Fun on the water is one of Brandenburg's attractions; as well as pleasure cruises, there's canoeing, sailing, water-skiing, festivals and regattas on the glorious network of waterways that links to the Oder in the east and the Elbe to the west.

407 H6 Tourist Information, Steinstrasse 66–67, 14776 Brandenburg ☎ 03381 208769 May–end Sep Mon–Fri 9–7, Sat, Sun 10–3; Oct–end Apr Mon–Fri 9–7, Sat, Sun 10–2 Brandenburg

COLDITZ

www.fremdenverkehrsamt-colditz.de

This little old town stands on a bend in the Mulde, a picturesque stream winding through the attractive countryside of central Saxony. The river passes countless castles along the way, including Thalwitz, Wolkenburg, Rochlitz and Podelwitz.

All of them are worth a visit, but none of them have quite the resonance of Schloss Colditz (guided tours Apr–end Oct daily 10–5; Nov–end Mar daily 10–4; tel 034381 43777). The fortress, high above the town, won notoriety in World War II, when it served as a supposedly 100 per cent secure prison for Allied officers identified by their captors as incorrigible would-be escapers. Perhaps inevitably, it became a university of escape, the exploits of its inmates subsequently celebrated in dozens of books and a TV series. The guided tour through courtyards and claustrophobic interiors reveals the astonishing ingenuity exercised by the prisoners in their attempts—10 per cent of them successful—to extricate themselves from the confines of the castle.

407 H9 Tourist Information, Markt 1, 04680 Colditz ☎ 034381 43519 Apr–end Oct Tue–Fri 9–5, Sat, Sun 10–4; Nov–end Mon–Fri 10–4

COTTBUS

www.cottbus.de

Cottbus has a reputation for taking work seriously, perhaps dating from when industrious Huguenot weavers settled here in the 17th century. The lovely woods and waterways of the Spreewald (▷ 234) are nearby and Cottbus is one of Germany's greenest cities, with a chain of parks and open spaces along the River Spree.

There's the Goethepark, the Spreeauenpark (lavishly laid out for the 1995 National Garden Festival) and the sublime landscape created in the mid-19th century by the eccentric Prince Pückler-Muskau as a setting for his ancestral home, Schloss Branitz (Apr–end Oct daily 10–6; Nov–end Mar daily 11–5; tel 0355 75150). The castle's exotic interiors evoke the prince's travels in Africa and the Orient, while the romantic park reflects his admiration for all things English. At the western end of this landscape, rising from the lake, is a great earthen pyramid, which is the Prince's mausoleum.

407 K8 Cottbus-Service, Berliner Platz 6/Stadthalle, 03046 Cottbus ☎ 0355 75420 Mon–Fri 9–6, Sat 9–1 Cottbus

Opposite *The Prisoners Courtyard at Colditz Castle*

Below *The picturesque town of Bautzen*

INTRODUCTION

Rebuilt after its wartime destruction, and home to some of Europe's finest art and architecture, Dresden heads the list of Germany's most beautiful cities. The capital of Saxony is on a broad bend of the Elbe, and its famous silhouette of baroque towers, spires and domes is once more intact, the result of decades of devoted reconstruction following the infamous Allied bombing raid of 13 to 14 February 1945.

Few places in Germany are so well endowed with galleries and museums, their paintings, sculptures and other objets d'art accumulated by extravagant rulers over the years. Most of the museums are within easy walking distance of each other. Cultural life, from opera to cabaret, flourishes. The 18th-century Neustadt largely escaped the effects of the bombing, and it is here that the city's heart beats most strongly in the evenings, with an array of pubs, bars, restaurants and places of entertainment. The Elbe, plied by the famous White Fleet of pleasure steamers, forms a link between city and countryside, its banks lined by palaces, vineyards and the astonishing rocky landscapes of Saxon Switzerland (▷ 233).

From a modest riverside settlement of Slav fishermen and farmers, Dresden evolved in the 15th century into the residence of the rulers of Saxony. Its glory days began in the reign of August der Starke (Augustus the Strong; 1670–1733), so-called because of his prodigious siring of children. King of Poland as well as Elector of Saxony, Augustus spent lavishly on buildings and works of art, and he and his immediate successors gave the city its predominantly baroque character.

In the 19th and early 20th centuries, Dresden expanded, but remained a city of art, escaping the worst effects of industrialization. This, so reasoned its inhabitants as World War II drew to its close, was why it had not been bombed to destruction like other German cities. They were wrong; on the 13–14 February 1945, the firestorm unleashed by British and American planes laid waste to a vast area, killing tens of thousands. The devastation was so great that shocked city planners thought seriously about abandoning the site altogether and building a new Dresden elsewhere.

INFORMATION

www.dresden-tourist.de

407 J9 General Info: Dresden-Werbung und Tourismus GmbH, Ostra-Allee 11, 01067 Dresden 0351 4919 2100 Tourist-Information, Prager Strasse 2, 01069 Dresden 0351 4919 2100; Mon–Sat 10–7 Tourist-Information, Schinkelwache (Theaterplatz) 0351 4919 2100 Thu 10–6, Fri 10–7, Sat, Sun 10–5 The Dresden-City-Card, valid for 48 hours, costs €21 and affords free use of public transportation and free or reduced admission (also for an accompanied child) to museums and other attractions; the family card costs €42 Dresden Hauptbahnhof and Dresden Neustadt

Opposite *The Semper Opera House, Hofkirche cathedral and Dresden Schloss at night*

Above *The moated outer wall of Dresden's Zwinger*

TIPS

» Take the No. 11 tram past the opulent villas along Bautzener Strasse to the suburban Waldschlösschen stop and enjoy the classic vista of the city's skyline rising over the Elbe.

» Few cities list a car factory as one of their attractions, but Dresden's ultra-modern Volkswagen works, known as the Gläserne Manufaktur (Transparent Manufactory) and built on a prominent site on the edge of the Grosser Garten park, has to be seen to be believed.

» Take a short cruise on the Elbe aboard one of the antique steamers of the Weisse Flotte (White Fleet), operated by Sächsische Dampfschiffahrt (tel 0351 866090; www.saechsische-dampfschiffahrt.de) from docks along Terrassenufer.

Below *Part of the Zwinger group of buildings*

WHAT TO SEE

ZWINGER

www.skd-dresden.de

Arranged around a spacious courtyard with lawns, pools and fountains, the spectacular group of baroque buildings known as the Zwinger was built from 1709 onwards by Saxony's most flamboyant ruler, Augustus the Strong, and his court architect, Matthäus Daniel Pöppelmann. Augustus had recently acquired the additional title of King of Poland, and the Zwinger was intended as a setting for the lavish pageants and festivities appropriate to his greatly enhanced status, as well as becoming a home for the royal collections of art and porcelain.

It remains one of the great sights of Germany, attracting visitors from around the world who fill it with something of the animation it was originally conceived for. Many are on their way to see the artworks in the Old Masters Gallery, but the Zwinger is a great work of art in its own right. Enter through the magnificent Kronentor, topped by the golden crown of Poland, or through the Glockenspielpavillon, with a carillon made from Meissen porcelain. Opposite is Pöppelmann's masterpiece, the Wallpavillon, a building of almost unbelievable exuberance with decoration by the sculptor Balthasar Permoser (1651–1732), who was also responsible for many of the delightful figures in the adjoining Nymphenbad (Nymphs' Bathing Place).

Augustus and his successors amassed huge quantities of art, most of which survived the 1945 bombing and temporary exile in the Soviet Union 'for safe keeping'. The pictures in the Gemäldegalerie Alte Meister (Old Masters Picture Gallery) make up one of the world's great collections. The gallery's most outstanding painting is Raphael's *Sistine Madonna* (*c* 1514), the tenderest possible evocation of maternity, and the cheeky cherubs at the foot of the picture have become almost as well known as the serene Madonna herself. There are other first-rate Italian Renaissance canvases as well, such as Giorgione's *Sleeping Venus* (1510), which shows the goddess as an earthly looking young woman slumbering in an open landscape. There are also fine examples of Dutch art like Jan Vermeer's *Girl Reading a Letter at an Open Window* (1657). Meticulously detailed townscapes by Canaletto show Dresden at the summit of its beauty in the 18th century.

The Zwinger has other fabulous collections, among them the Rüstkammer (Armoury) and the Porzellansammlung (Porcelain Collection). The Mathematisch–Physikalischer Salon (Mathematical–Physical Sciences Salon), with its array of finely crafted scientific instruments is closed for restoration until 2010.

215 A2 Theaterplatz 1, Dresden 01067 0351 4914 2000 Tue–Sun 10–6 Gemäldegalerie Alte Meister, Rüstkammer and Skulpturensammlung: adult €7, child (6–18) €4.50, under 6 free, family €15; Porzellansammlung: adult: €6, child (6–18) €3.50, under 6 free, family €13; Zwinger combined ticket: adult €12, child (6–18) €7, under 6 free, family €25 Tram 4, 8, 9

KATHEDRALE SS TRINITATIS

www.bistum-dresden-meissen.de

Overlooking the Elbe, the elegant Holy Trinity Cathedral—formerly the Hofkirche (Court Church)—of 1751 was the last great baroque edifice to be completed in Dresden. In this otherwise solidly Protestant city, it is a Catholic place of worship, built by the Saxon rulers who changed their religion in order to qualify for the crown of Poland. No local architect could be found for the task, so an Italian master builder, Gaetano Chiaveri, was brought in, along with his workforce, which was housed in the Italienisches Dörfchen (Italian Village), now a popular riverside restaurant. Despite its size—it is the largest church in Saxony—the cathedral is a joyful and elegant edifice, the parade of sandstone saints along its balustrades giving it a particular air of gaiety. Inside, the organ is the masterpiece of the great Saxon organ-builder Silbermann, while the crypt houses the sarcophagi of Saxon rulers.

✚ 215 B2 ✉ Schlossplatz, 01067 Dresden ☎ 0351 484 4712 ◷ Mon, Tue 9–6, Wed, Thu 9–5, Fri 1–5, Sat 10–5, Sun 12–4 ✋ Free 🚊 Tram 4, 8, 9

RESIDENZSCHLOSS

www.skd-dresden.de

The palace of the Saxon rulers began as a medieval fortress commanding the crossing of the Elbe and was extended and modified in Renaissance and neo-Renaissance styles right up to the abdication of the last king of Saxony in 1918. Comprehensively destroyed in 1945, it is still being rebuilt and is destined to house a number of museums. It is already home to the Grünes Gewölbe (Green Vault), a fabulous array of jewels and the exquisitely crafted objects to which Augustus the Strong seems to have been particularly addicted. The most extraordinary item is the 'Court of Delhi on the Birthday of the Great Moghul', an utterly over-the-top tableau of gold, silver, enamel and precious stones that cost Augustus twice the price of a princely palace. You can climb the 100m (328ft) to the top of the palace's tower (Tue–Sun 10–6, summer only), but its most striking feature is the famous frieze on an outside wall; made up of 25,000 Meissen porcelain tiles, it is an impressive parade of the Saxon rulers' 800-year dynasty.

✚ 215 B2 ✉ Taschenberg 2, 01067 Dresden ☎ 0351 4914 2000 ◷ Fri–Wed 10–6 ✋ Adult €6, child (6–18) €3.50, under 6 free, family €13 🚊 Tram 4, 8, 9

BRÜHLSCHE TERRASSE

The best way to appreciate Dresden's wonderful setting is to take a stroll along this superb elevated terrace overlooking the Elbe. To one side are the historic buildings making up the city's famous skyline, and to the other the great river, graced by the white steamers along the quayside. Beyond the Neustadt on the far bank rise the gentle hills colonized by the city's affluent villa suburbs. Sometimes known as the Balcony of Europe, the terrace owes its official name

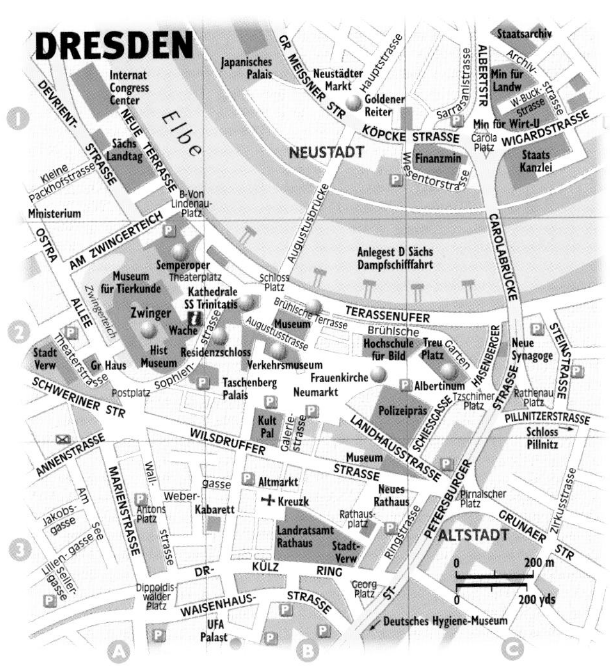

THE LAST KING

After the unification of Germany in 1871, Saxony remained a kingdom, though its monarch had no real power. The last Saxon king, a member of the Wettin dynasty, which had first come to prominence here 800 years earlier, was Friedrich August III, a popular figure with a common touch. Along with Kaiser Wilhelm II, he was forced to abdicate at the end of World War I. Dresdeners lined the streets to bid him farewell, but Friedrich August's comment—in broad Saxon dialect—was 'Macht Euren Dreck alleene!'—roughly translated as 'Now you'll have to make your own mess!'

Below *The view from Frauenkirche across the old city and the Elbe*

to the 18th-century Count Brühl, who converted the old fortifications here into a splendid garden for his palace.
215 B2 Tram 4, 8, 9

FRAUENKIRCHE

www.frauenkirche-dresden.org

No other building in Dresden embodies the city's history and beauty so poignantly as the glorious Frauenkirche (Church of Our Lady). A masterpiece of baroque architecture, it was consecrated in 1736 with music directed by Johann Sebastian Bach. The great building's lovely, bell-shaped dome formed the focus of Dresden's skyline. It withstood the bombs of 1945, but two days later, as the tortured stonework cooled, it collapsed.

For years the church remained a gigantic pile of rubble, a monument to disaster. Then the awesome decision was taken to rebuild, a process completed in 2005. The Frauenkirche has become a symbol of reconciliation between former enemies, with some of the costs of reconstruction funded by British contributions; the golden cross that will crown the dome was made in Coventry, itself severely damaged by German bombing, and was handed over by the Duke of Kent on 13 February 2000. Much of the original, blackened stonework has been reused, giving the edifice a patchwork appearance.
215 B2 Neumarkt, 01067 Dresden 0351 6560 6100 Mon–Fri 10–12, 1–6, Sat, Sun limited visits possible Hourly tours by prior arrangement Donation requested Tram 1, 2, 4

ALBERTINUM

www.skd-dresden.de

The sombre architecture of this late 19th-century palace gives little idea of the riches within, among them some of Dresden's finest artistic treasures. If you are a lover of modern art, head for the Galerie Neue Meister (Modern Masters), which is especially rich in German painting of the 19th and 20th centuries. Look out for evocative works by Romantic artists like Caspar David Friedrich (1774–1840) and Ludwig Richter, both inspired by Dresden and its surroundings, and marvel at the *1000-Jährige Reich* painted by Hans Grundig in 1938, an extraordinary prophecy of the horrors of war which were shortly to engulf Europe and lead eventually to Dresden's destruction.

The largest of its kind outside Italy, the Skulpturensammlung (Sculpture Collection) covers the whole history of European sculpture and is particularly rich in Classical Greek and Roman works. At the time of writing, the Albertinum was closed for renovations and was due to reopen in 2010.
215 C2 Georg-Treu-Platz 2, 01067 Dresden 0351 4914 2000 Tram 3, 7

MORE TO SEE

DEUTSCHES HYGIENE- MUSEUM

www.dhmd.de

Founded by the inventor of Odol, Germany's best-selling mouthwash, this unusual establishment tells you everything you could want to know about hygiene and health. The most popular exhibit is the famous Glass Human, with a nervous system made of 13km (8 miles) of wiring.
Off 215 B2 Lingnerplatz 1, 01069 Dresden 0351 484 6400 Tue–Sun 10–6 Adult €6, child (4–18) €3, under 4 free, family €11 Tram 1, 2, 4, 10, 12, 13

GOLDENER REITER

The imposing gilded figure greeting you as you enter the Neustadt district on the far bank of the Elbe is Augustus the Strong. He is shown in Roman dress on a rearing horse looking towards the city that he embellished so extravagantly, mostly at the expense of the townsfolk.
215 B1 Neustädter Markt Tram 4, 8, 9

SEMPEROPER

www.semperoper-fuehrungen.de

Dresden has one of the greatest opera houses in Europe, named for its architect, Gottfried Semper. Destroyed in 1945, it was rebuilt in exemplary fashion by the GDR authorities. It reopened in 1985.

A215 A2 Theaterplatz 2 0351 491 1496 Entry by guided tour only (times vary) Adult €7, students up to age 27 €3.50, under 6 free, family €12 Tram 4, 8, 9

SCHLOSS PILLNITZ

www.pillnitz.com

On the banks of the Elbe in its park among the vineyards, Pillnitz Palace was built by Augustus the Strong in mock-Chinese style. It houses a collection of decorative arts from earliest times to the 20th century.

Off 215 C2 August-Bockstiegel-Strasse, Pillnitz, 01326 Dresden 0351 261 3260 May–end Oct daily 10–6 Adult €3, child (6–18) €2, under 6 free 83

VERKEHRSMUSEUM DRESDEN

www.verkehrsmuseum-dresden.de

This major museum deals with all kinds of transportation. There are fascinating vehicles of all kinds, including Dresden's oldest surviving tram.

215 B2 Johanneum, Augustusstrasse 1, 01067 Dresden 0351 86440 Tue–Sun 10–5 Adult €3, child (5–16) €2, under 5 free, family €8 Tram 1, 2, 4

Above *Statue of Augustus the Strong*
Below *The Semperoper opera house*

INFORMATION

Dessau

www.dessau.de

407 H7 Tourist Information Dessau, Zerbster Strasse 2c, 06844 Dessau 0340 204 1442 Apr–end Oct Mon–Fri 9–6, Sat 9–1; Nov–end Mar Mon–Fri 9–5, Sat 10–1 Dessau

Wörlitz

www.woerlitz-information.de

407 H7 Wörlitz Information, Förstergasse 26, 06786 Wörlitz 034905 20216 Mar–end Oct daily 9–6; Nov–end Feb Mon–Fri 9–4, plus Sat, Sun 11–3 in Feb

TIPS

» In summer, the best way to arrive in Wörlitz is by train from Dessau. There's also a 40km (25-mile) circular bicycle tour—Fürst Franz Weg—taking in many of Prince Leopold's landscapes.

» If the gondolas are crowded, leave them behind and discover the park at your own pace on foot.

Above *The Walter Gropius Meisterhaus was the home of the Bauhaus movement*

DESSAU AND WÖRLITZ

Dessau was home to the Bauhaus movement, and many buildings from this period are dotted around the town. In the 14th century, the princes of Anhalt built their castle at a point where the River Mulde could be bridged just before it flows into the mighty Elbe. Four hundred years later, their descendant, Prince Leopold, inspired by the spirit of the European Enlightenment and by travels in England and Italy, landscaped great tracts of his lands, creating a garden realm, at the time the most fabulous in Europe. His parks, lakes, garden buildings and statuary remain, and have become one of the great visitor attractions of eastern Germany. Together with the ecologically rich biosphere reserve of the river floodplains, they are now protected as a UNESCO World Heritage Site.

AVANT-GARDE CITY

Leopold was a most progressive ruler, assembling an array of professional and artistic talent in his little court, giving the public free access to his parks and gardens and promoting education and welfare. His example was followed in the early 20th century, when Dessau became home to the Bauhaus school (▷ 21; daily 10–6; tel 0340 650 8251). Headed by Walter Gropius (1883–1969), this influential institution in the development of Modernism in design and architecture flourished until it was closed by the Nazis in the early 1930s. Its coolly contemporary buildings, designed by Gropius himself using steel, concrete and glass, still stand, and, well restored, are once more a design education facility that attracts architectural pilgrims from all over the world.

GARDEN PARADISE

The number of parks and palaces in and around Dessau can be daunting, so if time is short, you shouldn't miss Wörlitz, perhaps Germany's supreme achievement in landscape design. No fence separates the little town from the tree-rich Schlossgarten, the setting for Leopold's summer residence, Schloss Wörlitz (tours late Mar–end Apr and Oct Tue–Sun 10–5; May–end Sep Tue–Sun 10–6; tel 034905 20216), built for him by Friedrich Wilhelm von Knobelsdorff between 1769 and 1773. Beyond stretches the main lake, the Wörlitzer See, on its banks is a further series of delightful landscapes and garden features, among them a temple, a pantheon, a synagogue and the Gotisches Haus, one façade Venetian, the other a version of English Tudor. Equally extraordinary is the variety of bridges, which includes a mildly perilous-seeming suspension bridge. Experience the ever-changing vistas on foot, ferry or aboard a gondola.

EISENACH AND THE WARTBURG

▷ 220.

ERFURT

www.erfurt-tourismus.de

The cathedral city and capital of the *Land* of Thuringia, Erfurt escaped the worst that war damage and 40 years of Communism could do, and it is a pleasure to stroll through its old streets, with their fascinating mix of buildings of all ages.

Sooner or later you will find yourself at the River Gera, crossed by the medieval stone bridge known as the Krämerbrücke, a survivor from an age when bridges had to earn their keep by providing sites for shops and other buildings. This one supports an array of souvenir shops, and you can climb its tower.

Eventually you will arrive at the vast Domplatz, dominated by two great churches, the St. Marien Dom (Cathedral) and the St. Severikirche (Church of St Severus), rising from the opposite slope. Climb the monumental flight of steps to see the cathedral's treasures, including sculptures of the Wise and Foolish Virgins that grace the portal.

406 F9 Erfurt Tourist Information, Benediktsplatz 1, 99084 Erfurt 0361 66400 Apr–end Dec Mon–Fri 10–7, Sat 9–6, Sun 10–4; Jan–end Mar Mon–Sat 10–6, Sun 10–4 Erfurt

Below *The Kaisertrutz Tower in Görlitz is the unusual setting for temporary art exhibitions*

FREIBERG

www.freiberg.de

Spared wartime destruction, Freiberg owes its fame to its silver mines, the main source of Saxony's wealth for many years. Its mining connections gave it extra credibility in the eyes of the GDR's rulers, who spent scarce resources on restoring the patrician houses in the Altstadt. But the town's great treasure is its Dom, modest outside, but with one of the most glorious cathedral interiors in Germany. Come, if you can, on a Thursday evening, when the sublime sound of the great organ fills the space. It was built in the mid-18th century by Gottfried Silbermann, claimed by some to be the master organ-builder of all time.

Look, too, for the lavish mausoleums of Saxon rulers, happy to be buried in the town whose silver had financed their extravagant lifestyle in nearby Dresden (▷ 212–217). You can trace the story of silver mining at the Stadt- und Bergbaumuseum (Town and Mining Museum, Tue–Sun 10–5; tel 03731 20250) or follow in the footsteps of the old miners by descending the shaft of the Reiche Zeiche mine (three tours daily).

407 J9 Tourist-Information, Burgstrasse 1, 09599 Freiberg 03731 419 5160 Apr–end Dec Mon–Fri 9–6, Sat 9–12; Jan–end Mar Mon–Fri 9–5, Sat 9–12 Freiberg

GÖRLITZ

www.goerlitz.de

The Altstadt of Germany's easternmost town was miraculously spared by war, its wonderfully harmonious mixture of buildings ranging from medieval to modern. The town's suburbs on the far bank of the little River Neisse were detached from Germany in 1945 and are now the Polish town of Zgorelec. Far from seeing its frontier location as a disadvantage, Görlitz looks forward to a positive, bridging role in the era of eastward European Union expansion (▷ 24).

As you stroll from one square to another, Görlitz reveals its treasures, from remnants of fortifications to medieval churches and splendid Renaissance and baroque mansions. The most exquisite area is around the Untermarkt, with a Neptune fountain and arcaded townhouses; it is dominated by the Rathaus, which has a two-faced clock and an elegant outside stairway with a figure of Justice lacking her customary blindfold.

407 L9 Görlitzinformation, Obermarkt 32, 02826 Görlitz 03581 47570 Mar–end Dec Mon–Fri 9–7, Sat, Sun 9–6; Jan, Feb Mon–Fri 9–6, Sat 10–4 Görlitz

GOTHA

www.gotha.de

Celebrated in GDR times as a shrine to Socialism, Gotha's greater claim to fame is its aristocratic, even royal, past. For many years it was the seat of the Saxe-Coburg-Gotha dynasty, which included Prince Albert, Queen Victoria's husband, so the British Royal family were called Saxe-Coburg-Gotha until they changed it to Windsor in World War I. The town also gave its name to the *Almanac de Gotha*, the *Who's Who* of German nobility, and it remains a fascinating example of those little courtly cities so characteristic of Germany.

The town itself huddles respectfully at the foot of the steep slope leading up to Schloss Friedenstein, the imposing residence built in the mid-17th century by Duke Ernst the Pious. This formidable structure, with its arcaded courtyard and massive corner towers, stands in the middle of a vast park covering an area almost as extensive as the Altstadt itself. The austere exterior of the great building belies its contents: a succession of gorgeous rooms in every style from baroque to Empire, with collections reflecting the wealth and refined taste of successive dukes.

406 F9 Tourist Information, Hauptmarkt 33, 99867 Gotha 03621 5078 5712 Mon–Fri 9–6, Sat 10–3, Sun (May–end Sep) 10–2 Gotha

INFORMATION

www.eisenach-tourist.de
405 F9 Tourist-Information, Markt 9, 99817 Eisenach 03691 79230 Mon–Fri 10–6, Sat 10–4, Sun (Apr–end Oct) 10–4 Eisenach

TIPS

» The Wartburg attracts several million visitors a year. Parking is at a premium, and it is still quite a walk (or donkey ride) up to the castle. Why not start your walk from the town itself, beginning at the information point near the Predigerkirche?

» You don't have to go very far from Eisenach to get the feel of the dramatic landscapes of the Thuringian Forest. Just south of the town are a number of well-laid-out walks through rocky ravines like the Drachenschlucht and the Landgrafenschlucht.

Above *From its commanding position, the Wartburg castle watches over Eisenach*

EISENACH AND THE WARTBURG

A historic town, forming the gateway to the attractions of the Thuringian Forest. The Wartburg is the archetypal German castle. Crowning one of the wooded spurs of the vast Thuringian Forest, Wartburg Castle (Mar–end Oct daily 8.30–5; Nov–end Feb daily 9–3.30; tel 03691 2500) looks like a vision of the Middle Ages, with stone walls rising from the bare rock. At its foot spreads Eisenach, a fine little city in its own right, rich in associations with figures as diverse as Martin Luther (1483–1546) and Johann Sebastian Bach (1685–1750).

THE WARTBURG

The origins of the Wartburg go back to the 11th century, when it was founded by Count Ludwig of Thuringia. His successors built the splendid 12th-century *Palas*, one of the country's few surviving examples of a Romanesque palace. In 1521, the Protestant Duke Friedrich of Saxony, gave Martin Luther (▷ 33) a false identity, and provided him with lodgings where he could complete his translation of the Bible in peace. Soon, pilgrims were toiling up the slope to the castle, eager to see the mark on the wall where Luther is supposed to have hurled his ink-pot at the Devil. But the Wartburg's fame failed to halt its slide into decay. After patriotic students added their layer of symbolism to the castle at the end of the Napoleonic Wars (▷ 36), great efforts were made not just to repair it but to rebuild it from scratch where necessary. Much of what you see today dates from this time.

EISENACH

Once you have completed your visit to the Wartburg, descend to Eisenach, and enter the town through the imposing Nikolaitor, a formidable remnant of the old fortifications. Don't miss the tall-towered Georgenkirche (St. George's Church): Luther preached in the church, and it was here that J. S. Bach was baptized in 1685. Both are celebrated nearby. The rebuilt late-medieval residence of the Cotta family, where Luther lodged for several years as a schoolboy, is now the Lutherhaus (daily 10–5; tel 03691 29830), with displays on his life and work. A fine statue of the composer stands by the 600-year-old Bachhaus (daily 10–6; tel 03691 79340), which has a collection of contemporary musical instruments used for demonstrations and concerts. An equally interesting collection is at the Automobile Welt Eisenach (Tue–Sun 11–5; tel 03691 77212), which has examples of the cars that have been built here for over a century, among them the GDR's prestige model, the Wartburg.

HALLE

www.halle.de

This bustling place is the biggest city in Sachsen-Anhalt, but lost out to Magdeburg when the *Land* capital was chosen after reunification. Its prosperity was based on the extraction of salt, and one old saltworks—the Technisches Halloren- und Salinenmuseum (Tue–Sun 10–5; tel 0345 209 3230)—is now a museum. Such works were the forerunners of the vast, polluting chemical industry of the Communist era. Nowadays, Halle concentrates more on cultural offerings.

The city's greatest son was Georg Friedrich Händel (1685–1759). His life and work is evoked in the baroque Händel-Haus (daily 9.30–5.30; tel 0345 202 5034), where he was born, and where there are occasional chamber concerts, though the *Händelfest* is in June. Handel's statue is in the Marktplatz, which is dominated by the spires of the Marktkirche and the city's main landmark, the Roter Turm (Red Tower, 80m/260ft), which you can climb.

406 G8 Tourist Information Halle, Roter Turm, Marktplatz 13, 06108 Halle 0345 122 9984 Mon–Fri 9–7, Sat 10–4 , Sun (Apr–end Oct) 10–4 Halle

JENA

www.jena.de

Surrounded by high green hills, this old university city is in the beautiful valley of the River Saale. Wartime bombing and insensitive urban development in GDR times have left only fragments of Jena's former charm. The most prominent building now is the Universitätshochhaus, a cylindrical skyscraper (120m/395ft) dominating the central Eichplatz.

Nevertheless, there are plenty of reminders of an illustrious academic and cultural past, with houses and museums devoted to Johann Wolfgang von Goethe, Friedrich von Schiller and other luminaries, while contemporary Jena is a lively place, proud of the continuing high-tech traditions associated with the name of Carl Zeiss, who set up his optics workshop here in the 19th century.

In celebration of Zeiss's life, a formidable piece of optical equipment graces the Goethegalerie shopping mall, and you can visit the Zeiss Planetarium (daily 10–5, shows at variable times; tel 03641 885488), as well as the Optisches Museum (Optical Museum, Tue–Fri 10–4.30, Sat 11–5; tel 03641 443165), with the original Zeiss workshop.

406 G9 Jena Tourist-Information, Johannisstrasse 23, 07743 Jena 03641 498050 Apr–end Oct Mon–Fri 9.30–7, Sat 9.30–4, Sun 10–3; Nov–end Mar Mon–Fri 9.30–7, Sat 9.30–3 Jena

LEIPZIG

▷ 222–225.

MAGDEBURG

www.magdeburg-tourist.de

Magdeburg's fortunes took a turn for the better with the fall of Communism, when it became the capital of the re-created *Land* of Sachsen-Anhalt. It is now a thriving, forward-looking place, though still proud of the fragments of its past that survived an often catastrophic history. Of these fragments, the finest is the superb Dom (May–end Sep daily 10–6; Apr, Oct daily 10–5; Nov–end Mar daily 10–4; tel 0391 541 0436), one of Germany's greatest Gothic cathedrals, with a beautiful riverside setting. Built on foundations established in the 10th century by Emperor Otto the Great, it is not only an architectural jewel in its own right but has a wealth of sculpture, ranging from a 13th-century representation of a royal couple (possibly Otto and his consort Editha) to a poignant memorial to the victims of World War I by sculptor Ernst Barlach.

There's more sublime sculpture to be seen in the Romanesque Convent of Our Lady (Tue–Sun 10–5, tel 0391 565020).

406 G7 Tourist-Information-Magdeburg, Ernst-Reuter-Allee 12, 39104 Magdeburg 0391 19433 Apr–end Oct Mon–Fri 10–6.30, Sat 10–4; Nov–end Mar Mon–Fri 10–6, Sat 10–3 Magdeburg

Above *A modern sculpture set against the Romanesque buildings of Magdeburg's Convent of Our Lady*

MORITZBURG

www.moritzburg.de

Approached across a causeway and a gently rising ramp, the palace at Moritzburg is a formidable presence in the game-rich woods and heaths northwest of Dresden.

The area was one of the best-loved hunting grounds of the rulers of Saxony, one of whom, Elector Moritz, built a Renaissance hunting lodge here in 1542. In the 18th century, this building proved far too small for the expansive tastes of Elector Augustus the Strong, who extended it and added the huge corner towers with their domed caps.

The interior is equally grandiose, though most of the original furnishings disappeared in the chaos of 1945. Augustus' hunting trophies are still here; one set of horns is claimed to be the largest of its kind in the world; another monster specimen was acquired by Augustus from Friedrich the Great in exchange for a platoon of soldiers.

407 J9 Schloss Moritzburg, 01468 Moritzburg 035207 8730 Apr–end Oct daily 10–5.30 Nov–end Mar Tue–Sun guided tours only daily 10–4; Jan Sat, Sun guided tours only daily 10–4 Adult €6, child (6–15) €3, under 6 free, family €12

INFORMATION

www.leipzig.de
407 H8 Leipzig Tourist-Information, Richard-Wagner-Strasse 1, 04109 Leipzig 0341 710 4265 Mar–end Oct Mon–Fri 9.30–6, Sat 9.30–4, Sun, holidays 9.30–3; Nov–end Feb Mon–Fri 10–6, Sat 9.30–4, Sun, holidays 9.30–3 Hauptbahnhof

Above *Leipzig's über-modern trade venue, the Neue Messe*

INTRODUCTION

Saxony's second city may be smaller, more down to earth and less glamorous than the state capital, Dresden, but it is a bustling, forward-looking place of strong character, with a long and proud civic history. Its cultural life is second to none, not least because of its glorious musical tradition stretching back to the Middle Ages, which is still very much alive today. When Germans are asked how they feel about their native city, Leipzigers come out top in terms of affection and unwillingness to move elsewhere; after a stay here you will appreciate why. The city attracts plenty of visitors, but nowhere do they outnumber locals, a refreshing contrast to other popular destinations. A wealth of places to eat, drink, shop and be entertained more than makes up for the relatively small number of conventional monuments, though the ones that do exist are fascinating enough. The city is exceptionally compact and easy to explore on foot, its network of arcades providing all-weather cover. These are the successors to the traditional courtyards in which merchants from all over Europe once displayed their wares, the origin of the city's great trade fairs.

The fairs now take place in the Neue Messe, a state-of-the-art complex on the edge of the city, not far from the international airport, which has replaced Leipzig's famous railway station as the gateway for business visitors.

Leipzig's international profile traditionally depended on the markets and trade fairs whose origins go back to the 12th century, and perhaps even further. But the city has long played a key role in Germany's intellectual and cultural life. The book trade developed early, and many of the country's foremost publishers settled here. Musical life thrived, and many of the great masters of German music worked here, foremost among them Johann Sebastian Bach, Felix Mendelssohn and Robert Schumann. Even in GDR times, the famous Gewandhaus orchestra flourished under the inspired leadership of Kurt Masur. The university, founded in 1409, is only one of a number of academic institutions maintaining Leipzig's reputation as a hub of scientific achievement. While Dresden's life was focused on a royal court, Leipzig's depended on its citizens, whose sense of responsibility put the city in the vanguard of the movement that led to the fall of the Communist regime in 1989.

WHAT TO SEE

HAUPTBAHNHOF (MAIN STATION)

The area around Leipzig has one of the densest rail networks in the world, and its monumental main station is claimed to be the largest rail terminus in Europe. It was completed in 1913, at a time when the city was served by two state railways, the Prussian and the Saxon; consequently, the building had duplicated facilities—two main entrances, two great halls, two clocks and two waiting rooms. Prussian trains used platforms 1 to 13, and Saxon trains 14 to 26. Local people are proud to have such a grand gateway to their city, and there was much opposition to the post-unification idea of incorporating a huge shopping mall into the complex and converting some platforms for parking. Today, however, the shops of the Bahnhofspromenaden beneath the main concourse are an accepted part of the city (▷ 247).

✉ Willy-Brandt-Platz 5, 04109 Leipzig ☎ 0341 968 1055 🚌 72, 73, 89, 100, 131, 190, 191, 196, 197. Tram 1, 3, 9, 10, 11, 13, 14, 16

ALTES RATHAUS

www.stadtgeschichtliches-museum-leipzig.de

With its steep roof, six gables, arcades and splendid tower, the immensely long Old City Hall of 1556 is one of Germany's finest Renaissance civic buildings, expressive of local pride and of the need to impress visitors to the great trade fairs. It was completed in the interval between two fairs, in the extraordinarily short time of nine months, to designs by Hieronymus Lotter, the city's burgomaster. The interior has a superb ceremonial hall, and houses many of the treasures of the Stadtgeschichtliches Museum (City History Museum). To the west, the Rathaus dominates the marketplace, while to the east it overlooks one of Leipzig's most appealing historic buildings, the Alte Börse (Old Stock Exchange). This resplendent little baroque structure is now used for lectures and concerts. In front of it stands a statue of a youthful Johann Wolfgang von Goethe, gazing towards Auerbachs Keller, his best-loved watering hole and the inspiration for a famous scene in his *Faust* (▷ 35).

✉ Markt 1, 04109 Leipzig ☎ 0341 965 1320 🕒 Tue–Sun 10–6 ✋ Adult €4, child (6–18) €3, under 6 free 🚌 89. Tram 9

THOMASKIRCHE

www.thomaskirche.org

The church of St. Thomas goes back to the early 13th century, though the present structure dates largely from a Gothic rebuilding in the 15th century. But the building is less famous for its architecture than for its music. The angelic

TIPS

» Leipzig's trade fairs have an 800-year history, though the annual fair that brought the world here even in GDR times has now been replaced by a changing schedule of specialized events. They are held in the Neue Messe (New Trade Fair) on the northern outskirts, a spectacular complex of futuristic buildings that is the most up to date of its kind in the world. Check with the Leipzig Tourist Service about guided visits outside fair times.

» The Leipzig Card affords free use of public transportation in the city and reduced admission to concerts and other events, plus other reductions. Available from the tourist office, the card costs €8.90 for one day, €18.50 for three days and €34 for a family card for three days.

Below *Bach was the choirmaster at the Thomaskirche*

voices of the Thomaner, its boy choristers, were heard as long ago as the 13th century.

In 1723, they acquired a new choirmaster, none other than Johann Sebastian Bach, who as 'the cantor of cantors' directed the church's music until his death in 1750. He is buried inside the church, and his statue outside is a focal point for all visitors to Leipzig. The Thomaner usually sing at services on Fridays at 6pm and Saturdays at 3pm (▷ 247). Bach was a frequent visitor to one of the houses opposite, the house of his great friend and godfather to his children, Georg Heinrich Bose. Today the Bosehaus contains a Bach archive and a Bach Museum (daily 11–6; tel 0341 913 7200).

✉ Thomaskirchhof 18, 04109 Leipzig ☎ 0341 2222 4200 ⏲ Daily 9–6 ✋ Free 🚌 89. Tram 9

NIKOLAIKIRCHE

www.nikolaikirche-leipzig.de

With the simple sign *Offen für Alle* (Open to all) still hanging at its door, the church of St. Nicholas is indissolubly linked to the events of late 1989, when it was a focal point of the non-violent revolution which toppled the GDR's regime (▷ 46). Prayers for peace had been said here since 1981, and gradually the church became a place for those whose voices could not otherwise be heard in that oppressive society. On 9 October 1989, the 2,000 people leaving the church were greeted by tens of thousands of candle-holding demonstrators in the streets outside. In the face of this fearlessness, police and troops withdrew; a month later the regime opened the Berlin Wall.

✉ Nikolaikirchhof 3, 04109 Leipzig ☎ 0341 960 5270 ⏲ Daily 10–6 ✋ Free 🚌 Tram 4, 7, 8, 10, 11, 12, 15, 16

ZEITGESCHICHTLICHES FORUM

www.hdg.de

'Mr Gorbachev, open this gate.' Spoken in the shade of Berlin's Brandenburg Gate (▷ 80) when he visited Berlin in 1987, these words of the late US President Ronald Reagan greet visitors as they enter the Forum of Contemporary History. Other voices eerily evoke decades of Cold War and the division of Germany, among them John Kennedy's, with his famous cry of *'Ich bin ein Berliner!'* A branch of the Haus der Geschichte der Bundesrepublik Deutschland (▷ 166) in Bonn, the Forum brings to vivid life the realities of existence in eastern Germany under the dictatorship of the Socialist Unity Party, and is designed to appeal to visitors from abroad as well as to the local schoolchildren for whom it forms part of the curriculum. Posters, photographs, newsreels, uniforms and other exhibits recall key events like the uprising of 1953 and the regime's collapse in 1989, but there are plenty of reminders of the culture of everyday life, like a prominently displayed Trabant.

✉ Grimmaische Strasse 6, 04109 Leipzig ☎ 0341 22200 ⏲ Tue–Fri 9–6, Sat, Sun 10–6 ✋ Free 🚌 89. Tram 9

Below *Modern sculpted bronze figures above the central shopping area in the rebuilt Aldstadt*

VÖLKERSCHLACHTDENKMAL

www.stadtgeschichtliches-museum-leipzig.de

The colossal granite-clad memorial to the Battle of the Nations of 1813 looms like a manmade mountain over Leipzig's southeastern suburbs. Its intimidating presence is accentuated by the vast rectangular pool at its foot, by the broad steps by which it must be approached and by the gigantic figures gracing the summit. A dome soars an astonishing 68m (223ft) above the crypt. The monument was completed in 1913 on the 100th anniversary of the defeat of Napoleon by an alliance of mostly German armies (▷ 36). The battle, which raged around Leipzig for several days in October 1813, was the biggest and bloodiest hitherto in Europe, involving half a million soldiers. With its glorification of death in battle, the monument represents the militaristic values

that were to plunge Europe into the deadliest conflict of all time a century later (▷ 38–39). Nowadays, it offers a splendid panorama over Leipzig.
✉ Prager Strasse, 04299 Leipzig ☎ 0341 241 6870 🕐 Apr–end Oct daily 10–6; Nov–end Mar daily 10–4 🎫 Adult €5, child (6–18) €3, under 6 free, family €10 🚌 Tram 2, 15

MORE TO SEE

GEWANDHAUS

www.gewandhaus.de
Leipzig's symphony orchestra gave its first performances on the upper floor of the 'Clothmakers' Guild House' in 1781. Completed 200 years later, its present home is one of the GDR's prestige buildings, a modern structure, with lavish decoration and fine acoustics.
✉ Augustusplatz 8, 04109 Leipzig ☎ 0341 127 0280 🚌 Tram 4, 7, 8, 10, 11, 12, 15, 16

GRASSIMUSEUM

www.grassimuseum.de
The Bauhaus-style buildings of this famous museum house three separate facilities—the Museum für Angewandte Kunst (Decorative Arts), the Museum für Völkerkunde (Ethnography) and the Museum für Musikinstrumente (Musical Instruments).
✉ Johannisplatz 5–11, 04103 Leipzig ☎ 0341 222 9100 🕐 Tue–Sun 10–6 🎫 Combined ticket: Adult €12, child (6–18) €8, under 6 free, family €21; admission to individual museums costs less 🚌 Tram 4, 7, 12, 15

MENDELSSOHN-HAUS

www.mendelssohn-stiftung.de
With much evocative memorabilia, the family home of Felix Mendelssohn is a magnet for his admirers. As conductor of the Gewandhaus orchestra, Mendelssohn revived the reputation of composers, not least that of J. S. Bach.
✉ Goldschmidtstrasse 12, 04103 Leipzig ☎ 0341 127 0294 🕐 Daily 10–6 🎫 Adult €3.50, child (6–14) €1.75, under 6 free 🚌 Tram 4, 7, 12, 15

MUSEUM DER BILDENDEN KÜNSTE

www.mdbk.de
Leipzig has one of the finest art collections in Saxony, strong in Old Masters and in German art of the 19th century, as well as graphic works and sculpture.
✉ Katharinenstrasse 10, 04109 Leipzig ☎ 0341 216990 🕐 Tue, Thu, Sun 10–6, Wed 12–8 🎫 Adult €5, child (14–18) €3, under 14 free 🚌 89. Tram 9

MUSEUM IN DER RUNDEN ECKE

www.runde-ecke-leipzig.de
In December 1989, citizens stormed the headquarters of the Leipzig branch of the GDR's secret police (the Stasi), determined to preserve the vast records its occupants were shredding. The building now houses a compelling exhibition, Power and Banality, revealing the Communist regime's neurotic obsession with keeping track of everything about the public and private lives of its subjects.
✉ Dittrichring 24, 04109 Leipzig ☎ 0341 961 2443 🕐 Daily 10–6 🎫 Free 🚌 Tram 1, 9, 14

RUSSISCHE KIRCHE

www.russische-kirche-l.de
This extraordinary Russian Orthodox church, with its single tower (55m/180ft high) and richly decorated interior, would dominate the townscape of southeastern Leipzig were it not for the overwhelming presence of the Völkerschlachtdenkmal not far away. The church was built in memory of the 22,000 Russian soldiers who fell in the 1813 Battle of the Nations.
✉ Philipp-Rosenthal-Strasse 51a, 04103 Leipzig ☎ 0341 878 1453 🕐 Mar–end Nov daily 10–1, 2–5; Dec–end Feb daily 10–1, 2–4 🎫 Recommended donation €1 🚌 74. Tram 2, 16

Below *This Smart Car is the perfect size to allow the police to negotiate Leipzig's narrow streets*

INFORMATION

www.touristinfo-meissen.de

435 J9 Tourist Information, Markt 3, 01662 Meissen 03521 41940
Apr–end Oct Mon–Fri 10–6, Sat, Sun 10–4; Nov, Dec, Feb, Mar Mon–Fri 10–5, Sat 10–3; Jan Mon–Fri 10–5

TIP

» For the classic view of the castle and cathedral looking imperiously down on the town from their crag, cross the bridge over the Elbe to the far bank.

MEISSEN

Meissen is a well-preserved historic city, with a castle and cathedral overlooking the River Elbe and is the home of Meissen porcelain. Founded as a bulwark against the Slavs almost 1,100 years ago, the city still presents a defiant image of castle and cathedral on their rocky spur. Its red roofs are huddled defensively at the foot of the citadel, and, as one of eastern Germany's best-preserved little cities, its streets, squares and flights of steps are well worth exploring for their wealth of fine old buildings. But it is above all the reputation of its porcelain that makes Meissen an essential destination for visitors to this part of Saxony.

THE FIRST AND FINEST PORCELAIN

In the early 18th century, the court alchemist Johann Friedrich Böttger seemed on the point of cracking the age-old problem of how to convert base metal into gold. His master, Augustus the Strong, locked him up with instructions to get on with the job or else. Unsurprisingly, the wretched Böttger failed to produce gold, but his efforts yielded something almost as valuable and aesthetically far more pleasing—fine porcelain, up to then an impenetrable Oriental enigma. Determined to keep the process secret, Augustus decreed that production of porcelain should only take place within the secure walls of Meissen's citadel. It was only in 1863 that the factory moved to its present valley site on the edge of the town centre. Nowadays it's popular with all lovers of fine porcelain; you can view all the stages of production in the course of expertly guided tours.

THE BURGBERG

This is the name given to the crag crowned by the castle and cathedral. Regarded as the cradle of the Saxon state, there was a fortress here from the earliest times, but the present stronghold dates mostly from the late 15th or early 16th century. Following the removal of the porcelain works in 1863, the castle was given a thorough make-over, the aim being to give it what 19th-century taste considered to be an authentically medieval appearance. The walls were covered with paintings of heroic deeds from the Germanic past in an exaggerated style that soon went out of fashion, but that today is seen as historic in its own right. The lovely Gothic cathedral was begun in 1250 on the site of a Romanesque predecessor, and only completed in 1908, when the twin western towers were added.

Below *An example of Meissen porcelain*

Above *A peaceful inner courtyard at Mühlhausen's town hall in contrast to the town's role in the Peasants' Revolt of 1523–25*

MÜHLHAUSEN

www.muehlhausen.de

Seen from afar, miraculously preserved Mühlhausen still looks much as it did in the Middle Ages, with church spires rising over a ring of medieval walls and the red rooftops. Although dominated by kings and emperors in its early days, by the 13th century the town had won a degree of independence that was to express itself 200 years later in enthusiastic embrace of the radical ideas of the fiery Protestant preacher Thomas Müntzer, bitter opponent of Martin Luther (▷ 33).

Under Müntzer's leadership, the town became the focus of the Peasants' Revolt of 1523–25, but Müntzer himself met a tragic fate; after leading his followers to defeat, he was dragged back to Mühlhausen, tortured and executed. Inevitably, the GDR acclaimed him as a pioneer of Socialism, even renaming the town Thomas-Müntzer-Stadt after him. You can find out more in the Kornmarktkirche (Tue–Sun 10–4.30; tel 03601 404684). But even if you have little interest, interrupt your stroll through old streets and alleyways and look into the church where he preached, the lovely Marienkirche (daily 10–5; tel 03601 870023).

406 F8 Tourist-Information, Ratsstrasse 20, 99974 Mühlhausen 03601 404770 May–end Oct Mon–Fri 9–5, Sat, Sun 10–4; Nov–end Apr Mon–Fri 9–5, Sat 10–2

NAUMBURG

www.naumburg-tourismus.de

Overlooking the meeting point of the rivers Saale and Unstrut, this thousand-year-old little city is a real surprise: Europe's northernmost wine-growing area. The climate is dry, the soil good and the steep slopes of the riverbanks act as a suntrap as well as creating an unusually attractive landscape, though you will have to decide for yourself whether it quite justifies the epithet of 'Tuscany of the North'.

Visitors come this way not just for wine, but for art and architecture. Naumburg's attractive old streets and squares form the setting for one of Germany's great treasures: its cathedral, Dom St. Peter und Paul (Mar–end Oct Mon–Sat 9–6, Sun 12–6; Nov–end Feb Mon–Sat 10–4, Sun 12–4; tel 03445 230110), whose four-towered silhouette is recognizable from far away. Harmoniously combining Romanesque with Gothic, it contains an outstanding array of sculpture, much of it far in advance of its time. There are poignant scenes of Christ's Passion, but the outstanding figures are those of Margrave Ekkehardt and his consort, seen by generations as embodying the ideals of medieval chivalry.

406 G8 Tourist und Tagungsservice, Markt 6, 06618 Naumburg 03445 2731254 Apr–end Oct Mon–Fri 9–6, Sat 9–4, Sun 10–1; Nov–end Mar Mon–Fri 9–6, Sat 9–2 Naumburg

POTSDAM

▷ 228–232.

QUEDLINBURG

www.quedlinburg.de

Little Quedlinburg is perhaps the place where you come closest to Germany's deepest past, most of all in the Burgberg, the citadel of the country's earliest kings. Here, in the 10th-century crypt of St. Servatius' church, are the tombs of King Heinrich I and his wife, Mathilde, as well as the effigies of the abbesses who ruled the town for centuries. Gold and ivory objects and rare tapestries make the church's treasury one of Germany's richest.

The town itself, clustered beneath the citadel, is an unparalleled array of historic stone and timber-framed houses, just one of the reasons Quedlinburg was given UNESCO World Heritage Status in 1994. Some of the best buildings are in Breite Strasse and Steinweg, but almost every street and lane in the Altstadt is worth exploring. The Markt has a Renaissance town hall and customary statue of the knight Roland, guardian of civic liberties.

The corner known as the Finkenherd, just below the Burgberg, is particularly picturesque.

406 G7 Tourist Information, Markt 1, 06484 Quedlinburg 03946 90550 Apr–end Sep Mon–Fri 9–7, Sat 10–4, Sun 10–3; Oct–end Mar Mon–Fri 9.30–6, Sat 10–2

INFORMATION

www.potsdam.de
www.potsdamtourismus.de
www.spsg.de
403 J6 Brandenburger Strasse 3 (Am Brandenburger Tor), 14467 Potsdam 0331 275580 Apr–end Oct Mon–Fri 9.30–6, Sat, Sun 9.30–4; Nov–end Mar Mon–Fri 10–6, Sat, Sun 9.30–2 S-Bahn Potsdam Potsdam
An der Orangerie 1, 14469 Potsdam 0331 969 4202 Mar–end Oct daily 8.30–5; Nov–end Feb daily 9–4

Above *The theatrical entrance to Schloss Sanssouci*

INTRODUCTION

The capital of Brandenburg state, Potsdam is filled with art and architecture that embody the spirit of Prussia and imperial Germany, and has been dubbed Germany's Versailles. A small town just outside Berlin, it was transformed by successive monarchs into their idea of an earthly paradise. Potsdam stands on the River Havel, in the middle of a lavishly landscaped realm of lakes, forests, parks and ornamental gardens—a superlative setting for an extraordinary array of edifices, ranging from pompous palaces with sumptuous interiors, many restored to their original magnificence, to fanciful garden follies.

Potsdam is the most popular day-trip destination from Berlin as it is easily reached by S-Bahn train and by pleasure steamer. A day trip should be enough for a good impression of at least part of the town combined with a visit to a palace or museum, but two to three days is needed to do Potsdam justice.

Babelsberg, a suburb of Potsdam, enjoys worldwide fame as Germany's Hollywood, and was particularly prominent in the silent movie era of the 1920s. A variety of theme-park experiences have made Filmpark Babelsberg one of Germany's most popular visitor attractions.

Although founded in the tenth century on a site that had been occupied for centuries, Potsdam's rise to royal fame began after 1640, during the reign of the Great Elector, at a time when Prussia had been devastated by the Thirty Years' War. He revived the fortunes of his realm by bringing in industrious migrants from France and the Netherlands. His successors extended the city, making it their preferred residence after Berlin. As Prussia rose to European eminence as a military power in the 18th century, Potsdam took on the character of a garrison town, its citizens obliged to provide lodgings for the soldiers. More Dutch migrants arrived in the reign of the Soldier King, Friedrich Wilhelm I, who accommodated them in the brick-built houses of the Holländisches Viertel (Dutch Quarter).

The beautification of the town and its surroundings really began in the mid-18th century under his son, Friedrich II the Great, who built the palaces and laid out the parkland of Sanssouci. In the first decades of the 19th century, Friedrich's successors added to his vision, enlisting designers such as architect Karl Friedrich Schinkel and the great landscape architect, Peter Joseph Lenné.

Under both Nazism and Communism, the city's symbolic role in the nation's life continued. Hitler cosied up to Germany's military aristocracy with elaborate ceremonies focused around the Garrison Church. Schloss Cecilienhof hosted the Potsdam Conference of 1945, at which the leaders of the United States, Great Britain and the Soviet Union settled the political shape of occupied post-war Germany. The GDR took a negative view of Potsdam's superlative heritage, allowing much of it to moulder away and deliberately demolishing buildings like the Stadtschloss.

WHAT TO SEE

SCHLOSS SANSSOUCI

www.spsg.de

Crowning a terraced hillside, Friedrich the Great's summer retreat seems a modest affair. But it is a supreme achievement of 18th-century German architecture, a rococo jewel based on Friedrich's own designs, which he commanded his court architect, Knobelsdorff, to follow scrupulously. The King was an impatient client, and work was completed quickly; beginning in 1744, the terraces were laid out and planted with fruit trees and vines, while the palace itself was finished by 1746.

The best approach to the palace is from the park, up the splendid flight of steps in the middle of the terraces. The light-hearted tone desired by the King is set by the lively expressions and attitudes of the caryatids holding up the cornice, no doubt a reference to the wine produced by the terrace grapes. Friedrich's guests could saunter in and out of the palace through the doors beneath the dome, but today's visitors must go around the building and enter it from the colonnaded courtyard to the north. The guided tour leads through sumptuously decorated rooms that formed the setting for the monarch's private pleasures, principally music-making (he was a proficient flautist) and learned conversation with literary companions and other intellectuals. Among these was Voltaire, whom Friedrich hoped to persuade to stay here as his court philosopher. Despite all inducements, the Frenchman declined, and the affronted King took his revenge by decorating the guest room assigned to him with playful figures of apes and parrots. Other interiors include the circular Library with its collection of mostly French books, the gorgeous Marble Hall beneath the dome and the Concert Room. This riotous confection of rococo gilt and mirrors is in a famous painting by Adolph Menzel, *The Flute Concert of Frederick the Great at Sanssouci* (1852), in Berlin's Alte Nationalgalerie (▷ 77); it depicts Friedrich entertaining his guests in his role of flautist.

✉ Park Sanssouci, Maulbeerallee, 14469 Potsdam ☎ 0331 969 4200 🕓 Apr–end Oct Tue–Sun 10–6; Nov–end Mar Tue–Sun 10–5 ✋ May–end Oct: Adult €12, child (8–18) €8, under 8 free; Nov–end Apr: Adult €8, child (8–18) €5, under 8 free, by guided tour only 🚌 695, X15

PARK SANSSOUCI

The grand staircase and vineyard terraces making such a splendid formal approach to Schloss Sanssouci are a mere fragment of a vast park extending westward from the edge of the town centre to Friedrich's other, far larger residence, the Neues Palais. The park is gloriously varied, both in terms of buildings and landscape, a true reflection of how the tastes of Prussia's rulers changed over two centuries. It's a good idea to decide on priorities before setting out, as there is more than enough in the park to keep you busy for days on end. You can explore the parkland on either side of the long avenue and discover some of the fascinating buildings set among the generous greenery.

TIPS

» An economical alternative to a guided tour around Sanssouci is the very useful 695 bus, which connects Potsdam's railway station with several points around the edge of the park (Schloss Sanssouci, Neue Orangerie, Drachenhaus, Neues Palais). Hop on and off at will, using the *Tageskarte* (Day Ticket) unless you already have an ABC Berlin regional public transportation ticket, which is also valid for travel in Potsdam.

» Tram lines 92 and 96 from Potsdam Hauptbahnhof and S-Bahn station go north through the town. Transfer at Reiterweg/Alleestrasse to bus 692 to visit Schloss Cecilienhof. It's a pleasant walk back along the shore of the Heiliger See and through the Holländisches Viertel to Brandenburger Strasse to return to the station by tram.

Below *Detail of a lamp outside the Neues Palais, on the western side of the park*

BRIDGES

Of the seven bridges connecting the outside world to the island on which Potsdam is built, the Glienicker Brücke, marking the boundary with Berlin, is the best known. It carries what was once Reichstrasse (Imperial Highway) No. 1, which linked Aachen on the Belgian border to far-off Memel (now Klaipeda in Lithuania) in the east. As the Cold War boundary between West Berlin and the German Democratic Republic, it was closed to all but Allied military vehicles, making its then name, 'The Bridge of Unity' particularly ironic. On more than one occasion, the green-painted steel span was the scene of tense exchanges of valuable prisoners, the most sensational being that in 1962 of the American U2 pilot Gary Powers for the Soviet spy Rudolf Abel.

Below *One of two Communs buildings close to the Neues Palais*

If you have enough time, follow the circular walk beginning at Schloss Sanssouci, taking in most of the main features of the park. Flanking the Schloss is a pair of structures. To the east the Bildergalerie of 1764 (mid-May to mid-Oct Tue–Sun 10–6; tel 0331 969 4181), Germany's first purpose-built picture gallery, houses the royal collection of fine Old Master paintings. To the west is the Neue Kammern, originally an orangery, then a royal guest house. Farther west, the last edifice to be built in the park is the Neue Orangerie of 1864, still used to nurse tender plants through the winter. Farther west still on the high ground is the pagoda-like Drachenhaus, then the lovely rotunda of the Belvedere, built to offer a prospect over the whole area. After admiring the main façade of the Neues Palais, continue through the parkland south of the main axis, where you will find two of the park's most intriguing structures.

Schloss Charlottenhof was designed in 1826 in the form of an Italian Renaissance villa by the celebrated Berlin architect Karl Friedrich Schinkel as a summer palace for Crown Prince Friedrich Wilhelm IV. Nearby are the Roman baths, originally a gardener's residence, another attempt by Schinkel to implant the spirit of Italy in the heart of Prussia. But perhaps the most appealing of all the buildings in the park is the Chinesisches Haus of 1754 (May–end Oct Tue–Sun 10–6), a fantastical tent-like structure that exemplifies the 18th-century European passion for all things Chinese and which was used by Friedrich to show off his porcelain collection. Gilded figures sit and stand around the building, whose spreading roof is supported by columns in the form of palm trees. The circular lantern rising from the roof is topped by another gilded figure, a mandarin clutching a parasol. Inside, look up at the theatrically painted ceiling to see Chinese faces grinning down at you from the balcony.

NEUES PALAIS

www.spsg.de

What a contrast between little Schloss Sanssouci and this colossal edifice! By far the largest building in the park, it was completed in 1768 to celebrate Friedrich the Great's triumphs in the Seven Years War and proclaim Prussia's new-found status as one of the great powers of Europe, tasks it fulfils with overwhelming confidence. Behind the immensely long main façade with its cupola and its army of balustrade statues, there are some 200 rooms, many of them forming apartments originally intended to house Friedrich's guests. In addition, there is a superb baroque theatre and a number of richly ornamented cermonial halls and salons, among them the Marble Gallery and the Marble Hall with its magnificent inlaid floor. The most extravagant interior is the Grotto Hall; connecting palace to park, it is decorated with a mix of minerals, fossils, shells, glass and stonework.

On the far side of the palace, the west front consists of two wings partly enclosing a spacious courtyard and facing the so-called Communs, two sizeable blocks linked by a colonnade which housed the numerous staff.

✉ Park Sanssouci, Am Neues Palais, 14469 Potsdam ☎ 0331 969 4200 🕑 Apr–end Oct Wed–Mon 10–6; Nov–end Mar Wed–Mon 10–5 ✋ Apr–end Oct: Adult €5, child (8–18) €4, under 8 free, €1 extra for guided tour; Nov–end Mar: Adult €5, child (8–18) €4, under 8 free 🚌 605, 606, 695

NEUER GARTEN AND MARMORPALAIS

Potsdam's extensive 'New Garden' was laid out in the last years of the 18th century as a setting for the Marble Palace (May–end Oct Tue–Sun 10–6; Nov–end Apr Sat, Sun, holidays 1–5; tel 0331 969 4200), the summer residence of Crown Prince Friedrich Wilhelm. Eager to catch up on the latest fashions in landscaping, the Prince employed the garden designer Johann August Eyserbeck, fresh from working on the innovative English-style park at Wörlitz (▷ 218). The Neuer Garten benefits enormously from its lakeside setting, with cleverly contrived views across the water to other eye-catching features, such

Above *Frederick the Great's grandiose Neues Palais*

as the mock castle on Peacock Island far to the northeast. As at Sanssouci, the park is enhanced by a number of fanciful follies and other structures; they include a Gothic Library marking the boundary between town and park, a wonderful neo-Egyptian Orangerie, a splendid stone Pyramid, which served as an icehouse, and a group of brick buildings in Dutch style.

The Marble Palace itself is a modest neoclassical red-brick rectangle projecting out into the waters of the Heiliger See. It soon proved far too small for the Crown Prince and his family, and side wings were quickly added. It suffered bomb damage in 1945 and was ill-treated in GDR times, when it was used as the Museum of the People's Army. Its interior of lovely wall-paintings and gorgeous floors has now been restored.

SCHLOSS CECILIENHOF

www.spsg.de

The New Garden's main attraction is Schloss Cecilienhof, built for Crown Prince Wilhelm, Kaiser Wilhelm II's son. It is an extraordinary building, an early 20th-century reproduction of a half-timbered English Tudor manor house, all gables, steep roofs and a skyline of brick chimneys (most of which are purely decorative). It was completed in 1917, in the middle of World War I, a time when German admiration for things English was hardly at its height. At the end of the next war, in the summer of 1945, Cecilienhof was the setting for the Potsdam Conference, when US President Harry S. Truman, Soviet Political Leader Joseph Stalin and British Prime Minister Winston Churchill (later succeeded by Clement Attlee) met to shape the fate of the postwar world. The panelled interior has many mementoes of their deliberations. The GDR regime turned Cecilienhof into a luxury hotel, a role it continues to fulfil, playing host to eminent guests such as former American president George H. W. Bush.

✉ Neuer Garten, 14467 Potsdam ☎ 0331 969 4244 ◷ Apr–end Oct Tue–Sun 10–6; Nov–end Mar Tue–Sun 9–5 ✋ Apr–end Oct: Adult €5, child (8–18) €4, under 8 free, €1 extra for guided tour; Nov–end Mar: Adult €4, child (8–18) €3, under 8 free, by guided tour only 🚌 Tram 92 or 96, then bus 692

ALTER MARKT

Despite the disappearance of some of the buildings that once surrounded it, the Old Market is still the place where Potsdam presents itself to its public. The most prominent building is the Nikolaikirche (May–end Oct Mon 2–5, Tue–Sat

10–5, Sun 11.30–5; Nov–end Apr Mon–Sat 10–5, Sun 11.30–5; tel 0331 270 8602), with its portico, corner towers and its great dome. Begun in 1826, the church was a pet project of Friedrich Wilhelm IV while still Crown Prince; his stingy father, King Wilhelm III, refused to release money for the construction of the dome, and the building had to make do with an undistinguished flat roof until the old King passed away.

Flanking St. Nicholas' to the east is the baroque Altes Rathaus, Potsdam's old city hall, built in 1755 on the orders of Friedrich the Great, its tower topped by a gilded figure of Atlas. To the west is a huge and undistinguished megastructure of the 1970s, housing a variety of offices and institutions, including the tourist information centre, while to the south is a gap, only partly filled by the reconstructed Fortuna Portal. This is a fragment of the mostly 18th-century Stadtschloss (City Castle), which once dominated the square, and Potsdam itself. The principal Potsdam residence of Prussian kings, it was laid out around a great courtyard, but fell victim first to World War II bombing, then to the whims of GDR city planners, who considered it an unwanted symbol of Prussian militarism and demolished what was left of it in 1959.

14667 Potsdam Tram 90, 92, 93, 96, X98

MORE TO SEE

ALEXANDROWKA

www.alexandrowka.de

A charming group of Russian timber houses, authentic copies of those used to house Russian prisoners from the Napoleonic wars, were formed into a choir by Friedrich Wilhelm III. The choristers also had a Russian-style place of worship, the onion-domed Alexander Nevski Chapel.

Russische Kolonie Alexandrowka, 14469 Potsdam 691, 697. Tram 90, 92, 95

BELVEDERE AUF DEM PFINGSTBERG

www.pfingstberg.de

The monumental Roman-style Belvedere of 1863 provides one of the best views over Potsdam's surroundings.

Pfingstberg, 14469 Potsdam 0331 292468 Jun–end Aug daily 10–8; Apr, May, Sep daily 10–6; Oct daily 10–4; Nov, Mar Sat, Sun 10–4 Adult €3.50, child (6–16) €1.50, under 6 free, family €7.50 692

BRANDENBURGER TOR

Potsdam has a varied collection of city gates, but this is the most impressive. A triumphal arch, built on the orders of Friedrich the Great in 1770, it is actually older, though less famous, than Berlin's Brandenburg Gate, and forms a satisfying terminal feature to Brandenburger Strasse.

Am Luisenplatz, 14471 Potsdam X15, 695. Tram 94, 96

DAMPFMASCHINENHAUS

www.spsg.de

This lakeside pumping station, disguised as a mosque, is one of the city's most fanciful structures. Its minaret-like tower was built to conceal the chimney in the boiler hall.

Breite Strasse 28, 14471 Potsdam 0331 969 4225 May–end Oct Sat, Sun 10–6 Adult €2, child (8–18) €1.50, under 8 free (by guided tour only) Tram 94, 96

EINSTEINTURM

www.aip.de

An icon of modern architecture, the Einstein Tower was built in 1924 to house equipment investigating the Theory of Relativity, and is still in use today.

Wissenschaftspark Albert Einstein, Albert-Einstein-Strasse, 14473 Potsdam 0331 2880 Admission by guided tour only (tel 0331 291741) 691

Below *The Observatory in Wissenschaftspark (Science Park) Albert Einstein*

SÄCHSISCHE SCHWEIZ

Saxon Switzerland contains the most spectacular scenery in Saxony: A gloriously wooded sandstone upland through which the River Elbe has carved a winding course between Dresden and the border with the Czech Republic. The sandstone has been eroded into cliffs and ravines, and sculpted into fantastical shapes, including pinnacles, stacks, towers and natural bridges. In the past, few ventured deep into the Elbsandsteingebirge (Elbe Sandstone Mountains) except for woodmen and villagers seeking refuge in time of war. But in the late 18th century, the area's picturesque qualities were discovered by a pair of landscape painters from Switzerland (hence its popular name), as well as by Romantic artists like Caspar David Friedrich (1774–1840).

PIRNA AND KÖNIGSTEIN

Beneath its fortress, the old town of Pirna is the natural gateway to the area. The Markt remains almost as it was portrayed in a painting of 1755 by Canaletto. St. Marien's, the town's parish church, is a hall-church, which has particularly fine vaulting.

One of the most distinctive features of Saxon Switzerland is its table mountains—isolated massifs rising sheer from the countryside. One of the most spectacular, the Königstein, had its already formidable natural defences strengthened in the late 16th century by the addition of walls, ramparts and gateways, making Festung Königstein (Apr–end Sep daily 9–8; Oct daily 9–6; Nov–end Mar daily 9–5; tel 035021 64607) the strongest fortress in Germany.

BAD SCHANDAU AND THE BASTEI

Ever since visitors started coming to the area, the little riverside spa town of Bad Schandau has been a popular destination. Schandau has a wonderful open-air elevator that whisks 10 people at a time up to a high viewpoint, and also a rustic tramway running along the picturesque Kirnitzsch valley to the Lichtenhain waterfall.

Saxon Switzerland's best-known feature is the Bastei (Bastion), where a sheer cliff rises 190m (623ft) from the river. The spectacular rock formations here have attracted visitors ever since refreshment huts were built on the summit in 1826. Since then a network of paths, catwalks and bridges has been laid out, making it easy to experience this weird world without suffering from vertigo. And the refreshment huts have long since been replaced by a smart hotel, cafés and a panoramic restaurant.

INFORMATION

www.lanu.org
www.nationalpark-saechsische-schweiz.de
407 K9 Nationalparkhaus Sächsische Schweiz, Dresdener Strasse 2B, 01814 Bad Schandau 035022 50230 Apr–end Oct daily 9–6; Nov–end Mar Tue–Sun 9–5

TIP

» The Elbsandsteingebirge continue across the border into the Czech Republic, where they are known as Bohemian Switzerland. You can easily make day trips, either by steamer or by train, usually as far as the town of Děčin (Tetschen in German).

Above *A view of the River Elbe at Sächsische Schweiz*

SPREEWALD

www.spreewald-online.de

Downstream from Cottbus (▷ 211), the River Spree divides into countless tree-shaded channels, a tranquil inland delta designated a UNESCO Biosphere Reserve because of its extraordinarily diverse wildlife. The Spreewald is also home to Sorbs, an ethnic minority, whose ancestors cleared the once dense woodland to make a delightful mosaic of meadows, orchards and market gardens. The most famous crop is the gherkin, marinated in herbs to give it a special tang. Transport here is traditionally by punt, and there are some settlements still inaccessible by road; even the mail is delivered by boat. The appeal of the area to outsiders goes back a long way. It was discovered by Berlin artists and intellectuals early in the 19th century, and today it attracts millions, the majority of whom come to the little Spreewald capital of Lübbenau to enjoy a punt trip. Many of the villages have punt stations too, or you can avoid the crowds by walking or hiring a bicycle or canoe.

407 K8 Spreewald-Touristinformation, Ehm-Welk-Strasse 15, 03222 Lübbenau 03542 3668 Apr–end Sep Mon–Fri 9–7, Sat 9–4, Sun (May–end Jun) 11–3, (Jul–end Sep) 11–4; Oct Mon–Fri 9–6, Sat 9–4; Nov–end Mar Mon–Fri 10–4 Lübben, Lübbenau

WEIMAR

▷ 235.

WITTENBERG

www.wittenberg.de

This attractive small town on the River Elbe is also known as Lutherstadt Wittenberg: Of all the places that claim a connection with Martin Luther (▷ 33), this is the one most intimately associated with this leading figure of the Protestant Reformation. It was here Luther taught and preached, here in 1517 he nailed up his famous 95 theses denouncing church corruption, here he burned the papal bull condemning him, here he married and was buried. The central place of pilgrimage for Wittenberg's many visitors is the authentically furnished Lutherhaus (Apr–end Oct daily 9–6, Nov–end Mar Tue–Sun 10–5; tel 03491 42030), with its interesting museum of the Reformation, but there are many other sights connected with the great man.

Wittenberg is also home to a unique set of re-created interiors in the Haus der Geschichte (Mon–Fri 10–6, Sat, Sun, holidays, 11–6; tel 03491 409004) depicting everyday life under Communism.

407 H7 Wittenberg-Information, Schlossplatz 2, 06886 Lutherstadt Wittenberg 03491 498610 Mar–end Oct Mon–Fri 9–6.30, Sat, Sun 10–4; Nov, Dec Mon–Fri 10–4, Sat 10–2, Sun 11–3; Jan, Feb Mon–Fri 10–4 Lutherstadt Wittenberg

ZITTAU

www.zittau.eu

Separated from Poland only by the River Neisse, this attractive town once belonged to what is now the Czech Republic, the border with which is formed by the crest of the Zittauer Gebirge, the line of wooded hills a short distance to the south.

Zittau itself is not just a gateway to the hills but an atmospheric place of old streets, squares and fountains with more than a touch of Italy about it. For a fine view, climb the tower of the Johanniskirche (Mon–Fri 10–4.30, Sat 10–4, Sun 1–4; tel 03583 510933) and meet the watchman who marks the passing time with a blast from his trumpet. In the Kirche zum Heiligen Geist hangs the town's greatest treasure, the Zittauer Fastentuch (Lenten Veil, Apr–end Oct daily 10–6; Nov–end Mar Tue–Sun 10–5; tel 03583 500 8920). Dating from 1472, the veil (8.2m/27ft by 6.8m/22ft) shows 90 biblical scenes painted onto the cloth, an achievement of medieval story-telling comparable to France's Bayeux Tapestry.

407 K9 Tourist-Information Zittau, Rathaus, Markt 1, 02763 Zittau 03583 752137 Mon–Fri 9–6, Sat 9–1, Sun (May–end Oct) 1–4

Above *A tourist boat on the canal at Lubbenau in the Spreewald*

ZWICKAU

www.kultourz.de

A town identified with that icon of the GDR, the Trabant car, would seem a place to be avoided. But although Zwickau's recent fortunes were built on heavy industry, its traditions go back centuries to the silver mines in the Erzgebirge/ Ore Mountains to the south.

The town was mentioned as long ago as 1118. So as well as handsome structures from the 19th and early 20th centuries, there are plenty of fiNE older buildings. A must for music-lovers is the Robert-Schumann-Haus, the rebuilt birthplace of the composer Robert Schumann (Tue–Fri 10–5, Sat, Sun 1–5; tel 0375 215269).

Zwickau's most fascinating museum is the well-stocked August Horch Museum (Tue–Sun 9.30–5; first Thu in month to 9pm; tel 0375 271 7380) in the north of the town. It celebrates the name of the automobile pioneer who, in 1904, founded the works that turned out elegant limousines and classic racing cars as well as Audis, DKWs and, latterly, the Trabant, and is set in the former Audi works.

407 H9 Tourist Information Zwickau, Hauptstrasse 6, 08056 Zwickau 0375 271 3240 Mon–Fri 9–6.30, Sat 10–4 Zwickau

WEIMAR

This miniature ducal capital city is suffused with the atmosphere of the Golden Age of German culture. Otherwise just one of Germany's countless little courtly cities, Weimar occupies a special place in German life because of the unique flowering of literary and cultural life that took place here in the late 18th to early 19th centuries. It was started by Duchess Anna Amalia, who wanted to get the best education possible for her son. A search for tutors led to an invitation to the 26-year-old Johann Wolfgang von Goethe (1749–1832). The two young men got on well, forming an enduring partnership; Goethe served under Carl August for the rest of his life as a government official. His fame drew other luminaries here, including the playwright Friedrich von Schiller (1759–1805). Weimar acquired a Europe-wide reputation for intellectual excellence. Franz Liszt (1811–86) became musical director and Richard Wagner (1813–83) also visited. Henry van der Velde (1863–1957) founded the school of art and design that, under Walter Gropius (1883–1969), was to evolve into the Bauhaus (▷ 21).

In 1919, the government fled here from revolutionary chaos in Berlin, and the town gave its name to the short-lived democratic republic, destroyed by Hitler in 1933 (▷ 40). By then, Weimar was a stronghold of Nazism, whose aversion to the left-leaning ideas of the Bauhaus had forced the movement to relocate to Dessau (▷ 218).

THE GOLDEN AGE

Almost any of Weimar's streets and squares reveal something of the spirit of the city's Golden Age. The famous statue of Goethe and Schiller in front of the Deutsches Nationaltheater is a compulsory stop for every German visitor. Other Goethe shrines include his main residence, Goethes Wohnhaus (Apr–end Sep Tue–Fri, Sat 9–7, Sun 9–6; Oct Tue–Sun 9–6; Nov–end Mar Tue–Sun 9–4; tel 03643 545347), with a fine modern museum that deals with the phenomenon of Weimar Classicism. There's also the associated Goethes Hausgarten, the house garden that Goethe helped to landscape.

BUCHENWALD

Many visitors make the trip to Gedenkstätte Buchenwald (Apr–end Oct daily 10–6; Nov–end Mar daily 10–4; tel 03643 4300), the remains of Buchenwald concentration camp, 8km (5 miles) to the north of the town, where there are museums and memorials evoking the camp's use under the Nazis and during the Soviet occupation.

INFORMATION

www.weimar.de

406 G9 Tourist-Information Weimar, Markt 10, 99423 Weimar 03643 7450 Apr–end Oct Mon–Sat 9.30–7, Sun, holidays 9.30–3; Nov–end Mar Mon–Fri 9.30–6, Sat, Sun, holidays 9.30–2 Welcome-Center, Friedensstrasse 1, 99423 Weimar Mon–Sat 10–6 Weimar

TIP

» A walking tour with an English-speaking guide will enormously enhance your appreciation of the heritage of this delightful little city.

Below *Goethes Hausgarten at the rear of the Goethes Wohnhaus*

AROUND THE BROCKEN: INTO THE HARZ MOUNTAINS

This drive skirts the Harz Mountains, then climbs to give you a view of central Germany's highest point, the Brocken. For a closer look at its summit, you can leave your car and the 21st century behind and make an ascent by steam railway.

THE DRIVE
Distance: 100km (62 miles)
Allow: 2 hours
Start at: Quedlinburg
End at: Wernigerode

★ Drive west out of Quedlinburg and follow signs that take you along minor roads to Thale, where you should look for directions to the *Seilbahn* (cable car).

❶ Thale's early fortunes were based on the iron ore extracted from the Harz Mountains, which form a dramatic rocky backdrop to the town. The disused iron- and steelworks are now in an advanced state of decay, but Thale still provides its visitors with mineral water from its spa. A big attraction is the gorge of the River Bode (▷ 239), a cable car and chairlift and a summer toboggan run around the entrance to it. There are also children's play facilities.

Above *Schloss Wernigerode which you can visit early on in your drive, or towards the end of the journey*

Continue west, following signs to the town of Blankenburg, then taking the B6 towards Wernigerode.

❷ Wernigerode has one of Germany's most extravagant town halls—the extraordinary spiky towers of the Rathaus overlook the marketplace—and a wealth of timber-framed buildings. The Altstadt is a popular starting point for exploration of the Harz and is the northern terminus of the narrow-gauge railway which threads its way through the mountains (▷ 238).

Continue west along the B6, making a brief diversion south to go through the Altstadt of Ilsenburg, a pleasant, low-key resort popular with hikers. The B6 leads to Bad Harzburg.

❸ Bad Harzburg is one of the area's main resort towns, with plenty of spa facilities for its guests. The exhibits in the Haus der Natur provide a lively introduction to the natural riches of the mountains.

From Bad Harzburg, follow signs towards Braunlage, driving south along the B4 limited-access highway, which climbs into the heart of the Harz. After 11km (7 miles), turn east into the large car parking area at Torfhaus.

❹ Torfhaus, at 798m (2,618ft), is the most popular spot for viewing the

Brocken. From here there's a superb panorama over the forested foothills towards the mountain's rounded summit (1,142m/3,747ft), some 5km (3 miles) away. During the Cold War, Torfhaus, which was in the Federal Republic, was one of the places where West Germans could easily gaze into the forbidden territory of the German Democratic Republic. If you are unlucky with the weather, visit the Nationalparkhaus Altenau-Torfhaus on the far side of the road (take care in crossing). The multi-media exhibits give a virtual tour of the Brocken, and you can even hear the call of the lynx, one of the area's more elusive inhabitants.

Descend south along the B4 for 9km (5.5 miles), and take the exit signposted 'Braunlage Nord'.

❺ Braunlage is a busy upland resort, popular in both summer and winter, with a dense network of marked trails and a good range of visitor facilities. A cable car whisks visitors up to the top of the Wurmberg (972m/3,189ft), with fine views northwards.

Above *Wernigerode's 13th-century town hall*

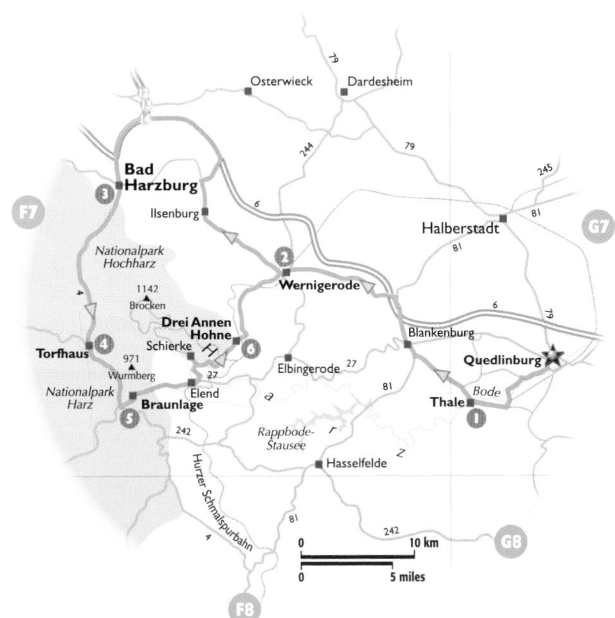

From Braunlage, drive northeast along the B27, following signs to Schierke. After 5km (3 miles), turn north in the village of Elend up a minor road, still following signs to Schierke, and after 2km (1.2 miles), turn east towards Drei Annen Hohne. In 4km (2.5 miles), the road crosses the Brocken railway. Drive past the station and turn south into the large parking area.

❻ Drei Annen Hohne station is busy in summer (though trains run all year round), as it is an intersection on the Harzer Schmalspurbahn (HSB), Germany's most extensive narrow-gauge rail system. Trains run north to Wernigerode and south to Nordhausen, as well as to the summit of the Brocken (⊳ 238).

From Drei Annen Hohne, drive north for 11km (7 miles) towards

Wernigerode. The road drops down through the forest and enters the town through extensive suburbs.

WHEN TO GO

This drive can be undertaken year-round, though it's best when clear weather gives good visibility. Snowfall may affect conditions, but the train ride to the summit of the Brocken up snow-covered slopes is a unique experience.

PLACES TO VISIT

HARZER SCHMALSPURBAHN
www.hsb-wr.de
✉ Friedrichstrasse 151, 38855 Wernigerode ✋ Brocken summit €24, child (6–11) €12, under 6 free

HAUS DER NATUR
www.haus-der-natur-harz.de
✉ Nordhäuser Strasse 2B, 38667 Bad Harzburg ☎ 05322 784337
🕒 Tue–Fri (and holiday Mondays) 10–5
✋ Adult €2, child (6–18) €1, under 6 free, family €5

NATIONALPARKHAUS ALTENAU-TORFHAUS
www.nationalparkhaus-altenau-torfhaus.de
✉ Torfhaus 21, 38667 Torfhaus ☎ 05320 263 🕒 Apr–end Oct daily 9–5, Nov–end Mar daily 10–4

NATIONALPARK-INFORMATIONSHAUS (BROCKENHAUS)
www.nationalpark-harz.de
☎ 039455 50005 🕒 Daily 9.30–5
✋ Adult €4, child (6–18) €3, under 6 free, family €8.50

WHERE TO EAT

DER KRÄUTERHOF
Elegant hotel/restaurant near the railway station in Drei Annen Hohne.
✉ 38875 Drei Annen Hohne/Schierke
☎ 039455 840

STEAMING UP THE BROCKEN

The station at Drei Annen Hohne is the most convenient starting point for a trip to the top of the Brocken by an HSB steam train—the Brockenbahn. Schierke, the next stop up the line, is nearer the summit, but lacks parking, while leaving from Wernigerode adds 40 minutes.

The ride is an exhilarating experience. A massive 2-10-2 locomotive, especially built for the line in the 1950s to tackle the steep 1:25 gradient, pulls the train, which consists of old-fashioned coaches (cars) with open platforms at each end. The 16km (10-mile) trip, including a 5-minute stop at Schierke, takes 45 minutes. At the top, there are cafés and the Brockenhaus, a modern museum devoted to explaining the mountain's history and ecology. Exhibits illustrate the GDR's treatment of its highest mountain as forbidden territory; from the early 1960s, the railway was only used to supply the listening posts.

If you have time, take the 2km (1.2-mile) walk laid out around the summit; it gives superb, ever-changing views over much of the Harz and the lowlands at its foot and takes you past the granite outcrops nicknamed the Witches' Altar and Devil's Pulpit, reminders of the Brocken's place in legend.

Below *The Brockenbahn steam engine on Brocken summit*
Opposite *Walking alongside the River Bode*

THE GORGE OF THE RIVER BODE

This mostly level walk penetrates deep into the core of the Harz massif along what has been justly described as the 'most rugged valley north of the Alps'. The walk follows part of a longer trail leading through the Bode gorge to the resort town of Treseburg and is waymarked with blue triangles on a white background.

THE WALK

Distance: 8km (5 miles)
Allow: 2 hours
Start/end at: *Seilbahn* (cable railway) parking area in Thale

HOW TO GET THERE

▷ 236.

★ From the *Seilbahn* parking area, walk south along the riverbank and turn west across two bridges towards the cable railway.

❶ The cable railway whisks you high over the river to Hexentanzplatz, named for the witches said to have danced there.

Continuing through the valley, turn south along the side of the cable railway terminus and walk through the wood alongside the river). The rocky scenery becomes more dramatic as you approach the footbridge known as the Katersteg (Tomcat Bridge).

❷ On the other side of the Katersteg are a large youth hostel and the Kleiner Waldkater restaurant and guest house.

Without crossing the bridge, continue upstream. Sheer rock walls rise 300m (1,000ft) and in places the path is aligned directly above the rushing river. It rounds a projecting rockface known as the Goethe-Felsen (Goethe Rock).

❸ The Goethe-Felsen was named in 1949 in honour of the great writer, who came here in 1784.

Carry on upstream to the Königsruhe restaurant, which has the figure of a witch on its roof.

❹ The Königsruhe stands on a spot where refreshments have been served since 1820.

Continue upstream through the Königsruhe group of buildings.

❺ Herr von Bülow, commemorated in the plaque here, was the forestry superintendent. A sign just beyond the plaque reminds you that you are on a *Wanderweg*—a hiking path with difficult stretches. However, with proper footwear you need not worry. A path leads up to the Rosstrappe viewpoint in 45 minutes, but our walk continues to the Teufelsbrücke (Devil's Bridge).

The Teufelsbrücke crosses the Bode at the narrowest point in the gorge. There were once plans to build a hydroelectric dam here.

Cross the bridge and continue walking for 70m (76 yards) on the far bank of the river to the Bodekessel (Bode Cauldron).

❻ The Bodekessel got its name from the turbulent water in the deep pool that the river has carved out of the granite.

Many walkers turn back at this point, but it is worth taking a deep breath and tackling the zigzag path that climbs up towards the rim of the plateau, just below the area known as the Prinzensicht. From the path's summit there is a commanding view over the ravine. Return to your starting point in Thale.

WHEN TO GO

This walk can get very crowded during the school holidays and in the summer months, especially on weekends.

PLACES TO VISIT

HEXENTANZPLATZ

www.seilbahnen-thale.de
Reached by road or cable railway (weekends only in winter). Spectacular viewpoint, zoo, open-air theatre, summer toboggan run.
☎ 03947 2500

ROSSTRAPPE

www.seilbahnen-thale.de
Reached by road or chairlift (weekends only in winter). Spectacular viewpoint.
☎ 03947 2500

WHERE TO EAT

GASTSTÄTTE KÖNIGSRUHE

Attractive, rustic restaurant and café overlooking the River Bode. Enjoy game, fish and home-made pastries.
✉ Hirschgrund 1, 06502 Thale ☎ 03947 2726

HIGHLIGHTS OF SAXONY

This drive starts off in lowland landscape, but the scenic highlight of the tour is the wooded valley of the Elbe known as Saxon Switzerland (▷ 233). The route also takes in several of the historic cities of Saxony, each with its own character. On either side of Dresden, the route forms part of the Saxon Wine Route.

THE DRIVE
Distance: 360km (224 miles)
Allow: 8 hours
Start/end at: Leipzig

★ Leave Leipzig eastwards on the B6 towards Wurzen. In Wurzen turn north into the Altstadt and park the car.

❶ Wurzen announces itself from far off with two huge grain elevators, but it's an old place with a stately market square. Although the cathedral dates from the 12th century, it is most remarkable for its 1932 refurbishment, which includes a Crucifixion scene in bronze.

Retrace your route along the B6 for 2km (1.2 miles), turning south onto the B107 to Grimma.

❷ The 800-year-old small town of Grimma calls itself the 'Pearl of the Mulde valley', but the river wrought havoc in terrible floods in 2002. The lovely baroque bridge designed by Mathaes Daniel Pöppelmann now lacks its central span, but has a splendid Saxon coat of arms adorning the parapet.

Continue south for 15km (9 miles) along the B107 through attractive countryside to Colditz. Here follow signs to *Zentrum.*

❸ The international fame of Colditz (▷ 211) rests on the role of its crag-top castle in World War II, when its massive walls imprisoned the most recalcitrant of Allied prisoners of war.

Drive east from Colditz along the B175 towards Döbeln. On the approach to this town follow signs to Dresden and the autobahn. Leave the autobahn at exit 78 and follow signs to *Zentrum.*

❹ Dresden's (▷ 212–217) historic heart was completely destroyed in the Allied bombing raids of 13 February 1945, but rebuilding has restored at least some of the charm of Saxony's venerable capital.

Take the B172 southeast from Dresden and follow signs to Pirna. In Pirna turn north and follow signs to *Historische Altstadt*.

5 Pirna has a charming market square that remains almost exactly as it was depicted in a famous painting of 1755 by Canaletto. The old town promotes itself as the gateway to Saxon Switzerland.

Return to the B172 and drive east for 12km (7.5 miles), turning south off the main road towards the parking area for Königstein.

6 The great fortress of Königstein (▷ 233) occupies the summit of one of Saxon Switzerland's strange tabletopped hills, a sandstone plateau that wind and water have eroded into fantastic shapes. There are superb panoramas from its ramparts.

Return to the B172 and continue east, dropping down to the River Elbe. In 5km (3 miles), the road crosses the Elbe into Bad Schandau (▷ 233), but before entering the town turn south off the bridge approach and follow signs to Hohenstein, driving north through a wooded gorge. Continue west through tiny Hohenstein, following signs to Bastei. Turn south in 2.5km (1.5 miles) towards the Bastei. Leave your car at the park-and-ride station, or continue south to the main parking area.

7 The Bastei (bastion) is a spectacular place, where rock columns and pillars plunge 190m (623ft) to the water's edge. The vertiginous views over the valley of the Elbe from the top of these sandstone formations equal those from the Königstein fortress.

Return to the road and turn west towards Pirna, but after 9km (5.5 miles) follow signs towards Pillnitz, then Dresden. You are now on the Saxon Wine Route, and the road runs for a while at the foot of the vineyards of a wine region now emerging from the obscurity it suffered under the GDR regime.

Back in Dresden, follow signs to Radebeul, then Coswig and Meissen. As you finally emerge from Dresden's extensive built-up area you will see, on the north side of the road, Schloss Wackerbarth, the revived Saxon state winery, its terraced vineyards rising steeply behind the castle. Continue northwest for 10km (6 miles) to Meissen, following signs to *Zentrum* and enjoying the view of castle and cathedral before crossing the Elbe into the heart of the city.

8 Meissen (▷ 226) has a well-preserved Altstadt worth a stroll, but highlights of a visit here are a walk up to the castle and a tour of the world-famous porcelain factory.

From Meissen, drive northwest along the B6 towards Oschatz, turning northeast after 20km (12 miles) towards Riesa. Avoiding the middle of Riesa, follow signs north to Torgau, which is reached in 39km (24 miles).

9 Torgau is proud of Schloss Hartenfels, its vast and splendid Renaissance castle. The town is also famous as the point where the American and Soviet armies met on the banks of the River Elbe in the closing days of World War II, splitting Hitler's Third Reich in half.

Return southwest to Leipzig (52km/32 miles) along the B87.

WHEN TO GO

This drive can be undertaken at any time of year, but take care when walking around the Bastei in icy conditions.

PLACES TO VISIT

PIRNA

www.pirna.de

Am Markt 7, 01796 Pirna ☎ 03501 46570 Apr–end Oct Mon–Fri 9–6, Sat 9.30–1, Sun 11–2; Nov–end Mar Mon–Fri 9–6, Sat 9.30–1

WHERE TO EAT

Berghotel und Panoramarestaurant Bastei (01847 Lohmen/bastei, tel 035024 7790) is a hotel complex with several restaurants, including one perched on the edge of the Bastei rocks with fabulous views. Near Dresden, you can enjoy refined but not expensive eating in Schloss Wackerbarth (Wackerbarthstrasse, 101445 Radebeul, tel 0351 89550), the spacious restaurant attached to the Saxon state winery.

Opposite *The Basteibrucke is in a spectacular setting over the River Elbe*

TO THE TOP OF THE PFAFFENSTEIN IN SAXON SWITZERLAND

This hike in Saxon Switzerland (▷ 233) gives you the chance to enjoy the bizarre beauty of this world of weirdly eroded sandstone. Protected by sheer 60m (200ft) cliffs, the Pfaffenstein, which rises to 434m (1,424ft), appears impregnable, but its formidable natural ramparts are split by fissures through which steps have been carved and metal stairways hung, making the great crag accessible to walkers.

THE WALK
Distance: 4.5km (3 miles); total ascent: 110m (360ft)
Allow: 1 hour 30 min
Start/end at: Pfaffendorf car parking area
How to get there: The village of Pfaffendorf is 3km (2 miles) south of Königstein town. From the roundabout (traffic circle) on the B172 in Königstein, drive south, turning left (east) at the sign for Pfaffendorf up a steeply climbing minor road. Turn right (south) into the parking area, which is just past the built-up part of the village.
Note: The sheer drops from the top of the Pfaffenstein are mostly unprotected and small children should not be allowed to run around unsupervised on the summit.

★ Walk south from the parking area, turning slightly right (southwest) up a path made of concrete slabs towards the wooded cliffs of the Pfaffenstein. At the edge of the woods, turn half-left (southeast) into the trees and climb across the boulder-strewn slope. This is the beginning of the Nadelöhr.

❶ The Nadelöhr (Eye of the Needle) is aptly named: At first sight it looks impossible to thread your way up through the narrow clefts in the cliffs. However, the fissures have been artificially enlarged in places, and steps, metal stairways and handrails make the ascent of this flank of the Pfaffenstein straightforward (if somewhat breathless). This approach was first opened in 1894.

At the top of the climb you reach the more-or-less flat summit of the Pfaffenstein.

❷ Much of the summit is covered with open woodland of silver birch and other trees, some apparently growing directly out of the bare rock. In places there is a substantial layer of loamy soil, up to 1.5m (5ft) thick, which retains water, and this made it possible for prehistoric people to set up permanent camp here.

Follow the timber railing around, turning left (southeast) at a sign indicating *Aussichtspunkt/ Goldschmidthöhle* (Viewpoint/ Goldsmith's Cave). The magnificent view extends beyond other table mountains, such as the Papststein straight ahead, to old volcanic peaks far away in the Czech Republic. Return the way you came and turn left (south) at the sign indicating 'Barbarine', then right (west) to 'Opferkessel-Dom-Luftballon'.

❸ 'Sacrificial Cauldron', 'Cathedral' and 'Air Balloon' are a few of the fanciful names given to the variously shaped rocks forming the western ramparts of the Pfaffenstein. There are popular climbing faces nearby and a fine view of the Königstein fortress (▷ 233).

Go back the way you came, turning right (south) to the Gaststätte (Restaurant) and the viewing tower.

The Pfaffenstein lodge/restaurant has been enlarged several times since it was established on this spot in 1880. The stone tower, 27m (89ft) high, built in 1904, replaced a timber structure erected in 1894. Its structural condition may mean that it is sometimes closed to the public.

As you continue south, you descend into a natural amphitheatre, climb through rocks and narrow clefts and ascend stone steps to reach a viewpoint facing southeast. The Pfaffenstein cliffs are at their most dramatic here—precipitous walls with great masses of fallen rock at their feet. Metal stairways lead down through the rocks to a flat area with extensive views to the southwest. A cleft to the east gives access to a narrow platform directly facing the Barbarine needle rock.

❹ The Barbarine, which is an immensely tall and thin rock, seems an impossible climb to the layman, but it was very popular until its dangerous state led to its closure to climbers in 1975. The precarious summit has now been stabilized by the injection of resins and silicon. The rock owes its name to a tall tale about a disobedient little girl who was turned to stone by her angry mother.

Go back towards the tower and lodge, turning left (west) where a sign indicates *Klammweg/ Bequemer Abstieg* (cleft path/ easy descent). The path goes down via steps and through a spectacularly deep cleft, eventually emerging into a flat open area.

❺ A medallion high on the rock-face commemorates Karl Gottlob Jäckel, a local landowner who was responsible for opening up the Pfaffenstein to the public in the 19th century.

Continue down, turning right (north) when you emerge from the trees. Follow the flank of the Pfaffenstein north, then east, turning left (north) in 650m (710 yards) to descend the concrete path to the parking area.

WHEN TO GO

This walk is best enjoyed when clear autumn weather gives good visibility.

PFAFFENSTEIN

The Pfaffenstein was inhabited in the Bronze Age, then served as a refuge for people from the valley. In the mid-19th century, one of its caves was a hideout for a counterfeiter who had escaped from the prison on the Königstein. Not long after his recapture, the rock's delights were discovered by walkers and climbers; in 1880 the refreshment hut was built, followed by the viewing tower in 1904. The Pfaffenstein's most famous feature, the needle rock called the Barbarine, was climbed for the first time by the alpinist Rudolph Fehrmann and Englishman Perry Smith.

WHERE TO EAT

Snacks may be available at the lodge on top of the Pfaffenstein. There are also places to eat in Königstein and Bad Schandau (5.5km/3 miles east). In Pfaffendorf village, next to the parking area, is the simple Gasthaus und Pension Zum Pfaffenstein (Pfaffesteinweg 1, 01824 Pfaffendorf, tel 035021 67951).

Clockwise from left to right *Steps up through the Eye of the Needle help to make the seemingly impossible ascent of the Pfaffenstein; the views from the summit are stunning*

THE THURINGIAN FOREST: A CIRCULAR TOUR FROM EISENACH

A glorious hilly area running some 100km (60 miles) southeast from Eisenach (▷ 220), the Thuringian Forest mixes deep beech and spruce woodland with open areas of field and meadow. This drive through the forest takes in a whole string of historic towns, beginning with Eisenach, the imperial city where this route begins and ends, while Goethe and J. S. Bach provide literary and musical associations.

THE DRIVE
Distance: 170km (106 miles)
Allow: 4 hours
Start/end at: Eisenach

★ From Karlsplatz in the middle of Eisenach, take the B19 southwards and follow signs towards Wartburg, turning east at the first set of traffic lights onto steep Johann-Sebastian-Bach-Strasse. Drive up, following small green signs towards the Burschenschaftsdenkmal and Berghotel. Park where the road ends and walk up to the memorial.

❶ The huge stone Burschenschaftsdenkmal (Fraternities Memorial) was built in 1902 to commemorate the great rally on the Wartburg in 1817, during which patriotic students called for freedom and national unity. The vast wooded panorama gives a foretaste of the landscapes of the Thuringian Forest.

Return to the heart of town, first following signs for *Alle Richtungen* (all directions), then signs towards Gotha and the B7. In 4.5km (3 miles), turn south onto the B88, and stay on this road following signs towards Ohrdruf and Ilmenau. After 19km (12 miles), at 2km (1.2 miles) beyond the spa town of Tabarz, turn south into the car parking area of the Marienglashöhle.

❷ The Marienglashöhle is one of the largest crystalline caves in Europe, featuring magical patterns formed by gypsum crystals as well as stalactites and stalagmites.

Continue 2km (1.2 miles) along the B88 to Friedrichroda.

❸ Like Tabarz, Friedrichroda is a summer resort and spa town, much developed in GDR days with oversize buildings for subsidized vacationers, but now recovering much of its attractive late 19th to early 20th-century character.

Continue along the B88 to Ohrdruf. When you exit the town, leave the

B88 and take the B247 towards Oberhof. To the east, in 1.5km (1 mile), you'll see the car parking area for the Tobiashammer.

❹ The Tobiashammer is a fascinating technical museum, with exhibits that include a monster 1920s steam engine.

Continue south along the B247 towards the winter resort of Oberhof. The resort, with its huge hotels and ski slopes, is to the west, while there are views to the southeast of the Schneekopf (978m/3,209ft). Beyond Oberhof, turn southeast onto a minor road signposted Schmücke. The road winds through the forest, close to the famous Rennsteig long-distance trail. After 16km (10 miles), turn north along the B4 towards Ilmenau. As the road descends to Stützerbach, there are fine views of houses hung with slate tiles. After 10km (6 miles) you'll reach the old town of Ilmenau.

❺ Ilmenau is known for its glass and porcelain, and above all for its associations with one of Germany's greatest writers, Johann Wolfgang von Goethe (▷ 35), who came here no fewer than 28 times, finding inspiration in the surrounding hills, woods, valleys and ravines.

Continue heading north on the B4 to Arnstadt, where the hills of the Thuringian Forest descend to the plain.

❻ Well-preserved Arnstadt is one of Germany's most venerable small cities. J. S. Bach was organist here between 1703 and 1707; the town museum pays tribute to him. But Arnstadt's great attraction is Mon Plaisir, a collection of 400 costumed dolls, assembled in the 18th century by the widowed Princess Augusta Dorothea and occupying a floor in the Neues Palais.

Continue north along the B4 for 19km (11.5 miles) to Erfurt. In the city, follow signs to 'Dom' and park on the Domplatz.

❼ In Erfurt (▷ 219), the capital of Thuringia, take time to appreciate its dramatically sited Gothic cathedral, old buildings and a horticultural exhibition at the Cyriaksburg castle, just outside town.

From the middle of Erfurt, follow the B7 for 21km (13 miles) to Gotha. On the approach to the town, look for signs to Schloss Friedenstein. Park in front of the castle, with its massive twin towers, and walk through the spacious courtyard for a wonderful view over the old city below.

❽ The princely city of Gotha has an old core focused on the high-gabled Town Hall, and rich art collections displayed in the 17th-century baroque Schloss Friedenstein.

Return to Eisenach along the B7.

WHEN TO GO

This drive can be undertaken at any time of year, but check on driving conditions in winter, when the mountian roads may be affected by snowfall as well as crowded with winter sports traffic.

PLACES TO VISIT

MARIENGLASHÖHLE

✉ 99894 Friedrichroda ☎ 03695 614101 🕐 Daily Apr–end Oct daily 9–5; Nov–end Mar daily 9–4 💶 Adult €4, child (6–16) €2, under 6 free

TOBIASHAMMER

✉ Suhler Strasse 34, 99885 Ohrdruf ☎ 03624 402792 🕐 Daily 9–5

WHERE TO EAT

Thuringian sausages are famed far beyond their place of origin, and in the most visited parts of the Forest you will find plenty of stands selling them. Halfway along the route is Gasthof Meyersgrund (Ilmenauerstrasse 7, 98714 Stützerbach; tel 036784 50235), a roadside restaurant specializing in trout.

Opposite *Flowers in front of scrubland stretching towards thick forest in the Thüringer Wald*

BAD SAAROW

SAAROWTHERME

www.bad-saarow.de/therme

At this little spa town you get the chance to bob around in an enclosed salt-water pool at a temperature of 35°C (95°F), then swim outside in an open-air pool. There are also saunas, mud baths and massages.

✉ Am Kurpark 1, 15526 Bad Sarow ☎ 033631 8680 🕐 Sun–Thu 9am–9pm, Fri, Sat 9am–11pm 🖐 Full-day treatments from €59

BAD SULZA

TOSKANA THERME

www.liquid-sound.com

A luxurious and unusual spa experience. Your immersion is accompanied by light and 'liquid sound' and, if you wish, by an 'Aqua-Wellness Bodyworker'.

✉ Wunderwaldstrasse 2a, 99518 Bad Sulza ☎ 036461 92000 🕐 Mon–Thu 10am–10pm, Fri, Sat 10am–midnight 🖐 Treatments from €12

BAUTZEN

SAURIERPARK

www.saurierpark.de

Lurking in this leafy park just 4km (2.5 miles) north of Bautzen are terrifying creatures from Jurassic times. There is also a playground.

✉ 02625 Bautzen (outside Kleinwelka) ☎ 035935 3036 🕐 Easter Friday–early Nov daily 9–6 (9–7 Jun–end Aug) 🖐 Adult €9, child (5–16) €5, under 5 free, family €22.50 ☕

COTTBUS

PARKEISENBAHN COTTBUS

www.parkeisenbahn-verein.de

Under Soviet-style Communism nearly all the work of getting narrow-guage trains to run to time was carried out by Young Pioneers. Their young successors still attend to the little trains that chuff (steam) or chug (diesel) for more than 3km (2 miles) through the town's parkland.

✉ Am Eliaspark 1, 03042 Cottbus ☎ 0355 756170 🕐 May–end Aug daily 10–5; Apr, Sat, Sun and holidays 10–5; Sep, Sat, Sun 10–5; service every 15–45 mins 🖐 Adult €3, child (3–14) €2 ☕

DRESDEN

GROSSER GARTEN

www.schloesser-dresden.de

The Great Garden has 34km (21 miles) of footpaths (and skating paths), a palace, a boating lake, an open-air theatre, a puppet theatre and the city zoo. One way of exploring it is to take the

Above *The picture-postcard Christmas Market held outside the Old Town Hall in Leipzig*

Parkeisenbahn (Park Railway, Apr–end Oct), which runs through the greenery past many of its features, including Volkswagen's 'transparent' factory (▷ 214).

✉ Hauptallee 5, 01219 Dresden ☎ 0351 445 6795 🕐 Daily 🚋 Tram 9, 10, 11 ☕

KULTURPALAST

www.kulturpalast-dresden.de
www.dresdnerphilharmonie.de

The Palace of Culture is the base of the renowned Dresden Philharmonic Orchestra and the venue for a range of entertainments. It comes into its own during the classical music festival and International Dresden Dixieland Jazz Festival (▷ 249).

✉ Kulturpalast am Altmarkt, 01067 Dresden ☎ 0351 486 6666 🕐 Mon–Fri 10–7, Sat 10–4 (concert weekends) 🖐 Varies 🚋 Tram 3, 7, 11 to Altmarkt

M.5 NIGHTLIFE

www.m5-nightlife.de

More sophisticated than your normal disco, M.5 has top DJs, go-go girls and boys, a fabulous range of drinks and good food.

✉ Münzgasse 5, 01067 Dresden ☎ 0351 496 5491 ⏲ Thu–Sat 9–late ✋ €7–€8, ladies free 🚋 Tram 1, 2, 4, 49 to Neumarkt; tram 3, 7, 9, 12 to Pirnaischer Platz

PFUNDS MOLKEREI

www.pfunds.de

This wonderful dairy shop is considered by local people (as well as by the *Guinness Book of Records*) to be the 'most beautiful dairy in the world'. Founded in 1880, it is embellished with more than 3,500 hand-painted tiles made by Villeroy & Boch. You can choose from a range of more than 100 different kinds of cheese, and there's a very pleasant café upstairs.

✉ Bautzner Strasse 79, 01099 Dresden ☎ 0351 808080 ⏲ Mon–Sat 10–6, Sun 10–3 🚋 Tram 11 to Pulsnitzer Strasse ☕

PUPPENTHEATERSAMMLUNG

www.skd-dresden.de

This wondrous collection contains marionettes, stage sets and all kinds of puppet theatre memorabilia. The puppets spring to life in shows on the last Sunday of every month.

✉ Jägerhof, Köpckestrasse 1, 01097 Dresden ☎ 0351 4914 4502 ⏲ Tue–Sun 10–6 ✋ Adult €3, child (6–16) €2, under 6 free, family €7

STRIEZELMARKT

www.striezel-markt.de

This is the name given to Dresden's Christmas market, held on the Altmarkt. Originally, in the 15th century, only *Stollen* (fruit bread) was allowed to be sold, but gradually other goods crept in, such as the famous wooden toys from the Ore Mountains (▷ 248).

✉ Altmarkt, Dresden ☎ 0351 160 9158 ⏲ Late Nov–24 Dec Sun–Thu 10–8, Fri, Sat 10–9 🚋 Tram 1, 2, 4, 6 to Altmarkt

GÖRLITZ

KARSTADT

www.karstadt.de

German retailers were among the pioneers of department stores, and some of those built in the early 20th century were architectural monuments in their own right. Most were destroyed in wartime, but the Karstadt *Jugendstil* (art nouveau) store escaped intact. Opened in 1913, it's a fabulous creation, with retail space opening off the central atrium beneath a stained-glass roof.

✉ An der Frauenkirche 5–7, 02826 Görlitz ☎ 03581 4600 ⏲ Mon–Fri 9.30–6.30, Sat 9–4 (sometimes 9–6)

SPIELZEUGMUSEUM

www.spielzeugmuseum-goerlitz.de

This little museum has a fascinating array of the wooden toys made in the region, some up to 150 years old, some new.

✉ Rothenburgerstrasse 7, 02826 Görlitz ☎ 03581 405870 ⏲ Wed–Fri 10–12, 2–4, Sat, Sun 2–5 ✋ Adult €2, child (4–16) €1

HALLE

TURM

www.turm-net.de

With its large student population, Halle is a young city, and the 'Tower' of the Moritzburg has had a hot reputation for decades. There is live music, plus disco, party nights and cabaret-type entertainment.

✉ Friedemann-Bach-Platz 5, 06108 Halle ☎ 0345 202 3737 ⏲ Events: Wed–Sun ✋ €2.50–€12 🚋 Tram 7 to Moritzburgring

JENA

ROSENKELLER

www.rosenkeller.org

Jena's ancient wine cellars were cleared out by voluntary student workers and turned into a lively and friendly place to meet, flirt and enjoy all sorts of cultural (lectures, discussions) and other (live bands, disco, jazz) offerings. There is a choice of drinks, and a beer garden.

✉ Johannisstrasse 13, 07743 Jena ☎ 03641 931190 ⏲ Tue–Sat from 9pm ✋ Events: €2–€8

LEIPZIG

BAHNHOFSPROMENADEN

The huge multi-level retail mall, which was cleverly inserted into Leipzig's main railway station in the 1990s, continues the city's tradition of all-weather shopping arcades.

✉ Hauptbahnhof Leipzig, Willy-Brandt-Platz 7, 04109 Leipzig ☎ 0341 141270 ⏲ Mon–Sat 6am–10pm, Sun 6–4 🍴 ☕

GEWANDHAUS

www.gewandhaus.de

Leipzig's great powerhouse is the Gewandhaus and its world-famous orchestra. The 600-plus annual events held here include orchestral concerts, organ recitals, choral and chamber music and other events

✉ Augustusplatz 8, 04109 Leipzig ☎ 0341 127 0280 ⏲ Mon–Fri 10–6 or to start of concert, Sat 10–2 and 1 hour before concert ✋ €9–€43

OPER

www.oper-leipzig.de

Leipzig has had an opera house since 1693, and its musical directors have included Gustav Mahler (1860–1911). The present building, completed in 1960, was one of the GDR's most prestigious cultural and architectural projects. It is also home to the Leipziger Ballett.

✉ Oper Leipzig, Augustusplatz 12, 04109 Leipzig ☎ 0341 126 1261 ⏲ Mon–Fri 10–8, Sat 10–4 ✋ €10–€55

THOMASKIRCHE

www.thomaskirche.org

www.thomanerchor.de

It's an unforgettable experience to listen to the choir of St. Thomas's Church. The boys perform twice a week, except during school holidays and when they are on tour.

✉ Thomaskirchhof, 04109 Leipzig ☎ 0341 2222 4200 ⏲ Motets: Fri 6, Sat 3 ✋ Free, but schedule purchase obligatory (€1)

WEIHNACHTSMARKT

The Christmas market on the square in front of Leipzig's Altes Rathaus is one of the oldest (from 1767) and largest in Germany.

✉ Markt, Leipzig ⏲ Stands: late Nov–Christmas Eve daily 10–8 🚋 Tram 9 to Thomaskirche

WERK II KULTURFABRIK

www.werk-2.de

This old gas-meter factory in Leipzig's southern suburb has been converted into a splendid 'social-cultural' venue, with a head-spinning line-up of parties, live music, performance, discos, dances, children's events and exhibitions.

Kochstrasse 132, 04277 Leipzig 0341 308 0140 7pm From €3 Tram 9, 10, 11 to Connewitzer Kreuz

ZOO LEIPZIG

www.zoo-leipzig.de

Leipzig Zoo plans to extend its range of habitats for the animals that live here. There is already the Tiger Taiga, the Valley of the Sloths and Pongoland, rocks, savannah and forest populated by gorillas, chimpanzees and orang-utans.

Pfaffendorfer Strasse 29, 04105 Leipzig 0341 593 3385 Nov–end Mar daily 9–5; Apr, Oct daily 9–6; May–end Sep daily 9–7 Adult €13, child (4–14) €9, family €34 Tram 12 to Zoo Leipzig

MEISSEN

MEISSENER PORZELLAN

www.meissen.de

Perhaps the most appropriate place to select an exquisite Meissen porcelain souvenir is in the exhibition hall of the factory itself. There's also an outlet at Burgstrasse 6.

Meissener Porzellan in der Schauhalle, Talstrasse 9, 01662 Meissen 03521 468332 May–end Oct daily 9–6; Nov–end Apr daily 9–5

NAUMBURG

NAUMBURGER WEIN UND SEKT MANUFAKTUR

www.naumburgerweinundsekt.de

In the heart of Europe's northernmost vineyards, the oldest *Sekt* (sparkling white wine) production site in Germany has been restored and reopened to visitors.

Blütengrund 35, 06618 Naumburg/ Henne 03445 202042 Mon–Fri 8–6, Sat, Sun 11–6

MODELLBAHN-WIEHE

www.mowi-world.de

The tiny town of Wiehe, 34km (21 miles) from Naumburg, is home to what is claimed to be the biggest model railway attraction in the world. There are various layouts, including a miniature version of the famous steam train that puffs its way to the top of the Brocken mountain.

Am Anger 19, 06571 Wiehe 034672 83630 Daily 10–6 (24–31 Dec daily 10–2) Adult €8.50, child (4–14) €4.50, family €20 Gastronomy Zone

POTSDAM

FILMPARK BABELSBERG

www.filmpark.de

Visit the vast studios in the suburb of Babelsberg, which were responsible for *Metropolis* (1927) and *The Blue Angel* (1930). .

August-bebelstrasse 26–53 (entrance on Grossbeerenstrasse), 14482 Potsdam 0331 721 2750 Apr–end Oct daily 10–6 Adult €19, child (4–14) €12.50, family €55 Bus 601 from Potsdam train station to 'Filmpark' Choice of eating places

SÄCHSISCHE SCHWEIZ

ARNOLDS BERGSPORTLADEN

www.bergsport-arnold.de

With around 400km (250 miles) of waymarked footpaths, Saxon Switzerland (▷ 233) is great for hikers, while there are no fewer than 700 rockfaces open to rock climbers. A good introduction to climbing opportunities (including courses) is offered by climber Bernd Arnold from his shop in Hohnstein.

Obere Strasse 2, 01848 Hohnstein 035975 81246 Mon–Fri 9–6, Sat 9–2 3-day introductory course €150

FELSENBÜHNE RATHEN

www.dresden-theater.de

This open-air theatre is reckoned to be one of the most beautiful and atmospheric of its kind. Check access details when reserving; it is on the opposite bank of the Elbe from the station and car park.

Amselgrund 17, 01824 Kurort Rathen 035024 7770 May–end Sep daily 9–7, and evening performances €6–€22 Kurort Rathen

SEIFFEN

ERZGEBIRGISCHES SPIELZEUGMUSEUM

www.spielzeugmuseum-seiffen.de

Visit the Erzgebirgische Spielzeugmuseum (Ore Mountains Toy Museum) or watch the woodcarvers at work in the village.

Hauptstrasse 73, 09548 Seiffen 037362 8239 Daily 9–5 Adult €3.50, child (4–16) €1.50, under 4 free, family €7

THÜRINGER WALD

OBERHOF

www.oberhof.de

At 800m (2,625ft), Oberhof has sports and recreational facilities and skiing. In summer, you can whizz along at nearly 80kph (50mph) on the 1,130m (1,235-yard) bobsleigh run (tel 036842 2920; www.rennsteigthermen.de).

Kurverwaltung/Oberhof-Information, Crawinkler Strasse 2, 98559 Oberhof 036842 2690 Oberhof, then by local bus to the resort

RENNSTEIG

www.rennsteigportal.de

The Rennsteig ridge walk atop the heights of the Thuringian Forest is the most famous of all Germany's many long-distance trails. Reserve a tour, which organizes your hotel and collects you at the end of each day.

Haus des Gastes, Bad Vilbeler Platz 4, 98599 Brotterode 036840 3333 Apr–end Oct Mon–Fri 9–5.30, Sat 10–2; Nov–end Mar Mon–Fri 10–4 (Thu 10–5.30) €70 for 3-day tour

THÜRINGENWALDBAHN

www.waldbahn-gotha.de

A ride aboard this rural tramway will give you a taste of the woods and mountains of the Thuringian Forest.

Thüringerwaldbahn und Strassenbahn Gotha GmbH, Waltershäuserstrasse 98, 99854 Gotha 03621 4310 Adult €1.20, child (6–14) 80¢

WEIMAR

DEUTSCHES NATIONALTHEATER WEIMAR

www.nationaltheater-weimar.de

Weimar's German National Theatre stages competent productions from the classical German repertory, such as Goethe's *Faust*. For non-German-speakers, there are operas, the occasional musical and concerts by the Weimar Staatskapelle.

Theaterplatz 2, 99423 Weimar 03643 755334 Mon 2–6, Tue–Sat 10–6 (Nov–end Mar Sat 10–1, 4–6), Sun 10–1 €10–€55

FEBRUARY/MARCH

KURT WEILL FEST

www.kurt-weill-fest.de

Among its sons Dessau numbers the composer Kurt Weill (1900–50), whose music for Bertolt Brecht's *Threepenny Opera* so tellingly evokes the decadent spirit of the Weimar era. This 10-day festival celebrates Weill's work in the context of its time with first-rate concerts, films, dances and other entertainments, including a lavish '1920s Berlin Ball'.

✉ Kartenservice Kurt Weill Dessau, Rossdeutscher & Bartel GbR, Tchaikowskistrasse 16, 04105 Leipzig ☎ 01805 564564

MARCH

TELEMANN FESTIVAL

www.telemann.org

Magdeburg celebrates composer Georg Philipp Telemann (1681–1767). A performance of one of Telemann's choral works in the 11th-century Convent of Our Lady, is a sublime experience.

✉ Magdeburger Telemann-Festtage, Telemann-Zentrum, Schönebecker Strasse 129, 39104 Magdeburg ☎ 01805 449449

MARCH/APRIL

OSTERREITEN

www.bautzen.de

The Sorbs, a minority of ethnic Slavs, celebrate Easter in a distinctive way. Villages stage an *Osterreiten* (Easter Ride), in which festively clad riders process around the parish proclaiming the tidings of the Resurrection. Bautzen has a display of the traditional craft of Easter egg painting.

✉ Sorbische Kulturinformation, Postplatz 2, 02625 Bautzen ☎ 03591 42105 🕑 Easter

APRIL

WALPURGISNACHT

www.harzer-walpurgisnacht.de

Virtually all the communities in and around the Harz Mountains make the most of the area's connection with *Walpurgisnacht*, the Witches' Sabbath, which attracts thousands of revellers. Some of the most outrageous happenings occur at the Hexentanzplatz above the resort of Thale, when the devil greets the witches who have arrived on brooms, pitchforks, goats and pigs, and weds the prettiest of them.

✉ Thale-Tourist-Information, Bahnhofstrasse 3, 06502 Thale ☎ 03947 2597 ✉ Walpurgisverein, Harz ☎ 03947 2324 🕑 Last weekend in April

MAY

INTERNATIONALES DIXIELANDFESTIVAL

www.dixieland.de

Dresden's five-day International Dixieland Jazz Festival is one of the most lavish events of its kind in the world. Far more bands wish to participate than there is room for, despite the variety of venues.

✉ Kulturpalast, Schlossstrasse 2, 01067 Dresden ☎ 0351 500 5321 🕑 Mid-May

ROLANDFEST

www.rolandfest.de

During *Rolandfest* the streets and squares of Brandenburg are given over to medieval festivities celebrating the knight Roland, guardian of civic liberties, who stemmed the advance of the Arabs into France. There are jugglers and other medieval characters, tournaments, ancient crafts on display, and a lively procession.

✉ Brandenburg Information: Hauptstrasse 51, 14776 Brandenburg ☎ 03381 19433 🕑 Third weekend in May

MAY/JUNE

MUSIKFESTSPIELE

www.musikfestspiele.com

Dresden's 17-day classical music festival stars first-rate performers and ensembles from around the world. Concerts are held in some of the city's finest interiors, and also in outdoor locations like the Grosser Garten, the grounds of Pillnitz Palace the banks of the Elbe and distant venues, like Meissen's cathedral.

✉ Ticketcentrale Kulturpalast Dresden, Schlossstrasse 2, 01067 Dresden ☎ 0351 486 6666 🕑 Late May/early June

JUNE

HÄNDEL-FESTSPIELE

www.haendel-in-halle.de

Halle's Handel Festival is a major event in the musical calendar, drawing not only fans but serious students of his music to the city where the composer was born. Ten days of works by George Frederick Handel (1685–1759) and his contemporaries are complemented by seminars and conferences.

✉ Direktion der Händel-Festspiele, Händel-Haus-Halle, Grosse Nikolaistrasse 5, 06108 Halle ☎ 0345 5009 0221 🕑 10 days in June

SANSSOUCI MUSIC FESTIVAL

www.musikfestspiele-potsdam.de

Midsummer concerts of classical music are held in some of the loveliest interiors of historic Potsdam, including Schloss Sanssouci itself, the Chinese Teahouse and the baroque theatre of the Neues Schloss. There is an extensive line-up of other events, plus guided walks and exhibitions.

✉ Wilhelm-Staab-Strasse 10/11, 14467 Potsdam ☎ 0331 288 8828 🕑 June

BERGSTADTFEST

www.freiberg.de

The silver miners of Saxony are proud folk, with traditions going back to medieval times. Freiberg's main festival is the Miners' Festival, held on the last weekend in June. The miners wear their distinctive uniforms and carry banners, making a splendid spectacle as they parade through the city streets on the Sunday on their way to worship in Freiberg's lovely cathedral.

✉ Fremdenverkehrsamt der Stadt Freiberg, Burgstrasse 1, 09599 Freiberg ☎ 03731 419 5160 🕑 Last weekend in June

EATING

PRICES AND SYMBOLS

The restaurants are listed alphabetically (excluding Le, La and Les) within each town. The prices given are the average for a two-course lunch (L) and a three-course dinner (D) for one person, without drinks. The wine price is for the least expensive bottle. All the restaurants listed accept credit cards unless otherwise stated.

For a key to the symbols, ▷ 2.

DESSAU-WÖRLITZ

KORNHAUS

www.kornhaus.de

The panoramic restaurant, in one of Dessau's key Modernist buildings with a striking glazed rotunda and view of the Elbe, was built by Bauhaus architect Carl Fieger in 1930. Brave souls should try the huge *Eisbein Franz Fürst Franz* (pork knuckle) or the less daunting *Räucherwurst* (smoked sausage).

✉ Kornhausstrasse 146, 06846 Dessau
☎ 0340 640 4141 ⏲ Daily 11.30am–11pm/midnight 🖐 L €16, D €22, Wine €14

DRESDEN

CAFÉ ZUR FRAUENKIRCHE

www.cafezurfrauenkirche-dresden.de

This Franco-German café claims that it is *the* place in Dresden to see and be seen throughout the day. It has an enviable location at the foot of the rebuilt Frauenkirche, and makes a fine place to take a break from sightseeing, whether you stop for a meal, a snack, a coffee, a beer or a cocktail.

✉ An der Frauenkirche 7, 01067 Dresden
☎ 0351 498 9836 ⏲ 8am–1am
🖐 L €16, D €30, Wine €12 🚋 Tram 1, 2, 4, 49 to Neumarkt; tram 3, 7, 9, 12 to Pirnaischer Platz

CAROUSSEL

www.buelow-residenz.de

This elegant establishment belongs to the Bülow Residenz, one of Dresden's most sophisticated small hotels. Its restaurant has gathered a wealth of commendations. A number of intimate side rooms lead off the main dining room. The tempting dishes are a satisfying blend of German and Mediterranean cuisine, prepared with an inventive use of seasonings.

The quality of the food and the place's reputation make advance reservations essential.

✉ Rähnitzgasse 19, 01097 Dresden
☎ 0351 80030 ⏲ Tue–Sat 12–2, 6.30–late 🖐 L €60, D €75, Wine €22
🚋 Tram 4, 8, 9, 49 to Neustädter Markt

Above *The terrace tables of the restaurant in the courtyard of the Brauhaus Wittenburg, which brews its own beers*

COSELPALAIS

www.restaurant-dresden.de

With a view of Dresden's great Frauenkirche, the rebuilt 1765 Coselpalais is one of the city's finest baroque mansions, its interior adorned with mirrors and tasteful furnishings. The restaurant serves meticulously prepared French and Italian dishes, as well as local cuisine such as pheasant breast wrapped in ham. Select your home-made delicacy from the pâtisserie counter of the Grand Café.

✉ An der Frauenkirche 12, 01067 Dresden
☎ 0351 496 2444 ⏲ Daily 10am–1am
🖐 L €25, D €60, Wine €16 🚋 Tram 3, 7, 9, 49 to Synagoge

ITALIENISCHES DÖRFCHEN

www.italienisches-doerfchen.de

The 'Italian Village', erected in the 18th century to house the workers who were building the nearby Hofkirche, has evolved into a complex of eating places with a spacious terrace overlooking the River Elbe. It has a Mediterranean feel, with a café-cum-pâtisserie and restaurants serving a choice of Italian dishes (in the Bellotto) or Saxon dishes (in the Kurfürstenzimmer).

✉ Theaterplatz 3, 01067 Dresden ☎ 0351 498160 🕐 Daily from 10am 🖐 L €18, D €25, Wine €14 Theaterplatz

PATTIS

www.pattis.net

The Pattis family were among the pioneers of contemporary cuisine in post-1989 eastern Germany and have received numerous commendations. The restaurant in their hotel in the Briesnitz suburb has two sections: The Gourmet is the place for a serious feast, while the Vitalis is for those seeking something lighter.

✉ Merbitzer Strasse 53, 01157 Dresden ☎ 0351 42550 🕐 6pm–midnight 🖐 Menus from €30, Wine €24 🚌 Bus 94 to Merbitzer Strasse

SÄCHSISCH-BÖHMISCHES BIERHAUS ALTMARKTKELLER

www.altmarktkeller-dresden.de

This atmospheric cellar establishment lies deep beneath the rebuilt Altmarkt. There's draught beer from Prague as well as from nearby Radeberg, both ideal for drinking with hearty dishes such as roast goose or suckling pig. For a musical accompaniment to your meal, come on Friday or Saturday evening, when Czech brass bands or jazz ensembles play live.

✉ Altmarkt 4, 01067 Dresden ☎ 0351 481 8130 🕐 11am–midnight 🖐 L €15, D €20, Wine €13 🚌 Tram 1, 2, 4, 49 to Altmarkt

VILLA MARIE

www.villa-marie.com

In an idyllic riverbank setting close to the 'Blue Wonder' bridge over the Elbe, this stylish restaurant in an Italianate villa serves creative cuisine, with fine wines to match. There is a laid-back atmosphere. It's a wonderful place to dine outside in the summer months.

✉ Fährgässchen 1, 01309 Dresden ☎ 0351 315440 🕐 11.30am–1am 🖐 L €22 D €27, Wine €12 🚌 Tram 6, 12 to Schillerplatz

EISENACH

THÜRINGER HOF

www.steigenberger.de

This is a long-established and sensitively modernized hotel with an excellent bistro-style restaurant overlooking Karlsplatz. There is a choice of Thuringian cuisine or European and Asian delicacies. In the bistro-style Leander's Küche & Wein, the show kitchen serves Mediterranean specialties.

✉ Karlsplatz 11, 99817 Eisenach ☎ 03691 280 🕐 Daily 11.30am–2am 🖐 L €15, D €35, Wine €20

DER ZWINGER

www.kaiserhof-eisenach.de

In the vaulted cellars of the old Kaiserhof hotel, this is one of the most venerable establishments in town. Great attention has been paid to the interior design, and the restaurant has a fine range of Thuringian dishes and a choice of beers from the world-renowned Paulaner brewery in Munich.

✉ Wartburgallee 2, 99817 Eisenach ☎ 03691 203343 🕐 Mon–Sat 11.30–11, Sun noon–10pm 🖐 L €14, D €22, Wine by the glass

ERFURT

ALBOTH'S

www.alboths.de

This is probably the best restaurant in Erfurt, with an original interior and a limited number of tables. The finest French- and Italian-inspired dishes, as well as regional specialties, are prepared under the supervision of a master chef. There is also a well-chosen wine list.

✉ Futterstrasse 15, 99084 Erfurt ☎ 0361 568 8207 🕐 Tue–Sat 6.30pm–midnight 🖐 Set-price menus €26–€60, Wine €28

GÖRLITZ

SCHNEIDER STUBE

www.tuchmacher.de

The intimate Tailor's Den restaurant, in the 16th-century Romantik Hotel Tuchmacher (▷ 255), has impeccable service and a carefully constructed menu listing Silesian dishes and international cuisine. Begin your meal with a slice of rabbit brawn, and continue with saddle of venison or the chef's special version of *Schlesisches Himmelreich*, accompanied by superb wines.

✉ Romantik Hotel Tuchmacher, Peterstrasse 8, 02826 Görlitz ☎ 03581 47310 🕐 Mon 6–10pm, Tue–Sun 11.30–3, 6–10 🖐 L €30, D €65, Wine €23

HALLE

WEINKONTOR

This converted brick warehouse near Moritzburg is a fine place in which to try wines from the little-known Saale-Unstrut region (and elsewhere) alongside your meal.

✉ Robert-Franz-Ring 21, 06108 Halle ☎ 0345 200 3351 🕐 Daily 6pm–late 🖐 D €15, Wine €8

LEIPZIG

APELS GARTEN

www.apels-garten.de

The sombre interior of this long-established restaurant still has something of the atmosphere of GDR days, but it's cheerful and friendly, with prompt service and an excellent choice of traditional local dishes. *Leipziger Allerlei* (young spring vegetables in sauce) features on the menu, as do game, fish, tasty pork dishes and delicious desserts. There is also a good selection of wines.

Children under 10 dine free of charge.

✉ Kolonnadenstrasse 2, 04109 Leipzig ☎ 0341 960 7777 🕐 Mon–Sat 11am–11pm, Sun 11am–3.30pm 🖐 Set-price menus from €29, Wine €16 🚌 Tram 9 to Thomaskirche

AUERBACHS KELLER

www.auerbachs-keller-leipzig.de

This basement establishment, just off Leipzig's most prestigious arcade, is one of the city's best-known sights; it was the setting for a scene in Goethe's *Faust*. The restaurant serves hearty food amid a bustling atmosphere. Try something satisfyingly Saxon, like stuffed venison roulade with red cabbage and mushrooms.

✉ Mädlerpassage, Grimmaische Strasse 2–4, 04109 Leipzig ☎ 0341 216100

Daily 11.30am–midnight L €18, D €36, Wine €14 Tram 9 to Thomaskirche; tram 4, 7, 9, 10, 11, 12, 15, 16 to Augustusplatz

BAYERISCHER BAHNHOF

www.bayerischer-bahnhof.de

Leipzig is home to a very special beer, the top-fermented Gose. The old Bavarian Station, built in 1842 and a rare survivor from the earliest days of train travel, has been converted into a pub/restaurant and a brewery. It is a fun place to sample Gose. There are also four restaurants, each with its own distinctive atmosphere, and a beer garden for warmer days.

Bayerischer Platz 1, 04103 Leipzig 0341 124 5760 Daily 11am–midnight L €10, D €16, Wine €19 Tram 16 to Bayerischer Platz

CAFÉ GRUNDMANN

www.cafe-grundmann.de

The long-established Café Günther reopened with this new name and its art deco grandeur carefully restored. Now catering for a varied clientele, the café has a select range of drinks, including fine wines, together with Italian, Spanish and French cuisine.

August-Bebel-Strasse 2, 04275 Leipzig 0341 222 8962 Mon–Fri 9am–1am, Sat 10am–1am, Sun 10–10 L €12, D €18, Wine €14 89 to Schenkendorfstrasse

CAFÉ KANDLER

An intimate establishment on two floors linked by a spiral staircase, Café Kandler has a fine view over the square in front of the city's famous Thomaskirche. It has an excellent range of teas as well as coffee. Try a *Leipziger Lerche*, a marzipan and strawberry jam confection. Alternatively, there's the equally delicious *Bachtaler* (Bach dollar), an unusual praline souvenir that is the Leipzig equivalent of Salzburg's *Mozartkugel*.

Thomaskirchhof 11, 04109 Leipzig 0341 213 2181 Tue–Sat 9am–10pm, Sun, Mon 9am–8pm Cakes and desserts from €3 Tram 9 to Thomaskirche

GOSENSCHENKE

www.gosenschenke.de

Now one of Leipzig's suburbs, Gohlis was a village in the 18th century and still has its own picturesque little castle, the Gohlisches Schlösschen. It is also home to this, the only surviving traditional pub serving the *Gose* beer. Enjoy your tipple in the rustic cellar or in the 500-seater beer garden. Food is also available.

Menckestrasse 5, 04155 Leipzig 0341 566 2360 5.30pm–1am D €16, Wine €17 Tram 12 to Fritz-Seeger-Strasse

LANDGASTHOF PODELWITZ

www.landgasthof-podelwitz.de

This friendly country inn on the northern outskirts of Leipzig was one of the first of a wave of gastronomic establishments to open after 1989. People still head out of the city to enjoy substantial meals here (such as goulash of wild boar), served in a variety of settings including a conservatory.

Wiederitzscher Strasse 10–14, 04519 Rackwitz (near Podelwitz) 034294 8240 Wed–Fri 4–11, Sat 11am–midnight, Sun 11–11 L €16, D €22, Wine €16

RATSKELLER DER STADT LEIPZIG

www.ratskeller-leipzig.de

Up to 700 diners can be served here in a variety of rooms, each of which has its own distinctive ambience. They include the *Ratskeller* itself, seating up to 200, a sophisticated wine restaurant, a 'clubroom' with leather armchairs, the rustic *Alte Wache* and others. At the entrance, look for the sculpture of the taxpayer being fleeced by a councillor.

Lotterstrasse 1, 04109 Leipzig 0341 123 4567 Mon–Sat 11–11, Sun 11–3.30 L €22, D €28, Wine €16 Tram 2, 8, 9 to Neues Rathaus

STADTPFEIFFER

www.stadtpfeiffer.de

Popular among concert-goers and with a deservedly high reputation is the Stadtpfeiffer restaurant, within the walls of the city's world-renowned Gewandhaus concert hall (▷ 225).

Augustusplatz 8, 04109 Leipzig 0341 217 8920 Tue–Sat 6pm–midnight Set menu from €88 per person, Wine €22 Tram 4, 7, 8, 10, 11, 12, 15, 16 to Augustusplatz

ZUM ARABISCHEN COFFE BAUM

www.coffe-baum.de

This is one of the most venerable of Leipzig's coffee houses, beautifully restored and covering several floors, with a pair of restaurants as well. In addition, there is a fascinating coffee museum.

Kleine Fleischergasse 4, 04109 Leipzig 0341 961 0061 Cafés: 10–6. Restaurants: 10am–midnight Set-price menus from €17 Tram 9 to Thomaskirche

MEISSEN

VINCENZ RICHTER

www.vincenz-richter.de

This 16th-century timber-framed building is one of the sights of old Meissen and has been a refined wine tavern since 1873. Wines come from the owners' vineyards, while the menu includes sophisticated versions of traditional Saxon dishes such as *Sauerbraten* of wild boar, in which the meat is braised. Reservations are advisable.

An der Frauenkirche 12, 01662 Meissen 03521 453285 Tue–Sun 12–12 L €28, D €34, Wine €14

MORITZBURG

RESTAURANT LAUBENHÖHE

www.laubenhoehe.de

Founded in 1900, this establishment has been run since 1977 by one of eastern Germany's leading catering families. Now the owners, they have completely modernized it in tasteful country-house style, and pride themselves on their friendly service and their delicious dishes, such as pigeon terrine and saddle of venison. The menu changes according to availability of ingredients. There is a good choice of open wines, available by the glass.

Köhlerstrasse 77, 01689 Weinböhla 035242 36186 Tue–Sun 12–3, 6–midnight L €16, D €24, Wine €15

NAUMBURG

WEINGUT LÜTZKENDORF

www.weingut-luetzkendorf.de

This model estate is near the little spa town of Bad Kösen, 7km (4.5 miles) upstream from Naumburg, and produces some of the finest wines of the picturesque Saale-Unstrut region. Phone in advance for a tasting beneath the vine-covered pergola on the summer terrace.

✉ Saalberge 31, 06628 Bad Kösen
☎ 034463 61000 🕒 Visits by appointment only 🖐 Wine-tasting (eight wines) with bread and cheese €13, cold meal (small side orders only) €6.50

POTSDAM

KRONGUT BORNSTEDT

www.krongut-bornstedt.de

Within easy walking distance of Schloss Sanssouci, the Crown Estate of Bornstedt is a beautifully restored Italianate complex of buildings laid out for King Friedrich Wilhelm IV in the mid-19th century. There are two cafés here, plus a brick-vaulted beer hall serving Brandenburg brews, as well as quality boutiques and craftspeople. The pleasant courtyard setting is enhanced by views of a lake.

✉ Ribbeckstrasse 6–7, 14469 Potsdam
☎ 0331 550650 🕒 Daily from 10am
🖐 Two-course meal €15, glass of wine (beer hall) €3.50 🚋 Tram 92 to Kirschallee terminus

MAISON CHARLOTTE

www.maison-charlotte.de

Potsdam's *Holländisches Viertel* (Dutch Quarter) has a great selection of pubs, bars and restaurants, including the agreeable Maison Charlotte. It has a cheerful bistro atmosphere and friendly service. The menu lists French dishes made from good German ingredients. Reservations are essential.

✉ Mittelstrasse 20, 14467 Potsdam
☎ 0331 280 5450 🕒 Daily 12–11pm
🖐 L €28, D €39, Wine €18 🚋 Tram 90, 92, 95 to Nauener Tor

VILLA KELLERMANN

www.villa-kellermann.de

This elegant Italian restaurant enjoys a privileged setting on the banks of the Heiliger See, with superb views across to the Marble Palace. The grand villa has an illustrious past as a guest house for visitors to the Prussian court. The menu consists of superior Italian dishes.

✉ Mangerstrasse 34–36, 14467 Potsdam
☎ 0331 291572 🕒 Apr–end Sep Tue–Sun noon–10pm; Oct–end Mar Fri 4pm–10pm, Sat, Sun noon–10pm 🖐 L €28, D €35, Wine €29 🚋 Tram 93 to Mangerstrasse

QUEDLINBURG

WEINSTUBE

www.hotelambruehl.de

In a stylishly furnished and decorated listed building beneath Quedlinburg's citadel is the Wine Cellar, a sophisticated restaurant belonging to one of this lovely town's best hotels. In summer, there is outdoor dining.

✉ Romantik Hotel am Brühl, Billungstrasse 11, 06484 Quedlinburg ☎ 03946 96180
🕒 Early Jan to mid-Mar daily noon–10pm; mid-Mar to early Jan Wed–Sat noon–10pm
🖐 L€30, D €38, Wine €15

SPREEWALD

ZUM GRÜNEN STRAND DER SPREE

www.spreewaldbrauerei.de

This country inn in the village of Schlepzig has won a reputation for fish, game and other dishes served in a refined ambience. It has its own brewery, which offers a tasting tour at a very reasonable price, and there are fruit brandies to sample as well. House specials from the River Spree include Wels catfish and *zander* (pike-perch), or you could try *Omas Grützwurst* (grandma's grits sausage) with Sorbian *sauerkraut*. There's a veranda and a terrace overlooking the surrounding countryside.

✉ Dorfstrasse 53, 15910 Schlepzig
☎ 035472 6620 🕒 Daily noon–10
🖐 L €23, D €28, Wine €16

WEIMAR

ALT WEIMAR

www.alt-weimar.de

This 150-year-old building was the home of Rudolf Steiner (1861–1925), the founder of anthroposophy. In 1909. It is now an exquisite small hotel with *Jugendstil* and Bauhaus touches. There is a wine bar, plus a bistro with a cosmopolitan wine list, refined versions of Thuringian cuisine and Tuscan dishes.

✉ Prellerstrasse 2, 99423 Weimar
☎ 03643 86190 🕒 Daily 11am–late
🖐 L €40, D €48, Wine €16

CAFÉ RESIDENZ

www.residenz-cafe.de

This stylish café in the middle of town is more than 160 years old. Come here for excellent breakfasts, snacks, cakes or full meals, which you can have with a choice from the full range of alcoholic and non-alcoholic drinks.

✉ Grüner Markt 4, 99423 Weimar
☎ 03643 59408 🕒 Daily 8am–1am
🖐 L €12, D €16, Wine by the glass

ZUM ZWIEBEL

www.zum-zwiebel.de

Rustic atmosphere and furnishings are complemented by hearty meals. Typical Thuringian dishes include game and poultry with dumplings to mop up the rich gravy, plus mouthwatering sausages and home-made apple strudel. The *Grillplatte*, comprising sausages, pork and turkey, and served with woodland mushrooms and roast potatoes, is a real challenge. Beer is served from the barrel and the wines come from all over.

✉ Teichgasse 6, 99423 Weimar ☎ 03643 502375 🕒 Mon–Fri 11.30am–1am, Sat, Sun 11am–1am 🖐 L €15, D €19, Wine €22

WITTENBERG

BRAUHAUS WITTENBERG

www.brauhaus-wittenberg.de

This atmospheric 16th-century brewery is built around a courtyard. The central feature of its main restaurant is the brewery itself. Satisfy your hunger with typical Germanic dishes such as *Grillhaxe* (grilled leg of pork or lamb) or home-smoked eel and trout.

✉ Markt 6, 06886 Lutherstadt Wittenberg
☎ 03491 433130 🕒 Daily 6am–11pm
🖐 Set-price menu from €16

Above *The Travel Charme Hotel Gothisches Haus in Harz-Wernigerode*

PRICES AND SYMBOLS

The prices are the lowest and highest for a double room for one night including breakfast, unless otherwise stated. All the hotels listed accept credit cards unless otherwise stated. Note that rates can vary widely throughout the year.

For a key to the symbols, ▷ 2.

BAUTZEN

GOLDENER ADLER

www.goldeneradler.de

With its flower-bedecked façade and steep dormer-pierced roof, this four-star hotel in a mansion dating from 1540 has all the character you'd expect. But while the granite vaults of the wine cellar evoke the past, the bedrooms are fully up to date. Saxon and international dishes are served in the restaurant.

✉ Hauptmarkt 4, 02625 Bautzen
☎ 035 914 8660 €99–€125 30

SPREE-HOTEL

www.spreehotel.de

This convenient, modern, four-star hotel enjoys a quiet location on the banks of a reservoir. It is only a few minutes' drive from town, and has pleasant, functional rooms, a restaurant with regional cuisine and a café-bar.

✉ An den Steinbrüchen 9, 02625 Bautzen
☎ 03591 21300 €72–€86 80

COLDITZ

WALD CAMPING

www.campingplatz-colditz.de

Colditz is well situated for exploring central Saxony. The campsite has an enviable location on the edge of the castle's former game park, near the town's heated outdoor swimming pool. There are plenty of facilities, plus chalets and caravans for rent.

✉ Am Waldbad 5, 04680 Colditz
☎ 034381 43122 Camping from €5 per night; caravan/mobile home from €14; bungalow €30 P

DESSAU-WÖRLITZ

LANDHAUS WÖRLITZER HOF

www.woerlitzer-hof.de

Absorb the delights of the Dessau-Wörlitz region by basing yourself at this attractive country hotel, right by the Schlossgarten and Schloss Wörlitz. The hotel's restaurant serves local dishes and stages themed evenings.

✉ Markt 96, 06786 Wörlitz ☎ 034905 4110 €97–€132 46 P

DRESDEN

IBIS

www.ibishotel.com

The three high-rises on Prager Strasse shopping esplanade (the Bastei, the Lilienstein and the Königstein) may look bleak, but they offer convenience and comfort. The location is central, but quiet. The Bastei is slightly more expensive.

✉ Prager Strasse 9, 01069 Dresden
☎ 0351 4856 6445 €65–€85 306
P Unsupervised Tram 3, 7, 8, 9, 10, 11 to Hauptbahnhof Nord

MARTHA HOSPIZ

www.martha-hospiz.de

This mid-range hotel belongs to the reliable Christian Hoteliers chain. The dignified 100-year-old building occupies a quiet position in Dresden's attractive Neustadt. The 15-minute walk to the heart of the city on the far bank of the Elbe is an experience in itself. Saxon dishes are served in the rustic Zum Kartoffelkeller restaurant.

✉ Nieritzstrasse 11, 01097 Dresden
☎ 0351 81760 €102–€118 50
P Tram 4, 8, 49 to Palaisplatz

PULLMAN DRESDEN NEWA
www.accorhotels.com
This skyscraper overlooking the Prager Strasse shopping mall dates from GDR times, but its interior has been transformed with generous public areas and tasteful bedrooms.
Prager Strasse 2c, 01069 Dresden
0351 48140 €135–€175
319 (169 non-smoking)
Garage Tram 3, 7, 8, 9, 10, 11 to Hauptbahnhof Nord

SCHLOSS ECKBERG
www.schloss-eckberg.de
Completed in 1861 on the heights overlooking the Elbe, this wonderful neo-Gothic stronghold has been transformed into one of Dresden's outstanding hotels. The castle has few rooms, but these are the ones to choose—for their clever combination of modern and antique furnishings, and for the river view. The extension has rooms with views over the castle's parkland. There is an excellent restaurant and a cellar with Saxon wines.
Bautzner Strasse 134, 01099 Dresden 0351 80990 Castle: €235–€295; Kavaliershaus (extension): €143–€190 Castle: 17; Kavaliershaus: 67 Tram 11 to Schloss Albrechtsberg

TASCHENBERGPALAIS KEMPINSKI DRESDEN
www.kempinski-dresden.de
This superb palace, built for Augustus the Strong (1670–1733), has been rebuilt with exquisite taste and converted into a luxurious hotel.
Taschenberg 3, 01067 Dresden
0351 49120 From €295 214
Indoor Sauna, solarium, massage Tram 1, 2, 4, 6, 8, 11, 12, 49 to Postplatz

EISENACH

BERGHOTEL
www.berghotel-eisenach.de
The comfortable, small and friendly Berghotel has a fabulous position high above the town, just below the Burschenschaftsdenkmal (Fraternities Memorial). From here you have views over the foothills of the Thuringian Forest to Wartburg castle.
An der Göpelskuppe 1, 99817 Eisenach
03691 22660 €88–€109 16

HOTEL AUF DER WARTBURG
www.wartburghotel.de
This luxury hotel nestles just below the walls of Wartburg castle, with some stunning views to the Thuringian Forest. Rooms are snug and the service is refined. The restaurant serves Thuringian fare.
99817 Eisenach 03691 7970
€315–€340 35

ERFURT

HOTEL UND GASTHOF NIKOLAI
www.hotel-nikolai-erfurt.com
Attractively decorated and stylish, this historic building is in the heart of old Erfurt, not far from the famous Krämerbrücke. It has a romantic atmosphere, a brasserie, a small restaurant and an outdoor terrace.
Augustinerstrasse 30, 99084 Erfurt
0361 598170 €85–€95 17

FREIBERG

ALEKTO
www.alekto.de
In this old mining and industrial town, why not stay in a former factory? The Alekto once turned out cutlery, but the art nouveau building close to the train station is now a hotel with plenty of facilities. There is a bar and a restaurant with meals at very reasonable prices.
Am Bahnhof 3, 09599 Freiberg
03731 7940 €85–€97 52
Free

GÖRLITZ

ROMANTIK HOTEL TUCHMACHER
www.tuchmacher.de
One of the Romantik group of individually run hotels, the Tuchmacher occupies one of the finest buildings in Görlitz, a Renaissance town mansion built in 1528 for the then mayor, the immensely rich Franz Schneider. Carefully restored, the building has period details, including late-Gothic vaulting otherwise found only in Prague. The restaurant serves refined versions of the cuisine of Silesia.
Peterstrasse 8, 02826 Görlitz
03581 47310 €147–€169 42
Sauna

GOTHA

HOTEL AM SCHLOSSPARK
www.hotel-am-schlosspark.de
Just above the old town and with direct access to spacious parkland, this four-star hotel has friendly service and comfortable, contemporary rooms. There is a choice of two restaurants, and the use of a Roman-style spa is included in the price of the room.
Lindenauallee 20, 99867 Gotha
03621 4420 €85–€125 95
Sauna

HALLE

MARTHA HAUS
www.stiftung-marthahaus.de
A member of the reliable VCH (Christian Hotels Association) chain, the Martha Haus is a carefully modernized baroque mansion in a quiet side street in the middle of the city.
Adam-Kuckhoff-Strasse 5–8, 06108 Halle 0345 51080 €65–€85
24

HARZ-ILSENBURG

LANDHAUS ZU DEN ROTHEN FORELLEN
www.rotheforelle.de
Ilsenburg is one of the smaller resorts of the Harz, and this country hotel in one of its most attractive buildings offers a luxurious, peaceful stay on the edge of the mountains. Rooms either face onto the mountains or overlook a little lake. Every comfort is provided, and after hiking in the hills you will be glad to relax in the sauna or in the lavish pool area. The hotel also has a gourmet restaurant and its own pâtisserie.
Marktplatz 2, 38871 Ilsenburg
039452 9393 From €231
52 Indoor Sauna

HARZ-WERNIGERODE

TRAVEL CHARME HOTEL GOTHISCHES HAUS

www.travelcharme.com

To stay here is like stepping back in time: The venerable 15th-century timber-framed building overlooks the main square in the most attractive town in the Harz Mountains, right next door to one of Germany's most picturesque medieval town halls. The rooms have been beautifully restored and furnished. There is a fully equipped spa with a range of beauty treatments, plus a piano bar, wine cellar and restaurant.

Marktplatz 2, 38855 Wernigerode 03943 6750 €59–€149 116 Spa

JENA

SCHWARZER BÄR

www.schwarzer-baer-jena.de

The names of those who have lodged within these walls range from Protestant reformer Martin Luther (1483–1546) and dramatist Johann Wolfgang von Goethe (1749–1832) to the celebrities and politicians of today. The hotel's restaurant prides itself on its cuisine and its range of wines (including rarities from around Jena) and beers.

Lutherplatz 2, 07743 Jena 03641 4060 €50–€95 66

LEIPZIG

BEST WESTERN PREMIER VICTOR'S RESIDENZ-HOTEL

www.victors-leipzig.bestwestern.de

Close to the middle of the city, this comprehensively renovated four-star establishment offers its guests every comfort, plus a choice of places to eat—including a traditional beer garden.

Georgiring 13, 04103 Leipzig 0341 68660 €110–€190 101 (75 non-smoking) Hauptbahnhof

FÜRSTENHOF LEIPZIG

www.starwoodhotels.com

An extremely luxurious, central hotel that occupies an 18th-century house. The Serpentine Salon is a princely setting for formal dining. Other special features of the hotel include a lavish, Mediterranean-style pool and a wine cellar.

Tröndlinring 8, 04105 Leipzig 0341 1400 €150–€305 92 Indoor Sauna Hauptbahnhof

HOTEL AM RATSHOLZ

www.hotel-am-ratsholz.de

This attractive hotel is on a direct tram route to the downtown area. Fresh, light furnishings contribute to the welcoming atmosphere. There is a choice of rooms, or stay in one of the apartments, which have kitchenettes. There is also a family-style restaurant.

Anton-Zickmantel-Strasse 44, 04249 Leipzig 0341 494 4500 €79–€120, excluding breakfast 113 Sauna Tram 3, 13 to Kunzestrasse or Huttenstrasse

LINDNER

www.lindner.de

This four-star establishment is on the edge of the Auenwald. Tranquillity is one of the hotel's draws, its distinctive architecture another. It is particularly popular with businesspeople, and has a choice of rooms and suites, or apartments for longer stays. The Am Wasserschloss serves Mediterranean-style meals.

Hans-Driesch-Strasse 27, 04179 Leipzig 0341 44780 €84–€129 200 S-Bahn to Leutzsch (10-minute walk)

MAGDEBURG

HERRENKRUG PARKHOTEL AN DER ELBE

www.herrenkrug.de

The English-style park here is a lovely setting for this complex, which features Jugendstil interiors as well as modern extensions. Most of the spacious, comfortable bedrooms overlook the park. Sample fine cuisine in the airy 19th-century dining room, in the winter garden or in the beer garden.

Herrenkrug 3, 39114 Magdeburg 0391 85080 €98–€158, excluding breakfast 147 Indoor Golf, sauna, solarium Tram 6

RESIDENZ JOOP

www.residenzjoop.de

In a quiet, leafy district, this 100-year-old villa within walking distance of downtown has been turned into a stylish hotel by the descendants of its original resident, Magdeburg's Swedish consul. It is regularly voted among Germany's top 10 in this class of hotel.

Jean-Burger-Strasse 16, 39112 Magdeburg 0391 62620 €96–€158 25 Am Fuchsberg/Erich-Wenert-Strasse Tram 3, 9

MEISSEN

WELCOME PARKHOTEL MEISSEN

www.welcome-hotel-meissen.de

This opulent villa on the Elbe was restored in 1993 to create a luxury hotel. You'll find peace and quiet among the trees, yet it is only a short walk from the town. The hotel operates a shuttle service to Dresden airport.

Hafenstrasse 27–31, 01662 Meissen 03521 72250 €120–€140, excluding breakfast 97 P

POTSDAM

RELEXA SCHLOSSHOTEL CECILIENHOF

www.relexa-hotels.de

An English-style manor in a wonderful lakeside setting, where the victorious 'Big Four' Allied powers met in 1945 to determine the shape of post-war Europe. The reason this exclusive hotel is not a five-star establishment is that its status as a listed (protected) building does not allow air conditioning.

Neuer Garten, 14469 Potsdam 0331 37050 €150–€175 41 Wellness P Cecilienhof

STEIGENBERGER HOTEL SANSSOUCI

www.steigenberger.com

This hotel is just outside one of the gates to Park Sanssouci. Facilities include bicycle rental and a complimentary pass for transportation in Potsdam and Berlin.

Allee nach Sanssouci 1, 14471 Potsdam 0331 90910 €130–€175 135 Sauna, cosmetic studio P €15 Tram 96/X98; bus 606/605

SÄCHSISCHE SCHWEIZ

BERGHOF LICHTENHAIN

www.berghof.li

A modest timber-built hotel in an area of sandstone rock formations and forest, popular with hikers and climbers. The main building has a modern annexe. There is a terrace with fine views, plus a restaurant.

Am Anger 3, 01855 Lichtenhain 035971 56512 €44–€68 27 Mountain bike rental and tours P

FORSTHAUS

www.weka-hotels.de

The valley of the River Kirnitzsch is one of the prettiest parts of Saxon Switzerland, and the restored timber-framed hotel has won awards for enhancing the surroundings.

Kirnitzschtalstrasse 5, 01814 Bad Schandau 035022 5840 €66–€88 29 P

ROMANTIK HOTEL DEUTSCHES HAUS

www.romantikhotel-pirna.de

A fine old gabled Renaissance building in a quiet, central position. The hotel has a barrel-vaulted cellar, an elegant first-floor salon and individually styled rooms.

Niedere Burgstrasse 1, 01796 Pirna 03501 46880 €92–€105 40 P

QUEDLINBURG

ROMANTIK HOTEL THEOPHANO

www.hoteltheophano.de

A lovely half-timbered, steep-roofed hotel with comfortable rooms, some with four-poster beds. Breakfast is served in the café opening onto the square; the cellar restaurant serves fine food.

Markt 13–14, 06484 Quedlinburg 03946 96300 €99–€140 22 P

SPREEWALD

SCHLOSS LÜBBENAU

www.schloss-luebbenau.de

This neoclassical mansion sits in an English-style park and has comfortable, tastefully furnished rooms and apartments.

Schlossbezirk 6, 03222 Lübbenau 03542 8730 €112–€162 46 Wellness P

SPREEWALDHOTEL LEIPE

www.spreewaldhotel.de

Get away from the crowds by staying at this small, modernized hotel. The restaurant serves local dishes. Boats and bicycles are available for guests.

Leiper Dorfstrasse 29, 03222 Lübbenau/Leipe 03542 2234 €50–€95 21 P

WEIMAR

DORINT AM GOETHEPARK

www.dorint.com

This five-star, central hotel combines contemporary comfort in the rooms with classic features.

Beethovenplatz 1–2, 99423 Weimar 03643 8720 €115–€264, excluding breakfast 143 Spa P

ELEPHANT

www.starwoodhotels.com

On Weimar's market place, this hotel has welcomed guests for more than 300 years. The opulent bedrooms and public spaces have art nouveau furnishings and contemporary art. Dine in the Michelin-starred Anna Amalia restaurant or the cellar restaurant.

Markt 19, 99423 Weimar 03643 8020 €129–€235 99 P

ROMANTIK HOTEL DOROTHEENHOF

www.dorotheenhof.com

This restored manor house has an idyllic setting among trees and there's a summer terrace and a herb garden.

Dorotheenhof 1, 99247 Weimar 03643 4590 €95–€165 60 P

WITTENBERG

LUTHER HOTEL WITTENBERG

www.luther-hotel-wittenberg.de

This Christian-run hotel in the heart of the town was built in the 1990s. The rooms are decent but plain, with modern furnishings. A still room affords space for prayer, meditation or just quiet relaxation, and a sauna and solarium back up this restful ethos.

Neustrasse 7–10, 06886 Wittenberg 03491 4580 €96–€122 165 (80 non-smoking) P €7 per day

Opposite *The entrance to the Welcome Parkhotel Meissen, on the banks of the River Elbe*

SIGHTS 260
WALKS 286
WHAT TO DO 290
EATING 294
STAYING 298

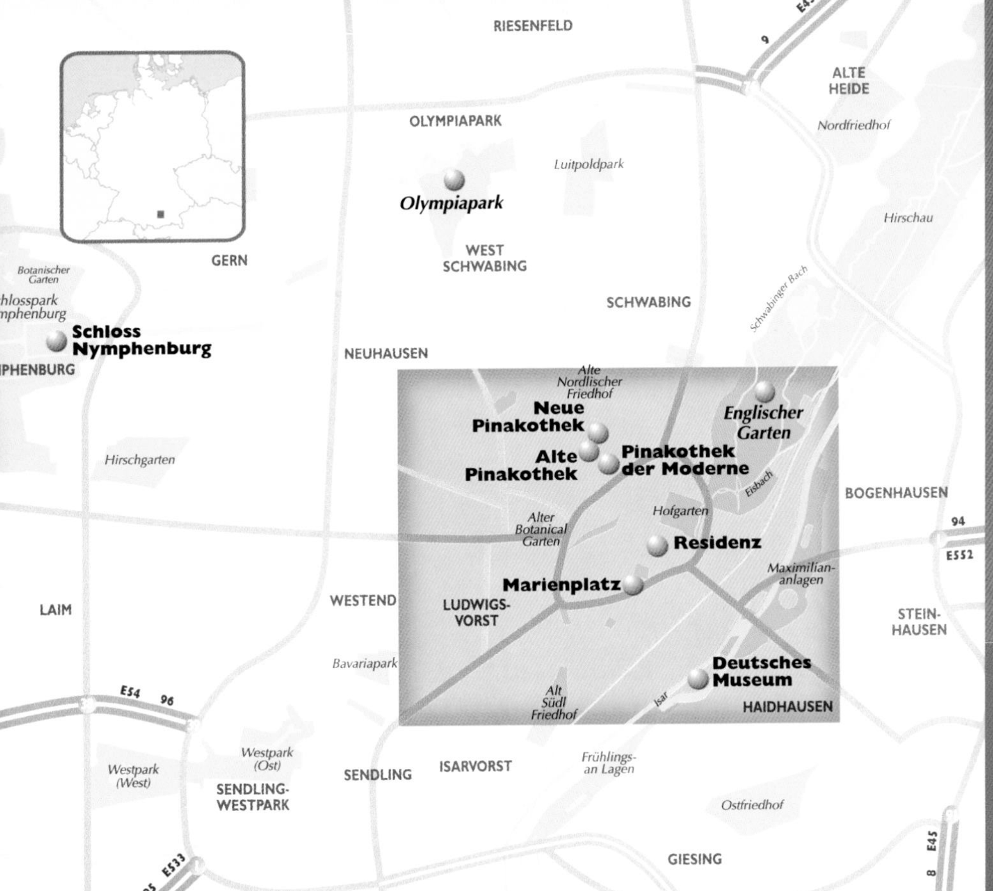

MUNICH

Historic München, Germany's 'beer capital', is extremely proud to be Bavarian. And while the traditional beer-and-Lederhosen image still exists, it doesn't reflect the city's superb art galleries, Italian-designer-clad citizens, and fashionable bars and restaurants. The best way to see Munich is on foot—many of the main attractions are within an area bounded by Odeonsplatz to the north, and the old city gates of Isartor to the east, Sendlingertor to the south and Karlstor to the west.

The city's coat of arms depicts a monk, a reminder that in the 10th century monks established a settlement on the banks of the River Isar, which became known as Munichen. In 1158, Duke of Saxony Heinrich der Löwe (Henry the Lion) took control. A century later, Munich became the main residence of the Wittelsbach dynasty. The Mariensäule was erected in Marienplatz to give thanks to God because the Swedes, who occupied Munich from 1618 until 1648, did not destroy the city. In the first half of the 19th century, Ludwig I commissioned the construction of many classical-style buildings, such as those in Königsplatz, leading to Munich's alternative name of Athens-on-the-Isar. Many of these have been turned into museums, such as the Glyptothek, and after suffering heavy bomb damage during World War II have been rebuilt.

Munich's heart is Marienplatz, where crowds gather to see the famous Glockenspiel come to life. For the best views, head out to Olympiapark and take the elevator up the Olympiaturm where, on a clear day, you can see as far as the Alps. The city has many beautiful (and free) places to walk and jog. Most locals go to stretch their legs in the Englischer Garten, but you are even allowed to jog through magnificent Schloss Nymphenburg's ornamental gardens. The famous Oktoberfest, a beer-drinker's idea of paradise, is held in late September in the Theresienwiese, an open green area.

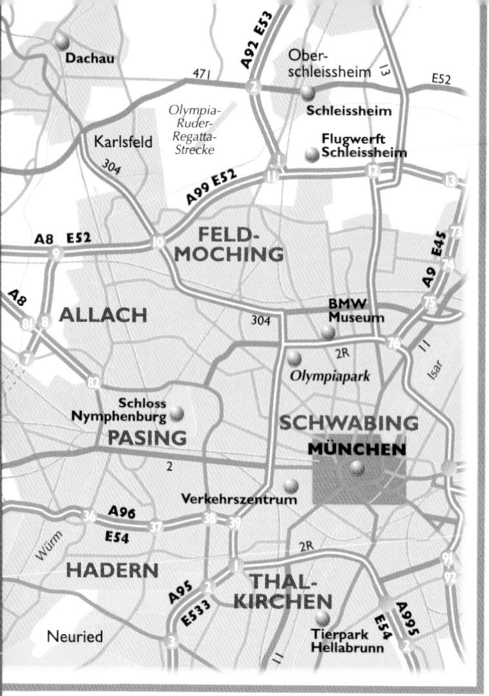
Dachau
Ober-
schleissheim
Schleissheim
Flugwerft
Schleissheim
Olympia-
Ruder-
Regatta-
Strecke
Karlsfeld
A92 E53
A99 E52
A8 E52
A8
A9 E45
E52
FELD-
MOCHING
ALLACH
BMW
Museum
Olympiapark
Isar
Schloss
Nymphenburg
PASING
SCHWABING
MÜNCHEN
Verkehrszentrum
A96
E54
Würm
HADERN
THAL-
KIRCHEN
A95
E533
A995
E54
Tierpark
Hellabrunn
Neuried

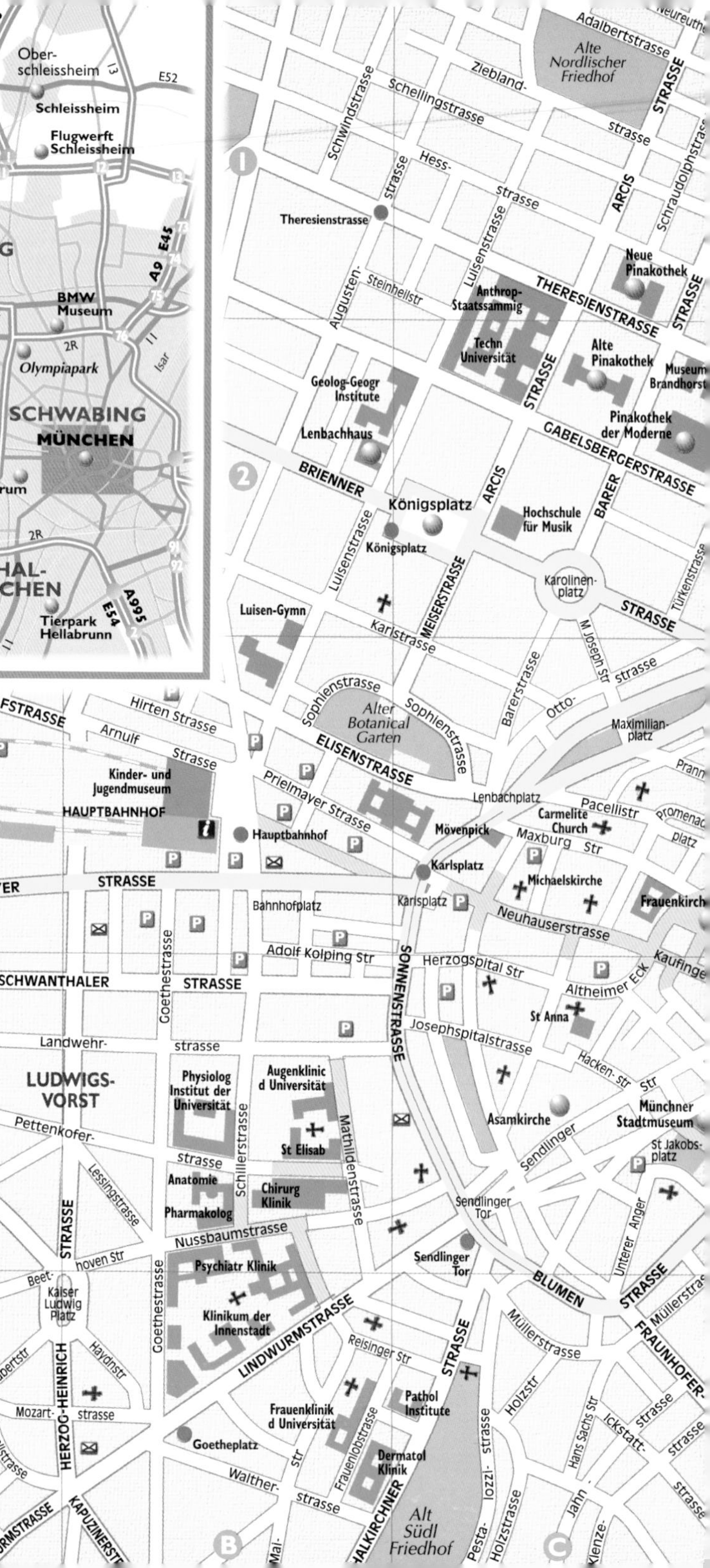
Adalbertstrasse
Alte
Nordlischer
Friedhof
Zieblandstrasse
Schellingstrasse
Schwindstrasse
Hess-strasse
Theresienstrasse
Luisenstrasse
ARCIS STRASSE
Schraudolphstrasse
Neue
Pinakothek
Augusten-strasse
Steinheilstr
Anthrop-
Staatssammig
THERESIENSTRASSE
Techn
Universität
Alte
Pinakothek
Museum
Brandhorst
Geolog-Geogr
Institute
Pinakothek
der Moderne
Lenbachhaus
GABELSBERGERSTRASSE
BRIENNER STRASSE
Königsplatz
Hochschule
für Musik
BARER STRASSE
Karolinen-
platz
MEISERSTRASSE
Luisen-Gymn
Karlstrasse
M Joseph Str
Türkenstrasse
Ottostrasse
Barerstrasse
Sophienstrasse
Alter
Botanical
Garten
Maximilian-
platz
ARNULFSTRASSE
Hirten Strasse
HACKERBRÜCKE
Arnulf Strasse
ELISENSTRASSE
Prielmayer Strasse
Kinder- und
Jugendmuseum
HAUPTBAHNHOF
Hauptbahnhof
Lenbachplatz
Pacellistr
Promenadeplatz
Carmelite
Church
Mövenpick
Maxburg Str
Karlsplatz
Michaelskirche
Frauenkirche
GRASSERSTR
Ammersee
BAYER STRASSE
Bahnhofplatz
Neuhauserstrasse
Kaufingerstrasse
GREITSTRMART
Theresienhöhe
Adolf Kolping Str
SONNENSTRASSE
Herzogspital Str
SCHWANTHALER STRASSE
Goethestrasse
Altheimer Eck
St Anna
Landwehrstrasse
Josephspitalstrasse
Hacken-str
BAVARIA-RING
LUDWIGS-
VORST
Physiolog
Institut der
Universität
Augenklinic
d Universität
Schillerstrasse
Mathildenstrasse
St Elisab
Asamkirche
Münchner
Stadtmuseum
Theresienwiese
Pettenkofer-strasse
Lessingstrasse
Anatomie
Pharmakolog
Chirurg
Klinik
Sendlinger Str
St Jakobs-
platz
Sendlinger
Tor
Unterer Anger
Theresienwiese
Bavariaring
HERZOG-HEINRICH STRASSE
Beethoven Str
Kaiser
Ludwig
Platz
Nussbaumstrasse
Psychiatr Klinik
Klinikum der
Innenstadt
BLUMEN STRASSE
Müllerstrasse
LINDWURMSTRASSE
Reisinger Str
FRAUNHOFER-STRASSE
Haydnstr
Schubertstr
Matthius-Pschorr-Strasse
Mozartstrasse
Frauenklinik
d Universität
Pathol
Institute
Holzstr
Hans Sachs Str
Ickstattstrasse
Kobellstrasse
Goetheplatz
Frauenlobstrasse
Dermatol
Klinik
Pestalozzistrasse
Walther-strasse
Alt
Südl
Friedhof
Holzstrasse
Jahnstrasse
Klenzestrasse
LINDWURMSTRASSE
KAPUZINERSTRASSE
Bavariaring
THALKIRCHNER STRASSE
A
B
C
1
2
3
4
5

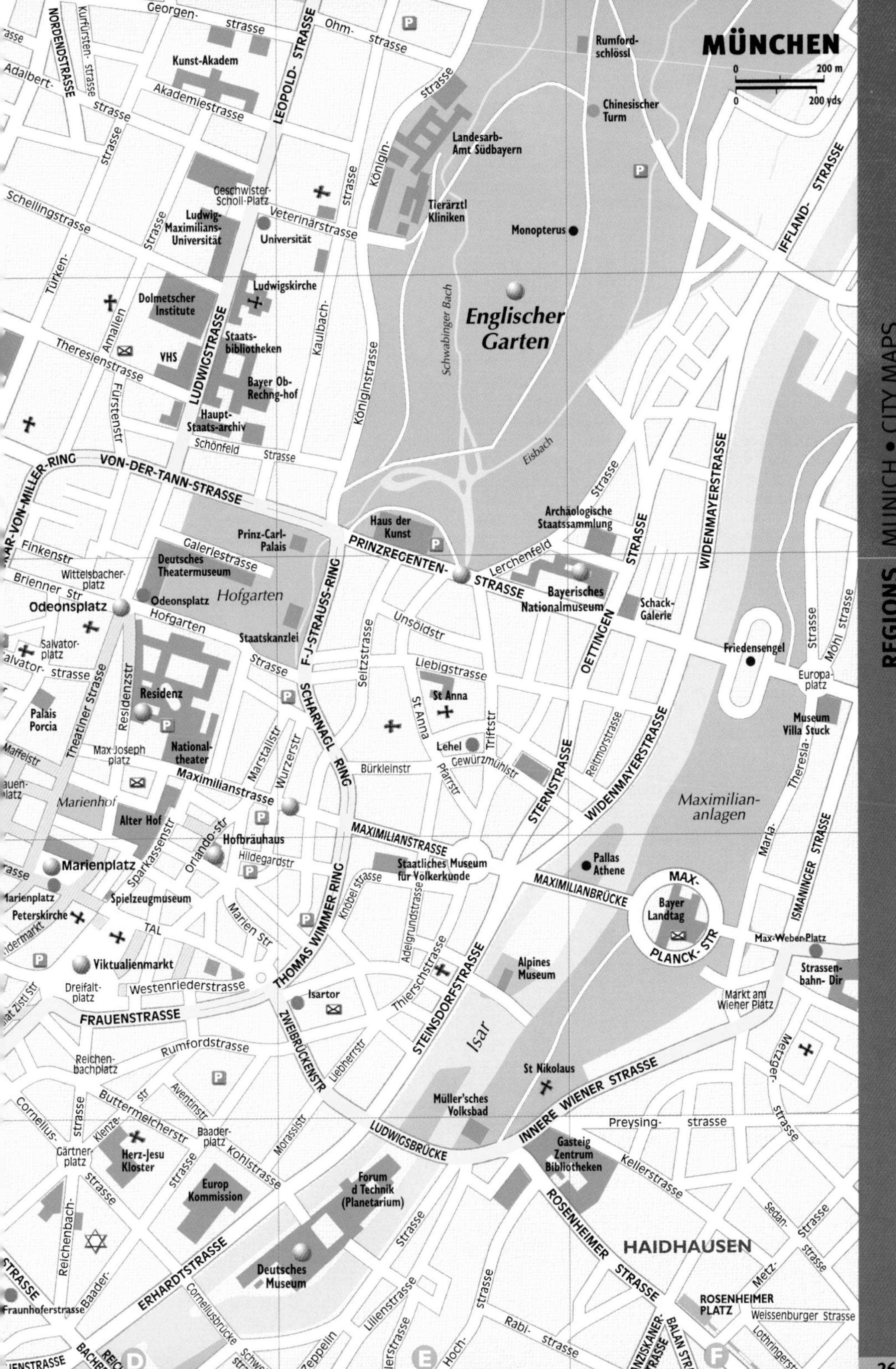
MÜNCHEN
0 200 m
0 200 yds
Georgen-strasse
Ohm-strasse
Kurfürsten-strasse
NORDENDSTRASSE
Adalbert-strasse
Kunst-Akadem
Akademiestrasse
LEOPOLD-STRASSE
Königin-strasse
Rumford-schlössl
Chinesischer Turm
Landesarb-Amt Südbayern
Schellingstrasse
Geschwister-Scholl-Platz
Ludwig-Maximilians-Universität
Universität
Veterinärstrasse
Tierärztl Kliniken
Monopterus
IFFLAND-STRASSE
Türken-strasse
Ludwigskirche
Dolmetscher Institute
LUDWIGSTRASSE
Staats-bibliotheken
Kaulbach-strasse
Schwabinger Bach
Englischer Garten
Theresienstrasse
Amalien-strasse
VHS
Bayer Ob-Rechng-hof
Königinstrasse
Fürstenstr
Haupt-Staats-archiv
Schönfeld Strasse
Eisbach
VON-DER-TANN-STRASSE
BARER-VON-MILLER-RING
Haus der Kunst
Archäologische Staatssammlung
Prinz-Carl-Palais
Galeriestrasse
Deutsches Theatermuseum
Finkenstr
Wittelsbacher-platz
Brienner Str
Odeonsplatz
Hofgarten
PRINZREGENTEN-STRASSE
Lerchenfeld-strasse
Bayerisches Nationalmuseum
STRASSE
WIDENMAYERSTRASSE
Schack-Galerie
OETTINGEN
Hofgarten Strasse
Staatskanzlei
F-J-STRAUSS-RING
Unsöldstr
Seitzstrasse
Liebigstrasse
Friedensengel
Möhl strasse
Europa-platz
Salvator-platz
Salvator-strasse
Theatiner Strasse
Residenzstr
Residenz
Palais Porcia
SCHARNAGL RING
St Anna
St Anna
Triftstr
Reitmorstrasse
Museum Villa Stuck
Maffeistr
Max-Joseph platz
National-theater
Marstallstr
Wurzerstr
Bürkleinstr
Pfarrstr
Gewürzmühlstr
Lehel
STERNSTRASSE
Theresia-
Maximilianstrasse
Marienhof
Alter Hof
Maximilian-anlagen
Hofbräuhaus
Orlando-str
Sparkassenstr
Hildegardstr
MAXIMILIANSTRASSE
Staatliches Museum für Völkerkunde
Pallas Athene
Maria-
ISMANINGER STRASSE
Marienplatz
Marienplatz
Spielzeugmuseum
Knöbelstrasse
Adelgrundstrasse
MAXIMILIANBRÜCKE
MAX-PLANCK-STR
Bayer Landtag
Peterskirche
TAL
Marien Str
THOMAS WIMMER RING
Max-Weber-Platz
Viktualienmarkt
Thierschstrasse
STEINSDORFSTRASSE
Alpines Museum
Strassen-bahn-Dir
Dreifalt-platz
Westenriederstrasse
Isartor
Markt am Wiener Platz
FRAUENSTRASSE
ZWEIBRÜCKENSTR
Liebherrstr
Isar
Metzger-strasse
Reichen-bachplatz
Rumfordstrasse
St Nikolaus
INNERE WIENER STRASSE
Cornelius-strasse
Buttermelcherstr
Aventinstr
Müller'sches Volksbad
Preysing-strasse
Klenze-str
Gärtner-platz
Herz-Jesu Kloster
Baader-platz
Kohlstrasse
Morassistr
LUDWIGSBRÜCKE
Gasteig Zentrum Bibliotheken
Kellerstrasse
Europ Kommission
Forum d Technik (Planetarium)
ROSENHEIMER STRASSE
Sedan-strasse
Reichenbach-strasse
HAIDHAUSEN
ERHARDTSTRASSE
Deutsches Museum
Baader-strasse
Corneliusbrücke
Lilienstrasse
Metz-strasse
STRASSE
Fraunhoferstrasse
ROSENHEIMER PLATZ
Weissenburger Strasse
Rabi-strasse
Hoch-strasse
Zeppelin
Lothringerstr
FRANZISKANER-STRASSE
BALAN STR
D
E
F
REGIONS MUNICH • CITY MAPS

MUNICH STREET INDEX

Street	Page	Grid
Adalbertstrasse	260	C1
Adelgrundstrasse	261	E4
Adolf Kolping Strasse	260	B3
Akademiestrasse	261	D1
Altheimer Eck	260	C4
Amalien Strasse	261	D2
Arcis Strasse	260	C2
Arnulf Strasse	260	A3
Auenstrasse	261	D5
Augustenstrasse	260	B2
Aventinstrasse	261	D4
Baaderplatz	261	D5
Baaderstrasse	261	D5
Bahnhofplatz	260	B3
Balan Strasse	261	F5
Barer Strasse	260	C2
Barerstrasse	260	C3
Bavariaring	260	A4
Bayer Strasse	260	A3
Beethoven Strasse	260	A5
Blumen Strasse	260	C4
Brienner Strasse	260	B2
Bürkleinstrasse	261	E3
Buttermelcherstrasse	261	D4
Corneliusbrücke	261	D5
Corneliusstrasse	261	D4
Dreifaltplatz	261	D4
Elisenstrasse	260	B3
Erhardtstrasse	261	D5
Europaplatz	261	F3
Finkenstrasse	261	D2
F-J-Strauss-Ring	261	E3
Franziskanerstrasse	261	F5
Frauenlobstrasse	260	B5
Frauenplatz	261	D3
Frauenstrasse	261	D4
Fraunhoferstrasse	260	C5
Fürstenstrasse	261	D2
Gabelsbergerstrasse	260	C2
Galeriestrasse	261	D2
Gärtnerplatz	261	D5
Georgenstrasse	261	D1
Gewürzmühlstrasse	261	E3
Goethestrasse	260	B5
Grasserstrasse	260	A3
Greitstrmart	260	A3
Hackenstrasse	260	C4
Hackerbrücke	260	A3
Hans Sachs Strasse	260	C5
Haydnstrasse	260	B5
Herzog-Heinrich Strasse	260	B5
Herzogspital Strasse	260	C4
Hessstrasse	260	C1
Hildegardstrasse	261	D4
Hirten Strasse	260	B3
Hochstrasse	261	E5
Hofgarten Strasse	261	D3
Holzstrasse	260	C5
Ickstattstrasse	260	C5
Ifflandstrasse	261	F1
Innere Wiener Strasse	261	E5
Ismaninger Strasse	261	F4
Jahnstrasse	260	C5
Josephspitalstrasse	260	C4
Kaiser Ludwig Platz	260	A5
Kapuzinerstrasse	260	B5
Karlsplatz	260	C3
Karlstrasse	260	B2
Karolinenplatz	260	C2
Kaufingerstrasse	260	C3
Kaulbachstrasse	261	E2
Kellerstrasse	261	E5
Klenzestrasse	260	C5
Knöbel Strasse	261	E4
Kobellstrasse	260	A5
Kohlstrasse	261	D5
Königinstrasse	261	E2
Königsplatz	260	C2
Kurfüstenstrasse	261	D1
Landwehrstrasse	260	A4
Lenbachplatz	260	C3
Leopoldstrasse	261	E1
Lerchenfeld Strasse	261	E3
Lessingstrasse	260	B4
Liebherrstrasse	261	E4
Liebigstrasse	261	E3
Lilienstrasse	261	E5
Lindwurmstrasse	260	A5
Lothringerstrasse	261	F5
Ludwigsbrücke	261	E5
Ludwigstrasse	261	D2
Luisenstrasse	260	B2
Maffeistrasse	261	D3
Malstrasse	260	B5
Mariatheresiastrasse	261	F4
Marien Strasse	261	D4
Marienplatz	261	D4
Markt am Wiener Platz	261	F4
Marstallstrasse	261	D3
Mathildenstrasse	260	B4
Matthiuspschorrstrasse	260	A5
Maxburg Strasse	260	C3
Maximilianbrücke	261	E4
Maximilianplatz	260	C3
Maximilianstrasse	261	D3
Max Joseph Platz	261	D3
Maxplanckstrasse	261	F4
Meiserstrasse	260	C2
Metzgerstrasse	261	F4
Metzstrasse	261	F5
M Joseph Strasse	260	C2
Möhl Strasse	261	F3
Morassistrasse	261	D5
Mozartstrasse	260	A5
Müllerstrasse	260	C5
Neuhauserstrasse	260	C3
Neureutherstrasse	260	C1
Nordendstrasse	261	D1
Nussbaumstrasse	260	B4
Odeonsplatz	261	D3
Oettingen Strasse	261	F3
Ohmstrasse	261	E1
Orlandostrasse	261	D4
Oskar-Von-Miller-Ring	261	D3
Ottostrasse	260	C3
Pacellistrasse	260	C3
Pestaiozzistrasse	260	C5
Pettenkoferstrasse	260	A4
Pfarrstrasse	261	E3
Prälat Zistl Strasse	261	D4
Prannerstrasse	260	C3
Preysingstrasse	261	E5
Prielmayer Strasse	260	B3
Prinzregentenstrasse	261	E2
Promenadeplatz	260	C3
Prüllerstrasse	261	E5
Rabistrasse	261	E5
Reichenbachbrücke	261	D5
Reichenbachplatz	261	D4
Reichenbachstrasse	261	D5
Reisinger Strasse	260	B5
Reitmorstrasse	261	F3
Residenzstrasse	261	D3
Rindermarkt	261	D4
Rosenheimer Strasse	261	E5
Rumfordstrasse	261	D4
St Anna	261	E3
St Jakobsplatz	260	C4
Salvatorplatz	261	D3
Salvatorstrasse	261	D3
Scharnagl Ring	261	E3
Schellingstrasse	260	B1
Schillerstrasse	260	B4
Schönfeld Strasse	261	D2
Schraudolphstrasse	260	C1
Schubertstrasse	260	A5
Schwanthaler Strasse	260	A4
Schweiger Strasse	261	D5
Schwindstrasse	260	B1
Sedanstrasse	261	F5
Seitzstrasse	261	E3
Sendlinger Strasse	260	C4
Sendlinger Tor	260	C4
Sonnenstrasse	260	C3
Sophienstrasse	260	B3
Sparkassenstrasse	261	D4
Steinheilstrasse	260	B1
Steinsdorfstrasse	261	E4
Sternstrasse	261	E3
Tal	261	D4
Thalkirchner Strasse	260	B5
Theatiner Strasse	261	D3
Theresienhöhe	260	A4
Theresienstrasse	260	C1
Theresienwiese	260	A4
Thierschstrasse	261	E4
Thomas Wimmer Ring	261	E4
Triftstrasse	261	E3
Türkenstrasse	260	C2
Unsöldstrasse	261	E3
Unterer Anger	260	C4
Veterinärstrasse	261	D1
Von-der-Tann-Strasse	261	D2
Waltherstrasse	260	B5
Weissenburger Strasse	261	F5
Westenriederstrasse	261	D4
Widenmayerstrasse	261	F4
Wittelsbacherplatz	261	D3
Wurzerstrasse	261	E3
Zeppelin Strasse	261	E5
Zieblandstrasse	260	C1
Zweibrückenstrasse	261	E4

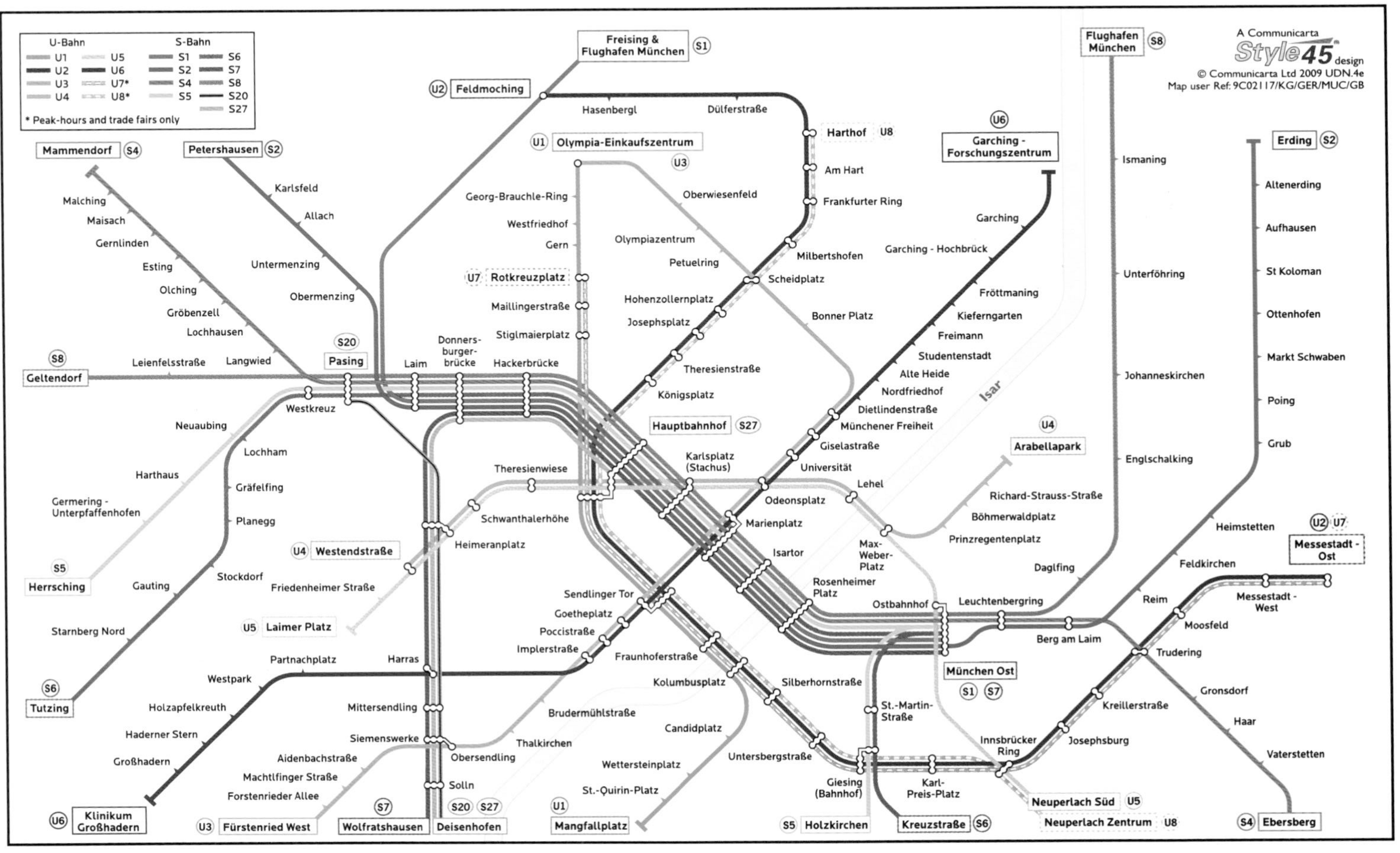
U-Bahn
U1
U2
U3
U4
U5
U6
U7*
U8*
S-Bahn
S1
S2
S4
S5
S6
S7
S8
S20
S27
* Peak-hours and trade fairs only
A Communicarta
Style45 design
© Communicarta Ltd 2009 UDN.4e
Map user Ref: 9C02117/KG/GER/MUC/GB
Freising & Flughafen München S1
U2 Feldmoching
Hasenbergl
Dülferstraße
Harthof U8
Am Hart
Frankfurter Ring
Milbertshofen
Scheidplatz
U1 Olympia-Einkaufszentrum
U3
Oberwiesenfeld
Olympiazentrum
Petuelring
Georg-Brauchle-Ring
Westfriedhof
Gern
U7 Rotkreuzplatz
Maillingerstraße
Stiglmaierplatz
Hohenzollernplatz
Josephsplatz
Theresienstraße
Königsplatz
Bonner Platz
Mammendorf S4
Malching
Maisach
Gernlinden
Esting
Olching
Gröbenzell
Lochhausen
Langwied
Petershausen S2
Karlsfeld
Allach
Untermenzing
Obermenzing
S8
Geltendorf
Leienfelsstraße
S20
Pasing
Laim
Donners-burger-brücke
Hackerbrücke
Hauptbahnhof S27
Karlsplatz (Stachus)
Westkreuz
Neuaubing
Lochham
Harthaus
Gräfelfing
Germering - Unterpfaffenhofen
Planegg
S5
Herrsching
Gauting
Stockdorf
Starnberg Nord
S6
Tutzing
Theresienwiese
Schwanthalerhöhe
Heimeranplatz
U4 Westendstraße
Friedenheimer Straße
U5 Laimer Platz
Partnachplatz
Westpark
Holzapfelkreuth
Haderner Stern
Großhadern
U6 Klinikum Großhadern
Harras
Mittersendling
Siemenswerke
Obersendling
Aidenbachstraße
Machtlfinger Straße
Forstenrieder Allee
U3 Fürstenried West
S7
Wolfratshausen
Solln
S20 S27
Deisenhofen
U1
Mangfallplatz
St.-Quirin-Platz
Wettersteinplatz
Candidplatz
Thalkirchen
Brudermühlstraße
Implerstraße
Poccistraße
Goetheplatz
Sendlinger Tor
Fraunhoferstraße
Kolumbusplatz
Silberhornstraße
Untersbergstraße
Giesing (Bahnhof)
S5 Holzkirchen
Kreuzstraße S6
Karl-Preis-Platz
St.-Martin-Straße
Marienplatz
Isartor
Rosenheimer Platz
Odeonsplatz
Universität
Giselastraße
Münchener Freiheit
Dietlindenstraße
Nordfriedhof
Alte Heide
Studentenstadt
Freimann
Kieferngarten
Fröttmaning
Garching - Hochbrück
Garching
U6
Garching - Forschungszentrum
Isar
Lehel
Max-Weber-Platz
Prinzregentenplatz
Böhmerwaldplatz
Richard-Strauss-Straße
U4
Arabellapark
Ostbahnhof
München Ost
S1 S7
Leuchtenbergring
Daglfing
Berg am Laim
Innsbrücker Ring
Neuperlach Süd U5
Neuperlach Zentrum U8
Josephsburg
Kreillerstraße
Trudering
Moosfeld
Messestadt - West
U2 U7
Messestadt - Ost
Flughafen München S8
Ismaning
Unterföhring
Johanneskirchen
Englschalking
Erding S2
Altenerding
Aufhausen
St Koloman
Ottenhofen
Markt Schwaben
Poing
Grub
Heimstetten
Feldkirchen
Reim
Gronsdorf
Haar
Vaterstetten
S4 Ebersberg

AMMERSEE

Just 34km (21 miles) southwest of central Munich and reached in about 50 minutes by S-Bahn train, Bavaria's third-largest lake (if you don't count those with waters shared by adjacent countries) is a popular jaunt for city denizens seeking fresh air, a sandy beach, or a waterfront fish restaurant. Active types will find watersports options, including swimming, sailing, windsurfing and angling, on the Ammersee. Tour boats—among them Bavaria's oldest paddle-steamer, the *Diessen* (1908)—from the Bayerische Seen-Schifffahrt line (tel 08143 94021; www.bayerische-seenschifffahrt.de) sail from Herrsching on the eastern shore to eight of the small towns and villages around the lake, which is 16km (10 miles) long and a maximum of 5km (3 miles) wide.

A worthwhile landward side-trip is to hilltop Kloster Andechs, a Benedictine monastery 3km (2 miles) south of Herrsching in the lush green countryside, its origins traceable back to the 10th century. The brewery and rustic restaurant here continue to attract 'pilgrims' to the Heilige Berg (Holy Mountain).

Off map 260 A3 S-Bahn Herrsching

ASAMKIRCHE

The narrow (9m/29.5ft) façade of this church gives little hint of the magnificence inside. Before entering, notice the unhewn rock on either side of the columns and, above the door, the statue of St. John Nepomuk, who gave the church its official name. It is commonly known as Asamkirche after the Asam brothers who designed, built and decorated it between 1733 and 1746. The brothers' efforts have resulted in a lavish rococo interior with sculptures of angels and gold leaf that makes the walls gleam. The church, only 30m (98ft) long, is crammed with ornamentation. Look out for the ceiling fresco by Cosmas Damian Asam, the portraits of the brothers and the gallery altar, which portrays the Holy Trinity.

Remember that the church is still a place of worship; when services are in progress, a sign is hung on the door asking you not to disturb those at prayer.

260 C4 Sendlinger Strasse 62, 80331 München (Altstadt) 089 260 9171 Mon–Fri 7.30–6, Sat 8–7, Sun 8–3 Free U-Bahn Sendlinger Tor 152. Tram 17, 18

BAYERISCHES NATIONALMUSEUM

www.bayerisches-nationalmuseum.de

The Bavarian National Museum is an art and cultural history museum with collections of arts and crafts from Bavaria and farther afield. You should pick up a plan of the museum, available in English. This is invaluable, as the museum has large collections spread over three floors. These include musical instruments, ceramics (including faience from Schloss Nymphenburg), suits of armour (look for the child-size suit), traditional clothes, furniture, baroque and rococo tapestries, Gothic sculpture and paintings from the 13th century through to art nouveau.

The museum is well known for its collection of 18th- and 19th-century German and Italian cribs (*Krippen*). There are temporary exhibitions on the upper floor, with themes such as The World in Miniature (toys).

The basement shop sells handcrafted Christmas decorations and ornaments with scenes of market stalls.

261 F3 Prinzregentenstrasse 3, 80538 München (Schwabing) 089 211 2401 Tue, Wed, Fri–Sun 10–5, Thu 10–8 Adult €7 (€1 on Sun), under 19 free U-Bahn Lehel 100. Tram 17

BMW MUSEUM

www.bmw-museum.de

Within walking distance of the Olympiapark (▷ 280, this unusual building, shaped like four cylinders and designed by Karl Schwanzer in 1970, is the headquarters of BMW. The windowless silver building shaped like a bowl next to it is the BMW Museum, the most popular company museum in the country. The 'Time Horizons' exhibition traces the company's history and technological developments in the last 80 years. There are plenty of models to admire, including rare and new sports cars and motorcycles. Just across Lerchenauer Strasse is the futuristic BMW Welt (World) building, where car buyers can take delivery direct from the factory.

260 (inset) Olympiapark 2, 80809 München (Olympiapark) 01802 118822 Tue–Fri 10–6, Sat, Sun 10–8 Adult €12, child (6–18) €6, under 6 free, family €24 U-Bahn Olympiazentrum 173

Opposite *The rich rococo interior of Asamkirche*
Below *The BMW Museum is an attraction for car lovers*

INFORMATION

www.alte-pinakothek.de
260 C2 Barer Strasse 27, 80333 München (Maxvorstadt) 089 2380 5216 Tue 10–8, Wed–Sun 10–6; closed Shrove Tue, 1 May, 24, 25, 31 Dec Adult €5.50 (€1 Sun), under 19 free U-Bahn Theresienstrasse Tram 27 Free audioguide (€4.50 on Sunday) Art books, postcards and things for children

Above Adoration of the Magi *(1502) by Hans Holbein the Elder*

INTRODUCTION

Containing more than 850 paintings by European artists from the 14th to the 18th centuries, the magnificent Alte Pinakothek is one of the oldest and most important galleries in the world. The gallery is arranged by schools—for example Room IX on the Upper Floor contains works by 17th-century Flemish artists such as Peter Paul Rubens—the Rubens collection is the world's finest—and Sir Anthony van Dyck. For all its high quality, the collection is a manageable size and it is possible to see everything in one visit—so long as you give yourself enough time.

Many of the works in the Alte Pinakothek used to be in a much smaller gallery in the Residenz [▷ 282–283], but when the collection outgrew it, Ludwig I commissioned his court architect Leo von Klenze (1784–1864) to design a new building. The gallery, which took 10 years to construct, was designed in the style of a Venetian Renaissance palace and was finished in 1836. Like many other buildings in Munich, the gallery suffered extensive bomb damage in World War II, but restoration work in the 1950s and 1990s revived it.

The entrance is set back from Theresienstrasse, opposite the entrance to the Neue Pinakothek. There are no explanatory notes next to paintings, so if you want to know more about what you're looking at, buy a gallery guide from the shop beforehand or make use of the audioguide.

WHAT TO SEE

RUBENS

The gallery houses the finest collection of paintings by the Flemish painter Peter Paul Rubens (1577–1640) in the world, so if you are a fan, you will not be disappointed. There's even a self-portrait of him with his first wife, Isabella Brant. The tender *Honeysuckle Bower* (*c* 1609) depicts the couple after his return from Italy and shortly after their marriage. They are both wearing the formal dress of Flemish aristocrats, while sitting in the shade of a honeysuckle plant, probably in the baroque garden of the artist's Antwerp home. The painting graces the walls of Room VII on the upper floor. Another highlight (and one to steer the children past) is the graphic, horrific depiction of *The Fall of the Damned into Hell* (1620), showing the bodies of the damned being sucked down into the everlasting fire. *Drunken Silenus* (1616–17), with the clear warning against the perils of too much wine, shows a ruddy-faced Silenus staggering along amid mythical animals and not-so-allegorical bunches of grapes. Rubens' range and versatility as an artist are evident in *Lion Hunt* (1621), an allegory of life and death.

ITALIAN PAINTING FROM THE 15TH TO THE 16TH CENTURIES

Renaissance masters such as Raphael (1483–1520), Titian (1488–1576), Leonardo da Vinci (1452–1519) and Sandro Botticelli (1445–1510) are all well represented. Raphael's *Canigiani Holy Family* (1505–06) shows the Holy Family arranged in the form of a pyramid, with angels looking down from clouds at the top of the painting. These angels were painted over and were only uncovered in 1983. If you look closely at Venetian artist Jacopo Tintoretto's *Vulcan Surprising Venus and Mars* (1555), you'll see Mars, the god of war, hiding under a table, trying to stop Venus' dog barking and revealing his presence.

17TH-CENTURY DUTCH PAINTING

This period is often referred to as the Golden Age of Dutch painting, as the success of the Dutch war of liberation against the Spanish brought about an independent middle class with a penchant for paintings by Dutch artists. One of the best-known painters of this time is Rembrandt (1606–69) and the gallery has a self-portrait (1629) painted when the artist was only 23, as well as two of his paintings with biblical themes—*The Raising of the Cross* (1633) and *Descent From the Cross* (1634).

Caravaggio fans will find something familiar in Gerrit van Honthorst's *The Prodigal Son* (1623), as the artist uses the chiaroscuro effect made famous by the Italian artist in his picture of a morally dubious group enjoying too much wine. Portraits were also popular at this time and you can see the arrogant stance of *Haarlem yarn-trader Willem van Heythuysen*, painted by Frans Hals in about 1625.

MORE TO SEE

Italian art from the 18th century is represented in elegant scenes of Venice's Canal Grande, Piazza San Marco and Rialto bridge by Venetian artists Canaletto (1697–1768) and Francesco Guardi (1712–93). There is only a fairly small collection of paintings by 16th- and 17th-century Spanish artists, although all the major artists are represented—Juan Pantoja de la Cruz (1553–1608), Diego Rodriguez de Silva (1599–1660), El Greco (1541–1614) and Bartolomé Esteban Murillo (1618–82). Murillo's representations of children in *Urchins Playing Dice* (*c*1675) and *Beggar Boys Eating Grapes and Melons* (*c*1645) show suspiciously healthy-looking beggars.

In the section devoted to French art, rococo artist François Boucher's *Portrait of Madame de Pompadour* (1756) depicts Louis XV's mistress reclining in her boudoir in a sumptuous green dress decorated with countless pink roses. She is surrounded by objects that represent her interests (sheet music, books and writing materials), and has her King Charles spaniel by her feet. The same artist's erotic *Reclining Girl* (1752) shows one of Boucher's models, Louise O'Murphy, who also later became the mistress of Louis XV.

Work by one of Rubens' contemporaries, Sir Anthony van Dyck (1599–1641), is in the Flemish section. There's van Dyck's self- portrait and a depiction of the Bible story from Daniel 13 of Susanna being surprised in her bath by two Elders. For an earlier, different depiction of the story, go to the Early German section to see the work by Albrecht Altdorfer (1480–1538).

TIPS

» You can't take bags or umbrellas into the gallery so make sure you have €2 for the deposit for the locker.
» You are allowed to take photographs as long as you do not use a flash.
» The greatly reduced cost of admission to the gallery on Sunday means it can get crowded.

GALLERY GUIDE

Ground Floor
Early German paintings, Brueghel paintings, temporary exhibitions, café and bookshop.
Upper Floor
Dutch, German, Italian, Flemish, French and Spanish paintings from the 14th to 18th centuries.

DACHAU

www.dachau.de

Until 1933, Münchners used to come to pretty Dachau to stroll along its picturesque cobbled streets and visit the Renaissance castle, but in that year, the Third Reich designated the town as the site of a concentration camp. Between 1933 and 1945, around 200,000 people were interned here, and about 32,000 of them died. Several of the camp's buildings have been turned into a museum and memorial, the KZ-Gedenkstätte (Tue–Sun 9–5; tel 08131 669970), which is at the eastern edge of town.

Schloss Dachau (Apr–end Sep Tue–Sun 9–6; Oct–end Mar Tue–Sun 10–4 ; tel 08131 87923), on a hill above the town and the River Amper, was a summer residence of the Bavarian royal family, the Wittelsbachs. The castle is known for the superb carved ceiling from the 16th century in the banqueting hall and for views of Munich and the Alps from the terrace.

260 (inset) 85221 Dachau 08131 669970 Tue–Sun 9–5 Tourist Information der Stadt Dachau, Konrad-Adenauer-Strasse 1, 85221 Dachau 08131 75286 Mon–Fri 9–6, Sat, Sun, holidays 9–1 S-Bahn Dachau

DEUTSCHES MUSEUM

▷ 270–274.

ENGLISCHER GARTEN

▷ 269.

FRAUENKIRCHE

The enduring image of Munich is the Italian Renaissance onion domes of the twin towers (100m/330ft high) of the city's cathedral, the Frauenkirche. The church was built between 1468 and 1488, although what you see today was rebuilt after the church was reduced to rubble in World War II. The distinctive green onion domes were originally added to the towers in 1524 as a temporary measure, but proved so popular that they remained. You can climb the south tower (Apr–end Oct Mon–Sat 10–5) for wonderful views of the city.

The cathedral is huge—109m (350ft) long and 41m (135ft) wide—and has a beautifully light interior with simple white walls and vivid stained-glass windows. Behind the choir, a staircase leads down to the crypt, where there are the tombs of Bavaria's rulers, the Wittelsbachs. At the front entrance you can see a footprint in the stone—legend has it that it was left by the Devil himself when he stamped his foot. For music recitals in the cathedral, pick up a leaflet inside, ask at the tourist office or see the website. www.muenchner-dommusik.de.

260 C3 Frauenplatz 1, 80331 München (Altstadt) 089 290 0820 Sat–Thu 7–7, Fri 7–6 Free U- or S-Bahn Marienplatz 52, 131, 152. Tram 19

HOFBRÄUHAUS

www.hofbraeuhaus.de

If you're looking for traditional dirndl-clad waitresses serving frothy steins of beer, and thigh-slapping oompah-band music, then this beer hall is where to go. The Hofbräuhaus is one of the world's most famous pubs, and certainly no visit to the city would be complete without a visit to this Munich institution. Just don't expect it to be full of locals.

The brewery was founded in 1589 when Wilhelm V wanted a dark beer to drink at court. The beer remained unavailable to the public until the brewery became an inn in 1828. The Hofbräuhaus also has a political history—the first mass meeting of the Nationalist Socialist Workers' Party (later the Nazi Party) took place here in 1920. Hitler spoke here, including an occasion that culminated in the Battle of the Hofbräuhaus. He finished his speech despite the throwing of steins and chairs going on around him.

261 D4 Platzl 9, 80331 München (Altstadt) 089 2901 3610 Daily 9am–midnight U-and S-Bahn Marienplatz 52, 131. Tram 19

KÖNIGSPLATZ

Königsplatz is a majestic square lined on three sides by neoclassical buildings, commissioned by Ludwig I in 1817. The Greek style of these buildings gave the square its alternative name, Athens-on-the-Isar. The Propyläen, on the west side of the square, is an imposing temple built for purely aesthetic reasons. It was based on the entrance to the Acropolis in Athens and was finished in 1862 by Leo von Klenze.

The Ionic-style building on the north side is the Glyptothek (Tue, Wed, Fri–Sun 10–5, Thu 10–8; tel 089 286100), a sculpture gallery with more than 160 Greek and Roman statues. Among the finest are the *Barberini Faun*, the bust of Augustus and Tenea's *Apollo*.

On the square's south side is the Antikensammlungen (Tue, Thu–Sun 10–5, Wed 10–8; tel 089 5998 8830), the State Collection of Antiquities, with ancient bronzes, jewellery, Greek vases, ceramics and sculpture.

260 C2 Königsplatz, 80333 München (Maxvorstadt) U-Bahn Königsplatz 100

Left *A metal watchtower among trees on the perimeter of the concentration camp at Dachau is dwarfed by a memorial*

ENGLISCHER GARTEN

The largest city park in Europe, ideal for sunbathing, surfing, rowing, having a beer or simply enjoying being outside. At 5km (3 miles) long and a kilometre (0.6 mile) wide, the Englischer Garten is more to the people of Munich than just a large park. Often referred to as 'the lungs of Munich', the English Garden is a place to relax, an aspect of life that is very important to Münchners, who flock here on weekends and sunny days. Prince Elector Karl Theodor commissioned the park, which had been the hunting grounds of the Wittelsbach dynasty, in the 18th century. The design was unusual for its time; it broke away from the fashion for more formal, manicured gardens and was instead an open, natural-looking *Volksgarten* (people's park), evident in the fields, woodland, lake, rivers and many kilometres of footpaths.

ACTIVITIES

With such large open spaces, the park is ideal for a range of activities, such as bicycling, jogging, having a picnic, feeding the ducks and boating or paddling in the lake. Some paths are suitable for pushchairs (strollers) and there are playgrounds, making this a great place for children. You should be aware that in summer it is not unusual (nor illegal) for Münchners to sunbathe nude by the river. You'll also see canoes on the Eisbach, and even surfers who challenge each other to stay upright as they surf against the flow of the crest of a permanent wave, which is at the stretch of water by Prinzregentenstrasse.

THINGS TO SEE

Most of the attractions are in the section south of the main road—the Isar Ring. Here is the Kleinhesseloher See, where you can rent a boat, or enjoy a beer or a meal at the Seehaus restaurant, where brass bands play and there's a festival atmosphere. If you follow the Eisbach creek south, you'll come to the Chinesischer Turm (Chinese Pagoda), where there's a 7,000-seater beer garden, as well as mulled wine stalls in winter and a children's playground. When you pay for your drinks at the supermarket-style cash desk in the beer garden, you must also pay a small deposit (*Pfand*) for each glass. (You are given a token that you hand back with your empty glass when you've finished your drink.) Close by stands the Monopteros (1837), a round Greek-style temple, that affords a fine view over Munich from atop the artificial hill on which it stands. At the very south of the garden is the Japanisches Teehaus, a teahouse that was a gift to the city of Munich from Japan on the occasion of the 1972 Olympic Games (▷ 45).

INFORMATION

www.schloesser.bayern.de

261 E2 Stretching from Prinzregentenstrasse in the south to the outskirts of the city in the north 089 3866 6390 Daily dawn to dusk U-Bahn Odeonsplatz, Universität, Giselastrasse, Münchner Freiheit 100, 144, 180, 181, 187, 231, 232. Tram 17 Seehaus restaurant and beer garden, Chinesischer Turm restaurant and beer garden, Japanisches Teehaus, Aumeister restaurant and beer garden

TIP

» You can rent bicycles at Kleinhesseloher See to explore more of the gardens.

Below *The Monopteros on a hill in Englischer Garten offers fine views across the city*

INFORMATION

www.deutsches-museum.de
261 E5 Museumsinsel 1, 80538 München (Haidhausen) 089 21791 Daily 9–5; closed 1 Jan, Shrove Tuesday (usually last Tue in Feb), Good Friday, 1 May, 1 Nov, 24, 25 and 31 Dec; closes at 1pm on second Wed in Dec Adult €8.50, child (6–15 and school students) €3, under 6 free, family €17; Tower lift €2. Planetarium €2 (evenings €3). Combined ticket for Deutsches Museum, Flugwerft Schleissheim, Verkehrszentrum and shuttle bus to Verkehrszentrum €17 S-Bahn Isartor; U-Bahn Fraunhoferstrasse 131. Tram 18 Guided tours in German only Guidebook €4 Internet café on 3rd floor, self-service restaurant Large book and giftshop outside

Above *It takes a large building to house the exhibits in this museum*

INTRODUCTION

This is Germany's most visited attraction and one of the largest science and technology museums in the world, but you don't need to be a science buff or have any specialist knowledge to appreciate the cars, planes, helicopters, model railway or re-creation of a mine, to name just a few of the 18,000 exhibits—a number that guarantees it's not possible to see everything, so you'll need to be selective. The museum was founded in 1903 by engineer Oskar von Miller (1855–1934), a leading light in the German energy industry. The collection moved to its present home on an island in the Isar (accessible from either side of the river) in 1925. In September 1992, the museum opened a separate branch, dedicated to aircraft and flying, at a former airfield at Schleissheim, 13km (8 miles) outside town. Expansion continued with the opening of the Vehrkehrszentrum, a museum devoted to transportation and mobility, in 2003. The Centre for New Technologies, which opened in 2005, focuses on genetic engineering and nanotechnology as well as hosting temporary special exhibitions.

Before you buy your ticket, decide whether you also want to visit the other museums, as it may be worth getting a combined ticket, which gives you entry to the main museum, the Verkehrszentrum (Transport Museum), which is in town, and the Flugwerft Schleissheim (Museum of Flight),. There is a free shuttle bus from the main museum to the Verkehrszentrum, but not to the Flugwerft. If you want to visit the Planetarium (sixth floor) or the Museumsturm (Tower), which cost extra, you'll need to buy your tickets at the Deutsches Museum.

WHAT TO SEE

MINE, BASEMENT

You reach this re-creation of a mine via a staircase past the cloakroom, and the museum recommends that you allow an hour to follow the underground route. The mine is sufficiently realistic that very small children and those who are claustrophobic may find the dim tunnels a little unnerving. Piles of coal and rock, pistons and pulleys and life-size models of miners, pick-axes in hand, add to the experience. Diagrams and models explain (mostly in German) the mining process as well as what life is like for miners.

AERONAUTICS, ROOM 17 (GROUND FLOOR) AND ROOM 26 (FIRST FLOOR)

Even if you're not particularly fond of planes, you should be impressed by the huge collection of aircraft in this hangar-like exhibition room. There are hang-gliders, helicopters, jet fighters and even a rocket, with information on the German space programme. You can get into a Junkers Ju 52 transportation plane and into the front section of a Lufthansa Boeing 707 with its 1970s-style interior decoration. One fascinating exhibit is the cross-section of a passenger aircraft suspended from the ceiling, which makes you realize exactly how little there is separating you from the outside when you are flying. If it all gets to be a bit much, you can sit down on (what else?) aircraft seats. Make sure you go upstairs to room 26, where you can get a better view of the aircraft and see the old-style flying machines with canvas wings and even bicycle wheels.

SHIPS AND BOATS (MARINE NAVIGATION), ROOM 10 (GROUND FLOOR)

If you can think of a way to travel across water, you are likely to find it in this well-stocked collection. When you enter the room, you are immediately struck by the dimensions of the 19th-century fishing wherry the *Maria* (60m/197ft long), which, despite its size, had a crew of only three. Other craft include a Venetian gondola, canoes from the Amazon, kayaks and many model ships.

If you go down the staircase next to the *Maria*, you'll find a huge area devoted to the sea. Here, there's the re-creation of a cruise liner, complete with sundeck, the noise of seagulls and officers' cabins. There are also many model sailing ships and war ships, huge anchors, old-fashioned diving suits, jet skis and a complete World War II German U-Boat. The side has been cut away so you can see exactly what's inside, including the engine room and the area where the seamen and officers slept when they were off duty.

TIPS

» The Deutsches Museum, unlike most other museums and galleries in Munich, is open on Mondays.

» You can bring your own food into the museum and there is a dining area on the ground floor where you can eat your picnic—particularly useful if you have young children with you.

» You are allowed to use video cameras and take photographs, even with a flash.

Below *Early cars are among the displays in the museum*

GALLERY GUIDE

Basement Mining, automobiles, Kids' Kingdom.

Ground floor Cloakroom, petroleum and natural gas, metal, welding and soldering, materials testing, machine tools, power machinery, machine components, electrical power, marine navigation (including canoes, boats and ships), buses and bicycles, vehicle engineering, trains and the model railway, tunnels, planes and helicopters, bridge building, hydraulic engineering, Foucault pendulum, snack bar and picnic area.

Mezzanine floor Self-service restaurant near the entrance.

Outside Exhibition area with lifeboat, windmill, train-carriage café (summer only), museum shop (in front of the museum).

First floor Energy technologies, physics, aeronautics, musical instruments, chemistry, pharmacology, special exhibitions, small coffee bar.

Second floor Altamira cave, ceramics, glass, paper and printing, astronautics, technical toys, textiles, the environment.

Third floor Astronomy, geodesy, computers, microelectronics, mathematical cabinet, telecommunications, agriculture, food technology, chronometry, weights and measures, internet café.

Fourth to sixth floors Amateur radio, astronomy, Zeiss Planetarium (buy tickets on the ground floor), sundial garden.

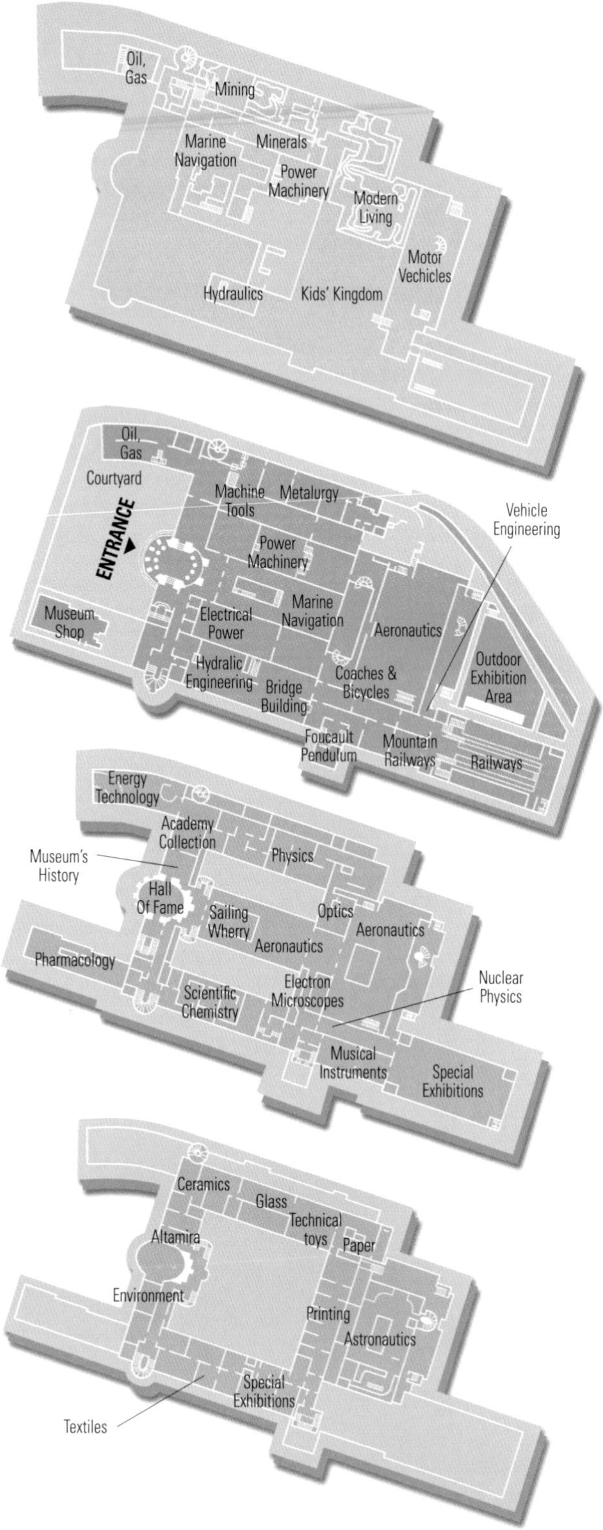

Oil, Gas
Mining
Marine Navigation
Minerals
Power Machinery
Modern Living
Motor Vechicles
Hydraulics
Kids' Kingdom

Oil, Gas
Courtyard
ENTRANCE
Machine Tools
Metalurgy
Vehicle Engineering
Power Machinery
Museum Shop
Electrical Power
Marine Navigation
Aeronautics
Outdoor Exhibition Area
Hydralic Engineering
Bridge Building
Coaches & Bicycles
Foucault Pendulum
Mountain Railways
Railways

Energy Technology
Academy Collection
Physics
Museum's History
Hall Of Fame
Sailing Wherry
Optics
Aeronautics
Aeronautics
Pharmacology
Electron Microscopes
Nuclear Physics
Scientific Chemistry
Musical Instruments
Special Exhibitions

Ceramics
Glass
Technical toys
Paper
Altamira
Environment
Printing
Astronautics
Special Exhibitions
Textiles

KEY

Basement

Ground Floor

First Floor

Second Floor

Third Floor

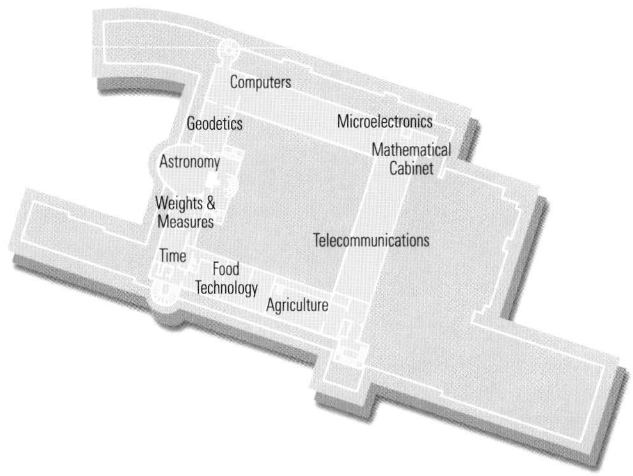

TRAINS AND AUTOMOBILES, ROOM 13 (GROUND FLOOR) AND ROOM 22 (BASEMENT)

See huge, shiny steam trains in the Railways exhibition room, although unfortunately you can't go inside any of them. In summer, you can go outside to an old-fashioned railway car that has been converted into a café. Other modern trains include the prototype of a train that runs above the track on an electromagnetic cushion. Nearby is a very steep mountain railway used in the Alps and a large model railway, which is always popular with children.

If trains aren't for you, head down the escalator to the automobiles, which include Carl Benz's 1886 motorized tricycle, 1920s American automobiles that wouldn't look out of place in a gangster film, VW Beetles and, of course, BMWs. If you want to get into a car, go to the end of the corridor, with its displays of coaches and bicycles, where you can climb inside a BMW or test your skills in a driving simulator (€2). If you still haven't had enough cars, take the free shuttle bus to the Transport Museum (part of the Deutsches Museum) or go to the BMW Museum (▷ 265).

FOR CHILDREN

There are plenty of exhibits that will entertain children. The Planetarium on the sixth floor (not suitable for children under 6) has a commentary in German but is still an exciting visual experience. The model railway will be particularly appealing to children and it runs at 11, 2 and 4. For smaller children, the Kids' Kingdom in the basement is a great place to play and run around. Older children may appreciate the driving simulator (€2) or getting into a BMW or fork-lift truck. In summer, the Outdoor Exhibition is the best place to be; you can go on board an ocean-going lifeboat and into a windmill. There are baby-changing facilities on the ground floor near the entrance.

The Deutsches Museum also has two other museums—the Verkehrszentrum and Flugwerft Schleissheim.

VERKEHRSZENTRUM (TRANSPORT AND MOBILITY MUSEUM)

www.deutsches-museum.de

The Verkehrszentrum is a transportation museum designed from a 21st-century point of view, and it contains every kind of car and bicycle imaginable, as well as buses and steam locomotives. The museum explores the concept of motion, with exhibits on engineering, city travel and journeys.

260 (inset) Theresienhöhe 14a, 80339 München (Westend) 089 5008 6762 Daily 9–5 Adult €6, child (6–15 and students) €3, under 6 free, family €12 U-Bahn Schwanthalerhöhe 134; shuttle bus from Museumsinsel (the main Deutsches Museum)

Below *Blimp models surround an old ship display*

FLUGWERFT SCHLEISSHEIM (AIRCRAFT MUSEUM)

If you like anything to do with flight, this extension of the Deutsches Museum's collection of civil, military and sport flying machines is for you. The site, on an old airfield at Schleissheim, 13km (8 miles) from downtown Munich, was originally built for the Bavarian Royal Flying Corps. There are helicopters (including one used by the police), gliders, planes, including a MiG fighter jet, and even a rocket. If you want to feel as if you are flying, try out the flight simulator. Keep your children entertained by letting them loose on the model planes. For good views, go up the control tower.

260 (inset) Effnerstrasse 18, 85764 Oberschleissheim 089 315 7140 Daily 9–5 Adult €12 S-Bahn Oberschleissheim Take the A99 to the Neuherberg exit

MORE TO SEE

» Take the elevator (65m/213ft) to the top of the tower (€2, under 6 free) at 10, 11, 12, 2, 3 and 4 for views of the city and, on a clear day, the Alps.

» The Environment exhibition on the second floor shows how much rubbish (garbage) the average German family produces in a year and how Germany's production of waste compares with that of other countries.

» On the third floor, the Agriculture section is in a room created to look like a barn, and is filled with tractors, ploughs and other farm machinery.

» To see what a traditional wooden mountain chalet looks like, go to the Food Technology exhibits on the third floor, although unfortunately you can't actually go inside the chalet.

» Although only a reconstruction, the Altamira cave is very dark. The exhibition shows the paintings of wild animals and hunting scenes that archaeologists found in this Spanish cave, and explains what they discovered about these hunters from their cave art.

» Look out for special temporary exhibitions.

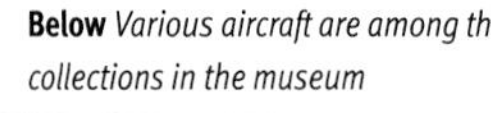

Below *Various aircraft are among the collections in the museum*

LENBACHHAUS

www. lenbachhaus.de

The Städtische Galerie im Lenbachhaus is in a beautiful dark yellow Florentine High Renaissance-style building with a small formal garden, with statues and a fountain. It was built in 1887 for the Bavarian painter Prince Franz von Lenbach. After his death, the building became the property of the State and was converted into an art gallery, which now charts the development of painting in Munich.

If you turn left when you reach the top of the stairs on the upper floor, you'll see the gallery's collection of Bavarian landscapes, with many paintings showing how Munich used to look. However, most people come for the paintings by the Munich-based expressionist group Der Blaue Reiter, founded by Wassily Kandinsky (1866–1944) and Franz Marc (1880–1916). There are many vibrant, abstract paintings by Kandinsky, his partner Gabriele Münter (1877–1962), and August Macke (1887–1914), as well as some by Paul Klee (1879–1940).

260 B2 Luisenstrasse 33, 80333 München (Maxvorstadt) 089 2333 2000 Tue–Sun and holidays 10–6 Adult €5, child (6–18) €2.50, under 6 free, family €7.50 U-Bahn Königsplatz 100. Tram 27

MARIENPLATZ

▷ 276–277.

MAXIMILIANSTRASSE

Maximilianstrasse, named for its creator King Maximilian II, begins with Munich's opera house, the Nationaltheater (▷ 292), and ends on the other side of the Isar with the Renaissance-style Maximilianeum building, which became the Bavarian State Parliament in 1949.

These grand buildings set the tone for the avenue, where Munich's designer-clad citizens shop. Window-shop (or indulge) at Gucci, Dior, Bulgari, Gianfranco Ferré, Versace and Hermès, or watch VIPs unload their Louis Vuitton luggage outside the Kempinski Vier Jahreszeiten.

261 E3 Maximilianstrasse, 80539 München (Maxvorstadt) West end: Marienplatz, Lehel Tram 17, 19

Above *The formal Italian garden to the rear of the Lenbachhaus, now an art museum*

MÜNCHNER STADTMUSEUM

www.stadtmuseum-online.de

The Stadtmuseum, in what was Munich's armoury, traces the city's history with a permanent exhibition and changing special exhibitions. It covers Munich's royal history through to the devastation of the city in World War II. You'll find paintings, furniture, toys, costumes, ancient weaponry and Bavarian handcrafts, as well as hundreds of musical instruments and a photography and film museum. Well-known aspects of the collections include Erasmus Grasser's Gothic Moriske dancers, which he made in the 16th century. They were originally carved for the Altes Rathaus in Marienplatz.

The puppet theatre museum (Münchner Marionettentheater) is one of the biggest in the world, with mechanical toys and glove puppets. Its collection covers Bavaria's important role in the production of puppets and toys. Alongside this is the fairground museum. When you're finished, head for the museum café, the Stadtcafé, with its delicious cakes and international newspapers.

260 C4 St.-Jakobs-Platz 1, 80331 München (Altstadt) 089 2332 2370 Tue–Sun 10–6 Adult €4, child (6–15) €2, under 6 free, family €6; free for all on Sun S-Bahn Marienplatz; U-Bahn to Marienplatzm Sendlinger Tor 52, 131, 152

NEUE PINAKOTHEK

▷ 278.

ODEONSPLATZ

This grand square, with wide Ludwigstrasse leading off to the north, is surrounded by impressive buildings. The most striking is the mustard yellow baroque Theatinerkirche which was designed by several Italian architects, including Agostino Barelli (1627–87), and was commissioned by Bavarian Elector Ferdinand Maria (1636–79) to celebrate the birth of his son. The church was based on, and takes its name from, the home of the Theatine order in Rome, Sant'Andrea della Valle, and has an arrestingly light interior decorated with white stuccowork.

On the south side of the square is the Feldherrnhalle, or General's Hall, and on the east side behind the wall is the Hofgarten (Court Garden). This was designed in a baroque Italian style, with a pavilion in the middle and arcades with frescoes depicting Bavarian history. If you head south along Residenzstrasse, you'll come to the entrance to the opulent Residenz (▷ 282–283), which takes up the entire block and was the home of the Wittelsbach dynasty and government for centuries.

261 D3 80539 München (Maxvorstadt) U-Bahn Odeonsplatz 100

INFORMATION
261 D4 Marienplatz, 80331 München (Altstadt) U-and S-Bahn Marienplatz 52, 131, 152 Plenty of restaurants and cafés, including the Glockenspiel Café (▷ 296) and Ratskeller (▷ 297) Marienplatz Mon–Fri 10–8, Sat 10–4; Sun, holidays 10–2

Above *Looking down onto the buildings surrounding the Marienplatz*

INTRODUCTION

This central square is surrounded by historic buildings and is home to the world-famous Glockenspiel. If the Englischer Garten represents Munich's lungs, then Marienplatz is surely its heart. The square has many roles, not least as a central point where people meet with friends, but also as the place where citizens converge to hold political demonstrations. In times past, tournaments, festivals, public ceremonies and executions took place here. The Viktualienmarkt was here until it grew too big and was moved to its present site nearby. Today the square has a lively buzz about it, with visitors taking photos of the Rathaus (City Hall) and the Glockenspiel, locals sitting outside enjoying a beer in summer and, in December, the traditional Christmas market.

WHAT TO SEE

MARIENSÄULE

Marienplatz takes its name from the Mariensäule, the golden figure of the Virgin Mary on a column, 11m (36ft) high, in the middle of the square. It was created in 1593 by the Dutch-born sculptor Hubert Gerhard and moved to Marienplatz at the request of Elector Maximilian in 1638. It marks the saving of the city during the period of Swedish occupation in the Thirty Years' War. On the statue's pedestal are four winged children who represent the fight against the sorrows of humankind—Heresy, War, Plague and Famine.

NEUES RATHAUS

The neo-Gothic Neues Rathaus (New City Hall), begun in 1867 and completed in 1909, fronts the north side of the square. It is built around six courtyards and its façade is a lavish confection of towers, turrets and sculptures (including gargoyles). Under the eaves at the front is a tourist information office, and at basement level is the Ratskeller, a huge restaurant and beer house. You can climb the tower (May–end Oct daily 10–7; Nov–end Apr Mon–Fri 10–5; tel 089 23300) for outstanding views of the city.

GLOCKENSPIEL

Get here at 11am, noon or (except Nov–end Feb) 5pm to see and hear the Glockenspiel (carillon) on the front of the Neues Rathaus's main tower. The mechanical clock is one of Europe largest carillons, counting 43 bells of different timbres. It chimes out four tunes, accompanying a parade of 32 brightly painted, almost life-size figures representing Bavarian blue-bloods, saints and characters from local folklore, which present scenes from Munich's history, such as the jousting tournament at the marriage of Duke Wilhelm V of Bavaria with Renata of Lorraine in 1568. Chirps from a golden cuckoo end the performance.

FISCHBRUNNEN

The Fischbrunnen (Fish Fountain) nearby, created in 1865 by sculptor Konrad Knoll, is named for the fish market that stood here. It is said that if you wash your wallet here on Ash Wednesday, it will never be empty. Munich takes this tradition seriously and the Lord Mayor still douses the city purse in the fountain every year.

ALTES RATHAUS

At the east side of the square is the Altes Rathaus (Old City Hall), which dates from the 15th century but was reconstructed after bomb damage during World War II. It contains the Spielzeugmuseum (Toy Museum, daily 10–5.30; tel 089 294001) and its collections of teddy bears, dolls, dolls' houses and model railways.

MORE TO SEE

COOPERS' DANCE

One of the events presented by the Glockenspiel figures is the Schäfflertanz (Coopers' Dance), which recalls the barrel makers who in 1517 danced through the streets to celebrate the end of the Black Death. Real-life dancers re-enact the Schäfflertanz every seven years during Fasching (Carnival): the next one is in 2012.

TIPS

» You'll probably pass through Marienplatz several times during your stay. Be there at 11, 12 or 5 (no 5pm performance Nov–end Feb) to see the Glockenspiel chime.

» For good views of the city, climb up the City Hall tower or the Alter Peter in Peterskirche nearby.

Left *Detail of the entrance of the Neues Rathaus*

Below *The statue atop the Mariensäule (Mary's Column)*

INFORMATION

www.neue-pinakothek.de
260 C1 Barer Strasse 29, 80799 München (Maxvorstadt) 089 2380 5195 Thu–Mon 10–6, Wed 10–8; closed 24, 25, 31 Dec, 1 May Adult €9.50 (€1 Sun), under 19 free U-Bahn Theresienstrasse Tram 27 Free audioguide (€4.50 on Sun)

TIPS

» Entry to all Munich's Pinakotheks is just €1 on Sunday, and so the gallery and restaurant can get very busy, particularly in the afternoon.

» Bear in mind that visiting all three Pinakothek galleries in one day may test the staying power of even the most artistically minded.

Above *The Neue Pinakothek is at the heart of the student quarter*

NEUE PINAKOTHEK

The largest post-war art gallery in Germany is packed with outstanding works of European art and sculpture from the late 18th to the early 20th centuries. The Neue Pinakothek is in a glass, granite and concrete building designed by Munich architect Alexander von Branca, and is sometimes referred to as Palazzo Branca. It contains hundreds of European paintings and sculptures from the late 18th to the early 20th centuries, focusing on the development of German art. There are particularly fine collections of 19th-century German art, landscapes by French, English and Spanish painters and a sizeable French Impressionism section. Throughout the gallery are sculptures, including works by Auguste Rodin, Edgar Degas and Pablo Picasso.

LANDSCAPES AND PORTRAITS BY EUROPEAN PAINTERS

Several rooms are devoted to landscapes by European artists, with English painters particularly well represented. *Landscape with Shepherd, Sheep and Cattle* (1783) was inspired by a visit Thomas Gainsborough made to the Lake District in the north of England. In his day, Gainsborough was a well-known painter of high-society figures, and here you can see examples of his portraits such as *Mrs Thomas Hibbert* from 1786. Other paintings to look out for include the unpretentious depiction of the *Marquise de Sorcy de Thélusson* by French portraitist Jacques Louis David (1748–1825) and still lifes and portraits by the Spanish painter Goya (1746–1828).

19TH-CENTURY GERMAN ART

The art in this gallery focuses on German Romanticism, Realism and Impressionism, with works by Caspar David Friedrich, Wilhelm von Kaulbach and Carl von Piloty, among others. Highlights include *The Schmadri Falls* (1822) by Joseph Anton Koch, which depicts dramatic snow-covered mountains and waterfalls, and German Impressionist Max Liebermann's *Munich Beer Garden* (1884), a scene that, apart from the style of dress, could be found in Munich today.

IMPRESSIONISM ONWARDS

Rooms 19 to 22 contain paintings by the French Impressionists. Highlights include Édouard Manet's painting *The Boat* (1874), which shows his friend Claude Monet painting a picture while on a boat with his wife. In rooms 21 and 22 you'll find examples of more modern art, notably Vincent van Gogh's *Sunflowers* (1888) and the beautifull, vibrant blues and greens of his *View of Arles* (1889).

PINAKOTHEK DER MODERNE

The collection brings together four key elements of 20th- and 21st-century art and design, complementing less well-known pieces and genres with works by the greatest names in modern art.

The city's museum of modern art's stellar collection of paintings and sculpture, architecture, design and graphic art ranges from the early 20th century until the most recent times. Displayed in a delicate-seeming, rectangular concrete building (2002) with a central glass rotunda, designed by Munich architect Stephan Braunfels, it stands right across the street from the venerable Alte Pinakothek (▷ 266–267). You enter on the ground floor, which is Level 2.

ART

On Level 3 you'll find a superb collection of modern and contemporary art. The most influential movements of the 20th century are represented here, among them cubism by Pablo Picasso (1881–1973), surrealism by Salvador Dalí (1904–89) and pop art by Andy Warhol (1928–87). Several rooms are devoted to expressionism—look out for Emile Nolde's *The Dance Round the Golden Calf* (1910). Paintings by members of the Blaue Reiter movement, which started in Munich, include *The Full Moon* (1919) by Paul Klee and *Dreamy Improvisation* (1913) by Wassily Kandinsky.

DESIGN

The exhibition in the basement (Level 1), traces the history of design, taking in the avant garde of the 1920s and pop art design along the way. Areas are dedicated to automobile design, computer culture (huge computers from the 1980s), and design of everyday objects such as furniture—there is a strong focus on the chair. Other exhibits to look out for include the perpetual motion machines full of designer sport shoes, and video installations. The huge, bright, jellyfish-like sculpture on the staircase to Level 3 is an arresting sight.

INFORMATION

www.pinakothek.de

260 C2 Barer Strasse 40, 80333 München 089 2380 5360 Tue 10–8, Wed–Sun 10–6 Adult €9.50 (€1 Sun), under 19 free U-Bahn Theresienstrasse Tram 27 Free audioguide (€4.50 on Sun)

Below *Items on display in the Pinakothek der Moderne*

INFORMATION

www.olympiapark-muenchen.de
260 (inset) Spiridon-Louis-Ring 21, 80809 München (Olympiapark)
089 30670 Stadium: mid-Apr to mid-Oct daily 8.30–8.30; mid-Oct to mid-Apr daily 9–4.30. Olympiaturm: daily 9am–midnight. Tours: Apr–end Oct daily
Entrance to the site free. Tower: adult €4.50, child (6–16) €2.80, under 6 free, family €14. For pool and ice skating ▷ 292 U3 Olympiazentrum, then 10-min walk Revolving restaurant Self-service café, beer garden and ice-cream stalls in summer Daily 9.30–7

TIPS

» When you arrive at the U-Bahn station, follow signs for Eissportzentrum, Olympiastadion, Besucherdienst or Olympiahalle, rather than Olympiadorf, which is on the wrong side of the motorway.

» Bring your swimming costume and a towel, so you can have a swim or use the sauna and steam room after the tour.

OLYMPIAPARK

The hub of Munich's sporting life and home of the Olympic stadium has views as far as the Alps from the Olympic Tower. When it was announced that the 1972 Olympic Games were to be held in Munich, the city set about building a comprehensive set of sports facilities on the site of the old airport (▷ 45). The site, which you can tour on the park train in the summer, is known for its unusual roof, which looks like a spider's web. It covers the Olympic Hall, where rock and pop concerts are held, the Olympic swimming pool and the stadium, which is home to Munich's two soccer teams, FC Bayern München and TSV 1860. Other facilities include the ice-rink, gym and spa complex, which are all open to the public.

If you prefer spending time outside, you can walk around the artificial lake, the Olympiasee, or climb 53m (174ft) up the man-made hill, made of rubble from World War II and now covered with alpine vegetation.

TOURS

There are several different tours you can take at the Olympiapark. The soccer tour, which lasts an hour, is at 11am and takes in the Olympic stadium, changing rooms and VIP area of Munich's soccer teams. The tour costs €6 for adults and €4 for children (6–15). The Adventure Tour, Apr–end Oct at 2pm and lasting an hour and a half, takes in the sights that you see on the soccer tour, the Olympic Hall and swimming pool, and includes a ride on the park train. It costs €8 for adults and €5.50 for children (6–15). If you're not afraid of heights, there's the Roof Climb Tour at 2.30, which involves climbing up to the roof of the Olympic stadium (wear rubber-soled shoes), where a guide explains the stadium's architecture and you get a different view of the Frauenkirche (▷ 268). This tour costs €25 during the week and €35 on weekends for adults, and €25 for children (10–15).

OLYMPIATURM

Built between 1965 and 1968, and standing 290m (951ft) high, the Olympic tower is now as much part of the Munich skyline as the twin onion domes of the Frauenkirche. You whizz up to the top in a matter of seconds in the high-speed lift (elevator), and it is certainly worth the trip as, on a clear day, you can see as far as the Alps. When you get to the top, make sure you go outside for unimpeded views over the whole city and fantastic photo opportunities. There's also a (very slowly) revolving restaurant which is open in the summer only.

PRINZREGENTEN-STRASSE

This long avenue, laid out in the 19th century, begins at the Englischer Garten (▷ 269) and ends in Prinzregentenplatz in the fashionable Bogenhausen district, where many Munich celebrities have their homes (Boris Becker lives here). By the Englischer Garten is the Haus der Kunst art gallery (daily 10–8, Thu 10–10; tel 089 2112 7113), which used to display German art of the Third Reich, but now houses changing exhibitions of contemporary art. Just beyond the gallery is a stretch of river where surfers surf against the flow of water.

Farther on is the Bayerisches Nationalmuseum (▷ 265), which contains items relating to Bavarian history. Heading east along the avenue, cross the River Isar and go down the underpass to cross the road. You come out at the golden Friedensengel (Angel of Peace), which faces towards Paris and was erected to commemorate the 25th anniversary of the Treaty of Versailles (▷ 40). Farther along, art lovers have another treat in the elegant, white Villa Stuck (Tue–Sun 11–6; tel 089 455 5510), which specializes in art nouveau.

261 E3 U-Bahn Lehel (west end) or Prinzregentenplatz (east end) Tram 17 to Haus der Kunst and Nationalmuseum

RESIDENZ

▷ 282–283.

SCHLEISSHEIM

www.schloesser.bayern.de

To the north of Munich are the three palaces and gardens that make up Schleissheim. The original palace was built in the late 16th century for Duke Wilhelm V and was expanded considerably by Maximilian I.

The more flamboyant palace is the Neues Schloss (New Palace), begun in 1701 by Prince Elector Maximilian Emanuel as 'the Bavarian Versailles'. The cost of building the palace drained Bavaria's resources, but resulted in an impressive building in baroque and rococo styles, with stuccowork and frescoes by François Cuvilliés (1696–1768) and the Asam brothers, whose work you can also see in Asamkirche (▷ 265). Prince Maximilian Emanuel was also a great collector of paintings, and in the Grand Gallery there are works by Anthony van Dyck (1599–1641) and Peter Paul Rubens (1577– 1640), among others.

The Lustheim Palace was built by Max Emanuel as a grand hunting lodge to celebrate his marriage to Maria Antonia, the daughter of the Austrian emperor. It is worth visiting for the Ernst Schneider Meissen porcelain collection alone.

Once you've seen the palaces, you can take time to enjoy the formal baroque gardens, which follow the strict rules set down by Versailles garden designer André Le Nôtre.

260 (inset) Max-Emanuel-Platz 1, 85764, Oberschleissheim 089 315 8720 Palace: Apr–end Sep Tue–Sun 9–6; Oct–end Mar Tue–Sun 10–4. Fountains: Apr to mid-Sep daily 10–4 Altes Schloss: adult €2.50; Neues Schloss: adult €4; Schloss Lustheim: adult €3; combined ticket: adult €6; child (under 18) free at all venues; gardens: free S-Bahn Oberschleissheim 292

SCHLOSS NYMPHENBURG

▷ 284–285.

TIERPARK HELLABRUNN

www.zoo-munich.de

Hellabrunn is different from many other city zoos in that it has been created as a 'geo-zoo', which means that the animals live in surroundings that are intended to be as close as possible to their natural habitat. The way the enclosures are designed means that you very often get a view of the animals without looking through a cage or a fence.

The zoo has a coral reef, a primate house with monkeys and gorillas, a South American area with anteaters and vicuñas and an Australian area with wallabies and kangaroos. There are plenty of activities for children, such as camel or pony rides, elephant shows and the seal show.

At the Isar entrance there is an enclosure where children can touch non-threatening animals, such as dwarf goats.

260 (inset) Tierparkstrasse 30, 81543 München (Thalkirchen) 089 625080 Apr–end Sep daily 8–6; Oct–end Mar daily 9–5 Adult €9, child (4–14) €4.50, under 4 free U-Bahn Thalkirchen 52

VIKTUALIENMARKT

The Viktualienmarkt (the name has a Latin derivation meaning 'food market') is the main food market in Munich. It used to be in Marienplatz but grew so big that it was moved to its present site by Peterskirche 200 years ago.

Anything and everything you could want to eat is here: Fruit, vegetables, fish, meat, sausages, cheese, honey, bread, cakes and wine are just some of the things on sale. There is also plenty of non-German produce available, including Italian cheeses and French wines, and in recent years more exotic stalls and shops have opened, such as the South American shop and the kosher shop where you can buy kosher red wine and soups as well as filled bagels for about €4.

The freshly squeezed juice stands are a must—choose from any combination of raspberry, orange, apple, carrot, pineapple and celery, to name a few, with a small juice costing upwards of €1.50.

The market is a good place to come for a quick bite to eat, with stalls selling pork sandwiches, pretzels, soup and *weissbier* (a pale, refreshing beer).

Don't leave without admiring the tall, brightly painted maypole in the middle of the market.

261 D4 Viktualienmarkt, 80331 München (Altstadt)z Mon–Fri 7–6, Sat 7–4; closed Sun U- or S-Bahn Marienplatz 52, 131. Tram 17, 18 Plenty of stalls selling take-away food and drinks

Opposite *The Olympiapark with the Olympiaturm in the foreground*

INFORMATION

www.residenz-muenchen.de
261 D3 Max-Joseph-Platz 3, 80333 München (Altstadt) 089 290671 Apr to mid-Oct daily 9–6; mid-Oct to end Mar daily 10–4 Schatzkammer: Adult €6, child (under 18) free; Residenzmuseum: Adult €6, child (under 18) free; combined ticket €9 U- or S-Bahn Marienplatz; U-Bahn Odeonsplatz 51. Tram 12, 16, 17

Above *The Antiquarium was built to house Duke Albrecht V's antiques*

INTRODUCTION

The largest building in Munich's Altstadt (old town), the Residenz started out as a small castle in 1385, and later was the residence of the dukes and kings of Bavaria for more than 400 years, from the beginning of the 16th century to the early 20th century. It includes the Antiquarium (a large Renaissance hall), a rococo theatre, royal apartments in the Königsbau (Royal Palace), museums and the Treasury, filled with priceless jewels, crowns, chains and ornaments.

The Wittelsbach dynasty, which ruled Bavaria for nearly 800 years, added to the original building over the years until it became the palace, with more than 130 rooms, that exists today. They used it as their luxurious private home, and for 400 years also as the seat of government. The complex is built around seven courtyards, decorated in a number of different styles (Renaissance, baroque, rococo and neoclassical) and filled with valuable paintings and sculptures, furniture, clocks, tapestries, porcelain and even sacred vestments.

Decide before you arrive what you would like to see and what you realistically have time for. You have the option of buying a ticket for the Treasury only, the Residenz only, or a combined ticket, which lets you see both. In the Residenz itself, about half the rooms are open to the public in the morning, then closed in the afternoon, when the rest of the rooms are open. This means that to see all the rooms you will have to visit before and after lunch or go straight through at the changeover time (12.30 in winter and 1.30 in summer). You should allow at least an hour for each set of rooms. In addition, you will need at least half an hour to see the Treasury. Pick up a free floor plan (available in English), which has a plan of the complex and numbers for each room.

WHAT TO SEE

TREASURY

The Wittelsbachs' Treasury (Schatzkammer) is in 10 rooms of the Königsbau, opposite the cloakroom, and contains hundreds of precious and priceless crowns and insignia, jewels, shrines, religious art and tableware. An audioguide (available in German, English, Italian and French) is included in the price of your ticket and gives a detailed commentary on most of the pieces in the Treasury. You'll need to be selective, as the commentaries cover so many of the items that the running time of the tape is several hours!

Highlights include the magnificent statuette of St. George, the patron saint of the Wittelsbach family. The stunningly detailed statuette, which shows St. George on horseback slaying the dragon, is exquisitely decorated in gold, silver, precious stones and large pearls. Other pieces to look out for include the rock crystal shrine with scenes from the Old Testament in room 6 and the beautiful table in room 7, commissioned by Elector Maximilian I and his first wife, Augusta-Wilhemine. The table is inlaid with gold, agate, lapis lazuli and jasper, and has a landscape picture in the middle, made from flat slices of precious stones.

ANTIQUARIUM (HALL OF ANTIQUITIES)

This magnificent hall, the largest Renaissance hall north of the Alps, was built by Duke Albrecht V between 1568 and 1571 to house his collection of antiques and later became a banquet hall. It's 66m (216ft) long, with a beautiful, low, barrel-vaulted ceiling, painted with scenes of old Bavarian towns and allegories of Fame and the Virtues. As you walk through the hall you have an eerie sensation of being watched by the collection of more than 100 busts, which are mostly from Rome and Venice.

ALTES RESIDENZTHEATER (CUVILLIÉS THEATRE)

Said by some to be the finest rococo theatre in the world, the Italian-style Old Residence Theatre was built between 1751 and 1755 by François Cuvilliés, and for this reason is also known as the Cuvilliés Theatre. One claim to fame is that in 1781 it hosted the world premiere of Mozart's *Idomeneo*. The building was destroyed after it was bombed in World War II, but the tiers of boxes had been removed for safekeeping beforehand, and you can still see them today. The theatre continues as a performance venue and so it is sometimes closed for rehearsals.

MORE TO SEE

The Residenz has a dizzying array of styles of interior decoration. Other interesting pieces to look out for include the Grottenhof, which you pass before going into the Antiquarium, with its unusual fountain encrusted with shells, and the Ancestral Gallery filled with portraits. On the upper floor is the Schwarzer Saal (Black Room), named after the black marble that surrounds the doorways. It has a beautiful trompe l'oeil ceiling painted by Hans Werl, which gives the illusion of an upper gallery supported by pillars. In the Green Gallery of the Rich Rooms, strategically placed mirrors make the rooms look as if they go on forever.

The Kaisersaal, which you'll come to at the end of your visit, is large and impressive with its marble floor, chandeliers, tapestries and ornate ceiling. The light pastel ceilings of the Royal Apartments, such as Maximilian II's living room (Wohnzimmer) are a pleasant antidote to the heavy opulence of rooms such as Ludwig I's sumptuous gold and deep red Throne Room. Also on the upper floor is the Rich Chapel, Maximilian I's private oratory, which lives up to its name by being richly decorated. The highlights are the oval-shaped tambour with stained-glass windows and the walls, which appear to be made of red marble, but are in fact lined with stucco, designed to simulate marble.

TIPS

» The Residenz is large, so why not make a day of it? After visiting the rooms that open in the morning, have a leisurely lunch before going back to see the afternoon rooms.

» There is a free cloakroom for bags and coats, although you may want to keep your coat on in winter; some of the larger rooms are quite cold.

GALLERY GUIDE

Ground Floor

The Treasury, Ancestral Gallery, Grotto Courtyard, Antiquarium, Nibelungen Halls, Court Chapel, Sacred Vestment Rooms, bookshop and cloakroom.

Upper Floor

Black Hall, Porcelain Chambers, Rich Rooms, Reliquaries Chamber, Rich Chapel, Stone Rooms, Four White Horses Hall, Imperial Hall, Royal Apartments.

Below *Look out for the variety of decorated ceilings in the Residenz*

INFORMATION

www.schloesser.bayern.de

260 (inset) Schloss Nymphenburg, 80638 München (Nymphenburg)

089 179080 Apr to mid-Oct daily 9–6, mid-Oct to end Mar daily 10–4; closed 1 Jan, Shrove Tue, 24, 25, 31 Dec; Pagodenburg, Badenburg and Magdalenenburg closed mid-Oct to end Mar Palace only: adult €5; Marstallmuseum (Carriage Museum) and Porcelain Museum: adult €4; Amalienburg only: adult €2; combined ticket for palace, carriage museum and porcelain museum: adult €10, child (under 18) free 51. Tram 12, 16, 17 Schlosscafé im Palmenhaus

INTRODUCTION

One of Germany's largest baroque palaces, Schloss Nymphenburg is set in beautiful parkland, yet within easy reach of the city. The kings of Bavaria used it as a summer residence in the days when the journey from Munich took two hours (nowadays it's a 15-minute tram ride). There is plenty here to fill a day, including visiting the palace rooms, filled with frescoes, paintings, chandeliers and fine furniture, along with three museums and landscaped parkland with four pavilions, each of which merit a visit. In addition, the palace is the home of the famous Nymphenburg porcelain factory.

The palace was begun by Elector Ferdinand Maria (ruled 1651–79) in 1664 to celebrate the birth of his son and heir Maximilian Emanuel, who himself later added a gallery and side wings to the original building. Between 1664 and 1757, five rulers from the Wittelsbach family—Ferdinand Maria, Maximilian II Emanuel, Karl Albrecht, Maximilian III Joseph and Maximilian IV Joseph—contributed to the construction. It was based on designs by the Italian architect Agostino Barelli, who also worked on the Theatinerkirche in Odeonsplatz and who was succeeded in 1673 by Enrico Zuccalli. From 1714 the German architect Joseph Effner took over, adding the pavilions Pagodenburg, Badenburg and Magdalenenklause (Hermitage of Mary Magdalene).

WHAT TO SEE

THE MAIN PALACE

The first thing you notice when you enter the palace is the large ceiling fresco in the Great Hall or Steinerner Saal (Stone Room), which was painted by Johann Baptist Zimmermann between 1755 and 1757 and was commissioned by Max Joseph, who wanted a fresco with themes of peace and reconciliation. In the middle is Apollo's sun chariot, with Olympian gods riding over a rainbow, and to the right is Diana, goddess of hunting, whose presence reflects the palace's role as a hunting lodge.

Other rooms you can see in the palace, most of which have a board with explanatory notes in German, English and Italian, include the Queen's Bedroom, where Ludwig II was born in 1845, and, in the south wing, Ludwig I's Gallery of Beauties, with paintings that were originally on show in the Residenz (▷ 282–283). Ludwig I (ruled 1825–48) was a great admirer of beauty and commissioned the artist Joseph Stieler to paint the portraits of many beautiful young women. Between 1827 and 1850 Stieler painted 36 portraits of women from various countries, including England, Italy and Bavaria, and his subjects included the daughter of a shoemaker as well as Ludwig I's sister and daughter.

On the ground floor you will find lockers, giftshop, ticket desk, toilets while the upper floor contains the palace rooms, including the Steinerner Saal (Stone Room) and the Schönheitsgalerie (Gallery of Beauties).

PARK AND PAVILIONS

The park, 300ha (740 acres) in size, is a wonderful place to walk at any time of the year. Originally in Italian style, the park was relaid in French baroque style. In the 19th century, it was transformed into an English park with waterways, a large and a small lake, the Monopteros (a Greek-style temple), statues and the long central canal, which ends in a waterfall. Amalienburg is the little pink-and-white rococo hunting lodge designed by the architect François Cuvilliés the Elder in 1734 and built by Karl Albrecht for his wife Electress Maria Amalia. It has a grand circular Hall of Mirrors with gold stuccowork, and its Hunting Room is full of landscape paintings.

Other than Amalienburg the pavilions in the park are Badenburg, with a large Banqueting Hall and a two-floor Bathing Hall, the octagonal Pagodenburg, with a beautiful domed ceiling, and Magdalenenklause, designed and built as a ruin, and in the grounds you will also see greenhouses and a fountain, and there is a café for refreshments.

MUSEUMS

At Schloss Nymphenburg there are three museums, each with a different themed collection. The Marstallmuseum (Coach Museum) is in the former stables: The large building is needed to show the sumptuous coaches (including some designed for children), sleighs and portraits of the royal thoroughbred horses. The ornate gold New Dress Coach of King Ludwig II has to be seen to be believed.

The Porcelain Museum, above the stables, displays the exquisite porcelain manufactured at the Nymphenburg porcelain factory, founded in 1761. There are plates, ornaments and urns, paintings and, surprisingly, an extensive collection of porcelain bridles. Both museums have the same opening hours as the palace.

In the north wing is the Museum Mensch und Natur (Museum of Man and Nature, Tue, Wed, Fri 10–7, Thu 9–8, Sat, Sun, holidays 10–6; tel 089 179 5890), which, unusually for a palace museum, does not showcase objects from the royal household. It explains how the Earth was created and traces the origin of species. It's designed as a 'hands-on' museum, and so should appeal to children.

TIPS

» The Badenburg, Pagodenburg and Magdalenenklause pavilions are closed in winter.

» The park is a wonderful place to explore, so bring your walking shoes and a camera. You can even go jogging here.

» The atmospheric café/restaurant Schlosscafé im Palmenhaus (▷ 297) is a great place for a coffee or lunch between museums.

» Classical music concerts are held at the palace. Ask at the tourist office or call 089 179 08444 for details.

» If you arrive by tram (which is more convenient than taking the U-Bahn), you'll need to walk to the palace, past the ornamental ponds, which takes about 10 minutes. Head towards the shop in the main palace building (the tall square building in the middle), where you buy your entrance ticket. Then head outside and up the steps to the palace entrance.

Opposite *The main palace at the middle of the Schloss Nymphenburg complex includes the ticket office*

MUNICH'S OLD TOWN

The walk starts on Munich's grand square, Odeonsplatz (▷ 275), and ends in the heart of the city on Marienplatz. It takes in several churches, including the twin-towered Frauenkirche, which has become emblematic of the city. En route you also pass one of Munich's grandest hotels and walk through one of the former gates to the city.

THE WALK
Distance: 2km (1.2 miles)
Allow: 2 hours
Start at: Odeonsplatz
End at: Marienplatz

HOW TO GET THERE
U-bahn Odeonsplatz.

★ Begin at Odeonsplatz and walk west along Brienner Strasse, where exclusive shops sell antiques, jewellery and designer clothes. Most shops here don't open until 10am, so if you come before then, it'll be window-shopping only. Very soon you'll come to Wittelsbacherplatz.

❶ Wittelsbacherplatz, named after the dynasty that ruled Bavaria from 1180 until 1918, has an impressive equestrian statue of Elector Maximilian I.

Opposite Wittelsbacherplatz, on the other side of the road, is Amiraplatz. Go down here past the Literaturhaus.

❷ The Literaturhaus is the home of Munich's literary scene, with book readings and a wonderful café. Opposite is the Hugendubel bookstore (▷ 290): Nearby is the Greek Orthodox Salvatorkirche.

Continue straight on to Kardinal Faulhaberstrasse, where you have a good view of the distinctive green onion domes of the Frauenkirche at the end of the street.

❸ The Palais Porcia on Kardinal Faulhaberstrasse has been the residence of the archbishops of Munich and Freising since 1818. Also in this street a grille (grate) on the pathway, in the shape of a dead man's body marks where Bavaria's first prime minister, Kurt Eisner, was assassinated in February 1919.

At the end of Kardinal Faulhaberstrasse, turn right into Promenadeplatz. Walk past one of Munich's glamorous hotels, the five-star Bayerischer Hof (▷ 298), with its costumed doorman outside.

❹ On Karmeliterstrasse, on the other side of Promenadeplatz, is the Carmelite church, the earliest baroque church in the city. Almost opposite on Pacellistrasse is the Dreifaltigkeitskirche (Church of the Holy Trinity), with its ornate gold and green door.

Continue to the end of Pacellistrasse. Opposite you, in the middle of the main road in Lenbachplatz, is the 1885 Wittelsbach Fountain. Don't cross the road—stay on the same side and turn left. On the left you'll pass the gleaming BMW showroom, which has 4x4 models from Munich's most popular car manufacturer. Cross over Maxburgstrasse to reach Mövenpick.

❺ Mövenpick is well known in Munich for its enormous breakfast buffet and Sunday brunch, which are served in the café. It also has a cocktail bar, a restaurant and even a cigar smoking room, and it's a good place to stop for coffee and cake.

When you come out of Mövenpick, turn left and continue along the main road until you come to Karlstor, formerly the west gate to the city, on the left. Go through the gate into the pedestrianized shopping area on Neuhauserstrasse. Pass Michaelskirche and, at the statue of a wild boar, turn left up Augustinerstrasse to the Frauenkirche.

❻ The mighty Frauenkirche (Church of Our Lady) acts as Munich's cathedral. Its twin towers, topped by distinctive green onion domes, which can be seen from all over the city, are the symbol of Munich.

Go down Thiereckstrasse and continue into Marienplatz, where there are plenty of options for lunch.

WHEN TO GO

You can do this walk at all times of the year.

PLACES TO VISIT

SALVATORKIRCHE

✉ Salvatorplatz 17, 80333 München
☎ 089 2280 7676 ⏲ Daily 10–5 ✋ Free

WHERE TO EAT

For a quick bite standing up, go to one of the food stands at the Viktualienmarkt (▷ 281), or for good traditional Bavarian fare, try Spatenhaus an der Oper (▷ 297). To get there, walk up Dienerstrasse to Max-Joseph-Platz. For something more exclusive (and expensive), indulge yourself at Dallmayr (▷ 296) on Dienerstrasse.

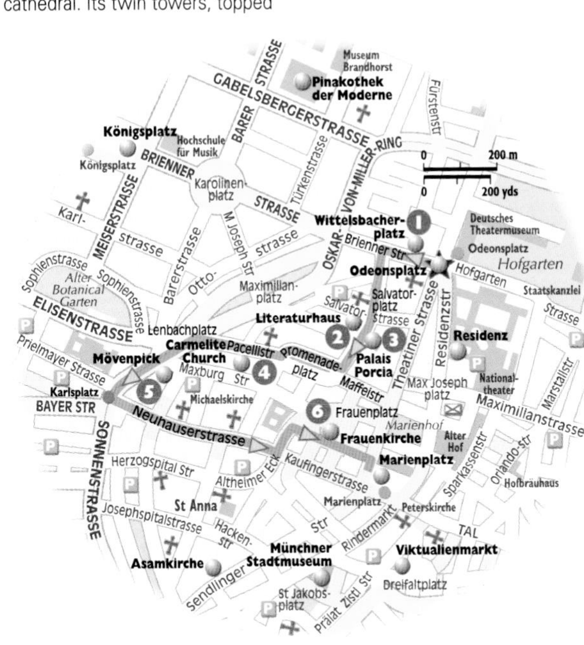

Opposite *The late Gothic Frauenkirche (Cathedral of Our Lady)*

MAXVORSTADT, SCHWABING AND THE ENGLISCHER GARTEN

Skirting the northern edge of the old town, this tour takes you through an area filled with art museums and galleries, before reaching the lively university district, then slicing through part of the Englischer Garten. It ends at a restful retreat in the heart of town.

THE WALK
Distance: 5km (3 miles)
Allow: 3 hours (excluding stops)
Start at: Königsplatz
End at: Odeonsplatz

HOW TO GET THERE
U-Bahn Königsplatz.

★ Take a turn around grassy Königsplatz (▷ 268), known as 'Athens-on-the-Isar' for its monumental neoclassical buildings: the Staatliche Antikensammlung on the south side, the Propyläen in the middle of a traffic circle on the west, and the Glyptothek on the north. Just off the square's northwest side, on Luisenstrasse, is the Lenbachhaus (▷ 275), a Tuscan-style villa with a fountain in the garden.

Leave Königsplatz on Brienner Strasse, passing by the Hochschule für Musik und Theater, on the way to Karolinenplatz.

❶ The obelisk, 29m (95ft) high, at the heart of Karolinenplatz, is a memorial (1833) to 30,000 Bavarian soldiers who fell in the Napoleon's invasion of Russia. From this circular 'square', the Kunstareal (art district), rich in public and private galleries, fans out through the surrounding streets.

Turn left on Barer Strasse and go north to the Alte Pinakothek (▷ 266–267) (entrance on Theresienstrasse).

❷ One of the world's great art galleries, the Alte Pinakothek is worth a visit of at least a half day. As if that isn't enough to delay you, also on Barer Strasse are its almost equally stellar sister galleries the Neue Pinakothek (▷ 278) and the Pinakothek der Moderne (▷ 279), which together bring the city's premier art collections right up to contemporary times.

Continue north on Barer Strasse, and turn right on Schellingstrasse. This street behind the university is one of many in the area that are vibrant with student cafés, bookstores and offbeat stores.

❸ At the end of Schellingstrasse rise up the twin towers of the Ludwigskirche (Ludwig Church; 1844), an Italianate basilica with colonnades along Ludwigstrasse. Among the notable decorative works is a fresco, *The Last Judgement* (1840), by Peter von Cornelius.

Go north a short way on Ludwigstrasse to Geschwister-Scholl-Platz.

❹ The entrance to Munich's university, the Ludwig-Maximilians-Universität, is marked by twin fountains. Geschwister-Scholl-Platz is named after brother and sister Sophie and Hans Scholl, members of the student Weisse Rose (White Rose) non-violent resistance movement against the Nazis, who were executed in 1943.

Turn right on Veterinärstrasse and continue along to the end, to enter the Englischer Garten (▷ 269).

❺ A short clockwise loop from this entrance, curving past the Chinesischer Turm (▷ 269) and the Monopteros (▷ 269), affords a brief introduction to Munich's vast main park, with little risk of getting lost among its myriad paths.

❻ Exit the park close to the Japanisches Teehaus (▷ 269), at the south end of Königinstrasse, at its junction with Prinzregentenstrasse. A short way along this elegant street is the Haus der Kunst (▷ 281), a neoclassical art gallery (1937) designed by architect Paul Ludwig Troost.

Turn around and cross over Königinstrasse to the south side of Von-der-Tann Strasse, passing a large fountain and the Prinz-Carl-Palais (1806), the office of Bavaria's Minister-President (prime minister). Go through the Dichtergarten (Poets' Garden) and cross over Galeriestrasse to enter the Hofgarten (1617).

❼ Stroll among the baroque Hofgarten's fountains and geometric lawns, and around the circular Dianatempel (Temple of Diana) at the nexus of its paths—or just take in the graceful scene while relaxing on a park bench.

Exit the garden on the west side, on Odeonsplatz.

WHEN TO GO

You can do this walk at all times of the year. If you wish to visit any of the museums or galleries along the way, remember that many are closed on Monday.

PLACE TO VISIT

LUDWIGSKIRCHE

✉ Ludwigstrasse 20, 80539 München
☎ 089 288334 🕐 Daily 8–6 ✋ Free

WHERE TO EAT

Offering everything from breakfast through lunch and dinner, and with snacks and coffee and cake for fillers, Café Puck (▷ 295) is a flexible option. One of the most popular eateries and beer gardens in the Englischer Garten is the Restaurant am Chinesischen Turm, easily identified by the pagoda dating from 1789 (▷ 295).

Opposite *Alte Pinakothek was built in Venetian Renaissance style*

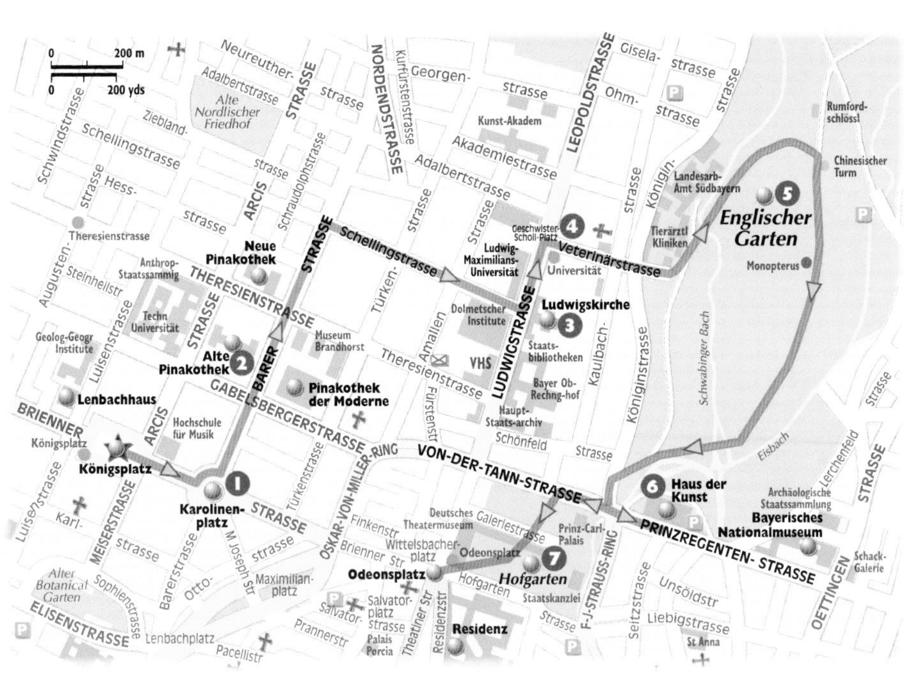

SHOPPING

ALLES AUS HOLZ

www.holz-leute.de

Everything in this store is made out of wood. Items that might fit in your suitcase include chess sets, toys, pens, large bowls and salad servers.
Viktualienmarkt 2, 80331 München (Altstadt) 089 268248 Mon–Fri 10–7, Sat 10–6 Marienplatz

BASIC

www.basic-ag.de

This supermarket-style shop is packed with organic fruit and vegetables, pasta, beer, wine, fruit juices, bread and even doughnuts (*krapfen*) and cosmetics. You can buy unbleached cotton clothes for children, and accessories. There's also a vegetarian restaurant (▷ 294), a health and beauty clinic (▷ 293) and a snack and juice bar.
Westenriederstrasse 35, 80331 München (Altstadt) 089 242 0890 Mon–Sat 8–6 Isartor

DALLMAYR

www.dallmayr.de

This traditional high-quality delicatessen has separate counters that sell beautifully decorated cakes, cold meats and sausages, chocolate, tea, coffee beans and fruit. There is also a restaurant (▷ 296).
Dienerstrasse 14–15, 80331 München (Altstadt) 089 21350 Mon–Sat 9.30–7 Marienplatz

GALERIA KAUFHOF

www.galeria-kaufhof.de

Kaufhof department store has three branches, and is not as expensive as the more classy Ludwig Beck and Loden Frey. Head to the basement for the best bargains.
Marienplatz (Kaufingerstrasse 1–5), 80331 München (Altstadt) 089 231851 Mon–Sat 9–8 Marienplatz

HUGENDUBEL

www.hugendubel.de

There are several other branches of this large bookstore chain in the city.
Marienplatz 22, 80331 München (Altstadt) 01801 484484 Mon–Sat 9.30–8 Marienplatz

KARE CITYHAUS

www.kare.de

This store sells funky accessories and items such as cushions, blankets, Italian Alessi kitchen implements, psychedelic ashtrays and even business-card holders. The Yambai Thai Garden downstairs serves delicious dishes.
Sendlinger Strasse 37, 80331 München (Altstadt) 089 230 8735 Mon–Sat 10–8 Sendlinger Tor

Above *The National Theatre is the home of the Bavarian State Opera and is a popular venue for opera-lovers*

LODEN FREY

www.loden-frey.de

An extremely elegant department store where designer-clad women shop for Armani, Dolce & Gabbana, Escada, Burberry, Valentino and Ralph Lauren.
Maffeistrasse 7, 80333 München (Altstadt) 089 210390 Mon–Sat 10–8 Marienplatz

LUDWIG BECK

www.ludwig-beck.de

A Munich store of choice with several floors of clothes, lingerie, expensive cosmetic brands, handbags and accessories. Don't miss the music department on the top floor, where you can listen on headphones before you buy. There are several cafés.
Marienplatz 11, 80331 München (Altstadt) 089 236910 Mon–Sat 10–8 Marienplatz

MAX KRUG

www.max-krug.com

Lined from floor to ceiling with beer steins, musical boxes, toys, Christmas decorations and wooden cuckoo clocks, handmade in Bavaria's Black Forest, this is the shop if you're looking for a cute Bavarian gift.

Neuhauser Strasse 2, 80331 München (Altstadt) 089 224501 Mon–Sat 9.30–8 Karlsplatz Stachus, Marienplatz

OBERPOLLINGER

www.oberpollinger.de

This huge department store sells a wide range of items.

Neuhauserstrasse 18, 80331 München (Altstadt) 089 290230 Mon–Sat 9.30–8 Karlsplatz

7 HIMMEL

www.siebterhimmel.com

Siebter Himmel (Seventh Heaven) is a women's clothing store with bright, funky, individual clothes at reasonable prices. Across the street is Schuhhimmel (Shoe Heaven).

Hans-Sachs-Strasse 17, 80469 München (Isarvorstadt) 089 267053 Mon–Fri 11–7, Sat 10–6 Sendlinger Tor

SPORT-SCHECK

www.sportscheck.com

Here you will find six floors of clothing and equipment, as well as anything else you could ever possibly need for just about any sport. You can buy gear for surfing, tennis, golf, running or the gym or fit yourslef out for skiing or snowboarding. The store also organizes day trips to the snow for winter sports.

Sendlinger Strasse 6, 80331 München (Altstadt) 089 21660 Mon–Sat 10–8 Marienplatz

VIKTUALIENMARKT

▷ 281.

WORDS'WORTH

www.wordsworth.de

There's a large selection of English-language literature, audio-books, videos, DVDs and postcards at this Schwabing store.

Schellingstrasse 3, 80799 München (Schwabing) 089 280 9141 Mon–Sat 10–7 Universität

ENTERTAINMENT AND NIGHTLIFE

ATOMIC CAFÉ

www.atomic.de

A strict door policy ensures that only the beautiful people get into this club, so it's a good idea to dress up. It is known for playing plenty of Britpop, as well as reggae, punk, soul and hip-hop.

Neuturmstrasse 5, 80331 München (Altstadt) 089 5481 8181 Tue–Thu, Sun 10pm–3am, Fri, Sat 10pm–4am €3 before 11.30pm Tram 19 to Kammerspiele

BAR CENTRALE

www.bar-centrale.com

Centrale is a small, intimate Italian bar, great for a late-night coffee or grappa. The room at the back is full of conversation and it gets very smoky.

Ledererstrasse 23, 80331 München (Altstadt) 089 223762 Mon–Sat 8am–1am, Sun 11am–1am Isartor

CHINESISCHER TURM

www.chinaturm.de

You can't beat the setting of this beer garden. There are plenty of people and there's always a good atmosphere, even in winter.

Englischer Garten 3, 80538 München (Schwabing) 089 383 8730 Daily 10am–midnight Bus 54, 154 Giselastrasse

CINEMA

www.cinema-muenchen.com

One screen shows English-language movies. Be sure to arrive early (or reserve by phone) for Sunday evening screenings and also on 'Cinema Days' (Monday and Tuesday), when movies starting before 5.30pm are €4 and after 5.30pm €5. You can take your drinks into the cinema.

Nymphenburger Strasse 31, 80335 München (Neuhausen) 089 555255 Box office noon–11pm €4–€8 Stigmaierplatz

COCCODRILLO

www.caffe-florian.de

This bar is in the atmospheric cellar of Caffè Florian in the university area of Schwabing, and has live music on Tuesdays and Thursdays. Happy hour is 8pm–9pm every evening.

Hohenzollernstrasse 11, 80801 München (Schwabing) 089 336639 Sun–Thu 8pm–1am, Fri, Sat 8pm–3am. Live music: Tue and Thu from 8pm (from 9pm Sep–end May) Giselastrasse, Münchner Freiheit Tram 12, 27 to Kurfürstenplatz; bus 33

DEUTSCHE EICHE

www.deutsche-eiche.de

This hotel is home to Munich's oldest gay bar, where Freddie Mercury used to have a beer when he was in Munich.

Reichenbachstrasse 13, 80469 München (Glockenbach) 089 231 1660 Daily 7.30am–1am Tram 17, 18 to Reichenbachstrasse

DEUTSCHES MUSEUM

▷ 270–274.

DEUTSCHES THEATER

www.deutsches-theater.de

The Deutsches Theater hosts ballet performances, musicals and revues, and during *Fasching* (Carnival; ▷ 293) many fancy-dress balls and events are held here. These are temporary premises while the theatre in Schwanthalerstrasse is being renovated.

Werner-Heisenberg-Allee 11, 80939 München (Schwabing-Freimann) 089 5523 4444 Box office: Mon–Fri 12–6, Sat 10.30am–1.30pm €19–€69 U-Bahn Fröttmaning Karlsplatz

ENGLISCHER GARTEN

▷ 269.

GASTEIG

www.gasteig.de

www.mphil.de

This huge complex is the home of the Munich Philharmonic Orchestra and it also hosts visiting orchestras. Many other different kinds of performances are also held here, from the Chinese State Circus to Frank Sinatra tributes.

Rosenheimer Strasse 5, 81667 München (Haidhausen) 089 480980 Box office: Mon–Fri 9–9, Sat 9–4, Sun 10–4 Varies Tram 18 to Am Gasteig; tram 15, 25 to Rosenheimerplatz

HIRSCHGARTEN

www.hirschgarten.de

The 200-year-old Hirschgarten is Munich's largest beer garden.

Hirschgarten 1, 80639 München (Nymphenburg) 089 1799 9119 Daily 9am–11.30pm Tram 17; bus 41, 68, 83

JAZZCLUB UNTERFAHRT

www.unterfahrt.de

Big names from around Germany and across the world, along with occasional proficient locals, perform jazz in a variety of styles in the vast cellar of a former brewery

Einsteinstrasse 42, 81675 München (Haidhausen) 089 448 2794 Sun–Thu 9.30pm–1am, Fri, Sat 9.30pm–3am €5–€32 Max-Weber-Platz

MATHÄSER

www.mathaeser.de

Munich's latest cinema complex is near the main train station (Hauptbahnhof). It has 14 screens, one or two of which usually show the latest blockbusters in English.

Bayerstrasse 5, 80335 München (Hauptbahnhof) 089 515651 Box office: 10.30am–10.50pm €7–€9 Karlsplatz Stachus

MÜNCHNER KAMMERSPIELE

www.muenchner-kammerspiele.de

This theatre company is housed in three locations in Munich. It stages high-quality productions, including contemporary plays and updated interpretations of Shakespeare.

Schauspielhaus: Maximilianstrasse 26–28, 80539 München. Neues Haus: Falckenbergstrasse 1, 80539 München. Werkraum: Hildegardstrasse 1, 80539 München 089 2339 6600 Box office: Mon–Fri 10–6, Sat 10–1 €8–€45 Tram 19 to Maximilianstrasse

NATIONALTHEATER

www.staatstheater.bayern.de

www.bayerisches.staatsoper.de

The Nationaltheater is home to the Bavarian State Opera and stages performances of Verdi, Wagner and Strauss during the opera season.

Max-Joseph-Platz 2, 80539 München (Altstadt) 089 2185 1920 Box office: Mon–Fri 10–6, Sat 10–1 Tours: 2pm €6–€240 Marienplatz, Odeonsplatz Bus 100 to Marienplatz; bus 53 to Odeonsplatz; tram 19 to Nationaltheater

NEKTAR

www.nektar.de

An evening in Nektar is a unique experience, starting with the slippers you are given to wear to your dinner, which you eat horizontally, lying down on cushions. Expect films, cabaret and live music.

Stubenvollstrasse 1, 81667 München (Haidhausen) 089 4591 1311 Sun–Thu 7pm–2am, Fri, Sat 7pm–3am Tram 15, 25 to Rosenheimerplatz

SCHUMANN'S

www.schumanns.de

This is a good-looking bar frequented by good-looking people drinking cocktails served by staff in old-fashioned white coats. Dress up.

Odeonsplatz 6–7, 80331 München (Altstadt) 089 229060 Mon–Fri 5pm–3am, Sat, Sun 6pm–3am Odeonsplatz

TIERPARK HELLABRUNN

▷ 281.

SPORTS AND ACTIVITIES

MIKE'S BIKE TOURS

www.mikesbiketours.com

You can tour the city by bicycle with an English-speaking guide. The four-hour ride, almost entirely on bicycle paths includes a stop at the beer garden in the Englischer Garten. There are bicycles for children, and trailers and child seats. Meet at the Altes Rathaus in Marienplatz.

Hochrukenstrasse, 80331 München 089 2554 3987 Mar to mid-Apr, Sep to mid-Nov 12.30; mid-Apr to end May, Aug 11.30, 4; Jun, Jul 10.30, 11.30, 3, 4, plus 6-hour tour departing at 12.30 with two breaks at Olympiapark and Schloss Nymphenburg Adult €24, child (6–14) €12, under 6 free

OLYMPIAHALLE

www.olympiapark-muenchen.de

This huge venue stages concerts by big names such as Pink and Phil Collins, as well as performances like *Lord of the Dance*. For tickets, contact Olympiapark's ticket service kiosk (opposite the ice-rink).

Olympiapark, Spiridon-Louis-Ring 21, 80809 München (Olympiapark) 089 30670 7pm–11pm Varies (tickets from München Ticket, tel 01805 481 8181) Olympiapark

OLYMPIASTADION

www.fcbayern.t-online.de

www.tsv1860.de

Watch one of Munich's two soccer teams (Bayern München and TSV 1860) play at the Olympiastadion, north of downtown Munich.

Olympiapark, Spiridon-Louis-Ring 21, 80809 München (Olympiapark) 089 699310 (FC Bayern München), 01805 601860 (TSV) Aug–end May €10–€60 Olympiazentrum

OLYMPIA-SCHWIMMHALLE

www.olympiapark-muenchen.de

If you're visiting the Olympiapark, bring your swimming costume and towel, as you may be tempted by the Olympic-size pool.

Olympiapark, Spiridon-Louis-Ring 21, 80809 München (Olympiapark) 01801 796223 Pool: daily 7am–11pm. Sauna: Mon 10am–11pm, Tue–Sun 8am–11pm (women only on Tue). Ticket office: closes at 10pm Pool (up to 3 hours): adult €3.60, child (6–14) €2.80, under 6 free; day tickets: adult €6.80, child (6–14) €4.80, under 6 free, family €14.40; Sauna plus swim: €13.50 (up to 4 hours), €20.30 (day ticket) Olympiazentrum

RIKSCHA-MOBIL

www.rikscha-mobil.de

If walking or bicycling seems a bit strenuous, hop into the back of a rickshaw, and create your own itinerary. Tours start at the Fish Fountain in Marienplatz.

Am Einlass 3, 80469 München (Marienplatz) 089 2421 6880 Apr–end Nov 30-minute tour from €37; 45-minute tour from €49; 60-minute tour from €52 Marienplatz

JANUARY/FEBRUARY

FASCHING

www.muenchen-tourist.de

Many balls are held across the city during *Fasching* (Carnival). You'll see people dressed in their finery for the classic evening balls, and entire families dressed in fancy dress for less formal events. On the third Sunday in February (*Fasching Sonntag*), there is music and dancing in the heart of the city.

Second week in January–end of February

APRIL/MAY

AUER DULT

www.muenchen-tourist.de

The *Dult* street market and funfair is held three times a year, with an antiques market and traditional Bavarian food and beer stands. Also late July to early August and the third week in October.

Mariahilfplatz, München Late April–beginning of May Tram 27; bus 52, 56

JUNE/JULY

MÜNCHNER FILMFEST

www.filmfest-muenchen.de

Munich is a major focus of film-making and home to numerous film production companies. During the week-long Munich Film Festival, international movies—particularly German and European productions—are premièred in some of the city's 84 cinemas.

Late June–early July

AUGUST

SOMMERFEST IM OLYMPIAPARK

www.olympiapark-muenchen.de

This family-friendly festival offers activities and attractions such as fishing competitions on the lake and beer stands for the parents, then when the sun goes down there are fireworks and live bands.

Olympiapark, Spiridon-Louis-Ring 21, 80809 München (Olympiapark) 089 30670 Two weeks in August Olympiazentrum

SEPTEMBER/OCTOBER

OKTOBERFEST

www.muenchen-tourist.de

Munich's legendary *Oktoberfest* is for all ages. Here you'll find the world's biggest funfair, and, of course, 14 vast beer tents serving up beer and Bavarian food to the sound of brass oompah bands. You will need to make sure you reserve your accommodation months in advance.

Theresienwiese, 80336 München (Theresienwiese) Mid-September to beginning October Theresienwiese

OCTOBER

DIE LANGE NACHT

www.die-lange-nacht.de

For one night only, more than 70 churches, museums and galleries stay open very late and organize concerts, guided tours and performances. To obtain information see the website, and to buy tickets contact München Ticket (tel 01805 481 8181; www.muenchenticket.de).

089 3061 0041 One night in mid-October

NOVEMBER/DECEMBER

CHRISTKINDLMARKT

www.muenchen-tourist.de

Dating from the 14th century, Munich's Christmas market is legendary—visitors come especially to spend the weekend here. There are more than 140 stands, where you can buy Christmas tree decorations, crafts, wooden toys and even figures from the Crib Market. There's also live music, Advent music at 5.30pm on the balcony of the town hall, and food stands selling baked apples, Glühwein (hot spiced wine) and roasted almonds.

Marienplatz, München (Altstadt) Last Friday of November–24 December Marienplat

HEALTH AND BEAUTY

BEAUTY AND NATURE

www.beautyandnature.de

This spa is on the first floor of the organic supermarket Basic (▷ 290).

Westenrieder Strasse 35, 80331 München (Altstadt) 089 2423 1233 Mon–Sat 8am–8pm 50-minute aromatherapy massage €47.50; other treatments €7–€98.50 Isartor

SANTA MARGARITA SCHÖNHEITSSALON

www.santa-margarita.de

Uses Aveda and Vagheggi products.

Reichenbachstrasse 24, 80469 München (Glockenbach) 089 201 0961 Mon by appointment only, Tue–Fri 9–7, Sat 10–2 1-hour body massage €74; 1-hour Aveda mood massage €68; pedicure €65 Fraunhoferstrasse

FOR CHILDREN

BAVARIA FILMSTADT

www.filmstadt.de

A huge Film City for children with elaborate street sets as well as a stunt show and motion cinema.

Bavariafilmplatz 7, 82031 München (Geiselgasteig) 089 6499 2000 Mar–end Oct daily 9–4; Nov–end Feb daily 10–3 90-minute tour: adult €11, child (5–14) €8, family €34; Stunt show: €8.50; 3D cinema: €4.50. Tram 25 to Bavariafilmplatz Tours in English: Mar–end Nov daily 1pm. 3D cinema: Mar–end Oct daily 9–5; Nov–end Feb daily 9–4

MARIONETTENTHEATER

www.muenchner-marionettentheater.de

There are puppet shows and storytelling held here all year round.

Blumenstrasse 32, 80331 München (Sendlinger Tor) 089 265712 Wed, Sat, Sun show times 3pm, 8pm Afternoon shows: adult €9, child €7. Evening shows: adult €18, child €10 Sendlinger Tor

Above *Diners in the News Bar café and bar in the Schwabing area, which serves Bavarian as well as international dishes*

PRICES AND SYMBOLS

The restaurants are listed alphabetically (excluding Le, La and Les). The prices given are the average for a two-course lunch (L) and a three-course dinner (D) for one person, without drinks. The wine price is for the least expensive bottle. All the restaurants listed accept credit cards unless otherwise stated.

For a key to the symbols, ▷ 2.

AUGUSTINER

www.augustiner-restaurant.com

This 14th-century beer hall and restaurant belongs to the Augustiner brewery. Here 200 members of staff cater for up to 1,500 people. Try Bavarian top-sellers such as suckling pig roasted in dark beer and served with dumplings, meatloaf, boiled beef with potato salad or sausages.

✉ Neuhauserm Strasse 27, 80331 München (Altstadt) ☎ 089 2318 3257 🕐 Beer hall: Daily 9am–midnight. Restaurant: Daily 10am–midnight 🖐 L €14, D €21, Wine €12 🚇 Karlsplatz, Marienplatz

AYINGERS

www.platzl.de

Enjoy Bavarian food and six different draught beers from the Aying family brewery (which owns the Platzl Hotel and the Pfistermühle restaurant, ▷ 296). The set-price lunch menu gives you the option of a Bavarian dish such as fried duck with blue cabbage and potato dumplings, or a lighter meal.

✉ Platzl 1a, 80331 München (Altstadt) ☎ 089 2370 3666 🕐 Daily 11am–1am 🖐 L €13, D €20, Wine €20 🚇 Marienplatz

BARISTA

This cocktail bar and restaurant is in the fashionable Fünf Höfe covered shopping area in the middle of town. The menu is short, with light dishes such as breast of duck with raspberry vinegar and swordfish served with peppers and sautéed potatoes. The three-course set-price dinner menu is particularly good value.

✉ Kardinal-Faulhaber-Strasse 11, 80333 München (Altstadt) ☎ 089 2080 2180 🕐 Mon–Thu 10am–1am, Fri, Sat 10am–2am, Sun 3pm–1am 🖐 L €20, D €27, Wine €22 🚇 Odeonsplatz, Marienplatz

BASIC BISTRO

www.basicbio.de

As an antidote to all those heavy Bavarian dishes, go light at this organic, vegetarian café upstairs from the organic food store Basic (▷ 290). You can help yourself to the couscous, hummus and olives at the salad bar—although don't get too carried away because these items are sold by weight. There are delicious fresh juices or bottles of organic beer to go with your meal. Credit cards are not accepted.

✉ Westenriederstrasse 35, 80331 München (Altstadt) ☎ 089 242 0890 🕐 Mon–Fri 9–8, Sat 8.30–6 🖐 L €6, D €8 🚇 Marienplatz

BENJARONG

The exotic décor and furniture stay on the right side of kitsch in this fabulous Thai restaurant. Eat in the main room, with its plush red seats and teak tables, or in a separate room with low tables and cushions on the floor. Dishes to try include chicken satay, fishcakes, spicy chicken soup with coconut milk and fried duck with pineapple.

✉ Falckenbergstrasse 7, 80539 München (Altstadt) ☎ 089 291 3055 🕐 Mon–Fri 12–2.30, 6–11.30, Sat, Sun 6–11.30 🖐 L €19, D €28, Wine €15 🚇 Marienplatz

BODEGA DALI

www.bodega-dali.de

Enjoy Spanish food and a great selection of full-bodied Riojas by the glass or bottle in this atmospheric wine cellar. Dishes go beyond tapas—there's tuna fish salad with tomatoes, paella and robust stews with tuna, potatoes and stuffed peppers (capsicums).

Tengstrasse 6, 80799 München (Maxvorstadt) 089 2777 9696 Daily 5pm–1am D €19, Wine €14 Josephsplatz Bus 53 to Josephsplatz

CAFÉ AM BEETHOVENPLATZ

www.mariandl.com

With its high-ceilinged rooms and chandeliers, this café, dating from 1899, is like a Viennese coffee house by day, while at night it is a restaurant serving international food. It's also a music bar, with classical, jazz or blues bands playing live almost every night.

Goethestrasse 51, 80336 München (Hauptbahnhof) 089 552 9100 Daily 9am–1am L€7, D €13, Wine €11 Goetheplatz

CAFÉ IM MÜLLER'SCHEN VOLKSBAD

If you've been to the Gasteig or Deutsches Museum and would like to eat in a place with atmosphere, this café/bar in the art nouveau Müller'sches Volksbad bathhouse is ideal. It's like being in a covered courtyard, with conservatory-style furniture, red leather sofas and tables made from old-fashioned sewing machines. The café specializes in large salads, while a typical dish of the day is pasta with courgette (zucchini) and salmon. There's a long drinks menu with wine, champagne and cocktails, and the café serves cakes until 11.30pm.

Rosenheimerstrasse 1, 81667 München (Haidhausen) 089 4453 9250 Daily 10am–1am L €7, D €12, Wine by the glass Tram 18 to Deutsches Museum

CAFÉ PUCK

www.cafepuck.de

The huge breakfast menu is available weekdays until 6pm and on Sundays and holidays until 8pm. Alternatively, choose from salads, burgers or pasta dishes, or have an ice-cream or a milkshake.

Türkenstrasse 33, 80799, München (Schwabing) 089 280 2280 Daily 9am–1am (food until 11.45pm) L€9, D €13, Wine €14 Universität Bus 53, tram 27

CAFÉ VOILÀ

www.cafe-voila.de

This friendly bar and café has long opening hours. It's the sort of place where you can order food in the middle of the afternoon. The breakfast menu is long, and there is a set-price lunch menu. You'll find it hard to resist the cake cabinet and the generous happy hours (5–8pm and 11pm–1am). There's a selection of magazines and an internet kiosk.

Wörthstrasse 5, 81669 München (Haidhausen) 089 489 1654 Daily 7am–1am (food until 12.30am) L €7, D €10, Wine by the glass Tram 15, 19, 25 to Wörthstrasse

CAFFE' FLORIAN

www.caffe-florian.de

Arguably Schwabing's best-known café, this has a real Italian feel and is a great place for coffee and cake or a filling plate of pasta. The menu changes every day and there are lunch specials. There is an extensive wine list. The Coccodrillo bar is downstairs (▷ 291).

Hohenzollernstrasse 11, 80801 München (Schwabing) 089 336639 Sun–Thu 9am–1am, Fri–Sat 9am–3am L €9, D €16, Wine €15 Giselastrasse, Münchener Freiheit Tram 12, 27 to Kurfürstenplatz; bus 23

CHINESISCHER TURM

www.chinaturm.de

The setting here in the Englischer Garten is beautiful; the pagoda dates back to 1789 when the gardens were created. There is a dining room inside as well as plenty of seats outside. Expect soups, salads, Bavarian dishes, fish and some vegetarian options too. The apfelstrudel is hard to resist.

Englischer Garten 3, 80538, München (Schwabing) 089 383 8730 Mon–Sun 10am–midnight L €13, D €21, Wine €12 Universität

COMERCIAL BAR

www.barcomercial.de

Run by an Italian family, this bar in the Fünf Höfe shopping area is a great place for a mid-shop cappuccino or lunch. The menu includes a good range of pizzas plus some tempting cakes and puddings; wine and cocktails are also available.

Theatinerstrasse 16, 80333, München (Altstadt) 089 2070 0266 Mon–Sat 9am–1am, Sun 12–12 L €9, D €17, Wine by the glass Odeonsplatz Tram 19

CONTI BISTRO

www.conti-bistro.de

The ground floor is light and airy, with changing collections of modern art on the walls, while downstairs in the basement you'll find yourself in an alpine chalet with wooden floor, walls and ceiling. Dishes include mushroom and truffle ravioli with grilled courgette (zucchini), and grilled chicken breast with pesto.

Haus der Bayerischen Wirtschaft, Max-Joseph-strasse 5, 80333, München (Altstadt) 089 5517 8684 Mon–Fri 10am–1am L €19, D €29, Wine €18 Odeonsplatz Tram 27

CONVIVA

www.convivamuenchen.de

The contemporary feel to this restaurant is reflected in some of its light Italian-influenced dishes. Try ricotta cheese flan with balsamic vinegar, and follow it with saffron risotto with white fish. There's a three-course set-price lunch menu.

Hildegardstrasse 1, 80539 München (Altstadt) 089 2333 6977 Mon–Sat 11am–1am, Sun 5pm–1am L €15, D €24, Wine €12 Tram 19 Isartor

DALLMAYR

www.dallmayr.de

This historic restaurant is the place for a first-class meal. Start with quail salad with marinated pumpkin, and follow it with braised pork in sherry

vinegar accompanied by chervil and parmesan biscuits..
Dienerstrasse 14–15, 80331 München (Altstadt) 089 213 5100 Tue–Sat 12–3, 7–11 L €24, D €38, Wine €25 Marienplatz

EDERER

www.restaurant-ederer.de

Fresh and light, speckled with works of modern German art, this restaurant at the Fünf Höfe gallery is one of Munich's most bankable eating prospects. Ace chef Karl Ederer is grounded in his regional roots, yet knows how to work in other European and international influences.
Kardinal-Faulhaber-Strasse 10, 80333 München (Altstadt) 089 2423 1310 Mon–Sat 12–3, 6.30pm–1am L €22, D €46, Wine €23 Odeonsplatz, Marienplatz

LA FAMIGLIA

www.torbraeu.de

La Famiglia is owned by an Italian family and serves Tuscan cuisine. Try quail breast in balsamic vinegar with grilled artichokes, and follow this with home-made tagliatelle with asparagus or veal fillet with mushrooms and roast potatoes.
Hotel Torbräu, Tal 41, 80331 München (Altstadt) 089 2280 7523 Daily 11–11 L €16, D €30, Wine €15 Isartor

FRAUNHOFER

www.fraunhofertheater.de

The relaxed atmosphere at this traditional tavern, with its heavy wooden tables, makes it a great place to dine on hearty Bavarian meat dishes. After, watch a performance at the theatre in the courtyard or at the on-site cinema.
Fraunhofer Theater, Fraunhoferstrasse 9, 80469 München (Isarvorstadt) 089 266460 Daily 4.30pm–1am L €20, Wine €15 Fraunhoferstrasse

GLOCKENSPIEL CAFÉ

www.cafe-glockenspiel.de

Squeeze into the tiny elevator and head up to the fifth floor for a drink or a meal with a view of Marienplatz. Sit inside or on the terrace.
Marienplatz 28 (entrance at Rosenstrasse Passage), 5th floor, 80331 München (Altstadt) 089 264256 Daily 10am–1am (meals are served until 7pm) L €10, D €14, Wine €15 Marienplatz Bus 52 Marienplatz

HACKERHAUS

www.hackerhaus.de

This large traditional restaurant retains an intimate atmosphere. The building dates from 1738 and has a beautiful interior, with vaulted ceilings. Tables in the courtyard fill up quickly—the area is heated in the winter and is covered when it rains. Choose from dishes such as liver-dumpling soup, roast pork and eight types of sausage.
Sendlinger Strasse 14, 80331 München (Altstadt) 089 260 5026 Daily 9am–midnight L €12, D €18, Wine by the glass Sendlinger Tor, Marienplatz

HOFBRÄUHAUS MÜNCHEN

www.hofbraeuhaus.de

You're more likely to come here for the beer, atmosphere, singing and oompah bands than for the cuisine. However, it's always good to have something hearty to eat with your beer, so try the sausages.
Platzl 9, 80331 München (Altstadt) 089 290 1360 Daily 9am–11.30pm L €10, D €14, Wine €15 Marienplatz

LAST SUPPER CLUB

www.lastsupper.de

Mediterranean food is served in Bavarian surroundings. Try rocket (arugula) salad with tomatoes and parmesan, and follow it with chicken with potato cakes and a mushroom sauce, or suckling pig with artichoke ravioli and sausage.
Fürstenstrasse 9, 80333, München (Schwabing) 089 2880 8809 Mon–Sun 7pm–1am L €26, Wine €16 Odeonsplatz

LUTTER & WEGNER

www.l-w-muenchen.de

This establishment is famed for its vast Sunday brunch buffet, served 10.30–2. It's an amazing place for breakfast too, served from 8 until 11. Under the same roof is the Venecia restaurant, the cocktail bar Sir Hyke's Place and another restaurant called Grappa's.
Lenbachplatz 8, 80333, München (Altstadt) 089 545 9490 Mon–Fri 8am–midnight, Sun 9am–midnight L €32, D €40, Wine €25 Karlplatz Stachus

NEWS BAR

www.newsbarmunich.de

This popular bar and café is a good place for a coffee or a meal at any time of day—they serve Bavarian dishes as well as burgers, baked potatoes, crêpes, salads, omelettes, pasta and vegetarian options.
Amalienstrasse 55, 80799, München (Maxvorstadt) 089 281787 Daily 7.30am–2am L, D €8, Wine by the glass Universität

PFISTERMÜHLE

www.platzl.de

Pfistermühle is an elegant restaurant in the vaults of a 16th-century former mill near Marienplatz and the Hofbräuhaus. The food is high-quality Bavarian fare, and there's an excellent selection of wines, as well as draught beer from the Aying family brewery (▷ 294). In summer, dine outside in the little beer garden.
Pfisterstrasse 4, 80331, München (Altstadt) 089 2370 3865 Mon–Sat 11.30am–midnight L €15, D €25, Wine €20 Marienplatz

PRINZ MYSHKIN

www.prinzmyshkin.com

This vegetarian restaurant is in a 450-year-old brewery with a high, white, vaulted ceiling that gives the place a monastic feel. You'll still feel virtuous even after tucking into dishes like spinach gnocchi, Indian curries, sushi, tofu stroganoff and pasta filled with pumpkin and tomatoes. There are also dairy- and egg-free dishes.
Hackenstrasse 2, 80331, München (Altstadt) 089 265596 Daily 11am–12.30am L €15, D €21, Wine €18 Sendlinger Tor, Marienplatz

RATSKELLER

www.ratskeller-muenchen.de

This traditional restaurant (seating 1,200) underneath the Rathaus has lots of booths and quiet corners where you can enjoy an intimate meal. Specialties include *Lammhaxl* (braised lamb shank with rosemary sauce) and *Entenbraten* (roast Bavarian duck with red cabbage and potato dumplings). Wines are from the award-winning Juliusspital Würzburg vineyards.

✉ Marienplatz 8, 80331, München (Altstadt) ☎ 089 219 9890 🕐 Daily 10am–midnight 🖐 L €10, D €18, Wine €14 Ⓤ Marienplatz

RISTORANTE ALBARONE

The fresh, light dining room at this Italian restaurant leads to a lovely garden. Expect Italian dishes with a twist, such as pheasant ravioli with sheep's milk cheese and slices of wild boar with a fig confit.

✉ Stollbergstrasse 22, 80539 München (Altstadt) ☎ 089 2916 8687 🕐 Mon–Fri 12–2.30, 6.30–11, Sat 6.30–11 🖐 L €24, D €39, Wine €20 Ⓤ Marienplatz

RIVA

www.rivabar.com

The pizzas at this bar and pizzeria are cooked in a wood-fired oven and range from the traditional margharita to ginger or curried chicken varieties.

✉ Tal 44, 80331 München (Altstadt) ☎ 089 220240 🕐 Daily 8am–1am 🖐 L €16, D €21, Wine €15 Ⓤ Isartor

SCHLOSSCAFÉ IM PALMENHAUS

www.palmenhaus.de

You'll find this elegant café in a glasshouse at the Nyphenburg Palace. Try the pork in a cream sauce with vegetables from the royal garden, and ricotta ravioli with tomatoes and pancetta, or you can have something lighter.

✉ Schlosspark, Nymphenburg Eingang 43, 80638 München (Neuhausen) ☎ 089 175309 🕐 Apr–end Nov daily 10–6; Dec–end Mar daily 10–5 🖐 Snacks and light meals €6–€14 🚌 Tram 17, bus 41 to Schloss Nymphenburg; tram 16 to Romanplatz (less convenient)

SCHWABINGER KARTOFFELHAUS

Potatoes (*Kartoffeln*) are the central ingredient in every dish. Choose from potatoes with shrimp and mushrooms, with spinach baked in a creamy cheese sauce or with herring in a sour cream sauce.

✉ Hohenzollernplatz 4, 80796, München (Schwabing) ☎ 089 303677 🕐 Mon–Sat noon–1am, Sun 5.30pm–1am 🖐 L €16, D €20, Wine by the glass Ⓤ Marienplatz, Isartor

SPATENHAUS AN DER OPER

www.kuffler-gastronomie.de

Come here for high-quality Bavarian food on the ground floor, while upstairs they serve international cuisine. Expect Bavarian specials such as *Wiener schnitzel*, *Schweinebraten* (crispy pork in a dark beer sauce) and boiled beef, as well as fish and unexpected dishes such as coconut curry soup.

✉ Residenzstrasse 12, 80333 München (Altstadt) ☎ 089 290 7060 🕐 Daily 9.30am–1am 🖐 L €24, D €32, Wine €22 Ⓤ Marienplatz, Odeonsplatz 🚌 Tram 19 🚆 Marienplatz

STADTCAFÉ

www.stadtcafe-muenchen.de

This friendly café/bar in the Stadtmuseum is good for a late breakfast or an early lunch.

✉ St.-Jakobs-Platz 1, 80331, München (Altstadt) ☎ 089 266949 🕐 Sun–Thu 10am–midnight, Fri, Sat 10am–1am 🖐 Daily menu, from €7 per person, Wine by the glass Ⓤ Marienplatz, Sendlinger Tor 🚌 Bus 52, 56 to Blumenstrasse

TERRINE

www.terrine.de

For an alternative to Bavarian dishes, try this excellent Parisian bistro. For starters, try asparagus in vinaigrette, rabbit with oyster mushrooms or salmon with leeks and rocket (arugula). Mains include venison with cabbage and plaice with spinach in a chervil sauce.

✉ Amalienpassage, Amalienstrasse 89, 80799 München (Schwabing) ☎ 089 281780 🕐 Tue–Fri 12–3, 6.30–1, Sat 6.30–1 🖐 L €25, D €45, Wine €24 Ⓤ Universität 🚌 Bus 53 to Universität

VILLANIS CAFÉ

www.villanis.com

This traditional-style café is popular with Munich's gay community.

✉ Kreuzstrasse 3b (at Sendlinger Strasse), 80331 München (Asamhof) ☎ 089 260 7972 🕐 Sun–Thu 10am–midnight, Fri, Sat 10am–1am 🖐 Snacks €6.50–€10, Wine €15 Ⓤ Sendlinger Tor

WEINHAUS NEUNER

www.weinhaus-neuner.de

Expect a high standard of cooking and service at the Wine House, with a huge list of wines. The cuisine leans towards Italy and France, with starters such as rocket (arugula) salad with ham and Parmesan, and veal cannelloni with spinach and tomato. Main courses include duck in a cognac and pepper (capsicum) sauce, and roast rabbit with a chervil and mustard sauce.

✉ Herzogspitalstrasse 8, 80331 München (Altstadt) ☎ 089 260 3954 🕐 Mon–Sat 11.30–3, 5.30–midnight. 🖐 L €18, D €44, Wine €20 Ⓤ Karlsplatz Stachus

ZUM FRANZISKANER

www.zum-franziskaner.de

In this traditional Bavarian restaurant, from the 14th century, each room has a different name. The meat is supplied by the restaurant's own butcher. Try the suckling pig roasted in dark beer and served with those most Bavarian of accompaniments—potato dumplings and sauerkraut.

✉ Perusastasse 5, 80333, München (Altstadt) ☎ 089 2318 1218 🕐 Daily 8am–midnight 🖐 L €18, D €23, Wine €16 Ⓤ Marienplatz, Odeonsplatz 🚌 Tram 19; Bus 52

ZUM SPÖCKMEIER

www.zum-spoeckmeier.de

You're by Marienplatz here, and when the Glockenspiel strikes at 11am people start coming in for lunch. This large restaurant has been around for more than 500 years. Expect hearty Bavarian dishes.

✉ Rosenstrasse 9, 80331, München (Altstadt) ☎ 089 268088 🕐 Daily 9.30am–midnight 🖐 L €11, D €19, Wine €13 Ⓤ Marienplatz

Above *The Bayerischer Hof is one of Munich's leading luxury hotels and has three restaurants*

PRICES AND SYMBOLS

The prices are the lowest and highest for a double room for one night including breakfast, unless otherwise stated. All the hotels listed accept credit cards unless otherwise stated. Note that rates can vary widely throughout the year.

For a key to the symbols, ▷ 2.

ACANTHUS

www.acanthushotel.de

Carola and Jörg Günther have run the hotel for 16 years. Rooms are decorated in either an English-floral style with antique furniture or in pastel shades with modern furniture.

An der Hauptfeuerwache 14, 80331 München (Altstadt) 089 231880 From €115 36 €15 Sendlinger Tor

ADMIRAL

www.hotel-admiral.de

The rooms in this four-star hotel, close to the River Isar and the Deutsches Museum, are extremely comfortable—chocolates on the pillow and a bowl of fruit await you.

Kohlstrasse 9, 80469 München (Isarvorstadt) 089 216350 €160–€310 33 (8 non-smoking) €12 Isartor

AM SIEGESTOR

www.hotel-siegestor.de

This pension, opposite the university's art school, has a wonderful old-fashioned Parisian-style elevator. The English-speaking owner, Frau Clauss, is proud of the building, which dates from 1879. Guest rooms don't have a private bathroom (some have a basin).

Akademiestrasse 5, 80799 München (Schwabing) 089 399550 €60–€100 20 Universität

APOLLO

www.apollohotel.de

Rooms in this three-star hotel are quiet considering the location is so close to the Hauptbahnhof. About 25 have a balcony. There is a little bar, which is open in the evenings.

Mittererstrasse 7, 80336 München (Hauptbahnhof) 089 539531 From €85 74 (18 non-smoking) €6 Hauptbahnhof

BAYERISCHER HOF

www.bayerischerhof.de

The Volkhardt family has run this five-star hotel since 1897. You're in absolute luxury here with three restaurants, several bars, designer boutiques, a beauty and hair salon, a rooftop pool, a sauna and steam bath, a gym and a sun terrace. Rooms even have PlayStations.

Promenadeplatz 2–6, 80333 München (Altstadt) 089 21200 €249–€459 373 (half non-smoking) Outdoor Odeonsplatz, Marienplatz Tram 19

CARLTON

www.carlton-garni.de

This comfortable four-star hotel is near the Pinakothek galleries. The breakfast here is special, with salmon and champagne as well as cereals, meats and cheeses.

Fürstenstrasse 12, 80333 München (Schwabing) 089 282061 From €129 49 (one non-smoking floor) Sauna, massage Odeonsplatz

CORTIINA

www.cortiina.com

Rooms in this boutique hotel are minimalist, with high-quality materials. They do English afternoon tea on weekends in winter, and the breakfast is more Italian, with cappuccino and light pastries.

Ledererstrasse 8, 80331 München (Altstadt) 089 242 2490 €196–€266, excluding breakfast 33 (3 non-smoking floors) Marienplatz, Isartor

CVJM JUGENDGÄSTEHAUS

www.cvjm-muenchen.org/hotel

You don't have to be young to stay at this youth hostel near the main train station. The rooms are simple and clean, although none has a private bathroom. A filling breakfast is included in the price.

Landwehrstrasse 13, 80336 München (Hauptbahnhof) 089 552 1410 €26.50–€41 per person per night (€29–€44.50 for over age 26); Nov–end Feb 10% discount; Oktoberfest supplement €5 85 beds (all non-smoking) Karlsplatz, Hauptbahnhof, Sendlinger Tor

GÄSTEHAUS ENGLISCHER GARTEN

www.hotelenglishgarden.de

It would be difficult to find a place to stay with more charm than this 200-year-old converted watermill right by the Englischer Garten. There are only 12 rooms, so reserve early. For families, there are 17 furnished apartments in a building opposite. In summer, breakfast in the garden.

Liebergesellstrasse 8, 80802 München (Schwabing) 089 383 9410 €71–€180, excluding breakfast 29 €8 Münchner Freiheit

HOTEL AM VIKTUALIENMARKT

www.hotel-am-viktualienmarkt.de

Its position behind the Viktualienmarkt is this family-run hotel's main advantage; its main disadvantage is that, although it is on four floors there is no elevator. Guest rooms have two, three or four beds. Generous breakfasts are served in the pretty breakfast room.

Utzschneiderstrasse 14, 80469 München (Isarvorstadt) 089 231 1090 €85–€150 27 (2 non-smoking floors) Tram 17, 18

PENSION GEIGER

www.pensiongeiger.de

This bright, basic pension is close to the Pinakothek galleries. There are rooms with or without a shower, and rooms with three beds. Only six rooms have a television.

Steinheilstrasse 1, 80333 München (Maxvorstadt) 089 521556 €55–€60 17 Theresienstrasse

PENSION SEIBEL

www.seibel-hotels-munich.de

This wonderful pension has bags of charm thanks to its traditional Bavarian decoration. It also has a great location, just behind the Viktualienmarkt. All but two rooms have their own private bathroom, and at the top of the building are three apartments.

Reichenbachstrasse 8, 80469 München (Isarvorstadt) 089 231 9180 Rooms €59–€189 20 (12 non-smoking) Theresienwiese Tram 17 or 18

PLATZL HOTEL

www.platzl.de

The hotel has been in the same family for more than 50 years. The comfortable rooms are decorated in blue and yellow, and have double glazing. The Moroccan-themed Maurischer Kiosk has a mini gym, sauna, Jacuzzi, steam room with underfloor heating and a floor mosaic incorporating real gold.

Sparkassenstrasse 10, 80331 München (Altstadt) 089 237030 Rooms €190–€240 166 (65 non-smoking) Spa €18 per day Marienplatz Bus 52 to Marienplatz

ST. PAUL

www.hotel-stpaul.de

Ideally situated for the Oktoberfest ground, rooms have television, telephone, a safe and internet access. There are two breakfast rooms and you can eat outside in the courtyard in summer.

St.-Paul-Strasse 7, 80336 München (Theresienwiese) 089 5440 7800 €92 40 (20 non-smoking) €10 Theresienwiese

SAVOY

www.renner-hotel-ag.de

Note that some rooms have been redecorated more recently than others.

Amalienstrasse 25, 80333 München (Schwabing) 089 287870 From €119 74 (10 non-smoking) Odeonsplatz

SCHLICKER

www.hotel-schlicker.de

You're near Marienplatz here, though rooms that face onto the Tal have double-glazed windows. There are different grades of room. In summer breakfast in the little garden.

Tal 8, 80331 München (Altstadt) 089 242 8870 €118–€174 69 rooms, 2 suites €10 Marienplatz

SEIBEL

www.seibel-hotels-munich.de

The three-star Hotel Seibel is owned by the same family as Pension Seibel (▷ above), but is not as central because it is on the other side of the Theresienwiese. Rooms are large, with heavy Bavarian-style furniture.

Theresienhöhe 9, 80339 München (Theresienwiese) 089 540 1420 €79–€189 65 (30 non-smoking) Theresienwiese

SPLENDID-DOLLMANN

www.splendid-dollmann.de

The Splendid is in a 19th-century townhouse and has the atmosphere of an exclusive members' club. Rooms are elegantly decorated and there are also suites, rooms with extra-large beds and an apartment. There's an elegant sitting room and a secluded garden in which breakfast is served in good weather.

Thierschstrasse 49, 80538 München (Lehel) 089 23 80 80 €160–€200, excluding breakfast 33 Lehel Tram 17 to Thierschplatz

TORBRÄU

www.torbraeu.de

This historic hotel was founded in 1490 and it has been in the same family for more than 100 years. There are two types of double room, standard and deluxe. All rooms are air conditioned. There's also a café, and La Famiglia (▷ 296) next door.

Tal 41, 80331 München (Altstadt) 089 242340 €189–€380 91 (60 non-smoking)

SIGHTS 302
WALKS AND DRIVES 330
WHAT TO DO 344
EATING 348
STAYING 354

SOUTHERN GERMANY

Consisting of the two large states of Baden-Wütttemberg and Bayern (Bavaria), southern Germany boasts a virtually inexhaustible array of scenic, historic, cultural and sporting assets. Rising through densely forested uplands to the Alps, the landscape of southern Germany is nothing if not dramatic. How could it be otherwise when it takes in the Bayerischer Wald (Bavarian Forest), central Europe's largest single expanse of woodland; the enchanting Schwarzwald (Black Forest); Bodensee (Lake Constance), set against an Alpine backdrop; and the magnificent Berchtesgadener Land? Castles and country palaces speckle the hills and mountains, none more emblematic than Schloss Neuschwanstein, with its fairy-tale turrets, or more appealing than King Ludwig's lavish Schloss Linderhof.

Many places in this setting are open-air sports paradises, with Garmisch-Partenkirchen leading the way, especially when it comes to skiing. There are many waymarked bicycle and walking routes, excellent winter sports facilities throughout the mountain and forest regions, and water sports on lakes such as Bodensee and Chiemsee.

The big cities of Nürnberg (Nuremberg), which hosts the Christkindlesmarkt, Germany's finest open-air Christmas market, and Stuttgart, home to the Porsche and Mercedes-Benz museums, have their own vigorous scenes to rival, if not quite match, that of the south's premier city Munich (▷ 258–299). Among its smaller cities and large towns, the south's incredible urban diversity is apparent. Laden with history and culture, places like Augsburg, Bamberg, Freiburg, Karlsruhe, Passau, Ulm and Würzburg are all worth days of exploration in their own right. And that's before you even consider Baden-Baden, Germany's oldest spa town; romantic Heidelberg; Regensburg, which has Germany's greatest concentration of medieval buildings and Rothenburg, which has the finest medieval townscape; Bayreuth, the home of Wagnerian opera; and Oberammergau, where the famous Passion Play is performed every ten years. You'll find a varied choice of traditional handicrafts. Of special interest are the Schwarzwald's cuckoo clocks, quality Nuremberg toys, and crystal glassware from the Bayerischer Wald.

ALTMÜHLTAL AND EICHSTÄTT

www.naturpark-altmuehltal.info
www.eichstaett.de

Altmühltal is Germany's largest nature park. Castles and fortresses nestle on wooded hills, and rugged crags overlook the rolling river valleys with their lovely towns and villages. The pretty town of Solnhofen is noted for its quarries of Jurassic limestone, holding numerous fossils. Pappenheim is an old-world little town with the 15th-century Gothic Stadtkirche and Galluskirche, which dates from Carolingian times.

The elegant city of Eichstätt is an architectural showpiece. The spires of its 14th-century cathedral and other churches dominate the skyline, and remains of medieval fortifications sit alongside rococo mansions. A mix of Romanesque, Gothic and baroque, the cathedral of St. Willibald (first bishop of Eichstätt) houses the tomb of the saint and pictures and relics, including the Pappenheim Altar, a late medieval depiction of the Crucifixion.

410 F12 Naturpark Altmühltal, Notre Dame 1, 85072 Eichstätt, 08421 98760 Tourist Office, Domplatz 8, 85072 Eichstätt 08421 600 1400 Eichstätt

ANSBACH

www.ansbach.de

The city of Ansbach is more than 1,250 years old. Now the administrative and cultural hub of central Franconia, its historic old town has attractive houses moulded over the years by its history as a former residence of the margraves of Brandenburg-Ansbach. The Markgräfliche Residenz (Apr–end Sep Tue–Sun 9–5; Oct–end Mar Tue–Sun 9–3; tel 0981 953 8390), one of the most important 18th-century palaces in Franconia, is a superb Renaissance structure with a magnificent rococo interior. It now houses a faience and porcelain collection and the Staatsgalerie.

You can see art nouveau buildings on Judttstrasse and baroque façades at Karlsplatz. The tranquil Hofgarten has a magnificent 250-year-old lime tree alley. Its Orangerie is one of the most remarkable park palaces of Franconia, and there is a memorial to the foundling, Kaspar Hauser, who reputedly had royal connections and was murdered here.

In Johann-Sebastian-Bach-Platz, don't miss the three-towered Gumbertus Church, with a Romanesque crypt, the Schwanenritterkapelle (Chapel of the Swan Knight) and the burial vault of the margraves.

410 F12 Johann-Sebastian-Bach-Platz 1, 91522 Ansbach 0981 51304 Ansbach

ASCHAFFENBURG

www.aschaffenburg.de

Tucked away in the northwest corner of Bavaria, Aschaffenburg is on the banks of the River Main and bordered by the rolling hills of the Spessart. The town is dominated by the mighty Schloss Johannisburg (Apr–end Sep Tue–Sun 9–6; Oct–end Mar Tue–Sun 10–4; tel 06021 386570), a magnificent Renaissance palace built at the beginning of the 17th century by the bishop of Mainz. Inside are the State Art Gallery, Palace Museum and state departments. There are fine views of the Main from the Palace Gardens and from the Pompejanum, a reproduction of the Villa of Castor and Pollux in Pompeii.

In the middle of town is the Stiftskirche, with its late Romanesque cloister. The church has a number of important works of art, including *Lamentation* (1525) by Matthias Grünewald, with its tender portrayal of grief. In the former chapter house is the Stiftsmuseum, with church art and a collection of faience.

409 D10 Schlossplatz 1, 63739 Aschaffenburg 06021 395888 Aschaffenburg

BADEN-BADEN

▷ 305.

BAMBERG

▷ 306.

BAYERISCHER WALD

www.nationalpark-bayerischer-wald.de

The Bayerischer Wald (Bavarian Forest) is the largest stretch of woodland in Central Europe. It covers 6,000sq km (2,300sq miles) between the Danube valley and merges into the Bohemian Forest in the Czech Republic and Austria. This wonderful park shelters pretty towns and villages with pastel-tinted houses, cobbled squares and winding lanes, pavement cafés, museums and galleries.

Near the information centre at Neuschönau is the Tier-Freigelände nature park where wild animals roam, while Furth im Wald is noted for its annual Slaying of the Dragon and Drachenmuseum (Dragon Museum; Apr–end Oct Tue–Sun 10.15–6.45; tel 09973 50940),

From the 15th century, many glass factories were established in the Bavarian forest, where fuel was plentiful, and for centuries they produced *Waldglas* (forest glass). Places associated with this industry can be seen along the Glasstrasse (Glass Route; ▷ 330–331).

To the west, Amberg is a charming town with medieval walls.

411 H12 Hans-Eisenmann-Haus, Böhmstrasse 35, Neuschönau 08558 96150 Bayerischer Wald

Opposite *A castle in the Altmühltal*
Right *Statues and sentry box in front of Ansbach's Residenz*

AUGSBURG

Bavaria's oldest city is a cultural city, with 15 museums and art galleries to visit. Augsburg's cityscape has been formed by its 2,000-year history; within it you'll find styles of all the major architectural periods. In particular the Renaissance flourished here, and rococo became known as the Augsburg style. The city has many great buildings, monumental fountains and grand boulevards. Maximilianstrasse is the grandest of all: The impressive Renaissance and baroque façades of stately patrician mansions line this broad avenue leading to the pedestrianized Rathausplatz. The imposing spired twin domes of the Renaissance Rathaus dominate the square, and inside, the restored Goldener Saal (golden hall) is famous for its magnificent portals, coffered ceiling and mural paintings. On Frauentorstrasse is the Mozarthaus (Tue–Sun 10–5; tel 0821 324 3894), the birthplace of Leopold Mozart, father of Wolfgang Amadeus, and now a museum devoted to the composer's family. The Romanesque and Gothic Domkirche St. Maria (St. Mary's Cathedral) has impressive bronze doors with 35 relief panels presenting Old Testament scenes, a Romanesque crypt, medieval frescoes and the so-called Prophets' Windows from the 12th century.

HISTORY

Augsburg came to the fore in the 15th century when it became established as an important trading hub linking northern Europe to Italy. Augsburg enjoyed its heyday during this period, when the city was highly prosperous as a result of the international trade in gold, silver and copper. Also, the financial businesses of the wealthy Fugger and Welser merchant families evolved here, making Augsburg second only to London as a banking hub. Augsburg's three magnificent fountains were erected in 1594 on the occasion of the city's 1,600th anniversary in memory of its Roman founders.

FUGGER FAMILY

Augsburg owes much to the Fugger family. In 1516, Jakob Fugger founded the Fuggerei, the world's oldest welfare settlement for the poor, and it still houses around 200 residents in a picturesque gated complex with modernized apartments. Residents are expected to pray daily for the Fugger family and in return they pay a minimal rent. The gates of the complex are closed from 10pm until 6am (5am in summer), and residents returning late are fined. The former family town house, the 16th-century Fuggerhaus, sits alongside many grand houses on Maximilianstrasse.

INFORMATION

www.augsburg-tourismus.com
410 F13 Regio Augsburg Tourismus, Schiessgrabenstrasse 14, 86150 Augsburg 0821 502070
Apr–end Oct Mon–Fri 9–6, Sat 11–5, Sun 10–2; Nov–end Mar Mon–Fri 9–5, Sat 10–2 Augsburg

TIPS

» Augsburg is an ideal base from which to visit Munich, especially during the *Oktoberfest* (▷ 293). It's just a half-hour ICE train ride from Munich and there are also hourly non-stop regional trains, which are cheaper.

» Hire a bicycle or tandem to tour the city and see the sights. There are many good bicycle rental companies with a range of adult and children's bicycles to suit all requirements.

» Next to the Town Hall, the Perlachturm (Perlach Tower) offers a spectacular view of Augsburg. It is open from May to the end of October.

Below *The pine-cone on top of the Altes Rathaus is a city symbol*

BADEN-BADEN

The gateway to the Black Forest is renowned for its spa, casino and horse racing. It has a townscape of elegant villas, stately 19th-century hotels, tree-lined avenues and meticulously well-kept parks. Once known as the Summer Capital of Europe, Baden-Baden has for many years been a popular destination with the rich and famous. Renowned for its spa, casino and horse racing, the town attracts visitors from all over the world who come here to sample the waters or lose their fortunes. Despite its upper-class image, the elegant town has much to offer the casual visitor. Its temperate climate and wonderful location in the lush valley of the River Oos at the gateway to the Black Forest add much to its attraction.

In the suburb of Iffezheim is the racecourse that hosts the International Horse Races of Baden-Baden each September.

WHAT TO SEE

Today, Baden-Baden is a popular all-year resort with elegant villas and stately 19th-century hotels. With its tree-lined avenues and immaculate parks, you can see evidence of its noble and elegant past everywhere; the white neoclassical Kurhaus (spa building) and impeccably maintained Kurgarten are the hub of fashionable life. The casino's interior is as opulent as its visitors, and has attracted the glitterati for many years.

Close by, you can test the saline waters at the Trinkhalle and then follow the lovely Lichtentaler Allee, passing the magnificent Baden-Baden Theatre, Kunsthalle (state art gallery) and Alleehaus (City Museum) to the medieval Cistercian Lichenthal Abbey. The ruined castle (Old Palace), originally built in 1102, was the seat of the margraves of Baden-Baden. The Paradise is a complex of waterfalls, fountains and cascades.

SPAS

Baden-Baden is best known for its thermal springs, Europe's hottest with a temperature of 69°C (156°F). You can see the restored ruins of a 2,000-year-old Roman bath used by Roman emperor Caracalla in AD213 from below Römerplatz. Built on either side of Römerplatz are the 19th-century Friedrichsbad and modern baths, the Caracalla Therme (▷ 344). Friedrichsbad has stunning interiors, especially the circular pool ringed by columns and arcades. The Caracalla Therme has a variety of hot and cold water grottoes, indoor and outdoor pools, and whirlpools.

INFORMATION

www.baden-baden.de

408 C12 Tourist-Information, Schwarzwaldstrasse 52 ☎ 07221 275200 Mon–Sat 9–6, Sun, holidays 9–1 Tourist-Information i-Punkt, Trinkhalle (at Kurhaus), Kaiserallee 3 ☎ 07221 275200 Mon–Sat 10–5, Sun, holidays 2–5 Baden-Baden Baden-Baden

TIPS

» Dining out in Baden-Baden can be expensive; take a short trip across the Rhine into France, where you will find some excellent restaurants in small villages that serve fine French cuisine at very reasonable prices.

» Take the funicular railway to the top of Baden-Baden's own mountain, the Merkur. There are wonderful views of the town and the surrounding area, plus a nature trail and waymarked footpaths.

Above *Outside the modern Caracalla Spa*

INFORMATION

www.bamberg.info
406 F11 Tourismus und Kongress Service, Geyerswörthstrasse 3, 96047 Bamberg 0951 297 6200 Apr–end Dec Mon–Fri 9.30–6, Sat, Sun 9.30–2.30; Jan–end Mar Mon–Fri 9.30–6, Sat 9.30–2.30 Bamberg

TIPS

» The best way of seeing Bamberg's treasures and experiencing the city's history is to stroll through the romantic lanes of the old town on foot. Most sights of interest are within a comfortable walking distance.

» There are over 90 breweries in and around Bamberg, the highest density of breweries in the world. The local brew is Rauchbier, a dark red ale with a smooth, smoky taste that you will find served in Schlenkerla, a traditional inn in the old town. There's an interesting beer brewing museum, the Fränkisches Brauereimuseum, in rebuilt historic caves of the former Benedictine monastery's brewing cellars.

Above *The rococo gatehouse hangs over the River Regnitz*

BAMBERG

There are over 90 breweries in and around Bamberg. Bamberg has everything for those prepared to linger and inhale the magic of the past that still hangs in the air. A thousand years of turbulent history are on display in this city, with historic buildings that read like an encyclopedia of architecture. The list is endless, but pride of place has to go to the amazingly situated Altes Rathaus (Old Town Hall), an unusual, picturesque mixture of rustic half-timbering and rococo elegance in the middle of the Regnitz. In 1993, the old town was declared a World Heritage Site by UNESCO.

HISTORY

After Heinrich II, the Holy Roman Emperor, was elected King of Germany in 1002, he decided to found a diocese in Bamberg to consolidate his power. A trading settlement began to emerge on the Regnitz below the cathedral, and in the late 14th century the citizens built a town hall on an island in the river. In parts of the city today you can still see evidence of the imperial endowment Heinrich gave to the diocese and the cathedral, and the city's division into two distinct districts is evident; the Burgerstadt (merchants' town) is close to the river, and the Bischofsstadt (ecclesiastical quarter) is on the slopes above.

KAISERDOM

The Kaiserdom (Imperial Cathedral; daily 8–5; tel 0951 502330) sits majestically on one of Bamberg's seven hills, its four great towers piercing the skyline above the town. Built between the late Romanesque and early Gothic periods, its interior has some of the most remarkable sculpture to be found in Germany. In front of St. George's Choir is the impressive tomb of Emperor Heinrich II and his wife, Queen Kunigunde, by Tilman Riemenschneider, while on the left-hand-side pier of the choir is the mysterious Bamberger Reiter (Bamberg Knight), whose identity is still the subject of much speculation. The most intriguing feature outside is the Fürstentor (Prince's Portal), with a sculpture showing Christ and the Last Judgement.

Looking over the Domplatz is the Alte Hofhaltung, a fine example of German Renaissance construction, built as the Bishop's Palace in 1576: It now houses the Historisches Museum (Tue–Sun 9–5; tel 0951 519 0746). On the other side is the Neue Residenz, which has a superb baroque interior and cobbled courtyard.

BERCHTESGADENER LAND

Berchtesgadener Land protrudes into Austria from southeastern Bavaria, just 20km (12.5 miles) from Salzburg. Nationalpark Berchtesgaden, with its landmark Watzmann peak (2,713m/8,900ft), has unusual natural features.

KÖNIGLICHES SCHLOSS (THE ROYAL PALACE)

www.haus-bayern.com

An interesting tour here leads from the Romanesque cloisters through periods of Gothic, baroque, rococo and Biedermeier. Rooms have items from the Wittelsbach family's collection (mid-May to mid-Oct Sun–Fri tours on the hour 10–noon, 2–4; mid-Oct to mid-May Sun–Fri tours at 11, 2; tel 08652 947980).

KEHLSTEINHAUS (EAGLE'S NEST)

www.eagles-nest.de

Perched at 1,834m (6,017ft), this building near the parking area at Obersalzberg was given by Martin Bormann to Adolf Hitler for his 50th birthday as a holiday house. The Kehlsteinhaus restaurant (mid-May to end Oct daily 8.20–5; tel 08652 2969) opened in 1952 and the views are spectacular. The restaurant is accessed by elevator.

DOKUMENTATION OBERSALZBERG

www.obersalzberg.de

The exhibition documents the history of Obersalzberg (Salzbergstrasse 41, 83471 Berchtesgaden Apr–end Oct daily 9–5 (last admission 4); Nov–end Mar Tue–Sun 10–3 (last admission 2); closed 1 Jan, 1 Nov, 24 and 31 Dec; tel 08652 947960), a former home of Adolf Hitler, and links local historical aspects with the phenomenon of the National Socialist dictatorship. There is access from here to underground bunkers.

SALZBERGWERK (SALT MINES)

www.berchtesgaden.de

In this fascinating underground attraction (May to mid-Oct daily 9–5; mid-Oct to end Apr daily 12.30–3; tel 08652 60020) tours are given by knowledgeable guides. You will need to wear warm clothing and good walking shoes on the tour and you will be given miner's clothing to wear over your own. A film sets the scene and fills you in on the techniques of salt mining.

INFORMATION

www.berchtesgadener-land.com

411 H15 Tourismusregion Berchtesgaden-Königssee, Königsseer Strasse 2, 83471 Berchtesgaden 08652 9670 Late May to mid-Oct Mon–Fri 8.30–6, Sat 9–5, Sun 9–3; mid-Oct to late May Mon–Fri 9–5, Sat 9–noon Berchtesgaden

TIPS

» Don't miss the 30-minute gondola ride to the summit of the Jenner, and its attractive mountaintop Marktrestaurant, even if it's just for a coffee or ice cream.

» Take the cruise across Königssee on electric-powered boats and hear the famed Königssee echo.

Above *The 17th-century pilgrimage chapel of St. Bartholomew, on the banks of the Königssee*

INFORMATION

www.bodensee-tourismus.com
410 D14 International Bodensee Tourismus, Hafenstrasse 6, 78462 Konstanz 07531 90940 The Lake Constance Card (Bodensee Erlebniskarte) allows free travel on ferries and cableways, and free entrance to 195 attractions around the lake, including those in Austria and Switzerland. The card comes in three variations; the prices are for adults and children ages 6–15, respectively. Landrattenkarte (does not permit free ferry travel) 3 days: €39,€21; 7 days: €49, €27; 14 days: €59, €31 Seebärenkarte 3 days: €69, €37; 7 days: €89, €47; 14 days: €121, €61 Sparfuchskarte 3 days: €49, €27; 7 days: €71, €37; 14 days: €109, €51

Above *Lindau harbour on Lake Constance*

INTRODUCTION

Often called the Swabian Sea because of its enormous size, the Bodensee (Lake Constance) is central Europe's third-largest lake. It has 273km (170 miles) of shoreline shared between three countries: Germany, Austria and Switzerland. At 173km (107 miles), Germany has the largest shoreline, and from here the panoramic backdrop of the Alps is breathtaking. It gets very busy here during the high season, but the rewards far outweigh the inconvenience of heavy traffic and crowded towns. Part of the area's attraction is the temperate climate; the mild, dry weather is ideal for visitors and the surrounding orchards and vineyards. The historic city of Konstanz, with its bustling Altstadt (old town), has many interesting places to visit. Around the lake, Mainau is a paradise island of tropical plants with a fairy-tale castle; Reichenau Island has three Romanesque churches; in Singen you can explore the largest castle ruins in Germany; a prehistoric lake dwellers' village has been wonderfully reconstructed in Unteruhldingen; Meersburg has two formidable castles; in Friedrichshafen there's the interesting Zeppelin Museum; and the island town of Lindau has many nooks and crannies to explore.

Lake Constance could be considered Germany's largest stretch of inland water (but it takes second place to the Müritzsee] as a lake lying entirely inside German territory) and is Europe's largest reservoir, supplying water to most of southern Germany. The vineyards and orchards on the northern side thrive in the mild climate, while from the southern banks you get spectacular views of the snow-capped Alps. The Rhine enters the lake at its southeastern corner and flows out through Untersee into Switzerland before crashing over the largest waterfall in Europe, the mighty Rhine Falls (23m/75ft high and 150m/490ft wide) in Schaffhausen. This spectacular expanse of water has served trade, culture and leisure for centuries, and today it continues to offer a wide range of opportunities to all its visitors.

WHAT TO SEE

KONSTANZ

www.konstanz.de

This historic city sits on a spit of land separating Obersee, the main area of the lake, from Untersee, where the mighty Rhine flows from the lake into Switzerland before beginning its long journey north through Germany.

Konstanz escaped bombing during World War II because of its close proximity to neutral Switzerland, so the city's historic buildings were spared. At the harbour, you can see *Imperia*, a massive female figure by sculptor Peter Lenk, which rotates on the base of a former light tower, enabling onlookers to view the provocatively clad woman from all angles. Initially the cause of much controversy but now widely accepted, the figure symbolizes the power of the courtesans who followed the male participants to Konstanz at the time of the Council of Constance. Nearby, the former warehouse known as the Konzil is where the 1417 papal election was held. The historic part of the city holds many delights: Don't miss the Marktstätte and Kaiserbrunnen (Emperor's Fountain, 1897), the 16th-century Rathaus, St. Stephen's Church, the five-floor Hohe Haus and the oldest building in Konstanz, the Cathedral.
Bahnhofplatz 13, 78462 Konstanz 07531 133030 Apr–end Oct Mon–Fri 9–6.30, Sat 9–4, Sun 10–1; Nov–end Mar Mon–Fri 9.30–12.30, 2–6 Konstanz

LINDAU

www.lindau-tourismus.de

The tiny island town of Lindau is linked to the mainland by a bridge on the northeastern corner of the lake. Owing to its location on a major trading route, Lindau was a bustling trading post in the Middle Ages, and consequently wealthy merchants built grand, gabled, Italian-style houses on the town squares. Half-timbered buildings from all eras lean over the narrow streets, and Maximilianstrasse, with its patrician houses, fountains and shaded walks, is particularly beautiful. Stroll around the Altstadt and see the Old Town Hall with its stepped gables and garish murals, the Diebsturm (Thieves' Tower) and the Peterskirche (St. Peter's Church), with fine frescoes showing scenes from the Passion story. Parking is a big problem here, so try leaving your car on the mainland and taking the free shuttle bus to the island.
Prolindau, Ludwigstrasse 68, 88131 Lindau 08382 260020 Mid-Mar to mid-Jun and mid-Sep to mid-Oct Mon–Fri 9–1, 2–6, Sat 2–6; mid-Jun to mid-Sep Mon–Fri 9–1, 2–6, Sat 2–6, Sun 10–2; mid-Oct to mid-Mar Mon–Fri 9–12, 2–5 Lindau

MEERSBURG

www.meersburg.de

Beautifully baroque, Meersburg is often described as a jewel of European architecture. The Unterstadt (Lower Town) consists of only two streets, which are sandwiched between the shore and the towering Altes and Neues Schloss (old and new castles) above. At the western end is the Seetor (Lake Gate) and at the eastern side the promenade is dominated by the massive tithe barn. The narrow streets in the historic Oberstadt (Upper Town) are lined with half-timbered houses and stately baroque buildings. Try to visit the Altes Schloss, Neues Schloss (which houses the Municipal Gallery) and Weinbaumuseum (Museum of Wine-Making).
Meersburg Tourismus, Kirchstrasse 4, 88709 Meersburg 07532 440400 Mon–Fri 9–12.30, 2–6, Sat 10–1

FRIEDRICHSHAFEN

www.friedrichshafen.de

Although an industrial town, its association with the Zeppelin airships make this a worthwhile place to visit. The Friedrichshafen Zeppelin Museum (May–end Oct Tue–Sun, also Mon Jul–end Sep, 9–5; Nov–end Apr Tue–Sun 10–5; tel 07541 38010) is housed in the former port railway station, and has the world's largest exhibition on airships. Also visit the twin onion-domed Schlosskirche, built in 1695 in the early baroque style by Christian Thumb.
Tourist-Information, Bahnhofplatz 2, 88045 Friedrichshafen 07541 30010 Apr, Oct Mon–Thu 9–noon, 2–5, Fri 2–5; Nov–end Mar Mon–Thu 9–noon, 2–4, Fri 2–4 Friedrichshafen

TIPS

» The best time to visit Lake Constance is during April or May, when the fruit trees are in blossom, or during the autumn wine harvest. The whole area around the lake is very busy during July and August.

» The most enjoyable way of seeing the sights around the lake is by boat. From March to early November, ferries call at most of the larger towns several times a day.

» The car ferry between Konstanz and Meersburg runs frequently (every 15 minutes during the daytime), seven days a week throughout the year. Fares for cars range from €6.40 to €10.80 (depending on length) plus €2 per adult and €1 per child.

Below *A great day's fishing at Meersburg*

BAYREUTH

www.bayreuth-tourismus.de

Bayreuth's history can be traced to the late 12th century, but it was from 1735 to 1763, during the rule of Margrave Friedrich and his enterprising wife, Wilhemine (the older sister of Friedrich II the Great), that the town came to prominence. Wilhemine was the force behind the construction of the magnificent palaces and gardens you can see in Bayreuth today.

Although you can still see traces of Bayreuth's medieval past—the original residence of the margraves, the Altes Schloss (Old Palace), dates back to the 14th century—the baroque age contributed most to the town's architectural character. The Neues Schloss (New Palace), built in 1753, houses several museums and has an interesting grotto and garden rooms.

Composer Richard Wagner (1813–83) is responsible for Bayreuth's eminence today; his former home, Villa Wahnfried, is now the Richard Wagner Museum (Apr–end Oct Mon, Wed, Fri–Sun 9–5, Tue, Thu 9–8; Nov–end Mar daily 10–5; tel 0921 757280), dedicated to his life and works. It is also the site of the annual Bayreuth Wagner Festival. In the gardens are the graves of Wagner and his wife.

406 G11 Luitpoldplatz 9, 95444 Bayreuth 0921 88588 Bayreuth

BERCHTESGADENER LAND

▷ 307.

BODENSEE

▷ 308–309.

CHIEMSEE

www.mychiemsee.de

Bavaria's largest lake is a popular resort with two principal islands and surrounded by pretty towns and villages. Chiemsee has good hiking, bicycling, boating and bathing facilities, as well as many museums and galleries.

Herreninsel (Men's Island) and Fraueninsel (Women's Island) are both interesting places. On the mostly wooded Herreninsel is the magnificent Schloss Herrenchiemsee (guided tours Apr to mid-Oct daily 9–6; mid-Oct to end Mar daily 9.40–4.15; tel 089 1790 8165), an unfinished palace of Ludwig II, a replica of Versailles. What does exist is impressive, especially the long Hall of Mirrors, palatial rooms and museum. The smaller Fraueninsel has a Benedictine nunnery, founded in the eighth century, and a picturesque little fishing village.

411 H14 Felden 10, 83233, Bernau am Chiemsee 08051 965550 Prien, Bernau

COBURG

www.coburg-tourist.com

The stark exterior of the massive Veste towers above this lively town. For many years this fortress was the seat of the dukes of Saxe-Coburg and a popular meeting place of the European aristocracy.

Known as the Crown of Franconia because of its hilltop position and towers, the castle was founded in the 11th century and much rebuilt during the Renaissance. This impressive stronghold, with its double ring of defensive walls, was never taken by force. Today, there is a display of weapons and copperplate engravings, plus a world-renowned art collection.

The Hofgarten (Court Garden) owes a lot to Coburg's ducal heritage. The garden stretches from the castle to Schloss Ehrenburg, which has an impressive baroque Riesensaal (Giants' Hall).

406 F10 Herrngasse 4, 96450 Coburg 09561 74180 Coburg

DINKELSBÜHL

www.dinkelsbuehl.de

Dinkelsbühl is a cultural monument: a distinctive townscape, perfectly preserved town walls and superb patrician houses. The Hezelhof, with its tiered balconies, and the Renaissance half-timbered Deutsches Haus are a reminder of the glorious era in the 15th and 16th centuries, when the town's craftsmen and flourishing trading activities enhanced its wealth.

There are four gates in the town walls, the most impressive being the Rothenburger Tor on the north side. Martin Luther Strasse leads to the Marktplatz and the late gothic Münster St. Georg, one of the most beautiful hall churches in Germany. The tower of the Münster offers the best panoramic views of the town. Behind the church is the Altes Rathaus (Old Town Hall) with prison cells and courtyard. A walk around the ramparts at night is an ideal way to experience the town's vibrant ambience, especially in the company of the nightwatchman as he does his rounds.

409 E12 Marktplatz, 91550 Dinkelsbühl 09851 90240 Dinkelsbühl

Left *The decorated Stadhaus, built in 1599, with market stalls in the square in Coburg*

FREIBURG IM BREISGAU

The capital of the Schwarzwald (Black Forest), Freiburg sits neatly in the midst of lush green hills and vineyards close to the borders of France and Switzerland. The historic Altstadt, with numerous historical monuments, museums, theatres and lively squares with intimate restaurants and quaint bars, all make this vibrant city popular with students and visitors alike. Look out for the Freiburg Bächle, the small streams of water that flow through the streets in open gullies. Nearby are the vineyards and wine villages of the Margrave, Kaiserstuhl and Tuniberg regions.

FREIBURG MÜNSTER

The magnificent Gothic Cathedral (Mon–Sat 10–5, Sun, holidays 1–7.30; tel 0761 218 8243) takes pride of place as Freiburg's main landmark. It took over 300 years to build and it ranks among the masterworks of Gothic architecture. The unique 116m (381ft) tower dominates the city, and if you are fit enough, you can climb to the viewing platform for magnificent views. The highlights of the lavish interior are its high altar with a famous altarpiece by Hans Baldung Grien, the choir chapels with their 16th-century windows, fine altars and monuments and the wonderful 14th-century stained glass in the aisles.

OTHER SIGHTS

The Augustiner Museum is a former monastery of the Augustinian hermits, with artistic and historical collections of the city and Upper Rhine region from the ninth to 20th centuries. The Museum for Town History is in the Wentzinger House, built in 1761 by the artist Johann Christian Wentzinger. The Adelshauser Kloster, an old convent now occupied by the Natural History Museum, has interesting geological, zoological and mineralogical collections. In the unusual Carnival Museum, the Breisgau Jesters' Guild shows the history of carnival from the Middle Ages to the present day.

Domplatz is surrounded by impressive buildings, the tallest of which is the historical Kaufhaus (Merchants' Hall), with statues of Habsburg rulers on its façade. Other sights worth seeing are the baroque Erzbischöfliches Palais (Archbishops' Palace), Haus zum Walfisch (House of the Whale) with its superb late Gothic portal, Basler Hof (Basle Court), the restored 15th-century Kornhaus (the original was destroyed in World War II) and the two medieval city gates, Martinstor and Schwabentor.

INFORMATION

www.freiburg.de
408 B13 Tourist Information, Rathausplatz 2–4, 79098 Freiburg
0761 388 1880 Jun–end Sep Mon–Fri 10–8, Sat 9.30–5, Sun 10–noon; Oct–end May Mon–Fri 10–6, Sat 9.30–2.30, Sun 10–noon Freiburg

TIPS

» The best way of seeing Freiburg is to take one of the many guided city tours with the Freiburg Kultur tour-guide team. They begin at the tourist office and cover a wide variety of sights and themes.
» Freiburg is an excellent base to tour the Black Forest and visit Germany's largest family theme park, the amazing Europa Park in Rust.
» The 1,284m (4,214ft) Schauinsland mountain provides the perfect platform for viewing both the city and the Rhine valley. The 15-minute Seilbahn (cable-car) ride from the valley station provides majestic views: the lush Black Forest spreads out below as you head for the top of the world.

Above *The sloping roofs and narrow streets of Freiburg*

INFORMATION

www.heidelberg-marketing.de
408 D11 Tourist Information Hauptbahnhof, Willy-Brandt-Platz 1, 69115 Heidelberg 06221 19433 Apr–end Oct Mon–Sat 9–7, Sun and holidays 10–6; Nov–end Mar Mon–Sat 9–6 Tourist Information Rathaus, Marktplatz, 69123 Heidelberg, tel 06221 19433 Mon–Fri 8–5, Sat 10–5 Heidelberg

Above *Although now in ruins, Schloss Heidelberg is worth a visit*

INTRODUCTION

Romantic Heidelberg is celebrated in song and poetry. An enchanting location on the meandering River Neckar at the point where the Neckar emerges from the wooded Odenwald hills and flows into the Rhine plain, amid wooded hillsides and sloping vineyards, does much to explain its appeal to artists, poets and visitors. The towers and bridges, Altstadt (old town) and majestic towering castle cast their magical spell on all who enter. This vibrant university town and former capital of the Palatinate has several theatres and private galleries, and concerts, festivals and other cultural activities going on throughout the year. Its sights attract visitors from around the world.

Heidelberg was destroyed during the Thirty Years' War and sacked again by invading French troops in the late 17th century. Careful rebuilding has created a city that has become one of Germany's most popular destinations. The magic of the castle, the Old Bridge and the old town has attracted such notable characters as Mark Twain and English artist J. M. W. Turner.

The main street, Hauptstrasse, is a pedestrianized shopping thoroughfare 1.6km (1 mile) long, with many narrow side streets full of offbeat shops, student pubs, bistros and intimate restaurants—it's a great place to explore but be prepared for the crowds. Perched high above this, the magnificent red sandstone Schloss Heidelberg, a castle that's among the finest examples of German Renaissance architecture, crowns the city. A highlight of exploring the town is walking through steep cobbled lanes from Kornmarkt up to the ruins.

Other places of interest include the university's Botanical Garden, one of Germany oldest, and the University Museum, which displays Heidelberg's academic history. Nearby is the Students' Prison, where from 1778 until 1914 students were imprisoned for so called Kavaliersdelikte (minor transgressions). The Palatinate Museum holds interesting regional items and works of art.

WHAT TO SEE

SCHLOSS HEIDELBERG AND SCHLOSSGARTEN

www.schloss-heidelberg.de

This impressive ruin on a granite rock 90m (300ft) above the city is one of Germany's finest examples of a Gothic-Renaissance fortress. Construction began in the 13th century and continued over a period of 400 years, with ramparts, buildings and palaces added in a variety of styles. The prince electors of the 16th and 17th centuries turned the fortress into a castle, and the two dominant buildings at the eastern and northern side of the courtyard are considered to be two of the most important buildings in German architectural history. The castle was destroyed during the Thirty Years' War and again in the late 17th century by invading French troops. Local people began using castle sandstone to build houses in Heidelberg, but fortunately this was stopped in 1800 by Count Charles de Graimberg. The King's Hall was added in 1934 and is used today for banquets, balls and theatrical performances.

During the Heidelberg Castle Festival, the amazing Renaissance courtyard is used for open-air musicals, operas, theatre performances and classical concerts, such as the famous Castle Serenades performed by the Heidelberg City Orchestra. From the terrace there are fantastic views across the town and Neckar valley: Look out for the huge footprint said to have been made by a knight who had to make a hasty escape from a third-floor window when caught by a prince in his wife's bedroom.

In former times, the geometrically designed terraces of the Renaissance garden stood out against the wooded background of Heidelberg Castle; before its destruction during the Thirty Years' War, contemporaries even considered the Hortus Palatinus to be the Eighth Wonder of the World. The remains of the Great Grotto, where the water flows in time with music, is amazing, and in the nearby pond is a great sandstone sculpture of Father Rhine.

✉ Schlosshof 1, 69117 Heidelberg ☎ 06221 538431 ⏲ Daily 8–5.30 ✋ Interior: adult €3, child (6–18) €1.50, under 6 free; Schlosshof, Grosses Fass and Deutsches Apothekenmuseum (combined): adult €3, child (6–18) €1.50, under 6 free; Castle interior (guided tours only) add: adult €4, child (6–18) €2, under 6 free, family €10; Garden: free 🚋 Bergbahn funicular

ALTE UNIVERSITÄT AND BOTANISCHE GARTEN

www.uni-heidelberg.de

www.botgart.uni-hd.de

Germany's oldest university was founded here in 1386. Dominating Universitätsplatz are the Old and New University buildings, along with the Löwenbrunnen, a fountain crowned by a lion symbolizing the power of the Palatinate. The ceiling in the Old Assembly Hall holds paintings depicting the four university faculties: philosophy, medicine, law and theology. The university museum explains Heidelberg's academic history and the library holds huge electronic archives. The Botanical Garden, one of the oldest in Germany, was originally established in 1593 as a *hortus medicus* for the cultivation of medical herbs. Nowadays, this institution is noted for plant biology and the greenhouses contain rare plant collections.

✉ Grabengasse 3, 69117 Heidelberg ☎ 06621 540 ⏲ Museum: Tue–Sat 10–4; Library: Mon–Sat 10–6; Botanical Garden: Mon–Thu 9–4, Fri 9–2.30, Sun 9–12, 1–4 ✋ Museum: adult €2.50, child (6–18) €2, under 6 free; Botanical Garden: free 🚌 31, 32

PHILOSOPHENWEG

Enjoy a stroll along the famous Philosophers' Walk and follow in the footsteps of Heidelberg's philosophers and university teachers. The views are outstanding, as are the exotic trees, shrubs, parks, gardens and memorial stones along the path.

TIPS

» For the best views of Heidelberg, take a stroll along the Philosophers' Path, one of Europe's most beautiful walks, high above the town and the River Neckar.

» Look out for the popular 'Made in Heidelberg' designs such as Lamy writing instruments and Gil Brett and Betty Barclay ladies' fashion.

HEIDELBERGCARD

Four variants of the HeidelbergCard are available from the tourist office, offering free or reduced travel on public transportation and admission to museums and other attractions. One-day card: €10; two-day card: €14; four-day card: €20; two-day family card: €28.

Below *Walking down a busy street in Heidelberg*

FURTWANGEN

www.furtwangen.de

The Schwarzwald (Black Forest) is the heart of the German clockmaking region, and Furtwangen is one of the industry's major towns. The Deutsches Uhrenmuseum (German Clock Museum; Apr–end Oct daily 9–6; Nov–end Mar daily 10–5; tel 07723 920 2800) is the place to go to see fine examples of timepieces from around the world. With over 5,000 exhibits, the museum has the largest collection of clocks in Germany, and the world's largest collection of Black Forest clocks, including Renaissance ones and examples of clockmasters' art. Many factories and workshops in the area are open to visitors.

If you are particularly interested in clocks, visit the nearby town of Villingen-Schwenningen and the Uhrenindustriemuseum, which housed the factory of the oldest clock company in Wurttemberg.

408 C13 Lindenstrasse 1, 78120 Furtwangen 07723 92950 Furtwangen

GARMISCH-PARTENKIRCHEN

www.garmisch-partenkirchen.de

Germany's winter sports capital comprises two villages that were merged together for the Winter Olympics of 1936, the older Partenkirchen and the more modern Garmisch. Garmisch is the ritzier of the two, with fashionable shops and cafés. Its Kurpark regularly hosts open-air concerts, and the Kurhaus contains a collection of Meissen porcelain and historic toys. Pfarrkirche St. Martin, built in 1733, has a rich baroque interior.

Partenkirchen is characterized by traditional painted houses, and one of these, a former merchant's residence at Ludwigstrasse 47, is the only house in the street not to have been devastated by a terrible fire in 1865. The house contains the Werdenfels Museum (Tue–Sun 10–5; tel 08821 2134), which vividly brings the region's distinctive culture to life. You are still likely to see country folk in traditional costumes and cattle being driven from their mountain grazing grounds through the streets here.

The towns straddle the River Partnach, surrounded by mighty mountain massifs. Most impressive is the Zugspitze, the highest mountain in Germany at 2,962m (9,724ft), easily conquered nowadays by rack railway from Garmisch. Another memorable ascent aboard the Eibsee Aerial Tramway from nearby Grainau.

410 F15 Richard-Strauss-Platz 1a, 82467 Garmisch-Partenkirchen 08821 180700 Garmisch-Partenkirchen

Below *Burg Trausnitz castle viewed through an archway at Landshut*

HEIDELBERG

⊳ 312–313.

LANDSHUT

www.landshut.de

This historical ducal town has retained much of the appearance and character of the provincial capital that it once was. The cobbled squares and town boulevards are ideal for exploring the cultural highlights of this medieval town. Landshut is on the banks of the River Isar, and the pattern of the town is set by two wide market streets, Altstadt and Neustadt, lined with late medieval townhouses. In Altstadt, the town's main street lined with late Gothic gabled houses, is the Stiftsbasilika St. Martin, its slender church tower rising to 133m (436ft), the highest brick steeple in the world.

Dominating the skyline is the imposing Burg Trausnitz (Apr–end Sep daily 9–6; Oct–end Mar daily 10–4; tel 0871 924110), founded by Duke Ludwig I in 1204. In the 16th century, the castle was rebuilt by Prince William of Bavaria in an Italian style. He retained the 13th-century chapel with its Romanesque statuary, and had the famous Narrentreppe, or Fools' Staircase, decorated with wall paintings. The castle terrace offers good views.

411 G13 Altstadt 315, 84028 Landshut 0871 922050 Landshut

LINDERHOF

www.linderhof.de

Set among magnificent mountain scenery and surrounded by forest, Schloss Linderhof is perhaps the most appealing of King Ludwig's castles. The Royal Villa of Ludwig II began as a hunting lodge belonging to his father, Maximilian II, and was based on the Petit Trianon at Versailles. Completed in 1878, the lavish interiors are not as spectacularly bizarre as Ludwig's Schloss Neuschwanstein (⊳ 322–325), but are nevertheless pretentious, with a large private bedroom, Hall of Mirrors and an enormous crystal chandelier weighing 500kg (1,000lb), all decorated in a mixture of Renaissance and baroque styles.

The formal French gardens, with fanciful fountains, pools and follies, are a wonderful place to explore. The grand cascade is a water jet that shoots higher than the palace itself, the grotto is an artificial stalactite cave inspired by the Venusberg of Wagner's opera Tannhäuser, and the oriental-style Moorish Kiosk has a grandiose peacock throne.

410 F15 Linderhof 12, 82488 Ettal 08822 920349 Apr to mid-Oct daily 9–6; mid-Oct to end Mar daily 10–4 Summer season (castle and gardens): adult €7, child (under 18) free; winter season (castle only): adult €6, child (under 18) free 9622 from Oberammergau

KARLSRUHE

Superb collections from the Baden State Museum are on display in the Schloss. In 1715, Margrave Karl Wilhelm decided to build a residential retreat close to the Rhine in the northern foothills of the Black Forest. Tired of living in a decaying medieval castle, the Margrave is said to have dreamed of building a city laid out in the shape of an oriental fan with a palace at the axis. When his son, Karl Friedrich, took up regency, he commissioned Albert Friedrich von Kesslau to build a new palace. Von Kesslau designed it in close consultation with his mentor La Guépière from Paris. The building work was completed in 1770. From the beginning, Karlsruhe was designed as a city without walls, and the unusual pattern of streets running in straight lines from the palace still exists today. Master builder and architect Weinbrenner created the numerous classical buildings around the city. In 1951, Karlsruhe lost its status as regional capital of Baden, but its importance is still recognized; today it is home to Germany's two highest courts, the Federal Constitutional Court and the Federal Supreme Court.

SIGHTS

The Marktplatz, designed by Weinbrenner in 1797, is a neoclassical square. A red sandstone pyramid (1825) that has become the emblem of Karlsruhe marks the burial vault of the town's founder. On either side of the square are the Stadtkirche, the municipal church for the state of Baden-Württemberg, and the Rathaus. The market fountain is a monument commemorating the merits of Grand Duke Ludwig in establishing the first spring water mains in Karlsruhe. Naturkundemuseum (Natural History Museum), Staatliche Kunsthalle (State Art Gallery), Städtische Galerie (Municipal Gallery) and Museum für Neue Kunst (Museum of Modern Art) all have wide ranges of interesting exhibits. Kaiserstrasse, the first main street running parallel to the Schloss, is a popular spot on a sunny day.

SCHLOSS

The Margraves' magnificent palace (Tue–Thu 10–5, Fri–Sun 10–6; tel 0721 926 6514) displays superb collections of the Baden State Museum: Greek, Roman and near-Eastern art, the Margrave of Baden's treasure chamber, a famous collection of Turkish trophies and art and cultural history from the Middle Ages to the modern era. Behind the palace, in the extensive Schlossgarten, is the Orangery, with exhibits, paintings and sculptures from the end of the 19th century through to the more contemporary, and the Botanic Garden.

INFORMATION

www.karlsruhe.de

408 C12 Tourist-Information, Bahnhofplatz 6, 76137 Karlsruhe 0721 3720 5383 Mon–Fri 9–6, Sat 9–1 Karlsruhe

TIPS

» The best vantage point from which to see the layout of this fan-shaped city is the palace tower. Here you are standing right at the axis and can look over the whole town from a height of 42m (138ft).

» Many German cities have a Christmas craft market, but the Karlsruhe Christkindl Markt is exceptional. Beginning in November, a small village of stalls takes over the market square and the smell of *Glühwein* (mulled wine) and *Lebkuchen* (gingerbread) fills the air.

Below *Looking up the wide footpath leading through the formal gardens of the Schloss*

INFORMATION

www.tourismus.nuernberg.de
410 F11 Nürnberg Info, Hauptmarkt 18, 90403 Nürnberg 0911 23360 May–end Oct Mon–Sat 9–6, Sun 10–4; Nov–end Apr Mon–Sat 9–6; during Christkindlesmarkt Mon–Sat 9–7, Sun 10–4 Nürnberg Info, Königstrasse 93, 90402 Nürnberg 0911 23360 Mon–Sat 9–7, Sun 10–4 Walking tours of the old town (in English) May–end Oct, late Nov–early Jan: Adult €9 plus €2 admission to Kaiserburg, child (under 15, accompanied by parents) free Nürnberg

Above *Many of Nürnberg's buildings have been reconstructed*

INTRODUCTION

Bavaria's second-largest city, after Munich, and one of southern Germany's leading industrial and commercial towns, Nuremberg is an interesting mix of the quaint and the cosmopolitan. The River Pegnitz divides the Altstadt (old town) into its Sebald and Lorenz districts, named after the main church in each district. This central medieval walled city criss-crossed by narrow streets and alleys—many of them pedestrians-only walkways that make ideal places to explore and for shopping—is lined with timber-framed houses.

Nuremberg was Germany's greatest surviving medieval city and, thanks to careful reconstruction, it has not only risen from the rubble of wartime destruction, but recaptured much of its former elegance and appeal. It's unfortunate, however, that the city is associated in many people's minds with its links to the Nazis in the 1930s, the infamous Nuremberg Laws on 'racial purity' and the post-World War II Nuremberg Trials, because it has far more to its history than this dismal period. The painter Albrecht Dürer lived here from 1509 to 1528, in a house that's now a museum, through which an actress dressed as Dürer's wife leads guided tours.

Three main churches—the Frauenkirche, the St. Lorenz Kirche and the St. Sebaldus Kirche—are prominent city landmarks adorned with magnificent works of art. The climb to the Kaiserburg (Imperial Castle), which dates back to the city's foundation in the 11th century, is well worth the effort. Try to visit the cellars and bunkers here, especially the World War II Kunstbunker (Art Bunker) and the labyrinth of underground cellars below the castle.

In November, the Marktplatz is invaded for the famous open-air Christkindlesmarkt, Germany's most highly regarded Christmas Market. Apart from the enormous variety of Christmas decorations on offer, don't miss the

Glühwein (warm spiced wine) and *Lebkuchen* (similar to gingerbread), both of which are dispensed in great quantities.

WHAT TO SEE

KAISERBURG (EMPEROR'S CASTLE)

www.schloesser.bayern.de

The Kaiserburg is an important medieval imperial palace: From 1050 to 1571 a variety of kings and Holy Roman Emperors stayed in it during their reign. You can visit the Romanesque Doppelkapelle (Double Chapel), the upper floor of which was reserved for the emperor and court, while the lower floor was for the lower ranks. In the Brunnenhaus (covered well), 48m (157ft) deep, you can watch lighted candles being lowered to demonstrate the depth of this rocky chasm. The mighty Sinwellturm (Sinwell Tower) dominates the courtyard, and there are great views of the city's pointed rooftops and towering churches from here.

Also here is the Kaiserburg Museum, which documents the castle's history and the evolution of weapons and defensive techniques.

Auf der Burg 13, 90403 Nürnberg 0911 244 6590 Apr–end Sep daily 9–6; Oct–end Mar daily 10–4 Adult €5, child (under 18) free. The rooms can only be visited on a guided tour, which takes about 1.5 hours. Combination ticket for Palace with Double Chapel, Deep Well, Sinwell Tower and Kaiserburg Museum: adult €6, child (under 18) free Tram 4

GERMANISCHES NATIONALMUSEUM

www.gnm.de

Allow plenty of time to visit this, the largest and most important museum of Germanic art and culture, spanning the centuries from prehistoric times to the present. Founded in 1852, the museum illustrates the high points of German art and history. Highlights include works by Albrecht Dürer and Veit Stoss, the world's earliest globe, and a self-portrait by Rembrandt.

Kartäusergasse 1, 90402 Nürnberg 0911 13310 Tue, Thu–Sun 10–6, Wed 10–9 Adult €6, child (6–18) €4, under 6 free, family €9 U-Bahn Lorenzkirche, Opernhaus

HISTORISCHER KUNSTBUNKER

www.museen.nuernberg.de

It is hard to imagine Nuremberg nowadays without the famous works of art that decorate its churches and fill its streets and museums. The devastating bombing attacks during World War II levelled 90 per cent of the architecture of the old town, but thanks to the foresight of town officials, much of Nuremberg's artistic heritage survived. At the start of the war, they transformed the former beer cellars, 24m (79ft) beneath the castle hill, into a secure art shelter with a simple but effective system of air conditioning and moisture-proof storage cells.

The original installations can still be seen on the tour. Dress warmly because even in summer it's cool in the rock-cut cellars.

Obere Schmiedgasse 52, 90403 Nürnberg 0911 227066 Guided tours daily 2pm (except public holidays). Tours only run if there are three or more adults. In German only Adult €4.50, child (10–18) €3.50, under 10 free

TIERGARTEN (ZOO)

www.tiergarten.nuernberg.de

This magnificent landscaped zoological garden with large open-air enclosures is a great place for a stroll. There are animal houses, aviaries and a children's zoo, plus the Adler miniature train, a model of Germany's first railway, which operates from Easter to end October.

Am Tiergarten 30, 90480 Nürnberg 0911 54546 Apr–end Sep daily 8–7.30; Oct daily 9–6; Nov–end Mar daily 9–5 Adult €7.50, child (4–13) €3.70, under 4 free, family €18 65. Tram 5

TIPS

» The Nürnberg Card (adult €19, child under 13 free) gives you two full days of unrestricted use of public transportation and free admission to 34 museums and sights. It also entitles you to 10–20 per cent off theatre tickets.

» You will get good views of Nuremberg from the Sinwell Tower, but as an alternative, go into the Castle Garden, turn left and follow the garden down to a door that leads onto a walkway: The views from here are equally spectacular.

» You cannot visit Nuremberg without sampling the famous Bratwurst. Try the Bratwursthäusle, Rathausplatz (next to the Church of St. Sebaldus). Sausages are made fresh every day in the factory below the restaurant.

Above *In the gardens in Ludwigsburg's Residenzschloss there are a number of attractions for the many visitors*

LUDWIGSBURG

www.ludwigsburg.de

Picturesque Ludwigsburg is on a plateau above the River Neckar. In 1704, it was chosen as the location for a royal summer residence, but under the rule of Duke Eberhard Ludwig this plan quickly expanded. It became a city of palaces, and the magnificent Residenzschloss (Residential Palace; guided tours mid-Mar to end Oct Mon–Fri 1.30, Sat, Sun 11, 1.30, 3.15; Nov to mid-Mar daily 1.30; tel 07141 182004), is the largest surviving baroque palace in Germany. Often called the Swabian Versailles, it has 452 rooms in 28 buildings. On the ground floor are examples of fine porcelain still being produced by the factory first established in the palace in 1758.

In the beautiful park there's an aviary and a Märchengarten (Fairy-tale Garden), where mechanical figures act out fairy-tales. North of the palace is the Favoritepark (a game park and nature reserve), with the baroque Favorite palace, the summer residence built by Ludwig for his mistress. The lakeside Monrepos palace is the former hunting lodge of Duke Eberhard Ludwig; it is a rococo masterpiece, with the interior decorated in the style of the Napoleonic era.

409 D12 Marktplatz 6, 71634 Ludwigsburg 07141 910 2252 Ludwigsburg

MANNHEIM

www.tourist-mannheim.de

The city was founded in 1606 by the Prince Elector Friedrich IV to establish a strong commercial base for the collection of taxes. He built a formidable fortress, with residential blocks that stretch out from its base like the squares on a chessboard. Streets define the 144 squares, each of which is designated by a letter and a number, a logical system unique in Germany.

Mannheim is the second-largest river port in Europe and a commercial and industrial hub. Little of the city survived World War II, and most of the rebuilding was practical rather than aesthetic.

In Friedrichsplatz stands the symbol of the city, the Wasserturm (water tower), built in 1886 and rising over 60m (200ft) high. It is watched over by a statue of Amphitrite, wife of the sea god Poseidon. Also worth visiting are the Kunsthalle (Tue–Sun 11–6; tel 0621 293 6413), housing one of Germany's leading displays of 19th- and 20th-century art; the Mannheimer Schloss (Palace), with more than 400 rooms (now the main campus of Mannheim University); and the huge Jesuitenkirche (Jesuit Church), a fine baroque building, now restored.

408 C11 Willy-Brandt-Platz 3, 68161 Mannheim 0621 101012 Mannheim

MAULBRONN

www.maulbronn.de

The little town of Maulbronn is in the vine-covered foothills of the Stromberg. It grew up around the Zisterzienserkloster, one of the earliest and most beautiful of Cistercian monasteries to survive in Germany. According to folklore, a group of monks stopped here in 1147 to water their mules (the name originally meant 'mule well') and stayed on to found the abbey. This story is depicted in sketches for a fresco on the wall of the Brunnenkapelle (Well Chapel).

Half-timbered buildings surround the abbey courtyard, inside which are the kitchens, inner chambers and cloisters. You can also see the Paradise, the porch of the church of St. Mary, which has a stone crucifix from 1473 and 15th-century choir stalls.

A pleasant place for a stroll is the Philosophers' Walk.

408 D12 Klosterhof 31, 75433 Maulbronn 07043 1030 Maulbronn

NÜRNBERG

▷ 316–317.

OBERAMMERGAU

www.oberammergau.de

World renowned for its fairy-tale houses and woodcarvings, but particularly for its Passion Play, Oberammergau is a popular resort year-round. The woodcarving tradition dates from the 17th century and fine examples can be seen in the town's many craft shops.

The Passion Play was first performed in 1634 in fulfilment of a vow made in 1633, when the village was stricken by plague. After months of suffering, the Oberammergauers swore an oath that they would perform the *Play of the Suffering, Death and Resurrection of Our Lord Jesus Christ* every 10 years. The next production is in 2010. Now, more than 2,000 actors, singers, instrumentalists and technicians are involved in the play. Policemen are even allowed to grow beards.

Many houses in the town are decorated with frescoes by Franz Zwirk (1748–92). Fine examples of painted façades include the Forsthaus and the magnificent Pilatushaus, with its ornate architectural fantasies. The Hänsel and Gretel House in Ettaler Strasse is a 20th-century creation.

410 F14 Eugen-Papst-Strasse 9a, 82487 Oberammergau 08822 922740 Oberammergau

PASSAU

▷ 328.

REGENSBURG

▷ 320–321.

ROTHENBURG OB DER TAUBER

At the intersection of the Burgenstrasse (Castle Road) and the Romantische Strasse (Romantic Road), Rothenburg Ob Der Tauber is ideally placed for touring the area. Visit the German Christmas Museum and Christmas Village, where it's Christmas every day. Rothenburg is a fascinating town at the intersection of the two most important tourist routes in Germany: the Castle Road and the Romantic Road. Completely ringed by ramparts, this is one of Germany's best-preserved medieval towns, and its silhouette high above the lush Tauber valley has earned Rothenburg the nickname of the 'Franconian Jerusalem'. A leisurely stroll through this delightful town will take you back in time, whether you choose to wander through the cobbled streets and winding alleys lined with picturesque, half-timbered houses with red-tiled roofs, or walk along the fortifications, with mighty battlements and towers.

ROTHENBURG'S TOWNSCAPE

Intricate wrought-iron signs on shops and restaurants are evidence of the craftsmanship that gave Schmiedgasse (Smithy's Lane) its name. Today, these signs still have to be made from wrought iron and approved by the town council. Plonlein (Little Square), with its changing street level and half-timbered house framed by Siebers Tower and the Kobolzell Gate, is one of the most famous places in the town. The Thirty Years' War is brought to life in the Historical Vaults of the Town Hall. Rothenburg's most powerful mayor, Heinrich Toppler, died in 1408 in the dungeons. St. Jacob's Church is the most important church in town, not only because of the towers, but also because of its interior with two altars by woodcarver Tilman Riemenschneider.

THE MARKET SQUARE

Marktplatz is the main focal point of the town and the beautiful Rathaus with its superb Imperial Hall is one of the finest in southern Germany. Ratstrinkstube (City Councillors' Tavern) is probably one of the most famous buildings in Rothenburg. Its main clock was installed in 1683, and since 1910, the two windows to the right and left open every hour between 11 and 3 and 8 and 10 to show the *Meistertrunk* (Master Draught). This commemorates an event in 1631 when Rothenburg was taken by Imperial troops, and only saved when the mayor was challenged to drink the welcome draught, more than 3 litres (almost 1 gallon) of wine.

INFORMATION

www.rothenburg.de
www.rothenburg-online.de
409 E11 Markplatz 2, 91541 Rothenburg ob der Tauber 09861 404800 May–end Oct Mon–Fri 9–6, Sat, Sun 10–3; Nov–end Apr Mon–Fri 9–5, Sat 10–1 (Dec 10–3), Sun (Dec only) 10–3 Rothenburg ob der Tauber

TIPS

» Visit the Deutsches Weihnachtsmuseum (German Christmas Museum; Apr–end Dec daily 10–5; Jan–end Mar Sat, Sun 10–5; tel 09861 409365), with fascinating exhibits that show Christmas in different eras, with explanations about ornaments and traditions.

» There are some lovely walks here, including a stroll along the Tauber valley to Detwang and St. Peter und Pauls Kirche. There's a good riverside beer garden and restaurant about halfway along. On a rainy day, you can still wander along the Wehrgang (Sentry walk), as it is roofed for over 2.5km (1.5 miles) between the Klingen Bastion and Kobolzell Gate.

Above *Even the fortifications have charm in this medieval town*

INFORMATION

www.regensburg.de

411 G12 Altes Rathaus, Rathausplatz 4, 93047 Regensburg 0941 507 4410 Apr–end Oct Mon–Fri 9–6, Sat 9–4, Sun 9.30–4; Nov–end Mar Mon–Fri 9–6, Sat 9–4, Sun 9.30–2.30 Regensburg

Above *The Stone Bridge crosses the River Danube*

INTRODUCTION

Germany's best-preserved medieval city, Regensburg is steeped in history and rich with relics. More than 1,300 medieval buildings are packed into an Altstadt (old city) barely 1km (0.6-mile) square. The cathedral city sits neatly beside the romantic Danube, its church spires sharing the skyline with the palaces of great noble families and patrician houses from the 13th and 14th-centuries. Remarkably, the city escaped the wartime devastation suffered by so many German cities, so its many historical buildings are unscathed, and its narrow cobbled streets and lively squares are a joy to explore. The Stone Bridge, as impressive today as it was when it was built in the 12th century, is the perfect platform to view the city's spires, towers and steep sloping roofs.

Regensburg's written history dates back to AD179, when the Roman legionary fortress Castra Regina was established at Celtic Radasbona. Following the Roman army's withdrawal, Regensburg became a frequent site for Imperial diets (councils) of the Germanic successor states and With this rise in its political fortune, the city enjoyed an economic boom. The officials of the Frankish kings became wealthy merchants. During the Middle Ages, the city's leading families, in competition with each other, built elaborate patrician houses in the style of Italian fortresses. Each showed off his wealth and prestige by building ever higher towers, of which 19 remain today to give the city its famous skyline. The most impressive is the Kastenmayerhaus, with its four-floor tower, and the Goldener Turm, with its imposing golden tower and Renaissance courtyard in Wahlenstrasse, the city's oldest street.

Buildings around the central marketplace are part of the Altes Rathaus (Old Town Hall), which was begun in the 13th century and evolved through additions and alterations. Its central zone is formed by the old Patrizierburg (Patrician Castle), consisting of the Tower and the Great Hall. To the left is the historic Reichssaal and the baroque town hall is on the right.

WHAT TO SEE

THURN UND TAXIS-MUSEUM

www.bayerisches-nationalmuseum.de

In the 18th century, the princes of Thurn and Taxis, founders of the first large-scale postal service in Europe, created a magnificent palace here built around a former eighth-century monastery. The apartments are adorned with magnificent 19th-century furnishings, as well as some brought from the family's older residences. There's a branch of the Bayerisches Nationalmuseum in the palace, with art collections of the Thurn and Taxis dynasty. The Cloisters are considered to be among the most impressive in Germany.

Emmeramsplatz 6, 93047 Regensburg 0941 504 8133 Apr–end Oct Mon–Fri 11–5, Sat, Sun 10–5; Nov–end Mar Sat, Sun 10–3 Adult €4.50, child (under 18) free 2

DOM ST. PETER (ST. PETER'S CATHEDRAL)

www.bistum-regensburg.de

Considered to be Bavaria's finest example of Gothic architecture, the cathedral originates from the 13th century, although the distinctive spires are a 19th-century addition by King Ludwig I. The 13th- and 14th-century stained-glass windows are sublime.

Unter den Schwibbögen 17, 93047 Regensburg 0941 586 5500 Apr–end Oct daily 6.30–6; Nov–end Mar 6.30–5 Adult €3, child (6–18) €1.50, under 6 free, family €6 A

DOMSCHATZMUSEUM (CATHEDRAL TREASURY)

www.bistumsmuseen-regensburg.de

In the Cathedral Treasury, the former bishop's residence, there's an assortment of 11th- to 18th-century church treasures on display. These include gold plate, vestments and tapestries.

Krauterermarkt 3, 93047 Regensburg 0941 57645 Apr–end Oct Tue–Sat 10–5, Sun, holidays 12–5; Nov–end Mar Fri, Sat 10–4, Sun 12–4 Adult €2, child (under 14) €1 , family €4 A

DOCUMENT NEUPFARRPLATZ

During excavations in the Altstadt, archaeologists unearthed the remains of cellars belonging to the houses and buildings of the Jewish quarter, as well as sections of the Roman legionary fortress Castra Regina. Visit this underground site to see the relics from the Roman age and the medieval Jewish quarter.

Neupfarrplatz, Regensburg 0941 507 1442 Thu, Fri, Sat by guided tour only Adult €5, child (11–18) €2.50, under 11 free, family €10; Tickets and information from Tabak Götz, Neupfarrplatz 3 A

TIPS

» The compact Altstadt and an extensive pedestrianized zone make Regensburg perfect for walking. Early mornings are the best time to explore and shop before the crowds arrive.

» Take the boat trip from the Steinerne Brücke to Walhalla, the imposing Greek-style marble temple built for King Ludwig I on a hillside overlooking the Danube. (Boats run Apr–end Oct daily 10.30 and 2. Adult €10, child (5–14) €4.50, under 5 free, family €23. The trip takes around three hours, including a stay at Walhalla.

» You cannot visit Regensburg without sampling the famous Bratwurst at the Historische Wurstkuche (Historic Sausage Kitchen). They serve more than 100,000 Regensburger Bratwurst every day.

» Take a tour in English, starting at the City Hall and taking in patrician houses, restored areas, Stone Bridge, Porta Praetoria, St. Peter's Cathedral and Old Town Hall. (May–end Sep Wed, Sat; adult €6). Buy your tickets at the Tourist Information Office.

Below left *Regensburg enjoys an attractive riverside setting*
Below *One of the unique tower houses dating from the 14th and 15th centuries*

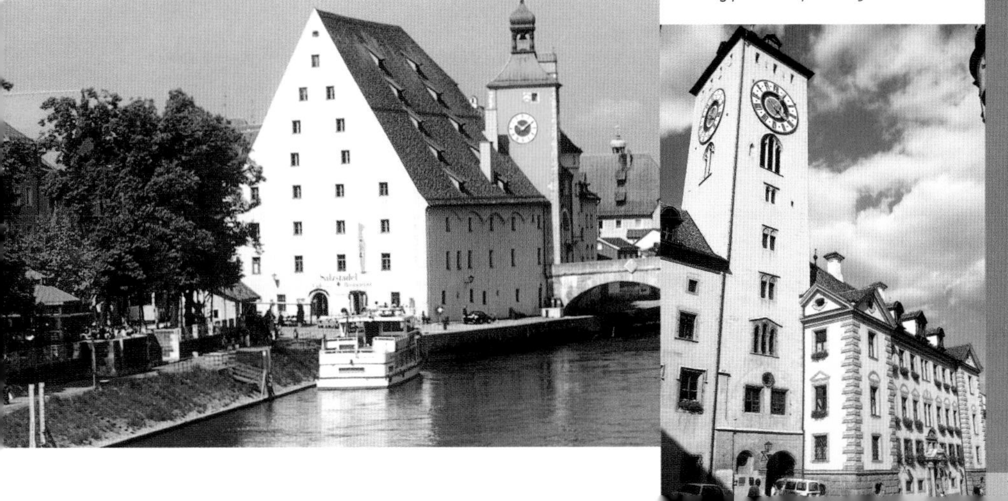

Above *George and the Dragon depicted in a painting of Wagner's opera 'The Mastersingers', in Neuschwanstein Castle*
Opposite *Fairy-tale Schloss Neuschwanstein in Bavaria*

INTRODUCTION

A fairy-tale come true, and inspiration for the castle in Walt Disney's *Sleeping Beauty*, King Ludwig's most famous castle stands 200m (650ft) above the valley floor. Magnificent Schloss Neuschwanstein is one of the most popular of all the castles in Europe and is always busy: 1.3 million people visit annually, and in the summer around 6,000 visitors a day stream through its rooms.

Prinz Otto Ludwig Friedrich Wilhelm was just 18 when he ascended the Bavarian throne in 1864. Although initially an enthusiastic leader, he became merely a puppet king following the creation of the German empire in 1871. He was introduced to the world of German sagas and legends through Wagner's operas, and this, combined with his love of French culture, led to the creation of three fantastical palaces: Linderhof (▷ 314) was built in the French style and Herrenchiemsee (▷ 310) was inspired by Versailles, but Neuschwanstein was King Ludwig's own personal fantasy. Its turrets and mock-medievalism were based on the Wartburg (▷ 220), and the interior styles range from Byzantine to Gothic and Romanesque.

The imposing structure was built between 1868 and 1886 but only about a third of it was actually completed. Its fairy-tale appearance is because the original designs were painted by Christian Jank, a scenery designer at the Court Theatre, and later translated into architectural plans by Eduard Riedel. Loved by his people but despised by his ministers, Ludwig was declared insane and deposed in 1886. He was taken from Neuschwanstein to Berg Palace on the banks of Lake Starnberg where he died in suspicious circumstances, along with his doctor—both men apparently having drowned. Just seven weeks after his death, Neuschwanstein was opened to the public to pay off the enormous debts he had incurred building it.

You can visit only 15 of the castle's rooms; the rest lie bare and eerie. On the second floor in particular you wander through empty room after empty room: Even the throne room doesn't have a throne in it. However, the rooms on view are amazing and once inside the castle you will appreciate the building's sheer size and understand why it is known as the Fairy-tale Castle

INFORMATION

www.neuschwanstein.de

410 F15 ✉ Neuschwansteinstrasse 20, 87645 Schwangau ☎ 08362 939880 ⌚ Apr–end Sep 9–6; Oct–end Mar daily 10–4 ✋ Adult €9, seniors and students €8, under 18 free; Königsticket (combined day ticket covering Hohenschwangau and Schloss Neuschwanstein): Adult €17, seniors and students €15, under 18 free; non-refundable ticket reservation fee, per ticket: €1.80 (Schloss Neuschwanstein), €3.60 (Königsticket) 🚌 Horse carriage from outside Ticket-Center. Bus from Schlosshotel Lisl to Jugend/Marienbrücke observation point (not suitable for disabled or elderly visitors): uphill €1.80, downhill €1.00, round-trip €2.60 (buses do not run in snow or ice) ❓ Entrance tickets can only be bought at the Ticket-Center, Alpseestrasse 12, 87645 Hohenschwangau, tel 08362 930830. You must therefore buy your ticket in this village below the castle before you start the approximate 30-minute walk to the castle, or in advance by phone or on the internet. The time can only be changed or the ticket cancelled up to two hours before the start of the tour (can be done by phone) 🚆 Füssen, then by bus to Hohenschwangau

TIPS

» An ideal base for your visit is Füssen, a renowned holiday and health resort in the eastern Allgau. It has a lovely historical Altstadt, and stands at the southernmost end of the Romantic Road.

» You can go through the automated entrance system's gates only at the allotted time, so if you miss your slot, you miss your tour. The 30-minute walk up the winding hill to the castle is very enjoyable, but if the weather is bad or you don't wish to tackle the climb there are other options. The horse-drawn carriage ride is a pleasant alternative, or there's a bus that will take you to the spectacular Marienbrücke observation point, leaving you with just a 10-minute walk to the castle entrance.

WALKS

There are some beautiful walks around the grounds, none more so than across Marienbrücke (Mary's Bridge) from where you can enjoy Ludwig's best-loved view. The bridge spans a deep gorge, and from the path between it and the castle is a lovely view of Hohenschwangau and the Alpsee. In fine weather, take the cable car up the Tegelberg (1,720m/ 5,645ft) from where you get outstanding views of the Alps.

Below *The exterior of Neuschwanstein Castle*

of a Fairy-tale King. The architecture and decoration are an interesting mixture of historical styles: Byzantine for the Throne Hall, Romanesque for the private apartments and Gothic for the impressive Singers' Hall. In every room you will see tributes to the Wagner operas: Look out for taps shaped like swans, illustrations from the Lohengrin saga and amazing stalagmites in the Grotto based on the Venusberg in Tannhäuser.

WHAT TO SEE

THE SÄNGERSAAL (SINGERS' HALL)

The heart of the castle is the lavish Singers' Hall, the first room to be planned, which was created so Ludwig could feed his obsession with Wagner. It is based on the Singers' Hall in the Wartburg (▷ 220), which was supposedly the setting for the singing contest in Wagner's opera *Tannhäuser*. Wall frescoes in the hall depict scenes from the opera, and on the end wall you will see a magnificent mural portraying Klingsor's magic garden from the opera *Parsifal*. Wagner concerts are held here every September, and even if you are not fortunate enough to get tickets, you will be able to imagine how wonderful they are when held in such a magnificent setting.

THRONE ROOM

The Byzantine Throne Room resembles the Court Chapel in Munich's Residenz (▷ 198–199), and is the most sumptuous room in the castle. Of particular interest are the wall paintings showing royalty performing holy acts, and a large image of Christ surrounded by nine canonized kings from the Middle Ages in the apse. Ludwig's throne was to be placed under this huge painting, but sadly it was never built. Even without a throne, this room was probably the most expensive to create, and savings were made by using mosaics instead of paintings and tinted stucco instead of marble for the pillars.

From the balcony, there are magnificent views of the gardens.

SERVANTS' ROOMS

Moving upstairs, the tour takes you through five of the servants' rooms, each simply fitted out with oak furniture and designed for two people. Between 10 and 15 servants were employed to look after the castle on a day-to-day basis, but if the King was in residence, double this number was needed.

DINING ROOM

The small dining room, connected to the kitchen three floors below by way of a dumb waiter (an elevator or lift used to transport food and drink), is indicative of King Ludwig's solitary existence. The interesting wall pictures show the world of the Minnesingers, German lyric poets and singers in the troubadour tradition who flourished between the 12th and 14th centuries. A magnificent gilt bronze sculpture portraying Siegfried's fight with the dragon Fafnir dominates the room.

BEDROOM

When you enter the bedroom the first thing you see is the King's huge bed, carved with spires and intricate tracery windows that resemble a late Gothic church. The elaborate oak carvings in the chamber took 14 woodcarvers over four years to complete. Ludwig was in this room when he was arrested on the night of 11 June 1886, before he was taken to Berg Palace on the banks of Lake Starnberg.

DRESSING ROOM

When you enter the dressing room, look up at the *trompe l'oeil* ceiling, which creates the illusion of looking up through a garden bower, with a background of blue sky and birds and a trellis of vines.

SALON

After touring a series of small rooms, entering the enormous salon, the largest room in the King's apartments, has quite an impact. In the far corner there are four columns that separate the main room from a secluded area where the king could retreat to read, known as Swan Corner. Wagner's influence is in evidence here too, with numerous images from the *Lohengrin* saga, painted onto coarse linen so they look like tapestries, and the swan motifs on the textiles and doors. There is also a beautiful life-size swan made of china.

Above left *Detail from an illustration depicting the Parsifal legend*
Above *Candelabra and wall paintings in the Sängersaal (Singers' Hall)*

GROTTO

Next to the Salon, the artificial grotto is yet another allusion to *Tannhäuser*, and it even has a concealed opening in the ceiling that allowed the King to listen to music from the Singers' Hall, directly above. The door into the conservatory actually slides down into rock, but for safety reasons this exit is always open.

KITCHEN

Prepare to be amazed at the equipment in the basement kitchens, which demonstrates the technically high standard of the castle's facilities. The crockery was added later, but everything else you see is original and would still be serviceable in a large modern kitchen. It's equipped with hot and cold running water, automatic spits and cupboards that could be heated with hot air from the large kitchen stove. Its pristine condition is partly due to the fact that the kitchen was only in use for two years, from 1884 to 1886.

SCHLOSS HOHENSCHWANGAU

Less famous, but no less worth seeing, Hohenschwangau was the castle where Ludwig spent his happy childhood. It stands above the village, romantically enthroned between centuries-old yews and weeping beeches. At its foot are the emerald waters of the moody Alpsee. If you are planning to visit Hohenschwangau, come here first, as it pales next to Ludwig's fantasy castle.

Apr–end Sep 9–6; Oct–end Mar daily 10–4 Adult €9, senior/student €8, under 18 free; Königsticket (combined day ticket covering Hohenschwangau and Schloss Neuschwanstein): adult €17, senior/student €15, under 18 free; non-refundable ticket reservation fee, per ticket: €1.80 (Hohenschwangau), €3.60 (Königsticket) Horse carriage from outside Ticket-Center: uphill €3.50, downhill €1.50

STUTTGART

INFORMATION
www.stuttgart-tourist.de
409 D12 i-Punkt, Königstrasse 1a, 70173 Stuttgart 0711 22280 Mon–Fri 9–8, Sat 9–6, Sun, holidays 11–6 Stuttgart

Above *The imposing Schlossplatz at night*

INTRODUCTION

Baden-Württemberg's state capital is beautifully located deep in a valley, with streets climbing steeply to meet surrounding hills covered with orchards, vineyards, forests and meadows. Its associations with the automobile and electrical industries through such famous names as Daimler, Benz and Bosch give Stuttgart an image of industrialization, but in reality its inner city parklands and surrounding landscape—parks and wooded zones account for almost a quarter of the entire 'urban' area—make the city a very enjoyable place to be. Today the population is about 600,000, and unlike many large industrial cities, Stuttgart is no concrete jungle. Its association with the manufacture of high-class, stylish cars gives the city a refined air, which you'll find in its streets, squares, parks and gardens. For a large city of regional importance, it has a wonderful relaxed atmosphere; maybe this is connected with those vineyards!

The name Stuttgart originates from a stud farm (Stutengarten), established in the 10th century by the Duke of Swabia. By the 12th century the settlement had become a thriving trading hub, and by 1427 was the capital and residence of the counts of Württemberg. Its prosperity and fortune continued to grow through the centuries and by the turn of the 20th century the city had a population of 175,000. Stuttgart suffered badly from Allied bombing during World War II and none of its landmarks or historic buildings survived intact. After the war, buildings were quickly restored and Stuttgart became the capital of the newly formed state of Baden-Württemberg (although many still call it Swabia).

Mercedes has its star badge proudly adorning the Hauptbahnhof (main station) tower and the Mercedes platform is open to visitors. You can take a free tour of the Mercedes-Benz Museum and factory, while the Porsche Museum has a grand display of 'Toys for Boys'.

Aside from the motor industry, the city has some fine museums and galleries: The Staatsgalerie is one of Europe's great modern art galleries; the Stiftsfruchtkasten, a former wine depot, has a wonderful collection of musical instruments; the reconstructed Stiftskirche has two very different late-Gothic towers, each 61m (200ft) high; and the art nouveau Market Hall, (1914) is one of the most beautiful in Germany. A trip to the theatre is a must, and where better to go than the Stuttgart State Theatre, incorporating the world-famous Stuttgart Ballet and the Stuttgart State Opera?

WHAT TO SEE

ALTES SCHLOSS—LANDESMUSEUM WÜRTTEMBERG

www.landesmuseum-stuttgart.de

The Old Palace has one of the most beautiful inner courtyards in the Renaissance style. It is the venue for summer concerts, theatre performances and the opening ceremony of the Christmas Market. The Württemberg State Museum has a wide variety of interesting exhibits of the House of Württemberg; look out for the elks on the clocktower that ram their horns on the hour.

✉ Schillerplatz 6, 70173 Stuttgart ☎ 0711 279 3498 🕐 Wed–Sun 10–5, Tue 10–1 ✋ Adult €4.50, child (14–18) €7, under 14 free, family €7 🚌 42, 44. Tram 5, 6, 7, 15

SCHLOSSPLATZ

In the middle of Schlossplatz is the Jubiläumssäule (Jubilee Column), erected in 1841 to commemorate the silver jubilee of the reign of King Wilhelm I. Be sure to visit the two fountains dating from 1863, a cast-iron music pavilion and a number of pieces of modern sculpture. Also here is the Kunstmuseum (Tue, Thu, Sat, Sun 10–6, Wed, Fri 10–9; tel 0711 216 2188), with mainly German art, and the baroque Neues Schloss.

✉ Schlossplatz, 70173 Stuttgart 🚌 42, 44. Tram 5, 6, 7, 15

MERCEDES-BENZ MUSEUM

www.museum-mercedes-benz.com

Recorded commentaries tell the history of the Daimler-Benz merger as you wander around an amazing array of magnificent cars. Free tours of the factory (at Sindelfingen; tel 07031 907 0403) are given twice a day, Monday to Friday, in English and German. They must be booked at least three weeks in advance. Minimum age is 6 years.

✉ Mercedesstrasse 100, 70372 Stuttgart ☎ 0711 173 0000 🕐 Tue–Sun 9–6 ✋ Adult €8, child (15–18) €4, under 15 free 🚉 Gottlieb-Daimler-Stadion 🚌 51

WILHELMA ZOO

www.wilhelma.de

Germany's largest Zoological and Botanical Gardens, on the northern edge of Rosensteinpark, are some of the most beautiful in Europe. Laid out for King Wilhelm I of Württemberg between 1842 and 1853 as a Moorish garden, the zoo has more than 10,000 animals of around 1,000 species. The mix of animal and plant life is exceptional and with approximately 2 million visitors every year, the Wilhelma is one of the most popular places to visit in Baden-Württemberg.

✉ Neckartalstrasse, 70342 Stuttgart (Bad Cannstatt) ☎ 0711 54020 🕐 May–end Aug daily 8.15–6; Apr, Sep daily 8.15–6.30; Mar, Oct daily 8.15–5; Nov–end Feb 8.15–4 ✋ Adult €11.40 (Mar–end Oct) or €8 (Nov–end Feb), child (6–17) €5.70 (Mar–end Oct) or €4 (Nov–end Feb), under 6 free, family €17.10–€28.50 (Mar–end Oct) or €12–€20 (Nov–end Feb) 🚉 S-Bahn Bad Canstatt 🚌 52, 55, 56. Tram 13, 14

TIPS

» The Bohnenviertel (bean quarter) is so called because it was formerly the area where workers or poorer people lived, and they reputedly ate mainly beans. It is now filled with many excellent bars and restaurants that are not on the tourist trail.

» The Stuttcard Plus 3-day ticket is good value at €18. It entitles one adult and two children (6–14) to free entry to all public museums, discounts on admission charges to other attractions and city tours and free travel on all inner-city public transportation for 3 days. If you don't want to use public transportation, the standard Stuttcard costs €12.

» For the best panoramic view of Stuttgart, visit the Fernsehturm (Television Tower). It is 217m (712ft) high and has a four-floor complex with a gourmet restaurant and viewing platform at 150m (490ft). On a clear day there are wonderful views of the Black Forest and Swabian Alps.

Below *The Silver Arrows Gallery in the Mercedes-Benz Museum*

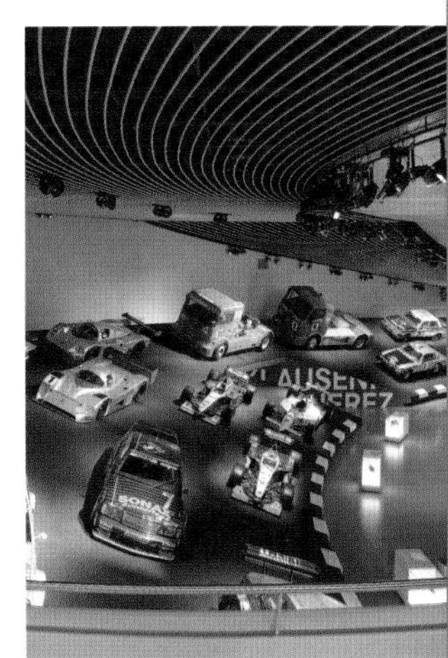

PASSAU

www.passau.de

This old Episcopal city is at the confluence of the blue Danube, green Inn and black Ilz rivers. Over the centuries, this spectacular setting has been responsible for many floods in the town, but it has also made it one of Germany's main river gateways to Austria and beyond.

The baroque design of Passau is dominated by large squares, riverside promenades and narrow winding lanes, framed by the Veste Oberhaus castle and the pilgrimage monastery Mariahilf. The old town lies on a narrow tongue of land between the Danube and the Inn, its houses huddled around a hill topped by the magnificent Dom St. Stephan (St. Stephen's Cathedral), from which narrow lanes spiral down to the two rivers. The cathedral houses the world's largest church organ, which is actually five organs played from one main keyboard.

411 J13 Rathausplatz 3, 94032 Passau 0851 955980 Passau

SCHLOSS NEUSCHWANSTEIN

▷ 322–325.

SCHWÄBISCH HALL

www.schwaebischhall.de

This is a popular little town on the north-eastern fringes of the Swabian Forest, overlooking the River Kocher. The buildings of the old town grow upwards from the river valley, and the sloping Marktplatz with its 16th-century fountain is one of the most impressive market squares in Germany. Around the square, the baroque Rathaus (Town Hall) has a magnificent clock and bell tower. An imposing flight of 54 stone steps, on which festival performances are given in summer, leads up to the Pfarrkirche (St. Michael's Church). The church interior has late-Gothic works of art, and the tower is the perfect place for panoramic views.

Hall, meaning 'place of salt', was a wealthy town in the 15th century because of its trade in salt, wine and corn. The Haller pfennig was minted here as early as the 11th century and gave its name to coins elsewhere in Germany and Austria. Schwäbisch was added to the name in 1934.

409 E12 Am Markt 9, 74523 Schwäbisch Hall 0791 751246 Schwäbisch Hall

STUTTGART

▷ 326–327.

TRIBERG

www.triberg.de

Triberg is in the heart of the cuckoo clock region. The business launched by Josef Weisser in 1824 gave the town the title of *Haus der 1,000 Uhren* (House of 1,000 Clocks). Triberg also has two of the largest cuckoo clocks in the world. The Gutach Falls, the highest waterfall in Germany (163m/535ft), are a spectacular sight after heavy rain or snow melt, as the water plunges in seven cascades down the mountain. The walk to the top of the falls is well worth the effort. In the Schwarzwaldmuseum (May–end Sep daily 10–6; Oct–end Apr daily 10–5; tel 07722 4434), a large collection of Black Forest clocks is on display, as well as local costumes and woodcarvings.

Deep in the Black Forest, Triberg is also renowned for the purity of its air and has become a popular health and spa resort.

408 C13 Schwarzwaldmuseum, Wallfahrt-Strasse 4, 78098 Triberg im Schwarzwald 07722 866490 Triberg

TÜBINGEN

www.tuebingen-info.de

Cobbled alleys, stone walls, half-timbered houses and pointed gables shape the university town of Tübingen. The Platanenallee (Avenue of Plane Trees) is a wonderful place to stroll along the picturesque bank of the Neckar. The Renaissance Hohentübingen Castle (now part of the university) gives the best views across the valleys of the Neckar and the Ammer and the red-tiled rooftops of the Altstadt and its surroundings. Burgsteige (Castle Way) has the oldest houses.

Holzmarkt (Timber Market) and St. George's Fountain give an excellent view of the late-Gothic Stiftskirche, with its handsome monuments commemorating members of the princely house of Württemberg. Beyond the church are the oldest parts of Karl Eberhard University and the Karzer (students' prison). On the banks of the Neckar is the Hölderlin Tower, and in the nearby Marktplatz are the Neptune fountain and Rathaus, a half-timbered building dating from 1435.

409 D13 An der Neckarbrücke 1, 72072 Tübingen 07071 91360 Tübingen

ULM

www.tourismus.ulm.de

The spire of Ulm's Münster is the tallest church spire in the world. Ulm is the birthplace of Albert Einstein.

Ulm's strategic location on the Danube brought it to prominence as early as the 12th century. Today, river traffic brings mainly tourists to this city divided by the blue water. Much of the old city was destroyed during a bombing raid in 1944, but many of the historic buildings have been carefully restored, making this an interesting place to visit.

Pride of place has to go to the Ulm Münster, the second-largest example of Gothic ecclesiastical architecture in Germany, and its spire, the tallest in the world. But it's not just the building that's worth seeing: There are many works of distinction inside the cathedral, too, particularly the 15th-century choir stalls by Jörg Syrlin the Younger, and Hans Multscher's life-size stone sculpture *Man of Sorrows* (1429) on the main portal. The Rathaus was built as offices in 1370 and has been the town hall since 1419. Inside is a replica of Albrecht Berblinger's flying machine. Berblinger built the machine in 1810 and, on 31 May 1811, he attempted, in the presence of the King, to glide over the Danube, but failed. However, in 1986, a replica was built and made the crossing successfully. The extensive Ulmer Museum (Tue–Sun

11–5; tel 0731 161 4312) has an emphasis on Gothic art in Upper Swabia, plus works by important 20th-century artists.

The legend of the Ulm Sparrow tells the story of citizens transporting wooden beams into the city for the construction of the Cathedral. The beams were loaded crosswise on the carriages, which meant that they were too wide to go through the narrow city gate. As the townspeople were wondering what to do, they suddenly noticed a sparrow carrying a long straw in its beak and observed it inserting this straw lengthwise into a niche of the tower. The citizens realized that if they repositioned the beams lengthwise on the carriages they would go through the gate, so in gratitude they placed a memorial to the sparrow on the Münster's roof.

409 E13 Tourist-Information Ulm, Stadthaus, Münsterplatz 50, 89073 Ulm 0731 161 2830 Apr–end Oct Mon–Sat 9–6, Sun 11–3; Nov–end Mar Mon–Fri 9–6, Sat 9–4 Ulm

Below *A group of statues surrounded by large basins in the central courtyard of the baroque Residenz in Würzburg*

WÜRZBURG

www.wuerzburg.de

The lively university city is surrounded by productive vineyards and dominated by the massive Festung Marienberg. The origins of this fortress date back to around 1000BC when Celtic tribesmen fortified the site, but it was in AD689 that the town really came to prominence with the martyrdom of three Irish missionaries, Kilian, Kolonat and Totnan, who tried to convert the local people to Christianity. Würzburg was severely damaged during World War II bombing, but after careful rebuilding, the city today has re-established itself as a popular destination renowned for its architecture, culture and wines.

Since the foundation of the Würzburg bishopric in AD742, the city has been the religious heart of the region. Würzburg is notable for its many churches, and one of the oldest is the Marienkirche, built on the site of the fortress in ad704 and surrounded by the first fortification in the 13th century. The Juliusspital, an impressive, castle-like baroque building dating back to 1576, was founded by Prince Bishop Julius Echter and contains a hospital, home for the elderly and a winery that supports both. The Marienkapelle on the Marktplatz is an interesting late-Gothic Bavarian church and the magnificent Dom St. Kilian is the fourth-largest Romanesque church in Germany.

Built for the prince bishops, the magnificent Fürstbischöfliche Residenz (1719–44) (Apr–end Oct daily 9–6; Nov–end Mar daily 10–4.30; tel 0931 355170) is the greatest baroque building of its kind in Germany. Designed by Balthasar Neumann (1687–1753), the palace has more than 300 baroque and rococo rooms, although many are still being renovated and may be closed. Their lavish decoration is breathtaking, especially the vast fresco painted by Giovanni Tiepolo on the ceiling above the grand staircase. Behind the Residenz, the terraced Hofgarten is filled with whimsical rococo sculptures.

409 E11 Falkenhaus, Am Markt, 97070 Würzburg 0931 372398 Apr–end Dec Mon–Fri 10–6, Sat 10–2; Jan–end Mar Mon–Fri 10–4, Sat 10–1 Würzburg

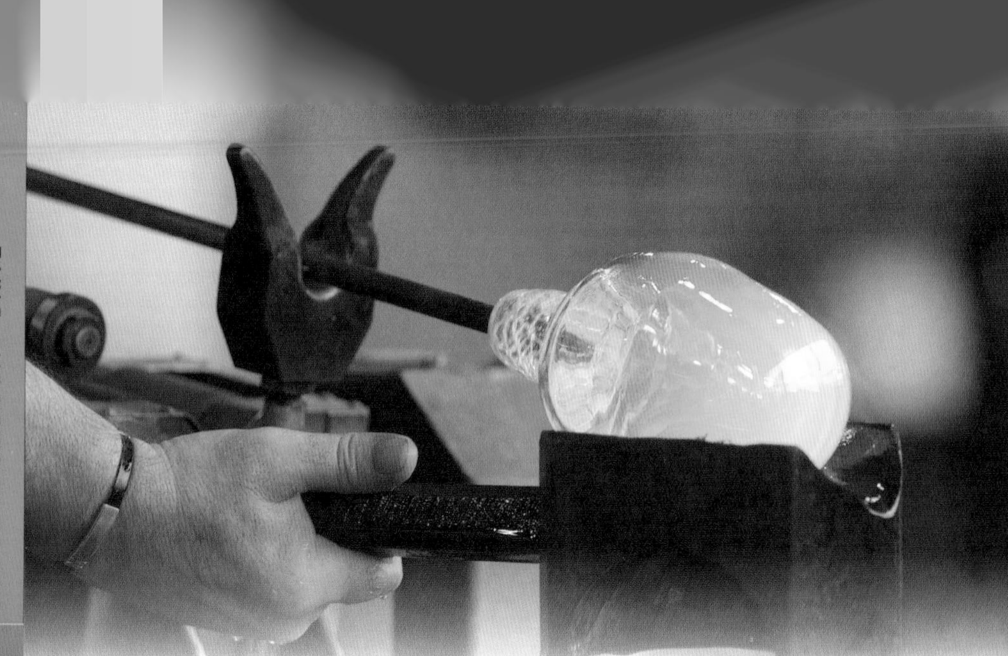

NORTHERN BAVARIA: THE GLASSTRASSE THROUGH THE BAYERISCHER WALD

Glass is the theme of this drive. From Passau (▷ 328), 'the city of three rivers', this route follows the 'Glass Route' through the Bavarian Forest National Park (▷ 303).

THE DRIVE
Distance: 267km (166 miles)
Allow: 10 hours
Start/end at: Passau

★ Leave Passau on the B85 and head north for 22km (13.5 miles) to Tittling.

❶ Tittling is the gateway to the Bavarian Forest. Visit the Museumsdorf Bayerischer Wald), where traditional life is portrayed.

Continue north along the B85 for a further 16km (10 miles), turn right onto the B533 and head northeast for 5km (3 miles) to Grafenau.

❷ Grafenau has an unusual snuff museum.

Leave Grafenau on the minor road, following signs to Spiegelau. To detour to the National Park's excellent visitor headquarters, look for a sign to turn right after 3km (2 miles). It's in the Hans-Eisenmann-Haus in Neuschönau, and has much information (including some in English) about the park.

Spiegelau is 8km (5 miles) from Grafenau. It has shops selling glasses of all shapes and sizes. From here, the Glass Route continues north through lush forests, passing old glassmaking towns, for a further 16km (10 miles) to Frauenau.

❸ Frauenau is the historic focus of glass production in the Bavarian Forest, with glass produced here since the 15th century.

From Frauenau continue northwest for 8km (5 miles) to reach the 'glass town' of Zwiesel.

❹ Zwiesel is dominated by the steeple of St. Nicholas's Church, where the *Jugendstil* (art nouveau) glass bears witness to the quality of the area's former plate glassworks.

When leaving Zwiesel, turn right at the intersection and head north to join the B27 for 16km (10 miles) to Bayerisch Eisenstein. As you approach the Czech border, take the left turn and follow the winding mountainous road for 26km (16 miles) to Lohberg and Lam. This is a spectacular drive along a ridge-top road. There are many lovely spots to stop and walk or admire the scenery. One of the best places for this is the Hindenberg viewpoint shortly before you descend into Lam. After leaving Lam, continue heading north for 23km (14 miles) towards Furth im Wald. You will soon pass through the small town of Engelshütt.

❺ Engelshütt's long history of glassmaking is enshrined in its name—En Glashutt (a glassworks).

The next town you come to after 10km (6 miles) is Neukirchen bei Heiligen Blut.

❻ Neukirchen bei Heiligen Blut is a place of pilgrimage after a Hussite (follower of the reformer Jan Hus) struck a venerated figure of the Virgin Mary with his sword in about 1450, and blood is said to have flowed from the wooden statue.

After a further 11km (7 miles) you reach the town of Furth im Wald.

❼ Furth im Wald is the home of the mirror-glass industry, and the Stadtmuseum has displays illustrating the history of glass.

From Furth im Wald head southwest along the B20 for 19km (11.5 miles) to Cham.

❽ In Cham every day at five minutes past noon, the French national anthem rings out from the town hall's tower in tribute to the town's best-known son, Nikolaus Graf von Luckner, who became a marshal in the French Army,.

Return to the B20 and head east for 2km (1.2 miles) before turning right onto the B85 and driving south through the heart of the Bayerischer Wald for 47km (29 miles) to Regen.

❾ Regen is noted for the production of optical glasses and lenses. Above the town in the direction of Passau the castle ruins of Weissenstein house the Museum Burgkasten collection of snuff bottles.

Continue south along the B85 for 59km (37 miles) to Passau.

WHEN TO GO

Except on public holidays and some weekends in the high season, this route is untroubled by hoards of visitors.

PLACES TO VISIT

GLASMUSEUM (FRAUENAU)

www.glasmuseum-frauenau.de
Am Museumspark 1, 94258 Frauenau
09926 941020 Mon–Fri 9–5, Sat, Sun 10–6; closed mid-Nov to mid-Dec
Adult €5, child (6–15) €2, under 6 free, family €11

GLASMUSEUM (PASSAU)

www.glasmuseum.de
Haus Wilder Mann, Am Rathausplatz, 94032 Passau 0851 35071 Daily 1–5
Adult €5, child (12–18) €3, under 12 free

VESTE OBERHAUS–OBERHAUSMUSEUM

www.oberhausmuseum.de
Veste Oberhaus 125, 94034 Passau
0851 493 3512 Mid-Mar to mid-Nov Mon–Fri 9–5, Sat, Sun 9–6 Adult €5, child (6–18) €4, under 6 free, family €10

Opposite *A glass-blower in Frauenau, a major historic centre for the production of glass*

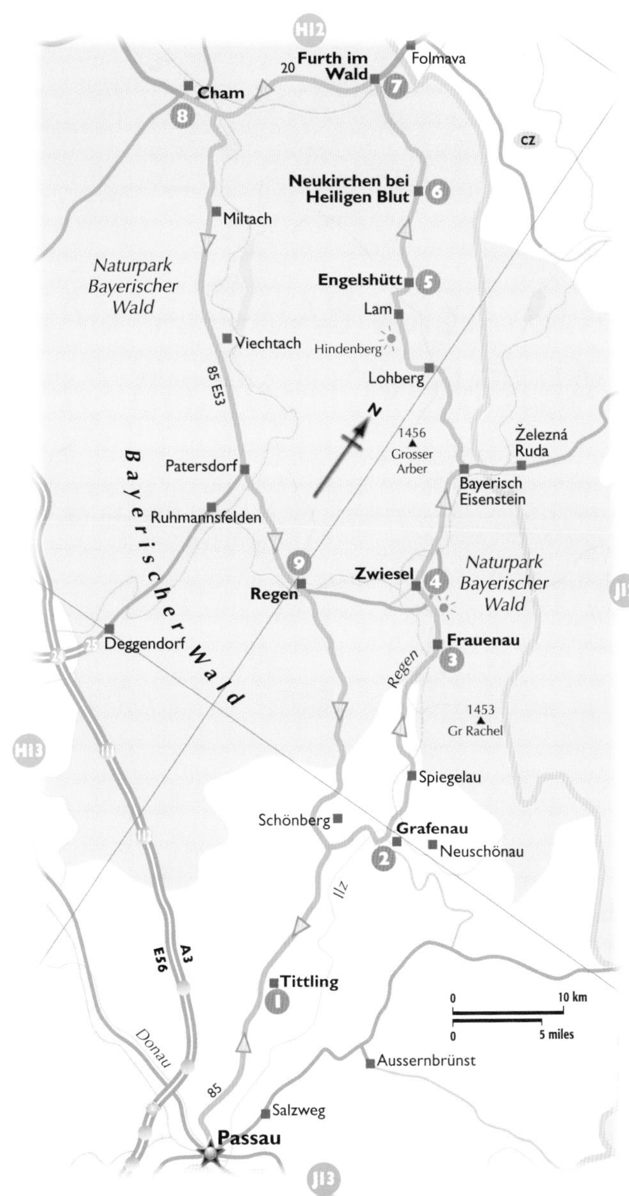

SOUTHERN BAVARIA: GARMISCH-PARTENKIRCHEN AND OBERAMMERGAU

This circular drive takes you from Garmisch-Partenkirchen (▷ 314), Germany's winter sports capital, to Oberammergau (▷ 318), a village renowned for its fairy-tale painted houses, woodcarvings and, above all, its Passion Play. The route also takes in Schloss Linderhof (▷ 314), one of the castles built by 'Mad' King Ludwig of Bavaria in the 19th century, and the Wieskirche, among the greatest rococo buildings in Europe.

THE DRIVE
Distance: 210km (130 miles)
Allow: 8 hours
Start/end at: Garmisch-Partenkirchen

★ From Garmisch-Partenkirchen head east past the Olympic Stadium and follow the B2 for 12km (7.5 miles) to Klais. From there, follow the signs to Schloss Elmau, which is a right turn onto a toll road (€6). This is a narrow, winding gravel road passing through forests; after 5km (3 miles) it opens out onto farmland.

❶ Schloss Elmau is now a private hotel open to residents only, with grounds that are worth seeing.

Return to Klais and head southeast from the village on a minor road for 5km (3 miles) to Mittenwald.

❷ Mittenwald is a photogenic small town surrounded by snow-capped Alpine peaks. Famous for violin-making, this busy visitor resort has retained much of its old-world charm. Look for the statue of violin-maker Matthias Klotz near the baroque church with its fine frescoes. The Geigenbau Museum has a good collection of old violins and other stringed instruments.

From Mittenwald go north on the B2. After 7km (4 miles) the road bends sharp left; from here continue straight ahead northwards onto the B11 and follow this road for 36km (22 miles). Look for the viewpoint over the Walchensee on your right to get wonderful views of the lake. Shortly before Bichl, turn left onto the B472 and continue for 18km (11 miles) to the intersection with the B2. Turn right then left, and after 3km (2 miles) rejoin the B472 west for 27km (17 miles) to the attractive small town of Schongau.

❸ Schongau, perched on a hill above the River Lech, is still partly surrounded by town walls. On Marienplatz are the Ballenhaus, a former warehouse from 1515, and the parish church of St. Mary of the Ascension, a Romanesque-Gothic building with a tower and choir dating from the 17th century.

Leave Schongau going west, and just outside town turn left at the B472 intersection, then head southeast for 7km (4 miles) before taking a right turn onto the B23. After 10km (6 miles), take a right

Opposite *Mittenwald nestles in the shadow of huge Alpine mountains*

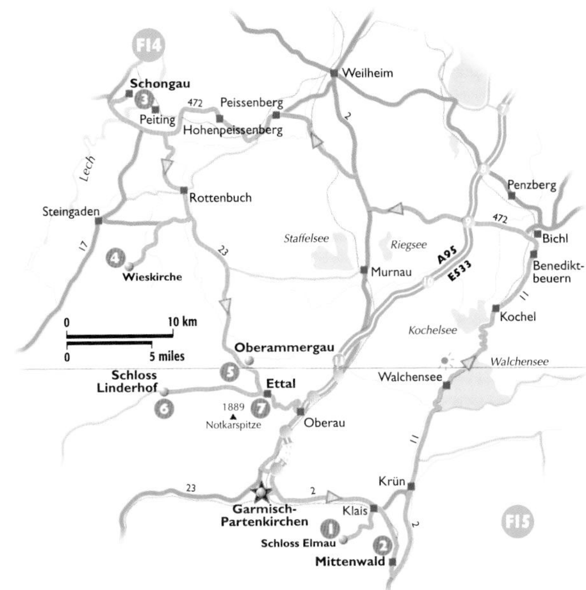

turn signposted to the Wieskirche and continue on this minor road for 9km (5.5 miles) before turning left again. Follow this narrow road through open countryside for 3km (2 miles). Suddenly, you will see the great dome of the Wieskirche.

❹ The Wieskirche ('Church in the Meadow') stands alone in the midst of green meadows, just as its name suggests, a plain white church embodying a perfect harmony of nature and architecture. This is one of the great rococo buildings of Europe, a pilgrimage church built to house a figure representing the scourged Christ, which had allegedly shed tears. This became known as 'the miracle in the meadows' and a surge of pilgrimages began. In 1745 the architect Dominikus Zimmermann built his masterpiece. The interior, flooded with light, is a glorious assemblage of stuccowork and fresco, notably the frescoed dome, the Gate to Paradise.

Leave the Wieskirche and return to the B23. Turn right and head south for 16km (10 miles) to Oberammergau. Turn left off the main road to enter the town.

❺ Oberammergau (▷ 318) is well described as a fairy-tale town: As soon as you enter, you are confronted by house façades painted with a varied mixture of religious, fairy-tale and secular themes. Although renowned for its Passion Play, Oberammergau is a popular resort all year.

Leave the town on the continuation of the minor road by which you entered, heading southwest for 8km (5 miles) to Schloss Linderhof.

❻ Schloss Linderhof (▷ 314), amid magnificent mountain scenery and surrounded by forest, is arguably the most pleasing of Ludwig II's castles.

Leave Linderhof on the minor road heading east across the wide valley floor at the foot of the Notkarspitze (1,889m/ 6198ft) for 11km (7 miles) to Ettal.

❼ Ettal is known for its Benedictine abbey and *Ettaler Klosterlikör*, a fragrant herb liqueur made by monks. The abbey, founded in 1330 by Emperor Ludwig the Bavarian and converted into a domed baroque church in the 18th century, has an unusual 12-sided nave and fine frescoes. The complex in front of the church is a boarding school.

From Ettal, head southeast along the B23 for 6km (3.5 miles) to Oberau, then turn right and follow the B2 south for 10km (6 miles) to Garmisch-Partenkirchen.

WHEN TO GO

Oberammergau, Garmisch-Partenkirchen and the Wieskirche attract large numbers of visitors and are exceptionally busy all year.

PLACES TO VISIT

GEIGENBAU MUSEUM (VIOLIN-MAKING MUSEUM)

www.geigenbaumuseum-mittenwald.de
✉ Ballenhausgasse 3, 82481 Mittenwald
☎ 08823 2511 ⏲ Feb to mid-Mar, mid-May to mid-Oct and mid-Dec to early Jan Tue–Sun 10–5; Jan, mid-Mar to mid-May and mid-Oct to end Oct Tue–Sun 11–4 ✋ Adult €4, child (6–14) €2, under 6 free

PASSIONSTHEATER, OBERAMMERGAU

www.passionstheater.de
✉ Passionswiese 1, 82487 Oberammergau
☎ 08822 92310 ⏲ Half-hourly guide tours: May–end Oct Tue–Sun (also holiday Mon) 10–12.30, 2–5 ✋ Adult €4, child (6–18) €1, under 6 free

SCHLOSS LINDERHOF

▷ 314.

WHERE TO EAT

This area is popular with visitors, so there's a wide choice of restaurants and cafés in the towns and villages around the route. In the Kurpark in Garmisch-Partenkirchen, the Adlwärth (Richard-Strauss-Platz 1, 82467 Garmisch-Partenkirchen; tel 08821 3177; May–end Oct) is an excellent café and restaurant in pleasant surroundings. One of the best places in Mittenwald is the Restaurant Arnspitze (Innsbrucker Strasse 68, 82481 Mittenwald; tel 08823 2425), which serves good local fare.

GARMISCH-PARTENKIRCHEN: THE PARTNACHKLAMM

This is a spectacular walk along a manmade path that snakes along the bottom of a ravine. The sheer walls of the Partnach gorge, near Garmisch-Partenkirchen (▷ 314), rise to 80m (260ft) and the foaming river roars through the narrow gorge. Tunnels have been cut into the rock to give safe access and views of the turquoise water below; in winter, spectacular ice formations cling to the rockfaces. Before following the path through the gorge, you can view it from above by taking a cable-car ride and walking back from the top of the gorge to one of the entrances.

THE WALK

Distance: 5km (3 miles)
Allow: 2 hours
Start/end at: Olympic Ski Stadium, Partenkirchen
Note: You will need good walking shoes and a jacket for this walk. Even in the height of summer the temperature drops dramatically in the gorge and water constantly drips from the high rocks above the walkway.

HOW TO GET THERE

The Olympic Ski Stadium is just off the B2 road in Partenkirchen and is well marked. There is ample free parking at the stadium. Admission to gorge: adult €2, child (6–16) €1, under 6 free.

★ You are not allowed to drive beyond the Olympic Ski Stadium. From here, you can either walk along the road (1.5km/1 mile) to the gorge entrance, or take a horse-drawn carriage ride (€3 per person). The road follows the course of the river, which flows quite sedately at this point in comparison to its furious passage through the narrow gorge.

❶ Opposite the Forsthaus Graseck hotel is the Graseckbahn automatic cable car, which will take you 130m (430ft) up to the small hamlet of Vordergraseck. The short cable-car ride takes you directly above the gorge, giving spectacular views of the sheer rockfaces and turbulent waters of the river Partnach below.

From Vordergraseck you can follow the signs to the Hohe Brücke (High Bridge), approximately 1km (0.6 mile) away, then follow the signs to take you downhill back to the lower gorge entrance, approximately 2km (1.2 miles). Alternatively, from the Hohe Brücke, follow the track up the valley for 1km (0.6 mile) to the top entrance.

From the lower gorge entrance, continue to the ticket gate (300m/330 yards) and enter the ravine. Almost immediately, you pass through a series of tunnels cut into the rockface. The noise of the water roaring through the narrow gorge below is deafening. The path is safe and the barriers are good, but you need to be cautious if you have young children with you, as the noise may frighten them. It's not feasible to take a pushchair (stroller).

❷ Early walkways through the gorge once helped forestry workers to float timber down to the sawmills, while the path visitors walk today involved the difficult task of blasting tunnels through the rockface.

After 700m (770 yards), you emerge from the gorge through another ticket gate into a wide valley where the river ambles serenely before being squeezed through the narrow gorge. This is a pleasant place to rest and relax before retracing your steps to the start of the walk.

WHEN TO GO

The path through the gorge is well maintained and open all year. During spring when the snow begins to melt, the water reaches its peak level and roars through the gorge, but summer is also a spectacular time to visit. Although the path is cleared of snow and gritted (salted) in winter, extreme care needs to be taken in icy conditions.

WHERE TO EAT

Hotel Leiner (Wildenauerstrasse 20, 82467 Garmisch-Partenkirchen; tel 08821 95280), just 200m (220 yards) from the Olympic Ski Stadium, is an ideal place to eat and stay. It has a restaurant, beer garden, terrace café, sauna and swimming pool. About halfway along the road between the stadium and the gorge entrance there's a café on the riverside, serving ice-cream, teas, coffee and snacks. At the entrance to the gorge is the Forsthaus Graseck hotel (Graseck 4, 82467 Garmisch-Partenkirchen; tel 08821 943240), where you can get good food and drink. There's also a beer garden between this entrance and the ticket gate.

ALONG THE SHORE OF LAKE CONSTANCE

The Bodensee (Lake Constance) is actually part of the course of the River Rhine. Konstanz, the largest town on the lake, sits on a spit of land separating the Obersee, the main area of the Bodensee, from the Untersee, where the Rhine leaves the lake to enter Switzerland. This walk follows the waterside promenade into the heart of the town. You will walk between grand houses that overlook the harbour and marinas filled with expensive yachts before you visit some of the town's historic sights and buildings. You can even put a foot in Switzerland!

THE WALK
Distance: 8km (5 miles)
Time: 3 hours
Start/end at: Bodensee Stadion, Konstanz

HOW TO GET THERE

Take the route marked to Meersburg and Mainau from Konstanz. About 500m (550 yards) after the Rhine bridge, turn right into Eichhornstrasse and follow this road to the Bodensee Stadion, where there is plenty of free parking.

★ This is a comfortable level walk. Leave the parking area from the east or south footpath and head for the promenade ahead. Turn right along the promenade and continue along this walkway to the Rhine bridge.

❶ From the promenade there are pleasing views across the lake; in the distance you will see Konstanz and the cathedral spire. The high, ugly building dominating the skyline is a residential building on the Swiss side of town. On your right are grand houses and hotels; on the left, you will pass the yacht marina.

At the Rhine bridge, turn right up the steps and left to cross the bridge. Keep to the left of the railway line and follow the promenade through the public gardens to the Konzil and the *Imperia* statue. There is a superb café/restaurant at the Konzil, ideal for coffee or lunch.

❷ The Konzil was built in 1388 as a grain store and warehouse for trade with southern Europe. It was here in 1417, during the Council of Constance, that the rift in Christendom known as the Great Schism (when rival popes had vied for power) was brought to an end. The *Imperia*, a massive female figure by sculptor Peter Lenk, rotates on the base of a former lighthouse. The figure symbolizing the power of the many courtesans who followed the male participants to Konstanz at the time of the Council of Constance.

Continue along the promenade for 500m (550 yards) and you will come to the Swiss border. Return to the Konzil, turn left over the railway line and take the underpass into the Marktstätte. Continue straight ahead through the market square and Kanzlestrasse, then turn right into Obermarkt, which becomes Wessenbergstrasse. Ahead of you is the Münster.

❸ The Münster Unserer Lieben Frau (Minster of Our Lady) stands on the site of a Roman fortress. If you have time, explore inside the impressive cathedral. Also worth seeing are St. Maurice's church, built around AD940, and the Silvesterkapelle (Silvester chapel) and Konradikapelle (Konrad chapel).

When you leave the cathedral, head back to the harbour and turn left along the promenade to retrace your route to the Bodensee Stadion.

Right *Bodensee (Lake Constance)*

WHEN TO GO

Although Lake Constance is a busy area in summer, especially on weekends, the promenade in Konstanz is reasonably quiet even in the height of summer. However, being flat and free of traffic, it is popular with local joggers and skaters. The town itself may be busy, but seeing the sights should not be a problem.

WHERE TO EAT

The ground-floor Konzil restaurant (Hafenstrasse 2, 78462 Konstanz; tel 07531 21221) is in a great position overlooking the harbour, and is a good place to stop for refreshments or a meal. Once you cross the road into the market square you will find plenty of excellent little coffee shops and restaurants with seating out on the square.

THE ALPS IN SOUTHERN BAVARIA

This drive follows the Alps along the Austrian border in southern Bavaria, from the southernmost end of the Romantic Road at Füssen to Isny, a border town between Bavaria and Baden-Württemberg.

THE DRIVE
Distance: 190 km (118 miles)
Allow: 7 hours
Start/end at: Füssen

★ The attractive mountain town of Füssen, with its handsome old quarter, stands at the end of the Romantische Strasse (Romantic Road), which links it with Würzburg 350km (215 miles) to the north. Nearby are Ludwig II's extraordinary medieval fantasies, the castles of Neuschwanstein (▷ 322–325) and Hohenschwangau (▷ 325).

Leave Füssen and head northwest along the B310 for 12km (7.5 miles) to join the B309 for 14km (8.5 miles) to Mittelberg, a tranquil village at the far end of the Kleinwalsertal valley. Continue northwest along the B309 for a further 16km (10 miles) to Kempten.

❶ Kempten, despite being a busy commercial town, has much that is worth seeing. The Archäologischer Park (Archaeological Park) occupies the former site of the Roman town of Cambodunum, and museums and galleries include the Allgäu-Museum (art and local history), Römisches Museum (the Romans), Alpinmuseum (people and mountains of the Alps) and the Alpenländische Galerie (Alpine arts). The Burghalde, one of the oldest parts of the town, was originally a Roman fort. Other sights are the Gothic church of St. Mang (1426) and a Jugendstil (art nouveau) fountain (1905), both in St. Mang-Platz; the Fürstäbtliche Residenz, a baroque palace with a magnificent rococo interior; and the St. Lorenz basilica, the first major church built in southern Germany after the Thirty Years' War (1652).

From Kempten, head west along the old B12 signposted to Wengen and Isny. Follow this scenic route for 25km (15.5 miles) as it climbs and twists to Wengen and the great Schwarzer Grat (Black Crest), before dropping down to Isny.

❷ Isny, a border town between Bavaria and Baden-Württemberg, is relatively quiet, ideal for a stop and a stroll. The clean air and climate around the town, an officially designated health resort, are known to be beneficial to your health and, although many people visit to take advantage of the resort's facilities, it doesn't get overrun. Main points of interest are the Rathaus, which has a massive tiled stove that reaches as high as the ceiling, and St. Nicholas's Church, with a library housed in its spire. Parking is reasonably easy to find and there are some pleasingly old-fashioned little cafés and restaurants in the squares and narrow streets.

From Isny, take the minor road marked with brown signs, which show it is a designated scenic route, south for 19km (11.5 miles) to join the Deutsche Alpenstrasse (German Alpine Highway) at Oberstaufen.

❸ Oberstaufen, a popular resort in the western Allgäu, is also noted for its *Schrotkur*, a cure for the effects of over-eating and drinking that involves fasting. A pleasant detour here is to visit nearby Steibis (2km/1.2 miles south) where you can take the cable car and walk to the summit of Hochgrat (1832m/5,023ft), from where there are stunning views.

Now head east along the B308 for 16km (10 miles) to Immenstadt.

❹ Immenstadt, idyllically positioned at the foot of the Immenstadter Horn, is another much-visited resort. The nearby Grosser Alpsee, an Alpine lake 3km (2 miles) long stretching below the towering mass of the Gschwendner Horn, is ideal for water sports and swimming. Sights in and around the town include the 17th-century ruins of Schloss Königsegg and the nearby Laubenbergstein castle.

Leave Immenstadt on the B19 and head southeast for 7km (4 miles) to Sonthofen, an attractive little town in the wide valley of the Iller noted for its winter sports facilities. Continue southeast along the B19 for another 13km (8 miles) to Oberstdorf.

❺ Oberstdorf has a famous ski jump and draws the crowds for its winter sports. In summer there's rock climbing, hiking, bicycling, hang-gliding and parasailing (a spectacular sight). The many cable cars (including the largest cable car in Germany, holding up to 100 passengers) take less active visitors to mountain summits for spectacular views and walks. The Sollereckbahn is Germany's longest continuous monocable elevator, with comfortable six-seater cabins allowing for tremendous views. No fewer than seven valleys join the Iller valley at Oberstdorf, each one with its own character and charm. The Heimatmuseum (Museum of Local History) in the town has some fascinating displays, including the largest shoe in the world, made by Oberstdorf shoemaker Josef Schatt, who used 18 cowhides to make it.

Return to Sonthofen along the B19, then turn right onto the B308 and head east for 15km (9 miles), via Hindelang, to Oberjoch. This road twists and winds with many hairpin bends; it is also a designated tourist route because of the stunning scenery, particularly along the stretch between Hindelang and Oberjoch. From Oberjoch take the B310 north for 16km (10 miles) to Mittelberg and continue along the B310 southeast for 24km (15 miles) back to Füssen.

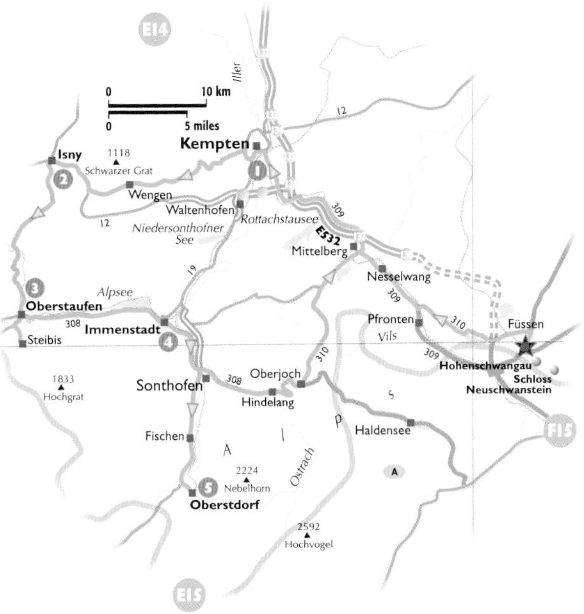

PLACES TO VISIT

ALLGÄU-MUSEUM

www.allgaeu-museum.de
✉ Grosser Kornhausplatz 1, 87439 Kempten ☎ 0831 540 2120 🕐 Tue–Sun 10–4 Adult €2.50, child (6–16) €1.25, under 6 free, family €5

MUSEUM HOFMÜHLE

✉ An der Aach 14, Immenstadt ☎ 08323 3663 🕐 Wed–Sun 2–5 Adult €2.50, child (6–16) €1.50, under 6 free

WHEN TO GO

The area around Oberstdorf gets extremely busy during the ski season, especially when there is a major ski-jump event scheduled. The Grosser Alpsee at Immenstadt is popular in summer and attracts water sports enthusiasts, so it is best avoided on weekends and during the high summer season. This also applies to certain parts of the route—the Deutsche Alpenstrasse and other roads designated for their stunning scenery.

WHERE TO EAT

The main towns along the route, such as Kempten and Oberstdorf, have a good choice of cafés and restaurants, but these are often busy. Look in the smaller towns and villages to find places to eat with local character. Try the Hotel Bistro Restaurant Bären (Obertorstrasse 9, 88316 Isny; tel 07562 2420), Hotel Restaurant Krone (Rottachbergstrasse 1, 87059 Immenstadt/Stein; tel 08323 96610) or, for its wonderful views, the Hotel Oberstdorf (Reute 20, Sesselweg 16, 87561 Oberstdorf; tel 08322 940770).

Opposite *Schloss Neuschwanstein provides a delightful diversion from the drive route*

THE BLACK FOREST: A CIRCULAR DRIVE FROM FREIBURG IM BREISGAU

This drive follows the southern fringes of the Schwarzwald (Black Forest) before heading into the heart of the German clockmaking region. Leaving behind the lush green hills and vineyards surrounding Freiburg, the route heads north deep into the forest before passing the Gutach Falls and the placid waters of the Titisee and Schluchsee lakes.

THE DRIVE
Distance: 184km (114 miles)
Allow: 6 hours
Start/end at: Freiburg im Breisgau

★ Take the busy B31 from Freiburg and head southeast for 25km (15.5 miles) to Hinterzarten. Turn north onto the quieter B500 and drive for 26km (16 miles) to Furtwangen, one of the major clockmaking towns in the Black Forest.

❶ In Furtwangen (▷ 314) you can visit the Deutsches Uhrenmuseum (German Clock Museum), which has the largest collection of clocks in Germany. In addition, many factories and workshops in the area open their doors to visitors, providing a great opportunity to see how clocks are made.

Continue north from Furtwangen along the B500 for 17km (11 miles) to Triberg.

❷ Triberg (▷ 328) is another place dominated by clocks—there are cuckoo clocks everywhere, including two of the largest in the world. The Schwarzwaldmuseum here has a large collection of Black Forest clocks on display, as well as local costumes, woodcarvings, ceramics and clockmaking memorabilia.

The roar of the nearby Gutach Falls (▷ 328), the highest waterfall in Germany (163m/ 535ft), is a welcome relief from the sound of cuckoos. This is a popular area for visitors at all times of year and finding somewhere to park can be difficult at times.

From Triberg take the B33 southeast for 25km (15.5 miles) to Villingen.

❸ The double town of Villingen-Schwenningen was founded in 1972. It's a curious hybrid of spa, medieval town and local industry—clockmaking, of course. You will find an interesting mix of attractions. Villingen is still surrounded by its original defensive walls and towers, and the old town is focused on the 12th-century Münster Unserer Lieben Frau (Minster of our Dear Lady). In Münsterplatz is the Altes Rathaus, which contains a museum with a collection of art and antiquities, and west of the old town is the Franziskaner Museum, in a former Franciscan monastery. In Schwenningen, you can visit the Uhrenindustriemuseum in what was the factory of the oldest clock company in Württemberg.

Continue south from Schwenningen along the B33/27 for 13km (8 miles) as the road gently climbs along the eastern fringe of the Black Forest to Donaueschingen.

4 Donaueschingen is where the rivers Breg and Brigach unite to form the source of the Danube. A monumental fountain in the Schlosspark marks the site of the Donauquelle (source of the Danube). From 1723 the baroque Schloss was the seat of the princes of Fürstenburg, whose territories passed to Baden and Württemberg in 1806. The castle was altered considerably during the 19th century, and the interior has fine furnishings. This is a pleasant small town and parking facilities are good. There are also agreeable walks through the Schlosspark and alongside the rivers.

Take the minor road south out of Donaueschingen for 5km (3 miles) to Hüfingen, then join the B31 west for 27km (17 miles) to Titisee. This road links the E41 and E35 autobahn routes and is also used by commercial vehicles.

5 Titisee is the resort village for the lake of the same name. Because of the easy direct access from a major road, it has become both busy and commercialized. The lake itself is attractive and the path around its shore makes a pleasant walk on a quiet day—if you can find one! There are plenty of recreational and water sports facilities around and on the lake itself, and equipment is available to rent. Schluchsee, about 10km (6 miles) south, off the B500, is a much quieter spot.

From Titisee, return to the B31, then take the B317 southwest for 21km (13 miles) to Todtnau.

6 The small town of Todtnau is tucked away in the southwest corner of the Black Forest, close to the borders of France and Switzerland. It is officially classified as a health resort, partly thanks to its spectacular setting surrounded by mountains, all of which exceed 1,000m (3,300ft) in height. Don't miss the opportunity to take the chairlift to the top of the Hasenhorn (1065m/3,495ft) to get fantastic views over the Alps and Black Forest. Just north of Todtnau, on the road to the village of Todtnauberg, is a dramatic waterfall that thunders down the mountainside from a height of 90m (300ft).

Leave Todtnau on the B317 and almost immediately turn right to follow a minor road for 25km (15.5 miles) and return to Freiburg. The scenery you pass through is a glorious mixture of towering mountains rising amid wooded ridges, alternating with peaceful valleys and meadows.

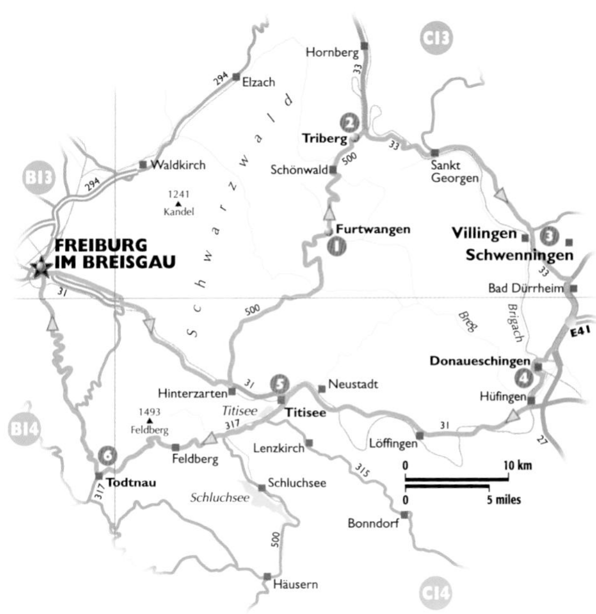

Opposite *Looking down onto the town of Freiburg*

WHEN TO GO

This is a busy area all year and in summer especially attracts hordes of visitors.

PLACES TO VISIT

DEUTSCHES UHRENMUSEUM

www.deutsches-uhrenmuseum.de
Robert-Gerwig-Platz 1, 78120 Furtwangen 07723 920 2800
Apr–end Oct daily 9–6; Nov–end Mar daily 10–5 Adult €4, child (6–18) €3, under 6 free, family €10

UHRENINDUSTRIEMUSEUM

www.uhrenindustriemuseum.de
Bürkstrasse 39, 78054 Villingen-Schwenningen 07721 38044
Tue–Sun 10–12, 2–6 Adult €3, child (6–16) €2, under 6 free

SCHWARZWALDMUSEUM, TRIBERG

▷ 328.

WHERE TO EAT

Being a university town, Freiburg has a good range of places to eat. Try the oldest inn, the Zum Roten Bären (Oberlinden 12; tel 0761 387870), or the Schlossbergrestaurant Dattler (Am Schlossberg 1; tel 0761 31729), just out of town, next to the upper cable station. In Triberg, the Bergcafe (Hermann-Schwerstrasse; tel 07722 866490) has good value and good views, and in Villingen, the Ratskeller (Obere Strasse 37; tel 07721 404794) has a satisfying menu.

THE NECKAR VALLEY AND THE BERGSTRASSE: A CIRCULAR DRIVE

From the romantic city of Heidelberg (▷ 312–313), you follow the winding Neckar valley with its attractive towns and castles before heading into the wooded hills of the Neckartal–Odenwald Nature Park, which stretches northwards from the Neckar. The route also takes in the historic Bergstrasse and the wine region of the Upper Rhine.

THE DRIVE
Distance: 242km (150 miles)
Allow: 9 hours
Start/end at: Heidelberg

★ Head east from Heidelberg along the B37 for 13km (8 miles) to Neckargemünd, an attractive town with 16th-century half-timbered houses. Just 5km (3 miles) farther on, take a right turn signposted Feste Dilsberg.

❶ The Keep of the mighty Feste (fortress) of Dilsberg towers over the rooftops of the Old Town, providing views of the Neckar valley.

From Dilsberg, return to the B37 and continue east along the river valley for 10km (6 miles) to Neckarsteinach.

❷ Neckarsteinach, known as the 'Town of Four Castles', is where the rivers Neckar and Steinach meet. It is the only town in Germany with four castles and you can enjoy a pleasant walk from one to another. Two of the castles are in ruins; the others are inhabited and private.

Still on the B37, after another 12km (7.5 miles) you'll come to Hirschhorn, a nice place to stop and watch boats pass through locks alongside the terraced Neckar dam. From here, the road follows a long bend in the river to Eberbach, for 10km (6 miles).

❸ Eberbach has some interesting places, and an enjoyable way to see them is by horse-drawn carriage.

You continue along the B37 for 29km (18 miles) southeast from Eberbach, passing by Zwingenberg and Neckargerach, before taking a left turn onto the B27 for Mosbach.

❹ Mosbach is a splendid town, sandwiched between the Neckar and the Odenwald range. This former free city of the Holy Roman Empire is more than 1,200 years old. Take time to see the Renaissance town hall and the Palm House (1610), a church since 1705 and considered one of the most beautiful half-timbered houses in Germany.

After leaving Mosbach follow the B27 for 21km (13 miles), then take a left turn onto a minor road signposted to Mudau and Amorbach. The scenery here is spectacular. Follow the road north for 20km (12 miles) to Amorbach. At the crossroads with the B47 go straight ahead along the B469 for 10km (6 miles) to Miltenberg, a pleasant small town. From Miltenberg, return along the B469 to the crossroads and turn right onto the B47 and continue west for 22km (13.5 miles) to Michelstadt and Erbach.

❺ Outstanding in Michelstadt is the picturesque Rathaus. In the Kellerie (a relic of the old castle) are the Odenwald Museum and the Toy Museum. Erbach is just south of the B47 and has a museum of ivory carving. The Schloss, with a round tower dating from 1200, has fine collections of art and weapons.

Leaving Erbach, continue west along the B47: You are now following a tourist route known as the Nibelungenstrasse, which runs between Worms and Würzburg. After 28km (17 miles) you will pass the village of Lindenfels, with its castle, and another 18km (11 miles) brings you to the intersection with the B3, known as the Bergstrasse. This historic route runs for 58km (36 miles) along the rift valley of the Upper Rhine. The region is famed for its mild climate, its fruit and its almond trees. The Bergstrasse is special in spring—a sea of blossom. Bensheim, the largest town in the region, lies at the intersection of the B47 and the Bergstrasse.

❻ Bensheim is a vibrant town, busy throughout the year. The drama productions in the international summer festival at Schloss Auerbach and Fürstenlager Park are recognized worldwide.

Opposite *Heidelberg is the starting point for this lovely drive*

It's a pleasant drive south along the B3 from Bensheim. For most of the year the surrounding slopes nurture various fruits, vines, figs, almonds and exotic trees. Just 3km (2 miles) from Bensheim is Heppenheim.

❼ Heppenheim is known for its drama festival and wine market. Visit the history and folklore museum at the Kurmainzer Amtshof and the state observatory in the castle ruins.

Still heading south along the B3, 13km (8 miles) from Heppenheim is Weinheim.

❽ Weinheim, a lovely little town, is the green heart of the Bergstrasse. It has castle gardens, parks and woodland with exotic plants and trees. The castle, old town hall, narrow Obertor arch and ruins of the town walls are all well preserved.

The final part of your journey continues south along the B3 for 18km (11 miles) to Heidelberg.

WHEN TO GO

The towns along the Bergstrasse get extremely busy from the end of April through to the end of September because of the blossom and the various festivals.

PLACES TO VISIT

MUSEUM FÜR STADTGESCHICHTE UND VOLKSKUNDE

✉ Kurzmainzer Amtshof, Amtsgasse 5, Heppenheim ☎ 06252 69112 ⏲ Wed, Thu, Sat 2–5, Sun and holidays 2–6 ✋ Adult €1, under 18 free

ODENWALD- UND SPIELZEUGMUSEUM

✉ Speicherbau der Kellerei, 64720, Michelstadt ☎ 06061 706139 ⏲ Daily 10–5 ✋ Adult €3, child (6–18) €1.50, under 6 free, family €7.50

WHERE TO EAT

All the towns along the Neckar have a choice of cafés and restaurants. Zum Schiff Restaurant in Neckarsteinach (Neckargemünder Strasse 2, 69239 Neckarsteinach; tel 06229 324) has a beautiful location on the banks of the Neckar. Eberbach's Café Viktoria (Friedrichstrasse 5–9, 69412 Eberbach; tel 06271 2018) is noted for its cakes. In the settlements between Amorbach and Bensheim the food is more traditional.

THROUGH THE MARGARETHENSCHLUCHT IN THE NECKAR VALLEY

This walk from the village of Neckargerach takes you high into the tree-lined slopes above the River Neckar, from where you will see the valley cutting its way through distant hills dominated by romantic castles. There is a choice of routes: For the more energetic, a spectacular scramble up the steep Margarethenschlucht gorge, with the alternative of a gentle stroll along the river for less adventurous walkers.

THE WALK

Distance: 4.5km (2.8 miles) for route 3; 7km (4.4 miles) for route 6 (see Note below)
Allow: 2 hours for route 3; 2 hours 30 min for route 6
Start/end at: Hotel Grüner Baum, Neckargerach
How to get there: Neckargerach is on the B37, 41km (25.5 miles) east of Heidelberg, 14km (9 miles) northwest of Mosbach. There's plenty of parking at the Hotel Grüner Baum on Neckarstrasse.
Note: *Ortsplan Neckargerach mit Wanderkarte* (in German only) is the small leaflet available from the tourist office. It includes a street plan and details of all the walking routes around Neckargerach, which are numbered. You will be following route 3 with an option to include part of route 6.

★ From Hotel Grüner Baum's parking area, walk along Neckarstrasse to the first intersection. Turn right, then take the second turn left into Bahnhofstrasse. As you continue uphill, the road bends right past the old railway station to a new bridge across the railway line. Cross the bridge and turn right along a tarmac path marked with green signs to the Margarethenschlucht, and follow it between houses and the railway line. Continue straight ahead along this path, which eventually becomes a gravel track, then a dirt path running between woodlands and the river below.

❶ There are spectacular views on your right of the river and its valley with the ruins of the 11th-century Minneburg peeping out of the trees. These ruins are accessible via a steep path through woodlands from near the village of Guttenbach, which became part of Neckargerach in 1973.

The path continues to climb gently away from Neckargerach. When you have walked 2km (1.2 miles) from the beginning of the route, you will come to an information board and the entrance to the Margarethenschlucht waterfall. The path, which climbs for 600m (660 yards) to the top of the waterfall, is very steep (ascent 100m/330ft) and slippery in places; good walking shoes are essential. Continue uphill on the narrow path and cross the lower waterfall. Approximately 50m (55 yards) later the path forks.

For a gentler route back to Neckargerach, continue straight ahead at this point and follow route 6 through the woods and along the river. Route 6 takes you right downhill, crosses the B37 and a small footbridge over the Neckar at the locks, then turns right and follows the river to Guttenbach before crossing the road bridge and river to return to Neckargerach.

To continue on route 3, head left at the fork, up the steps, and follow the narrow dirt path uphill. There is a double safety rope on one side of this path, but as you ascend into the gorge the drop down becomes very steep.

The path through the Margarethenschlucht zigzags across small waterfalls as it climbs high through the woodland to the top of the gorge.

At the top of the gorge you come out of the woodland into open countryside and join a narrow tarmac road. Turn left here and head downhill for approximately 300m (330 yards) to an intersection, then turn left again and follow this road to return to Neckargerach.

WHEN TO GO

Parts of this walk are possible at any time of year and it is not often busy. You should not attempt to walk through the gorge when there is ice or snow. Also be aware that after particularly heavy rainfall the volume of water over the falls may make the paths that cross them impassable. At such times, the walk along the river and through Guttenbach to Neckargerach is a pleasant alternative.

WHERE TO EAT

The hotel/restaurant Grüner Baum (Neckarstrasse 13, 69437 Neckargerach; tel: 0263 706) in Neckargerach is an excellent place to eat. The Greek owners provide a wide choice of refreshments, including Greek and German dishes.

Opposite *Waterfall in the Margarete Canyon*

BADEN-BADEN

CARACALLA THERME

www.carasana.de

Baden-Baden is renowned for its thermal springs, Europe's hottest at 69°C (156°F). The modern Caracalla Therme has a choice of relaxing and health-promoting treatment stations, including whirlpools and indoor and outdoor pools, all further enhanced with underwater jets and waterfalls. There is also a spacious, well-lit environment that has seven different types of sauna and an aromatic steam bath.

Römerplatz 1, 76530 Baden-Baden 07221 275940 Daily 8am–10pm, last admission 8pm €13 (2 hours), €15 (3 hours), €17 (4 hours)

FESTSPIELHAUS

www.festspielhaus.de

In 1998, Baden-Baden's neoclassical train station was transformed into the second-largest opera house in Europe. The modern concert hall has 2,500 seats and acoustics that are considered among the best in the world.

Beim Alten Bahnhof 2, 76530 Baden-Baden 07221 301 3101 Booking office: Mon–Fri 10–6, Sat, Sun and public holidays 10–2, and 2 hours before events Varies Special bus transfers (check website)

INTERNATIONALER CLUB

www.baden-galopp.de

The village of Iffezheim is home to the track that hosts the International Horse Races. The Spring Meeting (late May/early June), the Grand Festival Week (late August/early September) and the Sales and Racing Festival (late October) attract the rich and famous; these meetings are spectacular events.

Lichtentaler Allee 8, 76530 Baden-Baden 07229 187332 Meetings start 12.30 or 1.30 €7–€265

BERCHTESGADEN

WATZMANN THERME

www.watzmann-therme.de

This modern complex is an oasis of water fun, as well as a spa whose locally produced brine has curative and health-giving properties. Among the numerous pools, are indoor and outdoor ones enriched with brine from nearby salt mines, plus a sports pool and water slide.

Bergwerkstrasse 54, 83471 Berchtesgaden 08652 94640 Daily 10–10 €8.80 (2 hours), €11.40 (4 hours), €16.30 (day)

Above *Skiing in the mountainous area of Zügspitze; equipment can be rented and warm clothes are sold locally*

DINKELSBÜHL

CRAFT STORES

www.dinkelsbuehl.de

Dinkelsbühl is noted for its arts and crafts (ceramics), souvenirs and trendy clothes. Join the arts and crafts tour, which will take you to some of Dinkelsbühl's retail outlets.

Touristik Service Dinkelsbühl, Marktplatz, 91550 Dinkelsbühl 09851 902440

SUNDAY CONCERTS

A free concert is held in the town park music pavilion every Sunday from May to end September at 11.15am.

Town Park, 91550 Dinkelsbühl May–end Sep Sun 11.15am Free

FRAUENAU

GLASSHÜTTE EISCH

www.eisch.de

Frauenau is just one of numerous towns and villages along the famous Glasstrasse where you can buy glass or watch the craftsmen at work. At Glasshütte Eisch you can purchase products direct from

the factory outlet. The items are current or discontinued lines and remainders, which means they go for reduced prices.
Am Steg 7, 94258 Frauenau 09926 1890 Shop: Mon–Fri 9–6, Sat 9–4, Sun and holidays 10–4 Guided tours: Mon–Thu 9–11.30, 1–2.45, Fri, Sat 9–11.45

FREIBURG

EUROPA-PARK

www.europapark.de

With more than 100 attractions and shows, this is Germany's largest family theme park. Visit 11 European themed areas in one day, and you can also ride on the Silver Star, Europe's biggest roller-coaster.
Europa-Park-Strasse 2, 77977 Rust 01805 776688; ticket line 01805 788997 Apr–end Oct, Dec daily 9–6 (extended hours during peak season) Adult €31.50, child (4–11) €28, under 4 free

JAZZHAUS

www.jazzhaus.de

At this historic cellar traditional jazz nights are very popular, but there's also a varied line-up of other themed fun nights, such as a salsa night, reggae summer party, funky dance night and 1960s and 1970s nights.
Schnewlinstrasse 1, 79098 Freiburg 0761 292 3446 Fri, Sat 9pm–2am (doors open at 7pm on concert nights) €5–€20

THEATER FREIBURG

www.theaterfreiburg.de

Freiburg's largest theatre has four performance areas, where you can see opera, ballet, musicals and plays. Freiburg Philharmonic Orchestra concerts take place in the Konzerthaus.
Bertoldstrasse 46, 79098 Freiburg 0761 201 2853 (information and ticket office) Information and ticket office: Tue–Fri 10–6, Sat 10–1 €7–€50

GARMISCH-PARTENKIRCHEN

WINTER SPORTS

www.garmisch-partenkirchen.de

This is a paradise for winter sports enthusiasts, as there's something here to suit all levels of experience and preference. The skiing season begins in November with the Viva Winter Fun-Festival, a weekend of fun and action. There are ski trails and the glacier skiing region atop the Zugspitze. A delight for the family is sledging down the 3.9km (2.4-mile) run on Hausberg mountain.
Garmisch-Partenkirchen-Tourism, Richard-Strauss-Platz 2, 82467 Garmisch-Partenkirchen 08821 180700 Ski-pass from €88; sledge-trip details tel 08821 94 29 20 Garmisch-Partenkirchen

GÜNZBURG

LEGOLAND

www.legoland.de

Hugely popular with both children and adults,
Legoland Allee, 89312 Günzburg 08221 700700 Mid-Mar to early Nov daily 10–6, 7, 8, 9 or 10 (times vary with season and day of week; closed some days; see website for details) Adult €31.50, child (3–11) €27.50, under 3 free Günzburg (shuttle service)

HEIDELBERG

HEIDELBERGER MÄRCHENPARADIES

www.maerchenparadies.de

Translating as 'Heidelberg Fairy-tale Paradise', this recreational park provides lots of entertainment for both adults and children.
Königstuhl 5a, 69117 Heidelberg 06221 23416 Mar–end Jun, Sep–end Nov Mon–Fri 10–6, Sat, Sun 10–7; Jul, Aug daily 10–7; closed Dec–end Feb Adult €3, child (2–12) €2 Bergbahn ('mountain train') from Heidelberg

SCHWIMMBAD MUSIK CLUB

www.schwimmbad-musik-club.de

This excellent venue caters for all musical styles and is one of the most popular clubs in town.
Tiergartenstrasse 13, 69121 Heidelberg 06221 470201 Wed, Thu 10pm–3am, Fri, Sat 10pm–4am €2–€6

KARLSRUHE

FILMPALAST-AM-ZKM

www.filmpalast.net

This is the largest and most modern cinema multiplex in the city.
Brauerstrasse 40, 76137 Karlsruhe 0721 205 9200 Box office: daily 11am–midnight Adult €4.90–8.90, child under 12 €4.90–€6.50 Tram 6

POSTGALERIE

www.postgalerie.de

Karlsruhe's Postgalerie is a modern shopping mall in the pedestrian zone around Kaiserstrasse, an area with a varied choice of shops.
Kaiserstrasse 217, 76133 Karlsruhe 0721 180 5860 Mon–Sat

ZOOLOGISCHER GARTEN KARLSRUHE UND STADTGARTEN

www.karlsruhe.de/zoo

Karlsruhe Zoo is home to more than 1,000 animals of 150 species from all over the world. The beautiful Municipal Gardens have 800 large trees from a wide diversity of countries, as well as flowers, shrubs and climbing plants.
Ettlinger Strasse 6, 76137 Karlsruhe 0721 133 6815 May–end Sep daily 8–6; Feb–end Apr, Oct daily 9–5; Nov–end Jan daily 9–4 Adult €5.50, child (6–15) €2.50, under 6 free

KONSTANZ

BODENSEE-THERME

www.bodensee-therme-konstanz.de

This leisure and recreation area has a thermal bath with a temperature of 33°C (91°F), swimming pools with slides, a shallow pool for children, a solarium, a restaurant and a children's playground.
Wilhelm-von-Scholz-Weg 2, 78464 Konstanz 07531 363070 Daily 9–10 Adult €6.50, child €4.40 5

SEA LIFE KONSTANZ

www.sealife.de

At Konstanz's Sea Life centre, enormous glazed aquariums trace the aquatic life of the Rhine from its source in the Gotthard massif to the North Sea. It's an amazing world, with around 3,000 freshwater and saltwater fish. In the same building is the interesting Bodensee Naturmuseum (Lake Constance Natural History Museum).
Hafenstrasse 9, 78462 Konstanz 01805 6669 0101 Jul to mid-Sep daily 10–7; May, Jun, mid-Sep to end Oct

daily 10–6; Nov–end Apr Mon–Fri 10–5, Sat, Sun and holidays 10–6 Adult €12.95, senior €11.95, child (3–14) €9.50, under 3 free

WEINMARKT AN DER LAUBE
www.weinmarkt-konstanz.de
This wine market has a large selection of local and international wines to taste and buy.
Untere Laube 17, 78462 Konstanz 07531 22131 Tue–Thu 9–12.30, 2.30–6.30, Fri 9–6.30, Sat 9–1.30

NÜRNBERG

CINECITTA
www.cinecitta.de
Germany's largest multiplex cinema has 21 theatres that seat more than 5,000 people, three restaurants, cafés, bars and a film shop. Next door is an IMAX cinema.
Gewerbemuseumsplatz 3, 90403 Nürnberg 0911 206666 (box office) Daily 10am–midnight €5.90–€7.90

JAZZ-STUDIO
www.jazzstudio.de
The Jazz-Studio first opened in 1954 and has hosted many young, talented artists as well as regional and international stars.
Paniersplatz 27–29, 90403 Nürnberg 0911 935 0880 (tickets) Fri, Sat from 8.30pm (concerts begin at 9pm) €5–€15 46, 47

SPIELZEUGMUSEUM
www.spielzeugmuseum-nuernberg.de
Nuremberg has a long tradition of toy-making. Adults and children will enjoy the comprehensive collection of historic toys displayed on four floors of the Toy Museum.
Karlstrasse 13–15, 90403 Nürnberg 0911 231 3164 Tue–Fri 10–5, Sat, Sun 10–6 Adult €5, child (4–18) €2.50, family €5.50, €10.50 U1, U11 36 Guided tours €3.50

WMF-FACHGESCHÄFT
www.wmf.de
This shop specializes in wonderful Meissen porcelain.
Karolinenstrasse 27, 90402 Nürnberg 0911 206860 Mon–Sat 10–7

OBERAMMERGAU

PASSIONSTHEATER
www.passionstheater.de
Every year, opera performances are staged in the wonderful setting of Oberammergau's Passion Play Theatre. From May to the end of October you can also take a guided tour of this amazing venue. The next Passion Play will be performed in 2010. Tickets go on sale two years before each performance.
Oberammergau 08822 923158; 08822 92310 (info on 2010 Passion Play) Box office: Mon–Fri 10–6 €17–€240

WINTER SPORTS
www.ammergauer-alpen.de
Oberammergau has good skiing facilities to suit all standards.
Oberammergau Tourismus, Eugen-Papst-Strasse 9a, 82487 Oberammergau 08822 922740 Ski-lifts in winter 9–4.30 (every 30 mins) Ski-pass €21.50

RAVENSBURG

RAVENSBURGER VERLAGSMUSEUM
www.ravensburger-verlagsmuseum.de
The Ravensburg company is renowned throughout the world for its games, puzzles and children's books. Entry is free to the games museum and you can see old books, puzzles and games that have been produced since the company started up in 1883.
Marktstrasse 26, 88212 Ravensburg 0751 8860 Apr–end Sep Thu 2–6 (during holidays Tue–Fri 2–6, Sat, Sun 2–5) Free

ROTHENBURG OB DER TAUBER

WEIHNACHTSDORF
www.wohlfahrt.com
Rothenburg is fortunate to have a selection of the wonderful Wolfahrt shops. The Weihnachtsdorf, Käthe Wohlfahrt's Christmas Village, is where you will find an enormous selection of traditional German Christmas decorations and knick-knacks.
Herrngasse 1, 91541 Rothenburg ob der Tauber 09861 4090 Mon–Fri 8.30–7, Sat 9–6.30, Sun (May to mid-Oct) 9–6

FIGURENTHEATER AM BURGTOR
www.figurentheater-rothenburg.com
This is a wonderful little theatre with an entertaining puppet show that is ideal for all ages.
Herrngasse 38, 91541 Rothenburg ob der Tauber 09861 3333 May–end Aug, Dec 3pm, 8pm; Apr, Sep–end Nov 8pm Adult €7, child €5 (3pm); adult €9, child €7 (8pm)

STUTTGART

BREUNINGER
www.breuninger.de
Breuninger is a huge department store, set over six floors. The restaurant has a varied menu and is an ideal place to relax.
Marktstrasse 1–3, 70173 Stuttgart 0711 2110 Mon–Fri 10–8, Sat 9.30–8

MINERALBAD BERG
www.stuttgart.de/baeder
This bath complex has a nostalgic atmosphere reminiscent of the 1950s, and you take baths in copper tubs that are decades old. There are indoor and outdoor mineral swimming and therapeutic pools, a solarium and restaurant.
Am Schwanenplatz 9, 70190 Stuttgart 0711 216 7090 Mon–Thu 6am–8pm, Fri, Sat 6am–9pm, Sun 6–5 Adult €6.50, child (6–17) €5.30 U1, U2, U14 56, 402 S1, S2, S3

SI-ERLEBNIS-CENTRUM
www.si-centrum.de
This unique entertainment complex has two luxurious theatres showing successful musicals, six cinemas, a spa, a casino and two hotels. Also here are 19 themed restaurants.
Plieninger Strasse 100, 70567 Stuttgart 0711 7210 Contact/check website for details Varies U3, U5, U6 G74, 75, 77, 809, 826, 827

ZAPATA
www.zapata.de
With four dance floors and capacity for 1,600 people, this stylish disco is one of the largest in Stuttgart.
Pragstrasse 120, 70376 Stuttgart 0711 956 1544 Fri, Sat 10pm–5am €5

FESTIVALS AND EVENTS

MAY

DER MEISTERTRUNK

www.meistertrunk.de

According to legend, in 1631 Mayor Nusch of Rothenburg saved the town from being destroyed when he won the challenge to drain a tankard containing more than 3 litres (6 pints) of wine. This episode was first re-enacted as the festival play *Der Meistertrunk* (*The Master Draught*) in 1881.

☒ Rothenburg ob der Tauber ☎ 09861 976759 ◷ Whitsun (last Sun in May) ✋ Adult €6–€14, child (6–14) €3.50–€14

JUNE

RICHARD-STRAUSS-TAGE

www.richard-strauss-tage.de

Richard Strauss lived in Garmisch-Partenkirchen from 1908 until his death in 1949. Each June, Garmisch honours the composer with the Richard Strauss Festival. Artists from all over the world perform at this musical extravaganza.

☒ Garmisch-Partenkirchen-Tourism, Richard-Strauss-Platz 2, 82467 Garmisch-Partenkirchen ☎ 08821 180700 ◷ One week, mid-June ✋ €15–€60t

JUNE/AUGUST

SCHLOSSFESTSPIELE

www.schlossfestspiele-heidelberg.de

The ruins of Heidelberg Castle provide the picturesque setting for this world-famous festival. The courtyard is the site of open-air musicals, operas and theatre performances, as well as classical concerts performed by the Heidelberg City Orchestra.

☒ Friedrichstrasse 5, 69117 Heidelberg ☎ 06221 583 5020 ◷ End June to mid-August ✋ Adult €15–€50, reduction for child or senior depends on event

JULY

INTERNATIONAL ZELT-MUSIK FESTIVAL

www.zmf.de

This music festival has gained international recognition for its spectacular variety of presentations. More than 100 events over 19 days, with artists and stars from all over the world, contribute to a menu of classical, rock, jazz and circus.

☒ Rehlingstrasse 6e, 79100 Freiburg ☎ 0761 504030 (ticket hotline) ◷ Three weeks, late June to July ✋ Varies

DIE KINDERZECHE

www.kinderzeche.de

The historic festival play *Die Kinderzeche* (performed since 1897) is one of Germany's oldest and most interesting. According to legend, when Swedish troops laid siege to the town in 1632, the gatekeeper's daughter, Lore, together with the children of the town, pleaded for mercy and saved Dinkelsbühl from pillage and destruction. The event is accompanied by a diverse peripheral schedule, making it ideal for families.

☒ Bauhofstrasse 42, 91550 Dinkelsbühl ☎ 09851 589520 ◷ 10 days in July ✋ €2–€12

RUTENFEST

www.ravensburg.de

Ravensburg's local history festival begins every July with the firing of a small cannon from the Mehlsack tower, marking the start of a traditional event that attracts visitors from all over the world. The highlight is Monday's historical parade.

☒ Tourist Information Ravensburg, Kirchstrasse 16, 88212 Ravensburg ☎ 0751 82800 ◷ 5 days in July–August

AUGUST

KONSTANZER SEENACHTFEST

www.seenachtfest.com

www.konstanz.de

The Konstanzer Seenachtfest is the largest summer event held around Lake Constance, and takes place along the lakeshore of the city of Konstanz and the neighbouring Swiss city of Kreuzlingen. The Seenachtfest is mostly known for its fireworks on the lake, the biggest display in Germany. Events include street theatre, water-ski shows and live music on seven stages.

☒ Tourist Information Konstanz, Bahnhofplatz 13, 78462 Konstanz ☎ 01805 133030 ◷ Second weekend in August ✋ Adult €10, child under 14 free

SEPTEMBER

REICHSSTADT-FESTTAGE

www.rothenburg.de

The Imperial City Festival, a highlight of Rothenburg's calendar, sees the entire history of the town brought alive by more than 1,000 participants. On the Saturday, don't miss the spectacular fireworks display in the Tauber valley.

☒ Rothenburg ob der Tauber ☎ 09861 404800 ◷ 3 days end August–early September

SEPTEMBER/OCTOBER

CANNSTATTER VOLKSFEST

www.cannstatter-volksfest.de

This is one of the largest and best beer festivals in the world.

☒ Cannstatter Wasen, Stuttgart ☎ 0711 22280 (Stuttgart Tourist Office) ◷ End September/beginning October Mon–Fri noon–11, Sat, Sun 11–11 ✋ Free

NOVEMBER/ DECEMBER

CHRISTKINDLESMARKT

www.nuernberg.de

Nuremberg's Christmas Market is the oldest and one of the best in Germany.

☒ Hauptmarkt, Nürnberg ☎ 0911 23360 ◷ Last week in November–24 December

WEIHNACHTSMARKT

www.stuttgart-tourist.de

At Stuttgart's market, more than 200 brightly decorated stands sell a wide range of seasonal goods and culinary treats, including gingerbread, cinnamon waffles and mulled wine.

☒ Marktplatz and Schillerplatz, Stuttgart ☎ 0711 22280 (Stuttgart Tourist Office) ◷ Last week in November–23 December Mon–Sat 10–8.30, Sun 11–8.30

Above *A riverside restaurant terrace at Bodensee, where the catch of the day is a good menu option*

PRICES AND SYMBOLS

The restaurants are listed alphabetically (excluding Le, La and Les) within each town. The prices given are the average for a two-course lunch (L) and a three-course dinner (D) for one person, without drinks. The wine price is for the least expensive bottle. All the restaurants listed accept credit cards unless otherwise stated.

For a key to the symbols, ▷ 2.

AUGSBURG

BISTRO 3M

www.steigenberger.com

This is *the* place to find good French and Mediterranean cuisine. Bistro 3M is in the Steigenberger Drei Mohren hotel (▷354) and serves a good range of meals.

✉ Maximilianstrasse 40, 86150 Augsburg
☎ 0821 503 6650 ⌚ Sun–Tue 9am–midnight, Wed–Sat 9am–1am
✋ L €19, D €28, Wine €24

DIE ECKE

www.restaurantdieecke.de

This popular restaurant is in a pretty square in the heart of Augsburg, next to the Rathaus (Town Hall). The wonderful display of modern art helps to give it a relaxed bistro atmosphere. The food is excellent and includes classic Swabian and Bavarian dishes. Try the game served with *Spätzle*.

✉ Elias-Holl-Platz 2, 86150 Augsburg
☎ 0821 510600 ⌚ Daily 11.30–2, 5.30–1am ✋ L €16, D €23, Wine €20

BAD AIBLING

ROMANTIK HOTEL LINDNER

www.romantikhotel-lindner.de

Hotel Lindner is in a fairy-tale setting—the former Bavarian castle of Prantshausen. The restaurant offers a wonderful blend of Mediterranean and Bavarian cuisine. Special dishes include *Wiener schnitzel* with cranberries, spinach and ricotta ravioli with a ragout of tomatoes, and home-made cakes.

✉ Marienplatz 5, 83043 Bad Aibling
☎ 08061 90630 ⌚ Daily 11.30am–10pm
✋ L €20, D €25, Wine €21

BADEN-BADEN

KURHAUS

www.kurhausrestaurant.de

The beautiful Kurhaus spa building, with its stately rooms, casino, underground parking and restaurant, is the hub of Baden-Baden's social scene. This is a special place for a light lunch or coffee, but whatever you choose don't miss the Black Forest gateau, which has to be the best in the region. It's worth waiting for a table if you have the time. There's a tourist office in the same building.

✉ Kaiserallee 1, 76530 Baden-Baden
☎ 07221 9070 ⌚ Daily 10am–midnight
✋ L €36, D €44, Wine €22

BAMBERG

BRAUEREIGASTSTÄTTE KLOSTERBRÄU

www.klosterbraeu.de

This restaurant is in Bamberg's oldest brewery. Many of the dishes are cooked using the brewery's own beer—try the *Bierhaxe* (knuckle of veal or pork cooked with beer) or Franconian *Kummelbraten* (hot sliced pork with a crispy skin seasoned with caraway seeds). The brewery produces excellent beers to accompany your meal, and also makes schnapps.

✉ Obere Mühlbrücke 1–3, 96049 Bamberg
☎ 0951 52265 ⌚ Mon–Fri 10.30am–11pm, Sat, Sun 10am–11pm ✋ L €15, D €19

BRUDERMÜHLE

www.brudermuehle.de

Close to the river in the middle of Bamberg's historic old town, this former mill makes an attractive hotel (▷ 354) with an excellent restaurant. Eat in the intimate restaurant or on the pretty veranda, and you'll have a wide choice of Franconian dishes to choose from. Spring is a good time to eat here, when there's fresh carp and trout, lamb, asparagus and strawberries on the menu. In autumn and winter, the game dishes are excellent.

✉ Schranne 1, 96049 Bamberg ☎ 0951 955220 ◷ Daily 10am–midnight ✋ L €11, D €20, Wine €15

BAYREUTH

GOLDENER LÖWE

www.goldener-loewe-bayreuth.de

The beer is brewed on site in this restaurant right next to a brewery, and the sausages and *schnitzel* are also made here.

✉ Kulmbacher Strasse 30, 95445 Bayreuth ☎ 0921 746060 ◷ Mon–Sat 11.30–2, 5.30–10.30, Sun 11.30–2.30 ✋ L €17, D €22, Wine €15

COBURG

GOLDENE TRAUBE

www.goldenetraube.com

This superb hotel-restaurant (▷ 354) serves both regional and international cuisine; in season, the fish dishes in particular are very good. If you prefer something more informal, the hotel also has a wine tavern, the comfortable Weinstubla.

✉ Am Viktoriabrunnen 2, 96450 Coburg ☎ 09561 8760 ◷ Mon–Sat 12–2.30, 6–10.30, Sun 1–10pm ✋ L €18, D €26, Wine €19

DINKELSBÜHL

BRAUEREIGASTSTÄTTE ZUM WILDEN MANN

www.wilder-mann-dinkelsbuehl.de

In the restaurant here you will find a choice of excellent Franconian and international cuisine, plus a large selection of wines to accompany your meal. The *Braustube*, with its tiled floor and dark timber cladding, has a rustic feel and a pub atmosphere; it serves Franconian-Bavarian fare as well as local wines and beers. There is a beer garden.

✉ Wörnitzstrasse 1, 91550 Dinkelsbühl ☎ 09851 552525 ◷ Thu–Tue 10.30–2, 6–10 ✋ L €8, D €13, Wine €14

EBERBACH

CAFÉ VIKTORIA

www.cafe-viktoria.de

Although this superb café can get very busy, it's somewhere you just have to visit. Sit out on the terrace overlooked by a giant mural of Queen Victoria and enjoy live piano music as you sample the culinary delights. The café's signature dish is Viktoria gateau, which was created in 1962 by Heinrich Strohauer at a royal dinner and became so famous that it is now shipped throughout the world in special packaging.

✉ Friedrichstrasse 5–9, 69412 Eberbach ☎ 06271 2018 ◷ Sun–Fri 6am–6.30pm, Sat 6.30–6 ✋ Snacks €4–€8, L €13, Wine by the glass

ESSLINGEN

CAFÉ AM RATHAUS

This pretty little café is next to the old town hall in Esslingen, which is near Stuttgart. It's a lovely place to sit outside in the cobbled square and watch the world go by. The café has a great selection of mouthwatering cakes and pastries, plus a good-value lunch menu that is especially worth trying on weekends.

✉ Rathausplatz 8, 73728 Esslingen ☎ 0711 354411 ◷ Mon–Fri 9–6, Sat 8.30am–10pm, Sun 10–6.30 ✋ Cakes €3, pastries €4 , L €10

FÜSSEN

ALTSTADT-HOTEL ZUM HECHTEN

www.hotel-hechten.com

The popular restaurant on the first floor of this hotel has a wonderful choice of Bavarian dishes. If you are looking for a lighter meal, try the self-service buffet on the ground floor, where there's a choice of reasonably priced salads and hot dishes.

✉ Ritterstrasse 6, 87629 Füssen ☎ 08362 91600 ◷ Thu–Tue 11.30–2, 5–9 ✋ L €13, D €18, Wine €15

FREIBURG

ZUM ROTEN BÄREN

www.roter-baeren.de

Also a hotel (▷ 355), the Red Bear is housed in one of the oldest buildings in Freiburg and is the oldest inn in Germany. The chef here prepares an excellent selection of seasonal dishes using fresh local produce, including fish, game and wild mushrooms. Many tables are placed in individual booths, and together with the soft lighting this creates a relaxed atmosphere. Reservations are recommended.

✉ Oberlinden 12, 79098 Freiburg ☎ 0761 387870 ◷ Mon–Sat 12–2.30, 6.30–11 ✋ L €26, D €40, Wine €19

GARMISCH-PARTENKIRCHEN

GASTHOF FRAUNDORFER

www.gasthof-fraundorfer.de

This homey inn has been run by the same family for nearly 200 years (▷ 355). In the evenings there's Bavarian accordion music, *Schuhplattler* (Bavarian folk dancing), yodelling and singing. The restaurant has a marvellous atmosphere. One of the wooden tables is a *Stammtisch*, the exclusive territory of a group of regulars, each of whom always sits in the same place around it. Home-made Bavarian dishes accompanied by German beer and wine are served by traditionally dressed waitresses.

✉ Ludwigstrasse 24, 82467 Garmisch-Partenkirchen ☎ 08821 9270 ◷ Thu–Mon 7am–1am, Wed 5pm–1am ✋ L €16, D €22, Wine €14

RIESSERSEE

www.riessersee.de

The café-restaurant Riessersee is on a lakeside high above the towns of Garmisch and Partenkirchen. The restaurant has exposed beams and tiled floors and there are stunning views from the lakeside terrace. The menu includes fish and game dishes, and there are home-made cakes and pastries.

✉ Riess 6, 82467 Garmisch-Partenkirchen ☎ 08821 95440 ◷ 11.30am–9pm ✋ L €14, D €19, Wine €16

GIPFELALM
www.zugspitze.de
This is Germany's highest restaurant, on the peak of the Zugspitze. To get here, take the rack railway to the Sonn-Alpin restaurant, then the glacier railway (▷ 314) and enjoy the views. The restaurant serves Bavarian dishes, such as fresh pretzels with *Weisswurst* (white sausage) and *Leberkäse* (baked meatloaf made with minced meat, eggs and spices). The food apart, the journey up the mountain and the breathtaking views from the terrace into Germany, Austria, Switzerland and Liechtenstein make for an unforgettable experience.
✉ Zugspitze, 82475 Garmisch-Partenkirchen ☎ 08821 797252 ⌚ Daily 10am–4pm 🖑 Snacks €4–€8, L €15, Wine by the glass

HEIDELBERG

KULTURBRAUEREI
www.heidelberger-kulturbrauerei.de
The food and beer at the Kulturbrauerei are both excellent. There's a choice of traditional dining rooms all of which have plenty of atmosphere and character. The Biergarten is also a nice place to sit on a fine day to enjoy a traditional meal chosen from the comprehensive menu.
✉ Leyergasse 6, 69117 Heidelberg ☎ 06221 502980 ⌚ Sun–Thu 11–11, Fri, Sat 11am–midnight 🖑 L €18, D €28, Wine €24

SCHLOSSWEINSTUBE
www.schoenmehl.de
In the historic castle courtyard above the city, a choice of excellent food made from fresh seasonal ingredients is served in wonderful surroundings. Highly recommended is the duck, stuffed with apples and herbs and basted to create a crispy skin. Depending on the season, there's also a variety of other game to choose from. The wine list is extensive and includes many labels from the Bergstrasse region.
✉ Schlosshof, 69117, Heidelberg ☎ 06221 97970 ⌚ Thu–Tue 6pm–midnight 🖑 L €30, D €43, Wine €24

SIMPLICISSIMUS
www.restaurant-simplicissimus.de
This popular restaurant, in Heidelberg's historic quarter, has a great choice of food cooked in the French tradition. There's an excellent range of wines from prestigious vineyards and producers as well as bottles in the middle price range. The fillet of beef with wild mushrooms is particularly popular. In summer, try to get a table in the small courtyard.
✉ Ingrimstrasse 16, 69117 Heidelberg ☎ 06221 183336 ⌚ Tue–Sat 6pm–midnight 🖑 L €25, D €35, Wine €22

HOHENSCHWANGAU

SCHLOSSHOTEL LISL
www.lisl.de
The restaurant-café in Schlosshotel Lisl (▷ 355) is in the middle of the village between the fairy-tale castles of Neuschwanstein and Hohenschwangau. If it's a fine day you can sit out on the sun terrace with your coffee and enjoy the magnificent views. Inside, there's a spacious café with elegant white basket-weave furniture and a comfortable restaurant serving both regional and international cuisine. Both have large picture windows.
✉ Neuschwansteinstrasse 1–3, 87645 Hohenschwangau ☎ 08362 8870 ⌚ Daily 7am–10am, 11am–9pm; closed 19–26 Dec 🖑 L €15, D €20, Wine €22

KARLSRUHE

OBERLÄNDER WEINSTUBE
www.oberlaender-weinstube.de
This intimate wine bar is the oldest in town. It specializes in both French and regional cooking, producing such dishes as lamb with chanterelle mushrooms and pigeon with celeriac purée. There's an attractive courtyard where you can enjoy your meal on a fine day.
✉ Akademiestrasse 7, 76133 Karlsruhe ☎ 0721 25066 ⌚ Tue–Sat 11.45–2, 6–9.30 🖑 L €40, D €60, Wine €25

LADENBURG

FODY'S FÄHRHAUS
www.fodys.com
Part of a chain of restaurants already popular in Mannheim and Heppenheim, this branch of Fody's, 15km (10 miles) north of Heidelberg, is a big hit. The restaurant has a large terrace and beer garden, and the interior has a Mediterranean theme, which creates a warm and lively atmosphere. The menu includes a huge choice of soups, salads, regional and international dishes and drinks. Look out for the 'Eat as much as you like' buffet, which is great value.
✉ Neckarstrasse 62, 68526 Ladenburg ☎ 06203 938383 ⌚ Mon–Thu 11am–midnight, Fri, Sat 11am–1am, Sun 9am–midnight 🖑 L €6, D €12, Wine €14

LANDSHUT

STERNE
www.fuerstenhof.la
André Greul is the chef at this hotel restaurant, and he cooks fine international and organic regional dishes such as duck sausage and honey-glazed suckling pig. This is an ideal spot for a candlelit dinner. Less formal, and with a rustic Bavarian atmosphere, is the Herzogstueberl restaurant, which serves regional and international dishes.
✉ Fürstenhof Hotel, Stethaimer Strasse 3, 84034 Landshut ☎ 0871 92550 ⌚ Mon 6.30–9.30 Tue–Sat 12–2, 6.30–9.30 🖑 L €37, D €52, Wine €23

LINDAU

ZUM SÜNFZEN
www.suenfzen.de
This is a popular restaurant, and the food is exceptional. Fish dishes are made with catches from Lake Constance, while game is from the owners' own hunting grounds and the meat from their butchery. There's a range of Allgau Bavarian food and international dishes too. It's advisable to reserve in advance.
✉ Maximilianstrasse 1, 88131 Lindau (Bodensee) ☎ 08382 5865 ⌚ Daily 9.30am–midnight 🖑 L €15, D €20, Wine €14

MANNHEIM

DREHRESTAURANT SKYLINE
www.restaurant-skyline-mannheim.de
You will have magnificent views over the entire region when you dine

in this revolving restaurant in the Skyline Tower, 125m (410ft) above the city. The menu is varied, with a wide choice of regional cuisine, à la carte dishes and buffet meals. The grilled perch on dill mustard sauce with fresh spinach is highly recommended, as is the grilled chicken leg stuffed with tomatoes, mushrooms, herbs and cheese.
✉ Hans-Reschke-Ufer 2, 68165 Mannheim ☎ 0621 419290 🕐 Daily 10am–midnight 🖐 L €16, D €24, Wine €22

EICHBAUM BRAUHAUS

www.eichbaumbrauhaus.de
This excellent café-restaurant in Mannheim's largest brewery is an ideal refreshment stop at any time of the day, for breakfast, morning coffee, a quick lunch or an informal dinner. The restaurant is roomy and light, with traditional furnishings, beamed ceilings and carved wooden chairs. The food is good and there's a wide choice of menus; try the home-made *Spätzle*, North Sea crab on the home-baked brown bread or Nürnberg *Bratwurst*.
✉ Käfertaler Strasse 168, 68167 Mannheim ☎ 0621 35385 🕐 Daily 10am–midnight 🖐 L €10, D €14

MEERSBURG

HOTEL RESIDENZ AM SEE

www.hotel-residenz-meersburg.com
This restaurant has a beautiful setting. The hotel is surrounded by historic buildings and vineyards on three sides and overlooks Lake Constance, so it's a perfect place to stop for a meal or even just a coffee. The menu has a wide choice of regional dishes, including fish from the lake, local vegetables and wines.
✉ Uferpromenade 11, 88709 Meersburg ☎ 07532 80040 🕐 Wed–Mon 12–2, 5.30–9.30 🖐 L €38, D €60, Wine €22

MOSBACH

CAFÉ GRAMLICH

www.cafe-gramlich.de
The selection of home-made cakes and pastries here is exceptional, making it a great place to enjoy an indulgent break. Every imaginable type of cake is on display, so making a choice is a hard decision; if you really can't decide, try the Swiss cheesecake. The bread here is equally good.
✉ Haupstrasse 88, 74821 Mosbach ☎ 06261 2389 🕐 Wed–Sun 10am–9pm

NECKARGERACH

HOTEL GRÜNER BAUM

www.gruenerbaum-neckargerach.de
This hotel is owned and run by a Greek family, and in the restaurant you will find an amazing selection of fresh Greek dishes alongside popular local dishes. The salads in particular are exceptional. The restaurant's interior is typically Greek and has a casual style.
✉ Neckarstrasse 13, 69437 Neckargerach ☎ 06263 706 🕐 Mar–end Aug daily 11.30–2, 5–11; Sep–end Feb Mon–Sat 5–11, Sun 11.30–2, 5–11 🖐 L €17, D €25, Wine €12

NÜRNBERG

BRATWURSTHÄUSLE

www.die-nuernberger-bratwurst.de
The Bratwursthäusle is the place to try the famous *Bratwurst* (grilled sausages). Here, the traditional Nürnberg sausages are made fresh every day in the factory below the restaurant, then are taken upstairs to be grilled over beechwood and served on pewter plates with horse-radish, *Sauerkraut* and potato salad. This place is popular and gets very busy at lunchtimes and on weekends.
✉ Rathaus-Platz 1, 90403 Nürnberg ☎ 0911 227695 🕐 Mon–Sat 10am–10.30pm 🖐 L, D from €6, Wine by the glass

ESSIGBRÄTLEIN

History suffuses the sandstone walls and oak-beamed interior of an establishment that has been serving food since 1550. But this tiny Old Franconian gem close to the St. Sebald Church is not stuck in the past, and the traditional vinegar roast beef of the restaurant's name is by no means the only offering on the menu. Chef Andree Köthe's menu is limited in extent but not in sophistication or imagination.
✉ Weinmarkt 3, 90403 Nürnberg ☎ 0911 225131 🕐 Tue–Sat 12–3, 7pm–1am 🖐 L €22, D €40, Wine €21

GASTHAUS ROTTNER

www.rottner-hotel.de
The attractive black-and-white timber-framed former farmhouse that is now the Gasthaus Rottner (▷ 356) is in the village of Grossreuth on the outskirts of Nürnberg. The restaurant is welcoming, with traditional but innovative fare that includes fresh and seasonal produce. Dishes include tomato bread, herb pancakes, smoked venison and some amazing salads. In summer, ask for a table in the garden so that you can enjoy your dinner in the shade of the old lime trees.
✉ Winterstrasse 15–17, 90431 Grossreuth, Nürnberg ☎ 0911 612032 🕐 Mon–Fri noon–2pm, 6.30–9.30, Sat 6.30–9.30 🖐 L €18, D €25, Wine €21

OBERAMMERGAU

PARKHOTEL SONNENHOF

www.parkhotel-sonnenhof.de
This spacious hotel restaurant (▷ 356) is typically Bavarian in style. The chef cooks both regional and international dishes, so the menu offers a wide choice. Although the restaurant is large, it has plenty of character—many of the tables are tucked away in intimate corners. There is a good range of wines and beers, mainly from the wineries of Württemberg and the breweries of Ingolstadt.
✉ König-Ludwig-Strasse 12, 82487 Oberammergau ☎ 08822 9130 🕐 Daily 6.45am–9pm 🖐 L €22, D €30, Wine €14

ZUR TINI

This is a superb little restaurant in the heart of Oberammergau, where you can sit outside in the pedestrian area on a fine day and watch the world go by. The restaurant specializes in light Bavarian meals and snacks.
✉ Dorfstrasse 7, 82487 Oberammergau ☎ 08822 7152 🕐 Thu–Tue 10–2.30, 5.30–midnight 🖐 L €13, D €18, Wine by the glass

OBERSTDORF

BACCHUS STUBEN

www.bacchusstuben.de

This is a family-run restaurant serving fabulous traditional food. Seasonal dishes use fresh regional produce, including brown trout, *Zander* (pike-perch), salmon, asparagus, game and meat. The views of the mountains from the sun terrace are exceptional.

✉ Freibergstrasse 4, 87561 Oberstdorf ☎ 08322 4787 🕐 Tue–Sun 11.30–2, 5.30–8.30 ✋ L €17, D €27, Wine €16

RAVENSBURG

OBERTOR

www.hotelobertor.de

This historic hotel dates back more than 700 years (▷ 356), and has a restaurant serving typically Swabian food, creatively presented using seasonal produce. The wood-panelled dining room has beamed ceilings and beautiful objects—look for the special carved wooden lampshade holders that hang low over each table. History is everywhere around you at the Obertor, with its vaulted cellars and wooden ceilings—so much so that you feel that time stands still here.

✉ Marktstrasse 67, 88212 Ravensburg ☎ 0751 36670 🕐 Mon, Wed–Sat 5pm–midnight ✋ L €20, D €30, Wine €18

REGENSBURG

ORPHÉE

www.hotel-orphee.de

Once the largest in the Oberfalz region, this brewery was converted by a Hungarian Gypsy baron into a French-style café and wine bar, and no major changes have been made in the restaurant since 1896. The café was established to allow people to meet and enjoy a coffee or sit and read a newspaper in comfort; today, it is still an ideal place to relax and soak up the atmosphere, with its old wooden floor and antique furnishings. The menu has everything from pastries, baguettes, soups and crêpes to full meals.

✉ Untere Bachgasse 8, 93047 Regensburg ☎ 0941 52977 🕐 Daily 8am–1am ✋ L €12, D €22, Wine €12

HISTORISCHE WURSTKUCHL

www.wurstkuchl.de

This restaurant is beside the Danube, and on a fine day it's great to sit outside enjoying a plate of home-made sausages and *Sauerkraut* with a cool beer. The sausages are made fresh on the premises every day, and the cabbage for the *Sauerkraut* is fermented in the cellar vats.

✉ Thundorferstrasse 3, 93047 Regensburg ☎ 0941 466210 🕐 Daily 8am–7pm ✋ Sausages with *Sauerkraut* from €6.90, L €12.50, Wine by the glass

PRINZESS CONFISERIE

www.prinzess.de

This is the oldest café and chocolate manufacturing house in Germany. Choose from an amazing selection of home-made cakes, pastries and chocolates. The intimate seating areas on the upper floors have marble tables and comfortable armchairs.

✉ Rathausplatz 2, 93047 Regensburg ☎ 0941 595310 🕐 Mon–Sat 9.15am–6.30pm, Sun 11am–6.30pm

VITUS CAFÉ UND RESTAURANT

www.vitus-restaurant.de

This attractive restaurant and café is housed in a former chapel. Tables are well spaced, allowing plenty of room to admire the architecture in this historic building. It's a very popular place for morning coffee and mouth-watering pastries.

✉ Hinter der Grieb 8, 93047 Regensburg ☎ 0941 52646 🕐 Daily 9am–1am ✋ L €12, D €17, Wine €12

ROTHENBURG OB DER TAUBER

HOTEL RESTAURANT SCHRANNE

www.hotel-schranne.de

At this family-run hotel restaurant specializing in Franconian cuisine, the meat dishes are made with produce from the Schranne's own butchery. The large restaurant is bright and spacious. The staff are friendly and are always ready to help you with the menu or to recommend dishes. There's a good selection of local wines and beer.

✉ Schrannenplatz 6–7, 91541 Rothenburg ob der Tauber ☎ 09861 95500 🕐 Daily 11–9.30 ✋ L €18, D €24, Wine €12

ZUR HÖLL

www.romanticroad.com/hoell

The house is the oldest and one of the most beautiful in Rothenburg, and serves fine regional dishes and Franconian wines. The small menu complements the wines perfectly. Some of the tables are tucked away in secluded alcoves to create an intimate, old-fashioned atmosphere.

✉ Burggasse 8, 91541 Rothenburg ob der Tauber ☎ 09861 4229 🕐 Daily 5pm–1am ✋ D €25, Wine €18

SCHWÄBISCH HALL

CAFÉ ILGE

www.cafebar-ilge.de

This popular first-floor café is ideal for a relaxing coffee or beer. It has a friendly atmosphere, and good views from the two terraces that overlook the River Kocher and the ancient wooden bridge across it. There's a choice of snacks and pastries to enjoy with your drink. It's a popular and busy venue.

✉ Im Weiler 2, 74523 Schwäbisch Hall ☎ 0791 71684 🕐 Sun–Thu 11am–1am, Fri, Sat 11am–2am ✋ Snacks from €3, Wine by the glass

SPEYER

RESTAURANT BACKMULDE

www.backmulde.de

A popular place for regional dishes and wines where the dim lights and small rooms create an intimate atmosphere. Try the leg of goose and, when in season, the salads of fresh greens picked from the owner's garden.

✉ Karmeliterstrasse 11–13, 67346 Speyer ☎ 06232 71577 🕐 Tue–Sun 11.30–2.30, 7–11.30 ✋ L €21, D €34, Wine €23

STUTTGART

EMPORE

www.looss-kulinarisches.de

This lively Italian restaurant on the second floor above the busy market hall is perfect for a pasta lunch, a cappuccino or a bowl of delicious Italian ice cream.

Dorotheenstrasse 4, 70173 Stuttgart 0711 245979 Mon–Fri 9am–10pm, Sat 9am–6pm L €16, D €23, Wine €16

KACHELOFEN

A traditional restaurant specializing in Swabian dishes and very popular with locals. It's always busy, and the atmosphere is informal and jovial as waitresses squeeze between the closely spaced tables to serve the excellent food and wine. Each table has a small flag to indicate the nationality of the diner, so look around and see where everyone comes from.

Eberhardstrasse 10, 80173 Stuttgart 0711 242378 Mon–Sat 5pm–1am L €12, D €20, Wine €16

WEINSTUBE ZUR KISTE

www.zur-kiste.de

This quaint little restaurant, close to the Bohnenviertel (Bean Quarter), is the oldest in Stuttgart and probably its best-known and most popular wine tavern. It's a superb place to experience traditional Swabian dishes and regional wines, but it does get very busy and loud.

Kanalstrasse 2, 70182 Stuttgart 0711 244002 Mon–Fri 5pm–midnight, Sat 11.30–midnight L €15, D €24, Wine by the glass

TÜBINGEN

RESTAURANT MAUGANESCHTLE

www.mauganeschtle.de

Maultaschen, a ravioli-like stuffed pasta, is Tübingen's local dish and you can choose from 28 types of *Maultaschen*, as well as many other excellent dishes. If you like fish, try the *Zander* (pike-perch), which is available in season. The terrace overlooks the river.

Hotel Am Schloss, Burgsteige 18, 72072 Tübingen 07071 92940 Daily 11.30–3, 5.30pm–midnight. L €18, D €24, Wine €15

WEINSTUBE FORELLE

www.weinstubeforelle.de

In the middle of the old city, this little restaurant specializes in Swabian dishes. The lunch menu is good value and the small interior is welcoming. The game dishes, roasted duck liver and trout are all highly recommended.

Kronenstrasse 8, 72072 Tübingen 07071 24094 Daily 11.30–10.30 L €20, D €27, Wine €17

Above *Orphée is a French-style restaurant, housed in a former brewery*

VOLKACH

GASTSTUBE

www.schwane.de

The chef here specializes in Franconian cuisine. The cobbled courtyard is great in summer. There's a fine selection of wine from the hotel's own vineyard.

Hotel zur Schwane, Haupstrasse 12, 97332 Volkach 09381 80660 Tue–Sun 12–2, 6–9.30, Mon 6–9.30 L €18, D €27, Wine €18

WEINHEIM

SCHLOSSPARK RESTAURANT

www.hutter-im-schloss.de

In the wing of an historic building, this restaurant is the perfect place to enjoy a meal. The chef uses fresh seasonal produce to provide a varied menu that will suit all tastes; in spring, the lamb and *Zander* (pike-perch) are especially good. It's a very popular restaurant, so advance reservations are is advisable (Tuesday is the quietest day). Enjoy a walk through the park before or after your meal.

Obertorstrasse 9, 69469 Weinheim 06201 99550 Daily 11am–midnight L €31, D €38, Wine €18

WÜRZBURG

WÜRZBURGER RATSKELLER

www.ratskeller-wuerzburg.de

This elegant restaurant in the vaulted basement of the town hall is a special place for a special meal. The towered building is as impressive on the inside as it is from the outside, as room after room sprawls across the basement floors, each with its own distinctive style and ambience. The menu has both well-prepared local dishes and international cuisine.

Langgasse 1, 97070 Würzburg 0931 13021 Daily 10am–midnight L €24, D €30, Wine €12

ZUM STACHEL

www.weinhaus-stachel.de

A classy restaurant in a historic building in the middle of Würzburg's old town. The woodwork is highly polished, the lights are dim and tables are tucked away in alcoves, creating a relaxing, unhurried atmosphere. The terrace garden is wonderful on a fine summer's day. Zum Stachel is very popular with local businesspeople and gets busy at lunchtimes on weekdays. The menu has a variety of Franconian dishes, and the seasonal fish specials, such as *Zander* (pike-perch) and carp, are exceptional.

Gressengasse 1, 97070 Würzburg 0931 527 70 Daily 11am–midnight L €24, D €44, Wine €20

PRICES AND SYMBOLS

The prices are the lowest and highest for a double room for one night including breakfast, unless otherwise stated. All the hotels listed accept credit cards unless otherwise stated. Note that rates can vary widely throughout the year.

For a key to the symbols, ▷ 2.

AMORBACH

SCHAFHOF AMORBACH

www.schafhof.de

This hotel is in beautiful countryside next to a working farm. The main building dates from 1721. Some guest rooms have beamed ceilings, in both the main building and the barn. There are some lovely walks around the farm.

Otterbachtal, 63916 Amorbach
09373 97330 €135–€180 24
Spa

AUGSBURG

STEIGENBERGER DREI MOHREN HOTEL

www.steigenberger.com

In a historic building in the heart of Augsburg, this hotel offers luxury and comfort. In 1730 King Friedrich Wilhelm I of Prussia stayed here. The rooms overlook either the traffic-restricted Maximilianstrasse or the glass-roofed tea salon.

Maximilianstrasse 40, 86150 Augsburg
0821 50360 €150–€190 105 (plus 6 suites)

BAD AIBLING

ROMANTIK HOTEL LINDNER

www.romantikhotel-lindner.de

This hotel is in the fairy-tale setting of the former castle of Prantshausen with wood-panelled hallways and its large, elegant guest rooms. There's an excellent restaurant (▷ 348).

Marienplatz 5, 83043 Bad Aibling
08061 90630 €125–€165 26
Bicycles (free rental)

BADEN-BADEN

HOTEL AM MARKT

www.hotel-am-markt-baden.de

In this opulent town, this is an excellent, less expensive option. It is ideally located, tucked away in a quiet cobbled square close to the Old Town and Romerplatz. The rooms on the first two floors are spacious, with high ceilings, but not all rooms have a private bathroom.

Marktplatz 18, 76530 Baden-Baden
07221 27040 €62–€80 12
€4

Above *Parkhotel Sonnenhof in Oberammergau is popular with visitors for the plays*

BAMBERG

BRUDERMÜHLE

www.brudermuehle.de

A 14th-century former mill has been developed into this attractive hotel. Public rooms of the three-floor building, with its shuttered windows and steeply pitched red roof, are furnished with antiques. Guest rooms are in the original mill and in a house across the street. Reserve in advance and ask for a room overlooking the river or the stream and waterfall. The hotel has a restaurant (▷ 349)

Schranne 1, 96049 Bamberg 0951 955220 €120–€140 23 (all non-smoking)

COBURG

ROMANTIK HOTEL GOLDENE TRAUBE

www.goldenetraube.com

Goldene Traube has a history dating back to 1756. The hotel's guest rooms are comfortable and decorated in warm pastel shades, and there's a restaurant-cum-wine tavern (▷ 349).

Am Viktoriabrunnen 2, 96450 Coburg 09561 8760 €120–€160 72 Wellness

DINKELSBÜHL

GASTHOF GOLDNER HIRSCH

www.wunderle.claranet.de

The foundation walls of this house date back to the 14th century. Guest rooms are modern and spacious and breakfasts are exceptional.

Weinmarkt 6, 91550 Dinkelsbühl 09851 2347 €58–€110 14

ESSLINGEN-BERKHEIM

LINDE

www.linde-berkheim.de

This welcoming, family-run hotel is in a village near the autobahn leading into Stuttgart. Guest rooms are more like small apartments—spacious and comfortably furnished.

Ruiterstrasse 2, 73734 Esslingen-Berkheim 0711 345305 €93–€175 86 Indoor

FREIBURG

ZUM ROTEN BÄREN

www.roter-baeren.de

Zum Roten Bären is the oldest inn in Germany. Most of the guest rooms have their own character. Try to arrange a guided tour of the cellars. There is a restaurant (▷ 349).

Oberlinden 12, 79098 Freiburg 0761 387870 €149–€169 25

GARMISCH-PARTENKIRCHEN

GASTHOF FRAUNDORFER

www.gasthof-fraundorfer.de

This traditional hotel has been run by the Fraundorfer family since 1820. Guest rooms vary in size and the furnishings range from traditional in the main house to whimsically modern in the quieter Gästehaus Barbara, behind the hotel. Some rooms have a balcony. Every night except Tuesday, there's a Bavarian evening in the bar-restaurant (▷ 349).

Ludwigstrasse 24, 82467 Garmisch-Partenkirchen 08821 9270 €75–€125 30 Sauna, steam room and solarium

LEINER

www.hotel-leiner.de

The hotel, in a quiet area near the Olympic ski stadium, makes an ideal base for exploring this region.

Wildenauerstrasse 20, 82467 Garmisch-Partenkirchen 08821 95280 €112–€150 47 Indoor Sauna and solarium

RENAISSANCE RIESSERSEE

www.renaissance-riessersee-hotel.de

The Riessersee is on a beautiful lakeside high above Garmisch and Partenkirchen. Rooms and apartments are well appointed, and have stunning views.

Am Riess 5, 82467 Garmisch-Partenkirchen 08821 7580 €119–€144 155 Indoor

HEIDELBERG

MOLKENKUR

www.molkenkur.de

This beautifully located hotel is in peaceful surroundings with fine views, yet just a five-minute drive from the old town. Rooms are spacious and comfortably furnished. They have large windows leading onto balconies with amazing views.

Klingenteichstrasse 31, 69117 Heidelberg 06221 654080 €88, excluding breakfast 20 Spa Free

ZUM RITTER ST. GEORG

www.ritter-heidelberg.de

The stately façade of this Renaissance building dates from 1592. Many guest rooms have been renovated. If you don't want to be in a room over Hauptstrasse, request a quieter room in the wing at the rear of the hotel.

Hauptstrasse 178, 69117 Heidelberg 06221 1350 €144–€206, excluding breakfast 37

HOHENSCHWANGAU

SCHLOSSHOTEL LISL

www.lisl.de

From many of the rooms you get unobstructed views up to castles of Neuschwanstein and Hohenschwangau. The hotel dates back more than 100 years. Today, the stylish furnishings and spacious guest rooms make this the perfect place to enjoy a relaxing stay. The hotel has a restaurant (▷ 350).

Neuschwansteinstrasse 1–3, 87645 Hohenschwangau 08362 8870 €85–€125, excluding breakfast 35

KONSTANZ

RIVA KONSTANZ

www.hotel-riva.de

The Riva, which reopened in 2008 after being thoroughly modernized, is an elegant villa-style house in a quiet traffic-free area alongside Bodensee. Surrounded by wooded gardens, this is the ideal spot for visitors to Konstanz, which is just a 10-minute walk away. For the best views request a balcony room facing the lake.

Seestrasse 25, 78464 Konstanz 07531 363090 €220–€360 45 Outdoor Spa €15

LINDAU

LINDAUER HOF

www.lindauer-hof.de

This former granary store dating from the 17th century, directly on the harbourfront, has commanding views across Bodensee (Lake Constance). The smart, modern furnishings give a warm, welcoming feelings. Some guest rooms have pine ceilings and a separate sitting room with lake views, while others have their own terrace.

Seepromenade, 88131 Lindau 08382 4064 €150–€170, excluding breakfast 32 €10

MEERSBURG

GASTHOF ZUM BÄREN

www.baeren-meersburg.de

This 15th-century inn has been owned by the same family for five generations. Guest rooms are furnished with an interesting mixture of painted furniture and country pine pieces, along with antique touches.

Marktplatz 11, 88709 Meersburg 07532 43220 €82–€108 20 Indoor/outdoor

NECKARGERACH

GRÜNER BAUM

www.gruenerbaum-neckargerach.de

This pretty little hotel, run by the Greek Papadopoulos family, offers a warm welcome. Guest rooms are basic but comfortable. Request a room with a balcony, from where you will have stunning views. The hotel has a restaurant (▷ 351).

Neckarstrasse 13, 69437 Neckargerach 06263 706 €68 14

NÜRNBERG

BURGHOTEL STAMMHAUS

www.burghotel-stamm.de

Don't be put off by the external appearance of this hotel, because the facilities are adequate. Rooms are small but the terrace is the ideal setting for breakfast.

Schildgasse 14–16, 90403 Nürnberg 0911 203040 €82–€104 22 Indoor €5–€8

GASTHAUS ROTTNER

www.rottner-hotel.de

The spacious rooms here are beautifully furnished and decorated in pastel shades.

Winterstrasse 15–17, 90431 Grossreuth, Nürnberg 0911 658480 €148–€163 37

OBERAMMERGAU

PARKHOTEL SONNENHOF

www.parkhotel-sonnenhof.de

This hotel is in a quiet area. The modern guest rooms are spacious and light, with large windows leading out onto a balcony. The hotel has a restaurant (▷ 351).

König-Ludwig-Strasse 12–16, 82487 Oberammergau 08822 9130 €65–€85 59 (non-smoking) Indoor Wellness

Below *Schlosshotel Lisl in Hohenschwangau offers good views of Neuschwanstein castle from some guest rooms*

GÄSTEHAUS NEU

www.hotel-oberammergau.com

Stay in the traditional Bavarian family home of a woodcarver. The house is near the middle of town, and all the rooms are tastefully designed.

Passionswiese 3, 82487 Oberammergau 08822 6328 €44–€52 6

RAVENSBURG

OBERTOR

www.hotelobertor.de

Foundations here date from the 13th century, and during later centuries extra floors were added. The hotel has a restaurant (▷ 352).

Marktstrasse 67, 88212 Ravensburg 0751 36670 From €110 57 Wellness

REGENSBURG

BISCHOFSHOF

www.hotel-bischofshof.de

This is a historic hotel close to the Porta Praetoria, and to St. Peter's Cathedral. The rooms are quiet and face either the courtyard or the cathedral.

Krauterermarkt 3, 93047 Regensburg 0941 58460 €138–€148 55

ORPHÉE

www.hotel-orphee.de

This hotel has three floors of nooks and crannies. The French-style café and wine bar seems unchanged since the 19th century (▷ 352).

Untere Bachgasse 8, 93047 Regensburg 0941 596020 €120–€150 31

ROTHENBURG OB DER TAUBER

SCHRANNE

www.hotel-schranne.de

This family-run hotel is fronted by a large cobbled square. The comfortable rooms are modern, spacious and tastefully furnished. The breakfast and dining rooms are excellent (▷ 352).

Schrannenplatz 6–7, 91541 Rothenburg ob der Tauber 09861 95500 €65–€115 48

SCHÖNAU AM KÖNIGSSEE

ALPENHOTEL ZECHMEISTERLEHEN

www.zechmeisterlehen.de

Guest rooms are spacious and well appointed, with lovely views from the balconies across open meadows dotted with Alpine flowers and chalets to the distant mountains.

Wahlstrasse 35, 83471 Schönau am Königssee 08652 9450 €61–€106 14 Indoor and outdoor

SCHWANGAU-HORN

HOTEL CAFÉ HELMERHOF

www.helmerhof.de

You can stay in one of the hotel's spacious rooms or fully fitted apartments, each of which has a kitchen.

Frauenbergstrasse 9, 87645 Schwangau-Horn 08362 8069 €80–€94 20 Wellness

STUTTGART

BEST WESTERN HOTEL STUTTGART 21

www.stuttgart21.bestwestern.de

The hotel is modern, but the swimming pool adds a leisurely touch all by itself. The restaurant serves Swabian and international cuisine and has a sun terrace.

Friedhofstrasse 21, 70191 Stuttgart 0711 25870 €110–€220, excluding breakfast 89 (57 non-smoking) Indoor €7 Eckhartshaldenweg

ROMANTIK HOTEL TRAUBE

www.romantik-hotel-traube.com

The hosts describe their house as being comfortable, elegant and rustic. Guest rooms are attractive, with traditional furnishings and comfortable beds.

Brabandtgasse 2, 70599 Stuttgart-Plieningen 0711 458920 €149–€199 25

PRACTICALITIES

Practicalities gives you all the important practical information you will need during your visit from money matters to emergency phone numbers.

Essential Information 358

- Weather 358
- Documents 360
- Money 361
- Health 362
- Basics 364
- Finding Help 366
- Communication 367
- Opening Times and Tickets 369
- Tourist Offices 370
- Media, Books, Maps and Films 371
- Useful Websites 373

What to Do 374

- Shopping 374
- Entertainment and Nightlife 376
- Health and Beauty 379
- Sports and Activites 380
- For Children 384
- Festivals and Events 385

Eating 386

Staying 390

Words and Phrases 392

WEATHER

CLIMATE AND WHEN TO GO

Generally speaking, Germany enjoys a mild climate, with average temperatures reaching around 20°C (68°F) in July and August and dropping to around 0°C (32°F) in December and January. Average rainfall is also fairly seasonal, with most regions receiving up to 120mm (4.75in) a month in the height of summer and less than 20mm (0.75in) in the depths of winter. Having said that, however, the weather in Germany is also very changeable, not just from year to year, but also from month to month, week to week and even day to day. Likewise, good weather in, say, western Germany is no guarantee of similar weather in the north, south or east of the country. This can make packing something of a lottery, but so long as you're prepared for cold snaps in the winter and the odd day of rain in the summer you can't go far wrong (▷ 'What to Take', opposite).

In cold winters, snow is not uncommon, particularly in the south and southeast, where higher altitudes and a more continental climate contribute to a greater variation in seasonal temperatures. Western Germany tends to experience milder winters, while northern Germany usually feels a few degrees cooler than you might expect, thanks to bracing winds blowing in off the North Sea. In warm summers, temperatures in June and July have been known to reach a little above 30°C (90°F), with the weather often remaining relatively warm and dry until well into September.

The most reliable months for a visit in terms of weather are May to the end of September, although some areas, such as the Rhine and the Mosel, are probably best avoided in July and August, when the tourist tide is at its height. For those who are interested in winter sports, the ski slopes and cross-country trails in the Alps and the Black Forest are generally open from December to the end of March, while the slopes of the Harz (▷ 236) Eifel (▷ 167) and the Rothaargebirge further north enjoy a much shorter season.

WEATHER REPORTS

For up-to-date information in English on the weather forecast for Germany, log onto specialist websites such as www.met-office.gov.uk, www.weather.com and www.weatheronline.com or your local news network such as www.bbc.co.uk or www.cnn.com. Other. Germany's official tourist information website, www.germany-tourism.de, provides brief information on the current weather in all the country's major cities. For those who know a little German, there's

BERLIN

TEMPERATURE

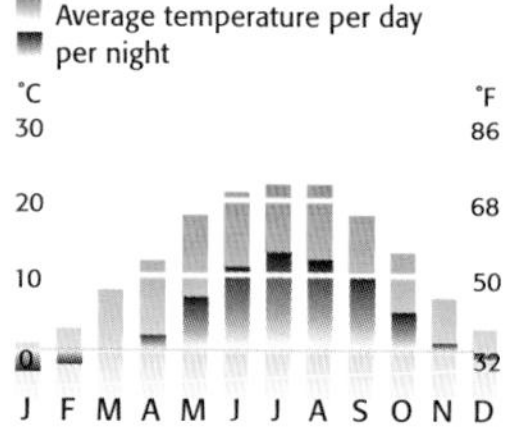

RAINFALL

www.wetteronline.de (the name doesn't necessarily mean it'll be 'wetter'!), and most national and local television networks provide regular forecasts, which should give you an idea of what to expect once you're there.

WHAT TO TAKE

Avoid packing too much, as anything you forget can invariably be bought almost anywhere in Germany. Having said that, however, be sure to pack enough clothes to cope with the sort of weather you can expect at the time of year you're planning to visit.

» Germans tend to dress quite casually, and jeans and athletic shoes are acceptable almost everywhere (with the exception of certain elegant restaurants, some nightclubs and some golf courses and so on). A tie is generally required only for casinos and business meetings. Visitors to cathedrals and other sights of religious importance should dress appropriately. If in doubt, dress as the locals dress.

» Light, waterproof jackets and/or umbrellas are useful back-ups at any time of year, while warm coats, hats and gloves will almost certainly be required in the winter months.

» Whether you're planning on trekking in the mountains or just wandering around the cities, be sure to pack a pair of sturdy, comfortable shoes.

» Electricity sockets in Germany require the standard, two-pin plugs that are used across most of mainland Europe, so visitors from the UK and the US will need to bring a travel adaptor for use with laptops and other electrical devices. Some appliances from the US may also need a transformer (check the user's manuals for details on what you need to take).

» If you are on any prescribed medication, make sure you take enough to last for your entire visit. However, many medicines—including some that are only available by prescription in other countries—can be obtained over the counter in a pharmacy (*Apotheke*; ▷ 363).

» It's a good idea to make photocopies of all important documents (passport, driver's licence and so on) and to ensure that these are kept separately from the originals. It's also a good idea to make a note of emergency phone numbers (such as those required for cancelling stolen credit cards), the serial numbers of traveller's cheques and the registration numbers of expensive items like computers, in case you need to report a loss or theft to police.

TIME ZONES

Germany is on Central European Time (CET), which is one hour ahead of Greenwich Mean Time (GMT). Daylight saving, when the clocks go forward an hour, runs from the last Sunday in March to the last Sunday in October. Compared to Germany, the time in other major cities is as follows:

CITY	TIME DIFFERENCE
Auckland	+11 hours
Dublin	-1 hour
London	-1 hour
Los Angeles	-9 hours
New York	-6 hours
Perth	+7 hours
Seattle	-9 hours
Sydney	+9 hours
Toronto	-6 hours
Vancouver	-9 hours

HAMBURG

TEMPERATURE

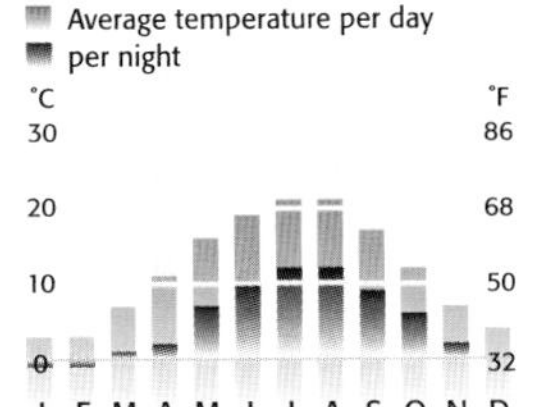

RAINFALL

KÖLN

TEMPERATURE

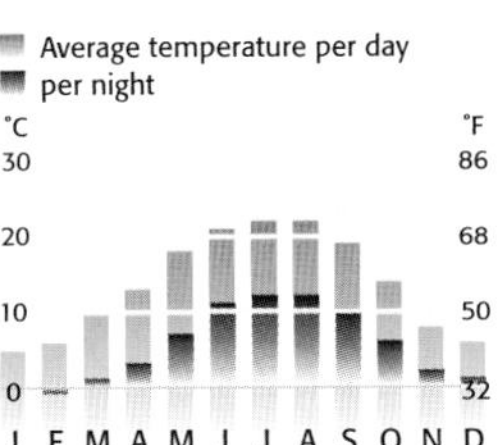

RAINFALL

Average rainfall

mm		in
120		4.5
80		3
40		1.5
0		0
	J F M A M J J A S O N D	

MÜNCHEN

TEMPERATURE

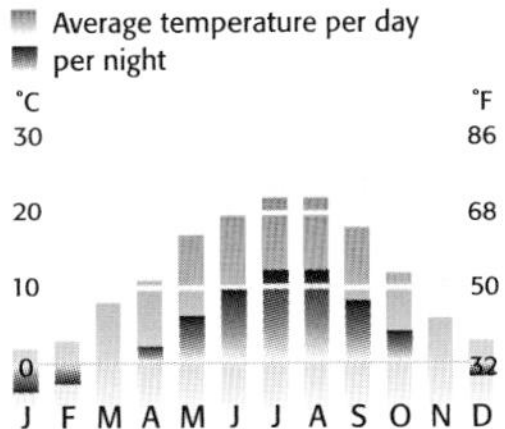

RAINFALL

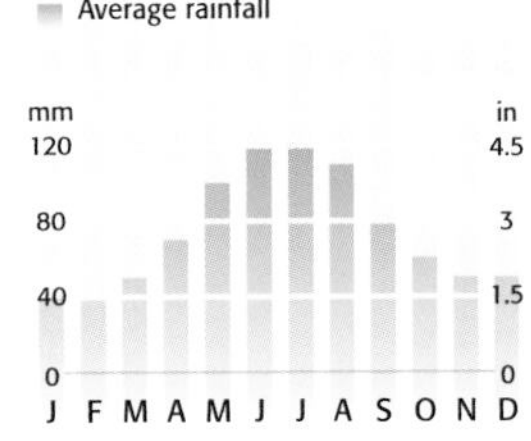

DOCUMENTS

PASSPORTS AND VISAS

» All visitors to Germany must carry a valid passport or, in the case of EU nationals, a national identification card or passport.

» EU visitors do not require a visa for entry into Germany, although for stays of more than 90 days either a residence permit or a work permit will need to be applied for.

» Visitors from Australia, Canada, New Zealand and the US require a visa only for stays exceeding 90 days. The same goes for visitors from around 40 other countries.

» Visitors from other countries require a three-month tourist visa, which can be obtained from German embassies or consulates. Fees vary depending on the country, and you may need to provide proof of having enough funds for your stay.

» The situation can change at short notice, so check with the German embassy in your home country before you travel.

TRAVEL INSURANCE

» In addition to covering the loss or theft of money and belongings, make sure your travel insurance covers repatriation in the event of an emergency.

» If you're planning to take part in any sports or adventurous activities, you should ensure you are covered for these.

» Report losses or thefts to the police as soon as possible (check individual insurance policies to see if there is a specified time limit), and be sure to obtain a signed and dated copy of your statement, as many insurance companies won't pay you any money without one.

HEALTH INSURANCE

» Visitors who live in a European Union country are advised to acquire a European Health Insurance

GERMAN EMBASSIES AND CONSULATES ABROAD

COUNTRY	ADDRESS	TELEPHONE
Australia	119 Empire Circuit, Yarralumla, A.C.T. 2600	02 6270 1911
	480 Punt Road, South Yarra VIC 3141	03 9864 6888
	13 Trelawney Street, Woollahra, NSW 2025	02 9328 7733
Canada	1 Waverly Street, Ottawa, Ontario, K2P OT8	613/232 1101
New Zealand	90–92 Hobson Street, Thorndon, Wellington	04 473 6063
Republic of Ireland	31 Trimleston Avenue, Booterstown, Blackrock, Co. Dublin	01 269 3011
UK	23 Belgrave Square, London, SW1X 8PZ	020 7824 1300
	16 Eglinton Crescent, Edinburgh, EH12 5DG	0131 337 2323
US	4645 Reservoir Road NW, Washington, DC 20007–1998	202/298-4000
	676 North Michigan Avenue, Suite 3200, Chicago, IL 60611	312/202-0480
	6222 Wilshire Boulevard, Suite 500, Los Angeles, CA 90048	323/930-2703
	871 United Nations Plaza, New York, NY 10017	212/610-9700

DUTY-FREE ALLOWANCES AND DUTY-PAID GUIDELINES

Visiting from another EU country

The amounts shown below are in line with other EU countries. There is no limit on the amount of foreign currency or euros that you can bring into Germany. Tax-paid goods for personal use (such as video cameras) can be brought in from other EU countries without customs charges being incurred. Guidance levels for tax-paid goods bought in the EU are as follows: Visiting Germany from outside the EU

» 3200 cigarettes or
» 400 cigarillos or
» 200 cigars or
» 3kg of smoking tobacco

» 10 litres of spirits or
» 20 litres of fortified wine (such as port or sherry) or
» 90 litres of wine (of which only 60 litres can be sparkling wine) or
» 110 litres of beer

You are entitled to these allowances only if you travel with the goods and do not plan to sell them. Check the latest position with the customs department in your home country.

» 200 cigarettes or
» 100 cigarillos or
» 50 cigars or
» 250g of smoking tobacco

» 1 litre of spirits or strong liqueurs
» 2 litres of still table wine or 2 litres of fortified wine, sparkling wine or other liqueurs
» 50cc of perfume
» 250cc/ml of eau de toilette

CONVERSION CHART

From	To	Multiply by
Inches	Centimetres	2.54
Centimetres	Inches	0.3937
Feet	Metres	0.3048
Metres	Feet	3.2810
Yards	Metres	0.9144
Metres	Yards	1.0940
Miles	Kilometres	1.6090
Kilometres	Miles	0.6214
Acres	Hectares	0.4047
Hectares	Acres	2.4710
Gallons	Litres	4.5460
Litres	Gallons	0.2200
Ounces	Grams	28.35
Grams	Ounces	0.0353
Pounds	Grams	453.6
Grams	Pounds	0.0022
Pounds	Kilograms	0.4536
Kilograms	Pounds	2.205
Tons	Tonnes	1.0160
Tonnes	Tons	0.9842

Card (EHIC) before leaving home. This entitles you to reciprocal healthcare in any EU country. In the UK, application forms can be obtained from any post office; the cards themselves are issued free of charge by the National Health Service.

In Ireland, application forms are available from local health offices, health centres and community care centres, and should be delivered to your local health office.

Without this card, you may be charged private rates, and your insurance company may not refund costs that you could have avoided with an EHIC. Even with an EHIC, private insurance is still recommended.

» For those visiting Germany from outside the EU, private health insurance is strongly recommended.

MONEY

THE EURO

Germany's currency is the euro (indicated by the symbol €), which at the time of writing it shares with 12 other EU countries (Austria, Belgium, Cyprus, Finland, France, Greece, Italy, Luxembourg, Malta, the Netherlands, Portugal, the Republic of Ireland, Slovenia and Spain). All euro coins have one side dedicated to their country of origin, while all euro notes are exactly the same across the euro zone. Both coins and notes can be used in any of the countries listed above, regardless of where they were minted or printed.

BEFORE YOU GO

It's a good idea to take a combination of cash, traveller's cheques and credit cards when travelling to Germany, so that you don't have to rely on any one means of paying for things in the event of an emergency. Change a small amount of cash before you go or when you get to the airport—enough to cover you for a day or two.

Traveller's cheques are a safe bet for the rest of your money, but make a note of the serial numbers and keep these in a safe place, separate from the cheques themselves.

Also check with your credit or debit card company whether you can withdraw money from ATMs (cashpoints); the exchange rate is usually quite good, although you may have to pay a fixed fee each time you withdraw money, so it makes sense not to take it out in small amounts. Make a note of the number you need to call if your card is stolen. Internationally recognized credit cards, in particular MasterCard and Visa, are accepted at major hotels, fuel stations, large shops and supermarkets, but it's always a good idea to check in advance in smaller hotels, restaurants and shops, as they may prefer cash.

EXCHANGE RATES

The exchange rate for the euro is subject to daily fluctuations. Please check before you travel.

BANKS

There are plenty of banks throughout Germany, and most will exchange foreign currency. International airports and many bigger cities also have currency exchanges (*Wechselstuben*).

ATMS

Automatic teller machines (ATMs, or cashpoints) are widespread throughout Germany, and can be found in all but the smallest towns and villages. Cards with a Maestro, Cirrus, Delta or Plus logo can be used to withdraw cash and pay for goods and services all over the country. Many credit and debit cards are now allocated a four-digit security number that can be used instead of a signature. If you don't have a security number, you may need to show another form of ID, such as a passport or driver's licence, when paying for goods over the counter.

EXCHANGING MONEY

Banks and currency exchanges (*Wechselstuben*) invariably charge a flat fee or a commission (typically €3 for amounts under €100, or 1 per cent—with a minimum charge of €5—for amounts above €100). Currency exchanges offer reasonable rates, and can be found at all international airports and main train stations throughout Germany. Money can also be changed at some of the bigger post offices in major towns and cities. Traveller's cheques can be changed in banks, currency exchanges and post offices, but they aren't usually accepted as payment in shops, restaurants and hotels.

WIRING MONEY

Money can be wired from home, but it's very expensive (as much as 10 per cent commission is charged for small amounts) and so is best avoided if at all possible. If you find yourself short of money, Western Union (www.westernunion.com) and MoneyGram (www.moneygram.com) can arrange instant cash transfers through many of Germany's major main street banks.

LOST OR STOLEN CREDIT CARDS	
American Express	0800 1012362
www.americanexpress.com	
Diner's Club	069 66166123
www.dinersclub.com	
MasterCard	0800 8191040
www.mastercard.com	
Visa	0800 8118440
www.visa.com	
These are the numbers to call from Germany	

10 EVERYDAY ITEMS AND HOW MUCH THEY COST	
Cup of tea or coffee	€1–€2
Bottle of water	25c–€2
Glass of wine	€2–€4
Glass of beer	€2–€3
Daily paper	60c–€1
20 cigarettes	€3.50–€4
Sandwich	€2.50–€4
Ice cream	€1–€1.50
Litre (0.26 US gallons) of petrol	€1.40

TAX REFUNDS

VAT, or sales tax, is called *Mehrwertsteuer* (MwSt) in Germany, and currently stands at 19 per cent (7 per cent on some goods and services).

Residents of non-EU countries can reclaim this tax on purchases at the higher rate (minus any administrative fees) when they leave the EU. Not all shops stock the necessary tax-free shopping cheques, so if you're planning on buying anything expensive, it's worth double checking this beforehand. (This facility is often indicated by a sign in the window saying 'tax-free for tourists' in English.) Participating shops will issue a cheque for the amount to be refunded, which can then be cashed at a VAT cash refund office (found at all international airports and sea ports). The cheque, along with the receipt, must be stamped by customs when you leave the country, and strictly speaking you're not allowed to use tax-free goods until you've left the EU.

Alternatively, tax can also be reclaimed through the Global Refund Tax Free Shopping Service, which is offered by major retailers all over the world. For more details, log onto www.globalrefund.com.

DISCOUNTS

Children, students and senior citizens can get substantial discounts for many services and attractions in Germany, from public transportation to museum admissions. With this in mind, it's always a good idea to carry some proof of age or status, such as a passport, International Student Identity Card (ISIC) or International Youth Travel Card (IYTC). You can get an ISIC from your student union or from ISIC issuing offices worldwide; information is available from the International Student Travel Confederation (www.istc.org). Both an ISIC and an IYTC cost US$22 or £7.

TIPPING

At restaurants, bistros and cafés, the service charge is always included in the bill, so tipping is not compulsory, although most people will round up the bill, perhaps adding 5 to 10 per cent. For other services, the following are rough guidelines:

Bar service	Change
Tour guide	Optional
Hairdresser	5–10 per cent
Taxi driver	5–10 per cent
Chambermaid	€3–€6

HEALTH

Germany's national health service works alongside the private sector, and hospitals and clinics are of a very high standard. Visitors from EU countries can claim free medical treatment, provided they have a European Health Insurance Card (EHIC, ▷ 361 and below for details). However, private health insurance is still recommended—and essential for visitors from non-EU countries.

BEFORE YOU GO

» No inoculations are required for visiting Germany, although it's a good idea to make sure your tetanus protection is up to date (boosters are required every 10 years).

» If you are on any medication and think you might need a prescription refill while you're away, ask for it from your own doctor well before you travel, and keep the packaging and/or the prescription in case you run out or lose your medication while you're in Germany and need a further supply.

» If you are planning to stay in Germany for a month or more, it may also be a good idea to have a full dental and medical check-up before you go.

WHAT TO TAKE

Although Germany hasn't got a reputation for scorching summers, the sun can still be quite fierce, so it's important to take plenty of high-SPF sunscreen. If you're travelling with children, it is best to use sunblock, and ensure they wear a hat and T-shirt if they are out in the sun for any length of time.

A basic first-aid kit is also useful, including:

» After-sun to soothe sore, sunburned skin.

» Wet wipes for cleaning and refreshment.

» Antihistamine cream for insect stings or bites.

» Antihistamine pills if you suffer from hay fever.

» Antiseptic cream, spray or wipes for cuts and grazes.

» Fabric plasters (Band Aids).

» Motion sickness remedies, if this is likely to be a problem.

» Painkillers such as paracetamol (acetominophen) for colds, and ibuprofen for muscular aches and pains.

IF YOU NEED TREATMENT

The quality of healthcare in Germany is comparable to that of the UK, US and Canada. Germany has an agreement with other EU countries that entitles all EU citizens to free reciprocal healthcare, including emergency hospital treatment. However, to take advantage of this, UK or Ireland residents must have a European Health Insurance Card (EHIC). The EHIC should not be seen as an alternative to adequate travel insurance, as (for example) reciprocal healthcare will not cover the costs of repatriation in the event of an emergency, or the cost of travel plans that have to be curtailed as a result of illness. Nor does it cover private treatment.

US visitors should check that their existing travel/health insurance is valid in Germany.

EMERGENCY TREATMENT

In the event of an emergency, go to the casualty department (Emergency Room) of the nearest hospital; for most minor ailments, visit a pharmacy (*Apotheke*) or a doctor (see below).

FINDING A DOCTOR

If you need a doctor (*Arzt*), ask at your hotel or your nearest pharmacy, who will be able to find one who is on call.

FINDING A HOSPITAL

Public hospitals are listed in the phone book under *Krankenhäuser*, although most hotels and guest houses should be able to point you in the right direction if required.

PHARMACIES

Pharmacies (*Apotheken*) can be found in every town and many villages in Germany. They are more common than they are in the UK or US, although in Germany they generally stock pharmaceuticals, toiletries and cosmetics, which are also available at a *Drogerie*.

German pharmacists are highly trained and can offer excellent over-the-counter advice; as such they're usually the first port of call for minor ailments, or if you're not sure whether or not you need to see a doctor. Generally speaking, you should be able to find someone who speaks at least some English to help you decide.

If you think you might need a prescription refill while you're away, ask your doctor for the chemical name (rather than the brand name) of the drug before you travel, as it may be marketed under a different name in Germany.

In larger towns, a rotation system ensures that there is always at least one pharmacy open 24 hours a day—which one it is on any given night is displayed in other pharmacy windows in the area.

WATER

It is completely safe to drink the tap water in Germany, although mineral water (*Mineralwasser*) is also widely available. It's sold *mit Kohlensäure* (carbonated) or *still* (still).

SUMMER AND WINTER HAZARDS

If you find yourself in the middle of a summer heatwave, take adequate precautions against sunburn and dehydration. Wear light, loose-fitting clothing and cover all exposed areas with high-SPF sunscreen. Drink at least 2 litres (4 pints) of water or other non-diuretic drinks a day (diuretic drinks such as tea and coffee actually contribute to dehydration by making you want to go to the toilet), and avoid doing anything too strenuous in the heat of the midday sun, particularly if you've got any children in tow.

In winter, it's important to stay wrapped up, especially if you're planning on skiing, trekking or mountaineering. Wear lots of thin layers rather than one thick one, carry a warm hat and gloves and take a waterproof jacket.

SUNBURN INDEX

INDEX	SKIN TYPE			
	Fair, burns	**Fair, tans**	**Brown skin**	**Black skin**
1/2	Low	Low	Low	Low
3/4	Medium	Low	Low	Low
5	High	Medium	Low	Low
6	Very high	Medium	Medium	Low
7	Very high	High	Medium	Medium
8	Very high	High	Medium	Medium
9	Very high	High	Medium	Medium
10	Very high	High	High	Medium

Low risk: The sun is not likely to harm you, but you should still use suncream.
Medium risk: Do not stay in direct sunlight for more than 1–2 hours.
High risk: You could burn in 30–60 minutes. Avoid direct sunlight, cover up and use sunscreen of SPF 15+.
Very high risk: You could burn in 20–30 minutes. Avoid direct sunlight, cover up and use sunscreen of SPF 15+.

HEALTHY FLYING

» Visitors to Germany from as far as the US, Australia or New Zealand may be concerned about the effect of long-haul flights on their health. The most widely publicized concern is Deep Vein Thrombosis, or DVT. Misleadingly called 'economy class syndrome', DVT is the forming of a blood clot in the body's deep veins, particularly in the legs. The clot can move around the bloodstream and could be fatal.

» Those most at risk include the elderly, pregnant women and those using the contraceptive pill, smokers and the overweight. If you are at increased risk of DVT see your doctor before departing. Flying increases the likelihood of DVT because passengers are often seated in a cramped position for long periods of time and may become dehydrated.

To minimize risk:
Drink water (not alcohol)
Don't stay immobile for hours at a time
Stretch and exercise your legs periodically
Do wear elastic flight socks, which support veins and reduce the chances of a clot forming

EXERCISES

1 Ankle Rotations
Lift feet off the floor. Draw a circle with the toes, moving one foot clockwise and the other counterclockwise

2 Calf Stretches
Start with heel on the floor and point foot upward as high as you can. Then lift heels high keeping balls of feet on the floor

3 Knee Lifts
Lift leg with knee bent while contracting your thigh muscle. Then straighten leg pressing foot flat to the floor

Other health hazards for flyers are airborne diseases and bugs spread by the plane's air-conditioning system. These are largely unavoidable but if you have a serious medical condition seek advice from a doctor before flying.

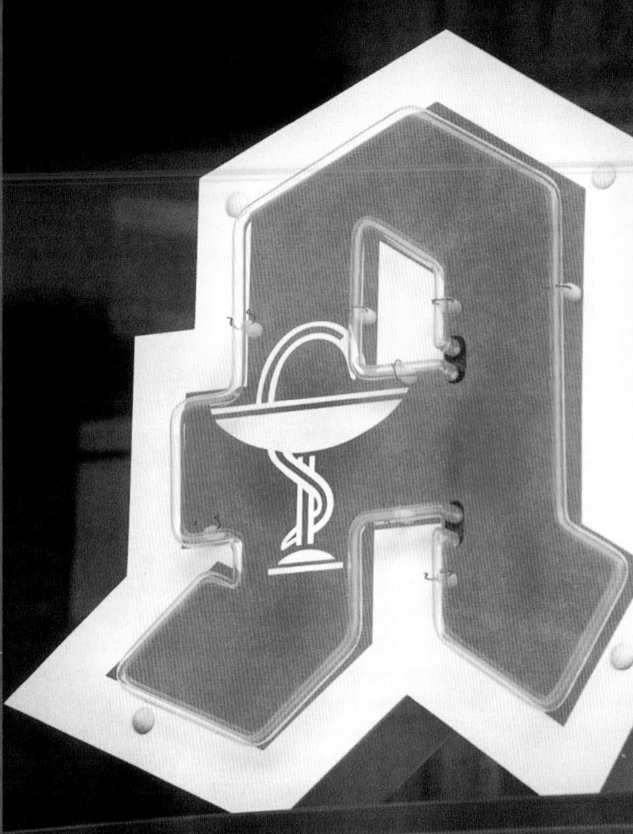

BASICS

ELECTRICITY

The power supply in Germany is 230V AC (which in practice means 220V–240V). Sockets take plugs with two round pins, so if you're planning on using your own electrical appliances such as hairdryers, laptops or radios, bring a travel adaptor with you (they don't cost very much and are sold at most international airports). Visitors from the US (where the power supply is 110V) should also bring a transformer from home, as these are harder to find in Germany.

LAUNDRY

All the major cities and many of the smaller towns in Germany have coin-operated laundrettes, or *Waschsalons*. Campsites often have their own washing facilities, and many hotels also offer a laundry service, although this is usually charged per item and so can get quite expensive when you start throwing in socks, underwear, T-shirts and the like.

MEASUREMENTS

The metric system is used throughout Germany. Distances and speed limits are given in kilometres and kph, fuel is sold by the litre, and food is sold by the gram or kilogram.

PUBLIC TOILETS

Finding a public toilet (*öffentliche Toilette*) in Germany isn't usually a problem, particularly in major towns and cities. Toilets in bars, restaurants and department stores are generally free, although it's impolite to use them without buying anything or asking first.

There are also public toilets at most train stations, bus stations and shopping malls, but there's often a charge for using them (from 30c to 50c). If there's an attendant on duty, it's polite to tip him or her around 20c–50c, but only if the toilet is clean. Major train stations, bus stations and international airports may also have shower facilities.

DENTAL TREATMENT

Dental treatment is expensive in Germany, so if you're having any problems with your teeth it makes sense to get them looked at before you travel. It's also a good idea to make sure your travel or medical insurance covers the cost of emergency dental care. If you need a dentist (*Zahnarzt*), again your hotel will be able to help, or ask at the pharmacy.

OPTICIANS

If you wear glasses or contact lenses, remember to take spares with you, and have a copy of your prescription handy in case you break or lose them. If you're going for a few weeks and don't want to carry lots of contact lens solution with you, it's easy enough to resupply at any *Apotheke* (pharmacy). Opticians (*Optiker*) are listed in the phone book.

COMMON AILMENTS

The two most common ailments you're likely to suffer from in Germany are diarrhoea (from eating unfamiliar foods) and dehydration (from not drinking enough on hot days or during periods of prolonged activity).

The former is unlikely to last more than a day or two, while the latter is easily treated with plenty of sugary drinks (water alone often isn't enough), or, in severe cases, a rehydration solution.

ALTERNATIVE MEDICINE

There is a long tradition of alternative medicine, or *Heilpraxis*, in Germany, particularly at spa resorts and towns.

For a list of practitioners, including osteopaths, chiropractors, homoeopaths and acupuncturists, look up '*Heilpraktiker*' in the local phone book.

SMOKING

In most of Germany's *Länder* (states), smoking is forbidden in bars, café-bars and restaurants, except in special smokers' rooms that (if they exist at all) must be sealed off from other guests. Among other places where smoking bans apply are dance clubs, public transportation and government buildings. There may be slight variations from state to state in the scope and implementation of their no-smoking laws.

LOCAL WAYS

If you're hoping to use your language skills, be aware that there are two forms of 'you' in German: the informal '*du*' and the more polite '*Sie*.' In general, you should always use *Sie* unless invited to do otherwise. Children, who are generally addressed as *du* by adults, are the only exception to this rule. Similarly, females should be addressed as *Frau* (Mrs) rather than *Fräulein* (Miss), and doctors should be addressed as *Herr Doktor*. Most Germans will be fairly forgiving if you get this sort of thing wrong, but they'll warm to you more quickly if they can see you're making an effort to get it right.

When being introduced to Germans, expect to shake hands with the men and sometimes to kiss the women on both cheeks—take your lead from the people you are being introduced to. If you're invited to someone's house for lunch or dinner, it's usually considered polite to take a small gift such as a bunch of flowers or a bottle of wine. Another thing to bear in mind about Germans is that they take a fairly relaxed view of nudity. It's not uncommon to see naked women in adverts or on the covers of mainstream magazines, and some beaches and spa baths encourage nude bathing.

CHILDREN

Germany is generally child-friendly, and family days out are commonplace throughout the country. There are numerous theme parks geared towards younger children (▷ 384), and most museums, theatres and zoos offer substantial discounts for younger visitors. Many hotels and guest houses also offer reduced rates for children, and public transportation, depending on the jurisdiction, is free for children under four, five, or six, and half-price for under-12s, under-13s, or under-14s.

Informal restaurants, bistros and cafés generally welcome children of all ages, particularly during the day or early in the evening, but if you do want to leave them behind, many hotels offer a babysitting service. Similarly, most tourist offices keep up-to-date lists of recommended babysitters and details of (usually very good) childcare facilities. Car-rental companies can supply child safety seats for a nominal fee, but these must be reserved in advance. Finally, all manner of baby foods, milks, nappies (diapers) and other infant essentials can be found in most German supermarkets.

VISITORS WITH A DISABILITY

Germany is quite a wheelchair-friendly country, although other disabilities (such as blindness) tend to be less well catered for. Many museums, theatres and cinemas, plus train and bus stations, are wheelchair accessible, as are autobahn rest stops. Most trains and U-Bahns are also wheelchair accessible, and trams and buses are slowly catching up. The government agency responsible for assisting people with a disability publishes a number of useful leaflets on places and hotels with suitable facilities. For further details, write to Hilfe für Behinderte (Help for the Disabled), Kirchfeldstrasse 149, 40215 Düsseldorf; tel 0211 310060; www.bag-selbsthilfe.de.

In the UK, Tourism for All (The Hawkins Suite, Enham Place, Enham Alamein, Andover SP11 6JS; tel 0845 124 9971; www.holidaycare.org.uk) has information on accessibility for visitors with disabilities. In the US, SATH (Society for Accessible Travel and Hospitality) has lots of tips for visitors with visual impairment or reduced mobility (www.sath.org). Mobility International USA (www.miusa.org) also offers advice (▷ 66).

PLACES OF WORSHIP

The two main religions in Germany are Catholicism and Protestantism, although there are also sizeable Muslim and Jewish communities—plus dozens of other religions—all over the country. The south of Germany is predominantly Catholic while the north and east are predominantly Protestant, although there are pockets of Catholicism in the far north. Religious tolerance is preached and (to a large extent) practised throughout Germany, and although religion is no longer as important as it was, say, 20 or 30 years ago, it still plays a large part in many people's lives. Most tourist offices (▷ 370) have information on local places of worship and service times, as do the places themselves.

FINDING HELP

If you have any concerns about your safety while you're in Germany, immediately talk to an English-speaking member of staff at your hotel or at your nearest tourist office, as they will almost certainly be able to advise you on where to go for help.

PERSONAL SECURITY

Germany is quite a safe country and crimes committed against visitors are rare, although some of the larger cities inevitably have areas that are best avoided (these are usually away from the main tourist areas, so shouldn't really present a problem). There are, however, some sensible precautions that are worth taking wherever you are:

» Never carry more cash with you than you need, and keep all valuable and irreplaceable items in your hotel room or, better still, in a hotel safety deposit box. Write down credit card and traveller's cheque numbers and keep them in a safe place.

» Carry bags and cameras slung diagonally across your chest rather than over one shoulder, and position them under one arm in busy places. Backpacks might seem like a good idea, but when they're worn using both straps it's almost impossible to keep an eye on them. If you must use a backpack, make sure that the zips are either lockable (i.e. with a miniature padlock) or hard to access. Again, if you're at all concerned about busy crowds, turn the backpack around and wear it on your front where you can see it.

» In public places, keep belongings close by: Try to get out of the habit of leaving wallets, mobile phones, sun-glasses and the like on tables, as this just increases the chances of them being stolen or forgotten. In busy eateries, particularly outside, make sure bags are securely closed, and put a chair leg through a strap to dissuade would-be thieves.

» Be wary of anyone who appears to invade your personal space, particularly if they bump into you. Avoid keeping wallets and other valuables in back pockets, where they're easy to get to. Similarly, never leave luggage or valuables on display in a parked car—in fact, even maps and other travel paraphernalia are a giveaway to a potential thief, so try to keep everything hidden whenever you're away from your car for any length of time.

» At night, stick to brightly lit, main streets whenever possible and avoid quiet areas.

LOST PROPERTY

If you lose money or valuables, inform the police and, depending on the small print of your policy, your travel insurance company as soon as possible (to be covered, lost or stolen belongings often have to be reported within 24 hours).

Similarly, if your traveller's cheques are lost or stolen, notify the issuing company and tell them the serial numbers of the missing cheques (for this reason, it's also a good idea to keep a note of their telephone number and the serial numbers of the cheques you have spent).

LOSS OF PASSPORT

» Always keep a copy of your passport number, and make a photocopy of the page that carries your details. Store both of these separately from your passport in case it is stolen.

» If you're really organized, you could also scan the relevant page of your passport and email it to an account that's accessible from any computer, such as at www.hotmail.com.

» Finally, if you do lose your passport or have it stolen, report it to the police as soon as possible, and contact your nearest embassy or consulate for assistance (▷ below).

EMERGENCY NUMBERS	
Ambulance/Emergency Doctor (Rettungsdienst/Notartz)	112
Fire Brigade (Feuerwehr)	112
Police (Polizei)	110
Roadside Rescue (ADAC—Allgemeiner Deutscher Automobil-Club)	01802 222222

CONTACTING YOUR EMBASSY OR CONSULATE

Many countries are represented by an embassy in Berlin, and may also operate consulates in major cities. In addition to the main embassies in Berlin, for example, there are British, American and Canadian consulates in Düsseldorf, Hamburg, Stuttgart and Munich, and British and Australian consulates in Frankfurt.

EMERGENCIES

In an emergency, phone 110 for the police and 112 for the fire or ambulance services. The latter number can be phoned from anywhere in the EU for any type of emergency. It's worth emphasizing, however, that 110 is an emergency number only, and should not be used for non-urgent calls, such as reporting a theft. Thefts should be reported to your nearest police station, where you should be able to find someone who speaks at least a little English. You will need to show some form of photo ID when reporting a theft. Many insurance companies won't pay out for lost or stolen goods without a police report, so for expensive items it's worth the trouble.

CONTACTING YOUR EMBASSY IN BERLIN

If you lose your passport or are arrested, contact your embassy at the address below:

Australia	Wallstrasse 76–79, 10179 Berlin	tel 030 880 0880
Canada	Leipziger Platz 17, 10117 Berlin	tel 030 203120
New Zealand	Friedrichstrasse 60, 10117 Berlin	tel 030 206210
Republic of Ireland	Friedrichstrasse 200, 10117 Berlin	tel 030 220720
UK	Wilhelmstrasse 70–71, 10117 Berlin	tel 030 204570
US	Neustädtische Kirchstrasse 4–5, 10117 Berlin	tel 030 83050

COMMUNICATION

With internet cafés springing up all over Germany and with email access now available in many hotels, keeping in touch while you're away has never been easier. Many mobile phones can be used all over Europe, although call charges can be expensive, and mobile companies also charge a premium for receiving a call from home.

Text messages are one way of keeping costs down, but if you're planning on phoning home a lot, it may be worth investing in a prepaid phone card.

AREA CODES WITHIN GERMANY	
Berlin	030
Bonn	0228
Dresden	0351
Düsseldorf	0211
Frankfurt	069
Hamburg	040
Köln (Cologne)	0221
Leipzig	0341
München (Munich)	089
Stuttgart	0711

POSTAGE RATES FOR LETTERS UP TO 20G	
Within Germany	55c
To western Europe	55c
To eastern Europe	55c
To Australia	E1.55
To America	E1.55
To Africa	E1.55
To Asia	E1.55

TELEPHONES

As you'd expect, the telephone system in Germany is fast, efficient and relatively inexpensive. The country code for Germany is 49, and the main phone company is Deutsche Telekom. To call the UK from Germany, dial 00 44, then drop the first 0 from the area code before dialling the rest of the number.
To call the US, simply preface the area code and number with 001.
To call Germany from abroad, dial the relevant international access code (i.e. 00 from the UK and 011 from the US) and the country code (49), followed by the local area code without the initial zero, and then the number.

PUBLIC TELEPHONES

Most pay phones in Germany accept only phone cards (*Telefonkarten*), which can be bought at tourist or post offices, fuel stations, newspaper kiosks and elsewhere. International calls can be made from all pay phones except for those marked *National*. Phone calls can also be made from main post offices, where the connection will be made for you; you pay after the call has been completed. If you're using a phone card to call abroad, shop around for the best rates (these are usually printed on the back of the cards), as these vary from company to company. Similarly, avoid using the phone in your hotel room for external calls, as this could well work out to be up to four times more expensive than using a pay phone. If you must call from your room, get the person at the other

INTERNATIONAL DIALLING CODES	
To call home from Germany, dial the international access code (00) followed by the country code:	
Australia	61
Canada	1
New Zealand	64
Republic of Ireland	353
UK	44
US	1

USEFUL TELEPHONE NUMBERS	
Directory enquiries (national)	11833
Directory enquiries (international)	11834
Directory enquiries (English-speaking)	11837

USING A COIN-OPERATED PHONE

1. Lift the receiver and listen for the dial tone.
2. Insert phone card or coins. The coin drops as soon as you insert it.
3. Dial or key in the number.
4. If you want to cancel the call before it is answered, or if the call does not connect, press the coin release lever or hang up and take the coins from the coin return.
5. Once your call is answered, the display will show how much money or units you have left. Unused coins will be returned after the call.

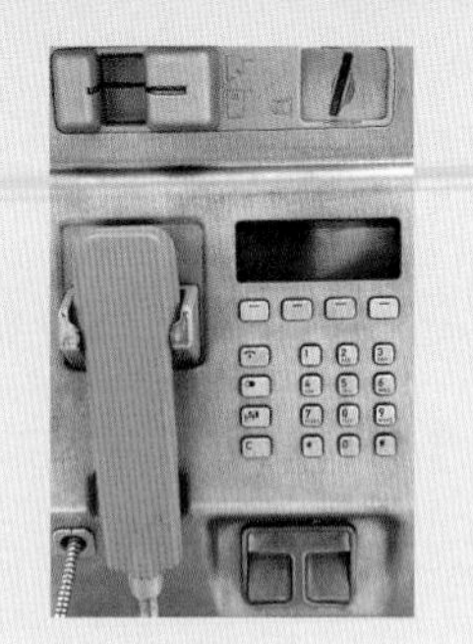

end to call you back, as they'll only be charged their standard national or international rate.

The number for directory questions is 11833 for domestic numbers, 11834 for foreign numbers and 11837 for English-language enquiries. Call rates from private phones are lower after 6pm and at weekends, but public phones cost the same no matter what time you call.

MOBILE PHONES

Check with your mobile supplier to see if your phone will work in Germany, and to find out what the charges will be to make and receive calls and text messages. Most phones bought in the UK are dual band, and should work all over Europe. For visitors from North America, only tri-band phones will work in Europe. Again, if you're unsure whether your phone is dual band or tri-band, check with your supplier. Don't forget to take a phone charger and a plug adaptor in case the batteries run low.

POSTAL SERVICES

Mail boxes in Germany are bright yellow and can be found outside and inside main post offices. Stamps (*Briefmarken*) can be bought from the post office counter or from stamp machines near the entrance—it's usually clear on these which stamps are required for postcards and/or letters abroad. In areas popular with visitors, some souvenir shops may also sell stamps, but don't count on it. Post offices (*die Post*) are normally found in the middle of towns and cities and are often at or near the train station. *Poste restante* letters and parcels can be sent to any German post office: Simply mark the item '*postlagernd—bitte halten*', and then write your surname in capitals followed by the address of the post office. You will usually be asked to show some ID, such as a passport or driver's licence, when collecting it. Officially, post offices will only hang on to uncollected mail for two weeks, so it's a good idea to plan any advance correspondence carefully. The postal service in Germany is generally quite quick: Letters sent within Germany usually arrive the following day, while letters to the rest of Europe may take three to four days. Letters sent to North America, Australia or Asia should take around a week, although they can take longer.

INTERNET ACCESS

There are plenty of internet cafés dotted all over Germany, so you shouldn't have any problem finding one in most major cities. Many hotels also offer internet access, either via a high-speed ISDN line in each room, or from a computer at or near reception. Expect to pay anything from €1 to €2 for every half-hour.

OPENING TIMES AND TICKETS

Germany's traditionally strict shopping laws have been relaxed in recent years, which means that shops can now stay open until 8pm from Monday to Saturday, although that's not to say they actually do so. For the most part, only bakeries are open on Sunday and even they may open up for only a few hours during the morning. Some *Länder* (states) are planning to permit longer opening hours.

BANKS

Banks tend to open from 8.30 or 9 and close at 4 (6 on Thursdays). Those in smaller towns may close for an hour or two at lunchtime. Banks are closed at weekends, although currency exchanges (particularly those at airports and train stations) may stay open from 6am to 10pm, seven days a week.

BARS, RESTAURANTS AND CAFÉS

Eateries and bars are generally open all day, although some live-music venues may open in the evening only. Bars tend to stay open until at least 1 or 2am, while many restaurants and cafés will close at midnight and will stop serving food at 10 or 11pm. Cafés usually open at 8 or 9am, while restaurants open for lunch at 11 or 11.30. In smaller towns and villages, particularly in the winter, restaurants may serve food only between 12 and 2pm and then again after 5 or 6.

CHURCHES

Churches have sporadic opening hours, but most—particularly the more famous churches and cathedrals—are open for at least a few hours every morning and a few hours every afternoon, six or seven days a week. There is rarely, if ever, a charge for entry and most publish a leaflet or fact sheet in English as well as German.

MUSEUMS

Museum opening hours vary, but they're generally from 9 or 10 until 5 or 6, with or without a one-hour break for lunch between 1 and 2. Many of the bigger art galleries, particularly in major cities, are open late (7 or 8) one evening a week. Most are closed for one day each week, usually Mondays.

TOURIST INFORMATION OFFICES

Tourist information offices also keep varying hours, but most of them are open from around 9 to 5 on weekdays and 10 to 1 on Saturdays. In the high season (April to the end of September) they may also be open on Sundays, and in major cities they will often stay open seven days a week (and occasionally well into the evening).

OFFICES

Standard business hours in Germany vary greatly, but are generally from 9 to 5 or 5.30. Government offices may close earlier, at 4 from Monday to Thursday, and as early as 1 on Fridays.

SHOPS

Shops in Germany tend to be open from 9 to 5 or 6 on weekdays and 9 to 4 or 5 on Saturdays. In smaller towns and villages, particularly in the winter, shops may close at 1 or 2 on Saturdays. Larger shops, such as department stores and supermarkets, may stay open later on weekdays and on Saturdays (i.e. until 7 or 8), while fuel stations are often open until 9 or 10pm, if not later.

ADMISSION CHARGES

Most visitor attractions in Germany charge an admission fee, and these can start to add up if you're paying for a whole family. To encourage you to visit more places, some cities sell welcome cards, which entitle you to significant discounts in museums, as well as free public transportation. If you're planning on packing it in, these cards are definitely worth the initial outlay. (See the individual sight entries for details.)

Some museums offer free or reduced-price entry on a certain day or after a certain time—again, check individual entries for details, or ask at your nearest tourist information office.

NATIONAL HOLIDAYS	
New Year's Day	1 January
Good Friday	March/April
Easter Monday	Monday after Good Friday
May Day	1 May
Ascension Day	May
Whit Monday	May/June
Unification Day	3 October
Christmas Day	25 December

YOUTH AND STUDENT DISCOUNTS

Full-time (but not part-time) students can buy an international student identity card, or ISIC (▷ 362), which provides proof of student status as well as entitling users to a wide range of reductions on everything from air fares to CDs. Under-27s can buy the International Youth Travel Card (IYTC) (▷ 362), which offers similar benefits, although at most attractions discounts are available only for full-time students or children aged 18 or under.

TOURIST OFFICES

Almost every town and village in Germany has a tourist information office, and the staff invariably speak at least some English. In larger towns and cities, staff members are likely to be pretty fluent, so getting hold of advice and information on your destination should never be a problem. Similarly, almost every tourist office has at least some printed information in English, even if it's just a map and a town guide; in bigger cities there's almost as much information available in English as there is in German.

Many tourist information offices also operate an accommodation reservation service, where you tell them your budget and the sort of place you're looking for, and they phone around to reserve a room for you. The service is free in many places, but even when there's a charge it's unlikely to be more than a euro or two. Even if you're not looking for somewhere to stay, tourist information offices make a great first point of contact when you've just arrived in a region or city. Many tourist information offices run a variety of guided tours, and although these might sound a bit touristy, a few hours in the company of a local expert will make the world of difference to how much enjoyment you get out of your stay.

Above *A couple consult a street map at a tourist infromation centre*
Below *A sign in Magdeburg*

TOURIST INFORMATION OFFICES IN GERMANY

Below are the contact details for tourist information offices in Germany's main towns:

Berlin	Am Karlsbad 11, 10785 Berlin	tel 030 264 7480
Bonn	Windeckstrasse 1, 53111 Bonn	tel 0228 775000
Dresden	Ostra-allee 11, 01067 Dresden	tel 0351 4919 2100
Frankfurt am Main	Hauptbahnhof, 60329 Frankfurt am Main	tel 069 2123 8800
Hamburg	Hauptbahnhof (Kirchenallee), 1300 Hamburg	tel 040 3005 1300
Köln (Cologne)	Kardinal-Höffner-Platz 1, 50667 Köln	tel 0221 2213 0400
Leipzig	Richard-Wagner-Strasse 1, 04109 Leipzig	tel 0341 710 4265
München (Munich)	Sendlinger Strasse 1, 80331 München	tel 089 2339 6500
Stuttgart	Königstrasse 1a, 70173 Stuttgart	tel 0711 22280

GERMAN NATIONAL TOURIST OFFICES ABROAD

Australia (also **New Zealand**)	P.O. Box 1461, Sydney, NSW 2001	tel 02 8296 0488
Canada	480 University Avenue, Suite 1410, Toronto, Ontario, M5G 1V2	tel 416/968 1685
UK (also **Ireland**)	P.O. Box 2695, London, W1A 3TN	tel 020 7317 0908
US	P.O. Box 59594, Chicago, IL 60659-9594	tel 773/539-6303
	122 E. 42nd Street, Suite 2000, New York, NY 10168	tel 212/661-7200
	1334 Parkview Avenue, Suite 300, Los Angeles Manhattan Beach, CA 90266	tel 310/545-1350

MEDIA, BOOKS, MAPS AND FILMS

TELEVISION

The two biggest state-run television networks in Germany are ARD (usually channel 1) and ZDF (usually channel 2), but there are a few smaller networks, most of them regional. These include BR (Bavaria), HR (Hessen), MDR (Central), NDR (North), RB (Bremen), RBB (Berlin-Brandenburg), SR (Saarland), SWR (Southwest), WDR (West). Various combinations of these stations operate the cultural stations Arte, Phoenix, and 3Sat. Although the excellent, ad-free children's channel KI.KA (Kinderkanal) is only in German, very young children might not notice this! Among private broadcasters are multiple RTL channels, Kabel Eins, MTV Germany, ProSieben, Sat.1, Viva and VOX. Many get all these channels plus CNN, Sky News, Eurosport and BBC World News.

RADIO

German radio broadcasts the same kind of material that you'll find anywhere in Europe, America, Australia or Asia. Mainstream pop and rock dominate the airwaves, with classics and oldies coming in a close second and classical music a distant third. If you're desperate to hear some English-speaking broadcasters there are a number of options: The BBC World Service can be found on both AM and FM (depending on where you are in the country), while BFBS (British Forces Broadcasting Service) airs music, news and chat across much of western Germany. The American Armed Forces Radio and Television Service broadcasts in the south of the country.

NEWSPAPERS AND NEWS MAGAZINES
Bild
Germany's most widely read daily, with a circulation of around 5 million. Tabloid sensationalism with a conservative slant.
Focus
Similar to Der Spiegel (see below) but with a more modern, eye-catching layout. Not unlike Time or Newsweek in the US.
Frankfurter Allgemeine Zeitung
National daily. One of Germany's most prestigious papers, with conservative views.
Der Spiegel
A highly respected weekly news magazine with a reputation for hard-hitting investigative journalism that's often highly critical of the incumbent government.
Die Zeit
A respected weekly with social democratic leanings and around half a million readers.

NEWSPAPERS AND MAGAZINES

The leading national dailies in Germany are the conservative *Frankfurter Allgemeine Zeitung* (published in Frankfurt am Main) and the more liberal *Süddeutsche Zeitung* (published in Munich). Less high brow are *Die Welt* and the sensationalist *Bild*, the two main papers of the Springer group. Also popular are weekly news magazines such as *Der Spiegel* and *Focus*, and women's weeklies such as *Brigitte*, which usually feature in-depth investigative reports alongside more light-hearted articles. English-language papers that can usually be found in the major cities include the *International Herald Tribune* (based in Paris), the *Financial Times* (based in London) and the *Wall Street Journal* (based in New York). The international editions of *Time* and *Newsweek* are widely available at airports, main train stations and large bookstores. Most towns and cities have their own dailies or weeklies, plus one or more listings magazines, which may be available in English.

SPECIALIST MAP SHOPS	
UK	
National Map Centre	22–24 Caxton Street, London SW1H 0QU (tel 020 7222 2466); www.mapsnmc.co.uk
Stanfords	12–14 Long Acre, London WC2E 9LP (tel 020 7836 1321); www.stanfords.co.uk
US	
The Complete Traveller Antiquarian Bookstore	199 Madison Avenue, New York, NY 10016 (tel 212/685-9007)
Map Link, Inc.	30 S La Patera Lane, Unit 5, Santa Barbara, CA 93117 (tel 805/692-6777); www.maplink.com

BOOKS

It's perhaps inevitable that some of the best writing on Germany focuses not on vineyards and olive groves, as seems to be the case for France and Spain, but on its history. Arguably the best novel ever written about World War I is Erich Maria Remarque's *All Quiet on the Western Front* (1929), which says more about the futility of war than anything written before or since. *The Rise and Fall of the Third Reich* (1960), written by journalist William L. Shirer, remains required reading for anyone interested in World War II, as does A. J. P. Taylor's *The Origins of the Second World War* (1961). *Escape from Sobibor* (1982), by Richard Rashke, and *Schindler's Ark (List)* (also 1982), by Thomas Keneally, both provide harrowing accounts of life in Nazi concentration camps. One of the most recent books to come out of this period is the highly recommended *My Wounded Heart* (2004) by Martin Doerry, based on letters smuggled out of Breitenau and Auschwitz concentration camps by the author's grandmother.

Less serious but no less intriguing is *Fatherland* (1992) by Robert Harris, a thriller that imagines

Left *A scene from Wolfgang Petersen's hugely successful television series* Das Boot *(1981)*

Europe if had Hitler won the war. For similarly gripping fiction, John le Carré's *The Spy Who Came in from the Cold* (1963) has a fantastic finale set at Checkpoint Charlie at the Berlin Wall.

For a more light-hearted read, try to get hold of a copy of *A Tramp Abroad* (1880) by Mark Twain, which includes two chapters on Germany and a hilarious postscript entitled 'The Awful German Language'. Another humorous glimpse into pre-World War I German life is provided in *Three Men on the Bummel* (1900) by Jerome K. Jerome, who sends the characters from his earlier novel *Three Men in a Boat* on a cycling tour through the Black Forest. Forecasting harsher times to come, *The Riddle of the Sands* (1903) by Erskine Childers, set among the West Frisian Islands, can lay claim to having invented the spy thriller genre.

Translated into English, Germany's own authors provide fascinating insights into people, places and character. A (very) short selection of the many titles worth chasing up might include Thomas Mann's *Buddenbrooks* (1901), the story of a Lübeck merchant family in decline; *Emile and the Detectives* (1929), a children's novel by Erich Kästner; *The Tin Drum* (1959) by Günter Grass, part of his Danzig Trilogy; and Heinrich Böll's *The Lost Honour of Katharina Blum* (1974), set during the Red Army Faction's terror campaign in the 1970s.

MAPS AND OTHER PUBLICATIONS

The Automobile Association in the UK publishes the *Big Road Atlas Germany*, which highlights scenic sites and routes, and which also has detailed maps of all major towns and cities. For a more general overview, the AA's 1:800,000 double-side map of the whole of Germany is great for planning your trip. A smaller-scale atlas of Germany can be found on pages 398–416 of this book.

Tourist offices have detailed maps of cities and nearby attractions. In addition, there are maps of the following cities in this book: Berlin (▷ 70–171), Hamburg (▷ 131), Köln (Cologne; ▷ 175), Dresden (▷ 215) and München (Munich; ▷ 260–261). There is also a map of Berlin's U-Bahn on page 53, 73. A regional map is on page 9. All of the drives in this book are also accompanied by a simplified map, as are the walks in Berlin and Munich.

MAPS FOR HIKERS

Specially designed tourist maps showing footpaths and bicycle routes in popular destinations are widely available throughout Germany (look for *Wanderkarte* or *Sonderkarte*).

For a complete list of available maps, contact Stanfords at 12–14 Long Acre, London, WC2E 9LP (tel 020 7836 1321), or log onto their website at www.stanfords.co.uk. Also try www.mapquest.com and www.mapsworldwide.com.

FILMS

A seminal film about World War I is Lewis Milestone's classic *All Quiet on the Western Front*, based on Erich Maria Remarque's novel of the same name (▷ 371). It was made in 1930, but has lost none of its meaning and power. Based on an award-winning 1966 Broadway musical, the movie *Cabaret* (1972) stars Liza Minnelli as a singer at Berlin's decadent Kit Kat Club in 1931, during the final chaotic years of the Weimar Republic, with Adolf Hitler and his violent, anti-Semitic Nazi Party preparing to seize power. Madness and death reign in *The Downfall* (2004), as Russian soldiers fight their way to Adolf Hitler's underground bunker, through a devastated Berlin defended by old men, Hitler Youth and fanatical Waffen SS troops. Among other fine German films that deal with this dark period in history are *The Bridge* (1959), *Stalingrad* (1993), and *Sophie Scholl—The Final Days* (2005). In Wolfgang Petersen's *Das Boot* (1981; ▷ 19), the fear and claustrophobia of life on a German U-boat is brought vividly to life.

Much more light-hearted is Wolfgang Becker's *Good Bye Lenin!* (2003), which hilariously documents a young man's attempts to keep the fall of Communism and the collapse of the Berlin Wall from his socialist mother (▷ 25).

USEFUL WEBSITES

GENERAL TOURIST INFORMATION

www.germany.info
German Embassy site, with an emphasis on politics, business and cultural affairs.

www.germany-tourism.co.uk
A superb website providing comprehensive information on all things German.

BACKPACKERS

www.backpackers.com
An excellent site for backpackers or those travelling on a budget.

DOCUMENTATION

www.fco.gov.uk
Up-to-the minute advice from the British Foreign Office about getting help abroad.

www.travel.state.gov
The website of the US Department of State Bureau of Consular Affairs.

DRIVING

www.aaa.com
No information on driving abroad, but you can order your International Driving Permit here.

www.adac.de
Website of Germany's equivalent of the AA in the UK and the AAA in the US. German only.

www.tank.rast.de
Provides a list of autobahn service stations, including those with facilities for visitors with a disability.

www.theaa.com
Up-to-date advice and information from the UK's leading motoring organization, plus a route planner to help you map out your itinerary in advance.

FESTIVALS

www.germany-tourism.co.uk
The official website of the German Tourist Board in the UK provides comprehensive information on festivals and events throughout the country.

FOOD AND DRINK

www.gaultmillau.de
This website is easy to navigate: Click on Unsere Besten for a list of recommended restaurants, which have been graded out of 20. There are links to those with their own websites.

www.schlemmer-atlas.de
Although not as easy for non-German speakers to navigate as the site above, you can search for restaurants regionally by clicking on the home page's map.

www.varta-guide.de
As well as listing selected hotels in Germany (see hotels below), this website provides information in German on the pick of the country's restaurants.

HEALTH

www.cdc.gov
Website of the Center for Disease Control, the US's leading authority on health and travel abroad.

www.dh.gov.uk
Contains travel-specific information from the UK's Department of Health.

www.who.int
The official website of the World Health Organization.

HOTELS

www.bed-and-breakfast.de
Provides a list of bed-and-breakfast options across Germany for those on a budget.

www.hotelguide.de
Features a selection of around 10,000 hotels in Germany, from pensions to palaces.

www.hotellerie.de and www.hrs.de
Online reservations for hotels across Germany, in English (the latter site is also available in 32 other languages).

www.varta-guide.de
A guide recommending hotels throughout Germany to suit all tastes and budgets.

MUSEUMS

www.icom.museum
The International Council of Museums website. Listings and virtual tours of some of the world's most famous museums, including a handful in Germany.

www.europeanmuseumguide.com
An excellent online directory providing information on the best museums in Europe.

VISITORS WITH A DISABILITY

www.access-able.com
A US-based website for people with a disability.

www.dircsa.org.au
An Australia-based website.

www.dpa.org.nz
A New Zealand-based website.

www.radar.org.uk
A UK-based website offering advice and information to people with a disability.

www.tourismforall.org.uk
Another UK-based organization dedicated to improving access to visitor attractions.

WEATHER

www.weather.com
Comprehensive worldwide weather forecasts.

www.metoffice.gov.uk
UK-based site offering one- and five-day forecasts for countries throughout Europe.

WORKING HOLIDAYS

www.workingholidayinfo.com
Information on working holidays all over the world.

SHOPPING

Shopping is practically a national pastime in Germany, and visitors keen to spend a few euros won't be disappointed by the quality and variety of goods available. Most towns are home to at least one major shopping mall and a handful of indoor *Passagen* (literally 'passageways') lined with shops. Commercial hubs like Frankfurt and Düsseldorf have some of the most exclusive and lucrative shopping districts in Europe, while cities such as Cologne and Berlin have a more eclectic feel. Bargains (and a great deal of junk) can be found at flea markets and Christmas markets all over the country, while souvenirs range from the distressingly tacky to the reassuringly expensive.

DEPARTMENT STORES

The biggest department store chain in Germany—and indeed the whole of Europe—is Karstadt, although you'll also find Galeria Kaufhof and other chain department stores in most major cities. All these stores sell an overwhelming range of high-quality goods, from clothes and kitchenware to sports equipment and electrical items. Many stores also have a restaurant or café in which shoppers can rest tired limbs, and where the food is usually reasonably good. The biggest department store on the European mainland, incidentally, is Berlin's famous KaDeWe (Kaufhaus des Westens), which has eight different levels, a legendary delicatessen and a tropical café on the top floor.

LOCAL MARKETS

All major towns in Germany have at least one weekly market (usually held on a weekday, but sometimes on a Saturday or Sunday), and many smaller towns do too. Berlin holds numerous flea markets at weekends, the most popular of which takes place in Charlottenburg every Saturday. Stuttgart hosts a number of markets at weekends and during the week; the biggest is probably its food market, which takes place two or three times a week. More popular than the weekly markets, however, are the Christmas markets. The best are in Nuremberg, Munich and Dresden, all three of which are famous for their handmade wooden toys and Christmas decorations.

Above *The brightly lit shopping mall of Freidrichstadt Passage in Freidrichstrasse, Berlin*

SUPERMARKETS

Until reunification in 1990, supermarkets in East Germany sold completely different brands from those in the West, but these days shops all over the country are stocked to the rafters with everything you could possibly need. Many of the bigger supermarkets, or hypermarkets, also sell things like clothes, basic sports equipment and electrical goods, and they're often part of a bigger retail complex. In smaller places, supermarkets are usually in or near the middle of town, while elsewhere they're more likely to be on the outskirts.

OPENING HOURS

Germany's shops used to be regulated by draconian laws covering opening times, but these days things are much more relaxed. Most shops in major cities stay open until 7 or 8pm on weekdays and 5 or 6pm on Saturdays. In smaller towns, shops tend to close at 6pm on weekdays. Markets usually end at around 4pm, apart from during the run-up to Christmas. Souvenir shops in resort towns may stay open later than usual in the high season, but will close earlier in the winter.

PAYMENT

Credit cards are not as widely accepted as they are in, say, the UK or US, although bigger shops and department stores will usually accept most major cards. If in doubt, ask before you buy to avoid disappointment. Personal cheques and traveller's cheques are not generally accepted, and smaller shops may refuse to change large-denomination notes (bills).

TAX REFUNDS

MwSt (sales tax or value-added tax/VAT) stands at 19 per cent (and a reduced rate of 7 per cent for some goods and services), and is added to most products. Non-EU citizens can request a tax-free shopping cheque for big purchases, which can then be cashed at customs on leaving the country. Not all shops offer this service, so check before you buy (participating shops should display a sticker saying 'tax-free for tourists' in the window; ▷ 362).

WHAT TO BUY

Beer Steins and Glasses

No trip to Germany would be complete without sampling the beer, and assuming you enjoy the experience, the stein the beer is served in makes an excellent souvenir. Steins are basically beer mugs, and they come in all shapes and sizes. Most are made from pewter or porcelain and have elaborate emblems on the side, and you can get them from department stores, beer halls and souvenir shops. Beer glasses in Germany are all very similar, but those that Cologne's *Kölsch* (▷ 387 is served in are unique, and are well worth searching out (*Kölsch* glasses are small and slender with completely straight sides).

Ceramics

Germany is well known for the quality of its porcelain. Its three most famous manufacturers are Villeroy & Boch, based in Mettlach, Meissen (▷ 181) based near Leipzig, and Fürstenberg, based in a palace dating from 1747 in the Weserbergland (▷ 150–151). The first two have outlets all over Germany (and throughout Europe), but the best place to pick up a bargain and see how everything is made is at the factory outlets in their home towns (worldwide delivery can be arranged at both). To see Villeroy & Boch's goods in use before you buy, look no farther than the vast mosaic that forms the choir floor of Cologne Cathedral (▷ 173), or the interior of the Pfunds Molkerei dairy shop in Dresden, which is made up of over 3,500 hand-painted tiles (▷ 247). High-quality porcelain is also produced in Thuringia.

Food and Wine

Every region of Germany has its local recipe when it comes to sausages, but unless they're cured or sealed, they're quite difficult to take home. The same is true for chocolates, particularly if you don't have access to a fridge while travelling—but do try them. Some of the best chocolate truffles in the world can be found at Fassbender & Rausch, in Berlin (▷ 106) and elsewhere, and the Belgian brand Leonidas Pralinen, which has outlets all over Europe, including Aachen (▷ 194).

The best places to try local wines are the Rhine and the Mosel valleys, which produce some excellent Rieslings. Also worth tasting if you're in the area is the velvety-smooth Spätburgunder from the Eifel's Ahr valley, and Sekt (Germany's answer to champagne) from Saale, Germany's northernmost wine-producing region. Other important wine-producing regions are Baden-Württemberg, Bavaria, Hessen, Rheinland-Pfalz, the Saarland and Sachsen.

Leather Goods

Look around any German main street in winter and you could be forgiven for thinking that everyone has shares in the country's cows. Leather jackets are available everywhere, although you may have to shop around to find a bargain. More traditional jackets (such as those worn by Bavarians in oompah bands) can be bought in Munich or its environs.

Shoes

You only have to look at a cross-section diagram of a pair of Birkenstock shoes to realize that the Germans take their footwear seriously. Layer after layer of felt and leather help to create shoes that shape themselves to your feet as you wear them. Look for a pair in one of the many outlets in major towns and cities.

Toys and Christmas Decorations

Christmas markets are a national institution in Germany, as are stalls selling seasonal decorations. These range in quality from tacky trinkets to handmade (and usually quite expensive) treasures crafted out of wood. Other items on offer include candles, chinaware and traditional wooden serving boards (used for cold meats and cheeses).

Toys are also a serious business. Seiffen, in the Erzgebirge Mountains near the Czech border, has 100 master craftsmen, and is the place to go for traditional wooden toys, as are Nuremberg, Dresden and Leipzig, particularly at Christmas time. The Harz Mountains are renowned for their wooden puppets, while the Black Forest is the place to head for cuckoo clocks.

ENTERTAINMENT AND NIGHTLIFE

The range of entertainment available in Germany is vast. From classical music and opera to rock and pop, from art house cinema to traditional cabaret, you're sure to find something appealing. Berlin is, of course, the best place for nightclubs and cutting-edge entertainment, but all Germany's cities have their highlights. Most cities have their own orchestra, theatre or opera companies, and many capitalize on famous citizens, such as Beethoven in Bonn or Wagner in Leipzig and Dresden. Cinema is popular with Germans, and you might even find an *original version* of the latest blockbuster. Despite their reputation for being a serious-minded lot, the Germans know how to have a good time, whether they're singing along with an oompah band at a traditional beer hall or immersing themselves in trance and techno at some hip new club.

CINEMA

Going to the cinema is a popular pastime (there are more than 80 cinemas in Munich alone) and most towns and cities have large multiplexes. The bad news is that films are usually dubbed in German, and even in bigger towns you may be hard pushed to find a film showing in its *original version*, or OV (O*riginal mit Untertiteln*, or OmU, means 'original language with subtitles'). If a film is showing in its original version, this should be indicated by OV or OmU on the poster outside the cinema, although if you can't see it, it's always worth asking. Major cities such as Berlin, Munich, Hamburg and Frankfurt all have cinemas that show original-language films, and Hollywood blockbusters are usually released at the same time as they are elsewhere in Europe.

Many cinemas also offer discounted admissions one evening a week—ask at the local tourist office for details.

CLASSICAL MUSIC AND OPERA

The Germans can't seem to get enough of classical music, which is hardly surprising given their track record. Germany has produced more famous composers than any other country in the world, among them Johann Sebastian Bach, Ludwig van Beethoven, Johannes Brahms, George Frederick Handel (born Georg Friedrich Händel), Richard Strauss and Richard Wagner, to name just a few. It goes without saying that the cities most closely associated with these names host internationally renowned music festivals every summer, but even smaller towns and villages put on regular classical concerts throughout the year.

The best time to catch a concert is during the summer, when most music festivals are in full swing, although the weeks leading up to Christmas are also well served with seasonal offerings. Details can usually be found at the local tourist information office.

The best-known concert venues in Germany are the Beethovenhalle in Bonn, the Sächsische Staatsoper (known as the Semperoper) in Dresden, the Gewandhaus in Leipzig and the Philharmonies in Berlin and Cologne. The best-known opera venues are the Nationaltheater in Munich and the Staatsoper in Berlin and Hamburg (see individual entries in the What to Do listings in each Regions chapter).

Churches and cathedrals also provide ideal venues for choral concerts—have a look at their notice boards or ask at the nearest tourist office for details of forthcoming events.

CONTEMPORARY LIVE MUSIC

Hard rock and heavy metal are extremely popular in Germany, as are mainstream pop and rock. Major international acts tend to perform in the bigger cities of Berlin, Cologne and Hamburg, but you'll find national and local rock bands performing just about anywhere, from the smallest pub to the biggest concert hall. Many cities also host an annual pop festival, such as the RheinKultur concert in Bonn. For information on what's on, check local listings magazines or at the nearest tourist information office.

JAZZ AND BLUES

Most jazz and blues music is performed in bars or clubs, but there are also a number of jazz festivals held in towns and cities throughout the country. Chief among these are the Stuttgart Jazz Days in April, the Dresden Dixieland Festival in May and JazzFest Berlin in early November, all of which attract the best in local and international talent.

FOLK AND REGIONAL MUSIC

Traditional regional music doesn't enjoy the same popularity in Germany as it does in, say, Spain, but there's no explaining the almost universal appeal of the ubiquitous oompah band. Although these brass and drum ensembles aren't popular with most of Germany's younger generation, older people invariably know all the words, and they generally don't need much encouragement to sing them. This can be a little overwhelming at first, but many songs have an easy-to-remember refrain that's repeated ad infinitum until the band members run out of breath. A few glasses of the local beer usually helps, but if you're still struggling, just stamp your feet and bang the table at the same time as everyone else. Oompah bands perform in pubs and beer halls year-round, but the best time to experience them is during the various Lenten carnivals that are held in January or February. Traditional folk festivals are also held across Germany in July and August.

THEATRE AND DANCE

Germany enjoys a rich and varied theatre scene, particularly in the larger cities. Unless you speak German, of course, you're unlikely to want to see a play, but that doesn't mean you can't take in a cabaret, a ballet or a dance performance. Check out Deutsche Oper in Berlin, the Deutsches Theater in Munich, the Niedersächsisches Staatstheater in Hannover or the Staatsoper in Hamburg for the best in ballet and the Tigerpalast in Frankfurt or the Friedrichstadtpalast in Berlin for the cream of cabaret. Many smaller cities and towns, especially those with a thriving university scene, are full of more intimate venues that stage mainstream and alternative acts all year round (see What to Do sections for listings).

If you do want to see something in English, Frankfurt's aptly named English Theatre is reputed to be the largest of its kind in mainland Europe, and puts on a full schedule of plays and musicals, many of them from Broadway and London's West End (▷ 196). There is also a smaller English-speaking theatre in Hamburg (▷ 153). For an authentic traditional German spectacle, look no farther than the famous puppet theatre in Cologne (▷ 198) or Lübeck (▷ 154).

BERLIN FILM FESTIVAL

The Berlin Film Festival (*Internationale Filmfestspiele Berlin*, or *Berlinale*) is one of the biggest celebrations of cinema in the world, and although it doesn't match the glitz and glamour of Cannes, it certainly enjoys a much bigger audience, with locals and visitors attending screenings in droves. During the decades before reunification, the *Berlinale* was one of the few forums where East and West came together, and because of this it was overtly political and often highly controversial. These days, of course, things are a bit calmer, but visitors can always be sure of seeing the very best in world cinema. The festival takes place in February each year. For more details check the website www.berlinale.de (in English and German).

TICKETS

Munich

Tickets for concerts and shows in Munich can be obtained from the venue's box office, or from München Ticket (tel: 0180 5481 8181; www.muenchenticket.de). The desk in the main tourist information office at Marienplatz also has information on last-minute tickets and deals.

Berlin

There are ticket outlets all over Berlin, although since most are likely to charge 15 per cent commission on top of the price of the ticket, it is a good idea to go to the relevant box office in person if you want to keep the cost down. You can also purchase tickets for most shows, concerts and sporting events online at the comprehensive and informative www.berlin.de (but note that, although this website does have an English listings section, the reservations facility is available only in German).

Given that Germany is a stronghold of techno, it's perhaps not surprising that clubs and discos are hugely popular in all of the major towns and cities, although even in smaller towns and villages the locals don't need much of an excuse to let their hair down and have a good time. Berlin and Hamburg are arguably the hottest of Germany's hotspots when it comes to cutting-edge clubs, but university cities such as Dresden, Leipzig, Münster and Cologne can certainly hold their own. You'll find music and venues to suit all trends and tastes. In addition to techno and trance clubs, there's no shortage of excellent jazz and blues bars in Germany, and most mainstream clubs put on at least one rock and pop night a week. Salsa, reggae and hard rock bands are also popular. Traditional music, which tends to be of the folk or brass band variety, is usually restricted to beer halls and pubs, and is particularly prevalent in smaller towns, where it's often the only form of after-hours entertainment. Most cities in Germany also boast a casino—one of the most luxurious is in Wiesbaden, where gamblers can place their chips beneath the crystal chandeliers and coffered ceilings of the city's magnificent neoclassical Kurhaus (▷ 189).

Germany goes to bed much earlier than many other European countries, with bars and clubs often closing as early as 1 or 2am, so if you're intent on pulling an all-nighter, your best bet is probably to head for Hamburg or Berlin.

Below *A bar in Berlin*

BARS

There are American-style bars in most major cities, but more traditional pubs (below) in Germany often double as something else, such as a restaurant, bistro or music venue. In smaller towns and villages, pubs and beer halls are the norm, with or without live music. They invariably serve traditional German food in addition to local dishes.

BERLIN'S GAY SCENE

The gay club scene in Berlin dates back to the early 1920s and originated in the dance halls and salons of Schöneberg. Along with London and Amsterdam, Berlin is one of the major gay capitals in Europe, home to about 300,000 gays and lesbians. The scene is a fully integrated part of mainstream culture and nightlife, so most clubs and bars are gay-friendly and many of the larger clubs have a gay night. The borough of Schöneberg should be the first place that visitors head for. There is a high density of clubs and bars welcoming gay visitors around the Fuggerstrasse, Motzstrasse and Eisenacher Strasse area. Lesbenberatung (Lesbian Advice Centre) on Kulmer Strasse has the latest details of lesbian-friendly parties and events (Kulmer Strasse 20a, 10783 Berlin (Schöneberg); tel 030 215 2000; www.lesbenberatung-berlin.de), while the gay shop Mann-O-Meter in Motzstrasse provides information and tips on the Berlin scene (Bülowstrasse 106, Berlin (Schöneberg); tel 030 216 8008; www.mann-o-meter.de).

Prenzlauer Berg is a popular student borough that attracts a very diverse crowd. Most of the cafés, bars and nightclubs are concentrated between Greifenhagener Strasse and Gleimstrasse. In Kreuzberg, the gay scene is focused around Oranienburger Strasse and parts of Mehringdamm, where you will also find the Schwules Museum (Gay Museum, Mehringdamm 61, 10961 Berlin (Kreuzberg); tel 030 6959 9050; www.schwulesmuseum.de; Sun–Fri 2–6, Sat 2–7). In Friedrichshain there is also a lively party scene near the East Side Gallery—the paintings are on the remains of the Berlin Wall. The Lesbian and gay City-Festival (▷ 111) takes place every year at the end of June around Nollendorfplatz and culminates with the CSD: Christopher Street Day gay and lesbian parade through the city.

HOW TO FIND OUT MORE

Most major towns and cities in Germany publish listings of what's on and local papers may also have up- to-date details in their entertainment sections. Tourist information offices are another good source of information, particularly in smaller towns.

Munich

» *München im...* (*München im Februar, München im März* and so on) is a free monthly paper with complete listings for museums, galleries, concerts, theatres and cinemas. The free fortnightly *In München* provides similar information. Both are in German only, but it's relatively easy to figure out what's what, and both are available in bars, restaurants and similar venues.

» Listings information in English can be found in *New in the City Today*, which is a free paper, and the more useful paid-for monthly magazine *Munich Found*. The latter contains restaurant reviews and other articles in addition to detailed listings.

Berlin

» The best paid-for listings magazines in Berlin are *Zitty* and *Tip*, both of which are packed with up-to-the-minute information on everything that's happening in Germany's capital city. They're published bi-weekly in German only. The monthly magazine *Berlin Programm* provides a more general overview of what's on where, while *Prinz*, another monthly magazine, picks out the month's best parties, gigs and concerts, and gives details of the latest film and music releases. It also reviews new restaurants, bars and club nights. In addition, *Prinz* publishes a yearly magazine that rates the top shops, restaurants, nightclubs, bars, health spas, gyms and hotels in the city.

» *030* is a free bi-monthly listings magazine, which you can pick up at tourist information offices, shops, bars, restaurants and hotels. It has all the latest information about the up-and-coming parties and club nights, plus reviews of recent gigs. It also has a good film review and cinema listings section.

HEALTH AND BEAUTY

Given the number of towns that have the world Bad (literally 'bath') in their names, it's perhaps not surprising that spas are something of a national obsession in Germany.

Unlike in the UK and the US, however, the term spa doesn't necessarily refer to an exclusive (and expensive) pamper palace—in fact, most spas in Germany are open to the general public and won't cost you much more than a trip to your local swimming pool. Facilities usually include numerous indoor and outdoor pools at various temperatures, plus water jets, Jacuzzis and extensive sauna areas. Changing facilities are invariably immaculate, and most spas also have at least one café or restaurant overlooking the main pool area (this is often open to bathers only). But the highlight of any spa experience has to be the water itself, which is usually salty and is supposed to work wonders on aching limbs. It's worth pointing out, however, that a few spas encourage what they call 'textile-free' (i.e. nude) bathing, so if you're at all concerned about this you might want to check before you go in. Massage, acupuncture and other therapies may also be offered at an additional cost.

Above *The grounds of the modern spa at Baden-Baden*

SPORTS AND ACTIVITIES

In general, Germans take good care of their health, and many take part in some kind of regular sports activity. Walking and bicycling are popular, and most cities have large parks where you can exercise without coming into contact with car fumes. Skiing and other winter sports are available in the mountainous south, while sailing is popular on the northern coastline, as well as on the many lakes and rivers. Soccer is the national sport, although abasketball also has a great following, as does motor racing—unsurprisingly for a country that produces so many top-flight cars.

BASKETBALL

Basketball is much more popular in Germany than it is elsewhere in Europe, with 11 professional teams from all over the country competing in the national Basketball Bundesliga (BBL). The season runs from the end of October until the end of June, with most games taking place on Friday, Saturday and Sunday nights. Alba Berlin were league champions for seven years in a row, between 1997 and 2003. They recovered their leading position in the season that ended in 2008. For schedules go to www.basketball-bundesliga.de.

BICYCLING

Bicycling is extremely popular in Germany and bicycles can be rented in most major towns. Berlin has more than 750km (465 miles) of bicycle paths. Bicycles can be rented in Berlin at the local *Fahrradstation*, which may also offer themed bicycle tours with English-speaking guides. Bicycle lanes are often separate from the road and tend to be much more user-friendly than those in the UK or the US.

Outside the cities, the most popular bicycle paths in Germany are those that line the Rhine and Mosel. These paths are continuous and run for most of the length of both rivers. The north of the country is generally quite flat and is well suited to family bicycling (again, bicycles can be rented in many towns). The south is hillier—even Alpine for those who have the stamina for this—but a popular and not-too-strenuous outing is the Bodensee-Radweg, a bicycling route that goes all the way around the Bodensee (Lake Constance).

The German tourist board (www.germany-tourism.co.uk) publishes the useful guide *Discovering Germany by Bike*. For those who wish to tour, the ADFC (German Bicyclists' Federation) offers a wealth of information on trails and routes; log onto www.adfc.de (but note that it is in German only).

FISHING

Germany has some of the most picturesque lakes, rivers and streams in Europe, and there is plenty to offer both the expert angler and the first-time fisherman. Trout fishing is popular, but other catches include pike, carp, salmon, perch and bream. The best areas for fishing are the Black Forest, the Harz Mountains, Bavaria and, of course, the Rhineland and North Rhine Westphalia. Hamburg and Kiel are well placed for sea fishing, as are many of the towns and villages along Germany's coastline.

An angling permit (*Angelschein* in German) is required, and can be obtained from the local rural district council (*Landratsamt*) on payment of a small fee (usually €5–€10). A similar fee may also be required for a local permit, payable to the owners of the fishing ground. For information on where to fish, and for advice on where to get the relevant permits, ask at your nearest tourist information office.

FORMULA ONE MOTOR-RACING

As befits the home of the legendary Schumacher brothers, Germany is the only country in the world to host two Grand Prix races per season: the European Grand Prix, held at the famous Nürburgring in western Germany (▷ 163), and the German Grand Prix, held at Hockenheim, near Heidelberg. Tickets for both these races are expensive. Of course, more minor motor-racing events take place at both tracks throughout the year and are much easier to get tickets for. For more information on events at both venues, go to www.nuerburgring.de or www.hockenheimring.de.

GOLF

German enthusiasm for golf is reflected in the number and quality of golf courses that are scattered throughout the country. The course at Gut Kaden, 47km (30 miles) north of Hamburg, and the Club Zur Vahr course in Bremen, former home of the German Open, are among the most famous, but equally impressive are the Klostermannshof course at Niederkassel, and the Hohen Wieschendorf on the Baltic Sea between Lübeck and Wismar. Many private clubs welcome non-members, although proof of your handicap (usually a minimum of 32) is often required. Clubs and carts can be rented at most courses. Green fees near major towns and cities such as Düsseldorf or Frankfurt are typically in the region of €60–€80 per round (although weekends are often cheaper), but clubs in the countryside charge a lot less. For a listing of selected courses in Germany, log onto www.golfeurope.com or www.linksgolf.co.uk.

HORSE RACING

Although not quite the national institution it is in England, horse racing in Germany continues to have an enthusiastic following, thanks to big weekend events at major race courses, such as the Mariendorf Derby in Berlin (▷ 109), Rennbahn Grafenberg in Düsseldorf (▷ 195), Rennbahn Verden near Bremen and the Internationaler Club at Baden-Baden (▷ 34). Dressing up is the order of the day at weekends, but Fridays tend to be a bit more relaxed, and are sometimes free.

ICE HOCKEY

Ice hockey in Germany is probably second only to soccer when it comes to the dedication and enthusiasm of its fans. It's also big business, with 14 professional teams competing in the national Deutschen Eishockey Liga (DEL), and dozens more taking part in the lesser leagues. The season runs from September through April, and games are usually played on Friday, Saturday and Sunday nights. In 2008, the Berlin Polar Bears won the national league championship. For a current schedule, look at www.del.org.

Clockwise from left to right *Ice hockey at the Olympiapark in Munich; playing golf near the Chiemsee*

IN-LINE SKATING

In-line skating is extremely popular in Germany, and an increase in demand in the last five years has resulted in the establishment of designated skating paths in a number of cities. In fact, skating is so popular that in many cities the downtown area is closed to traffic for one night a week to make way for those dashing about on eight wheels. Your nearest tourist information office can tell you the best places to skate, and advise on where to rent equipment.

SOCCER

Thanks to the success of its national team, soccer is arguably Germany's national sport. Dazzling performances by its young talent earned the team third place in the 2006 World Cup; less-dazzling performances were still good enough for them to reach the final of the European Football Championship in 2008. In addition to a (usually) strong national team, Germany also boasts one of the best leagues in Europe, with teams like Bayern München and Borussia Dortmund regularly battling it out on the national and international stage. The season lasts from August until late June, and games are usually played on Wednesday evenings or on weekends. For a full match schedule, log onto www.bundesliga.de and click on the link that says '*Spieltermine*'.

Many stadiums in Germany were renovated or rebuilt to stage the 2006 World Cup.

TENNIS

The biggest event of the country's tennis calendar is the German Masters in Hamburg, one of the key competitions on the international circuit. This is a popular event and tickets sell out quickly. Order yours through www.tennistours.com.

TREKKING AND CLIMBING

You could spend a lifetime trekking in Germany and you still wouldn't get close to covering all the country's marked paths. Popular areas include the Black Forest, with its well-signed trails and pretty, half-timbered villages; Upper Bavaria, with its fairy-tale castles and ancient monasteries; and the area known as Saxon Switzerland, which has around 700km (435 miles) of trails and no fewer than 700 different rockfaces for climbers of all abilities.

The Bavarian Alps form the heart of Germany's mountaineering scene, and the Zugspitze, the highest mountain in the country at 2,963m (9,721ft), is regularly tackled by experienced climbers in both summer and winter.

Well-established long-distance trails in Germany include the Rennsteig, a ridge walk through the Thuringian Forest, and the Oberlausitzer Bergweg, on the border with the Czech Republic. Culture buffs and wine aficionados may prefer the more romantic Rheinhöhenweg, which follows the right bank of the Rhine between Bonn and Oppenheim, or the Moselhöhenweg, which runs along both banks of the Mosel between Koblenz and Trier. And there's also the much shorter Rotweinwanderweg, between Altenahr and Bad Badendorf in the Ahr valley. An excellent resource for walks throughout Europe is www.walkingworld.com.

WATERSPORTS

Germany's coastline is awash with windsurfing and sailing opportunities: Sylt, Amrum and St. Peter-Ording are the best-known windsurfing spots on the North Sea coast, while the more sheltered Baltic coast towns are ideal for those with less experience. Kiel Bay, Lübeck Bay and Flensburg Firth are perfect for combining sailing with some city sightseeing. Elsewhere, Germany's numerous lakes provide plenty of potential for watersports in the summer: Bodensee (Lake Constance), in the far south of the country, is popular, as are Müggelsee in Berlin and Alster in Hamburg. Rafting, kayaking and canyoning are all available in the mountainous regions, with Berchtesgaden, Thuringia and the Harz Mountains offering the best white water rapids. Germany is also home to Europe's biggest scuba-diving venue, the DiveGasometer in Duisburg. It welcomes divers of all abilities, and its on-site facilities include an underwater wreck and an artificial reef. Lake Constance is another well-loved diving destination. For those with suitable experience and qualifications, however, the Baltic Sea offers some of the best wreck and cave diving in Europe.

WINTER SPORTS

Opportunities to enjoy winter sports abound in Germany, particularly in the south. The biggest and best-known skiing area in the country is at Garmisch-Partenkirchen (▷ 345) in the Bavarian Alps, an hour's drive from Munich. This resort has hosted the Winter Olympics, the Alpine World Ski Championships and numerous world cup winter sports events. Almost as impressive is Berchtesgaden National Park (▷ 307) in the southeast corner of the country, near Salzburg. Winterberg, in the Arnsberger Wald to the east of Düsseldorf, is Germany's northernmost ski resort, and is home to an Olympic bobsleigh run that is open to the public). There's also a bobsleigh run at Oberhof, the biggest resort in the Thuringian Forest. Other popular skiing areas include the Black Forest and the Harz Mountains. Ski rental is available in all areas, and the ski season usually runs from late November until late March (although it's generally shorter the farther north you go).

NATIONAL PARKS

There are 14 national parks, 14 biosphere reserves and no fewer than 90 nature parks in Germany. Below is a list of the parks, with a brief description of each. For more detailed information, visit the tourist board's website at www. germany-tourism.de.

MÜRITZ-NATIONALPARK
www.nationalpark-mueritz.de

An amazing and inviting landscape made up of dozens of small lakes in the northeast of Germany, and an important breeding ground for migratory birds. There are numerous hiking and bicycling paths.

NATIONALPARK BAYERISCHER WALD
www.nationalpark-bayerischer-wald.de

Near the Czech border, and characterized by densely forested mountains, central Europe´s largest protected closed woodland area has some good hiking trails.

NATIONALPARK BERCHTESGADEN
www.nationalpark-berchtesgaden.de

Rising more than 2,700m (8,860ft), Berchtesgaden is an important area for winter sports (▷ opposite) and is arguably Germany's most scenic national park.

NATIONALPARK EIFEL
www.nationalpark-eifel.de

Not far from Bonn and Cologne, the Eifel forms the westernmost of Germany's upland massifs, and comprises scenic river valleys and rolling, forested hills (also ▷ 96).

NATIONALPARK HAINICH
www.nationalpark-hainich.de

In the Thuringian mountains to the south of Weimar. It contains Europe's largest mixed deciduous forest and is rich in wildlife.

NATIONALPARK HAMBURGISCHES WATTENMEER
www.nationalpark-hamburgisches-wattenmeer.de

Straddles the banks of the Elbe River in the far north of Germany, and is rich in sea life and birdlife.

NATIONALPARK HARZ
www.nationalpark-harz.de

The park, southeast of Hannover, took over the former Nationalpark hochharz in 2006. It contains several spectacular caves and crags, plus the Brocken, northern Germany's highest peak at 1,142m (3,747ft).

NATIONALPARK JASMUND
www.nationalpark-jasmund.de

Comprises just 30sq km (11sq miles) of chalk cliffs and forested creeks on Rügen island, off Germany's northeast coast, but contains a variety of flora and fauna.

NATIONALPARK KELLERWALD-EDERSEE
www.nationalpark-kellerwald-edersee.de

Germany's newest national park is a haven of rolling hills and deciduous woodland just a short drive to the west of Kassel.

NATIONALPARK NIEDERSÄSCHSISCHES WATTENMEER
www.nationalpark-wattenmeer.niedersachsen.de

The national park protects some islands to the northeast of Bremen that are famed both for their beautiful and deserted beaches and for their fascinating birdlife.

NATIONALPARK SÄCHSISCHE SCHWEIZ
www.nationalpark-saechsische-schweiz.de

Just to the south of Dresden, near the Czech border. The park's craggy sandstone rock formations are popular with hikers and climbers alike. There are also boat tours on the River Elbe.

NATIONALPARK SCHLESWIG-HOLSTEINISCHES WATTENMEER
www.wattenmeer-nationalpark.de

Between Kiel and Lübeck. This park is known for its dunes, salt-marshes and Halligen (small islands that become flooded whenever there is a high spring tide or heavy storm).

NATIONALPARK UNTERES ODERTAL
www.unteres-odertal.de

Spilling over into Poland, this park is a unique wetland area offering some great birding opportunities, and is home to no fewer than 37 different types of fauna.

NATIONALPARK VORPOMMERSCHE BODDENLANDSCHAFT
www.nationalpark-vorpommersche-boddenlandschaft.de

On the coast between Rostock and Stralsund, this park is dominated by dunes, coves and Bodden (shallow bays cut off from the Baltic sea).

Below *Detail of a sign in the Sächsische Schweiz National Park*

FOR CHILDREN

A family day out is a common event for many Germans, so there's no shortage of things for kids to do. In addition to some world-class theme parks, Germany has plenty of excellent zoos, aquariums, planetariums and science sites, not to mention a handful of film museums, two or three car museums and even a chocolate museum with a working chocolate factory (▷ 198). More traditional are the various toy and puppet museums that are dotted around the country, which give an insight into the life and times of children in Germany.

THEME PARKS

There are dozens of different theme parks scattered throughout Germany. The biggest are described below, and more appear in the regional listings. Still others are mentioned on the German tourist board's website, www.germany-tourism.co.uk.

TAKING YOUR KIDS

» Children are welcome almost everywhere in Germany, as long as they're well behaved. German social life is very family-oriented, so pubs and beer halls are often frequented by families, particularly at lunchtime and in the early evening. Classier restaurants may be less amenable to welcoming children late at night, but on the whole it shouldn't be a problem. Most restaurants have a limited number of high chairs.

» Children's discounts are commonplace everywhere from museums to zoos, although the age limit varies both for very young children (who often get in free) and for school-age children. The upper age limit is normally 18, although 16 or even 14 is not uncommon. Children under 18 are also eligible for discounts on all public transportation.

» Infant products (baby food, milk formulas and so on) are widely available in supermarkets throughout Germany, but you might want to bring your own brand anyway.

» Most hotels are happy to put up additional beds in rooms for kids, and some of the bigger hotels have a babysitting service for parents who want an evening on their own.

GERMANY'S BIGGEST AND BEST THEME PARKS

Europa-Park, Freiburg

The aptly named Europa-Park allows you to travel around Europe in a single day, in addition to offering the usual rides, roller-coasters and other forms of family entertainment. It's also Germany's most popular leisure park and is probably best avoided during June, July and August. It's near Freiburg, in the south, and is open daily 9–6. More details can be found on pages 281–282 and at www.europapark.de.

Legoland, Günzburg

The fourth theme park of Danish toy manufacturer Lego is in Günzburg, near Ulm in southern Germany. More than 50 million Lego blocks have been used to create a miniature version of the world's greatest cities and landmarks. In addition to the park's 40 different attractions, there are entertainment shows for kids and adults alike. Closed early Nov to mid-March. For more details, ▷ 345 and see www.legoland.de.

Phantasialand, Brühl

Phantasialand near Cologne is one of Germany's most popular theme parks, with a range of white-knuckle rides and family entertainment. Among its annual highlights are the Festival of Lights in October and Winter Dream, a special performance put on during the weekends leading up to Christmas. Open daily Apr–end Oct 9–6. For more details, and for Christmas openings, visit the website, www. phantasialand.de.

Left *There are plenty of parks and gardens as well as special theme parks for children in Germany*

FESTIVALS AND EVENTS

A visit to any of the festivals listed here will show that not only do the Germans know how to have a good time, they know how to do it in style. Even the most raucous celebrations have a well-deserved reputation for being friendly and good natured, though, and visitors are made to feel especially welcome. As well as the major festivals, thousands more are held in every town, village and hamlet in the country: For details of these see individual entries in the What to Do sections in the Regions chapters. The list below is restricted to general festivals.

CARNIVAL, COLOGNE
February

Pre-Lenten celebrations take place all over Germany, but none is more spectacular than the week-long extravaganza held each year in Cologne. It includes endless parades, processions and brass bands, all enjoyed by millions of party-goers in fancy dress; the result is one of the world's biggest street parties.

DOM FESTIVAL, HAMBURG
Takes place three times a year, usually in March, July and August

Dating back to the 14th century, when traders and minstrels were offered refuge in St. Mary's Cathedral in bad weather, Hamburg's Cathedral Festival is one of the largest fairs in Germany. Thrill rides, beer tents, live music and family entertainment are all part of the fun. It attracts a staggering 9 million visitors.

RHINE IN FLAMES, BONN, BINGEN, KOBLENZ, OBERWESEL AND ST. GOAR
Summer; dates vary—see www.germany-tourism.co.uk

At five different venues throughout the valley on five different nights throughout the summer, the romantic Rhine provides the backdrop to one of the most spectacular fireworks displays in the world.

LOVE PARADE
July

One of the world's biggest raves, attracting around a million people. A procession is followed by two or three days of partying in clubs and on the streets. The event began in Berlin in 1989, but funding difficulties and controversy concerning the damage caused by the parade led it to relocate to the Ruhr, where it runs in a different city each year until at least 2011.

OKTOBERFEST, MUNICH
October

The most famous festival in Germany needs little introduction. An opening parade—in which everyone wears traditional regional costume and there is entertainment for all the family—is followed by 16 straight days of eating and drinking. Despite the fact that around 7 million litres (1.8 million US gallons) of Wies'n beer is consumed by the same number of visitors in a little more than two weeks, it's all very good natured.

WEINFESTE (WINE FESTIVALS)
Autumn; for information on individual festivals, see www.deutscheweine.de

Although Germany is better known for its beer festivals, the country also hosts hundreds of wine festivals to celebrate the annual grape harvest. The biggest are held in northern Bavaria, and in the Rhine and Mosel regions, and comprise the usual eating and drinking, accompanied by dancing and live music, but there are also smaller-scale parties in the wine-growing villages.

WEIHNACHTSMÄRKTE (CHRISTMAS MARKETS)
Last week of November–Christmas Eve

Mulled wine, roasted chestnuts and grilled sausages; market stalls festooned with carvings, candles and lambskin shoes; children clutching toys, gingerbread men and marzipan—these are the things that make Germany's traditional Christmas markets unique. They're held every year in cities, towns and villages throughout the country.

Below *Germany's Christmas markets, such as the one at Nuremberg are a popular wintern attraction for visitors to the country*

Eating and drinking well is more or less compulsory in Germany. Traditional dishes tend to be wholesome and hearty, with pork products—particularly sausages—a mainstay. Potatoes also feature highly, and *Sauerkraut* remains a popular—if no longer ubiquitous—item on German plates. But you will also find a wide variety of exquisite local dishes served alongside a growing range of international cuisine.

MEALTIMES

» Breakfast (*Frühstück*) typically includes a selection of rolls and sliced bread (light and dark), served alongside various cheeses, sliced meats and conserves, all washed down with a glass of juice and a cup of coffee or tea. Many hotels include a buffet breakfast in the room price—the quality of the spread can vary considerably, but it's usually pretty good.

» Alternatively, if breakfast isn't included in your room rate, try one of the dozens of mouthwatering pastries that are on display in every bakery in Germany.

» Lunch (*Mittagessen*) is traditionally the main meal in Germany, and most restaurants are open all day, not just in the evening. Many restaurants offer set-price menus, or *Tagesessen* (daily menu), at lunchtime, which is usually an excellent value for the money. A big, hearty meal and a beer or two, or a glass of sparkling water, is the norm rather than the exception here, although Germans don't seem to be too big on desserts, particularly at lunchtime. If this all sounds a bit heavy, light snacks can always be found at cafés and bistros, and all manner of sandwiches and sausage-based bites can be bought at bakeries *(Bäckerei)* and snack bars *(Imbissstube)*.

» Dinner *(Abendessen)* in many German homes consists of platters of breads, cheese and cold meats, accompanied by a chilled beer or a glass of wine. Restaurants, however, serve a full menu from 6pm onwards.

WHERE TO EAT

» Bakeries (*Bäckerei*) are usually the first eateries to open in the morning, so are useful if you are making an early start. They serve an overwhelming array of pastries, cakes and coffees, and sometimes rolls and sandwiches. All are freshly prepared and are at very reasonable prices. Nuts and/or fruit are high on the agenda when it comes to treats, while ham, cheese and salami are the staples of the sandwich scene. Many bakeries also have a small seating or standing area, so you can eat your purchases there.

» Snack bars (*Imbissstube*) usually serve a few varieties of sausage in a bread roll, and may also offer fries, burgers and kebabs. Most have a standing area. They're inexpensive, friendly, and great if you're in a hurry or on a tight budget.

» Cafés in Germany often open as early as 7 or 8am, and tend to serve a wide range of light snacks and hot and cold fast food, in addition to the ubiquitous coffee and cakes (*Kaffee und Kuchen*), which are usually enjoyed mid-morning or late in the afternoon.

» Bistros and restaurants are generally the last to open, but most will be up and running by midday at the latest. In bistros, snacks are served alongside main meals, and cocktails alongside coffee. Restaurants, meanwhile, follow the more traditional starter, main course and dessert format, and offer a similar range of beers, wines and spirits.

Opposite *A German* Kuchen *(cake) dusted with icing sugar*

» Beer halls (*Brauhäuser*) are the place to try traditional German food and sample some of the local beer. In most places, local dishes are served alongside countrywide staples. the beer might be brewed on the premises.

FAST FOOD

» The likes of McDonald's, Burger King and Pizza Hut can be found in Germany's larger towns and cities. There are also nationwide chains, such as Kamps bakery and Nordsee seafood, which serve value-for-money food.

INTERNATIONAL CUISINE

» Many parts of Germany are flush with foreign restaurants, of which Italian (serving pizza and pasta), Latin American (with tortillas and fajitas) and Greek (dishing up souvlaki and tzatziki) are the most popular. In the larger towns and cities, however, you'll find restaurants representing all regions of the globe, from Armenia to Vietnam. Thai and Chinese are particularly popular in the major financial hubs, such as Frankfurt and Düsseldorf.

SPECIAL REQUIREMENTS

» Vegetarians should look for the words *vegetarische Gerichte* (vegetarian dishes) on the menu, although vegetarianism isn't that widespread in Germany, so don't expect to be offered much by way of choice. In beer halls in particular, you may be lucky to find anything that doesn't include meat. Similarly, many seemingly innocuous options, such as soups, rice and vegetable dishes, might be prepared or spiced up with meat stock—if in doubt, ask. Things are changing, however, and in the major cities there are increasing numbers of restaurants catering specifically to vegetarians.

CHILDREN'S FOOD

» German children eat out with their parents from an early age, particularly in beer halls (*Brauhäuser*), which during the day and in the early evening are often patronized by the whole family.

» Smaller portions are offered as a *Kinderteller*. As a result, children tend to be well looked after. The food is often of the omelette or burger-and-fries variety, so you shouldn't get any complaints from your offspring, but if they (or you) are a bit more adventurous, starters or smaller portions of main meals are ideal. Even small children won't look out of place in many pubs and restaurants, although most places tend to be a bit more adult-oriented after 7 or 8pm.

WHAT TO DRINK

» Beer (*Bier*) is a national institution in Germany and throughout the country there are literally hundreds of breweries, beer halls and pubs producing their own. German beer traditionally tastes stronger than other European, American and Australian beers, and it can be light (*Helles*) or dark (*Dunkles*). Many regions take great pride in their particular special brew, such as *Altbier* (from the Rhine region) or *Kölsch* (from Cologne). Glasses are often smaller than they are in the UK or US, and in some cases they may contain only a few mouthfuls (although the price generally reflects this). German beer is almost always served cold.

» Wine (*Wein*) is not as popular a drink as beer at mealtimes, but that's not to say it isn't widely appreciated, particularly around the major wine-producing regions. Some 80 per cent of the wine produced in Germany is white, and the basic categories are *trocken* (dry), *halb-trocken* (medium) and *lieblich* (sweet). Wines are also further categorized into *Tafelwein* (table wine), *Qualitätswein* (quality wine) and *Qualitätswein mit Prädikat* (literally 'with distinctive features'). Among the most popular grape varieties are Riesling (a fresh, fruity white from the Mosel area), Silvaner (a full-bodied white from Pfalz) and Spätburgunder (a velvety-smooth red from the Ahr). A popular export wine is Liebfraumilch, originally named after the 14th-century Liebfrauenkirche convent in Worms and now produced throughout the Rhine region. Wine-tasting, which is usually a good value for money, is widely available in all the country's wine-producing areas.

» Ice wine (*Eiswein*) is made from specially selected grapes that are actually allowed to freeze on the vine in the autumn. It is considered to be something of a luxury, with half-bottle prices starting from around €30. *Sekt*, meanwhile, is Germany's version of champagne, and although it's not in the same league, some brands are of a very high quality. Finally, *Apfelwein* is a sweet, heady cider with a strong, sweet aftertaste. It is brewed particularly in Frankfurt and the southern Hesse palatinate.

» Schnapps (*Schnaps*) translates as 'spirits', and it is also used to describe sweet, fruit-based drinks that are taken as aperitifs or digestifs. Apple, pear and plum are the most common ingredients, and the drinks are traditionally downed in shots.

» Soft drinks can be found everywhere in Germany, as can bottles of mineral water—with the latter, be sure to ask for carbonated (*mit Kohlensäure*) or still (*still*), depending on what you prefer.

» Coffee (*Kaffee*) is served everywhere, and is relatively inexpensive (unless you're in a chain coffee shop, it which case you can easily pay a euro or more over the average). It usually comes in a cup (*Tasse*), and is served with sugar and milk or cream on the side.

» Tea (*Tee*) tends to be served in a glass, with the tea-bag left in the water, and sugar and/or lemon served on the side. If you want tea with milk (*Milch*), ask for it on the side, so that you can add it after the tea-bag has stewed a little.

USEFUL WORDS
Gerichte plate/dish
hausgemacht home-made
heiss hot
kalt cold
Speisekarte menu
Tageskarte specials menu
vegetarisch vegetarian

ESSEN—MEALS
Frühstück breakfast
Mittagessen lunch
Abendessen dinner

GANG—COURSES
Suppen soups
Vorspeise starter
Hauptgericht main
Nachtisch dessert

COOKING METHODS
nicht durchgebraten rare
frittiert fried
gebacken baked/roasted
gebraten (pan) fried
gedämpft steamed
gefüllt stuffed
gegrillt grilled
gekocht boiled
geräuchert smoked
geschmort braised
paniert breaded

FLEISCH—MEAT
Ente duck
Fasan pheasant
Gans goose
Gyros kebab
Hackfleisch mince (ground) beef
Hähnchen chicken
Kalbfleisch veal
Kaninchen rabbit
Kotelett (pork) chop
Lammfleisch lamb
Rindfleisch beef
Schaschlik kebab
Schinken ham (smoked or cooked)
Schnitzel escalope (scalloped meat)
Schwein pork
Speck bacon
Truthahn turkey
Wild game
Zunge tongue

WURST—SAUSAGES
Bierwurst beer sausage
Blutwurst black pudding (blood sausage)
Bockwurst boiled sausage
Bratwurst fried sausage
Brühwurst thick sausage
Currywurst spicy sausage
Knackwurst garlic sausage
Leberwurst liver sausage
Wiener frankfurters

FISCH—FISH
Barsch perch
Dorsch cod
Forelle trout
Hering herring
Karpfen carp
Lachs salmon
Makrele mackerel
Sardinen sardines
Schellfisch haddock
Scholle plaice
Seezunge sole
Tunfisch tuna

MEERESFRÜCHTE—SEAFOOD
Austern oysters
Hummer lobster
Krabben prawns
Miesmuscheln mussels
Muscheln shellfish

GEMÜSE—VEGETABLES
Artischocken artichoke
Bohnen beans
Erbsen peas
Gewürzgurken gherkins (pickles)
Grüne Bohnen green beans

Gurke cucumber
Karotten or **Möhren** carrots
Kartoffeln potatoes
Kohl cabbage
Paprika peppers
Pilze mushrooms
Spargel asparagus
Tomaten tomatoes
Zwiebeln onions

OBST—FRUIT

Apfel apple
Aprikose apricot
Banane banana
Brombeeren blackberries
Erdbeeren strawberries
Himbeeren raspberries
Kirschen red cherries
Mandarine mandarin
Melone melon
Orange orange
Pfirsich peach
Pflaumen plums
Trauben grapes
Zitrone lemon

SPECIAL DISHES

Bulette a type of meat pie that's typical of Berlin
Erbsensuppe mit Würstchen thick pea soup with frankfurter
Grünkohl mit Pinkel winter cabbage with a thick sausage and potatoes
Gulasch beef stew with paprika, often served up as a soup
Hackepeter German-style steak tartare, common in Berlin
Handkäse mit Musik medium-soft cheese from Frankfurt, served with pickled onions and bread
Jägerschnitzel escalope (scalloped meat) served in a mushroom and cream sauce
Kaiserschmarren pancakes with raisins, cinnamon and sugar
Kartoffelpüree mashed potato (often served with sauerkraut)
Kasseler Rippe mit Sauerkraut smoked saddle of pork with sauerkraut; a variation on knuckle of pork (▷ Schweinshaxe, right)
Labskaus sailor's stew, with cured beef, mashed potato, pickled beetroot (beet) and fish; from the north, where meat and fish are often combined
Matjeshering salted herring, another special dish in the north of Germany; often served pickled and rolled in sour cream as rollmops
Rippenbraten mit Backpflaumen spare ribs with prunes; this splendidly named dish is typical of the German tendency for combining sweet and savoury tastes
Rösti grated potatoes pan-fried with onion
Sauerkraut shredded white cabbage that's been pickled
Schlesisches Himmelreich literally 'Silesian heaven', a stew made of pork and dried fruits
Schwarzwälder Kirschtorte Black Forest gateau (literally 'Black Forest cherry cake')
Schwarzwälder Schinken Black Forest smoked ham, reputedly among the best in Germany
Schweinshaxe knuckle of pork. Available in regional variations in most parts of Germany; usually served with mashed potato and sauerkraut
Thüringer Rostbratwurst a coarse, fatty sausage that's typical of eastern Germany
Westfälischer Schinken fine ham from the Düsseldorf/ Westphalia region
Wiener Schnitzel practically synonymous with German cuisine; basically it is an escalope (scalloped meat) that's been pounded flat and then pan-fried in breadcrumbs

CONDIMENTS

Knoblauch garlic
Mayonnaise mayonnaise
Pfeffer pepper
Salz table salt
Senf mustard
Zucker sugar

SIDE DISHES

Brot bread
Bretzel pretzel (soft bread pastry in the shape of a knot)
Brötchen roll
Ei egg (uncooked)
gemischter Salat mixed salad
Kroketten (potato) croquettes
Nudeln noodles (also pasta)
Pommes frites chips/fries
Pumpernickel rye bread
Rührei scrambled egg
Spiegelei fried egg

NACHTISCHE UND KUCHEN—DESSERTS AND CAKES

Apfelstrudel apple and pastry
Berliner jam/jelly doughnut
Eierkuchen/Pfannkuchen pancakes
Eis ice-cream (also ice)
Käsekuchen cheesecake
Kekse biscuits /cookies (sweet)
Krapfen ring doughnut
Linzer Torte lattice tart
Obstsalat fresh fruit salad

GETRÄNKE—DRINKS

Apfelsaft apple juice
Bier beer (any sort)
Dunkles dark beer
Fruchtsaft fruit juice
Helles light beer
Kaffee coffee (black)
Kaffee mit Milch coffee with milk
Kaffee mit Sahne coffee with cream
Kölsch light, fizzy beer from Cologne
Limonade lemonade
Mineralwasser mineral water
Mineralwasser mit Kohlensäure carbonated mineral water
Pils strong-tasting lager
Schnaps strong spirit
(Zitronen) Tee (lemon) tea
Weinkarte wine list

WEIN—WINE

Apfelwein apple wine/cider
Glühwein mulled wine
Hauswein house wine
Roséwein rosé wine
Rotwein red wine
Sekt sparkling wine
Weisswein white wine

DIE RECHNUNG—THE BILL/CHECK

Wir möchten zahlen, bitte Can we have the bill, please?
Bedienung (nicht) inklusive service charge (not) included

Opposite *Freshly baked pretzels make a tasty snack*

Accommodation options in Germany range from luxury designer hotels with a sauna and spa to basic farm-stay rooms with clean sheets and hot and cold running water. You may be pleasantly surprised at the amount of luxury €150 will buy for two people.

HOTELS

Most hotels in Germany are assigned a star rating from one to five, and prices usually reflect this. However, bear in mind that higher prices are not necessarily a guarantee of quality: A hotel that claims three stars may be quite threadbare, while another hotel that has only one or two stars might be comfortable, clean and perfectly functional. For this reason, it's always a good idea to ask to see a room before reserving, or, if you're making a reservation online, to look at any pictures you can find. This is less of a problem with four- and five-star hotels, which are equivalent to their counterparts in the UK or US in terms of standards and amenities.

Budget accommodation (around €100 or less per room) is relatively easy to find if you're prepared to look around. Double rooms are a better value than singles: It's possible, for example, to find a comfortable double with private bathroom in the heart of a major city for as little as €85. Visitors with more to spend will be spoiled for choice, particularly in bigger towns. Most hotels include a buffet breakfast in the price, and most rooms will have a television with at least one or two satellite channels in English (such BBC World News and CNN International).

PENSIONS

Pensions tend to be small, privately run inns (with a restaurant) or hotels (without a restaurant), offering simple rooms and basic amenities. They're usually found outside the town or downtown city area, and charge prices that reflect their no-nonsense nature (€40 to €60 for a single and €60 to €85 for a double).

FARM STAYS

Staying on a farm is one of the best ways to experience rural Germany, but, as with pensions, it's not practical for those without their own transportation. Home stays and farm stays can be arranged by tourist information offices, sometimes for a small fee (this is never more than €2 or €3). Such accommodation tends not to be starred, and quality ranges from rustic but serviceable to downright luxurious.

HOSTELS

The Germans are crazy about hostels and hostelling, so it's unsurprising that there are more than 600 DJH (Deutsches Jugendherbergswerk or German Youth Hostel Association) hostels across the country, plus hundreds more independent ones. Facilities are generally good, but some hostels require visitors to vacate the building during the day, and others have a curfew (although this is usually late). Expect to pay anything from €20 to €35 for a bed in a shared room with breakfast, plus €4 to €6 for bed linen if you need some. For reservations and further information, log onto www.djh-ris.de (there's an English version).

CAMPING

As with many pensions, most campsites in Germany are well away from downtown city areas, and the majority are of the recreational vehicle (RV)/caravan sort. Most are open only from April to the end of September, although some open year round. Campers are often charged per tent, per person and per car, so the final price does add up, but it's an inexpensive option. A list of German campsites can be found at www.camping-club.de.

SELF-CATERING

Renting a room or an apartment for a few days is popular with holidaying Germans, and there's no reason why overseas visitors can't get in on the act. Quality varies from simple to sublime, but because the rent is shared it can be great value. Rented accommodation is ideal for families, particularly as it also offers a lot more privacy and flexibility. Local tourist offices can advise you, or you can visit www.germany-tourism.co.uk.

FINDING A ROOM

Rooms can be reserved in advance through most local tourism information websites (see Sight entries for details) or through the hotel finder at www.germany-tourism.co.uk. The best place to start your search in situ is at the local tourist office, which may offer a room-finding service for a nominal fee (usually €2 to €3). If the tourist office is closed, there's often a notice board outside with a list of nearby hotels.

It is always best to reserve ahead, particularly in the peak season. Check-out time is usually 11am or noon, although most hotels will be happy to store your luggage free of charge until later in the afternoon. In the chart below, (R) indicates that this is the number for reservations.

ROOM RATES

Rates vary considerably according to the season and whether or not there is a trade fair in town.

Hotels often quote their most expensive rate, so a little perseverance might elicit a better deal. By law, they must display a list of prices in every room, so you'll know you're not being ripped off. Extra beds can usually be added for a small charge (ideal for families with young children).

MAJOR HOTEL CHAINS		
Best Western	The world's largest hotel chain, offering four-star accommodation close to city downtown areas.	0800 212 5888 (R) www.bestwestern.de
Crowne Plaza	Part of the Inter-Continental group, with quality four-star hotels in Germany's big cities.	0800 181 6068 (R) www.ichotelsgroup.com
Dorint	Stylish and luxurious four-star spa hotels and resorts at locations throughout Germany.	0180 226 2524 (R) www.dorint.com
Ibis	Comfortable, great-value rooms in two- and three-star French-owned hotels, usually near city downtown areas.	06995 307595 (R) www.ibishotel.com
Hilton	US-based chain providing quality four-star accommodation, usually in central locations.	00800 8884 4888 (R) www.hilton.de
Holiday Inn	Part of the Inter-Continental group, offering four-star accommodation in main cities.	0800 181 6068 (R) www.ichotelsgroup.com
Inter-Continental	High-end, luxury hotel chain providing four- and five-star accommodation in cities.	0800 181 6068 (R) www.ichotelsgroup.com
Maritim	A German-based chain offering central four-star accommodation in many German cities.	0180 231 2121 (R) www.maritim.de
Marriott	A global group with luxury hotel and resort accommodation.	00800 1927 1927 (R) www.marriott.de
Mövenpick	Elegant and exclusive top-end hotels and resorts. Swiss owned.	0800 849 9999 (R) www.moevenpick.com
Novotel	Part of the Accor group, offering slightly classier versions of the Ibis hotels.	06995 307593 (R) www.novotel.com
Park Plaza	Modern, stylish designer hotels providing four-star accommodation.	0800 181 4442 (R) www.parkplaza.com
Radisson SAS	Part of the same group as Park Plaza, Radisson SAS provides accommodation in a series of large, stylish hotels in numerous cities across the world.	0800 181 4442 (R) www.radisson.com
Ramada	Part of the Marriott group, Ramada hotels provide four-star quality and service at affordable prices; they are centrally located in many German cities.	00800 8733 3737 (R) www.ramada.com
Sheraton	Mid- to high-end four- and five-star accommodation. (Note: international phone rates outside US.)	+1-888-625-5144 (R) www.starwoodhotels.com
Sofitel	The pinnacle of the Accor empire, offering luxury facilities in some splendid buildings.	06995 307595 (R) www.sofitel.com

There is one official standard German language, Hochdeutsch (High German), which is taught in school and which everyone in the country should be able to understand. However, regional dialects, with strong local accents, are widely spoken in many areas. The words and phrases that follow are High German, and the guide below should help you with the pronunciation.

Vowels:

a short as in h**a**nd, or long as in f**a**ther
e short as in b**e**t, or long as in d**a**y
i short as in f**i**t
o short as in l**o**st, or long as in c**oa**ch
u long as in b**oo**t
ä short as in w**e**t, or long as in w**ai**t
ö long as in f**u**r
ü long as in bl**ue**

Vowels are always short after double consonants, and long when followed by 'h'

Dipthongs:

ai as in m**i**ne
ie as in tr**ee**
ei as in sp**y**
eu as in b**oy**
au as in h**ow**
äu as in b**oy**

Consonants:

b is like **p** }
d is like **t** } at the end of a word or syllable
g is like **k** }
ch is either a throaty sound, like the Scottish lo**ch**, after a, o, u and au, or an exaggerated **h** sound after i, e ä, ö, eu, and ie
j is like **y** in **y**acht
s is either like **z** in **z**ip when it is the first letter of the word, or like **s** as in bu**s** if it goes before a consonant
sch is like **sh** as in **sh**ut
sp and **st** are pronounced **shp** and **sht**
v is like **f** as in **f**it when it is the first letter of the word
w is like **v** as in **v**ery

USEFUL WORDS

yes
ja

no
nein

perhaps
vielleicht

please
bitte

thank you
danke

thank you very much
danke schön

very kind of you
sehr freundlich (von Ihnen)

you're welcome
bitte schön

that's alright
ist schon in Ordnung

excuse me/sorry!
entschuldigung!

No, I'm sorry
Nein, es tut mir Leid

where
wo

here
hier

there
dort

when
wann

now
jetzt

later
später

why
warum

who
wer

may I/can I
darf ich/kann ich

what
was

how
wie

how much
wieviel

great!
ausgezeichnet!

not bad
nicht schlecht

I don't mind
es ist mir egal

I like ...
ich mag ...

CONVERSATION

Do you speak English?
Sprechen Sie Englisch?

I don't speak German
Ich spreche kein Deutsch

I don't understand
Ich verstehe nicht

Pardon?
Wie bitte?

Please repeat that
Wiederholen Sie das, bitte

Please speak more slowly
Sprechen Sie bitte langsamer

Write that down for me please
Schreiben Sie das bitte auf

Please spell that
Buchstabieren Sie das, bitte

What does that word mean?
Was bedeutet dieses Wort?

My name is ...
Ich heisse ...

What's your name?
Wie heissen Sie?

Hello, pleased to meet you
Guten Tag, freut mich

This is my friend
Das ist mein Freund (male)/ meine Freundin (female)

This is my wife/husband/ daughter/son
Das ist meine Frau/mein Mann/ meine Tochter/mein Sohn

Where do you live?
Wo wohnen Sie?

I'm from ...
Ich komme aus ...

Have you been here long?
Sind Sie schon lange hier?

A few days
Ein paar Tage

Good morning/afternoon
Guten Morgen/Tag

Good evening/night
Guten Abend/gute Nacht

Goodbye
Auf Wiedersehen

How are you?
Wie geht es Ihnen?

Fine, thank you
Sehr gut

What is the time?
Wie spät ist es?

See you sooon
Bis bald

See you later
Bis gleich

Have a nice holiday
Einen schönen Urlaub

I think so
Ich glaube schon

Do you know?
Wissen Sie?

I don't know
Ich weiss es nicht

Could you take a picture of me/ us please?
Könnten Sie bitte eine Foto von mir/ uns machen?

I don't have time
Ich habe keine Zeit

MONEY

Is there a bank/currency exchange office nearby?
Ist hier in der Nähe eine Bank/ Wechselstube?

I'd like to change sterling/ dollars into euros
Ich möchte Pfund/Dollars in Euro tauschen

What's the exchange rate?
Wie hoch ist der Wechselkurs?

Where can I cash this traveller's cheque?
Wo kann ich diesen Reisescheck einlösen?

Can I use my credit card to withdraw cash?
Kann ich mit meiner Kreditkarte Geld abheben?

POST

Where's the post office?
Wo ist hier ein Postamt?

Where's the postbox?
Wo ist hier ein Briefkasten?

What's the postage for a postcard/letter to ...?
Wieviel muss auf eine Postkarte/ einen Brief nach ...?

Are there enough stamps on it?
Sind genug Briefmarken darauf?

I'd like to send this parcel by air mail
Ich möchte dieses Päckchen per Luftpost schicken

IN TROUBLE

Help
Hilfe

Stop, thief
Haltet den Dieb

Can you help me, please?
Können sie mir bitte helfen?

Call the fire brigade/police/an ambulance
Rufen sie die Feuerwehr/ Polizei/einen Krankenwagen

Where is the police station?
Wo ist das Polizeirevier?

I need to see a doctor/dentist
Ich muss zum Arzt/Zahnarzt gehen

Please direct me to the hospital
Wie komme ich zum Krankenhaus?

I have lost my passport/ wallet/purse
Ich habe meinen Pass/meine Brieftasche/Geldtasche verloren

I have been robbed
Ich bin bestohlen worden

Is there a lost property office?
Gibt es hier ein Fundbüro?

I am allergic to ...
Ich bin allergisch gegen ...

I have a heart condition
Ich habe ein Herzleiden

HOTELS

Do you have a room?
Haben Sie ein Zimmer frei?

I have made a reservation for ... nights
Ich habe ein Zimmer für ... Nächte bestellt

How much per night?
Was kostet es pro Nacht?

Is the room air conditioned/ heated?
Hat das Zimmer eine Klimaanlage/ Heizung?

Is there an elevator in the hotel?
Hat das Hotel einen Fahrstuhl?

Do you have room service?
Haben Sie Zimmerservice?

When is breakfast served?
Wann gibt es Frühstück?

I need an alarm call at ...
Ich möchte um ... geweckt werden

May I have my room key?
Kann ich meinen Schlüssel haben?

Will you look after my luggage until I leave?
Kann ich bis zu meiner Abreise mein Gepäck hier lassen?

Where can I park my car?
Wo kann ich meinen Wagen parken?

Could I have another room?
Könnte ich ein anderes Zimmer haben?

We can't sleep due to the noise
Wir können durch den Lärm nicht schlafen

There's no hot water
Es gibt kein warmes Wasser

The room hasn't been cleaned
Das Zimmer ist nicht saubergemacht

The heater is not working
Die Heizung funktioniert nicht

The bed linen is dirty
Die Bettwäsche ist schmutzig

We're out of toilet paper
Das Toilettenpapier ist alle

What time should we vacate the room?
Wann müssen wir das Zimmer verlassen?

I am leaving this morning
Ich reise heute Morgen ab

Please can I pay my bill?
Kann ich bitte meine Rechnung bezahlen?

Thank you for your hospitality
Vielen Dank für Ihre Gastfreundschaft

RESTAURANTS

Waiter/waitress
Kellner/Kellnerin

I'd like to reserve a table for ... people at ...
Ich möchte einen Tisch für ... Personen um ... reservieren

A table for ..., please
Einen Tisch für ..., bitte

We have/haven't reserved
Wir haben/haben nicht reserviert

Could we sit there?
Können wir dort sitzen?

Are there tables outside?
Gibt es draussen Tische?

We'd like something to drink
Wir möchten etwas zu trinken

Could we see the menu/wine list?
Wir hätten gern die Speisekarte/ Weinkarte

Do you have a menu/wine list in English?
Haben Sie eine Speisekarte/ Weinkarte auf Englisch?

Is there a dish of the day?
Gibt es ein Tagesgericht?

What do you recommend?
Was empfehlen Sie?

I can't eat wheat/sugar/salt/ pork/beef/dairy
Ich vertrage keinen Weizen/ Zucker/kein Salz/Schweinefleisch/ Rindfleisch/keine Milchprodukte

I am a vegetarian
Ich bin Vegetarier

I'd like ...
Ich möchte ...

Could we have some salt and pepper?
Könnten wir etwas Salz und Pfeffer haben

May I have an ashtray?
Kann ich einen Aschenbecher haben?

Where's the toilet?
Wo ist die Toilette?

This is not what I ordered
Das habe ich nicht bestellt

The food is cold
Das Essen ist kalt

The meat is under/overcooked
Das Fleisch ist zu roh/verbraten

Can I have the bill, please?
Kann ich bitte die Rechnung haben?

The bill is not right
Die Rechnung stimmt nicht

I'd like to speak to the manager, please
Ich möchte mit dem Geschäftsführer sprechen

The food was excellent
Das Essen war ausgezeichnet

SHOPPING

Could you help me, please?
Können Sie mir helfen, bitte?

I'm looking for ...
Ich suche ...

When does the shop open/close?
Wann macht das Geschäft auf/zu?

I'm just looking, thank you
Ich sehe mich nur um, danke

Do you have anything less expensive/smaller/larger?
Haben Sie etwas Billigeres/ Kleineres/Grösseres?

How much is this?
Was kostet das?

Can you gift wrap this please?
Können Sie das bitte als Geschenk einpacken?

Do you accept credit cards?
Nehmen Sie Kreditkarten?

I'd like a kilo of ...
Ich möchte ein Kilo ...

I'd like .... grams please
Ich möchte ... Gramm bitte

Do you have shoes to match this?
Haben Sie dazu passende Schuhe?

My American/English size is ...
Meine amerikanische/ englische Grösse ist ...

This is the right size
Das ist die richtige Grösse

This doesn't suit me
Das steht mir nicht

Do you have this in ...?
Haben Sie das in ...?

Should this be dry cleaned?
Sollte das chemisch gereinigt werden?

I'll take this
Ich nehme das

ON THE ROAD

Can you direct me to ...?
Wie komme ich zum/zur/nach ...?

How many kilometres to ...?
Wie viele Kilometer nach/bis ...?

Is this the way to ...?
Ist dies der Weg nach ...?

Excuse me, I think I am lost
Entschuldigen Sie, ich glaube ich habe mich verlaufen/verfahren

You're going the wrong way
Da sind Sie hier nicht richtig

What is the quickest route to ...?
Was ist der schnellste Weg nach ...?

Could you point it out on the map?
Können Sie es mir auf der Karte zeigen?

Is there a(n)... around here?
Wissen Sie, wo hier in der Nähe ein(e) ... ist?

From there on you will see the signs
Da sehen Sie schon die Schilder

Go straight on
Gehen Sie geradeaus

Turn left
Biegen Sie links ab

Turn right
Biegen Sie rechts ab

Head north/south
Gehen/Fahren Sie nach Norden/ Süden

Cross over
Überqueren Sie

Traffic lights
Die Ampel

Roundabout
Der Kreisverkehr

Intersection
Die Kreuzung

Corner
Die Ecke

Tunnel
Der Tunnel

One-way street
Einbahnstrasse

Danger
Gefahr

Ice on road
Glatteis

Roadworks ahead
Baustelle

Services
Rasthofstätte

Entry
Einfahrt

Exit
Ausfahrt

No parking
Parken verboten

Restricted parking
Beschränktes Parken

Pedestrian zone
Fussgängerzone

GETTING AROUND BY PUBLIC TRANSPORTATION

Where is the train/bus station?
Wo ist der Bahnhof/ Busbahnhof?

Where is the information desk?
Wo ist die Auskunft?

Where can I buy a ticket?
Wo kann ich eine Fahrkarte kaufen?

Please can I have a single/return ticket to ... ?
Einmal einfach/hin und zurück nach ... bitte?

Can I come back on the same ticket?
Kann ich mit dieser Fahrkarte auch zurück?

Can I change on this ticket?
Kann ich mit dieser Fahrkarte umsteigen?

You have to change trains at ...
Sie müssen in ... umsteigen

How long is this ticket valid for?
Wie lange ist diese Fahrkarte gültig?

I would like a standard/first-class ticket to ...
Ich möchte eine Fahrkarte zweiter/erster Klasse nach ...

How much is the supplement for the intercity?
Wie hoch ist der IC Zuschlag?

Do you have a subway/bus map?
Haben Sie einen U-Bahn/Busplan?

Where is the timetable?
Wo ist der Fahrplan?

The train to ... has been delayed by ... minutes
Der Zug nach ... hat eine Verspätung von ... Minuten

The train now arriving at platform ... is the train to/from ...
Auf Gleis ... fährt ein der Zug nach/aus ...

Does this train/bus go to ...?
Fährt dieser Zug/Bus nach ...?

Does this train/bus stop at ...?
Hält dieser Zug/Bus in ...?

Is this seat free/reserved?
Ist dieser Platz frei/reserviert?

Your ticket please
Ihre Fahrkarte bitte

Where are we?
Wo sind wir?

Have we already passed ...?
Sind wir schon an/am/an der ... vorbei?

Do I have to get off here?
Muss ich hier aussteigen?

Can you let me know when we get to ...?
Würden Sie mir Bescheid sagen, wenn wir bei ... sind?

Could you stop at the next stop please?
Halten Sie bitten an der nächsten Haltestelle

We're now approaching ...
Wir nähern uns ...

Where can I find a taxi?
Wo bekomme ich ein Taxi?

Please take me to ...
Fahren Sie mich bitte zum/zur/nach ...

How much is the journey?
Was kostet die Fahrt?

Please turn on the meter
Stellen Sie bitte das Taxameter an

I'd like to get out here please
Ich möchte hier aussteigen

TOURIST INFORMATION

Where is the tourist information office/desk, please?
Wo ist die Touristeninformation, bitte?

Do you have a city map?
Haben Sie einen Stadtplan?

Where is the museum?
Wo ist das Museum?

Can you give me some information about ...?
Können Sie mir Informationen über ... geben?

What are the main places of interest here?
Was sind hier die Hauptsehenswürdigkeiten?

Please could you point them out on the map?
Können Sie sie mir bitte auf der Karte zeigen?

What sights/hotels/restaurants can you recommend?
Welche Sehenswürdigkeiten/Hotels/Restaurants können Sie empfehlen?

Is there an English-speaking guide?
Gibt es einen Führer, der Englisch spricht?

Are there organized excursions?
Gibt es organisierte Ausflüge?

Can we make reservations here?
Können wir hier buchen?

Is there a discount for senior citizens/students?
Gibt es eine Ermässigung für Senioren/Studenten?

Do you have a brochure in English?
Haben sie eine Broschüre auf Englisch?

DAYS, MONTHS AND SEASONS

Monday
Montag

Tuesday
Dienstag

Wednesday
Mittwoch

Thursday
Donnerstag

Friday
Freitag

Saturday
Samstag/Sonnabend

Sunday
Sonntag

January
Januar

February
Februar

March
März

April
April

May
Mai

June
Juni

July
Juli

August
August

September
September

October
Oktober

November
November

December
Dezember

Spring
Frühling

Summer
Sommer

Autumn
Herbst

Winter
Winter

NUMBERS

0.. null

1.. eins

2.. zwei

3.. drei

4.. vier

5.. fünf

6.. sechs

7.. sieben

8.. acht

9.. neun

10.. zehn

11.. elf

12.. zwölf

13.. dreizehn

14.. vierzehn

15.. fünfzehn

16.. sechzehn

17.. siebzehn

18.. achtzehn

19.. neunzehn

20.. zwanzig

21.. einundzwanzig

30.. dreissig

40.. vierzig

50.. fünfzig

60.. sechzig

70.. siebzig

80.. achtzig

90.. neunzig

100.. hundert

1000.. tausend

million.. million

quarter.. viertel

half.. hälfte

three quarters.. dreiviertel

COLOURS

black
schwarz

blue
blau

brown
braun

green
grün

grey
grau

orange
orange

pink
rosa

purple
lila

red
rot

turquoise
türkis

yellow
gelb

white
weiss

light
hell

dark
dunkel

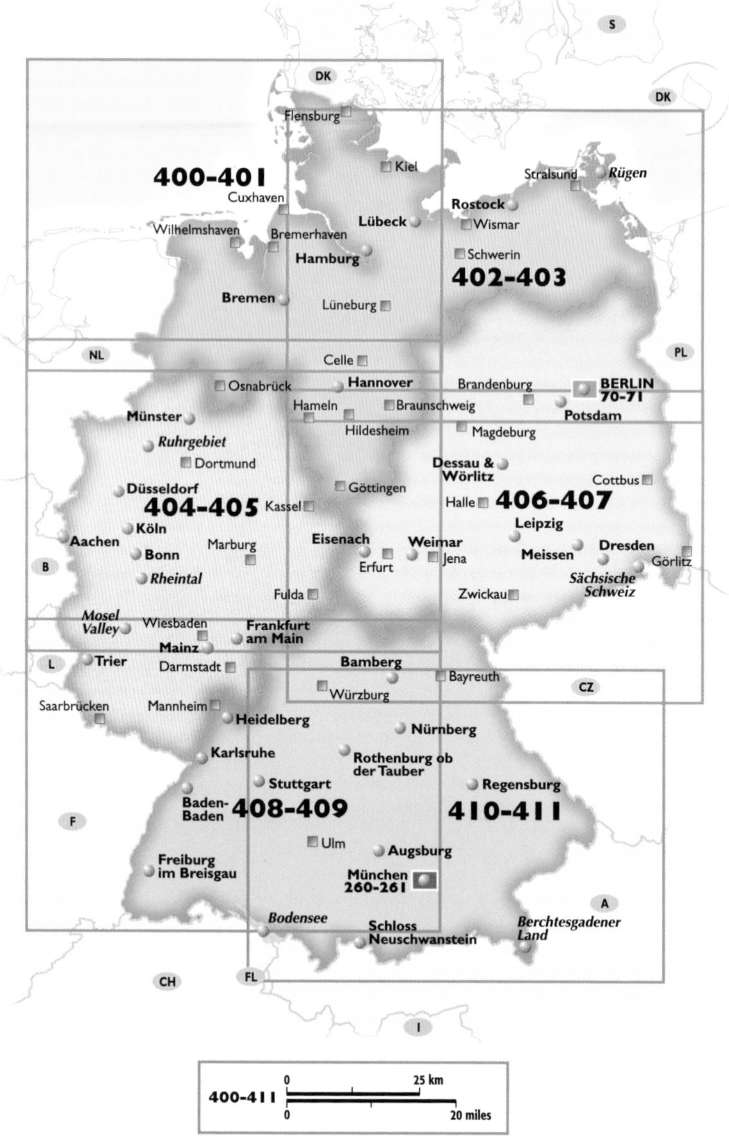

S
DK
DK
Flensburg
400-401
Kiel
Stralsund
Rügen
Cuxhaven
Rostock
Wilhelmshaven
Bremerhaven
Lübeck
Wismar
Hamburg
Schwerin
402-403
Bremen
Lüneburg
NL
Celle
PL
Osnabrück
Hannover
Brandenburg
BERLIN 70-71
Hameln
Braunschweig
Potsdam
Münster
Hildesheim
Magdeburg
Ruhrgebiet
Dortmund
Dessau & Wörlitz
Cottbus
Düsseldorf
Göttingen
404-405
Kassel
Halle
406-407
Köln
Leipzig
Aachen
Eisenach
Weimar
Marburg
Dresden
Bonn
Erfurt
Jena
Meissen
Görlitz
B
Rheintal
Sächsische Schweiz
Fulda
Zwickau
Mosel Valley
Wiesbaden
Frankfurt am Main
Mainz
L
Trier
Darmstadt
Bamberg
Bayreuth
Würzburg
CZ
Saarbrücken
Mannheim
Heidelberg
Nürnberg
Karlsruhe
Rothenburg ob der Tauber
Stuttgart
Regensburg
Baden-Baden
408-409
410-411
F
Ulm
Augsburg
Freiburg im Breisgau
München 260-261
A
Bodensee
Schloss Neuschwanstein
Berchtesgadener Land
CH
FL
I

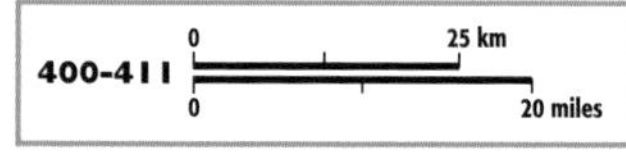

Toll motorway (Turnpike)

Motorway (Expressway)

Motorway junction with and without number

National road

Regional road

Railway

International boundary

Administrative region boundary

Built-up area

City / Town

National park

Featured place of interest

Airport

621 Height in metres

Viewpoint

Mountain pass

Ferry route

MAPS

Map references for the sights refer to the atlas pages within this section or to the individual town plans within the regions. For example, Hamburg has the reference 402 F4, indicating the page on which the map is found (402) and the grid square in which Hamburg sits (F4).

Maps	400
Atlas index	412

A
B
C
2
3
4
5
Deutsche
Ostfriesische Inseln
Juist
Norderney
Baltrum
Langeoog
Wangerooge
Spiekeroog
Borkum
Norddeich
Norden
Waddeneilanden
Terschelling
Ameland
Schiermonnikoog
Wittmund
Ogenbargen
Jever
Georgsheil
Aurich
Ems-Jade-Kanal
Roodeschool
Waddenzee
Appingedam
Leeuwarden
Buitenpost
Emden
Harlingen
Dollard
Neermoor
Hesel
Bergumer Meer
GRONINGEN
Siddeburen
Bolsward
Drachten
Leer
Loga
Eelde
Veendam
Sneek
Weener
Assen
Tjonger-Kanal
Heerenveen
Papenburg
Strücklingen
Smilde
Stadskanaal
Küsten-Kanal
IJsselmeer
Lemmer
Tieukemeer
Ems
Dörpenn
Musselkanaal
Dwingeloo
Enkhuizen
Hoogkarspol
Schoonoord
Ter Apel
Soeste
Emmeloord
Lathen
Meppel
Hoogeveen
Emmen
Haren
Cloppenburg
Nordradde
Lastrup
Klazienaveen
Coevorden
NL
Kampen
Schoonebeek
Meppen
Essen
Lelystad
Herzlake
Zwolle
Hardenberg
Emlichheim
Quakenbrück
Ommen
Hattem
Neuenhaus
Harderwijk
Uelsen
Fürstenau
Ankum
Bersenbrück
Lingen
Heerde
Raalte
Epe
Nordhorn
Vaassen
Nijverdal
404

D
E
F
G
Rømø
Skærbæk
Toftlund
Bevtoft
Hoptrup
Barsø
Lille Bælt
Ørbæk
Snarup
Gislev
Rødekro
Abenrá
Tyvsen
DK
Fåborg
Lyø
Svendborg
Tønder
Sæd
Tingley
Feldsted
Bovrup
Als
Fynshav
Avernakø
Tåsinge
Skarø
Spodsbjerg
Sylt
Nord-
Süderlugüm
Sønderborg
Ærø
Strynø
Rudkøbing
2
Föhr
Klixbüll
Leck
Flensburg
Risum Lindholm
Wallsbüll
Steinbergkirche
Langballig
Amrum
Friesische
Wanderup
Gelting
Langeness
Bredstedt
Hooge
Süderbrarup
Haselund
Hattstedt
Silberstedt
Schleswig
Schlei
Inseln
Husum
Busdorf
Nordstrand
Jagel
Kieler Bucht
Nationalpark Schleswig-Holsteinisches Wattenmeer
SCHLESWIG-
Tönning
Eider
Sorge
Helgoland
Rendsburg
KIEL
Heide
Tellingstedt
Hamdorf
Jevenstedt
Lütjenburg
Selent
3
Bucht
Ostsee-Kanal
Naturpark
Bordesholm
Preetz
Trischen
Meldorf
Hohenwestedt
Wankendorf
Plön
Nationalpark Hamburgisches Wattenmeer
Eutin
Nord-
Naturpark Holsteinische Schweiz
Scharhörn
Marne
Aukrug
Neumünster
Neuwerk
HOLSTEIN
Scharbeutz
Lübecker
Nationalpark Niedersächsisches Wattenmeer
Wilster
Kellinghusen
Rickling
Ahrensbök
Timmendorfer
Cuxhaven
Brunsbüttel
Elbe
Itzehoe
Bad Bramstedt
Bad Segeberg
Travemünde
Grosser Knechtsand
Lentföhrden
Neuhaus
Otterndorf
Cadenberge
402
Stockelsdorf
Schlutup
Dassow
LÜBECK
Bad Oldesloe
Quickborn
Weser
Hemmoor
Elmshorn
Pinnau
Elbe-Lübeck Kanal
Rehna
Jade
Ahrensburg
Naturpark
4
Himmelpforten
Oste
BREMEN
Schaalsee
Blexen
Fuhlsbüttel
Wilhelmshaven
BREMERHAVEN
Stade
Gadebusch
Jadebusen
Naturpark
HAMBURG
Nordenham
Mölln
Lützow
Horneburg
Lauenburgische
Varel
Beverstedt
Bremervörde
HAMBURG
Schaal-See
Rodenkirchen
Basdahl
Buxtehude
Schwarzenbek
Seen
Schil
Weser
Ovelgönne
Harburg
Hambergen
Kuhstedt
Selsingen
Geesthacht
Rade
Schaale
Hamme
Elsfleth
Zeven
Lauenburg
Horst
Pritz
Tostedt
Boizenburg
Hunte
Osterholz-Scharmbeck
Bockel
Bardowick
OLDENBURG
BREMEN
Welle
Naturpark Lüneburger Heide
Lüneburg
Scheessel
Elbe
Wümme
Sottrum
Naturpark
BREMEN
Rotenburg
Melbeck
Delmenhorst
Bremen
Hemslingen
Amelinghausen
Naturpark
5
Brinkum
Naturpark
Achim
Neuenkirchen
Bispingen
Elbufer-
Dannenberg
Wildeshauser
Zernien
Syke
Munster
Verden
Soltau
Uelzen
Drawehn
Jeetze
Bassum
Geest
Dörverden
Walsrode
Twistringen
Vechta
Barnstorf
Asendorf
Hassel
Aller
Bergen
Naturpark
Bergen
Weyhausen
NIEDERSACHSEN
Salzwedel
Sulingen
Südheide
Sprakensehl
Diepholz
Schwarmstedt
Rehden
Barenburg
Lemke
Eschede
Winterfeld
Nienburg
Rodewald
Wietze
Dümmer See
Kirchdorf
Landesbergen
405
Celle
Gross Oesingen
Stolzenau

Risum Lindholm
Leck
Flensburg
Langballig
Steinbergkirche
Ærø
Stokkemarke
Sakskøbing
E47
DK
Lolland
Rødbyhavn
Gelting
Wanderup
Süderbrarup
Bredstedt
Haselund
Hattstedt
Silberstedt
Schleswig
Schlei
Husum
Busdorf
Nordstrand
Jagel
SCHLESWIG-
Fehmarn
Kieler Bucht
Puttgarden
Landkirchen
Tönning
Eider
Sorge
Rendsburg
A210
KIEL
Grossenbrode
Tellingstedt
Hamdorf
Lütjenburg
Heide
Jevenstedt
Selent
Oldenburg
Ostsee-Kanal
Bordesholm
Preetz
Naturpark
Mecklenburger Bucht
Meldorf
Hohenwestedt
401
Wankendorf
Plön
Eutin
Naturpark Holsteinische Schweiz
Marne
Aukrug
Neumünster
Ba
Dobera
HOLSTEIN
Wilster
Kellinghusen
Rickling
Ahrensbök
Scharbeutz
Lübecker Bucht
Timmendorfer Strand
Poel
Brunsbüttel
Elbe
Itzehoe
Bad Bramstedt
Bad Segeberg
Travemünde
Neubukov
Neuhaus
Lentföhrden
Schlutup
Dassow
Cadenberge
Stockelsdorf
Wismar
LÜBECK
Grevesmühlen
Bad Oldesloe
Quickborn
Elmshorn
Hemmoor
Rehna
Pinnau
Ahrensburg
Elbe-Lübeck Kanal
Naturpark
Zickhusen
Brüel
Himmelpforten
Gadebusch
Stade
Fuhlsbüttel
Naturpark Schaalsee
Sternberg
ERHAVEN
HAMBURG
Lützow
Mölln
Schweriner-See
Horneburg
Lauenburgische
Schaal-See
Schwerin
Beverstedt
Bremervörde
HAMBURG
Basdahl
Buxtehude
Schwarzenbek
Seen
Schilde
Ovelgönne
Kuhstedt
Selsingen
Harburg
Rade
Geesthacht
Schaale
Hamme
Zeven
Horst
Lauenburg
Pritzier
Tostedt
Boizenburg
Redefin
Neustadt-Glewe
Parchim
Bockel
Bardowick
Sude
REMEN
Welle
Naturpark Lüneburger Heide
Lüneburg
Ludwigslust
Elbe
Scheessel
Wümme
Sottrum
Rotenburg
Naturpark
Grabow
Melbeck
Eldena
Naturpark
Karstädt
Hemslingen
Amelinghausen
Dannenberg
Achim
Bispingen
Neuenkirchen
Elbufer-
Elbetal
Munster
Zernien
Perleberg
Drawehn
Jeetze
Verden
Soltau
Uelzen
Wittenberge
Dörverden
Walsrode
Bergen
Alland
Hassel
Aller
Naturpark
Seehausen
Bergen
Weyhausen
Salzwedel
ACHSEN
Südheide
Sprakensehl
Schwarmstedt
Lemke
Eschede
Osterburg
Rodewald
Nienburg
Wietze
Winterfeld
Landesbergen
Celle
Gross Oesingen
Neustadt am Rübenberge
Milde
Leese
Wienhausen
Stendal
Steinhuder Meer
Hannover
Vinzelberg
Wunstorf
405
Aller
Gardelegen
Fischbeck
Oker
Mieste
Jävenitz
Lüderitz
Bad Nenndorf
Wolfsburg
Vorsfelde
Miesterhorst
Stadthegen
HANNOVER
Meine
Oebisfelde
Mittelland Kanal
Jerichow
Velpke
Dolle
Bückeburg
Peine
Pattensen
SACHSEN-
Naturpark
BRAUNSCHWEIG
Haldensleben
Colbitz
Oldendorf
Hachmühlen
Springe
Weserbergland-Fischbeck
Hildesheim
Königslutter
406
Erxleben
Burg
Wolmirstedt
Aller

H
J
K
L
Møn
Nykøbing
Falster
Marrebæk
Gedser
Kap Arkona
Nationalpark Jasmund
Sassnitz
Nationalpark Vorpommersche Boddenlandschaft
Rügen
E22/E251
Saaler Bodden
Stralsund
Samtens
Putbus
Ostseebäder
Biosphärenreservat Südost-Rügen
3
105
E22
Löbnitz
Ribnitz-Damgarten
Warnemünde
Rövershagen
Petersdorf
Abtshagen
Reinberg
Greifswalder Bodden
Sanitz
Grimmen
96
E251
Greifswald
ROSTOCK
Tessin
A20
103
110
Poggendorf
194
109
111
Zinnowitz
Koserow
Wolgast
Usedom
Recknitz
Gnoien
Trebel
Loitz
Laage
Naturpark Usedom
Bansin
Heringsdorf
Kamień Pomorski
Weitendorf
Dargun
Demmin
Jarmen
Ahlbeck
Świnoujście
Woliński Park Narodowy
108
A19
E55
Peene
Ziethen
MECKLENBURG-
Güstrow
Thürkow
Kummerower See
Anklam
Partówko
4
104
Teterow
Malchin
Golchen
Stettiner Haff
Zalew Szczeciński
Nebel
Malchiner See
Reuterstadt Stavenhagen
Tollense
Ueckermunder Heide
Krakow am See
Altentreptow
Friedland
Przybiernów
E65
Goldberg
192
Ferdinandshof
Babigoszcz
VORPOMMERN
Randow
Karow
Warren
Kl Plasten
A20
Elde
Neubrandenburg
Goleniów
Klink
Tollense See
Pasewalk
Lübz
Plau
Penzlin
E251
Woldegk
SZCZECIN
Plauer See
Müritz See
Müritz-Nationalpark
Jezioro Dąbie
198
Görlitz
Meyenburg
Möllenbeck
Naturpark Feldberger Seenlandschaft
Dabie
Neustrelitz
10
Morzycyn
E26
Müritz Nationalpark
A24
Mirow
Wesenberg
Prenzlau
A11
E28
A6
Ueckermarkische Seen
Stare Czarnowo
5
Pritzwalk
Ravensbrück
Naturpark Mittenwalde
Hassleben
Wittstock / Dosse
Gramzow
Gryfino
Fürstenberg
Jezioro Miedwie
Nationalpark Unteres Odertal
Szczeciński Park Krajobrazowy
Tüchen
Schönbeck
Milmersdorf
166
Dannenwalde
Biosphärenreservat
Pyrzyce
Schwedt
Gransee
2
PL
Gumtow
Kyritz
Schorfheide-Chorin
Angermünde
Lipiany
Glöwen
Neuruppin
Alt Ruppin
BRANDENBURG
Gross Schönebeck
Wusterhausen
Dosse
Löwenberg
Cedyński Park Krajobrazowy
Havelberg
Herzberg
Myślibórz
Liebenwalde
Naturpark
Eberswalde
Sandau
Friesack
Finow
Barnim
Bad Freienwalde
E65
Oranienburg
Biesenthal
167
Breisen
Havel
E26
Wriezen
Odra
Oder
Oderbruch
Klietz
A111
A10
Naturpark Märkische Schweiz
Witnica
6
Rathenow
188
Pessin
Bernau
132
BERLIN
Nauen
Tegel
Marxwalde
Spandau
Kostrzyn
Staaken
A100
BERLIN
Rudersdorf
Müncheberg
Seelow
Manschnow
Plaue
A115
Herzfelde
Genthin
POTSDAM
Brandenburg
E51
Schönefeld
A113
Fürstenwalde
Lebus
Ziesar
Frankfurt (Oder)

Zwolle
Ommen
Emlichheim
Quakenbrück
Harderwijk
Hattem
400
Uelsen
Neuenhaus
Naturpark Nördland
Ankum
Bersenbrück
NL
Heerde
Raalte
Lingen
Fürstenau
Epe
Vaassen
Nijverdal
Wierden
Almelo
Nordhorn
Freren
Teutoburger
APELDOORN
Amersfoort
Deventer
Oldenzaal
Denekamp
Lünne
Wald
Bramsche
Barneveld
Voorst
Hengelo
Bad Bentheim
Wiehengebirge
Zeist
Zutphen
Goor
ENSCHEDE
Ochtrup
Rheine
Lotte
Ede
Nat Park de Hoge Veluwe
Nat Park Veluwezoom
Dieren
Brummen
Lochem
Haaksbergen
Gronau
Epe
Wettringen
Tecklenburg
OSNABRÜCK
Amerongen
Velp
Doesburg
Eibergen
Heek
Emsdetten
Bad Iburg
Wageningen
ARNHEM
Groenlo
Ahaus
Steinfurt
Naturpark
Elst
Doetinchem
Lichtenvoorde
Altenberge
Teutoburger Wald
Zevenaar
Winterswijk
Stadtlohn
NORDRHEIN-
Glandorf
Wiehengebirge
Telgte
Coesfeld
Oss
NIJMEGEN
Isselburg
Bocholt
Borken
MÜNSTER
Grave
Cuijk
Kleve
Warendorf
Veghel
Uden
Gennep
Kalkar
Naturpark Raesfeld
Münsterland
Lembeck
Dülmen
Rheda
Goch
Xanten
Rhein
Hohe-Mark
Schermbeck
Wulfen
Drensteinfurt
Wiedenbrück
Ahlen
Beek en Donk
Venray
Weeze
Haltern
WESTFALEN
Wesel
Dorsten
Helmond
Well
Recklinghausen
Werne
HAMM
Lippstadt
Deurne
Geldern
Maas
Rheinberg
Kamp Lintfort
Dinslaken
Gladbeck
Lünen
Ruhrgebiet
EINDHOVEN
Horst
Bottrop
Gelsenkirchen
Castrop-Rauxel
Erwitte
Straelen
Kerken
Moers
Oberhausen
ESSEN
Unna
Werl
Soest
Venlo
DUISBURG
BOCHUM
DORTMUND
Tegelen
KREFELD
Mülhern
Ruhr
Witten
Menden
Belecke
Weert
Deutsch Niederlandischer Naturpark
Kettwig
Hattingen
Hemer
Naturpark Arnsberger Wald
Swaimen
Viersen
Düsseldorf
Velbert
Arnsberg
Warstein
Dülken
Ratingen
Hagen
Iserlohn
Beckum
Roermond
MÖNCHEN-GLADBACH
Neuss
DÜSSELDORF
WUPPERTAL
Meschede
Rheindahlen
Erkelenz
Rheydt
Lüdenscheid
Werdohl
Naturpark
Eslohe
Heinsberg
Grevenbroich
SOLINGEN
Remscheid
Halver
Homert
Sittard
Dormagen
Langenfeld
Naturpark
Geilenkirchen
Wermelskirchen
Lenne
Grevenbrück
Bergisch Gladbach
Naturpark
Brunssum
Mersch
LEVERKUSEN
Ebbegebirge
Sauerland
Maastricht
MAASTRICHT
Heerlen
Jülich
Naturpark
KÖLN (COLOGNE)
Olpe
AACHEN
Eschweiler
Köln/Bonn
Bergisches Land
Rothaargebirge
Düren
Rhein
Siegburg
SIEGEN
Rur
LIEGE (LUIK)
Herbesthal
Sieg
Eupen
Deutsch
Zülpich
BONN
Hennef
Verviers
Euskirchen
Altenkirchen
Dillenburg
(Nordeifel)
Königswinter
Theux
Monschau
Spa
Schleiden
Bad Münstereifel
Bad Honnef
Remagen
Belgischer
Nationalpark Eifel
Altenahr
Linz
Rennerod
Malmedy
Bütgenbach
Bad Breisig
Bad Hönnigen
Stavelot
Ligneuville
Brohl
Losheim
Blankenheim
Neuwied
Lahn
Wetzlar
B
Adenau
747
Naturpark
Stadtkyll
Nurburg
Montabaur
Koblenz
Naturpark
Kelberg
Mayen
Naturpark
Limburg
Wemperhaardt
(Sudeifel)
Prüm
Gerolstein
Eifel
Lahnstein
Diez
Hochtaunus
Pronsfeld
Schönecken
Burg Eltz
Brodenbach
Rhens
Braubach
Nassau
Camberg
Bastogne (Bastenaken)
Dasburg
Cochem
Treis
Boppard
RHEINLAND-
Mosel Valley
St Goarshausen
Naturpark Rhein-Taunus
Taunus
880
Bad Homburg
Deutsch-Luxemburgischer Naturpark
Alf
Oberwesel
St Goar
Alzette
Kastellaun
Kaub
Taunusstein
Wittlich
Bacharach
WIESBADEN
FRANKFURT AM MAIN
Diekirch
Bitburg
Zell
408
Ettelbruck
Simmern
Mülheim
MAINZ
A
B
C
6
7
8
9
10

NIEDERSACHSEN
D
E
F
G
401
402
406
409
Diepholz
Sulingen
Lemke
Rehden
Barenburg
Nienburg
Rodewald
Schwarmstedt
Weyhausen
Naturpark Südheide
Eschede
Sprakensehl
Salzwedel
Winterfeld
Dümmer See
Kirchdorf
Landesbergen
Stolzenau
Wietze
Celle
Gross Oesingen
Naturpark Dümmer
Uchte
Neustadt am Rübenberge
Leese
Steinhuder Meer
Hannover
Wienhausen
6
Bröckel
Aller
Oker
Bohmte
Petershagen
Wunstorf
Mieste
Lübbecke
Minden
Bad Nenndorf
Stadthagen
HANNOVER
Wolfsburg
Vorsfelde
Wiehengebirge
Melle
Bünde
Bad Oeynhausen
Bückeburg
Meine
Oebisfelde
Velpke
Peine
Naturpark
Hess Oldendorf
Hachmühlen
Weserbergland-
Pattensen
Springe
BRAUNSCHWEIG
Halden
Herford
Bad Salzuflen
Halle
Fischbeck
Coppenbrügge
Hameln
Hildesheim
Königslutter
Helmstedt
Erxleben
Wolfenbüttel
Lemgo
Lage
Schaumburg
Hameln
Elze
BIELEFELD
Detmold
Aerzen
Barntrup
Bodenwerder
Winnigstedt
Gütersloh
Stukenbrock
Blomberg
Polle
Eschershausen
Alfeld
Leine
Salzgitter-Bad
Schladen
Dardesheim
7
Hern
Naturpark Eggegeburge-
Stahle
Holzminden
Bad Gandersheim
Goslar
Seesen
Gröningen
Delbrück
Paderborn
Höxter
Einbeck
Harz
Bad Harzburg
Halberstadt
Salzkotten
Südlicher
Brakel
Godelheim
Naturpark Solling-Vogler
Nationalpark
Naturpark
Wernigerode
Blankenburg
Geseke
Lichtenau
Teutoburger Wald
Beverungen
Bad Karlshafen
Northeim
Osterode
Harz
Hochharz
Quedlinburg
Peckelsheim
Katlenburg-Duhm
Braunlage
Hasselfelde
Bode
Bad Wünnenberg
Scherfede
Gieselwerder
Gieboldehausen
Bad Lauterburg
Selke
Marsberg
Warburg
Reinhardshagen
GÖTTINGEN
Unter Herz
Diemelstadt
Brilon
Bredelar
Naturpark Münden
Hann-Münden
Duderstadt
Nordhausen
Breuna
Friedland
Olsberg
Naturpark Diemelsee
Bad Arolsen
KASSEL
Berga
Rossla
Ruhr
Korbach
Kaufungen
Witzenhausen
Heiligenstadt
Leinefelde
Sondershausen
8
Winterberg
Eder Stausee
Naturpark Habichtswald
Naturpark Meissner
Dingelstädt
Hallenberg
Helsa
Kaufunger Wald
Eschwege
Eigenrieden
Mühlhausen
Greussen
Eder
Nationalpark Kellerwald-Edersee
Hessich-Lichtenau
Wanfried
Bad Tennstedt
Staussfurt
Kölleda
Frankenberg
Battenberg
Sömmerda
Jesberg
Nationalpark Hainich
Bad Langensalza
Gebesee
Fulda
Münchhausen
Schwalm
Wartburg
Eisenach
Weimar
Cölbe
Bad Hersfeld
Gotha
ERFURT
Marburg
Kirchhain
Thüringer Wald
Valley
Ohm
Kirtorf
Alsfeld
Niederaula
Arnstadt
Ohrdruf
Barchfeld
9
HESSEN
THÜRI
Burghaun
Oberhof
Giessen
Lauterbach
Naturpark Hessische Rhön
Wasungen
Zella-Mehlis
Ilmenau
Grünberg
Vogelsberg
982 Gr Beerberg
Suhl
Saalfeld
Nidda
Fulda
Meiningen
Butzbach
950
Henneberg
Themar
Schleusingen
Neuhaus
Döllbach
Gersfeld
Eussenhausen
Bad Nauheim
Friedberg
Rhön
Mellrichstadt
Hildburghausen
Naturpark Hessischer Spessart
Bischofsheim
Naturpark
Eisfeld
Nieder-Wöllstadt
Heustreu
Rottenbach
Franken
Bad Neustadt
Bayerische
Bad Brückenau
10
Münnerstadt
Coburg
Wallenfels
Hanau
Rhön
Naturpark
Kronach
Offenbach
Hammelburg
Marktzeuln

HANNOVER
BRAUNSCHWEIG
402
Hildesheim
Wolfenbüttel
MAGDEBURG
Hameln
Goslar
Halberstadt
Wernigerode
Quedlinburg
GÖTTINGEN
Nordhausen
KASSEL
405
Mühlhausen
HALLE
Naumburg
Eisenach
Gotha
ERFURT
Weimar
Jena
GERA
THÜRINGEN
Fulda
Suhl
Plauen
Coburg
Schweinfurt
409
Bayreuth
Bamberg
WÜRZBURG
410
SACHSEN
ANHALT
Harz
Thüringer Wald
Frankenwald
Fichtel Gebirge

BERLIN
403
POTSDAM
Brandenburg
Plaue
Genthin
Rudersdorf
Müncheberg
Seelow
Manschnow
Herzfelde
Fürstenwalde
Lebus
Frankfurt (Oder)
Ziesar
A10
E30 E55
A12 E30
Swiecko
Torzym
Müllrose
Brieskow-
Finkenheerd
Beelitz
Görzke
Wiesenburg
Treuenbrietzen
Märkische
BURG
Heide
E36 E55
A13
Dahme
Biosphärenreservat
Spreewald
Naturpark
Schlaubetal
Beeskew
Eisenhüttenstadt
Trebatsch
Neuzelle
Nuthe
A9 E51
Marzahna
Kropstädt
Jüterbog
Biebersdorf
Lübben
Guben
Gubin
Rosslau
Coswig
Dessau
Wörlitz
Lutherstadt
Wittenberg
Dahme
Duben
Peitz
PL
Jessen
Brandis
Luckau
Eutzsch
Kemberg
Wüstermarke
Holzdorf
Dübener Heide
Herzberg
Schlieben
A15
E36
COTTBUS
Lubsko
Wolfen
Pretzsch
Dommitzsch
Drebkau
Tuplice
Langennaundorf
Döbern
Brehna
Wellaune
Bad Düben
183A
Delitzsch
Torgau
Schwarze
Bad Liebenwerda
Spremberg
Tschernitz
Senftenberg
Bad Muskau
Lauchhammer
Eilenburg
Belgern
Elbe
Spree
Gröditz
Elsterwerda
E55
A13
Hoyerswerda
Leipzig
Wurzen
Strehla
Spreewald
LEIPZIG
Markranstädt
A14
Mulde
Bernsdorf
Neisse
Oschatz
Riesa
Niesky
Königsbrück
Rötha
SACHSEN
Pegau
Colditz
A14
Moritzburg
A4
E40
Meissen
Borna
Döbeln
Radebeul
Dresden
Bautzen
Görlitz
Bischofswerda
Zgorzelec
Frohburg
Löbau
A4
E40
DRESDEN
Weisseritz
Herrnhut
Ebersbach
Pirna
Elbe
Sächsische
Schweiz
Rumburk
Neugersdorf
Ostritz
Freiberg
Frankenberg
Dippoldiswalde
Zittau
Elbsandsteingebirge
Schmilka
NP
České
Švýcarsko
Lužické
Hory
CHEMNITZ
Jizerské
Hory
Chrastava
Chko Labské
721
Česká
Kamenice
ZWICKAU
Zschopau
Altenberg
Lužické Hory
Liberec
E441
A72
Stollberg
Thum
Flöha
Cínovec
Piskovce
Děčín
Nový
Bor
Cvikov
Marienberg
956
Loučná
Dubí
1012
Ještěd
Olbernhau
Česká
Lipa
Aue
Annaberg-
Buchholz
Erzgebirge
Teplice
Chko
Ustí nad Labem
Hodkovice
nad Mohelkou
Reitzehain
Eibenstock
Hora Sv
Šebestiána
Bílina
České
837
Milešovka
Středohoří
Doksy
Turnov
Most
Bělá pod
Bezdězem
Vejprty
Chomutov
Oberwiesenthal
Chko
Kokořínsko
E442
Havraň
Klingenthal
Krušné Hory
1244
Klínovec
Jáchymov
Klášterec
nad Ohří
Postoloprty
Mladá
Boleslav
Louny
10 E65
Doupovské
CZ
Bad Brambach
Karlovy
Vary
Žatec
Schönberg
934
Hory
Slany
D8
E55
Vojtanov
Řevničov
Kladno
Nymburk
Bochov
E48
Slavkovský
Les
Chko
Bečov
nad Teplou
Slavkovský Les
PRAHA
(PRAGUE)
Cheb
Lubenec
Jesenice
D11
E67
20 E49
Tepelská plošina
Žďár
Chko
Úvaly
Velka Hleďsebe
Plasy
Kralovice
Kolín
Chodová
Planá
Křivoklátsko
D5
E50
Zbraslav
Planá
411
Úněšov
Kaznějov
Černošín
PLZEŇ
D1 E65
E59

RHEINLAND
Mosel Valley
404
A
B
C
Bastogne (Bastenaken)
Dasburg
Deutsch-Luxemburgischer Naturpark
Alzette
Bitburg
Wittlich
Zell
Mosel
Kastellaun
St Goarshausen
St Goar
Oberwesel
Bacharach
Kaub
Naturpark Rhein-Taunus
Taunusstein
Bad Homburg
FRANKFURT AM MAIN
WIESBADEN
MAINZ
Rüdesheim
Bingen
Rüsselsheim
Ettelbruck
Diekirch
10
L
Mersch
Echternach
Schweich
Mülheim
Traben-Trarbach
Simmern
Bernkastel-Kues
Trittenheim
Hunsrück
Arlon (Aarlen)
Wasserbillig
Trier
PFALZ
Bad Kreuznach
Wörrstadt
Gross-Gerau
DARMSTADT
LUXEMBOURG
Grevenmacher
Findel
Idar-Oberstein
Kirn
Nahe
Oppenheim
Meisenheim
Guntersblum
Ehnen
Saar
Birkenfeld
Alzey
Gemsheim
Remich
Glan
Esch-sur-Alzette
Hettange Grande
Mettlach
Nohfelden
Monsheim
Bensheim
Bürstadt
Sierck-les-Bains
SAARLAND
Altenglan
Winnweiler
Lohnsfeld
Grünstadt
Worms
Heppenheim
Weinheim
Thionville
Lebach
Uckange
Ottweiler
LUDWIGSHAFEN
11
Hagondange
Saarlouis
Neunkirchen
Landstuhl
Kaiserslautern
Bad Dürkheim
MANNHEIM
Auboué
Völklingen
St Ingbert
Homburg
Naturpark
Neustadt an der Weinstrasse
Mutterstadt
HEIDELBERG
Ensheim
Zweibrücken
673 Kalmit
Forbach
Pfälzerwald
METZ
SAARBRÜCKEN
Pirmasens
Edenkoben
Speyer
Wiesloch
St-Avold
Farébersviller
Hinterweidenthal
Sarreguemines
Landau
Frescaty
Puttelange
Parc Naturel Régional
Bitche
Bad Bergzabern
Neudorf
Bad Schönborn
Rohrbach-les-Bitche
Grostenquin
Bruchsal
Delme
des Vosges du Nord
Bretten
Dieulouard
Château-Salins
KARLSRUHE
Maulbronn
Parc Nat Rég de Lorraine
Ettlingen
12
NANCY
Sarrebourg
Haguenau
Soufflenheim
Rastatt
Pforzheim
Phalsbourg
Brumath
Neuves-Maisons
Hèming
Saverne
Lunéville
Baden-Baden
Bad Liebenzell
Blâmont
F
Marlenheim
Forbach
Strasbourg International
STRASBOURG
Calw
1009 Donon
Molsheim
1164
Raumünzach
Kehl
Renchen
Altensteig
Charmes
Baccarat
Appenweier
Schönmünzach
Herrenberg
Raon-l'Etape
Schirmeck
Oberkirch
Vosges
Offenburg
Kniebis
Nagold
Freudenstadt
Saales
Dompaire
St-Dié
Gengenbach
Bad Peterstal
Horb
Canal du Rhône au Rhin
Schwarzwald
Lossburg
Épinal
Brouvelieures
Biberach
Alpirsbach
13
Fraize
Rhin
Hausach
Schiltach
Haslach
Lapoutroie
Kaysersberg
Kenzingen
Oberndorf
Balingen
Parc Nat Régional
Hornberg
Remiremont
Gérardmer
Schramberg
Colmar
Elzach
Emmendingen
Triberg
Munster
Eschach
Rottweil
1202 Cornimont
des
Ballons
Breisach
Schönwald
1015
1241 Kandel
St Georgen
Rupt
Neuf Brisach
Villingen
Spaichingen
Luxeuil-les-Bains
Le Thillot
Bussang
Furtwangen
Soultz
Schwenningen
St Maurice-sur-Moselle
1250
FREIBURG IM BREISGAU
Tuttlingen
Bad Krozingen
Des Vosges
Thann
1414 Belchen
1493 Feldberg
Ronchamp
Geisingen
Feldberg
Lenzkirch
Lure
Müllheim
Bonndorf
MULHOUSE
Schönau
14
Belfort
Häusern
Sierentz
Riedern
Singen
Dannemarie
Zell
Altkirch
Montbéliard
Basel/Mulhouse
Schaffhausen
Waldshut
Lörrach
Berlingen
L'Isle-sur-le-Doubs
Delle
BASEL
Rheinfelden
Zurzach
Steckborn
CH
Reinach
Laufenburg (Baden)

Hanau
Offenbach
Aschaffenburg
WÜRZBURG
Schweinfurt
Bamberg
Coburg
Bayreuth
Erlangen
Fürth
NÜRNBERG
Ansbach
Heilbronn
Schwäbisch Hall
Ludwigsburg
STUTTGART
Esslingen
Aalen
Tübingen
Reutlingen
Ulm
AUGSBURG
Ingolstadt
MÜNCHEN (MUNICH)
Konstanz
Kempten
Rothenburg ob der Tauber
Dinkelsbühl
Nördlingen
Eichstätt
Heidelberg
Göppingen
Heidenheim
Kaufbeuren
Ravensburg
Friedrichshafen
405
406
410

406
409
WÜRZBURG
Bamberg
Bayreuth
Erlangen
Fürth
NÜRNBERG
Ansbach
Rothenburg ob der Tauber
Schwäbisch Hall
Ludwigsburg
STUTTGART
Esslingen
Aalen
Schwäbisch Gmünd
Göppingen
Heidenheim
Ingolstadt
Eichstätt
Naturpark Altmühltal (Südl Frankenalb)
Donauwörth
Ulm
AUGSBURG
MÜNCHEN (MUNICH)
Kempten
Kaufbeuren
Ravensburg
Friedrichshafen
Bodensee
Bregenz
St Gallen
Dornbirn
Oberammergau
Schloss Neuschwanstein
Schloss Linderhof
Garmisch-Partenkirchen
Füssen
Zugspitze
Bayerische Alpen

407
H
J
K
Žďár
Chko
Slavkovský Les
Tepelská Plošina
Chko
Křivoklátsko
PRAHA
(PRAGUE)
Gebirge
Naturpark
Kemnath
Steinwald
Waldnaab
Velka Hled'sebe
Chodová Planá
Planá
Kaznějov
Plasy
Úněšov
Erbendorf
Naturpark
Eschenbach
Hessenreuther
Manteler Wald
Tachov
Černošín
Stříbro
Kozolupý
PLZEŇ
(PILSEN)
Benešov
Weiden
Rozvadov
Waidhaus
Bor
Přimda
Stod
Líně
Příbram
Tok
Bystřice
Milín
Hirschau
Naturpark
Schnaittenbach
Horšovsky Týn
Přeštice
Staňkov
Sec
Votice
CZ
Oberpfälzer
Amberg
Oberviechtach
Orlícká přehr nádrž
Nepomuk
Lnáře
Wald
Klenčí
Draženov
Švihov
Kasejovice
Blatná
Tábor
Waldmünchen
Čerchov
Babylon
Schönthal
Folmava
Klatovy
Opařany
Sedlice
Bernartice
Bodenwöhr
Furth im Wald
Planá nad Lužnicí
Naturpark
Cham
Strakonice
Písek
Naab
Regen
Pancíř
Oberer
Bayerischer
Volyně
Protivin
Miltach
Bayerisch Eisenstein
Železná Ruda
Vodňany
Národní
Nittendorf
REGENSBURG
Viechtach
Wald
Chko
Ascha
Zwiesel
Naturpark Bayerischer Wald
Vimperk
Chko Třeboňsko
Patersdorf
Šumava
Pfatter
Regen
Gr Rachel
Park
ČESKÉ BUDĚJOVICE
Ruhmannsfelden
Horní Vltavice
Nationalpark Bayerischer Wald
Bayerischer Wald
Saal
Gr Laaber
Blanský Les
Straubing
Donau
Schönberg
Aiterhofen
Deggendorf
Philippsreut
Šumava
Knížecí Stolec
Velešín
Rohr i Niederb
Neufahrn
Ilz
Plattling
Chko Novohradské Hory
Pfeffenhausen
Ergoldsbach
Tittling
Vodní nádrž Lipno
Essenbach
Osterhofen
Aussernbrünst
Dolní Dvořiště
Vils
Arth
Isar
Haunersdorf
Salzweg
Wegscheid
Schläg
Novohradské Hory
Wullowitz
Landshut
Simbach
Rohrbach
Passau
Obernzell
Geisenhausen
Sandl
Vilsbiburg
Gangkofen
Pfarrkirchen
Neuburg
Schärding
Neufelden
Donau
Freistadt
Taufkirchen
Eggenfelden
Pocking
Mühlviertel
Neumarkt-St Veit
Novohradske
Taufkirchen
St Florian
Innviertel
Peuerbach
Obernberg
Dorfen
Simbach
Wilhering
Pregarten
Mühldorf
Altheim
Eferding
LINZ
Braunau
Alkoven
Linz
Inn
Grieskirchen
Asten
Perg
Haag
Alz
Ried im Innkreis
Garching
Burghausen
Uttendorf
Enns
Eberschwang
Strengberg
Saalach
Wels
Trostberg
Mattighofen
Lambach
Schwanenstadt
Kremsmünster
Tittmoning
Rott
Obing
Altenmarkt
Waginger See
Attnang-Puchheim
Aschbach Markt
Frankenmarkt
Sierning
Strasswalchen
Steyr
Neumarkt
Rosenheim
Chiemsee
Laufen
Kirchdorf an der Krems
Traunstein
Altersee
Gmunden
Freilassing
Traunsee
Micheldorf
Grassau
Raubling
Bernau
Grossraming
Traunkirchen
A
Marquartstein
Inzell
SALZBURG
Salzburg
Schafberg
Sengsengebirge
Bayrischzell
Stein Pass
Bad Reichenhall
St Gilgen
Salzkammergut
Kossen
Almsee
Gr Priel
Hallein
Reit im Winkl
Bad Ischl
Totes Gebirge
Altenmarkt
Berchtesgaden
Pötschen Pass
Kaisergebirge
Lofer
Berchtesgadener Land
Königssee
Strub Pass
Watzmann
Königssee
Lueg Pass
Bad Aussee
Pyhrn Pass
Hiefla
Söll
St Johann in Tirol
Nationalpark Berchtesgaden
Hallstätter See
Liezen
Admont
Wörgl
Pürgg
Stainach
Kitzbühel
Dachsteingruppe
Eisenerzer Alpen
Saalfelden
Kitzbüheler Alpen
Naturpark
Rottenmanner Tauern

Place	Page	Grid
Aachen	404	A8
Aalen	409	E12
Abtshagen	403	J3
Achim	401	E5
Adenau	404	B9
Adorf	406	H10
Aerzen	405	E7
Ahaus	404	B6
Ahlbeck	403	K4
Ahlen	404	C7
Ahrensbök	402	F3
Ahrensburg	402	F4
Aichach	410	F13
Aiterhofen	411	H12
Alf	404	B10
Alfeld	405	E7
Alpirsbach	408	C13
Alsfeld	405	D9
Altenahr	404	B9
Altenberg	407	J9
Altenberge	404	C6
Altenglan	408	B11
Altenkirchen	404	C9
Altenmarkt	411	H14
Altensteig	408	C13
Altentreptow	403	J4
Alt Ruppin	403	J5
Altshausen	409	D14
Alzey	408	C11
Amberg	411	G11
Amelinghausen	402	F5
Amorbach	409	D11
Angermünde	403	K5
Anklam	403	K4
Ankum	400	C6
Annaberg-Buchholz	407	J10
Ansbach	410	F12
Appenweier	408	C13
Arnsberg	404	C8
Arnstadt	406	F9
Arnstein	409	E10
Arth	411	G13
Ascha	411	H12
Aschaffenburg	409	D10
Aschersleben	406	G7
Asendorf	401	E5
Aue	407	H9
Auerbach	410	G11
Augsburg	410	F13
Aurach	410	F12
Aurich	400	C4
Aussernbrünst	411	J13
Babenhausen	409	D10
Babenhausen	409	E13
Bacharach	404	C10
Bad Arolsen	405	D8
Bad Bentheim	404	C6
Bad Bergzabern	408	C12
Bad Berneck	406	G10
Bad Bibra	406	G8
Bad Brambach	407	H10
Bad Bramstedt	401	F4
Bad Breisig	404	B9
Bad Brückenau	405	E10
Bad Doberan	403	H3
Bad Düben	407	H8
Bad Dürkheim	408	C11
Baden-Baden	408	C12
Bad Freienwalde	403	K6
Bad Friedrichshall	409	D12
Bad Gandersheim	405	E7
Bad Harzburg	406	F7
Bad Hersfeld	405	E9
Bad Homburg	404	D10
Bad Honnef	404	B9
Bad Hönnigen	404	B9
Bad Iburg	404	C6
Bad Karlshafen	405	E7
Bad Kreuznach	408	C10
Bad Krozingen	408	B14
Bad Langensalza	406	F8
Bad Lauterburg	406	F8
Bad Liebenwerda	407	J8
Bad Liebenzel	408	D12
Bad Mergentheim	409	E11
Bad Münstereifel	404	B9
Bad Muskau	407	K8
Bad Nauheim	405	D10
Bad Nenndorf	405	E6
Bad Neustadt	405	E10
Bad Oeynhausen	405	D6
Bad Oldesloe	402	F4
Bad Peterstal	408	C13
Bad Reichenhall	411	H14
Bad Salzuflen	405	D7
Bad Schönborn	408	D11
Bad Segeberg	402	F4
Bad Tennstedt	406	F8
Bad Tölz	410	G14
Bad Urach	409	D13
Bad Waldsee	409	E14
Bad Wünnenberg	405	D8
Balingen	408	D13
Bamberg	406	F11
Bansin	403	K4
Barchfeld	405	F9
Bardowick	402	F5
Barenburg	401	D6
Barnstorf	401	D5
Barntrup	405	E7
Basdahl	401	E4
Bassum	401	D5
Battenberg	405	D8
Bautzen	407	K9
Bayerisch Eisenstein	411	J12
Bayreuth	406	G11
Bayrischzell	411	G14
Beckum	404	C8
Beelitz	407	J7
Beerfelden	409	D11
Beeskew	407	K7
Beilngries	410	G12
Belecke	404	D8
Belgern	407	J8
Benediktbeuern	410	F14
Bennstedt	406	G8
Bensheim	408	D11
Berchtesgaden	411	H15
Berga	406	F8
Bergen	401	F5
Bergen	402	G5
Bergisch Gladbach	404	B8
Berlin	403	J6
Bernau	411	H14
Bernau	403	J6
Bernburg	406	G7
Bernkastel-Kues	408	B10
Bernsdorf	407	K8
Bersenbrück	400	C6
Besigheim	409	D12
Beverstedt	401	E4
Beverungen	405	E7
Biberach	408	C13
Biberach an der Riss	409	E14
Bichl	410	F14
Biebersdorf	407	K7
Bielefeld	405	D7
Biesenthal	403	J6
Bietigheim	409	D12
Bingen	408	C10
Birkenfeld	408	B11
Bischofsheim	405	E10
Bischofswerda	407	K9
Bispingen	401	F5
Bitburg	404	A10
Blankenburg	406	F7
Blankenheim	404	B9
Blaufelden	409	E11
Blaustein	409	E13
Blexen	401	D4
Blomberg	405	E7
Böblingen	409	D12
Bocholt	404	B7
Bochum	404	B7
Bockel	401	E5
Bodenwerder	405	E7
Bodenwöhr	411	H12
Böhmenkirch	409	E13
Bohmte	405	D6
Boizenburg	402	F5
Bonn	404	B9
Bonndorf	408	C14
Boppard	404	C10
Bordesholm	402	F3
Borken	404	B7
Borna	407	H9
Bottrop	404	B7
Brakel	405	E7
Bramsche	404	C6
Brandenburg	403	H6
Brandis	407	J7
Braubach	404	C10
Braunlage	406	F7
Braunschweig	402	F6
Bredelar	405	D8
Bredstedt	401	E2
Brehna	407	H8
Breisach	408	B13
Breisen	403	H6
Bremen	401	D5
Bremerhaven	401	D4
Bremervörde	401	E4
Bretten	408	D12
Breuna	405	E8
Brieskow-Finkenheerd	407	K7
Brilon	405	D8
Brinkum	401	D5
Bröckel	402	F6
Brodenbach	404	B10
Brohl	404	B9
Bruchsal	408	C12
Brüel	402	G4
Brunsbüttel	401	E4
Buchen	409	D11
Bückeburg	405	E6
Bünde	405	D6
Burg	406	G7
Burghaun	405	E9
Burghausen	411	H14
Bürstadt	408	C11
Busdorf	401	E3
Butzbach	405	D9
Buxtehude	401	E4
Cadenberge	401	E4
Calw	408	D12
Camberg	404	C10
Castrop-Rauxal	404	C7
Celle	405	F6
Cham	411	H12
Chemnitz	407	H9
Cloppenburg	400	D5
Coburg	406	F10
Cochem	404	B10
Coesfeld	404	B7
Cölbe	405	D9
Colbitz	402	G6
Coppenbrügge	405	E7
Coswig	407	H7
Cottbus	407	K8
Crailsheim	409	E12
Cuxhaven	401	D4
Dachau	410	G13
Dahme	407	J7
Dannenberg	402	G5
Dannenwalde	403	J5
Dardesheim	406	F7
Dargun	403	J4
Darmstadt	408	D10
Dasburg	404	A10
Dasing	410	F13
Dassow	402	G4
Dasswang	410	G12
Deggendorf	411	H13
Delbrück	405	D7
Delitzsch	407	H8
Delmenhorst	401	D5
Demmin	403	J4
Dessau	407	H7
Detmold	405	D7
Dieburg	409	D10
Diemelstadt	405	D8
Diepholz	401	D6
Diez	404	C9
Dillenburg	404	C9
Dillingen	410	F13
Dingelstädt	406	F8
Dinkelsbühl	409	E12

Dinslaken	404	B7
Dippoldiswalde	407	J9
Döbeln	407	J9
Döbern	407	K8
Döllbach	405	E9
Dolle	402	G6
Dommitzsch	407	H8
Donauwörth	410	F13
Dorfen	411	G13
Dormagen	404	B8
Dörpenn	400	C5
Dorsten	404	B7
Dortmund	404	C7
Dörverden	401	E5
Dörzbach	409	E11
Drebkau	407	K8
Drensteinfurt	404	C7
Dresden	407	J9
Duben	407	J7
Duderstadt	405	F8
Duisburg	404	B7
Dülken	404	A8
Dülmen	404	C7
Düren	404	B8
Düsseldorf	404	B8
Ebermannstadt	410	F11
Ebern	406	F10
Ebersbach	407	K9
Ebersberg	410	G14
Eberswalde	403	K6
Ebingen	409	D13
Edenkoben	408	C11
Egeln	406	G7
Eggenfelden	411	H13
Ehingen	409	E13
Eibenstock	407	H10
Eichstätt	410	F12
Eigenrieden	405	F8
Eilenburg	407	H8
Einbeck	405	E7
Eisenach	405	F9
Eisenhüttenstadt	407	K7
Eisfeld	406	F10
Eldena	402	G5
Ellingen	410	F12
Ellwangen	409	E12
Elmshorn	401	E4
Elsfleth	401	D5
Elsterwerda	407	J8
Elzach	408	C13
Elze	405	E7
Emden	400	C4
Emlichheim	400	B5
Emmendingen	408	B13
Emsdetten	404	C6
Emskirchen	410	F11
Engstingen	409	D13
Epe	404	B6
Eppingen	409	D12
Erbach	409	D11
Erbendorf	411	G11
Erfurt	406	F9
Ergoldsbach	411	G13
Erkelenz	404	A8
Erlangen	410	F11
Erwitte	404	D7
Erxleben	406	G7
Eschede	402	F6
Eschenbach	411	G11
Eschershausen	405	E7
Eschwege	405	E8
Eschweiler	404	A8
Eslohe	404	C8
Essen	404	B7
Essen	400	C5
Essenbach	411	G13
Esslingen	409	D12
Ettlingen	408	C12
Euskirchen	404	B9
Eussenhausen	405	F10
Eutin	402	F3
Eutzsch	407	H7
Feldberg	408	C14
Ferdinandshof	403	K4
Feuchtwangen	410	E12
Finow	403	J6
Fischbeck	405	E7
Fischbeck	402	H6
Flensburg	401	E2
Forbach	408	C12
Forchheim	410	F11
Frankenberg	405	D8
Frankenberg	407	J9
Frankfurt (Oder)	407	K7
Frankfurt Am Main	409	D10
Freiberg	407	J9
Freiburg Im Breisgau	408	B13
Freilassing	411	H14
Freren	404	C6
Freudenstadt	408	C13
Friedberg	405	D10
Friedberg	410	F13
Friedland	405	E8
Friedland	403	J4
Friedrichshafen	410	D14
Friesack	403	H6
Frohburg	407	H9
Fulda	405	E9
Fürstenau	400	C6
Fürstenberg	403	J5
Fürstenfeldbruck	410	F13
Fürstenwalde	407	K7
Fürth	410	F11
Furth im Wald	411	H12
Furtwangen	408	C13
Füssen	410	F14
Gadebusch	402	G4
Gaildorf	409	E12
Gammertingen	409	D13
Gangkofen	411	H13
Garching	411	H14
Gardelegen	402	G6
Garmisch-Partenkirchen	410	F15
Gebesee	406	F8
Geesthacht	402	F4
Gefrees	406	G10
Geilenkirchen	404	A8
Geisenfeld	410	G13
Geisenhausen	411	G13
Geisingen	408	C14
Geislingen	409	E13
Geldern	404	B7
Gelsenkirchen	404	B7
Gelting	402	F2
Gemsheim	408	C11
Gemunden	409	E10
Gengenbach	408	C13
Genthin	403	H6
Georgsheil	400	C4
Gera	406	H9
Gerolstein	404	B10
Gersfeld	405	E10
Geseke	405	D7
Gieboldehausen	405	F8
Gieselwerder	405	E8
Giessen	405	D9
Gladbeck	404	B7
Glandorf	404	C6
Glöwen	403	H5
Gnoien	403	J4
Goch	404	A7
Godelheim	405	E7
Golchen	403	J4
Goldbach	409	D10
Goldberg	403	H4
Gollhofen	409	E11
Gommern	406	G7
Göppingen	409	E12
Göritz	403	K5
Görlitz	407	L9
Görzke	407	H7
Goslar	406	F7
Gössweinstein	410	G11
Gotha	406	F9
Göttingen	405	E8
Grabow	402	G5
Gramzow	403	K5
Gransee	403	J5
Grassau	411	H14
Greifswald	403	J4
Greiz	406	H9
Greussen	406	F8
Grevenbroich	404	B8
Grevenbrück	404	C8
Grevesmühlen	402	G4
Grimmen	403	J3
Gröbers	406	H8
Gröditz	407	J8
Gronau	404	B6
Gröningen	406	G7
Grossenbrode	402	G3
Gross-Gerau	408	C10
Gross Oesingen	402	F6
Gross Schönebeck	403	J6
Grünberg	405	D9
Grünstadt	408	C11
Guben	407	K7
Gumtow	403	H5
Guntersblum	408	C10
Günzburg	409	E13
Gunzenhausen	410	F12
Güstrow	403	H4
Gütersloh	405	D7
Haag	411	G14
Hachmühlen	405	E7
Hagen	404	C8
Hahnbach	410	G11
Halberstadt	406	G7
Haldensleben	406	G6
Halle	405	D7
Halle	406	G8
Hallenberg	405	D8
Haltern	404	B7
Halver	404	C8
Hambergen	401	D4
Hamburg	402	F4
Hamdorf	401	E3
Hameln	405	E7
Hamm	404	C7
Hammelburg	409	E10
Hanau	409	D10
Hann-Münden	405	E8
Hannover	405	E6
Harburg	410	F12
Harburg	401	F4
Hardheim	409	E11
Haren	400	C5
Haselund	401	E2
Haslach	408	C13
Hassel	401	E5
Hasselfelde	406	F7
Hassleben	403	J5
Hattingen	404	B8
Hattstedt	401	E2
Haunersdorf	411	H13
Hausach	408	C13
Häusern	408	C14
Havelberg	403	H6
Hechingen	409	D13
Heek	404	B6
Heide	401	E3
Heidelberg	408	D11
Heidenheim	409	E13
Heilbronn	409	D12
Heiligenstadt	405	F8
Heilsbronn	410	F11
Heimertingen	409	E14
Heinsberg	404	A8
Helmstedt	406	G7
Helsa	405	E8
Hemau	410	G12
Hemer	404	C8
Hemmoor	401	E4
Hemslingen	401	E5
Henneberg	405	F9
Hennef	404	B9
Heppenheim	408	D11
Herbertingen	409	D14
Herford	405	D7
Heringsdorf	403	K4
Hern	405	D7
Herrenberg	408	D13
Herrnhut	407	K9
Hersbruck	410	G11
Herzberg	403	J6
Herzberg	407	J8

Herzfelde 403 K6
Herzlake 400 C5
Hesel 400 C4
Hessich-Lichtenau 405 E8
Hess Oldendorf 405 E6
Hettstedt 406 G8
Heustreu 405 E10
Hildburghausen 406 F10
Hildesheim 405 E7
Himmelpforten 401 E4
Hindelang 410 E15
Hinterweidenthal 408 C11
Hirschau 411 G11
Höchst 409 D11
Höchstädt 410 F13
Hof 406 G10
Hohenbrunn 410 G14
Hohenpeissenberg 410 F14
Hohenwestedt 401 E3
Holzdorf 407 J8
Holzkirchen 410 G14
Holzminden 405 E7
Homburg 408 B11
Horb 408 C13
Hornberg 408 C13
Horneburg 401 E4
Horst 402 F5
Höxter 405 E7
Hoyerswerda 407 K8
Husum 401 E3

Ichenhausen 409 E13
Idar-Oberstein 408 B10
Ilmenau 406 F9
Immenstadt 410 E14
Ingolstadt 410 G13
Inzell 411 H14
Iphofen 409 E11
Iserlohn 404 C8
Isny 410 E14
Isselburg 404 B7
Itzehoe 401 E4

Jagel 401 E3
Jarmen 403 J4
Jävenitz 402 G6
Jena 406 G9
Jerichow 402 H6
Jesberg 405 D8
Jessen 407 J7
Jevenstedt 401 F3
Jever 400 D4
Jülich 404 A8
Jüterbog 407 J7

Kaiserslautern 408 C11
Kaisheim 410 F12
Kalkar 404 B7
Kamp Lintfort 404 B7
Karlsruhe 408 C12
Karlstadt 409 E10
Karow 403 H4
Karstädt 402 G5
Kassel 405 E8
Kastellaun 404 B10
Katlenburg-Duhm 405 F7
Kaub 404 C10
Kaufbeuren 410 F14
Kaufering 410 F14
Kaufungen 405 E8
Kehl 408 B12
Kelberg 404 B9
Kellinghusen 401 E3
Kemberg 407 H7
Kemnath 406 G11
Kempten 410 E14
Kenzingen 408 B13
Kerken 404 B7
Kettwig 404 B8
Kiel 402 F3
Kirchdorf 405 D6
Kirchhain 405 D9
Kirn 408 B10
Kirtorf 405 D9
Kitzingen 409 E11
Kleve 404 A7
Klietz 403 H6
Klingenthal 407 H10
Klink 403 H5
Klixbüll 401 E2
Kl Plasten 403 J4
Kniebis 408 C13
Koblenz 404 C9
Kochel 410 F14
Kölleda 406 G8
Köln (Cologne) 404 B8
Königsbrück 407 K8
Königshofen 409 E11
Königslutter 406 F7
Königssee 411 H15
Königswinter 404 B9
Könnern 406 G8
Konstanz 409 D14
Korbach 405 D8
Koserow 403 K4
Köthen 406 H7
Krakow am See 403 H4
Krauchenwies 409 D14
Krefeld 404 B8
Kronach 406 G10
Kroppenstedt 406 G7
Kropstädt 407 H7
Krumbach 409 E13
Krün 410 F15
Kuhstedt 401 E4
Künzelsau 409 E11
Kupferzell 409 E12
Kyritz 403 H5

Laage 403 H4
Lage 405 D7
Lahnstein 404 C9
Landau 408 C11
Landesbergen 405 E6
Landkirchen 402 G3
Landsberg 410 F14
Landshut 411 G13
Landstuhl 408 B11
Langballig 401 E2
Langenfeld 404 B8
Langennaundorf 407 J8
Lastrup 400 C5
Lathen 400 C5
Laucha 406 G8
Lauchhammer 407 J8
Lauenburg 402 F5
Lauf 410 F11
Laufen 411 H14
Laufenburg (Baden) 408 C14
Lauffen 409 D12
Lauingen 410 E13
Lauterbach 405 E9
Lebach 408 B11
Lebus 403 K6
Leck 401 E2
Leer 400 C4
Leese 405 E6
Lehrberg 410 F11
Leinefelde 406 F8
Leipzig 407 H8
Leitzkau 406 H7
Lemgo 405 D7
Lemke 401 E6
Lentföhrden 401 F4
Lenzkirch 408 C14
Leverkusen 404 B8
Lichtenau 405 D7
Liebenwalde 403 J6
Limburg 404 C9
Lindau 410 D14
Lindenfels 409 D11
Lingen 400 C6
Linz 404 B9
Lippstadt 404 D7
Löbau 407 K9
Löbnitz 403 J3
Loga 400 C4
Lohnsfeld 408 C11
Lohr 409 E10
Loitz 403 J4
Lörrach 408 B14
Losheim 404 A9
Lossburg 408 C13
Lotte 404 C6
Löwenberg 403 J6
Lübbecke 405 D6
Lübben 407 K7
Lübeck 402 F4
Lübz 403 H5
Luckau 407 J7
Lüdenscheid 404 C8
Lüderitz 402 G6
Ludwigsburg 409 D12
Ludwigshafen 408 C11
Ludwigshafen 409 D14
Ludwigslust 402 G5
Lüneburg 402 F5
Lünen 404 C7
Lünne 404 C6
Lutherstadt Eisleben 406 G8
Lutherstadt Wittenberg 407 H7
Lütjenburg 402 F3
Lützen 406 H8
Lützow 402 G4
Magdeburg 406 G7
Mainz 408 C10
Malchin 403 J4
Mannheim 408 C11
Manschnow 403 K6
Marburg 405 D9
Marienberg 407 J9
Markranstädt 407 H8
Markt Bibart 410 F11
Marktoberdorf 410 F14
Marktzeuln 406 F10
Marne 401 E3
Marquartstein 411 H14
Marsberg 405 D8
Marxwalde 403 K6
Marzahna 407 H7
Maulbronn 408 D12
Mayen 404 B9
Meckenbeuren 410 D14
Meersburg 410 D14
Meine 402 F6
Meiningen 406 F9
Meisenheim 408 C11
Meissen 407 J9
Meitingen 410 F13
Melbeck 402 F5
Meldorf 401 E3
Melle 405 D6
Mellrichstadt 405 F10
Menden 404 C8
Mengen 409 D14
Meppen 400 C5
Mering 410 F13
Merkendorf 410 F12
Mersch 404 A8
Merseburg 406 G8
Meschede 404 D8
Messkirch 409 D14
Mettlach 408 A11
Metzingen 409 D13
Meyenburg 403 H5
Michelstadt 409 D11
Mieste 402 G6
Miesterhorst 402 G6
Milmersdorf 403 J5
Miltach 411 H12
Mindelheim 410 E14
Minden 405 D6
Mirow 403 J5
Mittenwald 410 F15
Mittenwalde 403 J5
Moers 404 B7
Möllenbeck 403 J5
Mölln 402 F4
Mönchen-Gladbach 404 A8
Monschau 404 A9
Monsheim 408 C11
Montabaur 404 C9
Moosinning 410 G13
Mosbach 409 D11
Muggendorf 410 G11
Mühlacker 409 D12
Mühldorf 411 H13
Mühlhausen 406 F8
Mülheim 408 B10

MAPS INDEX

Mülhern 404 B7
Müllheim 408 B14
Müllrose 407 K7
Münchberg 406 G10
Müncheberg 403 K6
München (Munich) 410 G14
Münchhausen 405 D9
Munderkingen 409 E13
Münnerstadt 405 E10
Munster 402 F5
Münster 404 C7
Murnau 410 F14
Mutterstadt 408 C11

Nagold 408 C13
Nauen 403 J6
Naumburg 406 G8
Neckargemünd 409 D11
Neermoor 400 C4
Neresheim 409 E12
Nersingen 409 E13
Nesselwang 410 E14
Neubrandenburg 403 J4
Neubukow 402 G4
Neuburg 410 F13
Neuburg 411 J13
Neudorf 408 C12
Neuenhaus 400 B6
Neuenkirchen 401 E5
Neufahrn 411 G13
Neuffen 409 D13
Neugersdorf 407 K9
Neuhaus 401 E4
Neuhaus 406 F10
Neumarkt 410 G12
Neumarkt-St Veit 411 H13
Neumünster 402 F3
Neunkirchen 408 B11
Neuruppin 403 J5
Neuss 404 B8
Neustadt 410 G12
Neustadt / Orla 406 G9
Neustadt am Rübenberge 405 E6
Neustadt an der Aisch 410 F11
Neustadt an der
Weinstrasse 408 C11
Neustadt-Glewe 402 G5
Neustrelitz 403 J5
Neuwied 404 B9
Neuzelle 407 K7
Niederaula 405 E9
Nieder-Wöllstadt 405 D10
Nienburg 401 E6
Niesky 407 L8
Nittendorf 411 G12
Nohfelden 408 B11
Norddeich 400 C4
Norden 400 C4
Nordenham 401 D4
Nordhausen 406 F8
Nordhorn 404 B6
Nördlingen 410 F12
Northeim 405 E7
Nurburg 404 B9
Nürnberg 410 F11

Nürtingen 409 D13
Oberammergau 410 F14

Oberau 410 F15
Oberhausen 404 B7
Oberhof 406 F9
Oberjoch 410 E15
Oberkirch 408 C13
Oberndorf 408 C13
Obernzell 411 J13
Ober-Roden 409 D10
Oberstaufen 410 E14
Oberstenfeld 409 D12
Oberviechtach 411 H11
Oberwesel 404 C10
Oberwiesenthal 407 H10
Obing 411 H14
Ochsenfurt 409 E11
Ochsenhausen 409 E14
Ochtrup 404 C6
Oebisfelde 402 G6
Oettingen 410 F12
Offenbach 409 D10
Offenburg 408 C13
Ogenbargen 400 C4
Ohrdruf 406 F9
Olbernhau 407 J9
Oldenburg 401 D5
Oldenburg 402 G3
Olpe 404 C8
Olsberg 405 D8
Oppenheim 408 C10
Oranienburg 403 J6
Oschatz 407 J8
Osnabrück 404 C6
Osterburg 402 G6
Osterhofen 411 H13
Osterholz-Scharmbeck 401 D5
Osterode 406 F7
Ostritz 407 L9
Otterndorf 401 E4
Ottweiler 408 B11
Ovelgönne 401 E4

Paderborn 405 D7
Papenburg 400 C5
Parchim 402 H5
Pasewalk 403 K5
Passau 411 J13
Patersdorf 411 H12
Pattensen 405 E6
Peckelsheim 405 D7
Pegau 407 H8
Peine 402 F6
Peissenberg 410 F14
Peiting 410 F14
Peitz 407 K7
Penzlin 403 J5
Perleberg 402 H5
Pessin 403 H6
Petersdorf 403 H3
Petershagen 405 D6
Pfaffendorf 406 F10
Pfaffenhausen 409 E14
Pfaffenhofen 410 G13

Pfarrkirchen 411 H13
Pfatter 411 H12
Pfeffenhausen 411 G13
Pforzheim 408 D12
Pfronten 410 E14
Philippsreut 411 J13
Pirmasens 408 B11
Pirna 407 K9
Plattling 411 H13
Plau 403 H5
Plaue 403 H6
Plauen 406 H10
Pleinfeld 410 F12
Plön 402 F3
Pocking 411 J13
Poggendorf 403 J4
Polle 405 E7
Pörnbach 410 G13
Pössneck 406 G9
Potsdam 403 J6
Pottenstein 410 G11
Preetz 402 F3
Prenzlau 403 K5
Pretzsch 407 H8
Pritzier 402 G5
Pritzwalk 403 H5
Pronsfeld 404 A10
Prüm 404 A9
Putbus 403 J3
Puttgarden 402 G3

Quakenbrück 400 C5
Quedlinburg 406 G7
Querfurt 406 G8
Quickborn 401 F4

Rade 401 E4
Radebeul 407 J9
Raesfeld 404 B7
Rastatt 408 C12
Rathenow 403 H6
Ratingen 404 B8
Raubling 411 G14
Raumünzach 408 C12
Ravensbrück 403 J5
Ravensburg 410 D14
Recklinghausen 404 B7
Redefin 402 G5
Regen 411 J12
Regensburg 411 G12
Rehden 401 D6
Rehna 402 G4
Reichenau 409 D14
Reichertshausen 410 G13
Reinberg 403 J3
Reinhardshagen 405 E8
Reit im Winkl 411 H14
Reitzehain 407 J10
Remagen 404 B9
Remscheid 404 B8
Renchen 408 C12
Rendsburg 401 E3
Rennerod 404 C9
Reuterstadt Stavenhagen 403 J4
Reutlingen 409 D13

Rheda 404 D7
Rheinberg 404 B7
Rheindahlen 404 A8
Rheine 404 C6
Rheinfelden 408 B14
Rhens 404 C10
Rheydt 404 B8
Ribnitz-Damgarten 403 H3
Rickling 402 F3
Riedern 408 C14
Riedlingen 409 D13
Riesa 407 J8
Risum Lindholm 401 E2
Rodenkirchen 401 D4
Rodewald 401 E6
Rohr i Niederb 411 G13
Rosenheim 411 G14
Rosshaupten 410 F14
Rossla 406 G8
Rosslau 407 H7
Rostock 403 H3
Rotenburg 401 E5
Roth 410 F12
Rötha 407 H8
Rothenburg ob
der Tauber 409 E11
Rott 411 G14
Rottenbach 406 F10
Rottenbuch 410 F14
Rottweil 408 C13
Rövershagen 403 H3
Rüdersdorf 403 J6
Rüdesheim 408 C10
Ruhmannsfelden 411 H12
Rüsselsheim 408 C10

Saal 411 G12
Saalfeld 406 G9
Saarbrücken 408 B11
Saarlouis 408 A11
St Georgen 408 C13
St Goar 404 C10
St Goarshausen 404 C10
St Ingbert 408 B11
Salzgitter-Bad 406 F7
Salzkotten 405 D7
Salzwedel 402 G6
Salzweg 411 J13
Samtens 403 J3
Sandau 403 H6
Sangerhausen 406 G8
Sanitz 403 H3
Sassnitz 403 K3
Sauerlach 410 G14
Saulgau 409 D14
Schäftlarn 410 F14
Scharbeutz 402 G3
Scheessel 401 E5
Scherfede 405 D8
Schermbeck 404 B7
Schiltach 408 C13
Schirnding 406 H10
Schladen 406 F7
Schleiden 404 A9
Schleswig 401 E2

Place	Page	Grid
Schleusingen	406	F9
Schlieben	407	J8
Schlutup	402	G4
Schmilka	407	K9
Schnaittenbach	411	G11
Schönau	408	B14
Schönbeck	403	H5
Schönberg	407	H10
Schönberg	411	J13
Schönecken	404	A10
Schönmünzach	408	C12
Schönthal	411	H12
Schönwald	408	C13
Schramberg	408	C13
Schrobenhausen	410	F13
Schwabach	410	F12
Schwäbisch Gmünd	409	E12
Schwäbisch Hall	409	E12
Schwarmstedt	401	E6
Schwarzenbek	402	F4
Schwedt	403	K5
Schweich	408	B10
Schwenningen	408	C13
Schwerin	402	G4
Seehausen	402	G5
Seelow	403	K6
Seesen	405	F7
Selent	402	F3
Selsingen	401	E4
Senftenberg	407	K8
Siegburg	404	B9
Siegen	404	C9
Silberstedt	401	E2
Simbach	411	H13
Simmern	408	B10
Sindelfingen	409	D12
Singen	408	C14
Sinsheim	409	D11
Soest	404	C7
Solingen	404	B8
Soltau	401	E5
Sömmerda	406	G8
Sondershausen	406	F8
Sottrum	401	E5
Spaichingen	408	C13
Spandau	403	J6
Speyer	408	C11
Sprakensehl	402	F6
Spremberg	407	K8
Springe	405	E6
Staaken	403	J6
Stade	401	E4
Stadthegen	405	E6
Stadtkyll	404	A9
Stadtlohn	404	B7
Stadtsteinach	406	G10
Staffelstein	406	F10
Stahle	405	E7
Starnberg	410	F14
Staussfurt	406	F8
Steinbergkirche	401	F2
Steinfurt	404	C6
Steingaden	410	F14
Stendal	402	G6
Sternberg	402	H4
Stockelsdorf	402	F4
Stollberg	407	H9
Stolzenau	405	E6
Straelen	404	A7
Stralsund	403	J3
Straubing	411	H12
Strehla	407	J8
Streitberg	410	F11
Strücklingen	400	C5
Stukenbrock	405	D7
Stuttgart	409	D12
Süderbrarup	401	F2
Süderlugüm	401	E2
Suhl	406	F9
Sulingen	401	D6
Sulzbach	409	D12
Süssen	409	E13
Syke	401	D5
Szczecin	403	K5
Tauberbischofsheim	409	E11
Taufkirchen	411	G13
Taunusstein	404	C10
Tecklenburg	404	C6
Telgte	404	C7
Tellingstedt	401	E3
Tessin	403	H4
Teterow	403	H4
Thannhausen	410	E13
Themar	406	F9
Thum	407	H9
Thürkow	403	H4
Timmendorfer Strand	402	G4
Tittling	411	J13
Tittmoning	411	H14
Tönning	401	E3
Torgau	407	J8
Tostedt	401	E5
Traben-Trarbach	408	B10
Traunstein	411	H14
Travemünde	402	G4
Trebatsch	407	K7
Treis	404	B10
Treuenbrietzen	407	J7
Triberg	408	C13
Trier	408	A10
Trittenheim	408	B10
Trostberg	411	H14
Tschernitz	407	K8
Tübingen	409	D13
Tüchen	403	H5
Tuttlingen	408	C14
Twistringen	401	D5
Überlingen	409	D14
Uchte	405	D6
Uelsen	400	B6
Uelzen	402	F5
Uffenheim	409	E11
Ulm	409	E13
Unna	404	C7
Varel	401	D4
Vechta	401	D5
Veitshöchheim	409	E11
Velbert	404	B8
Velpke	402	G6
Verden	401	E5
Viechtach	411	H12
Viersen	404	B8
Villingen	408	C13
Vilsbiburg	411	H13
Vinzelberg	402	G6
Völklingen	408	B11
Vorsfelde	402	F6
Waidhaus	411	H11
Walchensee	410	F15
Waldmünchen	411	H12
Waldshut	408	C14
Walldürn	409	D11
Wallenfels	406	G10
Wallerstein	410	E12
Wallsbüll	401	E2
Walsrode	401	E5
Wanderup	401	E2
Wanfried	405	F8
Wangen	410	E14
Wankendorf	402	F3
Warburg	405	D8
Warendorf	404	C7
Warnemünde	403	H3
Warren	403	H4
Warstein	404	D8
Wasseralfingen	409	E12
Wasungen	405	F9
Weener	400	C5
Weeze	404	A7
Wegscheid	411	J13
Weida	406	H9
Weiden	411	H11
Weilheim	410	F14
Weimar	406	G9
Weingarten	410	D14
Weinheim	408	D11
Weinsberg	409	D12
Weissenburg	410	F12
Weissenfels	406	G8
Weitendorf	403	H4
Wellaune	407	H8
Welle	401	E5
Werdohl	404	C8
Werl	404	C7
Wermelskirchen	404	B8
Werne	404	C7
Werneck	409	E10
Wernigerode	406	F7
Wesel	404	B7
Wesenberg	403	J5
Wettringen	404	C6
Wetzlar	404	D9
Weyhausen	402	F6
Wiedenbrück	404	D7
Wienhausen	402	F6
Wiesbaden	408	C10
Wiesenburg	407	H7
Wiesloch	408	D11
Wietze	405	E6
Wilhelmshaven	401	D4
Wilster	401	E4
Winnenden	409	D12
Winnigstedt	406	F7
Winnweiler	408	C11
Winterberg	405	D8
Winterfeld	402	G6
Wismar	402	G4
Witten	404	C8
Wittenberge	402	G5
Wittlich	404	B10
Wittmund	400	C4
Wittstock / Dosse	403	H5
Witzenhausen	405	E8
Woldegk	403	J5
Wolfen	407	H8
Wolfenbüttel	406	F7
Wolfratshausen	410	F14
Wolfsburg	402	F6
Wolgast	403	K4
Wolmirstedt	406	G7
Worms	408	C11
Wörrstadt	408	C10
Wörth	409	D11
Wriezen	403	K6
Wulfen	404	B7
Wunstorf	405	E6
Wuppertal	404	B8
Wurtberg	405	F9
Würzburg	409	E11
Wurzen	407	H8
Wusterhausen	403	H6
Wüstermarke	407	J7
Xanten	404	B7
Zeitz	406	H9
Zell	404	B10
Zell	408	B14
Zella-Mehlis	406	F9
Zerbst / Anhalt	406	H7
Zernien	402	G5
Zeven	401	E5
Zickhusen	402	G4
Ziesar	407	H7
Ziethen	403	J4
Zinnowitz	403	K4
Zittau	407	K9
Zorneding	410	G14
Zschopau	407	J9
Zülpich	404	B9
Zweibrücken	408	B11
Zwickau	407	H9
Zwiefalten	409	D13
Zwiesel	411	J12

A

Aachen 8, 10, 31, 163, 164–165, 192, 194, 199
accommodation 206
Carolus Thermen 194
Dom 165
restaurants 200
accommodation 390–391
Berlin 116–119
camping 391
eastern Germany 254–257
farm stays 390
hostels 390
hotels 390, 391
Munich 298–299
northern Germany 160–161
pensions 390
reservations and prices 391
self-catering 391
southern Germany 354–356
western Germany 206–207
admission charges 369
Ahlbeck 145
air travel 48–51
airport–city transfers 48–49
airports 48–51, 63
disabilities, visitors with 66
domestic 62–63
health hazards for flyers 363
Almanac de Gotha 219
Altenahr 167
Altmühltal 303
Amberg 303
Ammersee 265
Amrum 139, 152
Ansbach 303
Gumbertus Church 303
Hofgarten 303
Markgräfliche Residenz 303
architecture 20–21
Arnsberg 191
Sauerland-Museum 191
Arnstadt 245
Mon Plaisir 245
Aschaffenburg 303
Schloss Johannisburg 303
Stiftskirche 303
ATMs 361
Attila 29
Augsburg 304
accommodation 354
Domkirche St. Maria 304
Fuggerei 304
Mozarthaus 304
Perlachturm 304
Rathaus 304
restaurants 348
Augustus the Strong 35, 213, 214, 215, 216, 217, 221, 226
automobile industry 20, 22, 23, 44, 214, 234

B

Baabe 143
Babelsberg 228, 248
baby supplies 365
babysitting services 365
Bach, Carl Philipp Emanuel 131
Bach, Johann Sebastian 34, 35, 216, 220, 224, 245
Bad Bodendorf 167
Bad Doberan 149
Bad Fredeburg 190
Bad Harzburg 236
Haus der Nature 236, 238
Bad Karlshafen 151, 156
Deutsches Hugenottenmuseum 151
Bad Saarow 246
Bad Schandau 233
Bad Sulza 246
Baden-Baden 11, 12, 301, 305, 344
accommodation 354
casino 305
City Museum 305
Künsthalle 305
Lichenthal Abbey 305
Merkur 305
restaurants 348
spas 305, 344
Baden-Württemberg 9, 301
Baltic coast 148–149
Baltrum 140
Bamberg 306
accommodation 354
Altes Rathaus 306
Altstadt 306
breweries 306
Historisches Museum 306
Kaiserdom 306
Neue Residenz 306
restaurants 348–349
banks 361, 369
Bansin 145
Barbarine 243
bars and cafés 369, 378
Bastei 233, 241
Bastorf 149
Bauhaus 21, 78, 185, 218, 235
Bautzen 211, 249, 254
Gedenkstätte Bautzen 211
Saurierpark 246
Sorbski Musej 211
Bavaria *see* Bayern
Bavarian Alps 6, 336–337
Bayerischer Wald (Bavarian Forest) 301, 303, 330–331, 336–337, 383
Bayern (Bavaria) 9, 301, 330–333
Bayreuth 301, 310, 349
Altes Schloss 310
Neues Schloss 310
Richard Wagner Museum 310
Villa Wahnfried 310
Beatles 133
beers 12, 174, 387
breweries 152, 185, 268, 306
festivals 17, 385
Beethoven, Ludwig van 166
Bensheim 341
Berchtesgadener Land 11, 301, 307
Dokumentation Obersalzberg 307
Eagle's Nest 307
Kehlsteinhaus 307
Königliches Schloss 307
Salzbergwerk (salt mines) 307
Bergen-Belsen Konzentrationslager (Concentration Camp) 138
Bergstrasse 341
Berlin 8, 10, 68–119
accommodation 116–119
Ägyptisches Museum 75
airports 48, 50
Alexanderplatz 76
Alte Nationalgalerie 77
Altes Museum 78
Antikensammlung 90
Aquarium 101
Arsenal 102
Bauhaus-Archiv 78
Bebelplatz 102
Berlin Film Festival 377
Berlin Film Museum 96
Berlin Mitte 102–103
Berlin State Library 102
Berlin Wall 44, 45, 46, 81
Berliner Dom 78
Bode-Museum 78
Botanischer Garten 80
Brandenburger Tor (Brandenburg Gate) 10, 80
Bröhan-Museum 80
Centrum Judaicum 88
children's entertainment 109–110
Coin Cabinet 78, 90
Collection of Classical Antiquities 90
Denkmal für die ermordeten Juden Europas 80
Deutscher Dom 81
Deutsches Historisches Museum 80–81
Egyptian Museum 75
entertainment and nightlife 107–108, 377–379
Federal Chancellery 21
Fernsehturm 10, 76
festivals and events 18, 111
Französische Dom 81
Friedrichswerdersche Kirche 103
gay scene 378
Gemäldegalerie 10, 83–86
Gendarmenmarkt 81
German Historical Museum 80–81
Hamburger Bahnhof 81
Haus am Checkpoint Charlie 81
Haus der Kulturen der Welt 104
Hedwigskirche 103
Holocaust Memorial 80
House of World Cultures 104
Huguenot Museum 81
Jewish Museum 10, 87
Jüdisches Museum 10, 87
Kaiser-Friedrich-Gedächtniskirche 105
Kaiser-Wilhelm-

Gedächtniskirche 87
Kindertheater Charlottchen 109–110
Knoblauchhaus 88
Konzerthaus 81
Kunstgewerbemuseum 87
Marienkirche 76
Märkisches Museum 87
Marx-Engels-Forum 102
Mauer Museum 81
Metro 53, 73
Müggelsee 109
Münzkabinett 78, 90
Museum of the Ancient Near East 90
Museum Berggruen 88
Museum of Byzantine Art 78
Museum für Gegenwart Berlin 81
Museum of Islamic Art 90
Museum für Naturkunde 110
Museum of the Present 81
Natural History Museum 110
Neue Nationalgalerie 89
Neue Synagoge 88
Neue Wache 102
nightlife and entertainment 12
Nikolaikirche 88
Nikolaiviertel 88
Old National Gallery 77
Pergamonmuseum 10, 90–95
Potsdamer Platz 96
public transportation 52–53, 73
Reichstag 10, 20, 97, 104, 105
restaurants 112–115
river trips 109
Rotes Rathaus 76
Sankt-Hedwigs-Kathedrale 103
Schiller Monument 81
Schloss Bellevue 101, 104
Schloss Charlottenburg 98–99
Sea Life Berlin 110
shopping 106–107
Siegessäule 100–101, 104–105
Sony Center 96
Soviet Memorial 104
Sowjetisches Ehrenmal 104
spa 109
sports and activities 108–109
street map 70–72
Tiergarten 10, 100–101, 104–105
Topographie des Terrors 88
Tv Tower 10, 76
Vorderasiatisches Museum 90
walks 102–105
Wall Museum 81
Zeiss Grossplanetarium 110
Zoo Berlin 101
Beuys, Joseph 19, 168–169, 171
bicycling 61, 108, 198, 292, 380
Binz 143
Biosphärenreservat Südost Rügen 143
birdwatching 138, 142, 143
Bismarck, Otto von 38, 105
Black Forest *see* Schwarzwald
Blücher, Marshal 141
Bodekessel 239
Bodensee (Lake Constance) 9, 12, 301, 308–309, 335
shore walk 335
Bodenwerder 151
Münchhausen Museum 151
Boiensdorfer Werder 149
Boltenhagen 148
Bonn 163, 166, 194–195, 385
accommodation 206
Beethoven Archive and Library 194
Beethoven Festival 199
Beethoven-Haus 166
Beethovenhalle 166, 194
Bonner Münster 166
Haus der Geschichte der Bundesrepublik Deutschland 166
restaurants 200–201
Rheinaue Freizeitpark 195
Boppard 183
borders 6, 25, 51
Borkum 140
Bramwald 151
Brandenburg 8, 209
Brandenburg (town) 211, 249
Braunlage 237
Braunschweig 123, 156
Bremen 8, 10, 121, 124–125, 152–153
accommodation 160
casino 152
Focke-Museum 124–125
Kunsthalle Bremen 125
Marktplatz 125
Rathaus 125
restaurants 156–157
St. Petri Dom 125
Universum Science Center Bremen 153
Bremerhaven 153
Brocken 237–238
Brockenbahn 23
Brodtener Steilufer 146
Brook Forest Nature Reserve 148
Bruegel, Pieter 83
Buchenwald concentration camp 235
Buchholz 183
Burg Eltz 167
Burg Rheinfels 183
Burgenstrasse 319
buses, long-distance 61
Buxtehude, Dietrich 137

C

camping 391
Canossa 31
car rental 51
Castle Road 319
Celle 123, 157, 160
Chagall, Marc 177
Cham 331
Charlemagne 30, 31, 129, 165
Chiemsee 310
children 365, 384, 387
entertainment 109–110, 293, 384
Christmas markets 12, 111, 247, 315, 316–317, 347, 375, 385
church opening times 369
cinema 18, 19, 25, 96, 248, 372, 376, 377
classical music and opera 376–377
climate and seasons 358–359
Cloef 181
Clovis 29
Coburg 310, 349, 354–355
Cochem 179
Historisches Senfmühle (mustard mill) 179
Reichsburg Cochem 179
Wine Trail 179
Colditz 11, 211, 240, 254
Cologne *see* Köln
conversion chart 360
Cottbus 211
Parkeisenbahn Cottbus 246
Schloss Branitz 211
Spreeauenpark 211
credit and debit cards 361, 375
lost/stolen 361
crime 366
cuckoo clocks 328, 338
culture and the arts 18–19
currency exchange 361

D

Dachau 268
Dambusters 191
Darmstadt 167, 201
Artists' Colony Museum 167
Ludwigsmonument 167
Mathildenhöhe 167
Das Boot 19
Daun 167, 193
Eifel-Vulkanmuseum 167, 193
dental treatment 364
Dessau-Wörlitz 11, 218, 250, 254
Deutsch-Belgischer Naturpark 192
Deutsche Alpenstrasse 55, 337
Dietrich, Marlene 96
Dinkelsbühl 310, 344, 347, 349, 355
Munster St. Georg 310
disabilities, visitors with 66, 365
discounts and concessions 362, 369
Donaueschingen 339
Dortmund 185
breweries 185
Brewery Museum 185
Marienkirche 185
Petrikirche 185
Reinoldikirche 185

Steinwache 185
Drei Annen Hohne 237, 238
Dresden 11, 209, 212–217, 240, 241, 246–247
accommodation 254–255
Albertinum 216
Armoury 214
Brühlsche Terrasse 215–216
Christmas market 247
Deutsches Hygiene-Museum 216
festivals 249
Frauenkirche 216
Gläserne Manufaktur 20, 214
Goldener Reiter 216
Grosser Garten 246
Kathedrale SS Trinitatis 214–215
Kulturpalast 246
Mathematical–Physical Sciences Salon 214
Old Masters Picture Gallery 214
Porcelain Collection 214
Puppentheatersammlung 247
Residenzschloss 215
restaurants 250–251
river cruises 214
Schloss Pillnitz 217
Semperoper 217
Skulpturensammlung (Sculpture Collection) 216
Verkehrsmuseum Dresden 217
Zwinger 214
dress codes 359
drinking water 363
drives
Baltic coast 148–149
Bavaria 330–333
Bavarian Alps 336–337
Black Forest 338–339
Eifel 192–193
Garmisch-Partenkirchen and Oberammergau 332–333
Glasstrasse 330–331
Harz Mountains and the Brocken 236–238
Neckar Valley and Bergstrasse 340–341
Sauerland and Winterberg 190–191
Saxony 240–241
Thuringian Forest 244–245
Weserbergland 150–151
driving 55–57
accidents and breakdowns 56
autobahns 55, 56
car rental 51
car sharing 57
disabilities, drivers with 66
distances and journey times 57
documents 51, 55–56
fuel 57
own car 51, 55
parking 56–57
road network 55
road signs 56
rules of the road 56
speed limits 55
to Germany 51
tourist routes 55
Droese, Felix 19
Düne 125
Dürer, Albrecht 18, 316
Düsseldorf 12, 163, 168–169, 195
accommodation 206
airport 49, 50
Aquazoo 195
Düsseldorf WelcomeCard 168
Hofgarten 169
K20 168–169
K21 169
Medianhafen 169
North Rhine-Westphalia Art Collection 168–169
restaurants 201
Rheinturm 169
duty-free and duty-paid goods 360

E

Eagle's Nest 307
East Frisian Islands 8, 10, 140
eastern Germany 8–9, 11, 208–257
accommodation 254–257
drives 236–238, 240–241, 244–245
festivals and events 249
restaurants 250–253
sights 209–235
walks 239, 242–243
what to do 246–249
eating out 386–389
children's food 387
fast food 387
international cuisines 387
mealtimes 386
menu reader 388–389
vegetarians 387
what to drink 387
where to eat 386–387
see also restaurants
Eberbach 340
economy 7, 22–23, 24–25
Eibsee Aerial Tramway 314
Eichstätt 303
Eifel 167, 192–193, 195, 383
Eifel-Vulkanmuseum 167, 193
Einbeck 121, 157
Einruhr 193
Eisenach 220, 244
accommodation 255
Automobile Welt Eisenach 220
Bachhaus 220
Georgenkirche 220
Lutherhaus 220
restaurants 251
Wartburg 220, 244
Elbe Sandstone Mountains 233
Elbsandsteingebirge 233
electricity 359, 364
embassies and consulates
abroad 360
Berlin 366
emergencies 362, 366
Engelshütt 331
entertainment and nightlife 376–379
bars 369, 378
Berlin 107–108, 377–379
cinemas 376
classical music and opera 376–377
contemporary live music 377
folk and regional music 377
gay scene 111, 378
jazz and blues 377
Munich 291–292, 377
theatre and dance 377
ticket outlets 377–378
environmental issues 26
Erbach 341
Erfurt 9, 219, 245, 251, 255
Erresberg 193
Erzebirge Mountains 9
Essen 163, 185, 195
accommodation 206
Design Centre Nordrhein-Westfalen 185
Museum Folkwang 185
Red Dot Design Museum 185
restaurants 201–202
Zeche Zollverein 23, 185
Ettal 333
Europa-Park 311, 345, 384
Eye of the Needle 242

F

Fachwerkhaüser (half-timbered houses) 123, 126, 127, 145
farm stays 390
fashion shopping 12
Federal Republic of Germany (FDR) 6, 44
ferry services
domestic 64
international 51
riverboat services 64, 65
Feste Dilsberg 340
festivals and events 16, 17, 384
beer festivals 17, 385
Berlin 111
eastern Germany 249
Munich 293, 385
northern Germany 155
southern Germany 347
western Germany 199
wine festivals 385
see also Christmas markets
Festung Königstein 233
Filmpark Babelsberg 228, 248
Fischer, Joschka 26, 45
fishing 265, 380–381
Flensburg 123
Museumwerft 123
Rum-Museum 123
Schiffartsmuseum 123
Schloss Glücksburg 123
Föhr 139
folk and regional music 377
food and drink
beers 12, 174
Bratwurst 317, 321
coffee and tea 387
drinking water 363

Kaffee und Kuchen (coffee and cakes) 12
marzipan 137, 154–155
regional cuisines 121, 163
schnapps 17, 387
smoked eel 154
see also eating out; restaurants
Foster, Sir Norman 20, 97, 185
Frank, Anne 138
Frankfurt am Main 163, 170–171, 195–196
accommodation 206
airport 48, 50
Bundesbank 170
Deutsches Architekturmuseum 171
English Theatre 196
Explora Museum 196
Historisches Museum 171
Kaiserdom 171
markets 195
Museum für Moderne Kunst 171
Naturmuseum Senckenberg 196
public transportation 54
restaurants 201–202
Römerberg 170–171
Saalhof Chapel 171
Senckenberg Natural History Museum 196
Städel-Museum 171
Zoo Frankfurt 196
Frauenau 330, 344–345
Glasmuseum 330, 331
Fraueninsel 310
Freiberg 209, 219, 249, 255
Dom 219
Town and Mining Museum 219
Freiburg im Breisgau 311, 338, 345, 349
accommodation 355
Altstadt 311
Augustiner Museum 311
Basler Hof 311
Carnival Museum 311
Erzbischöfliches Palais 311
Europa-Park 311, 345, 384
Kaufhaus 311
Münster 311
Museum for Town History 311
Natural History Museum 311
Friedrich I (Barbarossa) 31, 129
Friedrich, Caspar David 18, 36, 77, 126, 130, 216, 233, 278
Friedrich August III of Saxony 216
Friedrich Wilhelm I of Prussia 34, 78, 98, 228
Friedrich Wilhelm II of Prussia 34, 35, 80, 99, 229
Friedrich Wilhelm IV of Prussia 101, 232
Friedrichroda 244–245
Friedrichshafen 308, 309
Schlosskirche 309
Zeppelin Museum 308, 309
Friedrichstadt 127
Fulda 167
Dom Schatzkammer 167
Furth im Wald 303, 331
Dragon Museum 303
Furtwangen 314, 338
German Clock Museum 314, 338
Füssen 324, 336, 349

G

Garmisch-Partenkirchen 11, 301, 314, 332, 345, 347, 382
accommodation 355
Partnachklamm 334
restaurants 349–350
Werdenfels Museum 314
Gastarbeiter (guest workers) 25
gay and lesbian scene 111, 378
Gedenkstätte Bautzen 211
Gedenkstätte Buchenwald 235
Gedenkstätte Burgen-Belsen 138
German Alpine Highway 55, 337
German Democratic Republic (GDR) 6, 44, 45
German-Belgian Nature Park 192
Gerolstein 167, 193
Glasstrasse (Glass Route) 303, 330–331
Glowe 143
Godelheim 151
Goethe, Johann Wolfgang von 35, 105, 221, 223, 235, 239, 245
Goethe-Felsen 239
Göhren 143
golf 154, 195, 196, 381
Görlitz 25, 219, 247, 251, 255
Toy Museum 247
Goslar 123, 157, 160
Altstadt 123
Bergbaumuseum Rammelsberg 123
Kaiserpfalz 123
Gotha 219, 245, 255
Schloss Friedenstein 219, 245
Göttingen 126
Gänseliesel-Brunnen 126
Georg-August-Universität 126
Grafenau 330
Snuff Museum 330
Grainau 314
Green Party 19, 23, 26, 45
Greifswald 126
Grieben 143
Grimma 240
Gropius, Walter 21, 218, 235
Grosser Alpsee 337
Grosser Arber 331
Grosser Jasmunder Bodden 142
Güstrow 126
Gutach Falls 328, 338
Gutenberg, Johannes 33, 177

H

Halle 221, 247
accommodation 255
Handel Festival 249
Händel-Haus 221
restaurants 251
Roter Turm 221
Technisches Halloren- und Salinenmuseum 221
Hamburg 8, 10, 12, 31, 121, 128–133, 153–154, 385
accommodation 160–161
airport 49, 50
Aussenalster 130
Beatles-Platz 133
Binnenalster 130
English Theatre of Hamburg 153
fish market 153
Galerie der Gegenwart 130
Hamburg Card 131
Hamburg Dungeon 154
Hamburgmuseum 132
harbour tours 130–131
Jacobkirche 133
Krameramtswohnungen 131
Kunsthalle 130
Landungsbrücken 130–131
Michaelskirche 131
Museum für Kunst und Gewerbe 132
Museum für Volkerkunde 132
Petrikirche 133
public transportation 54
Rathaus 132–133
red light district 132
Reeperbahn 132
restaurants 157
Tierpark Hagenbeck 154
Hameln 126, 147, 150
accommodation 161
glockenspiel 126, 147
Marktkirche St.-Nicolai 147
Museum Hameln 147, 151
Pied Piper's House 147
restaurants 158
walk 147
Wedding House 147
Hämelschenburg 150–151
Handel, Georg Friedrich 221, 249
Hannover (Hanover) 121, 134–135, 154
accommodation 161
Fürstenhaus Herrenhausen-Museum 134–135
Herrenhäuser Gärten 134–135
Leineschloss 135
Lower Saxony State Museum 135
Maschsee 135
Neues Rathaus 135
Niedersächsisches Landesmuseum 135
restaurants 158
Hannoversch Münden 151

Harz Mountains 8, 12, 236–238, 249
Harzer Schmalspurbahn 23, 237, 238
Hasenhorn 339
health 362–364
alternative medicine 364
common ailments 364
dental treatment 364
drinking water 363
European Health Insurance Card (EHIC) 361, 362
health hazards for flyers 363
inoculations 362
insurance 360–361
medical treatment 362–363
medications 359, 362
opticians 364
pharmacies 363
pre-travel preparations 362
summer and winter hazards 363
sun safety 362, 363
Heidelberg 11, 301, 312–313, 345, 347
accommodation 355
Alte Universität 313
Botanische Garten 313
festival 313
Heidelberger Märchenparadies 345
Palatinate Museum 312
Philosophenweg 313
restaurants 350
Schloss Heidelberg 312, 313
Schlossgarten 313
Students' Prison 312
Heilgendamm 149
Heilige Berg 265
Heinrich I 227
Heinrich II 306
Heinrich IV 31
Helgoland 12, 125
Hellenthal 192
Heppenheim 341
Heringsdorf 145
Hermann (Arminius) 29, 139
Herreninsel 310
Schloss Herrenchiemsee 310
Hessen (Hesse) 8, 163
Hexentanplatz 239
Heydrich, Reinhard 42, 43
Hiddensee 143
Grieben 143
Kloster 143
Neuendorf 143
Vitte 143
Hildesheim 127, 150, 158
Bakers' Guildhouse 127
Butchers' Guildhouse 127
Dom 127
Michaelskirche 127
Roemer und Pelizaeus-Museum 127
Hildesheimer Wald 150
Hirschhorn 340
history of Germany 28–46
Berlin Airift 43
Berlin Olympics (1936) 41
Berlin Wall 44, 45, 46, 81
Christian conversion 30
Cold War 44, 230
colonialism 38
Enlightenment 34, 35
First World War 39, 40
Franco-Prussian War 37, 38
Franks 29, 30, 31
Hanseatic League 31, 121, 129, 136, 145, 176
Holy Roman Empire 32
Huns 29
Munich Olympics (1972) 45
Nazism 40, 41, 42, 43, 88, 235
Peasants' War (1524-25) 33, 227
Potsdam Conference (1945) 229, 231
prehistory 28
Prussia 34, 35, 36
Reformation 32, 33
reunification 24, 46
revolution (1848) 37
Roman presence 28–29
Romanticism 36
Second World War 42–43
terrorism 45
Thirty Years' War 32, 139
unification 38
Weimar Republic 40, 41
Hitler, Adolf 40, 41, 42, 43, 183, 268, 307
Hohe Acht 167
Hohenstein 241
Holy Mountain 265
Holzminden 151
Hooge 139
horse-racing 155, 195, 305, 344, 381
hostels 390
hotels 390, 391
see also accommodation
housing-sharing communities 16
Höxter 151
Huertgen Forest 192
Hürtgenwald 192
Husum 127

I

Ilmenau 245
Ilsenburg 236, 255
Immenstadt 337
immigrants 24, 25
Industrial Heritage Trail 184
industries 22–23
inoculations 362
insurance 360–361
internet access 368
Isherwood, Christopher 41
Isny 336

J

Jena 209, 221, 247, 256
Optical Museum 221
Universitätshochhaus 221
Zeiss Planetarium 221
Jever 121, 127
Johan Wilhelm II 168
Jugendstil 20, 167, 330
Juist 140

K

Kahler Asten 181, 190
Kalkhorst 148
Kalkriese 139
Varusschlacht Museum und Park 139
Kampen 139
Kandinsky, Vassily 78, 275
Kap Arkona 142
Karlsruhe 315, 345, 350
Christmas market 315
Municipal Gallery 315
Museum of Modern Art 315
Natural History Museum 315
Schloss 315
State Art Gallery 315
Zoologischer Garten 345
Kassel 26, 176
Park Wilhelmshöhe 176
Kelly, Petra 26
Kempten 336
Allgäu-Museum 336, 337
Alpinmuseum 336
Archaeological Park 336
Fürstäbtliche Residenz 336
Römisches Museum 336
St. Lorenz basilica 336
Kiel 10, 127, 158
Kiel Canal 127
Kirchdorf 149
Kirnitzsch Valley 233
Klee, Paul 78, 88, 168, 174, 275
Kleiner Jasmunder Bodden 142
Kloster 143
Kloster Andechs 265
Kloster Corvey 151
Klütz 148
Klützer-Ostsee-Eisenbahn 148, 149
Koblenz 10, 176, 178, 179, 385
accommodation 206–207
Deutsches Eck (German Corner) 176
Mittelrhein-Museum 176
restaurants 202
Kohl, Helmut 46
Köln (Cologne) 8, 10, 163, 172–175, 196–198
accommodation 207
Chocolate Museum 174–175, 198
Claudius Therme 197
Deutsches Sport und Olympia Museum 175, 197
eau de Cologne 175, 197
festivals 17, 199
Fondation Corboud 174
Karneval 17, 385
Kölner Dom 173
Museum Ludwig 174
Puppenspiele (puppet theatre) 198
restaurants 202–203
Roman-Germanic Museum 172, 173–174
Schokoladenmuseum 174–175, 198
Wallraf-Richartz-Museum 174
Zoologischer Garten Köln 198

Königstein 233, 241
Konstanz 308–309, 335, 345–346, 347, 355
Imperia 309, 335
Konzil 309, 335
Minster of Our Lady 335
Sea Life Konstanz 345–346
Kühlungsborn 149

L

Lahn Valley 176
Lahr 25
Lake Constance *see* Bodensee
landscape 6
Landshut 314, 350
Burg Trausnitz 314
Stiftsbasilika St. Martin 314
Langeness 139
Langeoog 140
language
menu reader 388–389
words and phrases 392–397
laundry 364
Lauterbach 143
Legoland 345, 384
Leipzig 209, 222–225, 247–248, 249
accommodation 256
airport 49, 50–51
Altes Rathaus 223
Bach Museum 224
Battle of the Nations Memorial 224–225
Bosehaus 224
Christmas market 247
City History Museum 223
Decorative Arts Museum 225
Ethnography Museum 225
Forum of Contemporary History 224
Gewandhaus 225, 247
Grassimuseum 225
Hauptbahnhof (Main Station) 223
Leipzig Card 223
Mendelssohn-Haus 225
Museum der Bildenden Künste 225
Museum in der Runden Ecke 225
Musical Instruments Museum 225
Nikolaikirche 224
Old Stock Exchange 223
restaurants 251–252
Russische Kirche 225
Thomaner (boy choristers) 224, 247
Thomaskirche 223–224, 247
trade fairs 222–223
Völkerschlachtdenkmal 224–225
Zeitgeschichtliches Forum 224
Zoo Leipzig 248
Lemgo 176
House of the Witches' Mayor 176
Limburg 176
Dom St. Georg 176
Lindau 308, 309, 350, 355
Lindenfels 341
Linderhof 314
Liszt, Franz 166, 235
local ways 365
Lorelei Rock 182–183
Loreley Besucherzentrum 182–183
Losheim 192
lost property 366
Löwe, Heinrich der 123
Lower Saxony 8
Lübbenau 234, 257
Lübeck 10, 121, 136–137, 154–155
accommodation 161
Buddenbrookhaus 136
Holstentor 137
Marienkirche 137
puppet theatre 154
Rathaus 137
restaurants 159
Sea Captains' Guild House 137
Sea Life Timmendorfer Strand 155
Theaterfiguren Museum 155
Lübecker Bucht 146
Ludwig II 323
Ludwigsburg 318
Favoritepark 318
Märchengarten (Fairytale Garden) 318
Residenzschloss 318
Ludwigslust 138
Luise, Princess 35, 105
Lüneburg 138, 159
Deutsches Salzmuseum 138
Lüneburger Heide 138
Luther, Martin 32, 33, 189, 220, 234

M

Magdeburg 9, 33, 221, 249, 256
Convent of Our Lady 221
Dom 221
Mainau 308
Mainz 177, 203
Dom St. Martin 177
Gutenberg-Museum 177
St. Stephan Church 177
Mann, Thomas 136
Mannheim 318, 350–351
Jesuitenkirche 318
Kunsthalle 318
Mannheimer Schloss 318
Wasserturm 318
maps 372
for hikers 372
map shops, specialist 371
Marburg 181
Elisabethkirche 181
Margarethenschlucht 342, 343
Marienglashöhle 244, 245
Marx, Karl 187, 188
Mathildenhöhe 167
Maulbronn 318
Zisterzienserkloster 318
measurements 360, 364
Mecklenburg-Vorpommen 8, 121, 138, 140
Mecklenburgische Seenplatte 138
medical treatment 362–363
medications 359, 362
Meersburg 308, 309, 351, 355
Museum of Wine-Making 309
Meissen 226, 241
accommodation 257
Burgberg 226
Dom 226
porcelain factory 226, 248
restaurants 252
Mendelssohn, Felix 35, 225
Merkel, Angela 7, 46
Mettlach
Keramikmuseum 181
Villeroy & Boch 181
Michelstadt 341
Miltenberg 341
Mittelberg 336
Mittenwald 332
Violin-Making Museum 332
mobile phones 368
Modernism 20, 23, 218
Möhne Dam 191
Moholy-Nagy, László 78
money 361–362
ATMs 361
banks 361, 369
credit and debit cards 361, 375
currency 361
currency exchange 361
discounts and concessions 362, 369
everyday items and prices 361
tax refunds 361–362, 375
tipping 362
traveller's cheques 361, 366
wiring 361
Monschau 167, 192
Moritzburg 221, 252
Mosbach 340, 351
Mosel Valley 178–179
motor racing 14, 195, 381
Mühlhausen 227
München (Munich) 9, 11, 258–299
accommodation 298–299
Aircraft Museum 274
airport 49, 50
Alte Pinakothek 266–267, 288
Altes Rathaus 277
Ammersee 265
Angel of Peace 281
Antikensammlungen 268
Asamkirche 11, 265
Bavarian National Museum 265
BMX Museum 265
Chinesischer Turm 269, 289, 291
Coach Museum 285
Cuvilliés Theatre 283
Dachau 268
Deutsches Museum 11, 270–274
Dreifaltigkeitskirche 287
Englischer Garten 11, 269, 289
entertainment and

nightlife 291–292, 377, 379
festivals and events 277, 293, 385
Fischbrunnen 277
Flugwerft Schleissheim 274
Frauenkirche 268, 287
Friedensengel 281
Glockenspiel 277
Glyptothek 268
Haus der Kunst 281, 289
Hofbräuhaus 11, 268
Hofgarten 275, 289
Karolinenplatz 288
Königsplatz 268, 288
Lenbachhaus 275, 288
Literaturhaus 287
Ludwig-Maximilians-Universität 289
Ludwigskirche 288–289
Lustheim Palace 281
Marienplatz 11, 276–277
Mariensäule 276
Marionettentheater 275, 293
Maximilianstrasse 275
Metro 263
Monopteros 269, 289
Münchner Stadtmuseum 275
Museum of Man and Nature 285
Neue Pinakothek 278, 288
Neues Rathaus 276
Neues Schloss 281
Odeonsplatz 275, 287
Oktoberfest 17, 385
Olympiapark 15, 45, 280, 292
Olympiaturm 280
Palais Porcia 287
Pinakothek der Moderne 279, 288
Porcelain Museum 285
Prinzregenten-Strasse 281
Propyläen 268
public transportation 54, 263
Puppet Theatre Museum 275, 293
Residenz 275, 282–283
restaurants 294–297
Salvatorkirche 287
Schleissheim 281
Schloss Nymphenburg 11, 284–285
shopping 290–291
sports and activities 292
State Collection of Antiquities 268
street plan 260–262
Theatinerkirche 275
Tierpark Hellabrunn 281
Transport and Mobility Museum 273
Verkehrszentrum 273
Viktualienmarkt 281
Villa Stuck 281
walks 286–289
Wittelsbacherplatz 287
Münchhausen, Baron 151
Münster 180, 198
accommodation 207
All-Weather Zoo 198
Dolphinarium 198
Dom St. Paul 180
Graphikmuseum Pablo Picasso 180
Horse Museum 198
Rathaus 180
restaurants 203–204
State Museum and Planetarium 198
Müntzer, Thomas 33, 227
Müritz-Nationalpark 138, 383
museum opening times 369

N

Nadelöhr 242
Napoleon Bonaparte 36, 188, 224
national holidays 369
national parks 383
Nationalpark Altenau-Torfhaus 237, 238
Nationalpark Berchtesgaden 307, 382, 383
Nationalpark Hainich 383
Nationalpark Hamburgisches Wattenmeer 383
Nationalpark Harz 383
Nationalpark Jasmund 143, 383
Nationalpark Kellerwald-Edersee 383
Nationalpark Niedersächsisches Wattenmeer 140, 383
Nationalpark Sächsische Schweiz 383
Nationalpark Schleswig-Holsteinisches Wattenmeer 139, 383
Nationalpark Unteres Odertal 383
Nationalpark Vorpommersche Boddenlandschaft 143, 383
Naturpark Arnsberger 191
Naturpark Münden 151
Naturpark Rothaargebirge 181
Naturpark Tier-Freigelände 303
Naturschutzgebiet Brooker Wald 148
Naumburg 227, 248, 253
Dom St. Peter und Paul 227
Neckar Valley 340–343
Neckargemünd 340
Neckarsteinach 340
Nefertiti 75
Neubrandenburg 139
Neubukow 149
Neuendorf 143
Neukirchen bei Heiligen Blut 331
Neustrelitz 138
newspapers and magazines 371
Nibelungenstrasse 341
Niedersachsen (Lower Saxony) 8, 121
Nord-Ostsee-Kanal 127
Norderney 140
Nordfriesische Inseln 10, 139
Nordrhein-Westfalen 8, 163
Nordstrand 139
North Frisian Islands 10, 139
North Rhine-Westphalia 8, 163
northern Germany 8, 10, 120–161
accommodation 160–161
drives 148–151
festivals and events 155
restaurants 156–159
sights 121–145
walks 146–147
what to do 152–155
nuclear power 23
Nürburgring 163, 195
Nürnberg (Nuremberg) 11, 301, 316–317, 346
accommodation 356
Christmas market 316–317, 347
Frauenkirche 316
Germanisches Nationalmuseum 317
Historischer Kunstbunker 316, 317
Kaiserberg 316, 317
restaurants 351
St. Lorenz Kirche 316
St. Sebaldus Kirche 316
Tiergarten (zoo) 317
Toy Museum 346

O

Oberammergau 318, 333, 346, 351, 356
Passion Play 318
Oberhof 245, 248, 382
Oberkirchen 190
Oberstaufen 337
Oberstdorf 337, 352
office hours 369
Oktoberfest 17, 385
Oldenburg 139
Landesmuseum für Kunst und Kulturgeschichte 139
Olsberg 190
opening times 15, 369
opticians 364
Osnabrück 139
Ostfriesische Inseln 8, 10, 140
Ostseebäder 143

P

packing 359
Pappenheim 303
Passau 328, 330
Dom St. Stephan 328
Glasmuseum 331
Mariahilf 328
passports and visas 359, 360
lost/stolen passport 366
Peenemünde 145
Pellworm 139
Pelm 193
Pergamon Altar 90, 92–93
personal security 366
Pfaffendorf 242
Pfaffenstein 242–243
Phantasialand 384
pharmacies 363
Picasso, Pablo 88, 89, 168, 174, 180
Pied Piper of Hamelin 126, 147

Pirna 233, 241, 257
places of worship 365
Poel 149
police 366
politics 6–7, 24, 25
postal services 368
Potsdam 11, 209, 228–232, 249
accommodation 257
Alexandrowka 232
Alter Markt 231–232
Altes Rathaus 232
Belvedere auf dem Pfingstberg 232
Bildergalerie 230
Brandeburger Tor 232
Chinesisches Haus 230
Dampfmaschinehaus 232
Einsteinturm 232
Filmpark Babelsberg 228, 248
Glienicker Brücke 230
Marmorpalais (Marble Palace) 230, 231
Neuer Garten 230–231
Neues Palais 230
Nikolaikirche 231–232
Park Sanssouci 229–230
restaurants 253
Schloss Cecilienhof 231
Schloss Charlottenhof 230
Schloss Sanssouci 229, 249
Stadtschloss 232
Prüm 193
Fürstabtei (Princely Abbey) 193
public transportation
Berlin 52–53, 73
disabilities, visitors with 66, 365
Frankfurt 54
Hamburg 54
Munich 54
see also air travel; buses; ferry services; taxis; train services
Putbus 143

Q

Quedlinburg 227, 236, 253, 257
Burgberg 227

R

racoons 26
radio 371
Ravensburger Verlagsmuseum 346
reading, recommended 371–372
Regen 331
Regensburg 301, 320–321
accommodation 356
Cathedral Treasury 321
Document Neupfarrplatz 321
Dom St. Peter 321
Goldener Turm 320
Kastenmayerhaus 320
restaurants 352
Stone Bridge 320
Thurn und Taxis-Museum 321
Walhalla 321
regions of Germany 8–9
Reichenau Island 308
Reinhardswald 151
Remagen 183, 204
Friedensmuseum Brücke von Remagen 183
Remarque, Erich Maria 139
Rennsteig 248
restaurants
Berlin 112–115
eastern Germany 250–253
Munich 294–297
northern Germany 156–159
opening times 369
southern Germany 348–353
western Germany 200–205
Rheinland-Pfalz 8, 163
Rheintal (Rhine Valley) 11, 182–183
Rhine Falls 308
Rhineland-Palatinate 8, 163
River Bode gorge 239
Roetgen 192
Romantische Strasse (Romantic Road) 55, 319, 336
Römerstrasse 128 21
Rosstrappe 239
Rostock 8, 121, 141
accommodation 161
boat tours 141
Kulturhistorisches Museum 141
restaurants 159
St.-Marien-Kirche 141
Schiffbau- und Schiffahrtsmuseum 141
Zoo Rostock 155
Rothenburg ob der Tauber 301, 319, 346, 347
accommodation 356
City Councillors' Tavern 319
German Christmas Museum and Village 319, 346
Rathaus 319
restaurants 352
St. Jacob's Church 319
Rotweinwanderweg 167
Rügen 12, 142–143
accommodation 161
Baabe 143
Binz 143
Biosphärenreservat Südost Rügen 143
Glowe 143
Göhren 143
Jagdschloss Granitz 143
Kap Arkona 142
Königsstuhl 143
Lauterbach 143
Nationalpark Jasmund 143
Ostseebäder 143
Putbus 143
Sassnitz 143
Sellin 143
Vitt 142
Ruhrgebiet (the Ruhr) 8, 11, 23, 184–185
Dortmund 185
Essen 185
Industrial Heritage Trail 184
Rurberg 193

S

Saarbrücken 181, 207
Historisches Museum 181
Saarland 8, 10–11, 163, 181
Sachsen (Saxony) 9, 209, 216, 240–241
Sachsen-Anhalt (Saxony-Anhalt) 9, 209
Sächsische Schweiz (Saxon Switzerland) 11, 233, 241, 242–243, 248, 257
sailing 265
St. Boniface 30, 167
St. Goar 183, 204, 385
salt mining 138, 221, 307
Sassnitz 143
Sauerland 181, 190–191, 198–199
Sauerland-Bad 190
Saxon Switzerland *see* Sächsische Schweiz
Saxon Wine Route 241
Saxony *see* Sachsen
Schaffhausen 308
Schauinsland 311
Schiller, Friedrich von 81, 221, 235
Schlager music 19
Schlepzig 253
Schleswig 140, 161
Archäologisches Landesmuseum 140
Dom 140
Landesmuseum für Kunst und Kulturgeschichte 140
Schloss Gottorf 140
Schleswig-Holstein 8, 121
Schliemann, Heinrich 149
Schloss Bellevue 101, 104
Schloss Cecilienhof 231
Schloss Charlottenburg 98–99
Schloss Charlottenhof 230
Schloss Dachau 268
Schloss Friedenstein 219, 245
Schloss Gottorf 140
Schloss Güstrow 126
Schloss Hartenfels 241
Schloss Heidelberg 312, 313
Schloss Herrenchiemsee 310
Schloss Hohenschwangau 325
Schloss Jever 127
Schloss Johannisburg 303
Schloss Linderhof 301, 333
Schloss Ludwigslust 138
Schloss Neuschwanstein 11, 301, 322–325
Schloss Nymphenburg 11, 284–285
Schloss Sanssouci 229, 249
Schloss Wackerbarth 241
Schloss Wolfenbüttel 145
Schloss Wörlitz 218
Schluchsee 339
Schongau 332
Schumacher, Michael 14
Schumann, Robert 234
Schwäbisch Hall 328, 352
Schwarzer Mann 192

Schwarzwald (Black Forest) 6, 9, 204, 301, 338–339
Schwerin 121, 140, 159
Galeriegebäude 140
Schweriner Schloss 140
science and technology 22–23
Sea Life Berlin 110
Sea Life Konstanz 345–346
Sea Life Speyer 199
Sea Life Timmendorfer Strand 155
Sedan 37
Seiffen 248
Ore Mountains Toy Museum 248
self-catering 391
Sellin 143
shopping 374–375
Berlin 106–107
department stores 374
markets 374
Munich 290–291
opening hours 15, 369, 375
payment 375
Sunday trading 15
supermarkets 374
tax refunds 361–362, 375
what to buy 375
see also Christmas markets
Singen 308
smoking etiquette 365
soccer 14, 15, 109, 153, 195, 197, 382
social issues 24–25
Soest 181, 190, 204, 207
Wiesenkirche 181
Solnhofen 303
Sonthofen 337
Sorb ethnic minority 234, 249
southern Germany 9, 11, 300–356
accommodation 354–356
drives 330–333, 336–341
festivals and events 347
restaurants 348–353
sights 301–329
walks 334–335, 342–343
what to do 344–347
spas 15, 379
Aachen 165, 194
Bad Harzburg 236
Bad Karlshafen 151
Bad Saarow 246
Bad Sulza 246
Baden-Baden 11, 12, 301, 305, 344
Berchtesgaden 344
Berlin 109
Friedrichroda 244–245
Köln (Cologne) 197
München (Munich) 293
Sauerland-Bad 190
Tabarz 244
Thale 236
Triberg 328
Villingen-Schwenningen 338–339
Wiesbaden 189
Speyer 189, 199, 352
accommodation 207
Historisches Museum 189
Kaiserdom 189
restaurants 204
Sea Life Speyer 199
Technik Museum Speyer 199
Spiegelau 330
Spiekeroog 140
sports and activities 380–383
basketball 108, 380
bicycling 61, 108, 198, 292, 380
fishing 265, 380–381
golf 154, 195, 196, 381
hang-gliding 337
horse-racing 155, 195, 305, 344, 381
ice hockey 108, 381
in-line skating 382
motor racing 14, 195, 381
mountain biking 181
parasailing 337
rock-climbing 337
sailing 265
soccer 14, 15, 109, 153, 195, 197, 382
tennis 14, 153, 382
trekking and climbing 167, 181, 239, 242–243, 248, 372, 382
trotting meetings 109
watersports 382
windsurfing 152, 265
winter sports 181, 192, 198–199, 248, 314, 337, 345, 346, 382
Spreewald 11, 234, 253, 257
Stade 140
Schwedenspeicher-Museum 140
Stasi 46, 225
Stauffenberg, Count Claus von 43
Steibis 337
Steinhude 154
Steinhuder Meer 135
Störtebeker, Klaus 31
Stove 149
Stralsund 21, 145
Deutsches Meeresmuseum 145
Katharinenkloster 145
student travellers 362, 369
Stuttgart 11, 301, 326–327, 346, 347
accommodation 356
Altes Schloss 327
Fernsehturm 327
Jubilee Column 327
Kunstmuseum 327
Mercedes-Benz Museum 327
Porsche Museum 327
restaurants 352–353
Schlossplatz 327
Staatsgalerie 20, 327
Stiftskirche 327
Stuttcard Plus 327
Weissenhof Estate 21
Wilhelma Zoo 327
Württemberg State Museum 327
Stützerbach 245
sun safety 362, 363
sunburn index 363
Sylt 139, 161

T

Tabarz 244
tax refunds 361–362, 375
taxis 61
Telemann, Georg Philipp 249
telephones 367–368
television 371
reality television shows 17
tennis 14, 153, 382
Teutoberg Wald 8
Teutoburg Forest 8
Thale 236
theatre and dance 377
theme parks
Europa-Park 311, 345, 384
Legoland 345, 384
Phantasialand 384
Vogelpark Walsrode 155
Thüringen 9, 209
Thüringer Wald (Thuringian Forest) 9, 220, 244–245, 248
time zones 359
Timmendorfer-Strand 149
tipping 362
Titisee 339
Tittling 330
Tobiashammer 245
Todtnau 339
toilets 364
Tollensesee 139
Torfhaus 236–237
Torgau 241
Schloss Hartenfels 241
tourism 15
tourist information 369, 370, 373
Trabant 234
train services 58–60
disabilities, visitors with 66, 365
international services 51
journey times 60
narrow-gauge railways 23, 236, 237, 238, 246
overnight services 58
rail passes 59
steam trains 23, 143, 148, 246
tickets and fares 58–59
train information 59
train types 58
traveller's cheques 361, 366
Travemünde 137, 146, 148
trekking and climbing 167, 181, 239, 242–243, 248, 372, 382
Triberg 328, 338
cuckoo clocks 328, 338
Gutach Falls 328, 338
Schwarzwaldmuseum 328, 338
Trier 11, 163, 178, 186–188, 199
accommodation 207
Basilika 188
Dom 188
gladiatorial re-enactments 188
Imperial Baths 188
Kaiserthermen 188
Karl Marx Haus 188
Porta Nigra 187–188
restaurants 205

Roman ruins 187–188
Schlosspark Quint 188
Toy Museum 199
Tübingen 328, 353

U

Uhrenindustriemuseum 314
Ulm 328–329
Ulm Münster 328
Ulmer Museum 328–329
Unteruhldingen 308
Usedom 145
Ahlbeck 145
Bansin 145
Heringsdorf 145
Historisch-Technisches Informationszentrum 145
Peenemünde 145

V

Varusschlacht Museum und Park 139
vegetarians 387
Verden 155
Vierseenblick 183
Villingen-Schwenningen 314, 338–339
Uhrenindustriemuseum 314, 338–339
Vitt 142
Vitte 143
Vogelpark Walsrode 155
Voigt, Wilhelm 39
volcanic springs 167, 193
Völklinger ironworks 181
Volkswagen 20, 22, 44, 214
Vulkaneifel 167, 193

W

Wagner, Richard 18, 105, 189, 235, 310, 324
walks
Berlin 102–105
Bodensee shore 335
Brodtener Steilufer 146
Garmisch-Partenkirchen: the Partnachklamm 334
Hameln 147
Munich 286–289
Neckar Valley 342–343
Pfaffenstein 242–243
River Bode gorge 239
Wallenstein, Albrecht von 32
Walpurgisnacht 249
Walsrode 155
Wangerooge 140
Wannsee 43
Warnemünde 141
Wartburg 220, 244
watersports 382
Wattenmeer 140
Watzmann 307
weather reports 358–359
websites 373
Weilburg 176
Weill, Kurt 249
Weimar 9, 11, 209, 235
accommodation 257
Deutsches Nationaltheater Weimar 235, 248
Gedenkstätte Buchenwald 235
Goethe Wohnhaus 235
Goethes Hausgarten 235
restaurants 253
Weinheim 341, 353
Wernigerode 236, 256
Weserbergland 150–151
Westerland 139
western Germany 8, 10–11, 162–207
accommodation 206–207
drives 190–193
festivals and events 199
restaurants 200–205
sights 163–189
what to do 194–199
what to do
Berlin 106–111
eastern Germany 246–249
Munich 290–293
northern Germany 152–155
southern Germany 344–347
western Germany 194–199
see also children; entertainment and nightlife; festivals and events; national parks; shopping; spas; sports and activities
Wiehe, Modellbahn-Wiehe (model railway) 248
Wiesbaden 189, 205
casino 199
Kaiser Friedrich Therme 189
Kurhaus 189
Marktkirche 189
Museum Wiesbaden 189
Thermalbad Aukammtal 189
Wieskirche (Church in the Meadow) 333
wildlife 26
Wilhelm I 38
Wilhelm II 38, 39, 77, 176
Wilhelma Zoo 327
Wilhelmshaven 155
windsurfing 152, 265
wines 12, 387
Liebfraumilch 189
Red Wine Hiking Trail 167
Saxon Wine Route 241
Sekt 248, 387
Spätburgunder 167, 201
wine festivals 385
Winkhausen 190
winter sports 181, 192, 248, 337, 345, 346, 382
Winterberg 181, 190, 382
Wismar 21, 145, 148, 159, 161
Wittenberg 9, 33, 234
accommodation 257
Haus der Geschichte 234
Lutherhaus 234
restaurants 253
Wodorf 149
Wohlenberger Wiek 148
Wolfenbüttel 145
Fachwerkhaüser (half-timbered houses) 145
Herzog-August Bibliothek 145
Schloss Wolfenbüttel 145
Wörlitzer See 218
Worms 189
Dom 189
Liebfrauenkirche 189
Luther Memorial 189
Wurmberg 237
Würzburg 329, 353
Dom St. Kilian 329
Festung Marienberg 329
Fürstbischöfliche Residenz 329
Juliusspital 329
Marienkapelle 329
Marienkirche 329
Wurzen 240

Z

Zeche Zollverein 23, 185
Zittau 234
Lenten Veil 234
Zoo am Meer Bremerhaven 153
Zoo Berlin 101
Zoo Frankfurt 196
Zoo Leipzig 248
Zoo Rostock 155
Zoologischer Garten Köln 198
Zugspitze 6, 314
Zwickau 234
August Horch Museum 234
Robert-Schumann-Haus 234
Zwiesel 330

PICTURES

The Automobile Association wishes to thank the following photographers and organisations for their assistance in the preparation of this book.

Abbreviations for the picture credits are as follows – (t) top; (b) bottom; (l) left; (r) right; (c) centre; (AA) AA World Travel Library

2 AA/P Bennett;
3t AA/A Baker;
3ca AA/T Souter;
3cb AA/C Sawyer;
3b AA/S McBride;
4AA/M Jourdan;
5AA/J Smith;
6AA/A Kouprianoff;
7b AA/M Jourdan;
7t AA/P Bennett;
8 AA/S McBride;
10 Friedemann Vogel/Bongarts/Getty Images;
11 AA/J Smith;
12l AA/T Souter;
12r Juergen Henkelmann Photography/Alamy;
13 Tourismus + Congress GmbH Frankfurt am Main;
14 AA/M Jourdan;
15b AA/A Baker;
15t Mark Ralston/AFP/Getty Images;
16 AA/T Souter;
17r AA/T Souter;
17l Photolibrary.com/Frank Chmura;
18 Michaela Barth /Tilo Steffens © Bayreuther Festspiele GmbH / Enrico Nawrath;
19t Juergen Henkelmann Photography/Alamy;
20 AA/S McBride;
21l AA/M Jourdan;
21r AA/T Souter;
22 Siemens AG;
23l Daimler Chrysler Media Services;
23r SIPA Press/Rex Features;
24 Fotolia.com/Jan Kranendonk;
25 Action Press/Rex Features;
26r AA/A Kouprianoff;
26l AA/S McBride;
27 AA/C Sawyer;
28 AA/A Baker;
29r akg-images/Bildarchiv Steffens;
29l Yadid Levy/Robert Harding;
30 akg-images/Herve Champollion;
31b AA/D Traverso;
31t AA/P Bennett;
32 Mary Evans Picture Library;
33r AA/A Kouprianoff;
33l akg-images;
34 akg-images;
35t AA/A Kouprianoff;
35b akg-images/Sotheby's;
36 AA/P Bennett;
37b akg-images;
37t akg-images;
38 akg-images;
39l akg-images;
39r akg-images;
40 Mary Evans Picture Library;
41t akg-images;
41b imagebroker/Alamy;
42 akg-images;
43l AA/T Souter;
43r akg-images;
44 AA/T Souter;
45r AA/D Traverso;
45l akg-images;
46l akg-images/ullstein bild;
46r Reuters/Ralph Orlowski/Corbis;
47 Photolibrary.com/Elfi Kluck;
49 Tourismus + Congress GmbH Frankfurt am Main;
50 AA/T Souter;
51 AA/M Trelawny;
54 AA/C Sawyer;
58 AA/A Kouprianoff;
59 AA/M Trelawny;
60 AA/A Kouprianoff;
61 AA/M Jourdan;
62 Digital Vision;
63 istock/Alexander Wilms;
64 AA/T Souter;
65 AA/P Bennett;
66 AA/N. Lancaster;
67 AA/M Jourdan;
68 AA/S McBride;
74 AA/T Souter;
75 akg-images;
76 AA/S McBride;
77 AA/A Baker;
78 AA/C Sawyer;
79 Photolibrary.com/Henkelmann;
80 AA/A Baker;
81 AA/C Sawyer;
82 Gemaldegalerie, Berlin, Germany/ The Bridgeman Art Library;
84 Gemaldegalerie, Berlin, Germany/ The Bridgeman Art Library;
86 AA/J Smith;
87 Ruben Joye/Fotolia.com;
88 AA/C Sawyer;
89 AA/A Baker;
90 AA/J Smith;
91 AA/J Smith;
93 AA/S McBride;
94 AA/J Smith;
95 AA/J Smith;
96 AA/S McBride;
97 AA/S McBride;
98 AA/C Sawyer;
99 AA/A Baker;
100b AA/J Smith;
100t AA/T Souter;
101 AA/T Souter;
102 AA/S McBride;
104 AA/A Baker;
105 AA/A Kouprianoff;
106 AA/A Kouprianoff;
109 AA/J Smith;
110 AA/S McBride;
112 AA/A Kouprianoff;
116 Hotel Adlon, Berlin;
120 AA/P Bennett;
122 AA/D Traverso;
123 AA/D Traverso;
124 AA/D Traverso;
125 AA/P Bennett;
126 AA/A Kouprianoff;
127 AA/D Traverso;
128 Sergey Kelin/Fotolia.com;
129 AA/P Bennett;
130 AA/P Bennett;
132 Bildagentur Hamburg/Alamy;
133 AA/P Bennett;
134 AA/A Kouprianoff;
135 AA/A Kouprianoff;
136 AA/P Bennett;
137 Peer Frings /Fotolia.com;
138 AA/P Bennett;
139 AA/P Bennett;
140 AA/D Traverso;
141 AA/P Bennett;
142 AA/P Bennett;
143 Photolibrary.com/Fritz Poelking;
144 Photolibrary.com/Werner Otto;
145 AA/D Traverso;
146 AA/P Bennett;
148 AA/P Bennett;
150 AA/D Traverso;
152 Photolibrary.com/Targa;
154 AA/D Traverso;
156 imagebroker/Alamy;
158 AA/A Kouprianoff;
160 AA/P Bennett;
162 Tourismus + Congress GmbH Frankfurt am Main;
164 Lovrencg/Fotolia.com;
165 AA/A Kouprianoff;
166 Photolibrary.com/Atlantide

S.N.C.;
167 AA/A Kouprianoff;
168 Yadid Levy/Robert Harding;
169r akg-images;
169l Yadid Levy/Robert Harding;
170 Frankfurt Tourist+Congress Board, Fraport AG and Bünck + Fehse Visualisation and Animations Design GmbH, Berlin;
171 Tourismus + Congress GmbH Frankfurt am Main;
172 AA/A Baker;
173 AA/A Kouprianoff;
175 AA/P Enticknap;
176 AA/A Kouprianoff;
177 Bernd Kröger/Fotolia.com;
178 AA/A Baker;
179t AA/A Baker;
179b AA/A Kouprianoff;
180 AA/A Kouprianoff;
181 AA/A Baker;
182 AA/A Kouprianoff;
183 AA/A Kouprianoff;
184 AA/A Kouprianoff;
185 AA/A Kouprianoff;
186 Vitamin B/Fotolia.com;
187 AA/A Kouprianoff;
188 AA/A Kouprianoff;
189 AA/A Baker;
190 AA/A Kouprianoff;
192 Gavin Hellier/Robert Harding;
194 AA/A Kouprianoff;
197 Photolibrary.com/Fwagner;
200 AA/K Blackwell;
203 AA/A Kouprianoff;
205 AA/A Kouprianoff;
206 AA/A Kouprianoff;
208 AA/P Bennett;
210 Germany Images David Crossland/Alamy;
211 Bernd Kröger/Fotolia.com;
212 Photolibrary.com/Martin Rugner;
213 AA/P Bennett;
214 AA/P Bennett;
216 Photolibrary.com/JTB Photo;
217b AA/P Bennett;
217t Photolibrary.com/Ypps;
218 AA/P Bennett;
219 AA/P Bennett;
220 Roman M/Fotolia.com;
221 AA/D Traverso;
222 AA/P Bennett;
223 AA/P Bennett;
224 AA/D Traverso;
225 AA/P Bennett;
226 akg-images;
227 AA/A Kouprianoff;
228 AA/S McBride;
229 AA/A Kouprianoff;
230 AA/A Kouprianoff;
231 AA/J Smith;
232 AA/J Smith;
233 AA/P Bennett;
234 AA/A Kouprianoff;
235 AA/P Bennett;
236 Frank/Fotolia.com;
237 avatra images / Alamy;
238 AA/P Bennett;
239 AA/P Bennett;
240 Ole Jensen/Fotolia.com;
242 AA/P Bennett;
243 AA/P Bennett;
244 AA/D Traverso;
246 Photolibrary.com/Carlos;
250 AA/P Bennett;
254 AA/P Bennett;
256 AA/P Bennett;
258 AA/C Sawyer;
264 Pat Behnke/Alamy;
265 Photolibrary.com/Yadid Levy;
266 Alte Pinakothek, Munich/ Interfoto/Bridgeman Art Library;
268 AA/C Sawyer;
269 Niceshot/Fotolia.com;
270 AA/M Jourdan;
271 AA/M Jourdan;
273b AA/M Jourdan;
274 AA/C Sawyer;
275 AA/C Sawyer;
276 AA/A Baker;
277l AA/C Sawyer;
277r AA/T Souter;
278 AA/C Sawyer;
279 AA/M Jourdan;
280 AA/C Sawyer;
282 AA/T Souter;
283 AA/M. Jourdan;
284 AA/M Jourdan;
286 AA/P Davidson;
288 AA/T Souter;
290 Photolibrary.com/U & H Kolley;
294 AA/M Jourdan;
298 Photolibrary.com/Dirk Von Mallinckrodt;
300 Photolibrary.com/Knöll;
302 Photolibrary.com/Robert Knöll;
303 AA/A Baker;
304 AA/A Baker;
305 AA/M Jourdan;
306 AA/A Baker;
307 AA/T Souter;
308 Thomas Roth/Fotolia.com;
309 AA/M Jourdan;
310 AA/A Baker;
311 AA/M Jourdan;
312 AA/M Jourdan;
313 AA/M Jourdan;
314 AA/M Jourdan;
315 AA/A Baker;
316 AA/A Baker;
318 AA/M Jourdan;
319 AA/A Baker;
320 AA/M Jourdan;
321r AA/A Baker;
321l AA/M Jourdan;
322 AA/M Jourdan;
323 AA/T Souter;
324 AA/T Souter;
325r AA/T Souter;
325l AA/T Souter;
326 Henner/Fotolia.com;
327 Photolibrary.com/Nathan Willock;
329 AA/T Souter;
330 Photolibrary.com/Martin Siepmann;
332 AA/A Baker;
335 AA/A Baker;
336 AA/M Jourdan;
338 AA/M Jourdan;
340 AA/M Jourdan;
342 Tim Krieger/Alamy;
344 Photolibrary.com/Egebhardt;
348 Ruth Tomlinson/Robert Harding;
353 imagebroker/Alamy;
354 Parkhotel Sonnenhof;
356 AA/M Jourdan;
357 sculpies/Fotolia.com;
358 AA/M Jourdan;
364 AA/M Jourdan;
365 AA/T Souter;
367b "Jackie Ranken";
367t Imagestate;
368t AA/M Jourdan;
368b Vario Images/Alamy;
369 AA/M Jourdan;
370t AA/M Jourdan;
370b AA/P Bennett;
372 Photos 12/Alamy;
373 Digital Vision;
374 AA/S McBride;
376 Photolibrary.com/Torrione Stefano;
378 AA/A Kouprianoff;
379 AA/M Jourdan;
380 AA/T Souter;
381 AA/T Souter;
383 AA/P Bennett;
384 AA/M Jourdan;
385 Photolibrary.com/Frank Chmura;
386 fooddesign/Fotolia.com;
388 marcotogni/Fotolia.com;

390 AA/M Jourdan;
399 AA/A Baker.

Every effort has been made to trace the copyright holders, and we apologise in advance for any accidental errors. We would be happy to apply any corrections in the following edition of this publication.

CREDITS

Managing editor
Marie-Claire Jefferies

Project editor
Bookwork Creative Associates Ltd

Design
Drew Jones, pentacorbig, Nick Otway

Cover design
Chie Ushio

Picture research
Luped Picture Research

Image retouching and repro
Michael Moody

Main contributors
Margaret Campbell, Michael Ivory, Paul Grogan, Nicola Lancaster, Isla Love, George McDonald, Derek Mackenzie-Hook

Updater
George McDonald

Indexer
Marie Lorimer

Production
Karen Gibson

See It Germany
ISBN 978-1-4000-0387-7
Third Edition

Published in the United States by Fodor's Travel and simultaneously in Canada by Random House of Canada Limited, Toronto.
Published in the United Kingdom by AA Publishing.

Color separation by Keenes, Andover, UK
Printed and bound by Leo Paper Products, China
10 9 8 7 6 5 4 3 2 1

Special Sales: This book is available for special discounts for bulk purchases for sales promotions or premiums. Special editions, including personalized covers, excerpts of existing books, and corporate imprints, can be created in large quantities for special needs.
For more information, write to Special Markets/Premium Sales, 1745 Broadway, MD 6-2, New York, NY 10019
or e-mail specialmarkets@randomhouse.com
Important Note: Time inevitably brings changes, so always confirm prices, travel facts, and other perishable information when it matters. Although Fodor's cannot accept responsibility for errors, you can use this guide in the confidence that we have taken every care to ensure its accuracy.

Unleash the Possibilities of Travel With Fodor's

Read before you get there, navigate your picks while you're there – make your trip unforgettable with Fodor's guidebooks. Fodor's offers the assurance of our expertise, the guarantee of selectivity, and the choice details that truly define a destination. Our books are written by local authors, so it's like having a friend wherever you travel.

With more than 10 different types of guidebooks to more than 150 destinations around the world, Fodor's has choices to meet every traveler's needs.

Visit **www.fodors.com** to find the guidebooks and connect with a like-minded community of selective travelers – living, learning, and traveling on their terms.

Fodor's For Choice Travel Experiences.

Dear Traveler,

From buying a plane ticket to booking a room and seeing the sights, a trip goes much more smoothly when you have a good travel guide. Dozens of writers, editors, designers, and cartographers have worked hard to make the book you hold in your hands a good one. Was it everything you expected? Were our descriptions accurate? Were our recommendations on target? And did you find our tips and practical advice helpful? Your ideas and experiences matter to us. If we have missed or misstated something, we'd love to hear about it. Fill out our survey at www.fodors.com/books/feedback/, or e-mail us at seeit@fodors.com. Or you can snail mail to the See It Editor at Fodor's, 1745 Broadway, New York, New York 10019. We'll look forward to hearing from you.

Tim Jarrell
Publisher